Attack on Titan Omnibus 11 is a work o̶͟
dents are the products of the author's i̶͟
blance to actual events, locales, or pers̶͟

A Kodansha Trade Paperback Original

Attack on Titan Omnibus 11 copyright © 2020 Hajime Isayama
English translation copyright © 2023 Hajime Isayama

Published in the United States by
Kodansha USA Publishing, LLC, New York.

Publication rights for this English edition arranged through
Kodansha Ltd., Tokyo.

First published in Japan in 2020 by Kodansha Ltd., Tokyo
as *Shingeki no kyojin*, volumes 31 and 32.

ISBN 978-1-64651-492-2

Original cover design by Takashi Shimoyama/Manami Fukunaga (Red Rooster)

Printed in the United States of America.

9 8 7 6 5 4 3 2 1

Translation: Ko Ransom
Lettering: Dezi Sienty
Additional Lettering: Evan Hayden
Editing: Tiff Joshua TJ Ferentini
Kodansha USA Publishing edition logo and cover design by Phil Balsman

Publisher: Kiichiro Sugawara

Director of Publishing Services: Ben Applegate
Director of Publishing Operations: Dave Barrett
Publishing Services Managing Editors: Alanna Ruse, Madison Salters,
with Grace Chen
Senior Production Manager: Angela Zurlo

KODANSHA.US

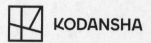

ATTACK on TITAN

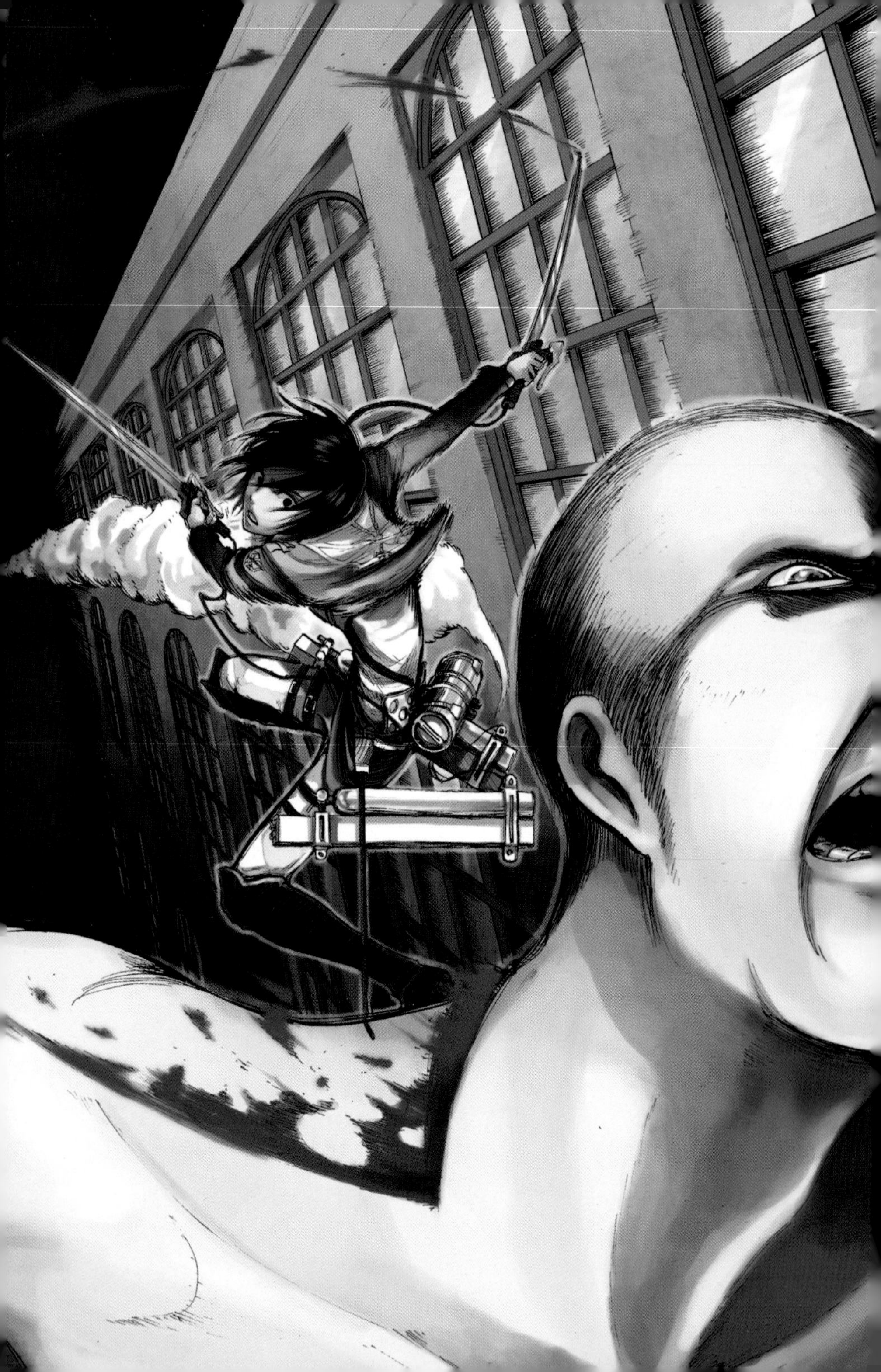

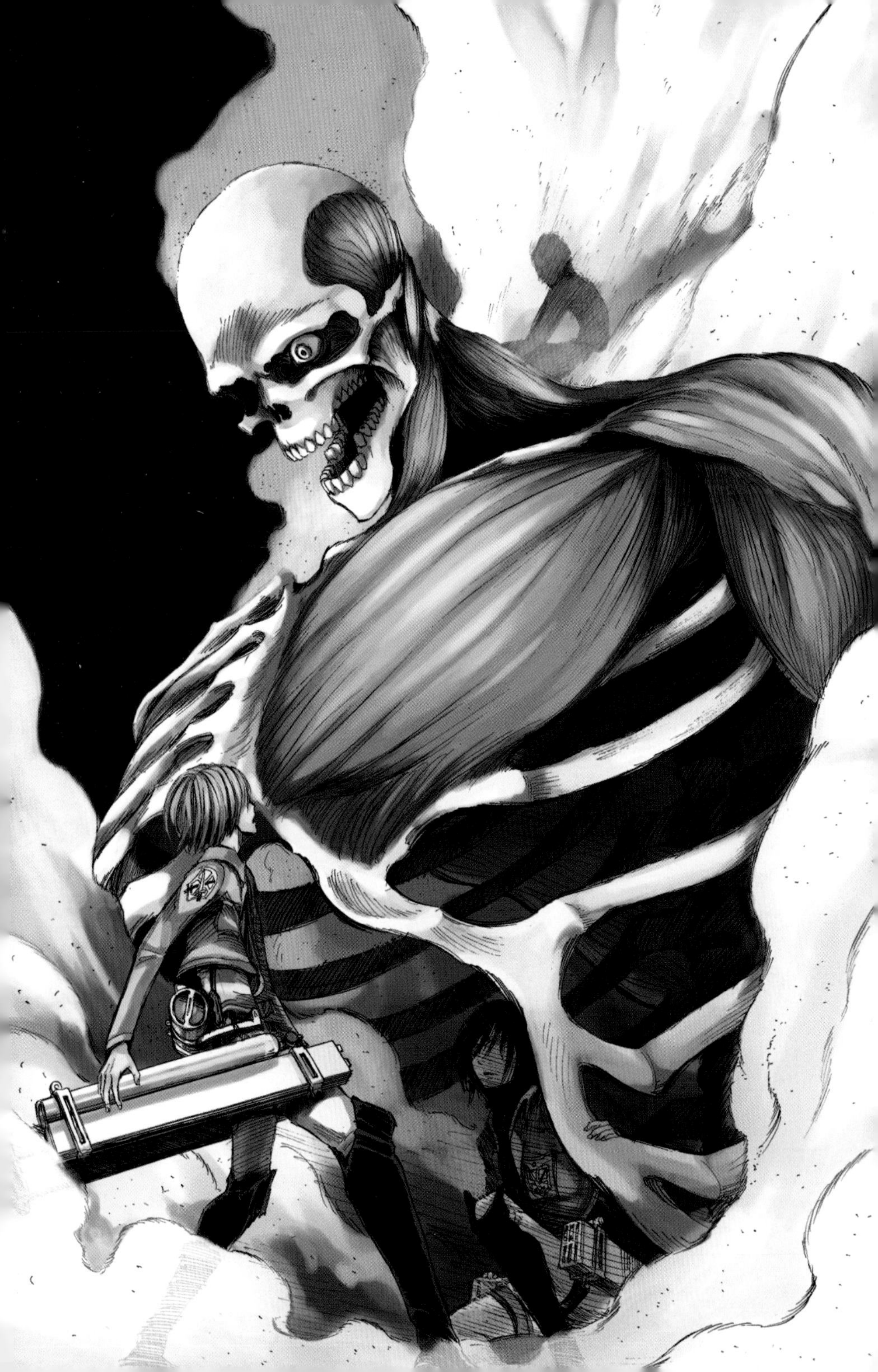

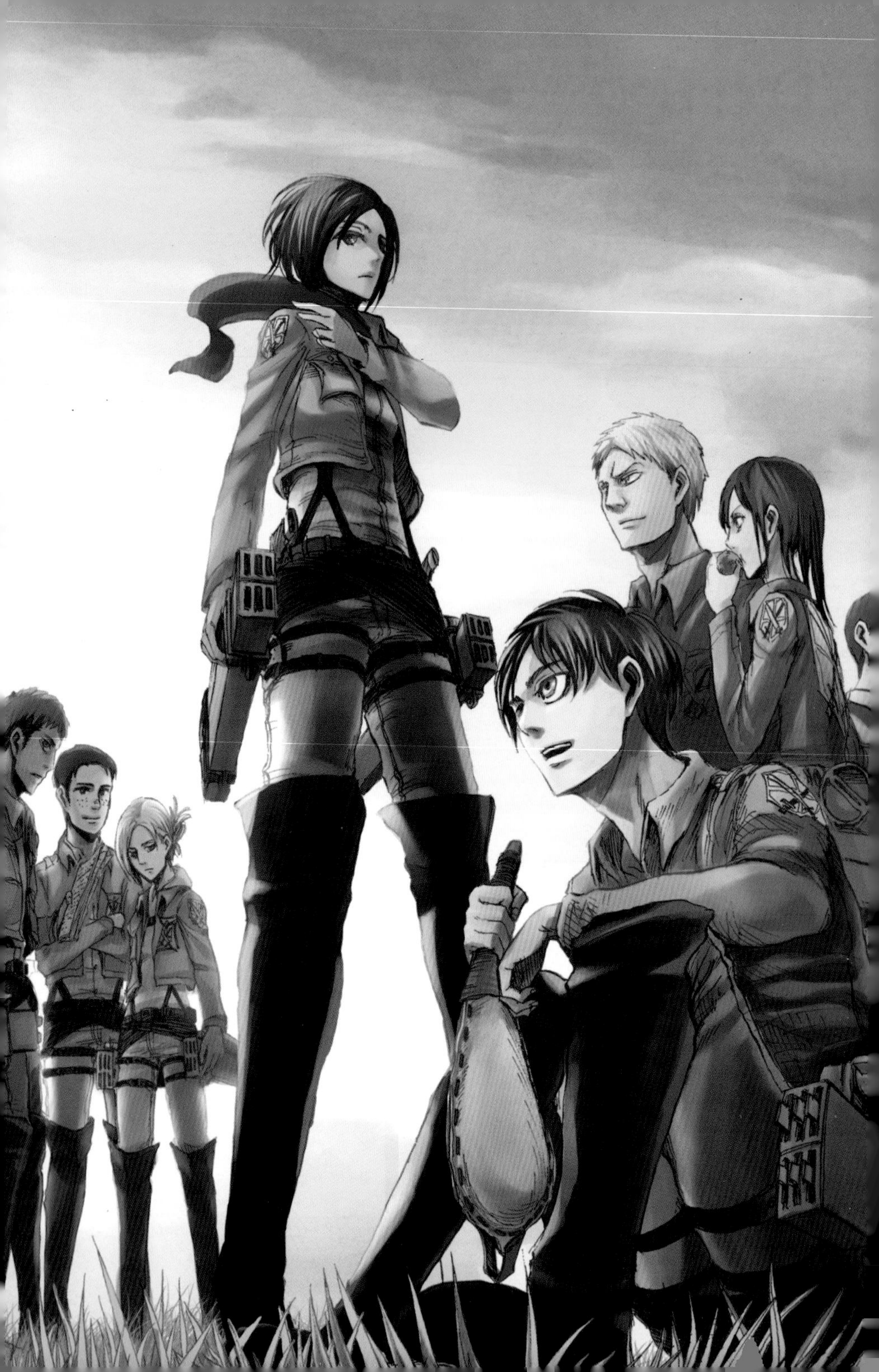

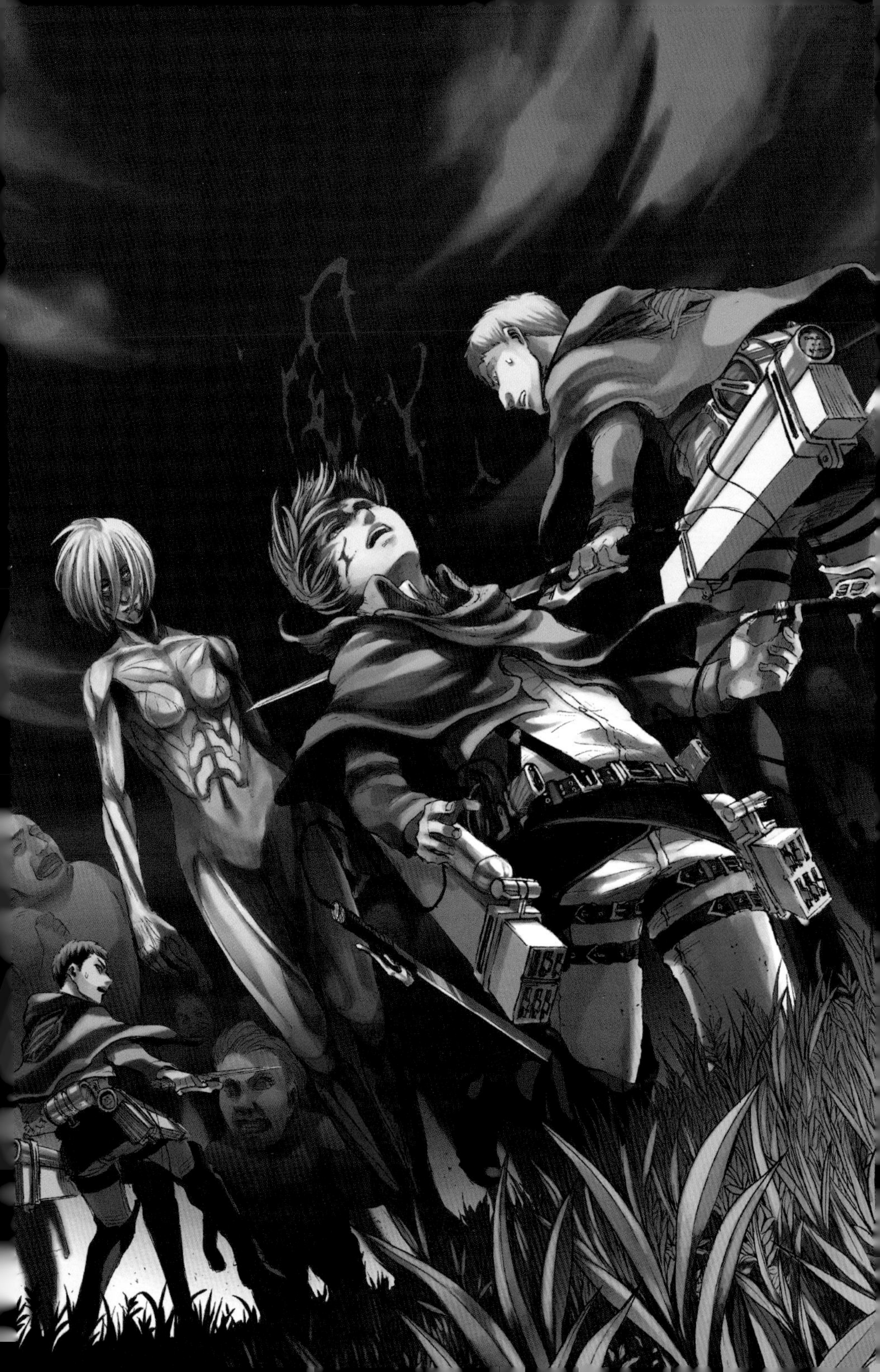

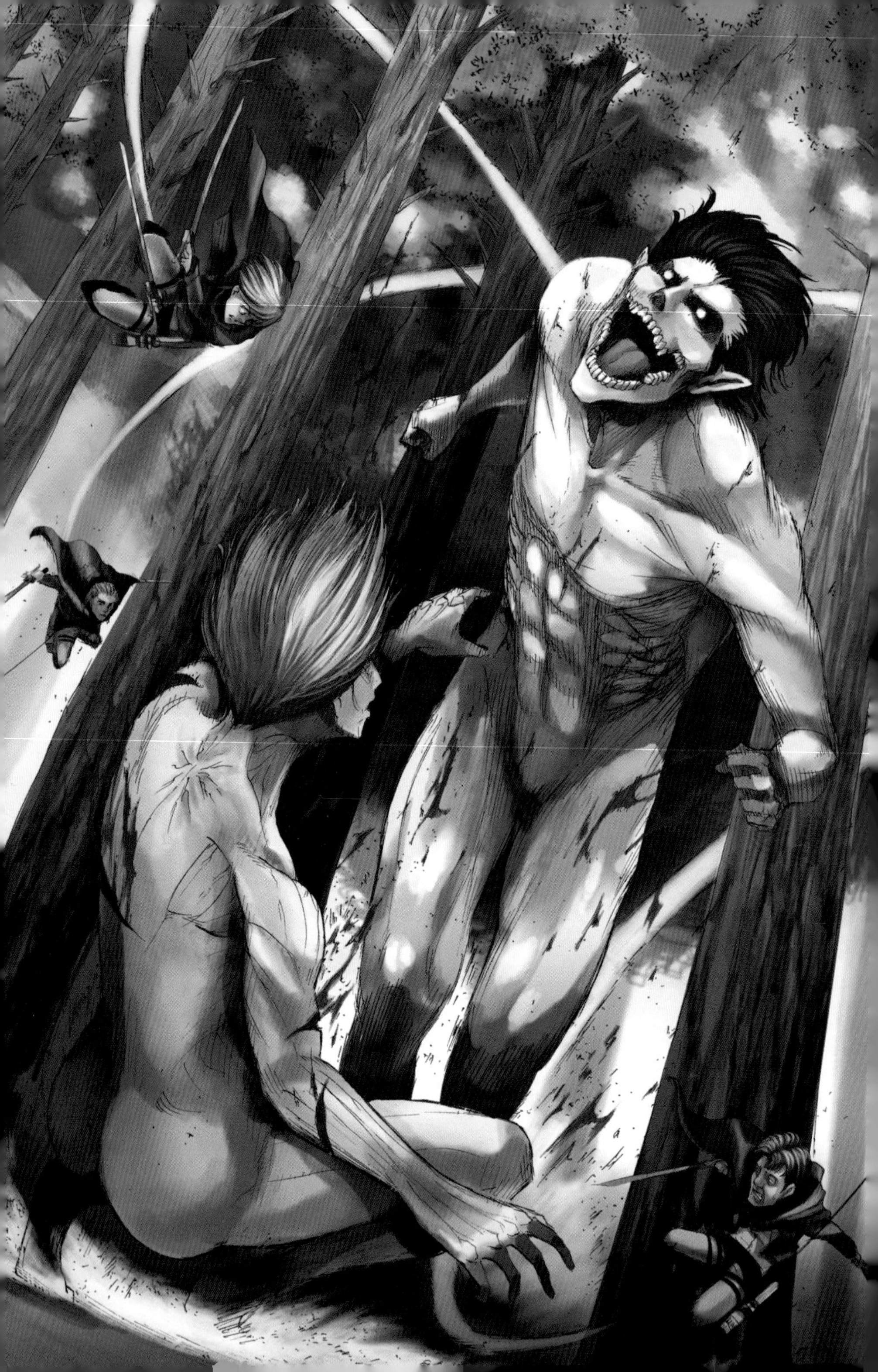

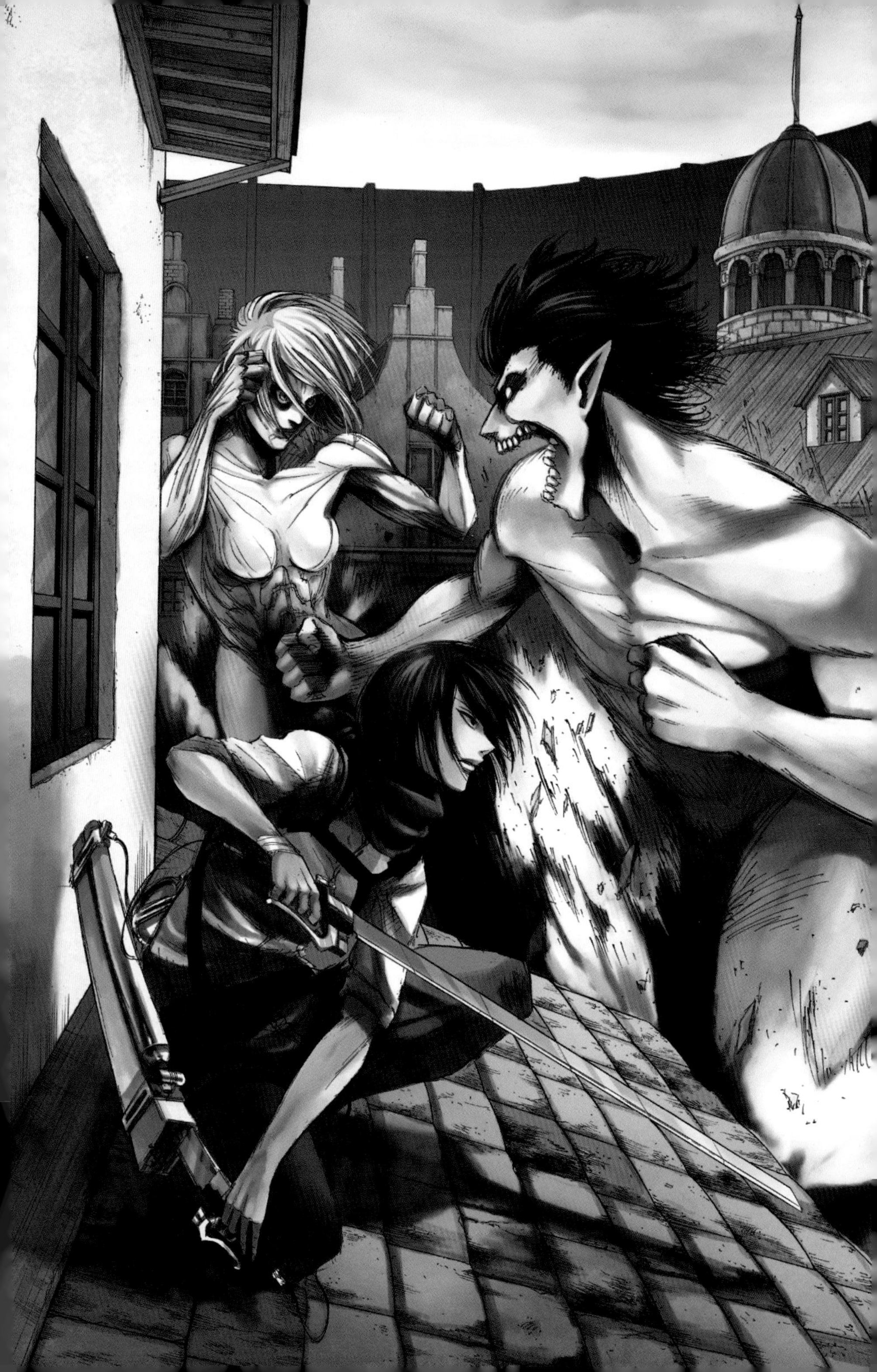

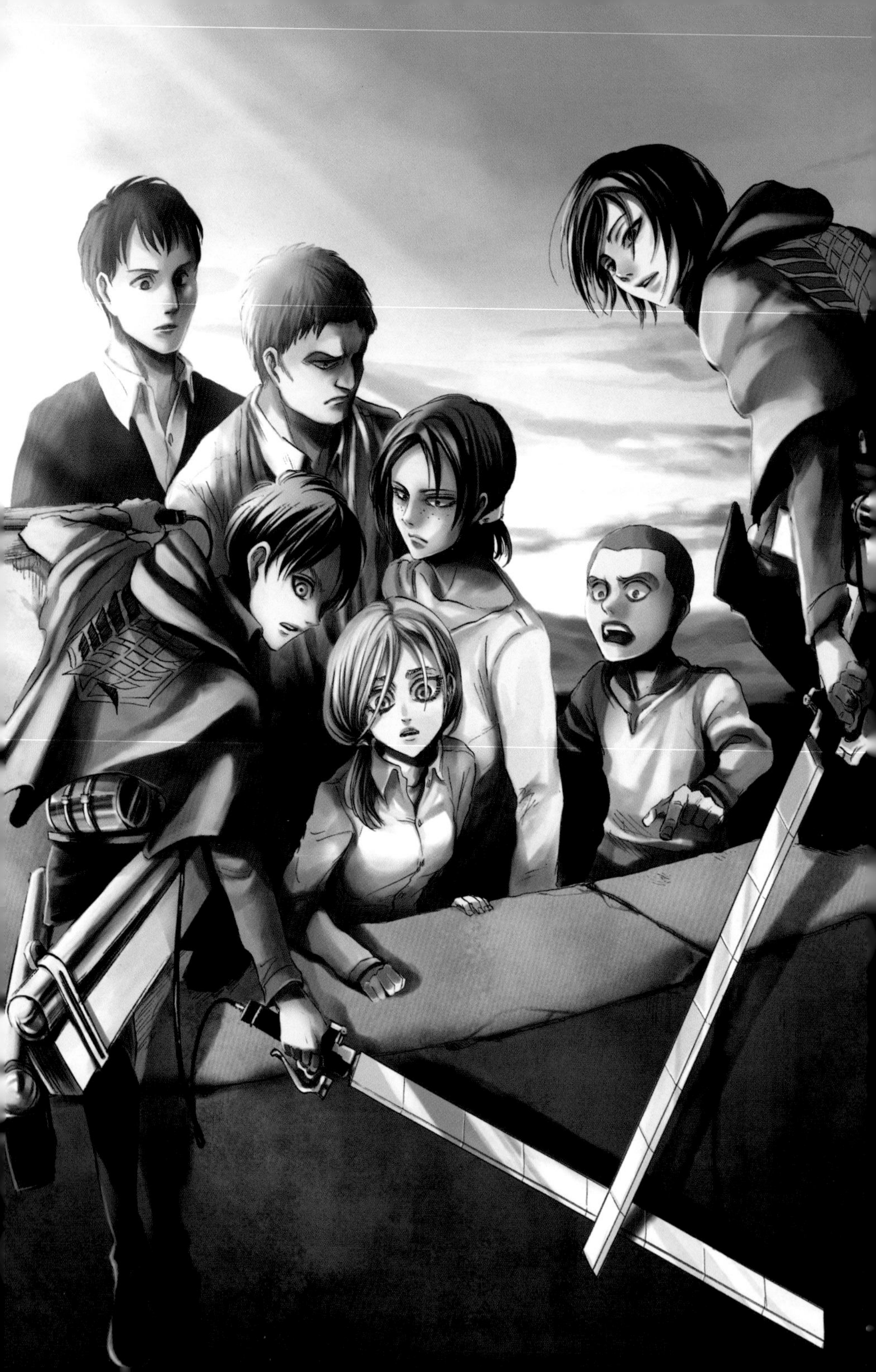

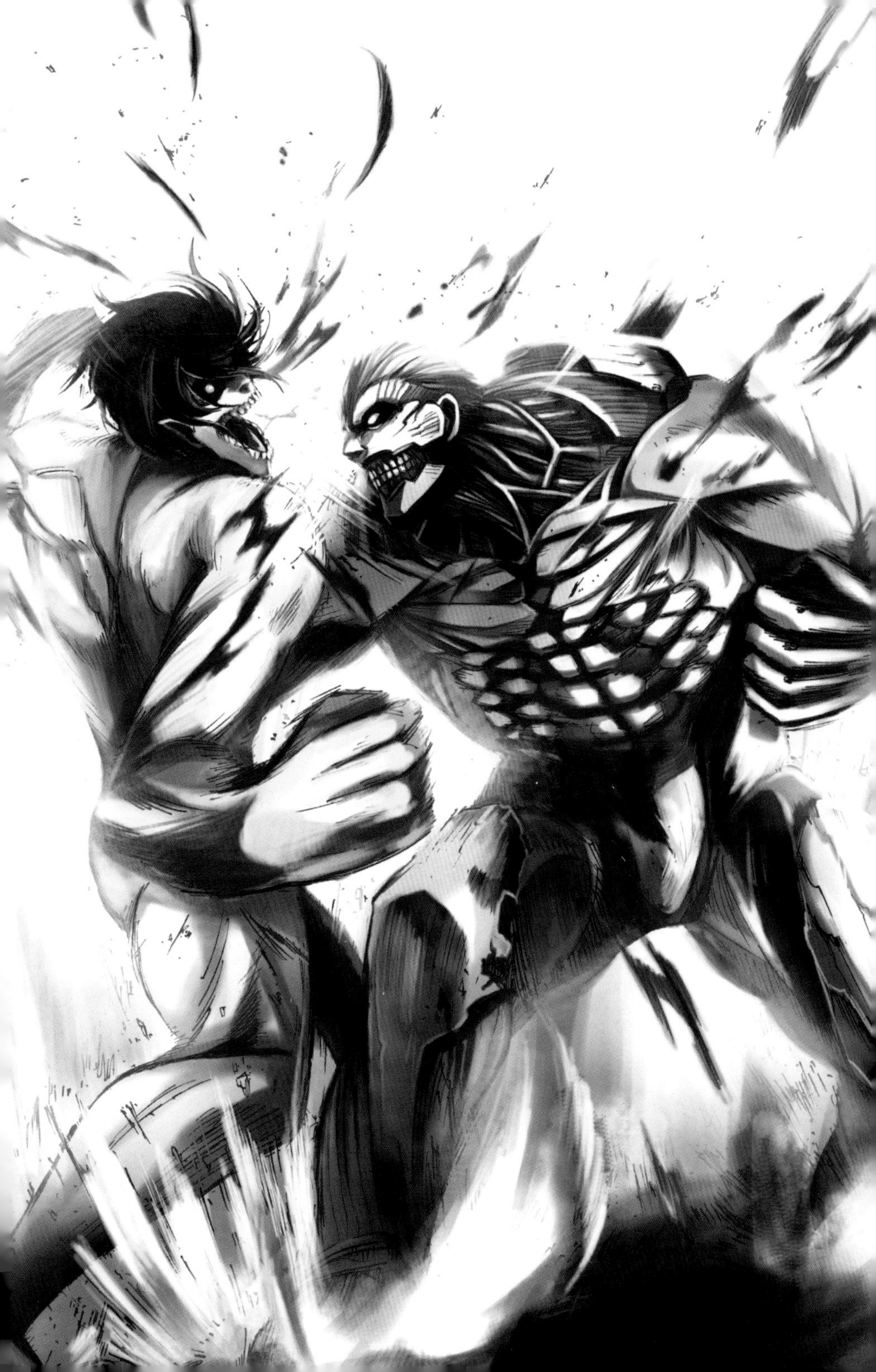

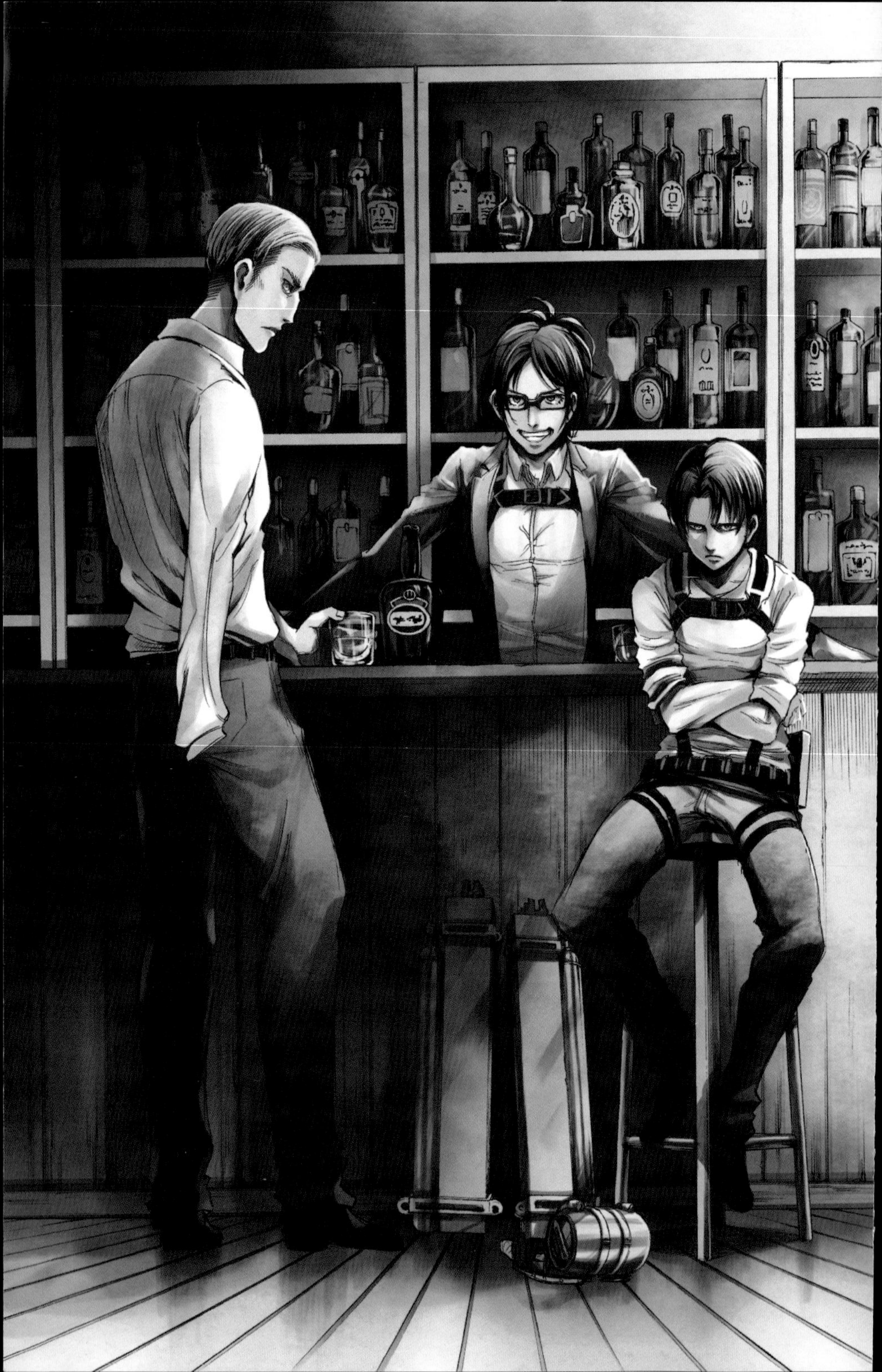

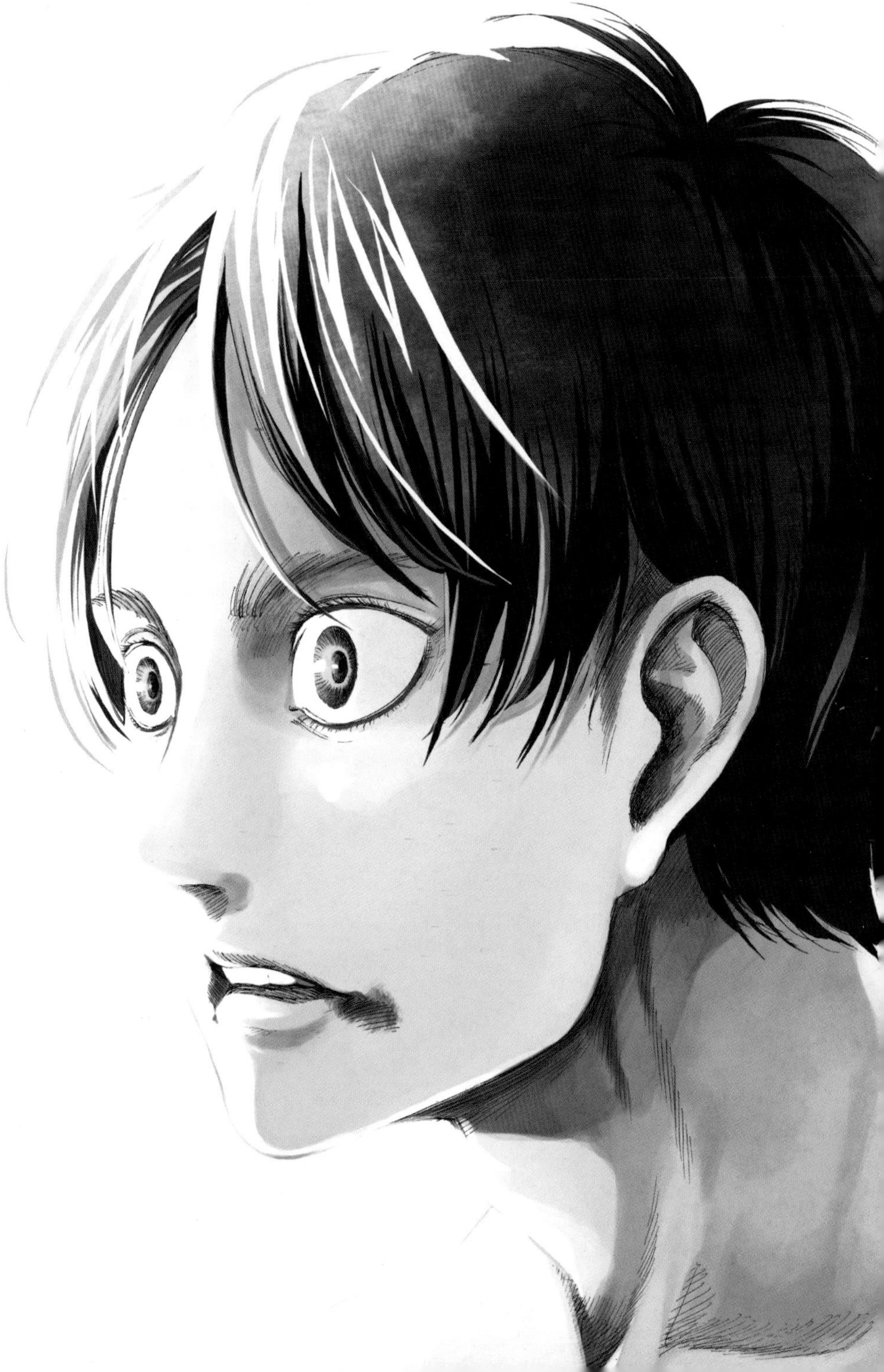

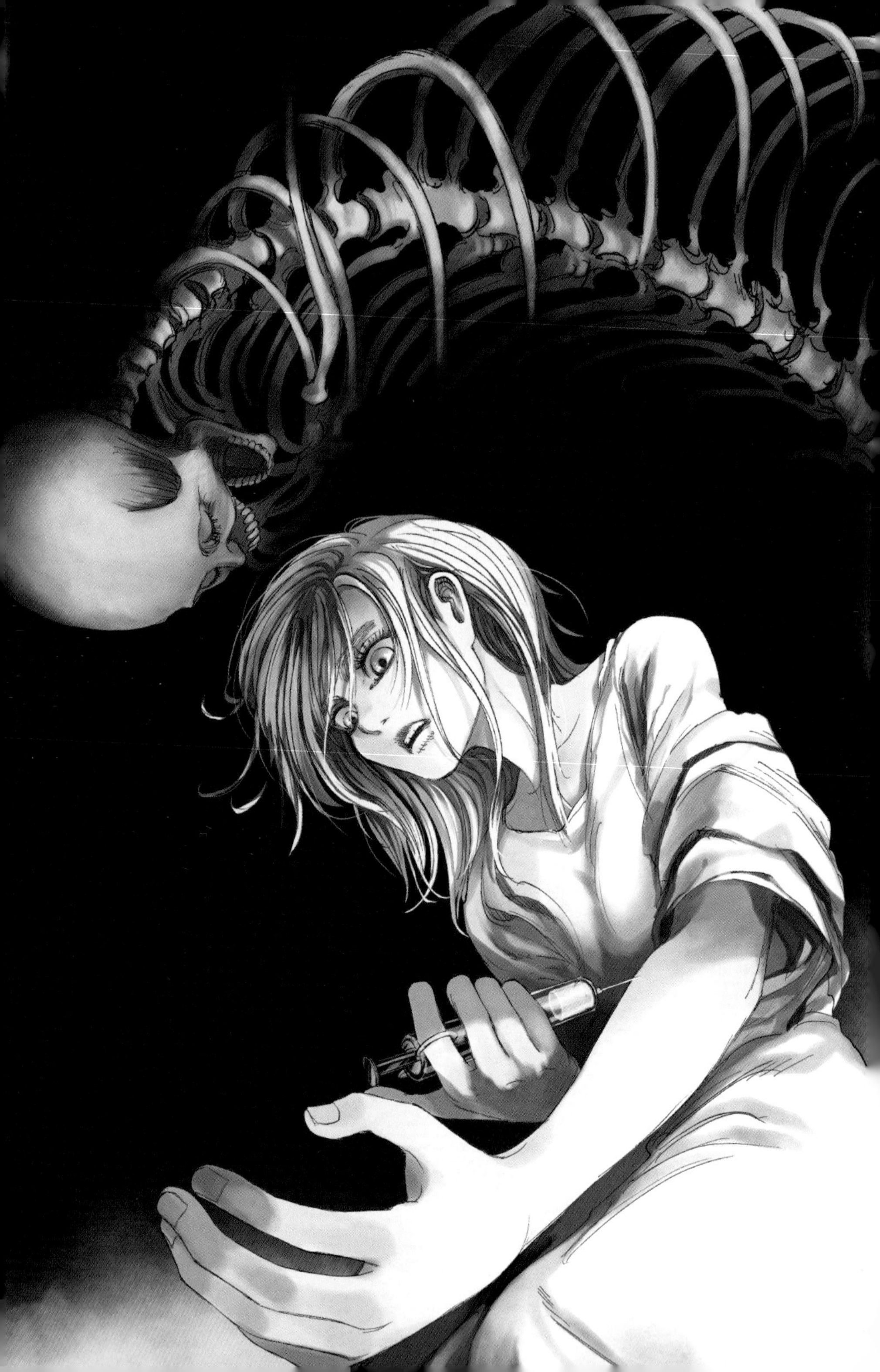

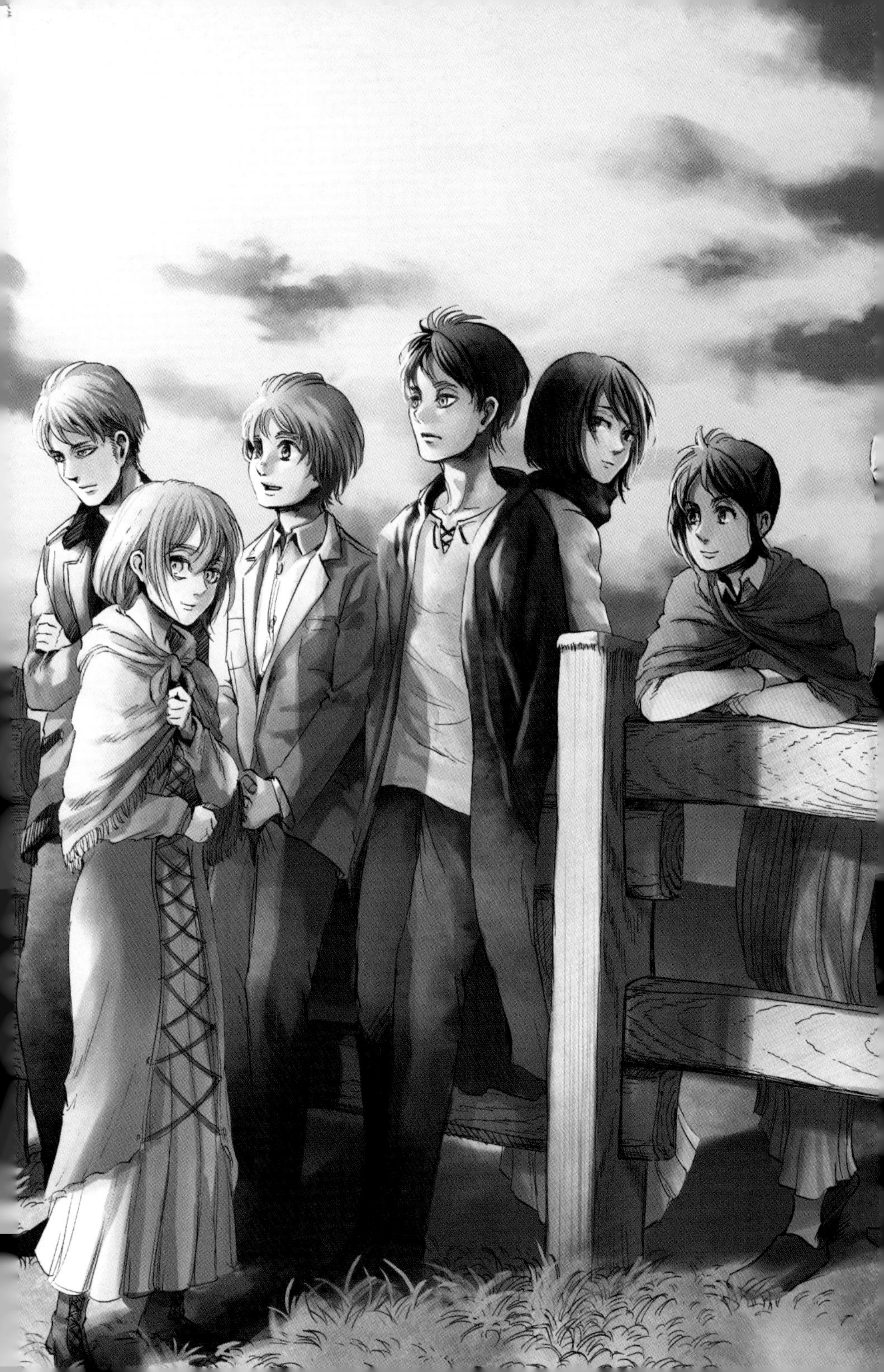

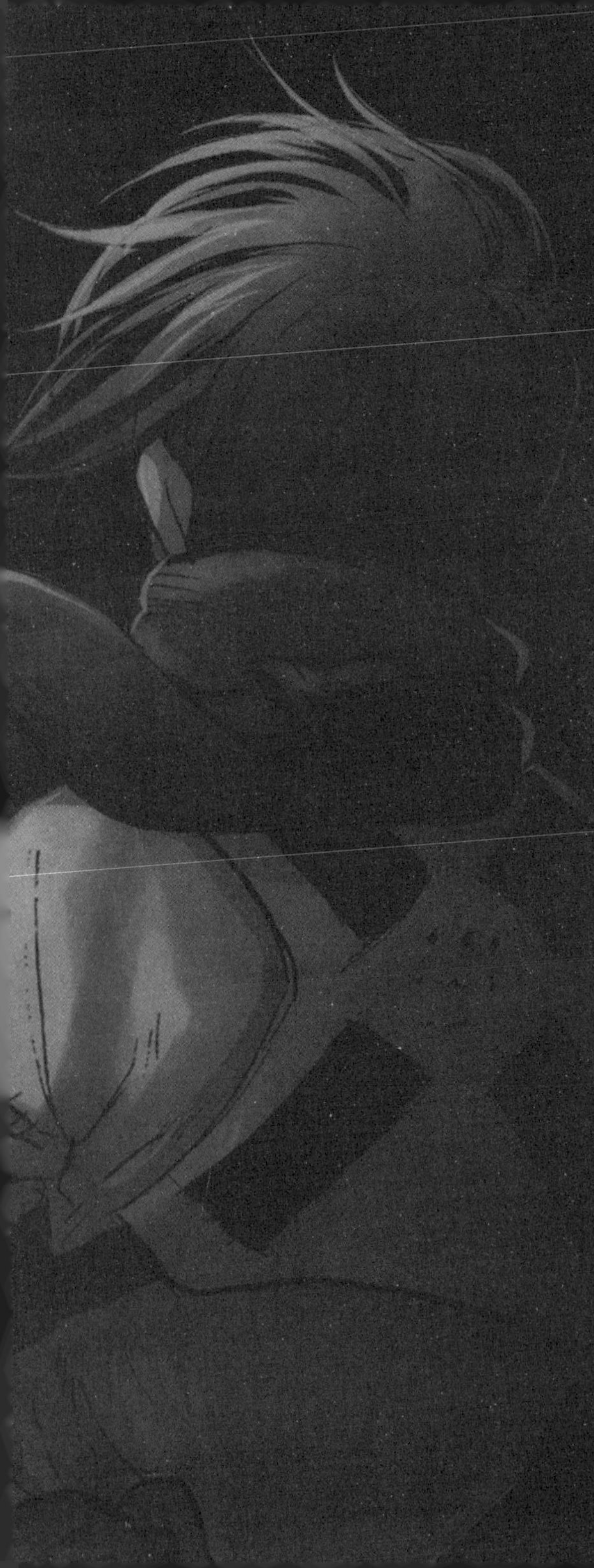

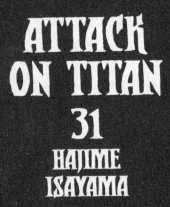

ATTACK ON TITAN

31

HAJIME ISAYAMA

THE CHARACTERS OF ATTACK ON TITAN

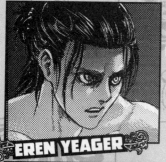

EREN YEAGER

FROM THE 104TH TRAINING CORPS; NOW IN THE SURVEY CORPS. HOLDS THE POWER OF THE ATTACK TITAN AND THE FOUNDING TITAN. BOLDLY INFILTRATED MARLEY ON HIS OWN.

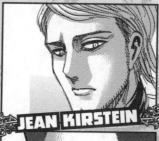

JEAN KIRSTEIN

FROM THE 104TH TRAINING CORPS; NOW IN THE SURVEY CORPS. ONCE KNOWN FOR HIS SARCASTIC PERSONALITY, HE HAS NOW GROWN INTO A LEADER FIGURE.

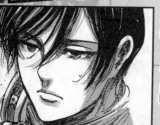

MIKASA ACKERMAN

FROM THE 104TH TRAINING CORPS; NOW IN THE SURVEY CORPS. SHE HAS SHOWN INCREDIBLE COMBAT ABILITIES EVER SINCE SHE WAS A RECRUIT. SHE SEES PROTECTING EREN AS HER MISSION.

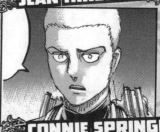

CONNIE SPRINGER

FROM THE 104TH TRAINING CORPS; NOW IN THE SURVEY CORPS. HE IS CHEERFUL IN PERSONALITY, BUT FINDS HIMSELF LOSING EVERYONE IMPORTANT TO HIM... ORIGINALLY FROM RAGAKO VILLAGE.

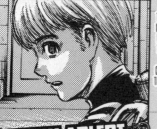

ARMIN ARLERT

FROM THE 104TH TRAINING CORPS; NOW IN THE SURVEY CORPS. HOLDS THE POWER OF THE COLOSSUS TITAN. HE HAS SAVED HIS COMRADES COUNTLESS TIMES WITH HIS SHARP INTELLECT AND BRAVERY.

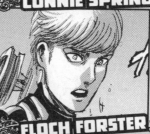

FLOCH FORSTER

A MEMBER OF THE SURVEY CORPS. A SURVIVOR OF THE DECISIVE BATTLE FOR SHIGANSHINA DISTRICT, WHICH CLAIMED MANY LIVES, INCLUDING ERWIN'S.

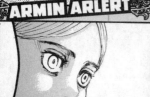

HISTORIA REISS

A DESCENDANT OF THE REISS FAMILY, THE TRUE ROYAL BLOODLINE, HISTORIA HAS NOW ASCENDED TO THE THRONE AS QUEEN. SHE ONCE BELONGED TO THE SURVEY CORPS UNDER THE NAME KRISTA LENZ.

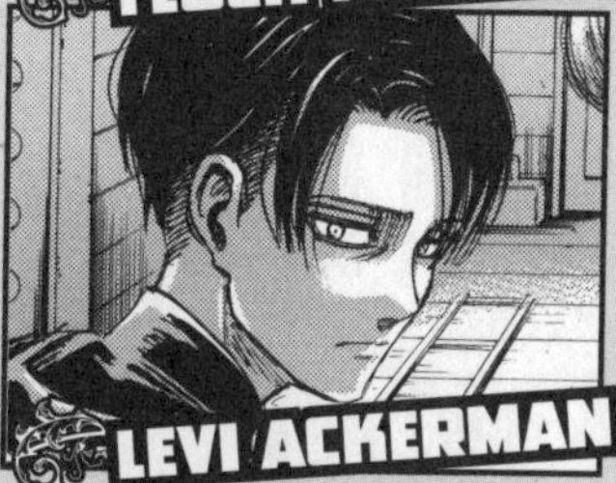

LEVI ACKERMAN

CAPTAIN OF THE SURVEY CORPS. KNOWN AS "HUMANITY'S STRONGEST SOLDIER." HE FIGHTS THROUGH HIS STRUGGLES IN ORDER TO CARRY ON HIS GOOD FRIEND ERWIN'S DYING WISHES.

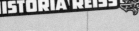

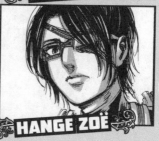

HANGE ZOË

COMMANDER OF THE SURVEY CORPS. DESPITE THE STRANGE WAY HANGE MAY ACT, THEIR KEEN POWERS OF OBSERVATION LED ERWIN TO NAME HANGE HIS SUCCESSOR.

THE NATION OF ELDIA [THE ISLAND OF PARADIS]

THE ELDIAN WARRIORS OF THE MARLEYAN ARMY

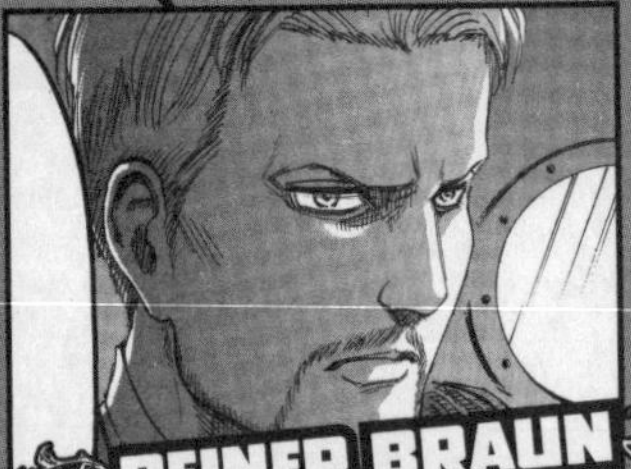

REINER BRAUN

HOLDS THE ARMORED TITAN WITHIN HIM. SINCE HE WAS THE ONLY ONE TO MAKE IT BACK FROM THE MISSION ON PARADIS, HE SUFFERS FROM A GUILTY CONSCIENCE.

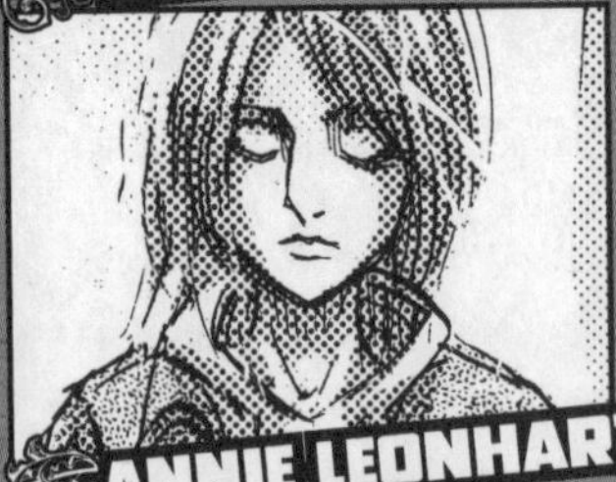

ANNIE LEONHART

HOLDS THE FEMALE TITAN WITHIN HER. A MEMBER OF THE 104TH. SHE HAS BEEN SLEEPING WITHIN A HARDENED CRYSTAL EVER SINCE HER TRUE IDENTITY WAS DISCOVERED.

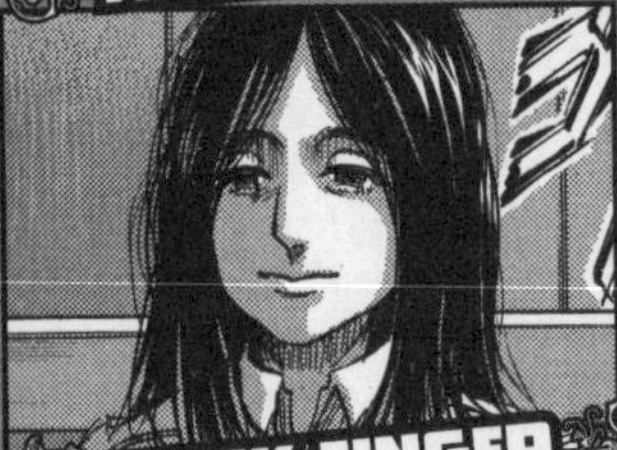

PIECK FINGER

HOLDS THE CART TITAN WITHIN HER, CARRYING THE PANZER UNIT ON THE BACK OF THE "CARTMAN" TO FIGHT. HIGHLY PERCEPTIVE.

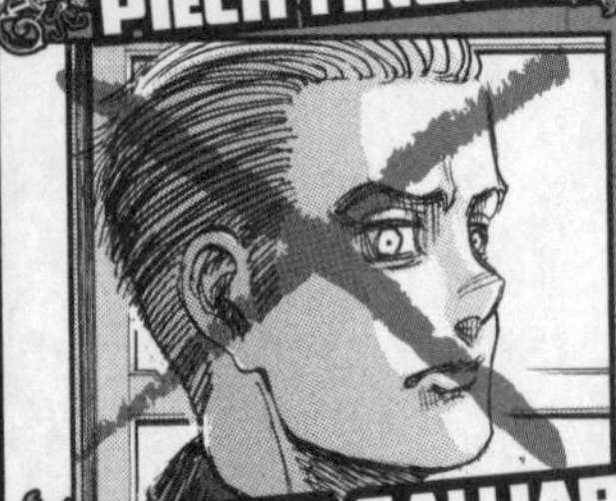

PORCO GALLIARD

HOLDS THE JAW TITAN WITHIN HIM. THERE IS STRIFE BETWEEN HIM AND REINER OVER BOTH THE INHERITANCE OF THE ARMORED TITAN AND THE DEATH OF HIS OLDER BROTHER, MARCEL.

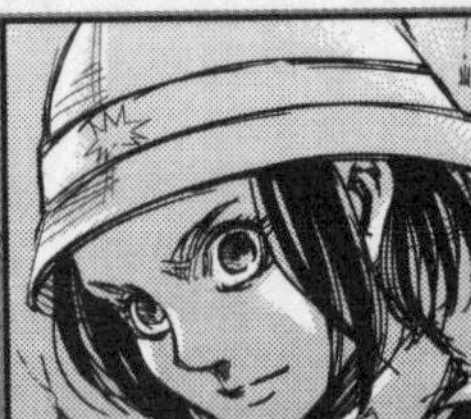

GABI BRAUN

BOLD DESPITE HER SMALL SIZE, GABI IS A DYNAMIC WARRIOR CANDIDATE. HER GOAL IS TO EVENTUALLY INHERIT THE ARMORED TITAN. REINER'S COUSIN.

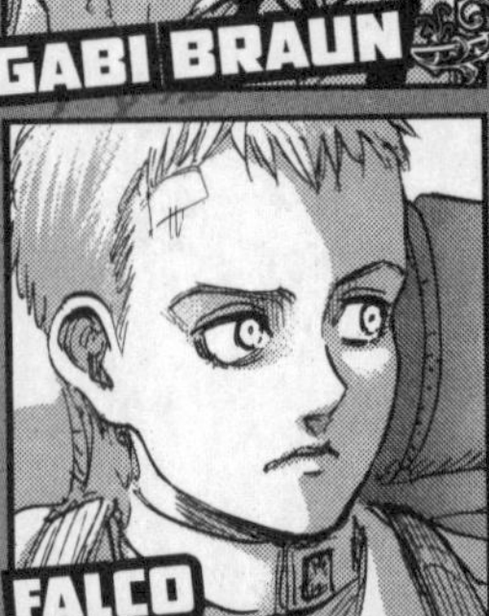

FALCO GRICE

A WARRIOR CANDIDATE. HE HAS AFFECTION FOR GABI AND WANTS TO PROTECT HER. DURING EREN'S TIME INFILTRATING MARLEY, FALCO COMES IN CONTACT WITH EREN WITHOUT REALIZING HIS TRUE IDENTITY.

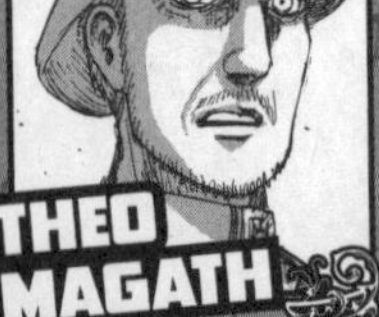

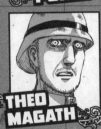

THEO MAGATH

LEADER OF THE WARRIOR UNIT. A MARLEYAN WHO LEADS A UNIT OF ELDIANS.

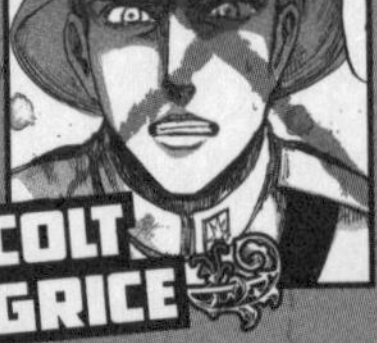

COLT GRICE

FALCO'S OLDER BROTHER. THE OLDEST OF THE WARRIOR CANDIDATES, AND, IN EFFECT, THEIR LEADER.

THE ANTI-MARLEYAN VOLUNTEERS

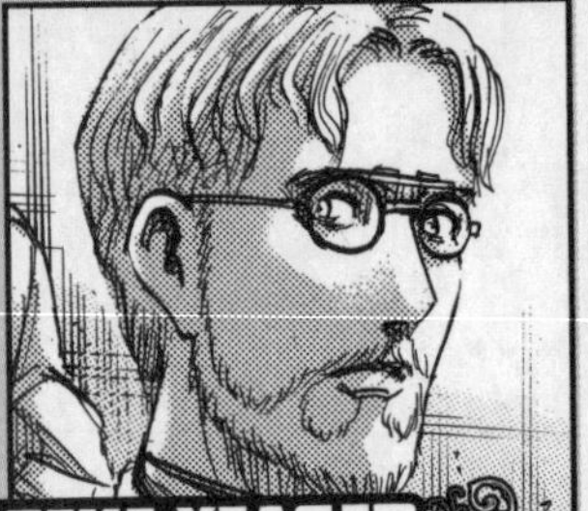

ZEKE YEAGER

HOLDS THE POWER OF THE BEAST TITAN. A LEADER OF THE WARRIORS, HE WAS ONCE KNOWN AS THE "WONDER CHILD." HIS MOTHER IS A DESCENDANT OF THE ROYAL BLOODLINE. HE IS ALSO EREN'S HALF-BROTHER.

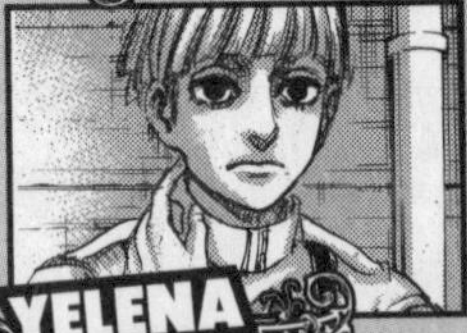

YELENA

YELENA COMMANDS THE VOLUNTEERS AND FOLLOWS ZEKE. SHE DRESSED AS A MAN DURING THE EXPEDITION TO MARLEY IN ORDER TO WORK IN SECRET.

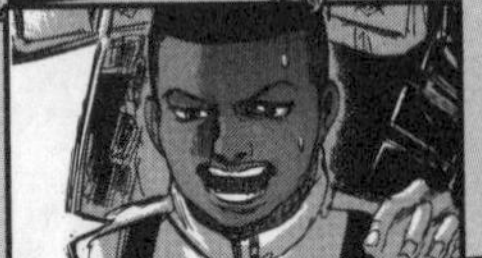

ONYANKOPON

AFTER TRAVELING TO PARADIS WITH YELENA, HE TELLS ITS INHABITANTS OF MARLEY'S ADVANCED CULTURE.

ATTACK on TITAN

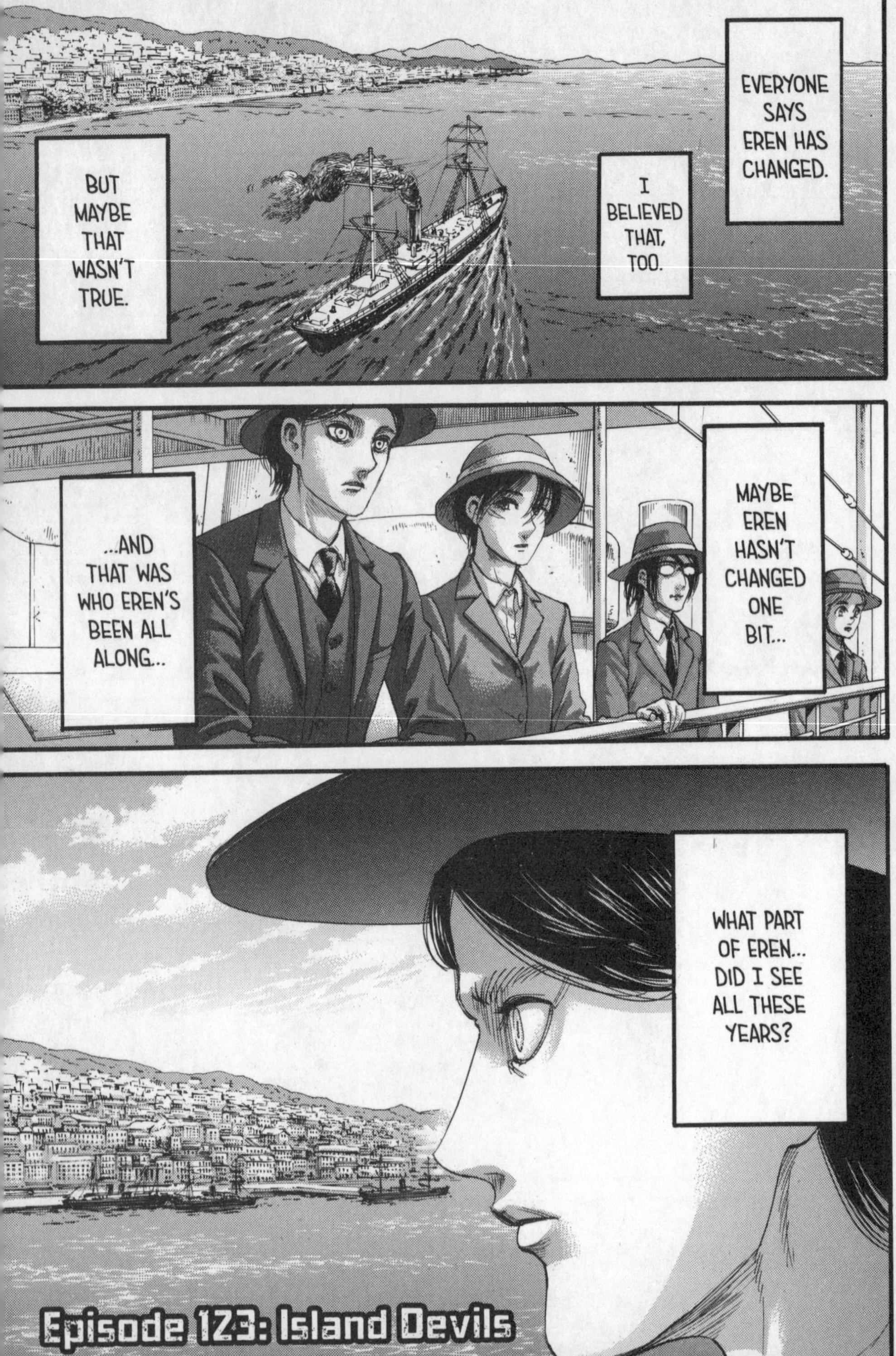
EVERYONE SAYS EREN HAS CHANGED.
I BELIEVED THAT, TOO.
BUT MAYBE THAT WASN'T TRUE.
MAYBE EREN HASN'T CHANGED ONE BIT...
...AND THAT WAS WHO EREN'S BEEN ALL ALONG...
WHAT PART OF EREN... DID I SEE ALL THESE YEARS?

Episode 123: Island Devils

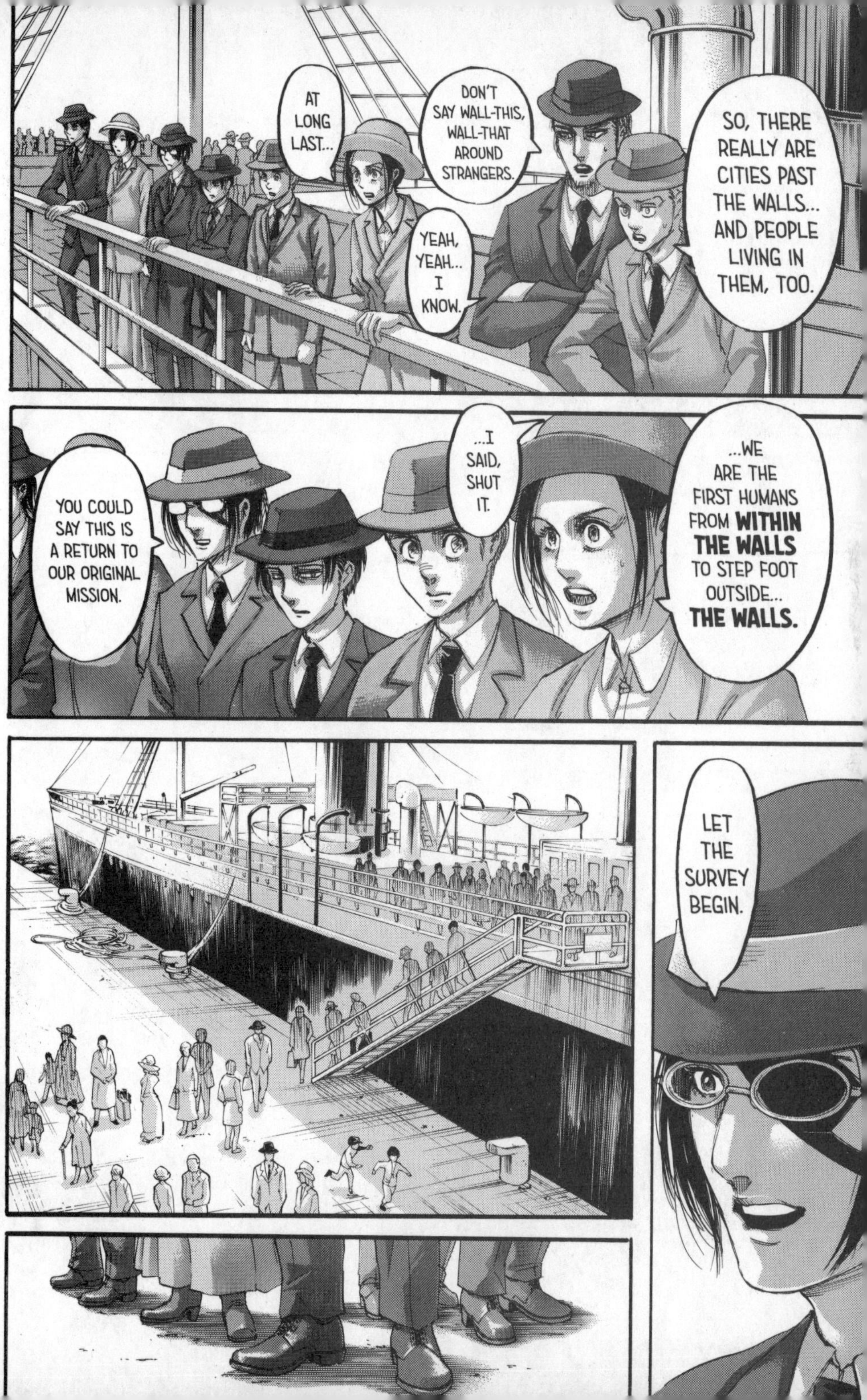
SO, THERE REALLY ARE CITIES PAST THE WALLS... AND PEOPLE LIVING IN THEM, TOO.
DON'T SAY WALL-THIS, WALL-THAT AROUND STRANGERS.
YEAH, YEAH... I KNOW.
AT LONG LAST...
...WE ARE THE FIRST HUMANS FROM **WITHIN THE WALLS** TO STEP FOOT OUTSIDE... **THE WALLS.**
...I SAID, SHUT IT.
YOU COULD SAY THIS IS A RETURN TO OUR ORIGINAL MISSION.
LET THE SURVEY BEGIN.

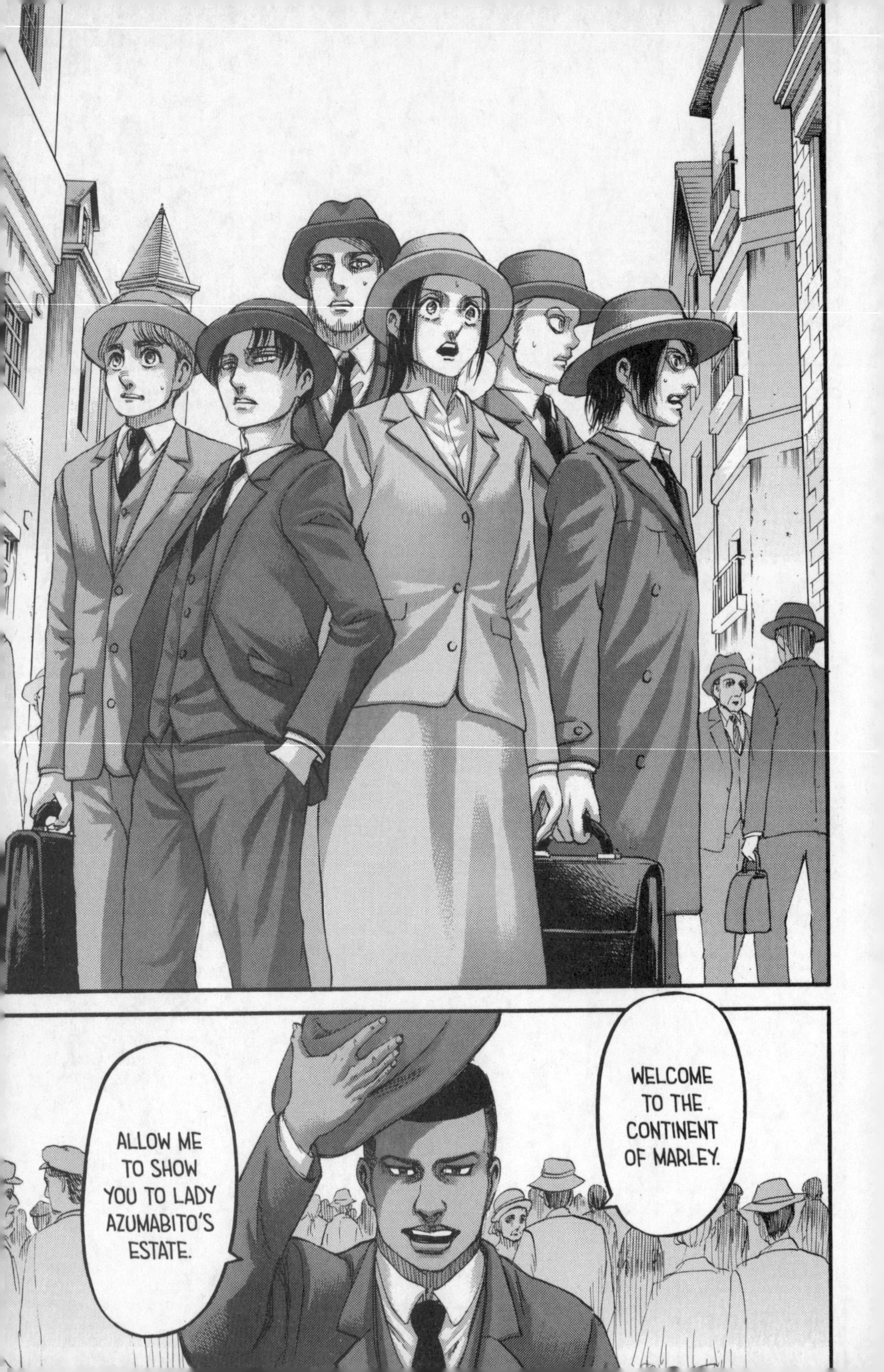
WELCOME TO THE CONTINENT OF MARLEY.
ALLOW ME TO SHOW YOU TO LADY AZUMABITO'S ESTATE.

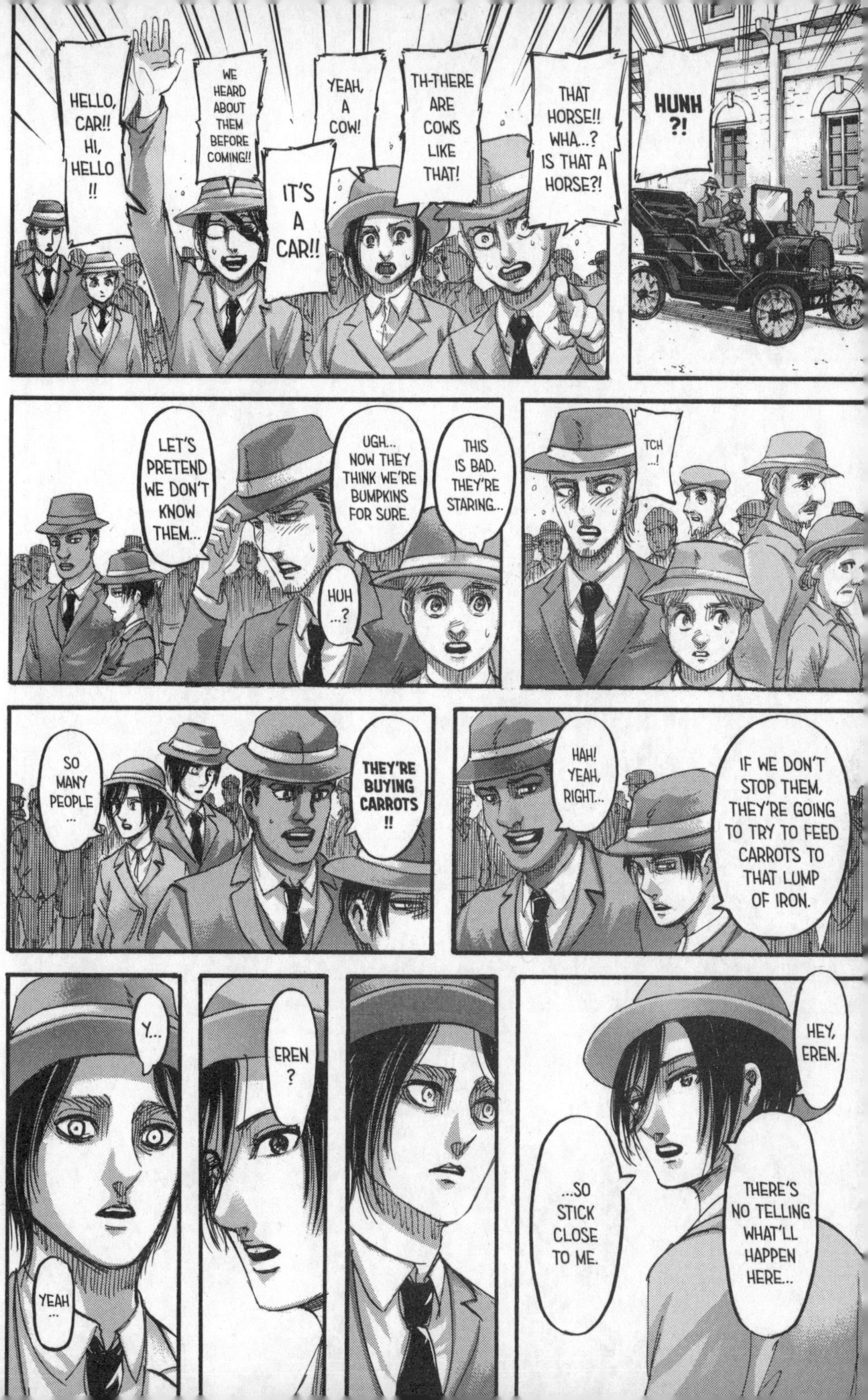
HUNH ?!
THAT HORSE!! WHA...? IS THAT A HORSE?!
TH-THERE ARE COWS LIKE THAT!
YEAH, A COW!
IT'S A CAR!!
WE HEARD ABOUT THEM BEFORE COMING!!
HELLO, CAR!! HI, HELLO !!
TCH ...!
THIS IS BAD. THEY'RE STARING...
UGH... NOW THEY THINK WE'RE BUMPKINS FOR SURE.
HUH ...?
LET'S PRETEND WE DON'T KNOW THEM...
IF WE DON'T STOP THEM, THEY'RE GOING TO TRY TO FEED CARROTS TO THAT LUMP OF IRON.
HAH! YEAH, RIGHT...
THEY'RE BUYING CARROTS !!
SO MANY PEOPLE ...
HEY, EREN.
THERE'S NO TELLING WHAT'LL HAPPEN HERE...
...SO STICK CLOSE TO ME.
EREN ?
Y...
YEAH ...

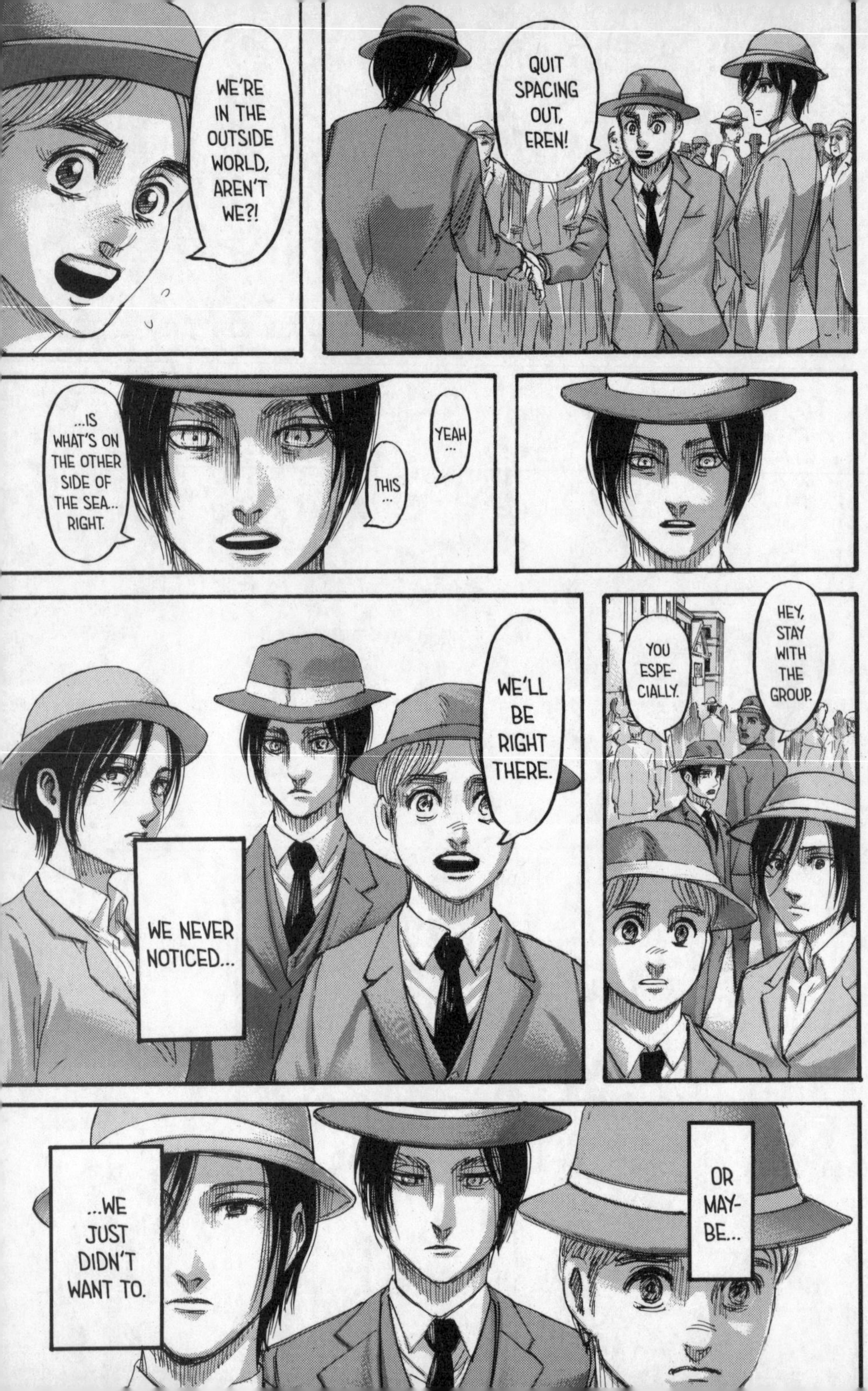
QUIT SPACING OUT, EREN!
WE'RE IN THE OUTSIDE WORLD, AREN'T WE?!
YEAH...
THIS...
...IS WHAT'S ON THE OTHER SIDE OF THE SEA... RIGHT.
HEY, STAY WITH THE GROUP.
YOU ESPECIALLY.
WE'LL BE RIGHT THERE.
WE NEVER NOTICED...
OR MAYBE...
...WE JUST DIDN'T WANT TO.

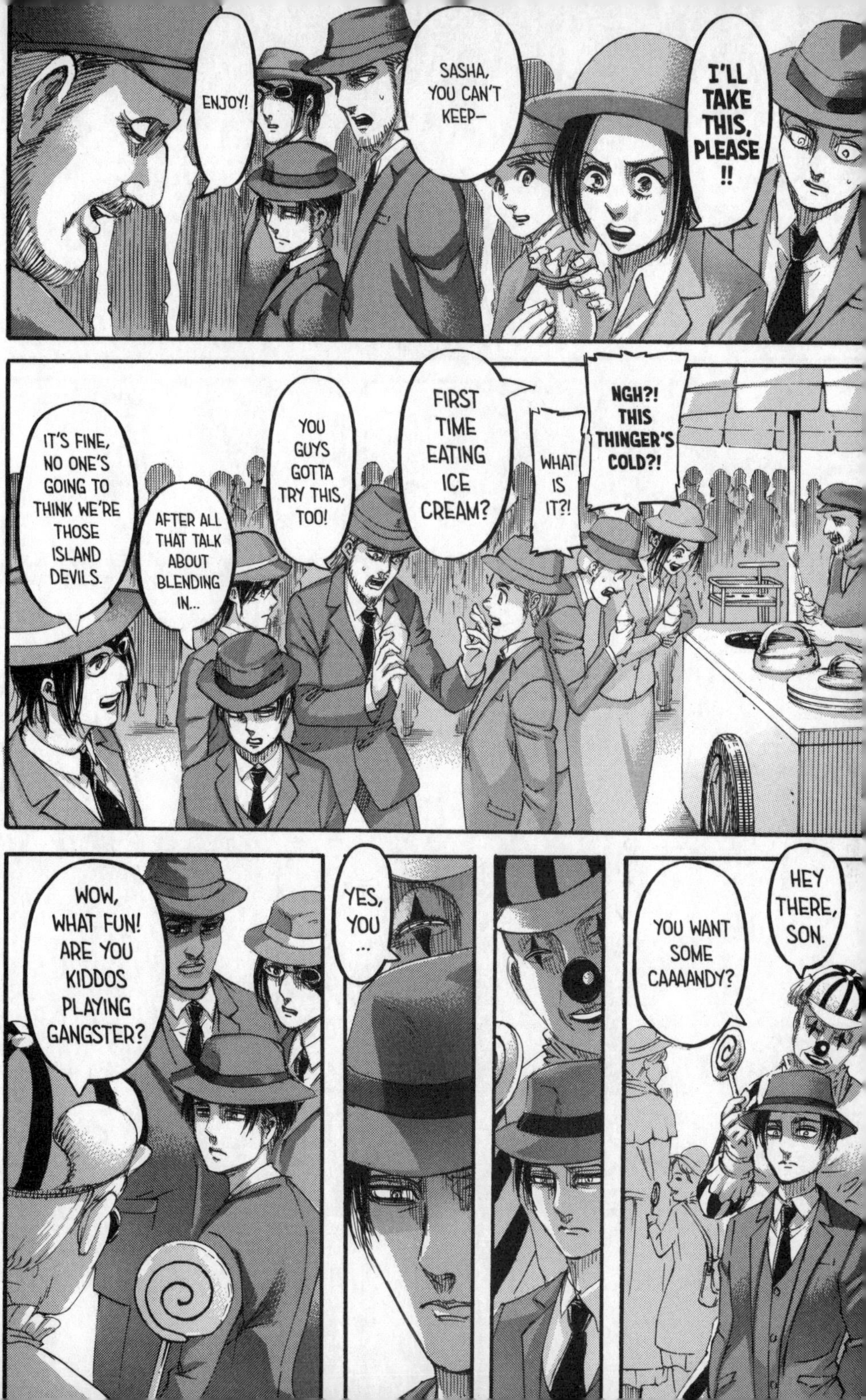
I'LL TAKE THIS, PLEASE!!
SASHA, YOU CAN'T KEEP—
ENJOY!
NGH?! THIS THINGER'S COLD?!
WHAT IS IT?!
FIRST TIME EATING ICE CREAM?
YOU GUYS GOTTA TRY THIS, TOO!
AFTER ALL THAT TALK ABOUT BLENDING IN...
IT'S FINE, NO ONE'S GOING TO THINK WE'RE THOSE ISLAND DEVILS.
HEY THERE, SON.
YOU WANT SOME CAAAANDY?
YES, YOU ...
WOW, WHAT FUN! ARE YOU KIDDOS PLAYING GANGSTER?

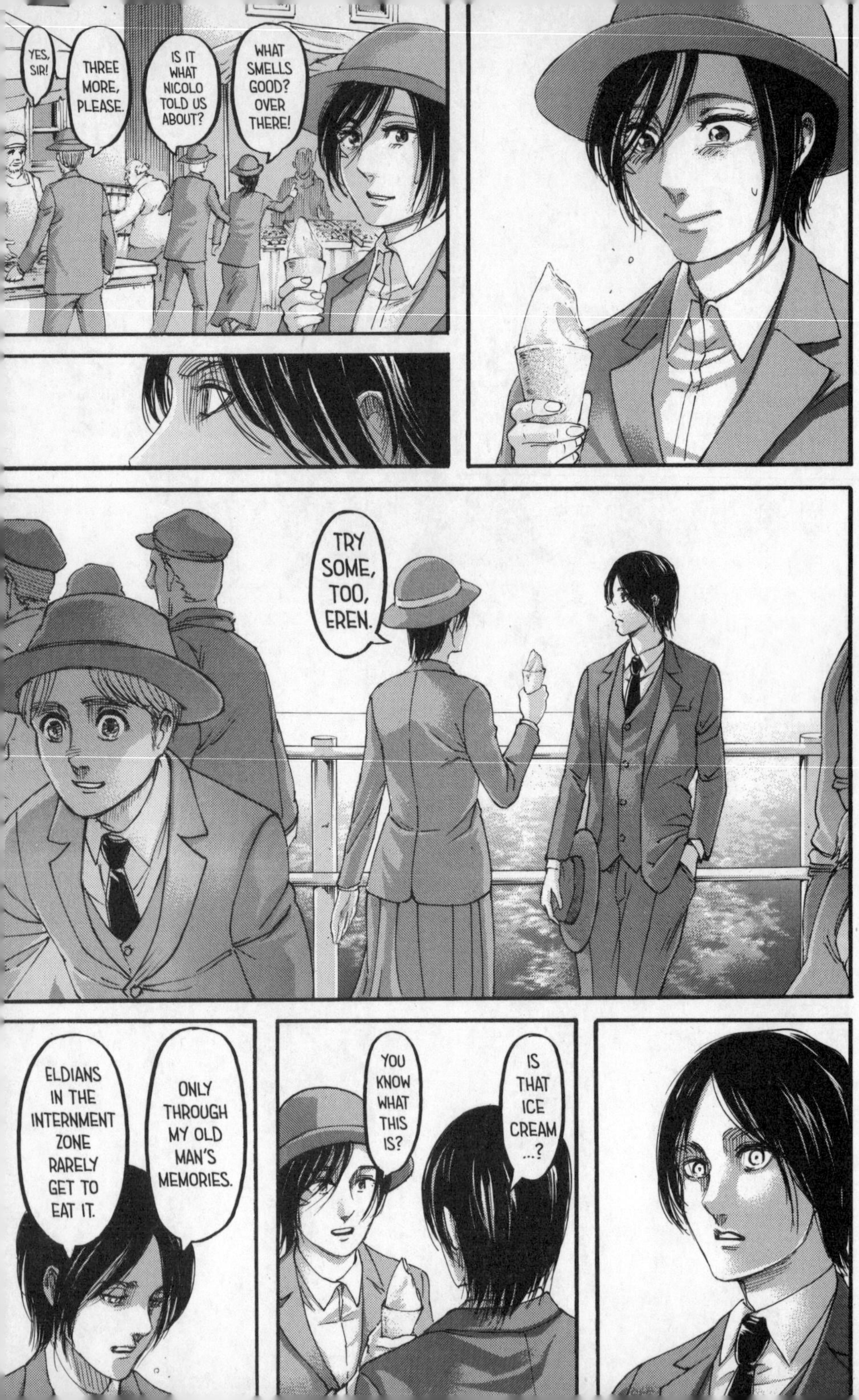
WHAT SMELLS GOOD? OVER THERE!
IS IT WHAT NICOLO TOLD US ABOUT?
THREE MORE, PLEASE.
YES, SIR!
TRY SOME, TOO, EREN.
IS THAT ICE CREAM ...?
YOU KNOW WHAT THIS IS?
ONLY THROUGH MY OLD MAN'S MEMORIES.
ELDIANS IN THE INTERNMENT ZONE RARELY GET TO EAT IT.

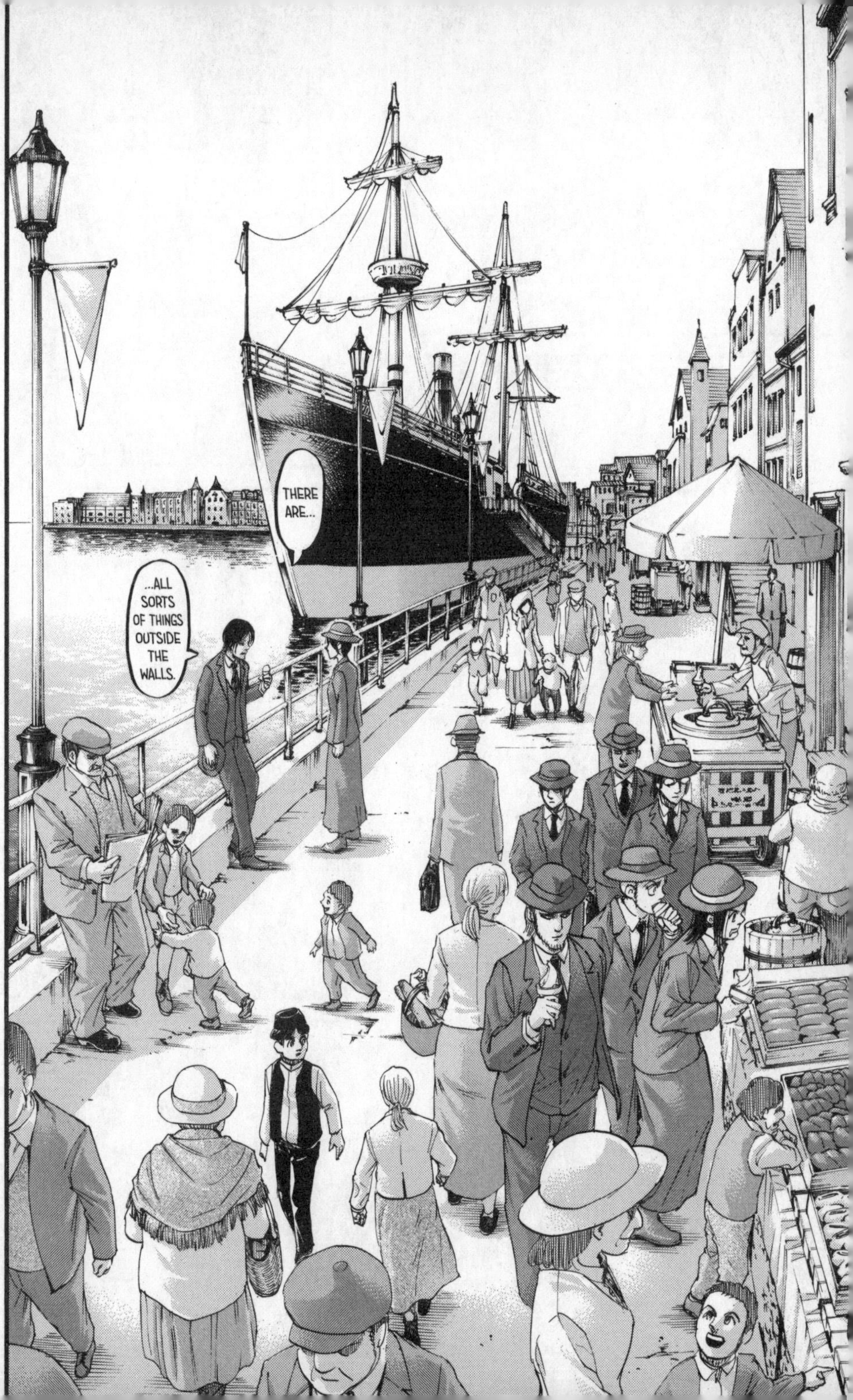
THERE ARE...
...ALL SORTS OF THINGS OUTSIDE THE WALLS.

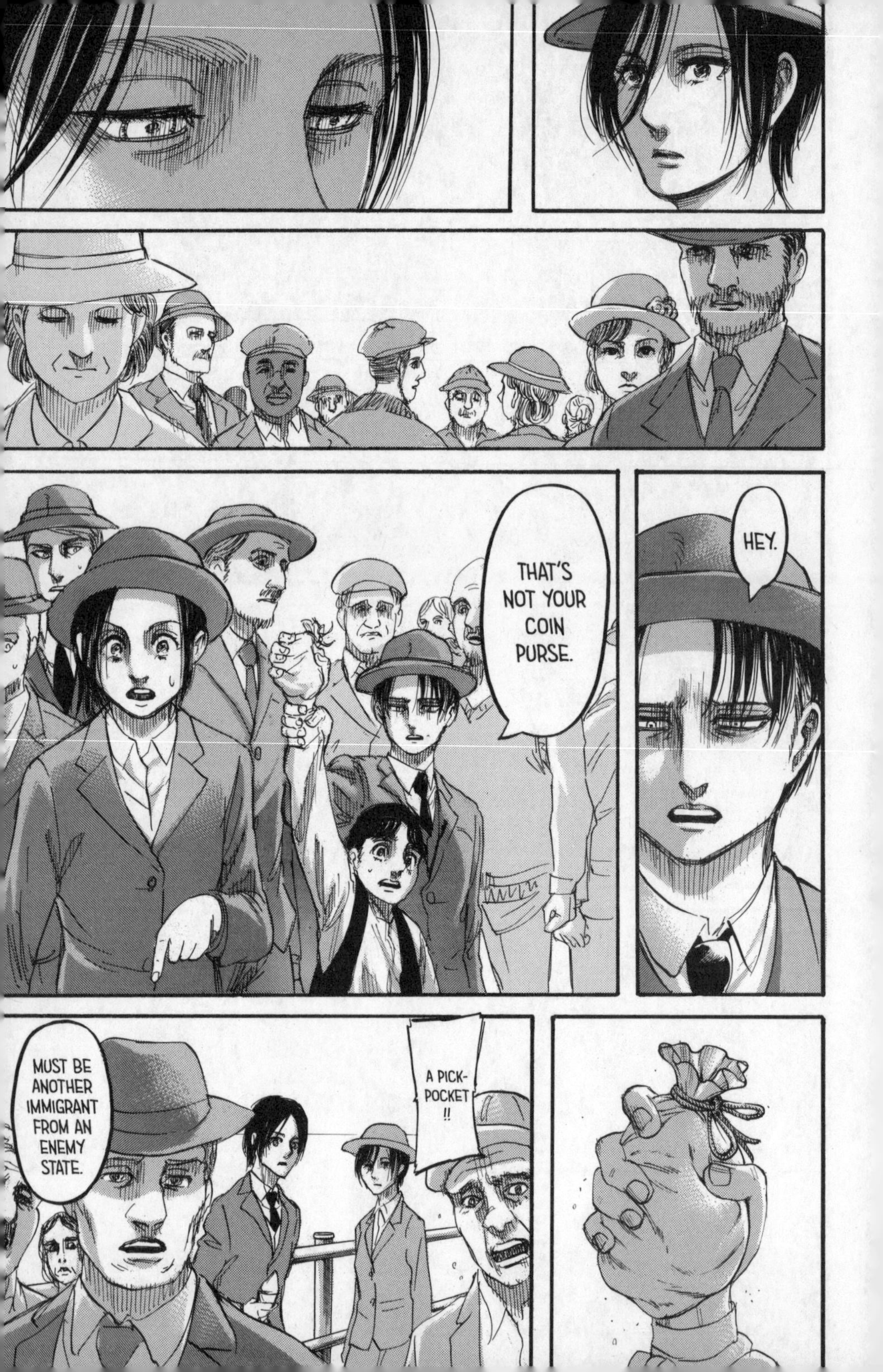
HEY.
THAT'S NOT YOUR COIN PURSE.
A PICK-POCKET !!
MUST BE ANOTHER IMMIGRANT FROM AN ENEMY STATE.

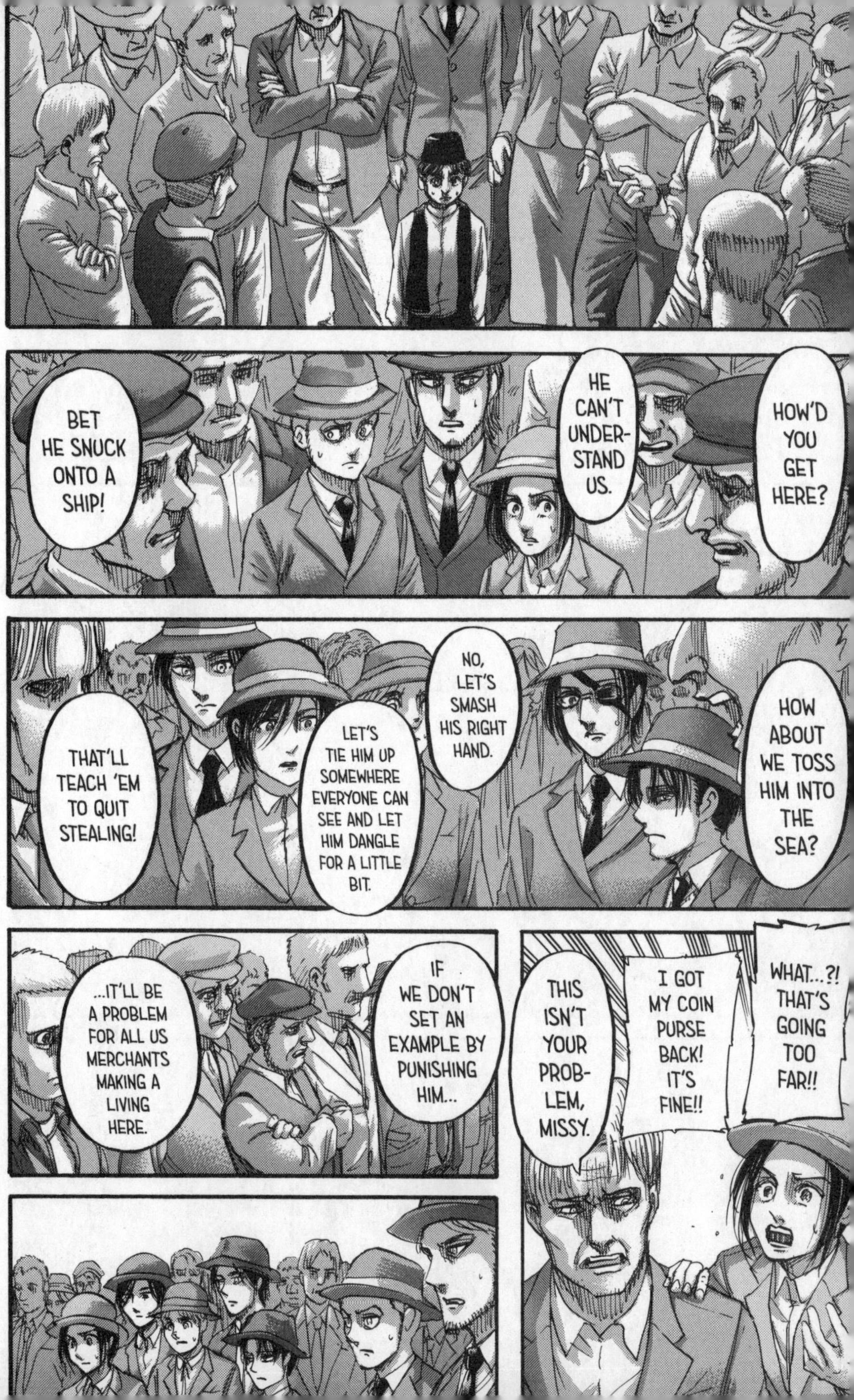
HOW'D YOU GET HERE?
HE CAN'T UNDER-STAND US.
BET HE SNUCK ONTO A SHIP!
HOW ABOUT WE TOSS HIM INTO THE SEA?
NO, LET'S SMASH HIS RIGHT HAND.
LET'S TIE HIM UP SOMEWHERE EVERYONE CAN SEE AND LET HIM DANGLE FOR A LITTLE BIT.
THAT'LL TEACH 'EM TO QUIT STEALING!
WHAT...?! THAT'S GOING TOO FAR!!
I GOT MY COIN PURSE BACK! IT'S FINE!!
THIS ISN'T YOUR PROB-LEM, MISSY.
IF WE DON'T SET AN EXAMPLE BY PUNISHING HIM...
...IT'LL BE A PROBLEM FOR ALL US MERCHANTS MAKING A LIVING HERE.

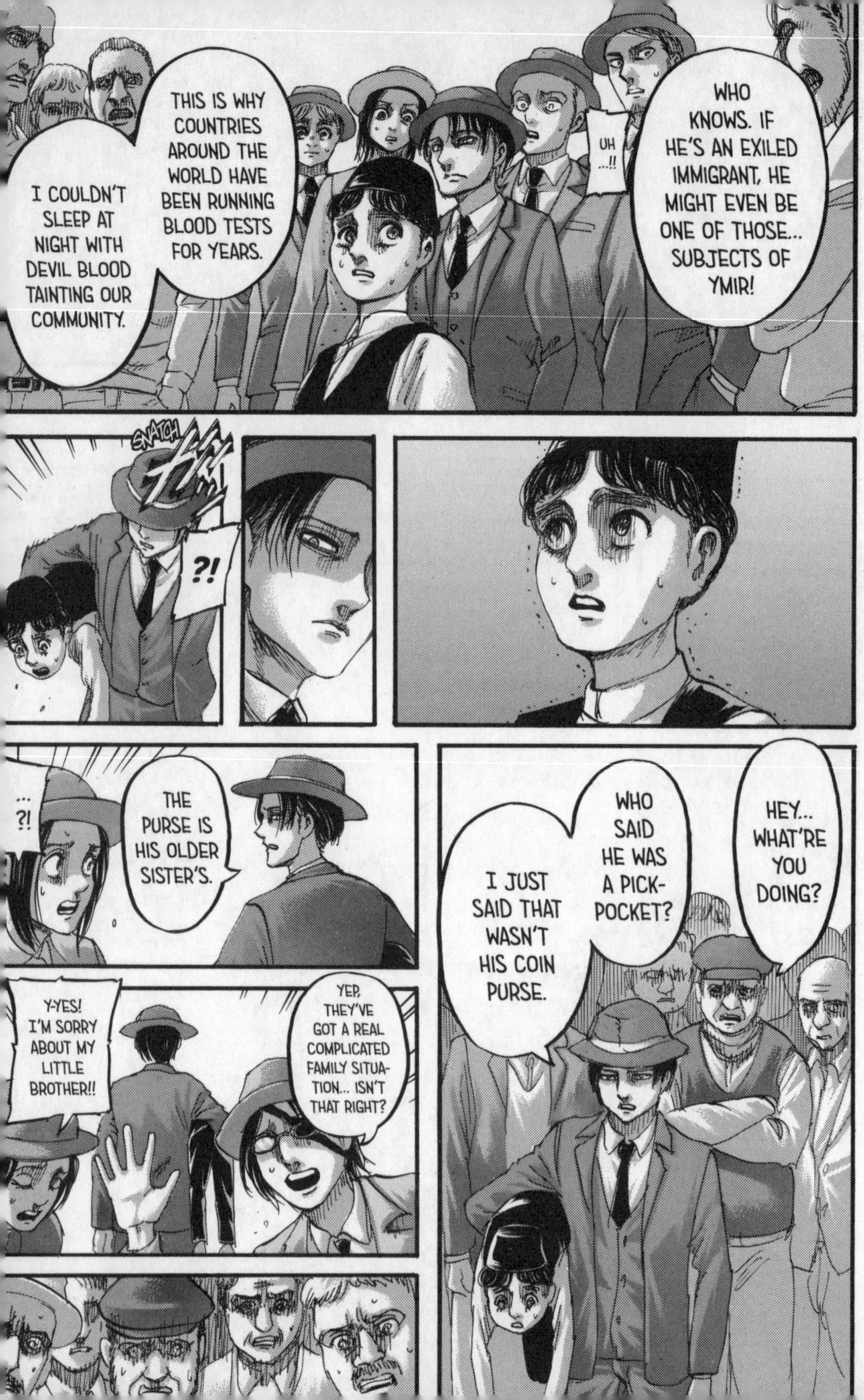
WHO KNOWS. IF HE'S AN EXILED IMMIGRANT, HE MIGHT EVEN BE ONE OF THOSE... SUBJECTS OF YMIR!
UH ...!!
THIS IS WHY COUNTRIES AROUND THE WORLD HAVE BEEN RUNNING BLOOD TESTS FOR YEARS.
I COULDN'T SLEEP AT NIGHT WITH DEVIL BLOOD TAINTING OUR COMMUNITY.
?!
SNATCH
HEY... WHAT'RE YOU DOING?
WHO SAID HE WAS A PICK-POCKET?
I JUST SAID THAT WASN'T HIS COIN PURSE.
THE PURSE IS HIS OLDER SISTER'S.
...?!
YEP, THEY'VE GOT A REAL COMPLICATED FAMILY SITUATION... ISN'T THAT RIGHT?
Y-YES! I'M SORRY ABOUT MY LITTLE BROTHER!!

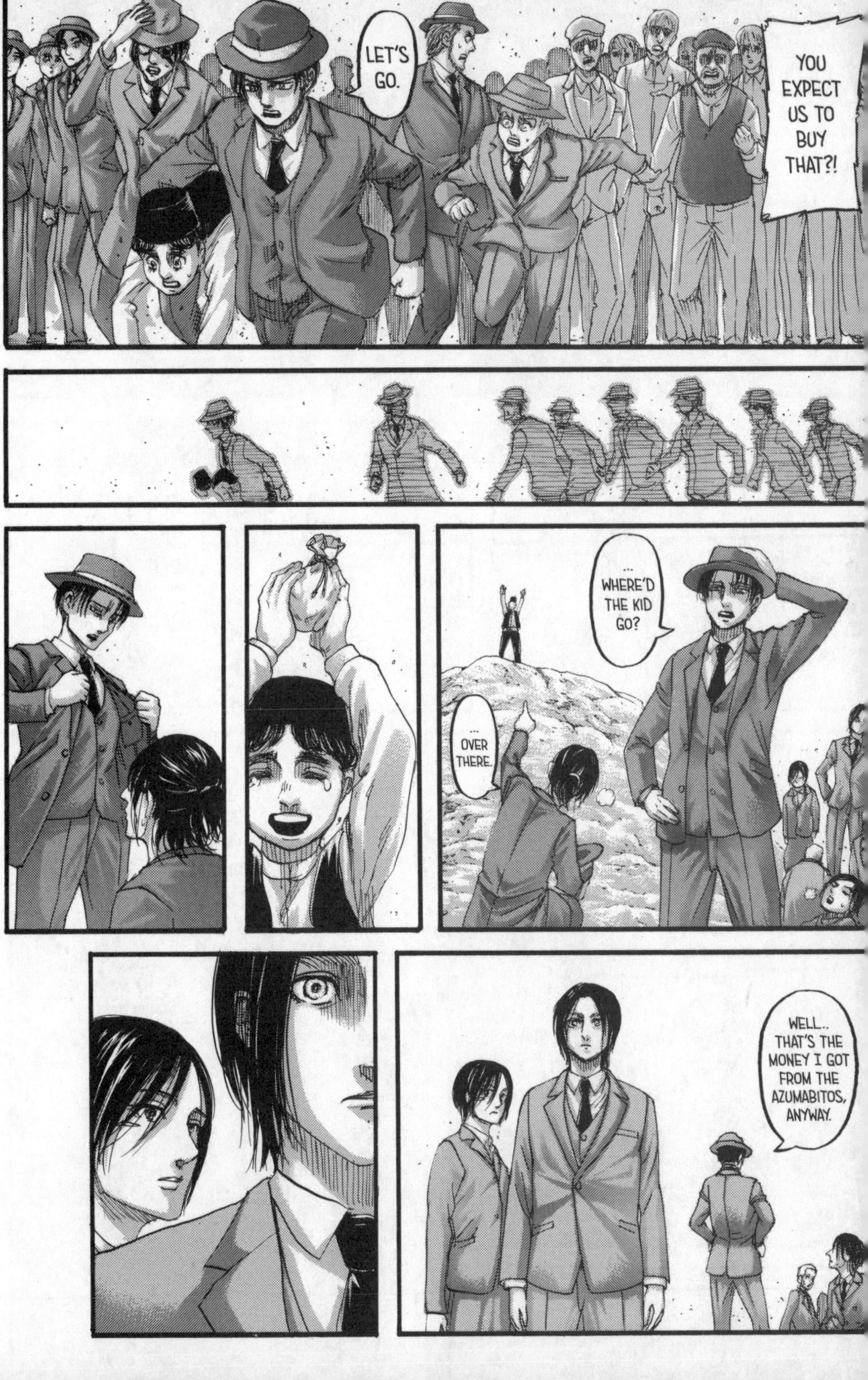
YOU EXPECT US TO BUY THAT?!
LET'S GO.
... WHERE'D THE KID GO?
... OVER THERE.
WELL... THAT'S THE MONEY I GOT FROM THE AZUMABITOS, ANYWAY.

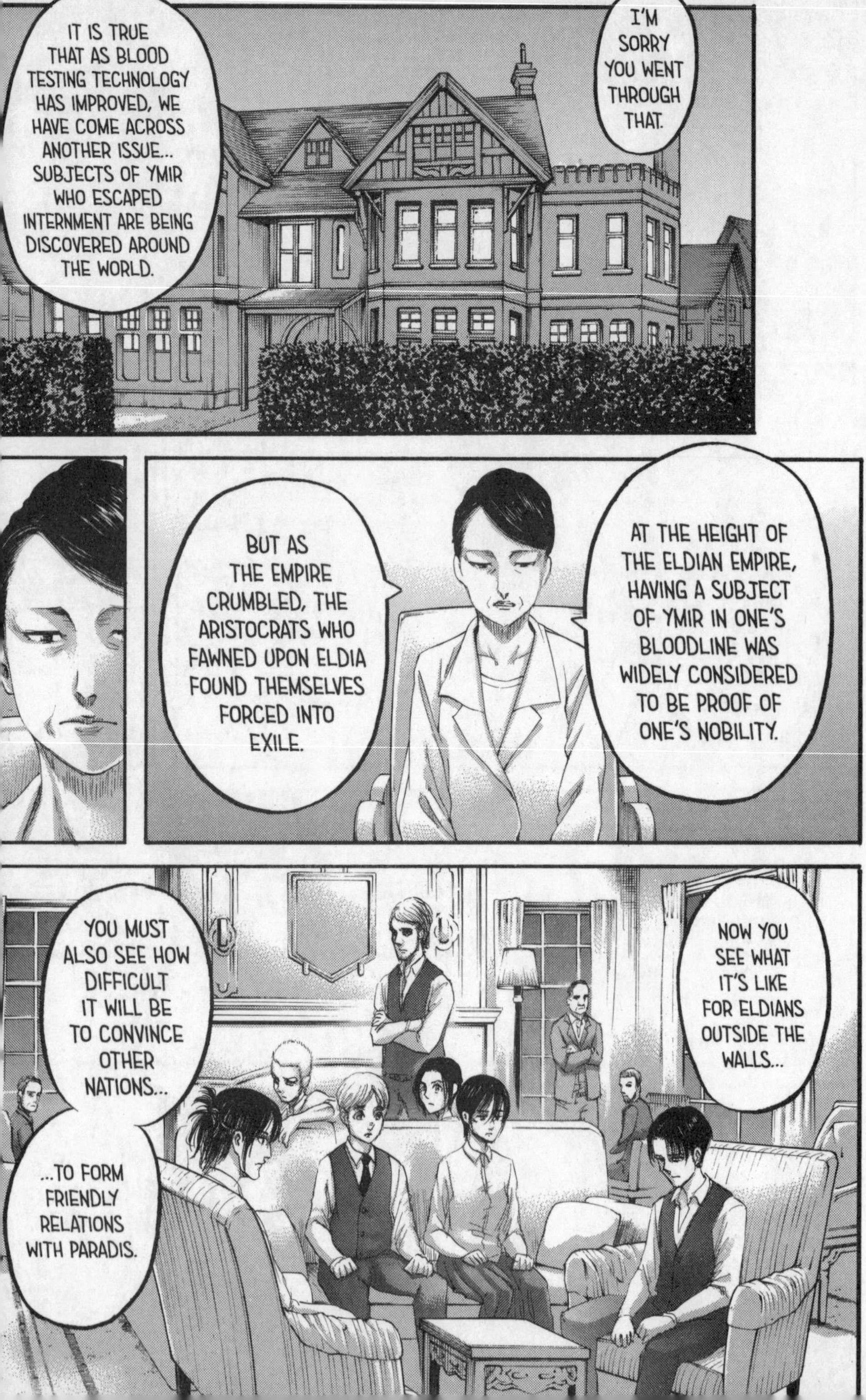
I'M SORRY YOU WENT THROUGH THAT.
IT IS TRUE THAT AS BLOOD TESTING TECHNOLOGY HAS IMPROVED, WE HAVE COME ACROSS ANOTHER ISSUE... SUBJECTS OF YMIR WHO ESCAPED INTERNMENT ARE BEING DISCOVERED AROUND THE WORLD.
AT THE HEIGHT OF THE ELDIAN EMPIRE, HAVING A SUBJECT OF YMIR IN ONE'S BLOODLINE WAS WIDELY CONSIDERED TO BE PROOF OF ONE'S NOBILITY.
BUT AS THE EMPIRE CRUMBLED, THE ARISTOCRATS WHO FAWNED UPON ELDIA FOUND THEMSELVES FORCED INTO EXILE.
NOW YOU SEE WHAT IT'S LIKE FOR ELDIANS OUTSIDE THE WALLS...
YOU MUST ALSO SEE HOW DIFFICULT IT WILL BE TO CONVINCE OTHER NATIONS...
...TO FORM FRIENDLY RELATIONS WITH PARADIS.

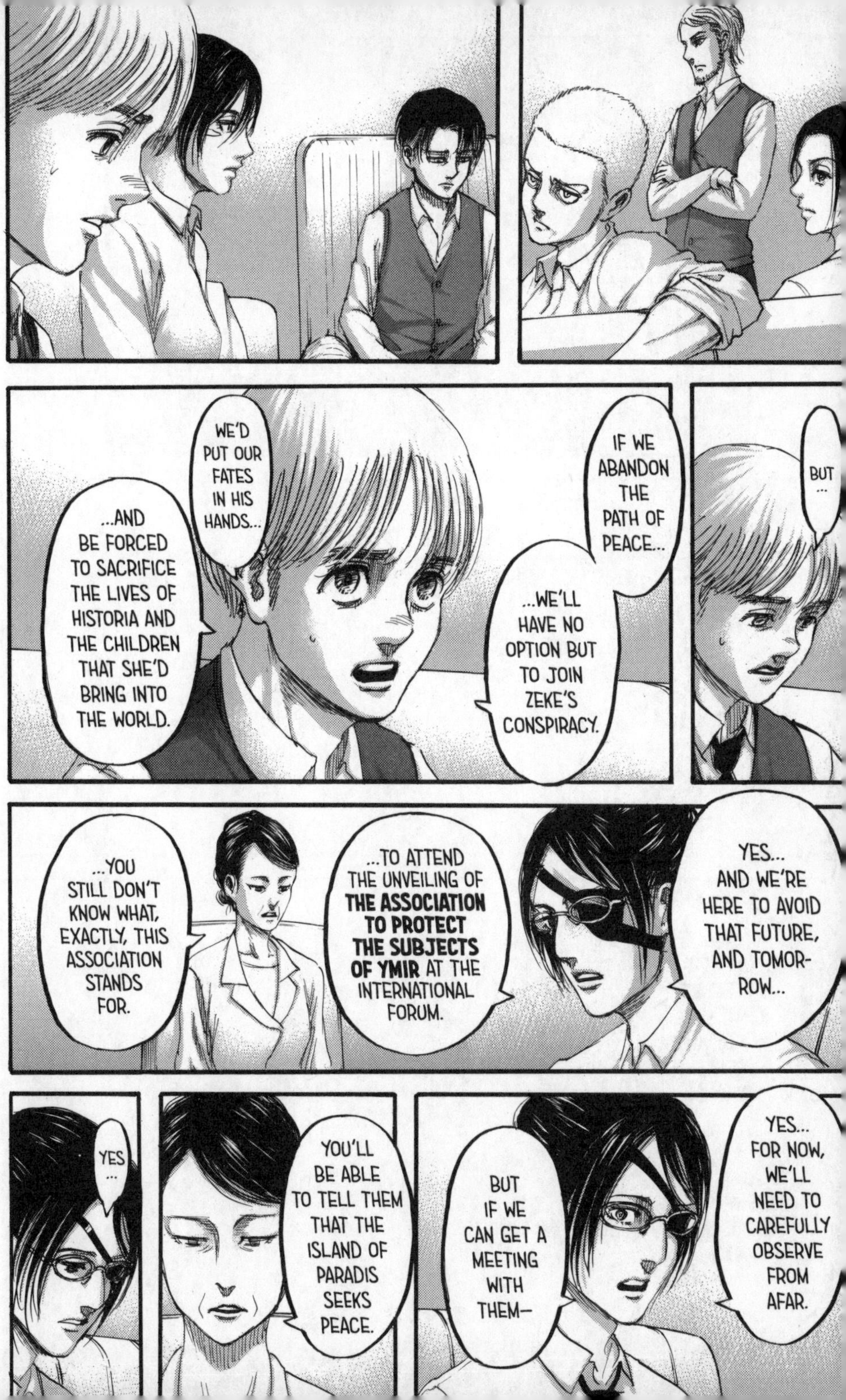
BUT ...
IF WE ABANDON THE PATH OF PEACE...
...WE'LL HAVE NO OPTION BUT TO JOIN ZEKE'S CONSPIRACY.
WE'D PUT OUR FATES IN HIS HANDS...
...AND BE FORCED TO SACRIFICE THE LIVES OF HISTORIA AND THE CHILDREN THAT SHE'D BRING INTO THE WORLD.
YES... AND WE'RE HERE TO AVOID THAT FUTURE, AND TOMOR-ROW...
...TO ATTEND THE UNVEILING OF THE ASSOCIATION TO PROTECT THE SUBJECTS OF YMIR AT THE INTERNATIONAL FORUM.
...YOU STILL DON'T KNOW WHAT, EXACTLY, THIS ASSOCIATION STANDS FOR.
YES... FOR NOW, WE'LL NEED TO CAREFULLY OBSERVE FROM AFAR.
BUT IF WE CAN GET A MEETING WITH THEM—
YOU'LL BE ABLE TO TELL THEM THAT THE ISLAND OF PARADIS SEEKS PEACE.
YES ...

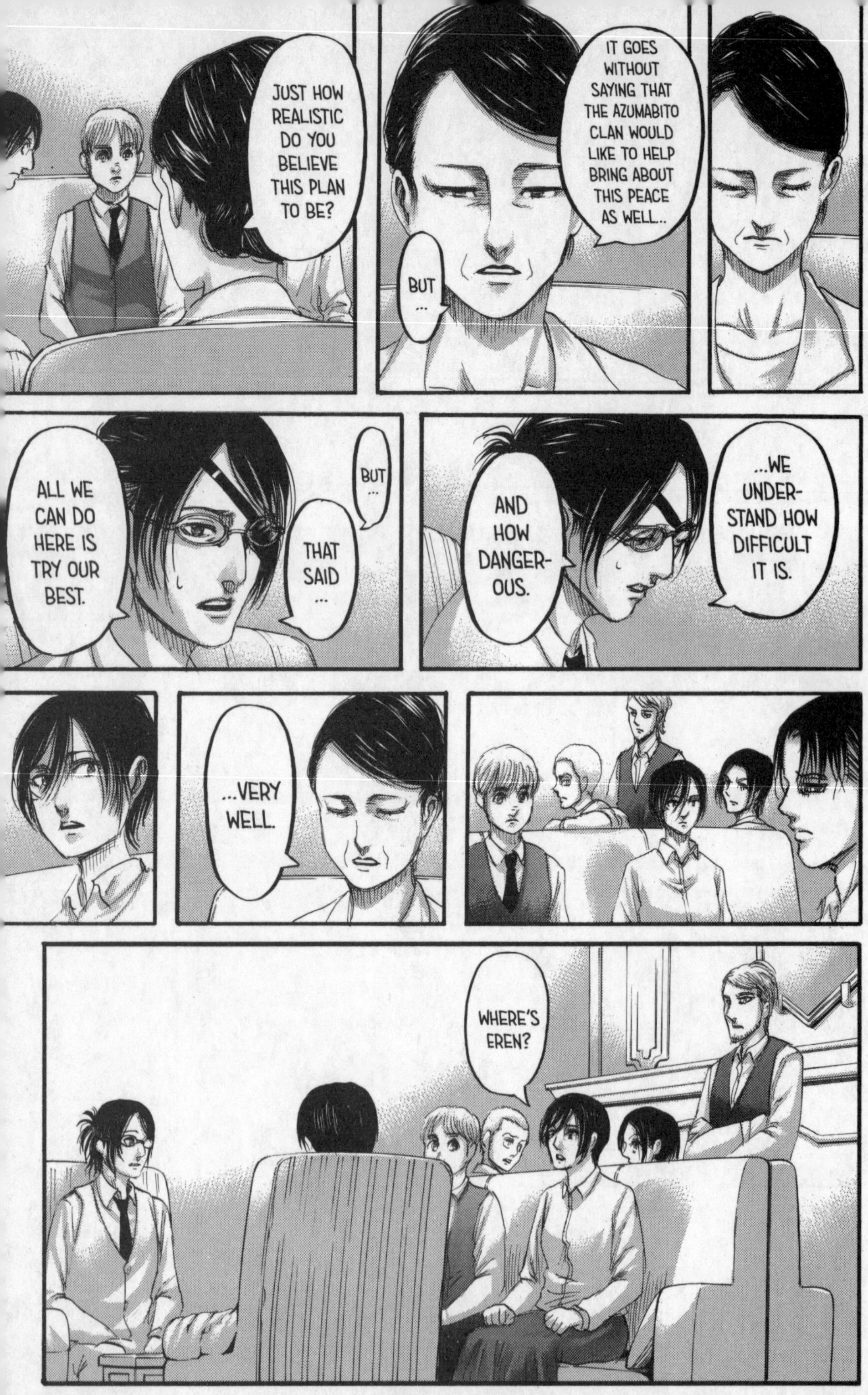
IT GOES WITHOUT SAYING THAT THE AZUMABITO CLAN WOULD LIKE TO HELP BRING ABOUT THIS PEACE AS WELL...
BUT ...
JUST HOW REALISTIC DO YOU BELIEVE THIS PLAN TO BE?
...WE UNDER-STAND HOW DIFFICULT IT IS.
AND HOW DANGER-OUS.
BUT ...
THAT SAID ...
ALL WE CAN DO HERE IS TRY OUR BEST.
...VERY WELL.
WHERE'S EREN?

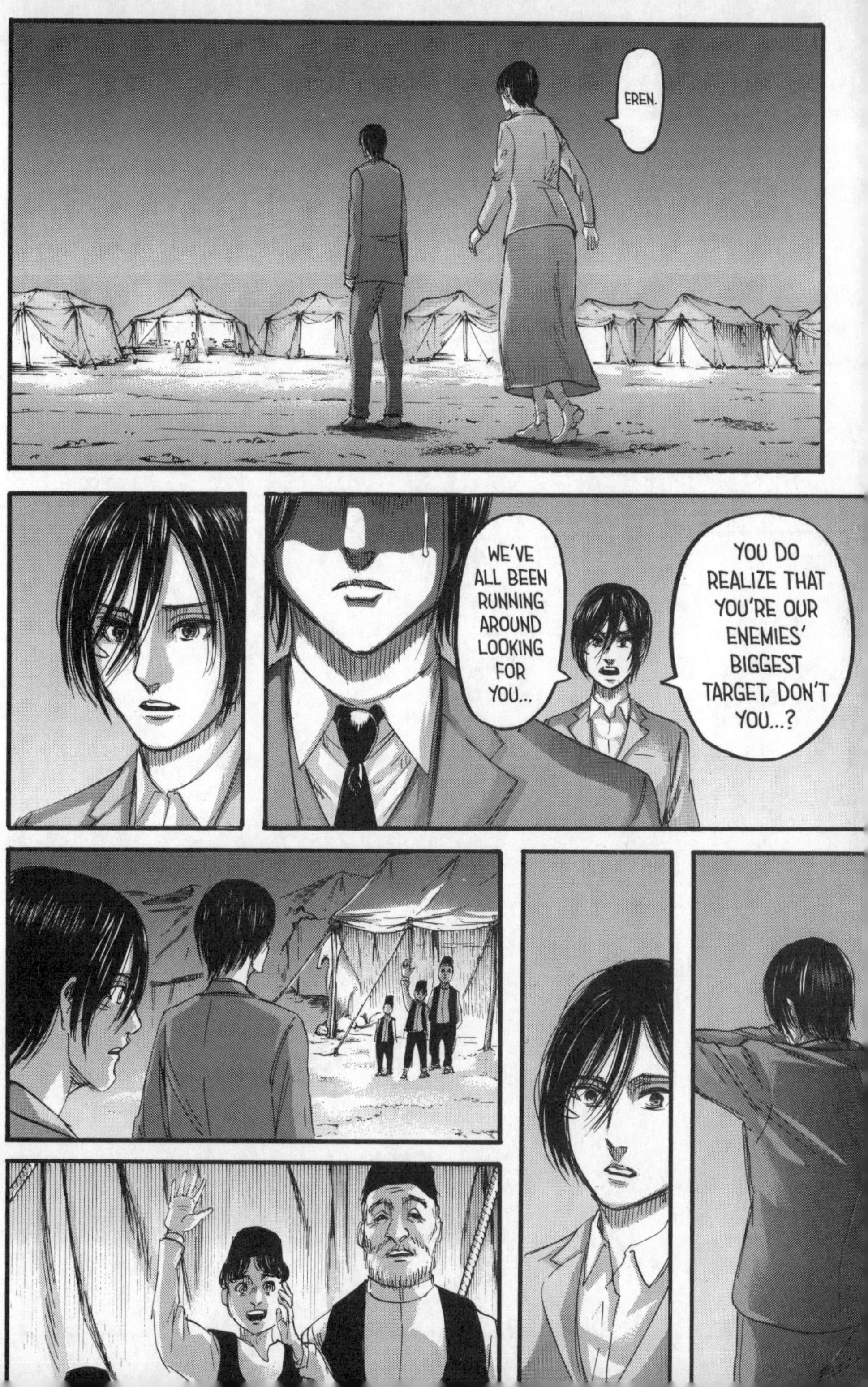
EREN.
YOU DO REALIZE THAT YOU'RE OUR ENEMIES' BIGGEST TARGET, DON'T YOU...?
WE'VE ALL BEEN RUNNING AROUND LOOKING FOR YOU...

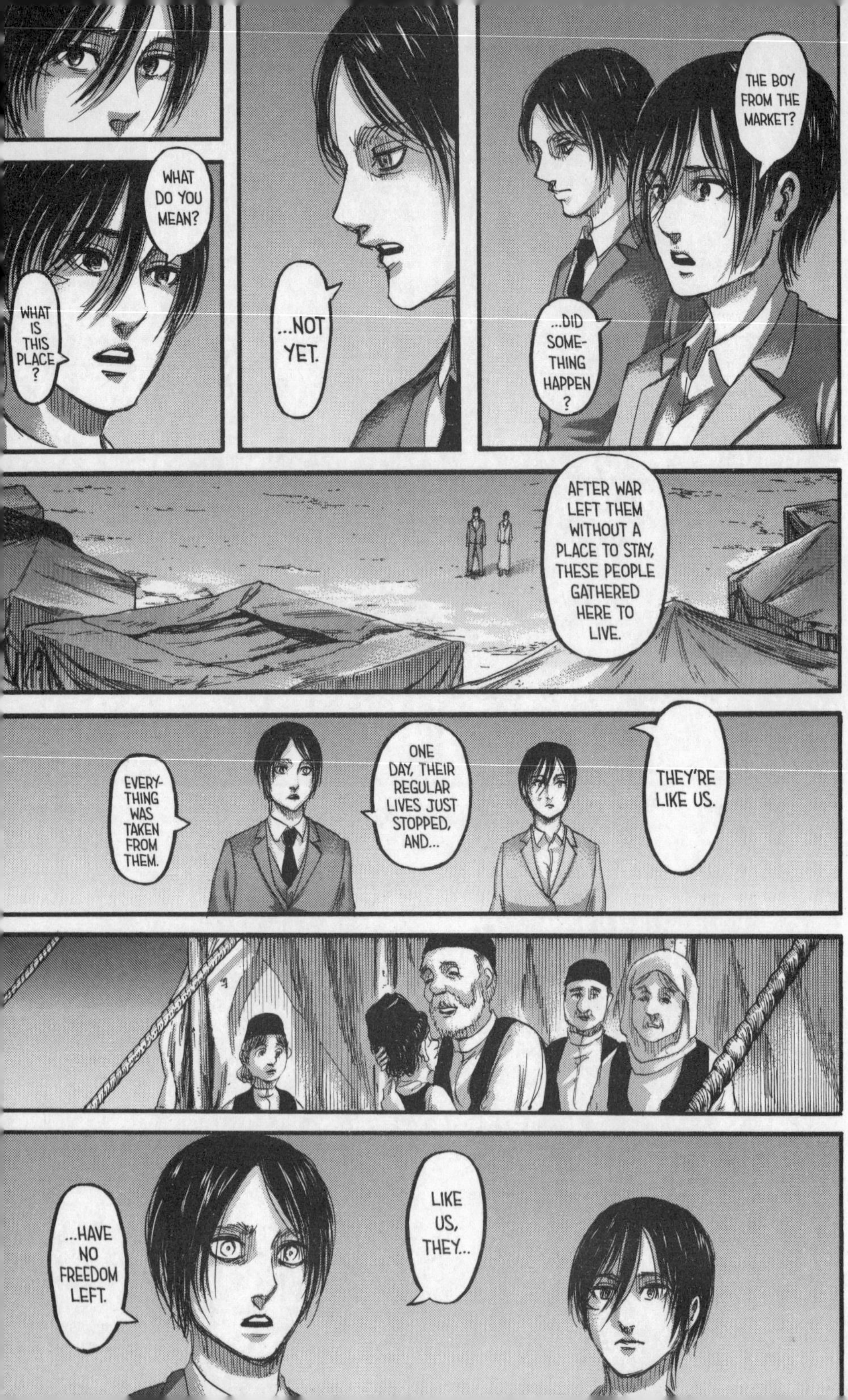
THE BOY FROM THE MARKET?
...DID SOMETHING HAPPEN?
...NOT YET.
WHAT DO YOU MEAN?
WHAT IS THIS PLACE?
AFTER WAR LEFT THEM WITHOUT A PLACE TO STAY, THESE PEOPLE GATHERED HERE TO LIVE.
THEY'RE LIKE US.
ONE DAY, THEIR REGULAR LIVES JUST STOPPED, AND...
EVERYTHING WAS TAKEN FROM THEM.
LIKE US, THEY...
...HAVE NO FREEDOM LEFT.

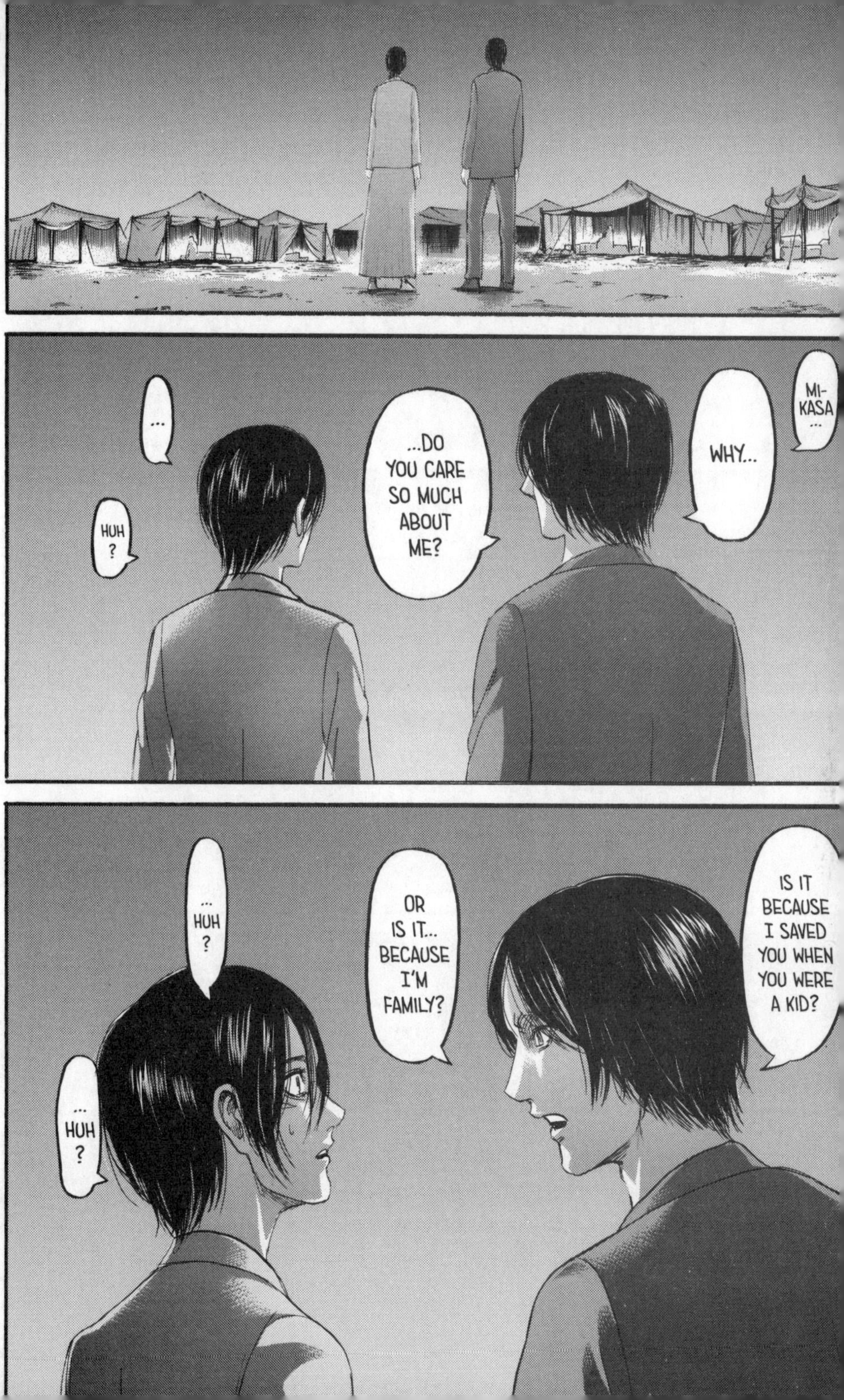
MI-KASA...
WHY...
...DO YOU CARE SO MUCH ABOUT ME?
...
HUH?
IS IT BECAUSE I SAVED YOU WHEN YOU WERE A KID?
OR IS IT... BECAUSE I'M FAMILY?
...HUH?
...HUH?

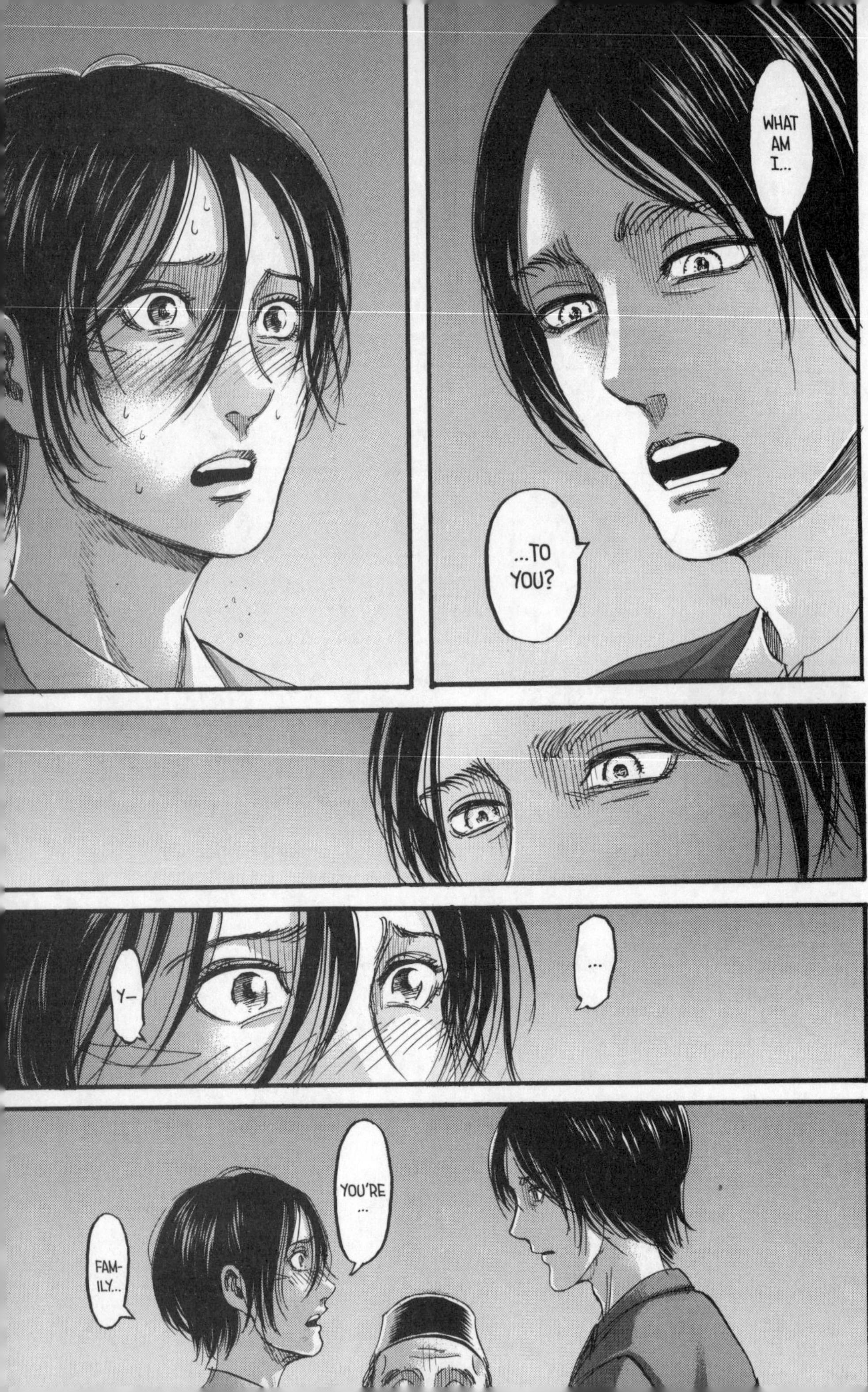
WHAT AM I...
...TO YOU?
...
Y—
YOU'RE ...
FAM-ILY...

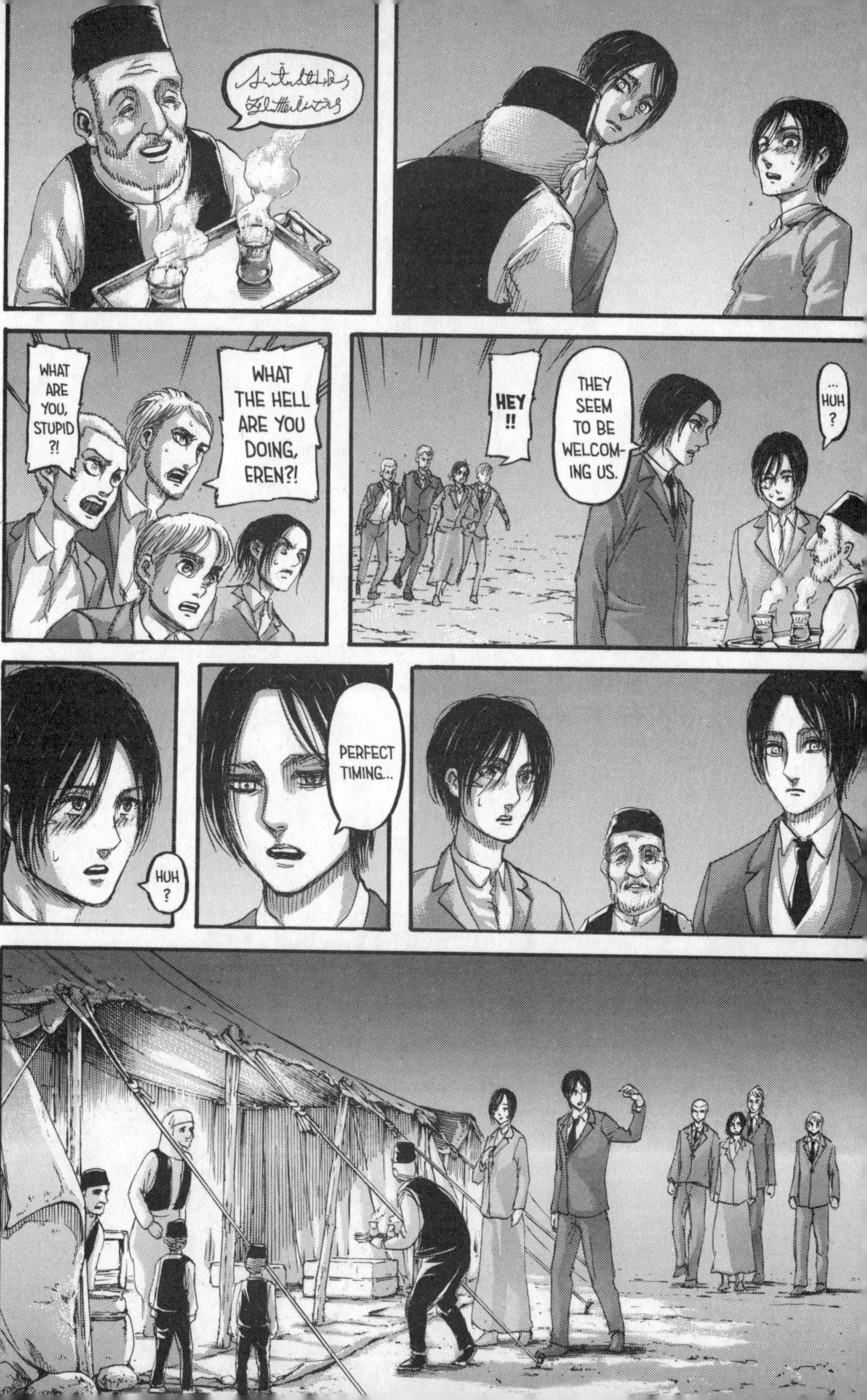
... HUH ?
THEY SEEM TO BE WELCOMING US.
HEY !!
WHAT THE HELL ARE YOU DOING, EREN?!
WHAT ARE YOU, STUPID ?!
PERFECT TIMING...
HUH ?

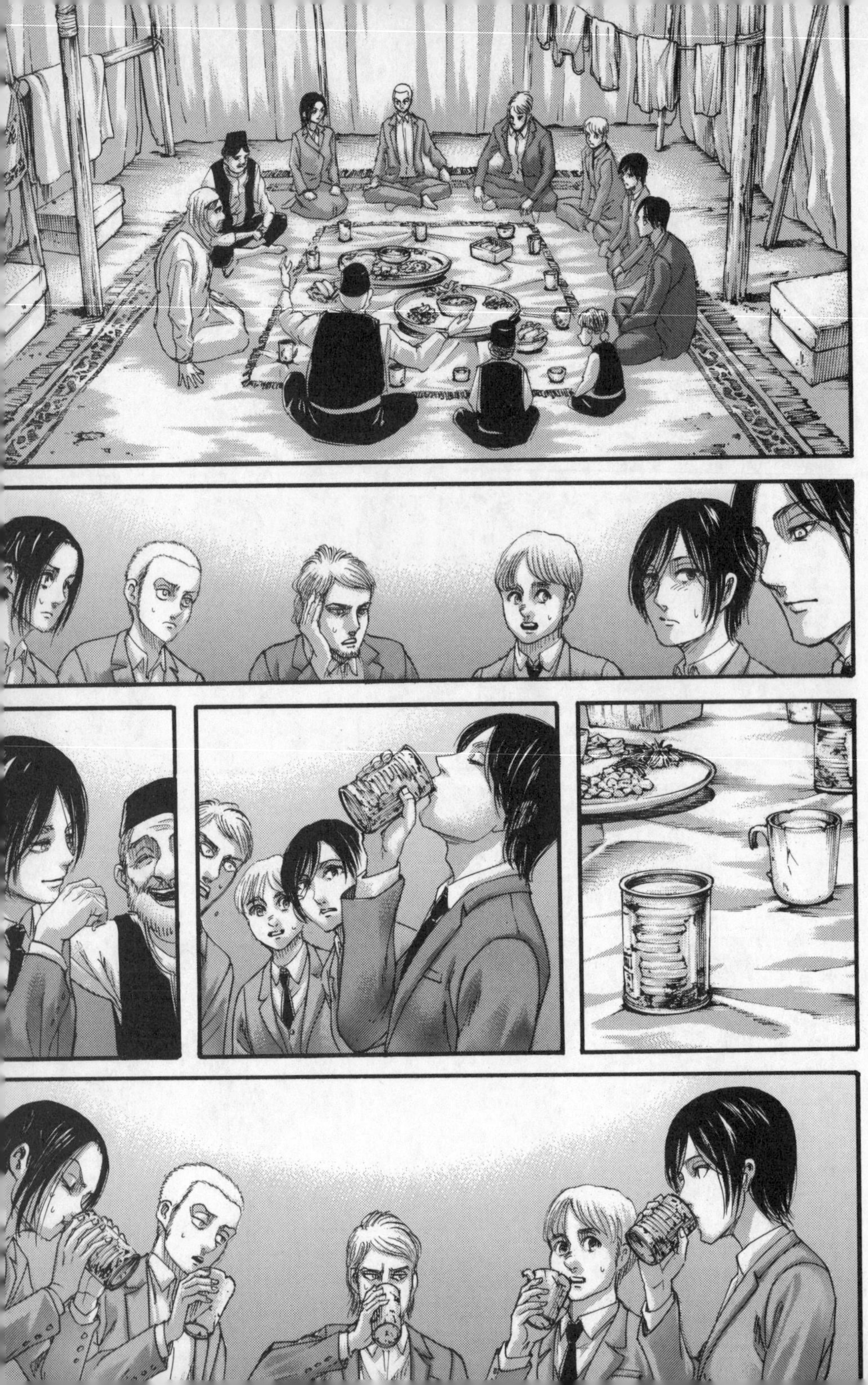

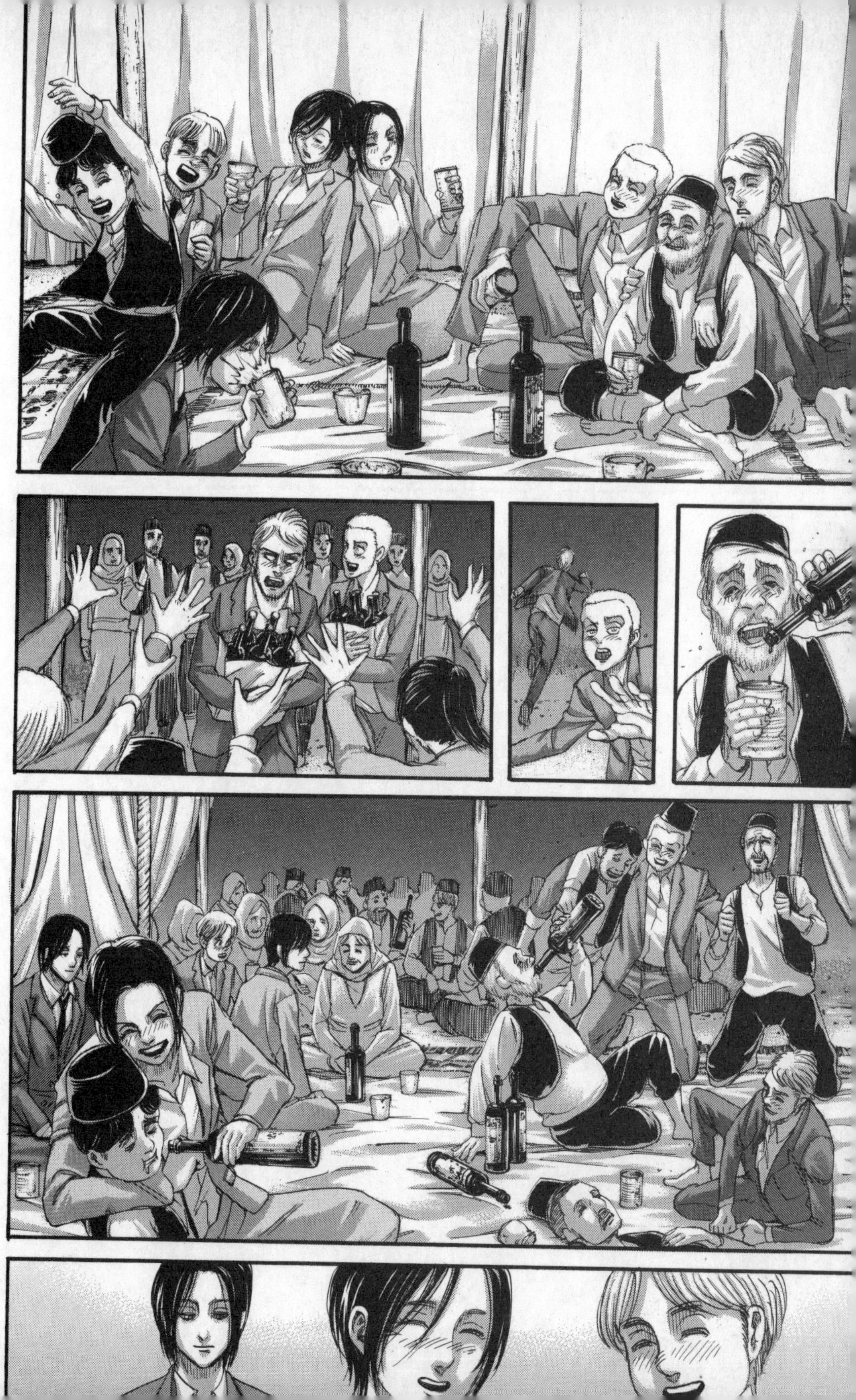

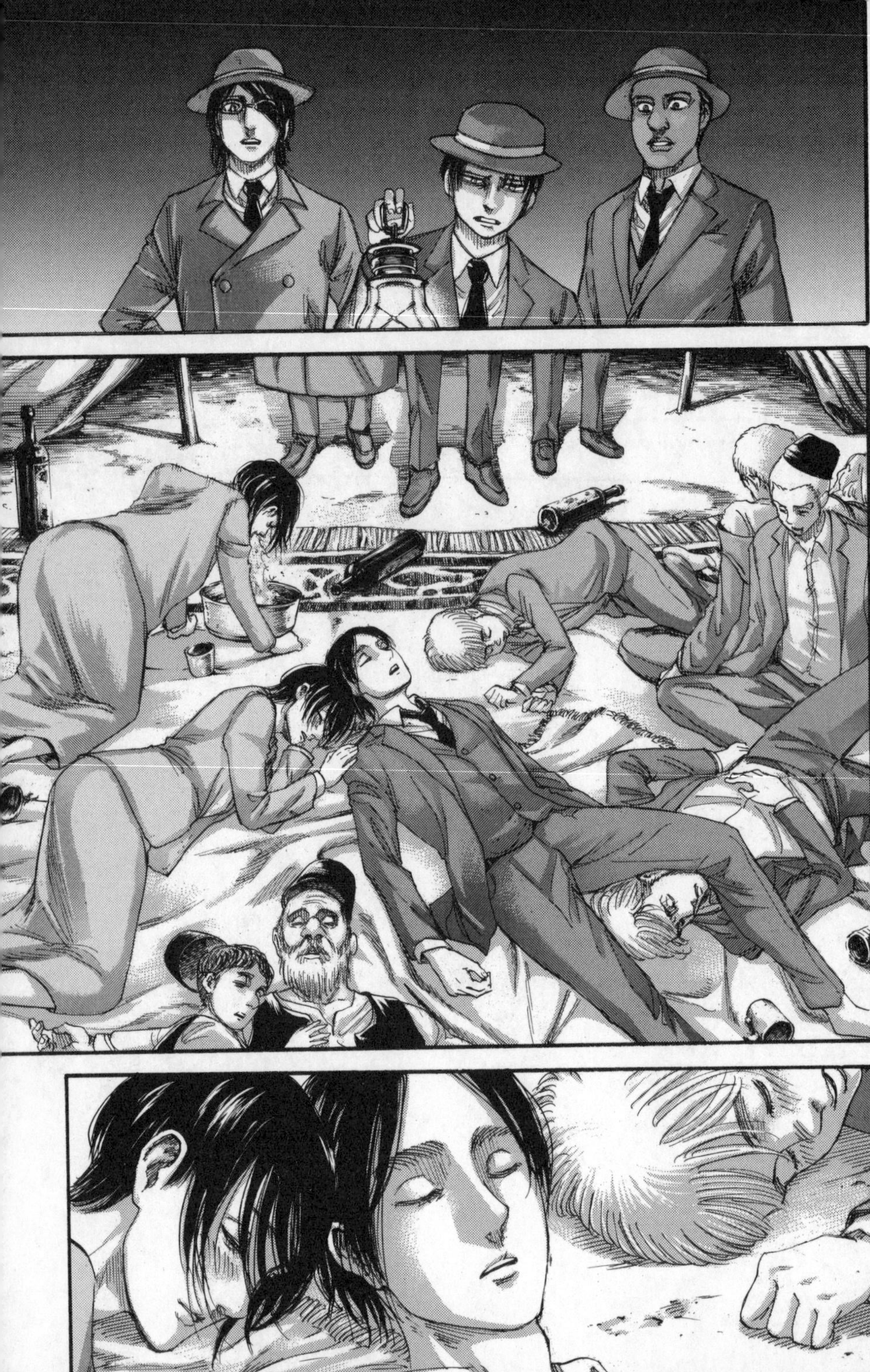

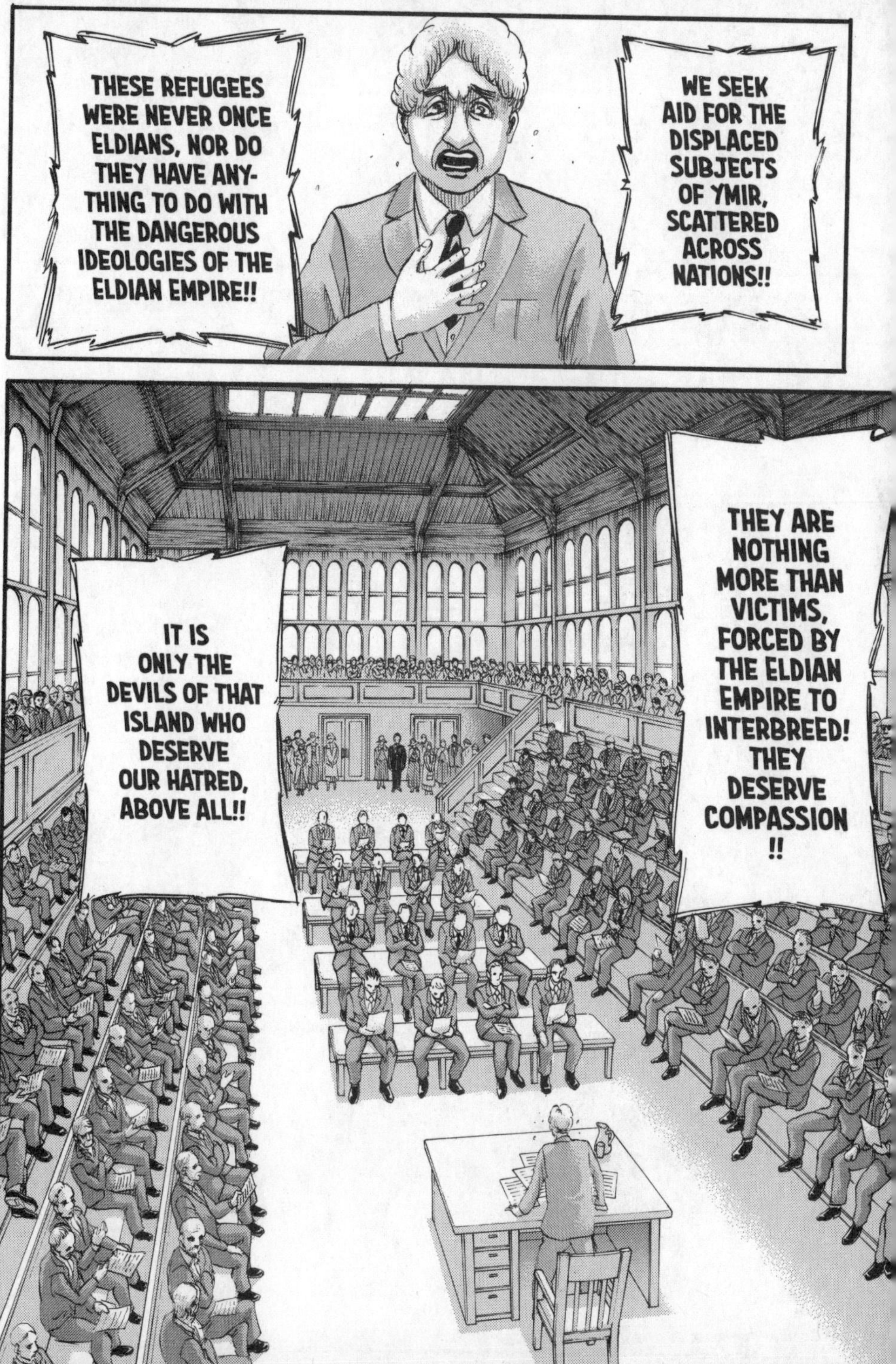
WE SEEK AID FOR THE DISPLACED SUBJECTS OF YMIR, SCATTERED ACROSS NATIONS!!
THESE REFUGEES WERE NEVER ONCE ELDIANS, NOR DO THEY HAVE ANY-THING TO DO WITH THE DANGEROUS IDEOLOGIES OF THE ELDIAN EMPIRE!!
THEY ARE NOTHING MORE THAN VICTIMS, FORCED BY THE ELDIAN EMPIRE TO INTERBREED! THEY DESERVE COMPASSION!!
IT IS ONLY THE DEVILS OF THAT ISLAND WHO DESERVE OUR HATRED, ABOVE ALL!!

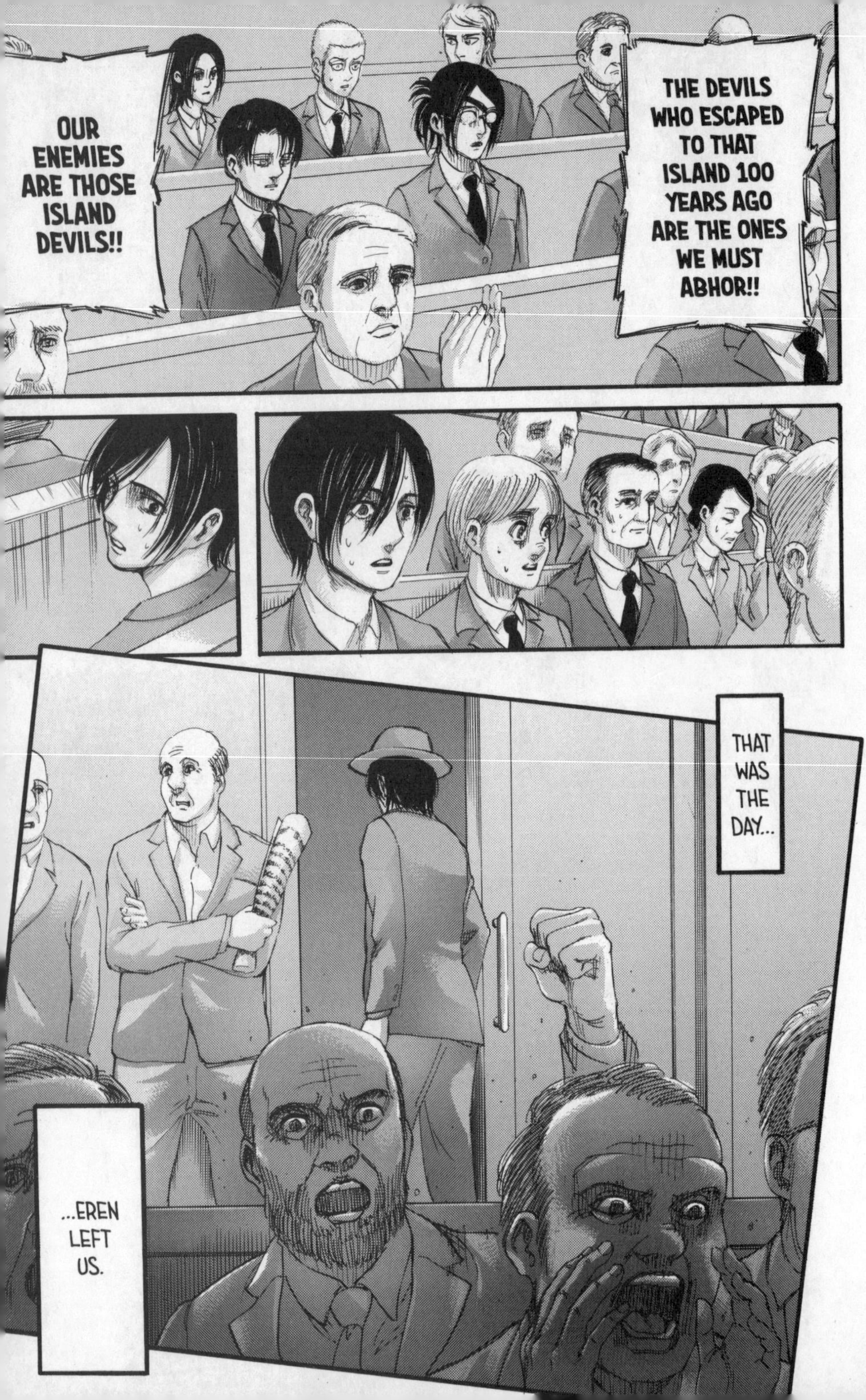
THE DEVILS WHO ESCAPED TO THAT ISLAND 100 YEARS AGO ARE THE ONES WE MUST ABHOR!!
OUR ENEMIES ARE THOSE ISLAND DEVILS!!
THAT WAS THE DAY...
...EREN LEFT US.

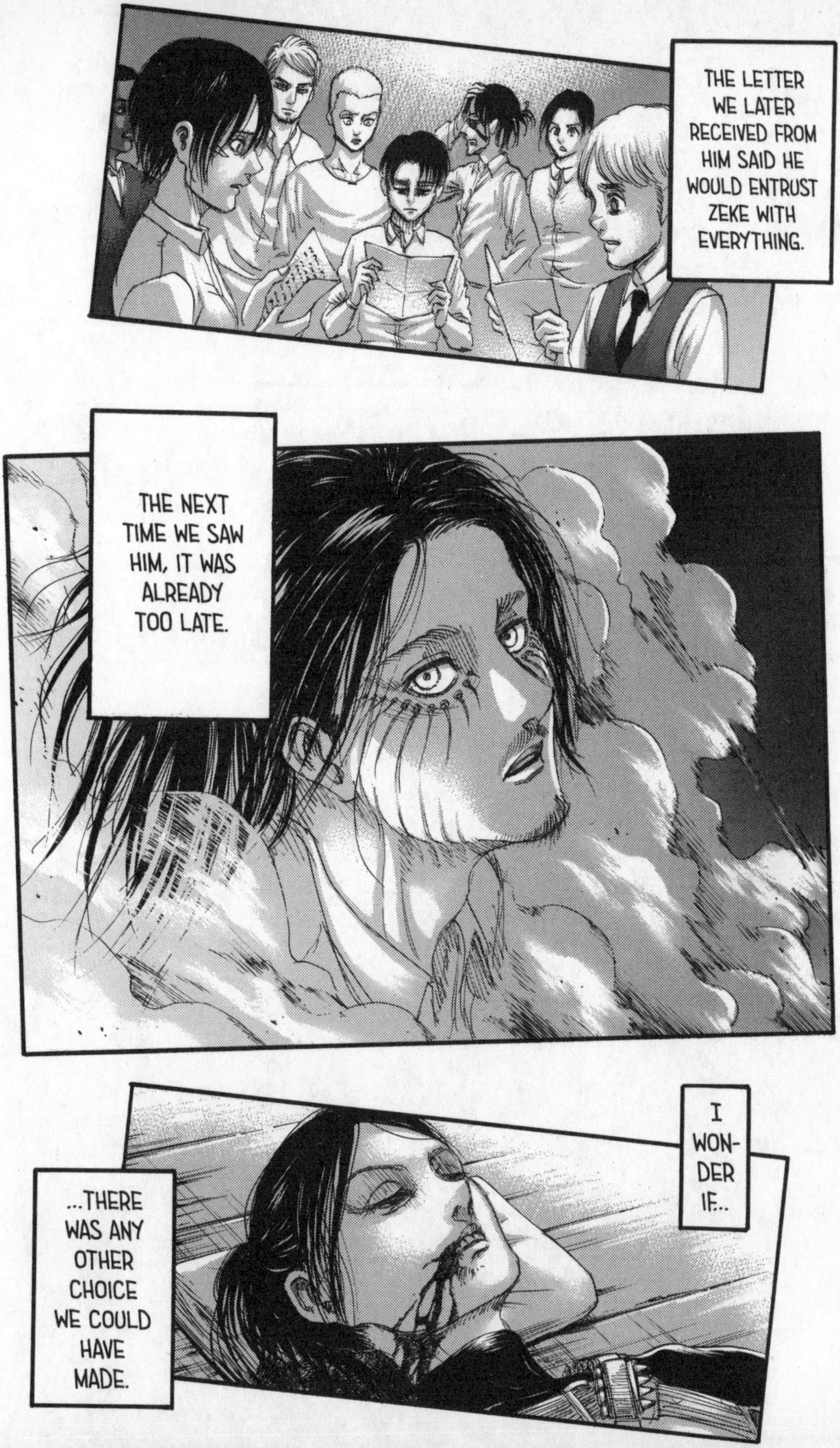
THE LETTER WE LATER RECEIVED FROM HIM SAID HE WOULD ENTRUST ZEKE WITH EVERYTHING.
THE NEXT TIME WE SAW HIM, IT WAS ALREADY TOO LATE.
I WON-DER IF...
...THERE WAS ANY OTHER CHOICE WE COULD HAVE MADE.

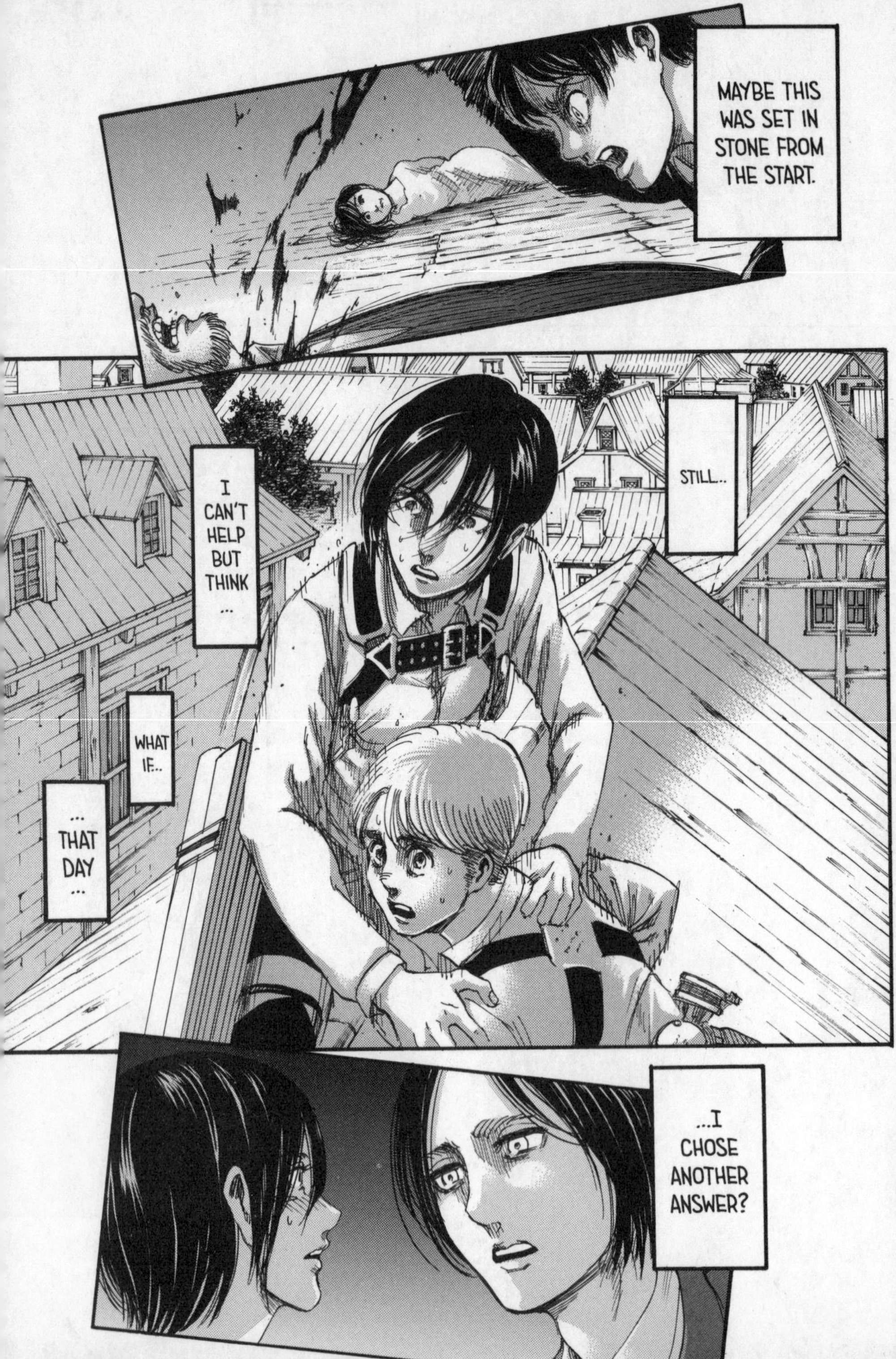
MAYBE THIS WAS SET IN STONE FROM THE START.
STILL..
I CAN'T HELP BUT THINK ...
WHAT IF..
... THAT DAY ...
...I CHOSE ANOTHER ANSWER?

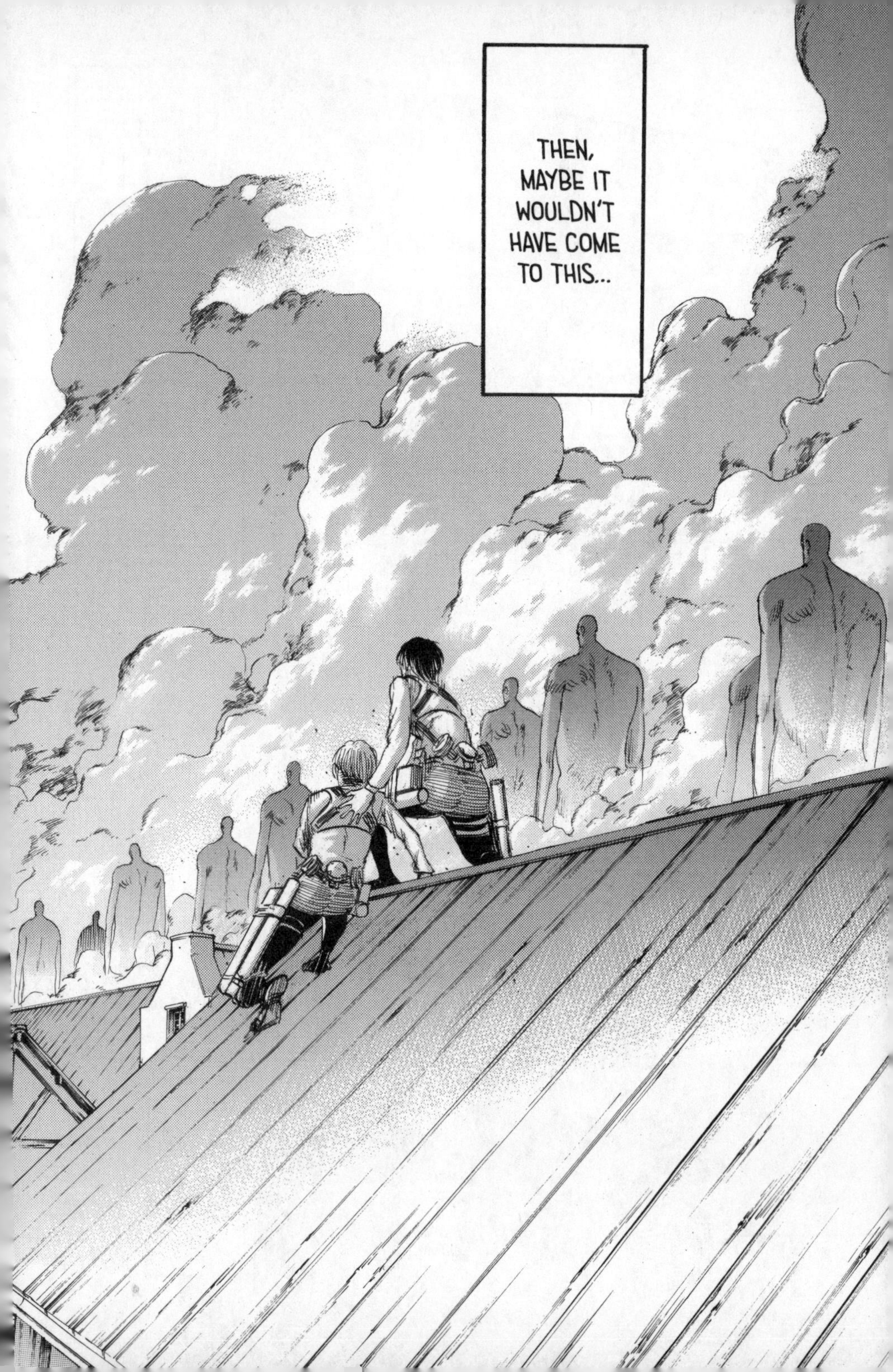
THEN, MAYBE IT WOULDN'T HAVE COME TO THIS...

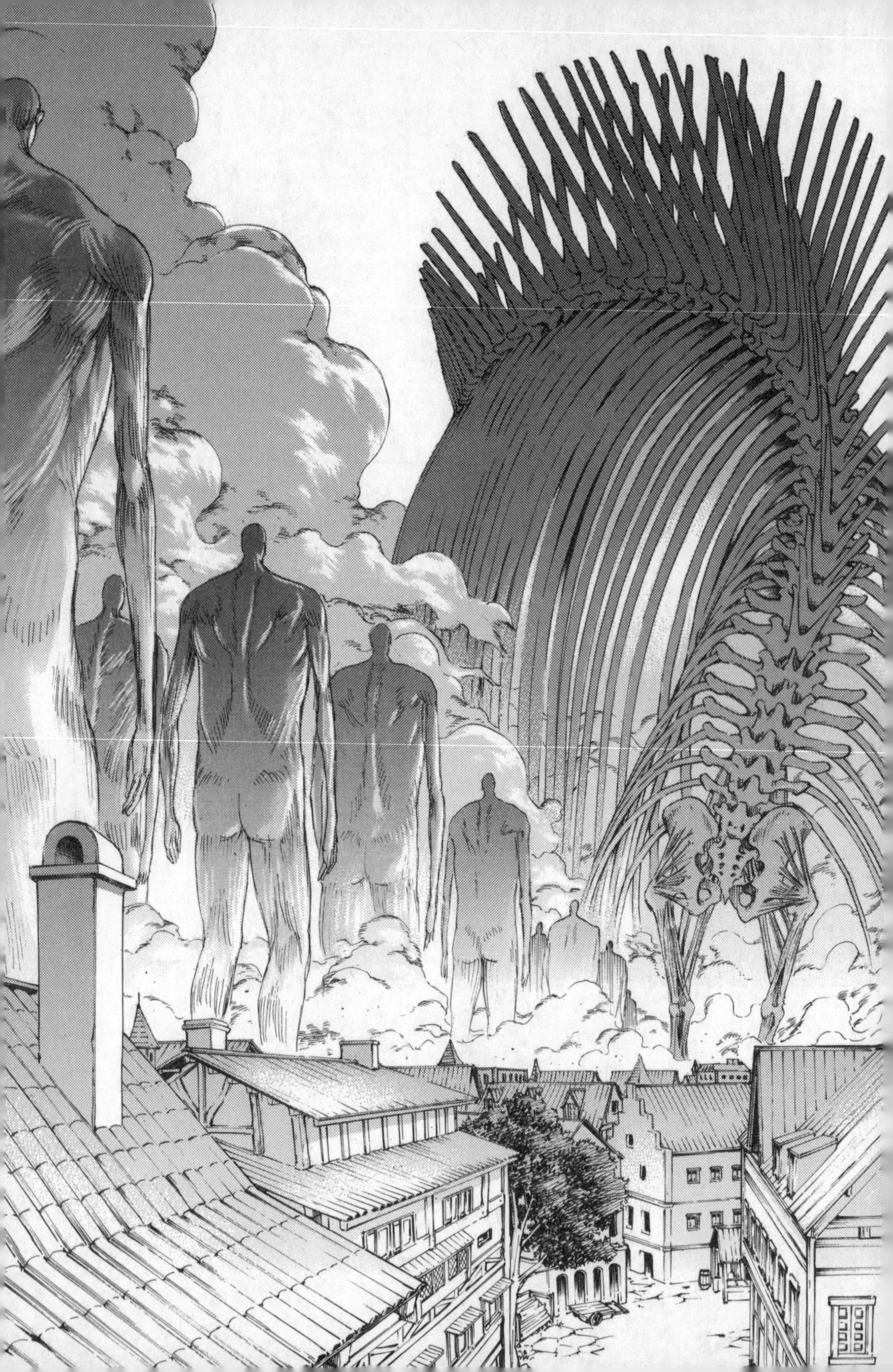

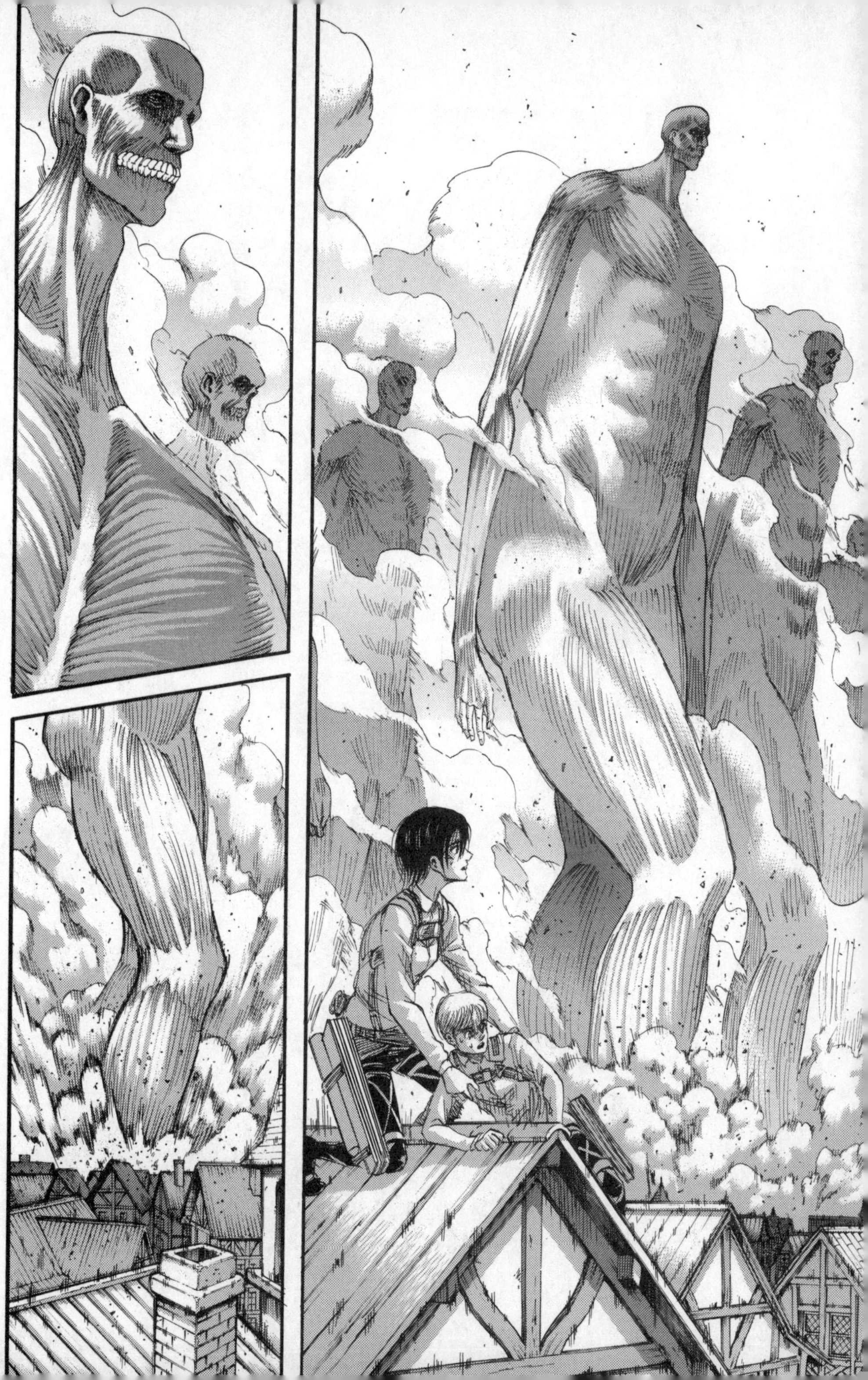

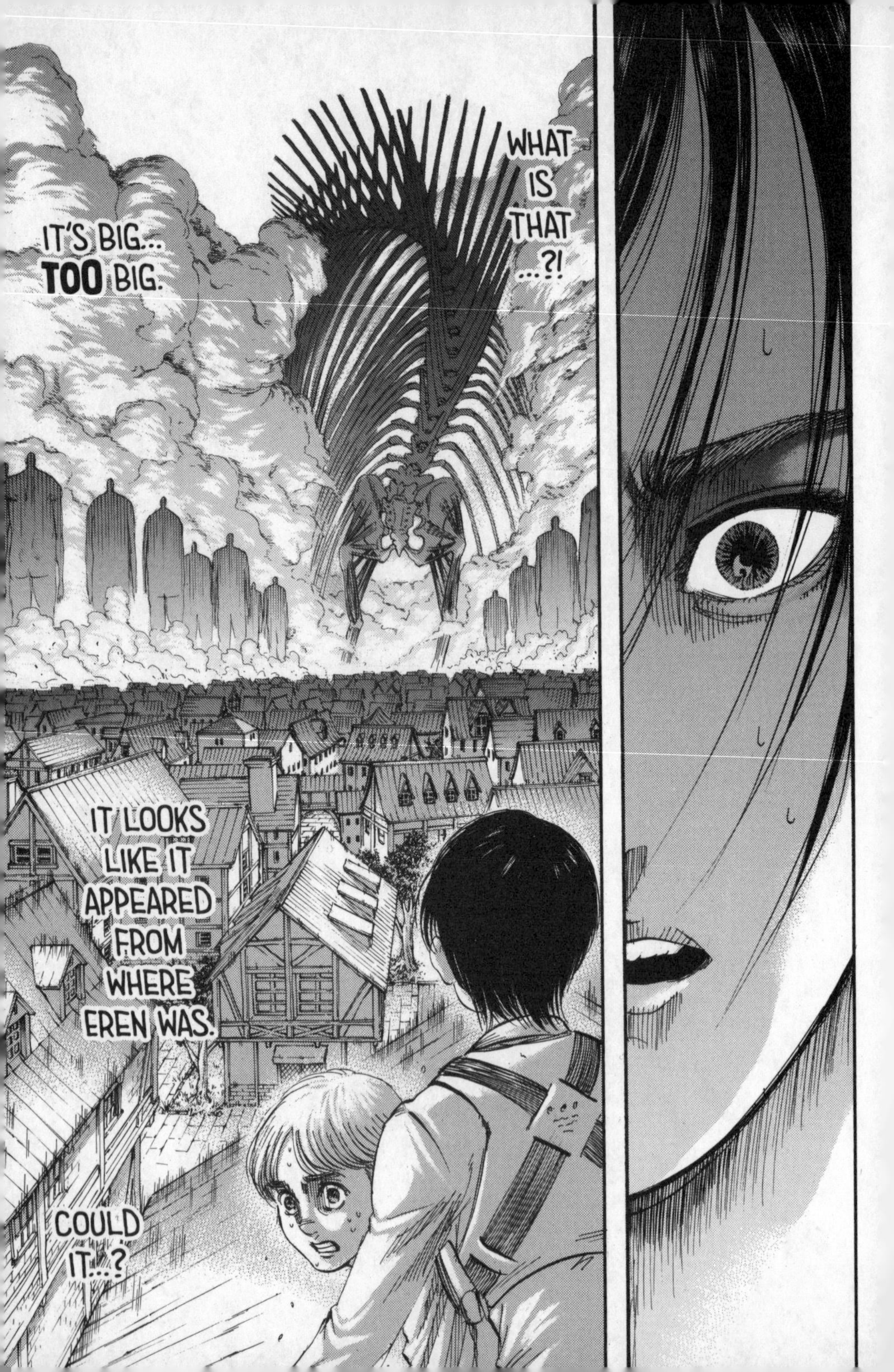
WHAT IS THAT ...?!
IT'S BIG... TOO BIG.
IT LOOKS LIKE IT APPEARED FROM WHERE EREN WAS.
COULD IT...?

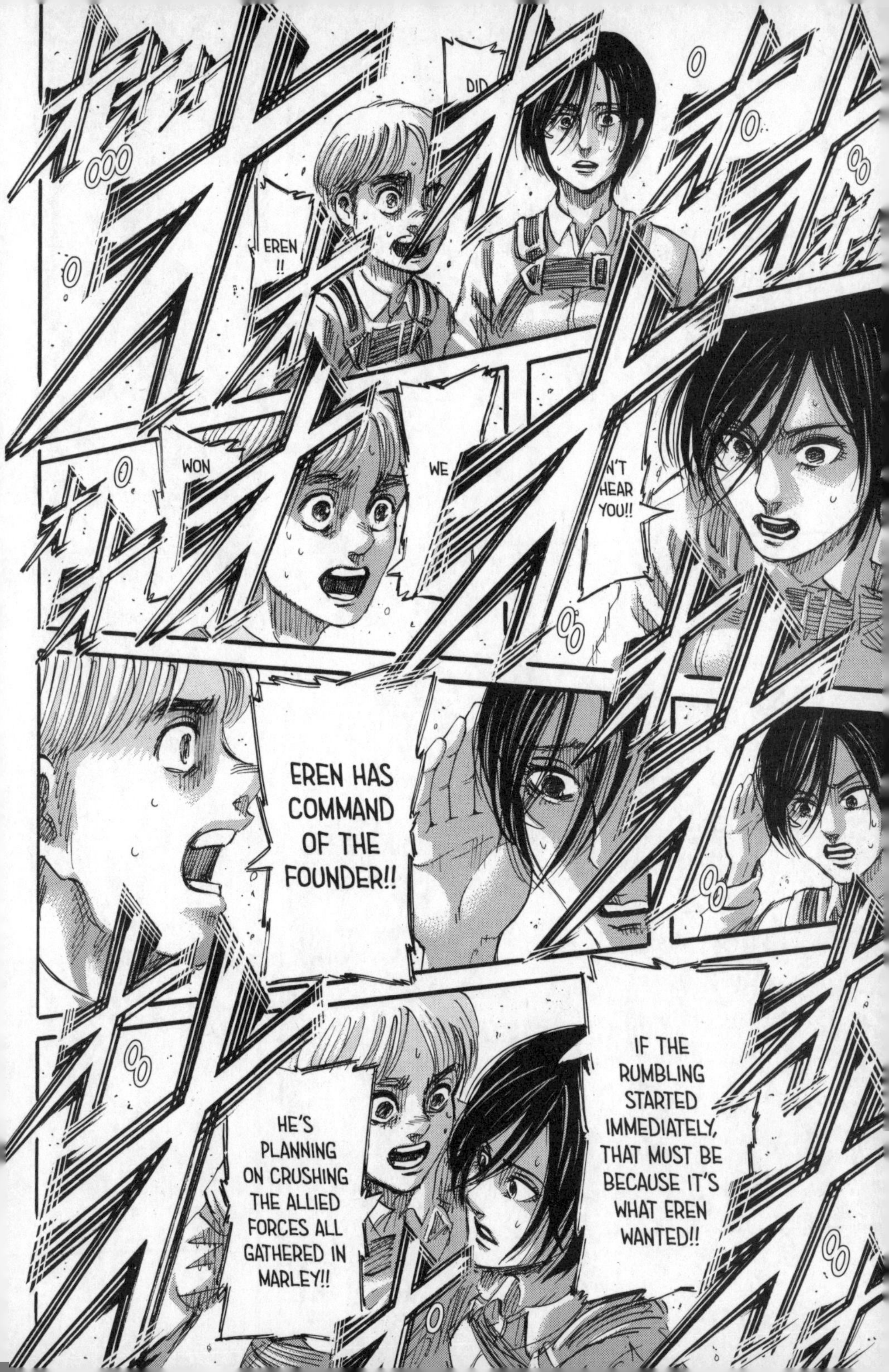
DID
EREN !!
N'T HEAR YOU!!
WE
WON
EREN HAS COMMAND OF THE FOUNDER!!
IF THE RUMBLING STARTED IMMEDIATELY, THAT MUST BE BECAUSE IT'S WHAT EREN WANTED!!
HE'S PLANNING ON CRUSHING THE ALLIED FORCES ALL GATHERED IN MARLEY!!

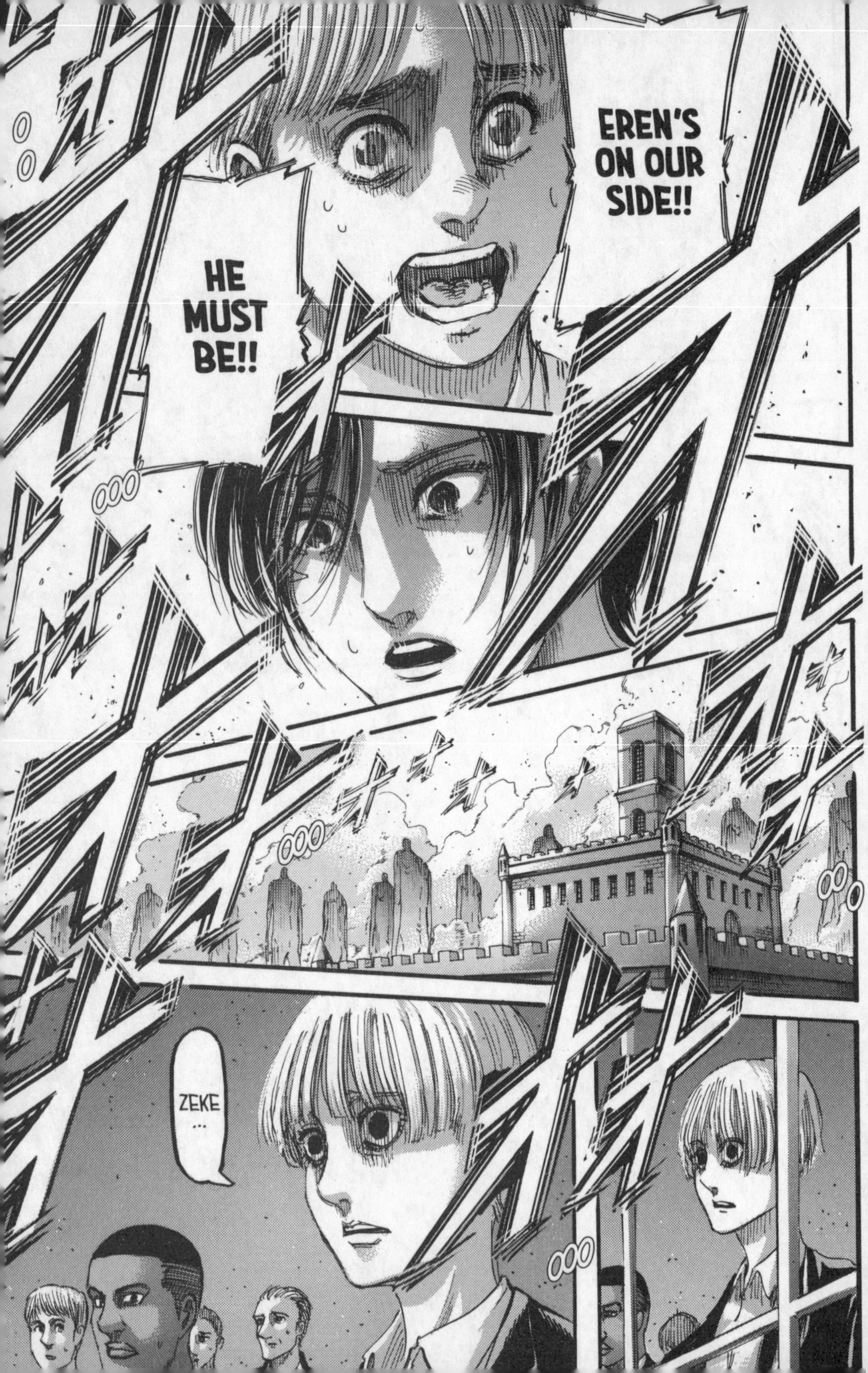
EREN'S ON OUR SIDE!!
HE MUST BE!!
ZEKE ...

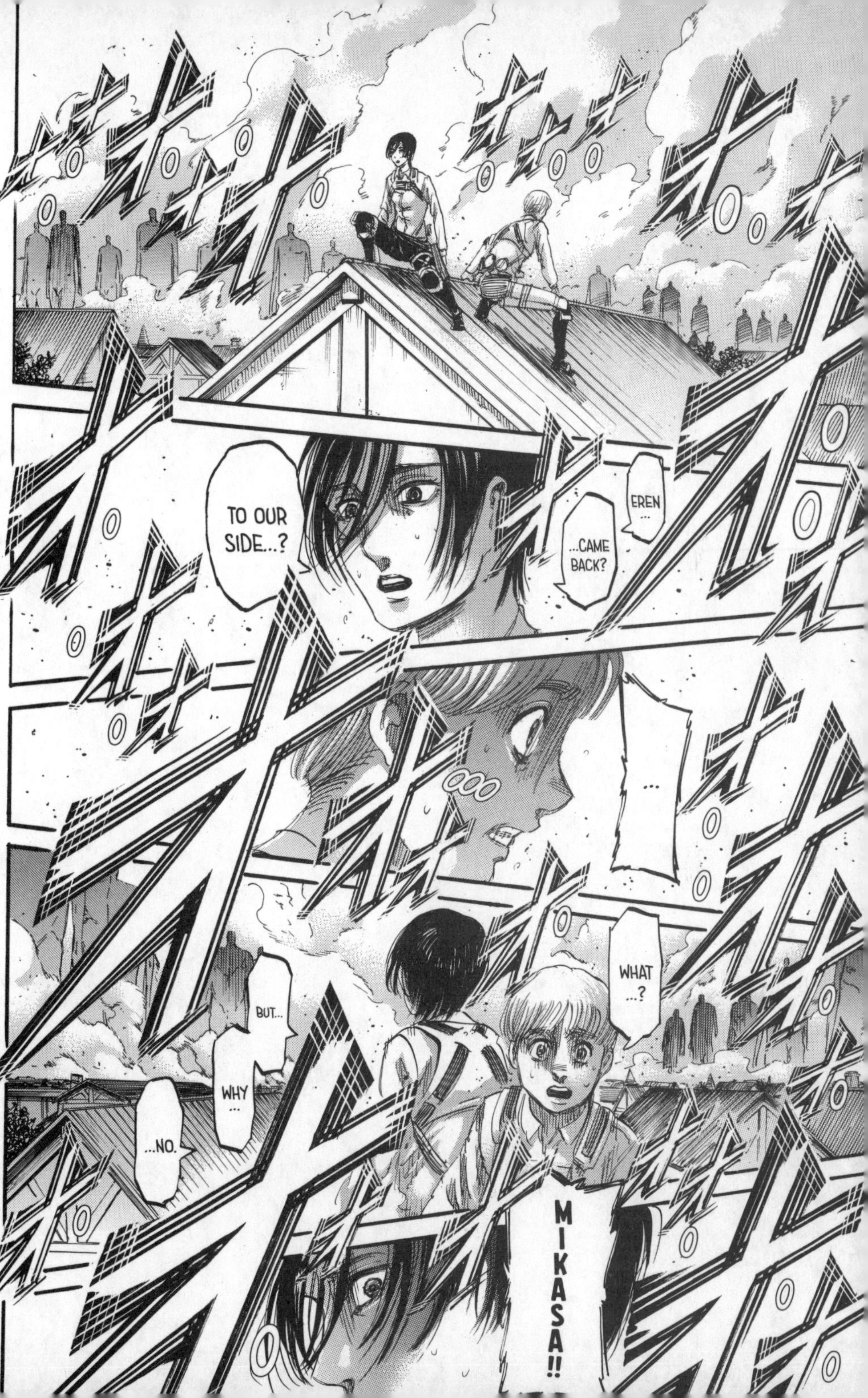
EREN ...
...CAME BACK?
TO OUR SIDE...?
...
WHAT ...?
BUT...
WHY ...
...NO.
MIKASA!!

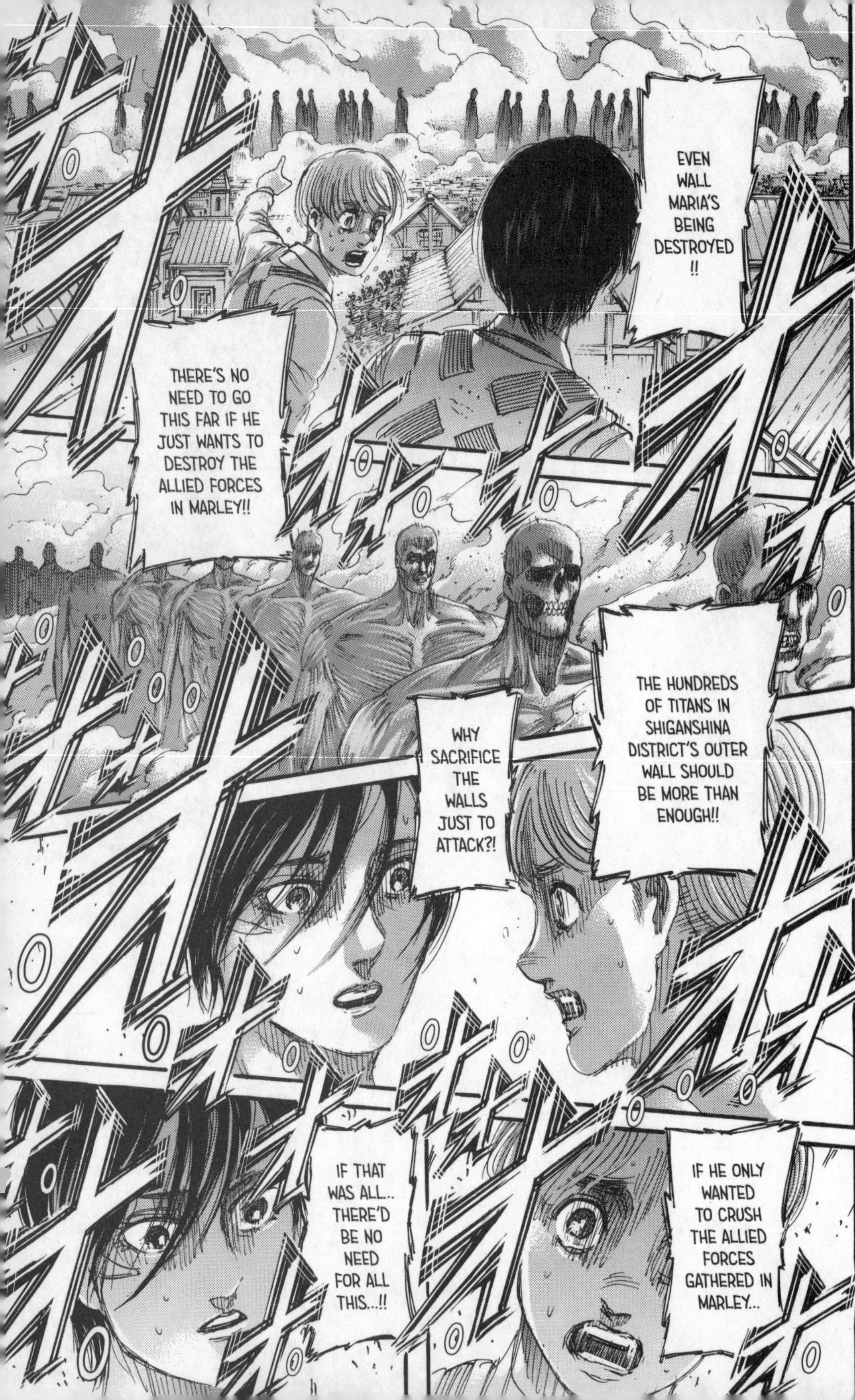
EVEN WALL MARIA'S BEING DESTROYED !!
THERE'S NO NEED TO GO THIS FAR IF HE JUST WANTS TO DESTROY THE ALLIED FORCES IN MARLEY!!
THE HUNDREDS OF TITANS IN SHIGANSHINA DISTRICT'S OUTER WALL SHOULD BE MORE THAN ENOUGH!!
WHY SACRIFICE THE WALLS JUST TO ATTACK?!
IF HE ONLY WANTED TO CRUSH THE ALLIED FORCES GATHERED IN MARLEY...
IF THAT WAS ALL.. THERE'D BE NO NEED FOR ALL THIS...!!

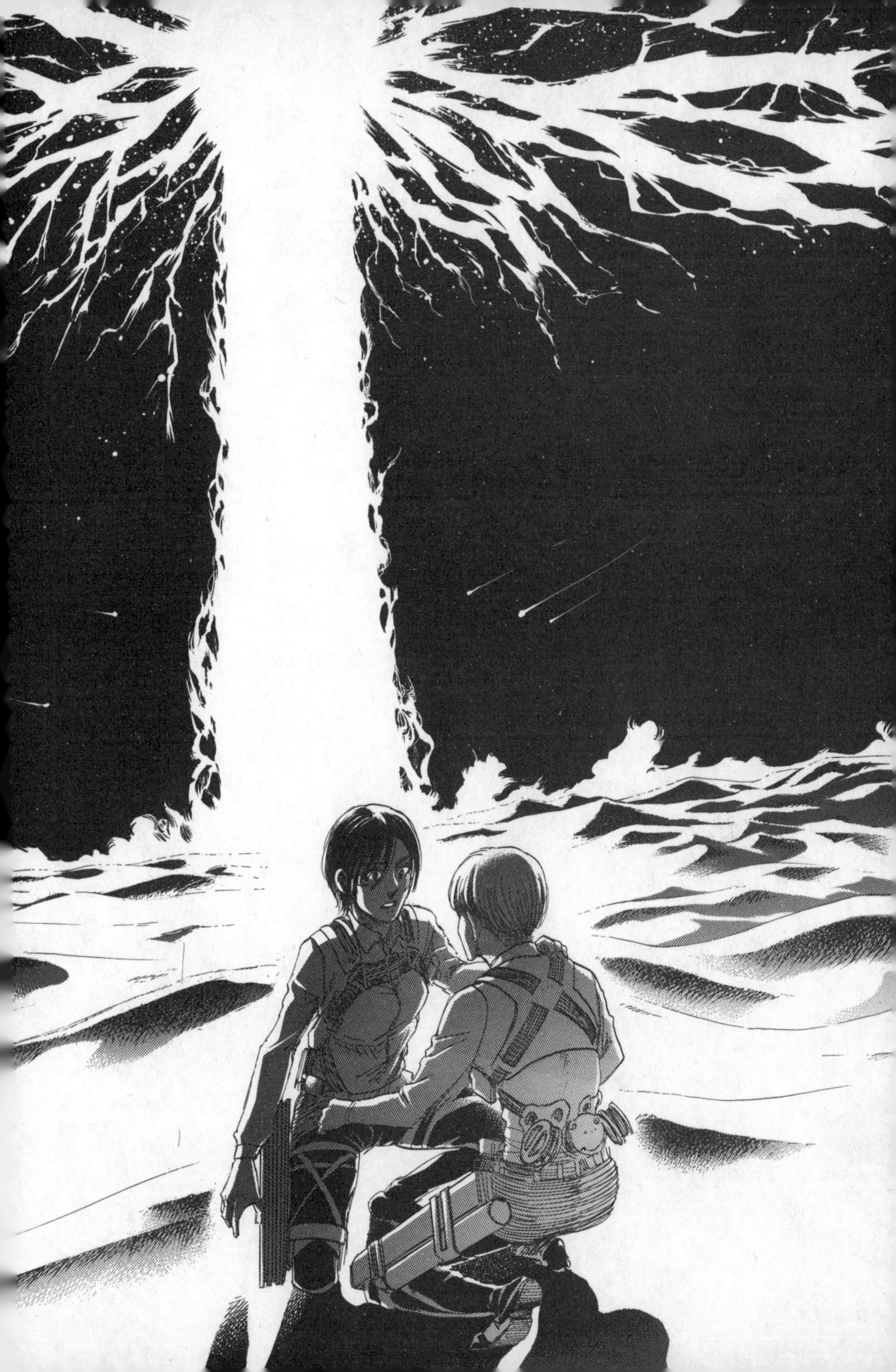

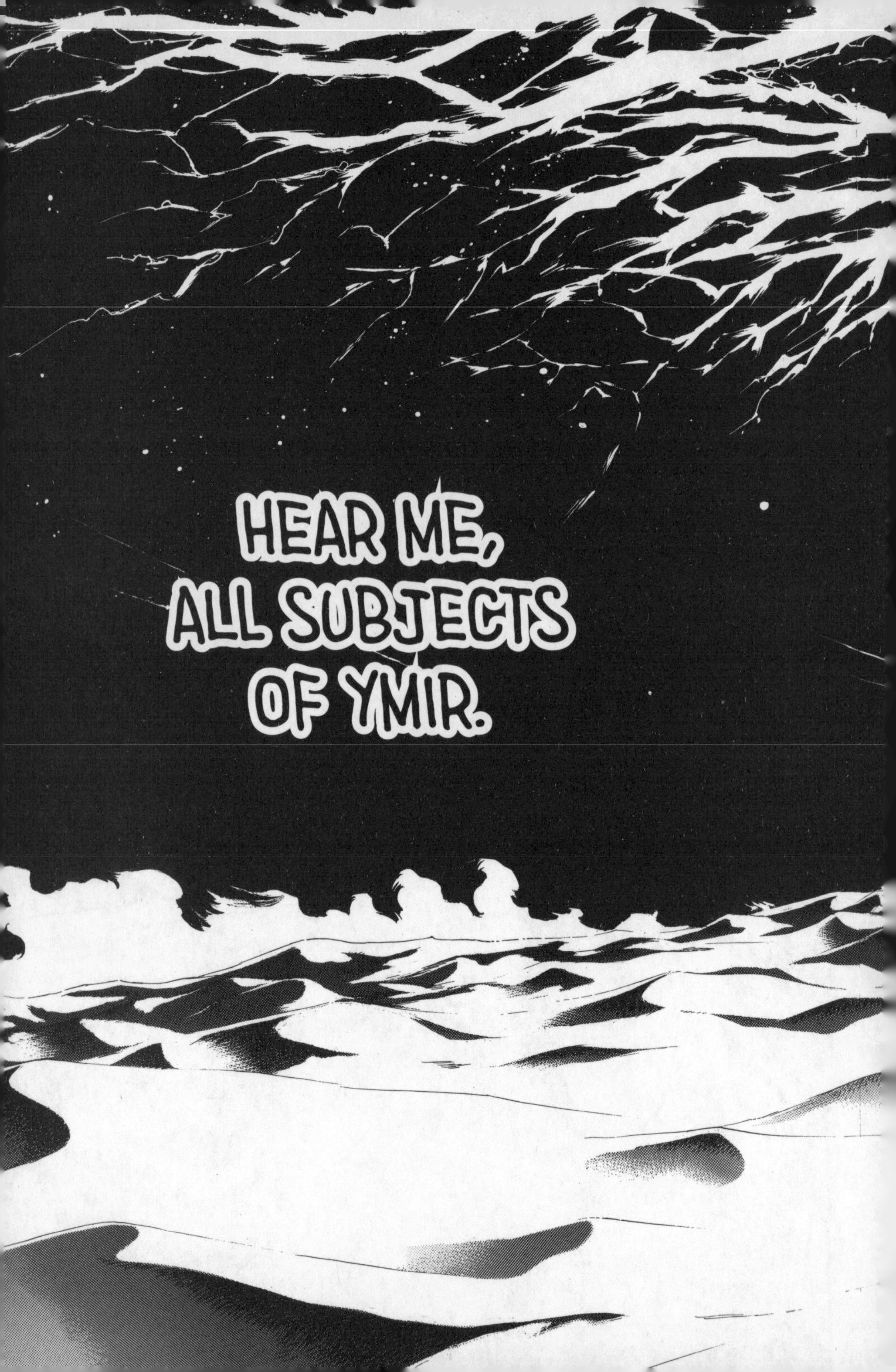
HEAR ME, ALL SUBJECTS OF YMIR.

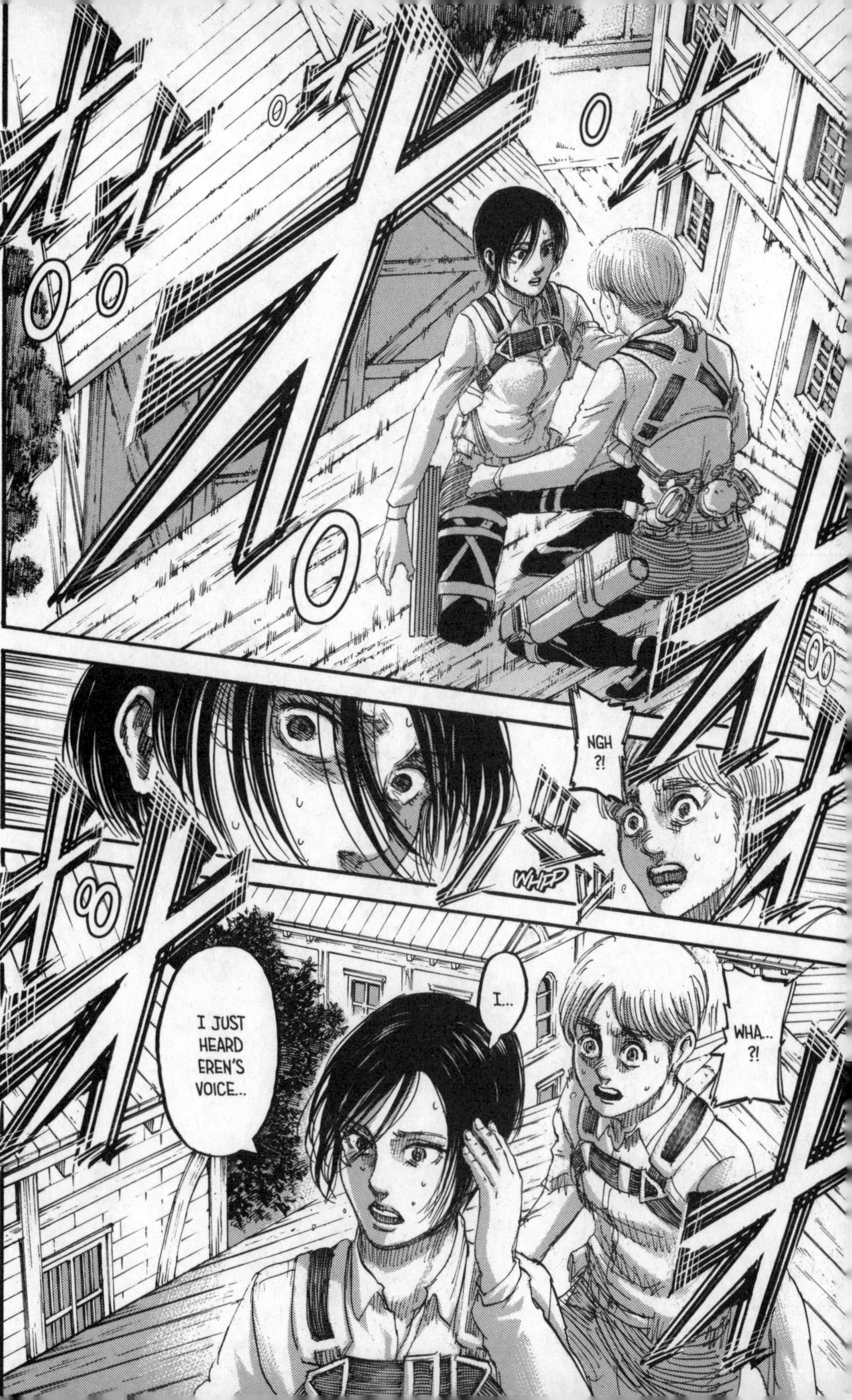
NGH ?!
WHIP
WHA... ?!
I...
I JUST HEARD EREN'S VOICE...

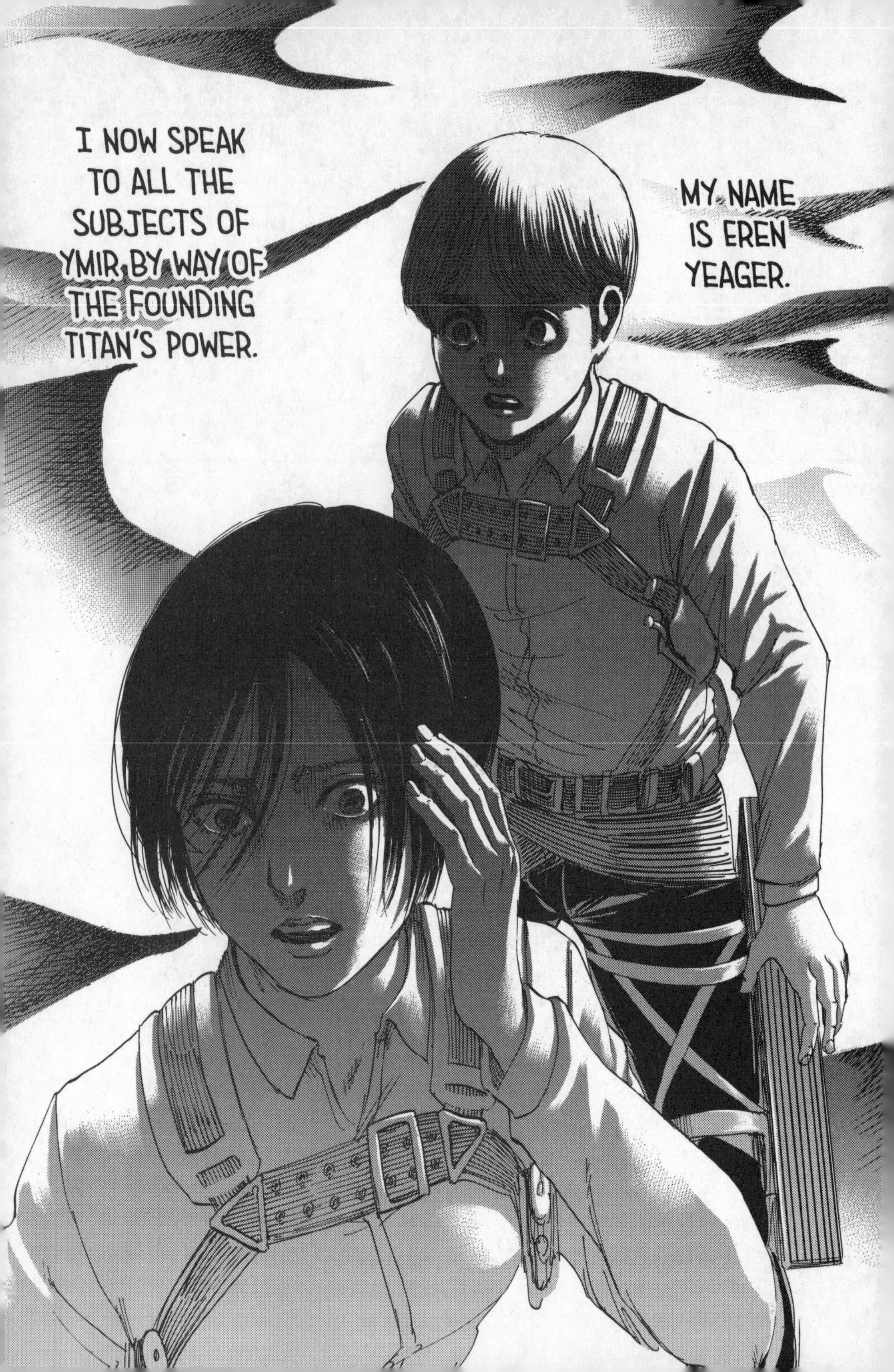
MY NAME IS EREN YEAGER.
I NOW SPEAK TO ALL THE SUBJECTS OF YMIR BY WAY OF THE FOUNDING TITAN'S POWER.

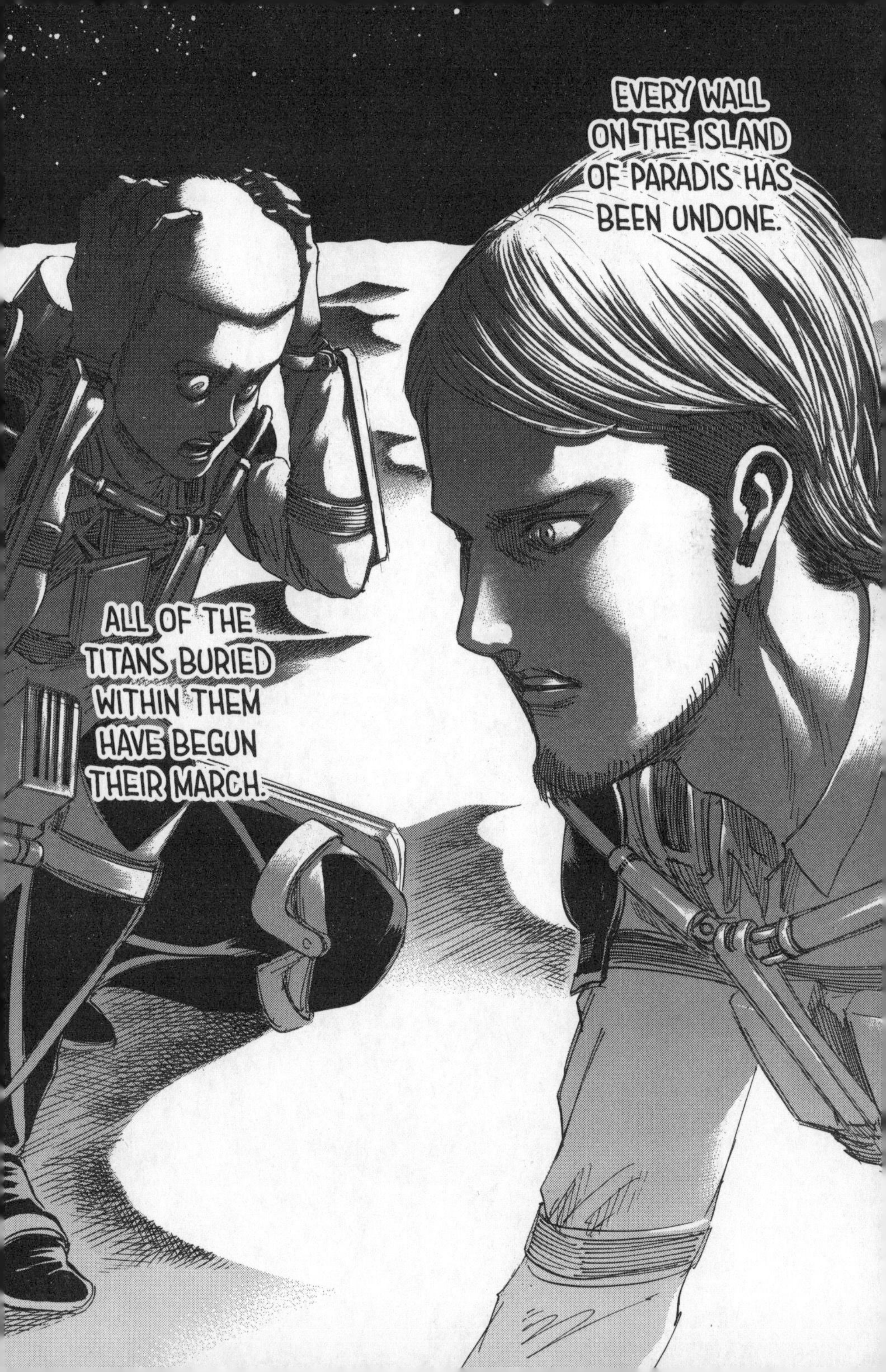
EVERY WALL ON THE ISLAND OF PARADIS HAS BEEN UNDONE.
ALL OF THE TITANS BURIED WITHIN THEM HAVE BEGUN THEIR MARCH.

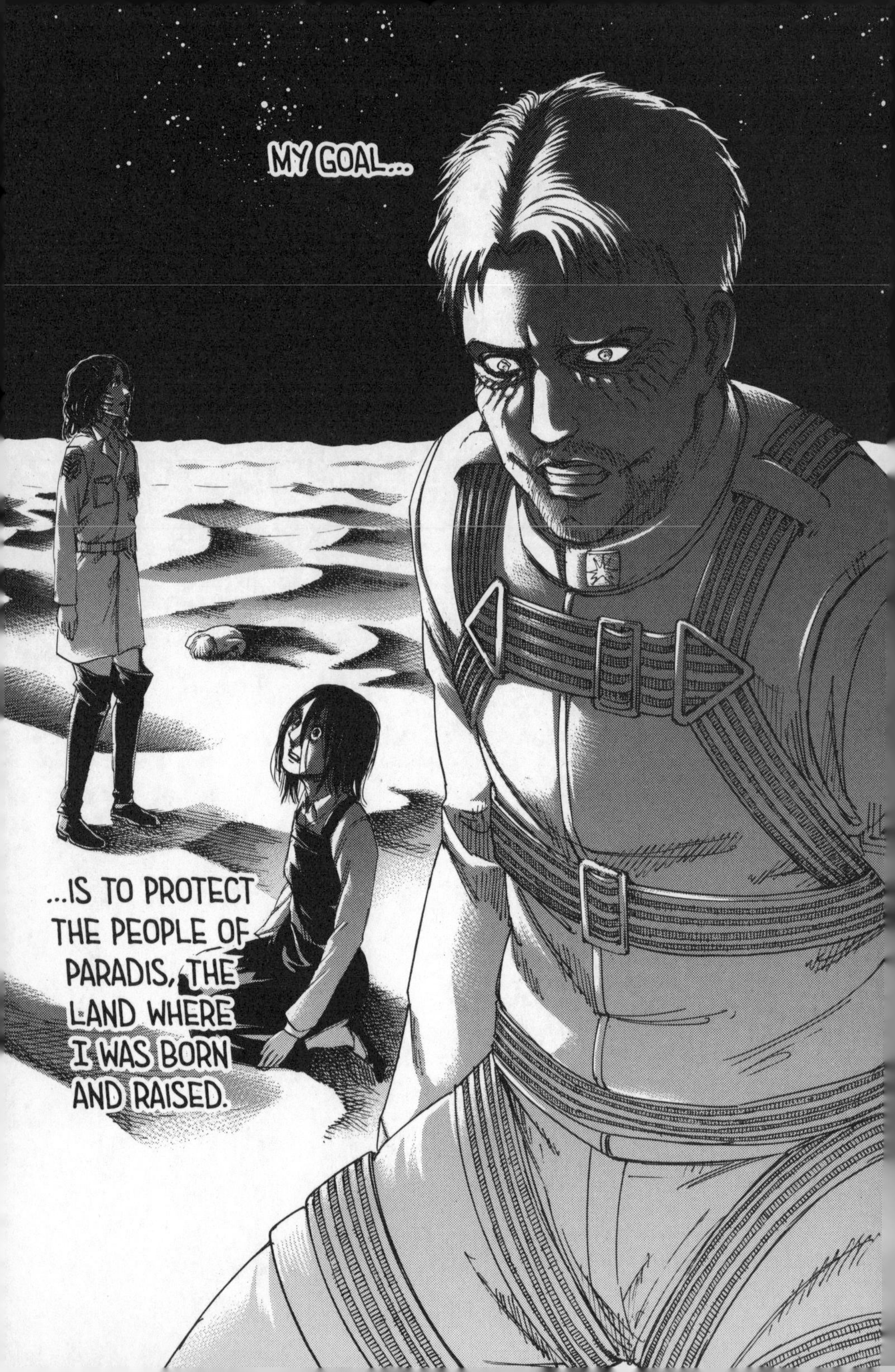
MY GOAL...
...IS TO PROTECT THE PEOPLE OF PARADIS, THE LAND WHERE I WAS BORN AND RAISED.

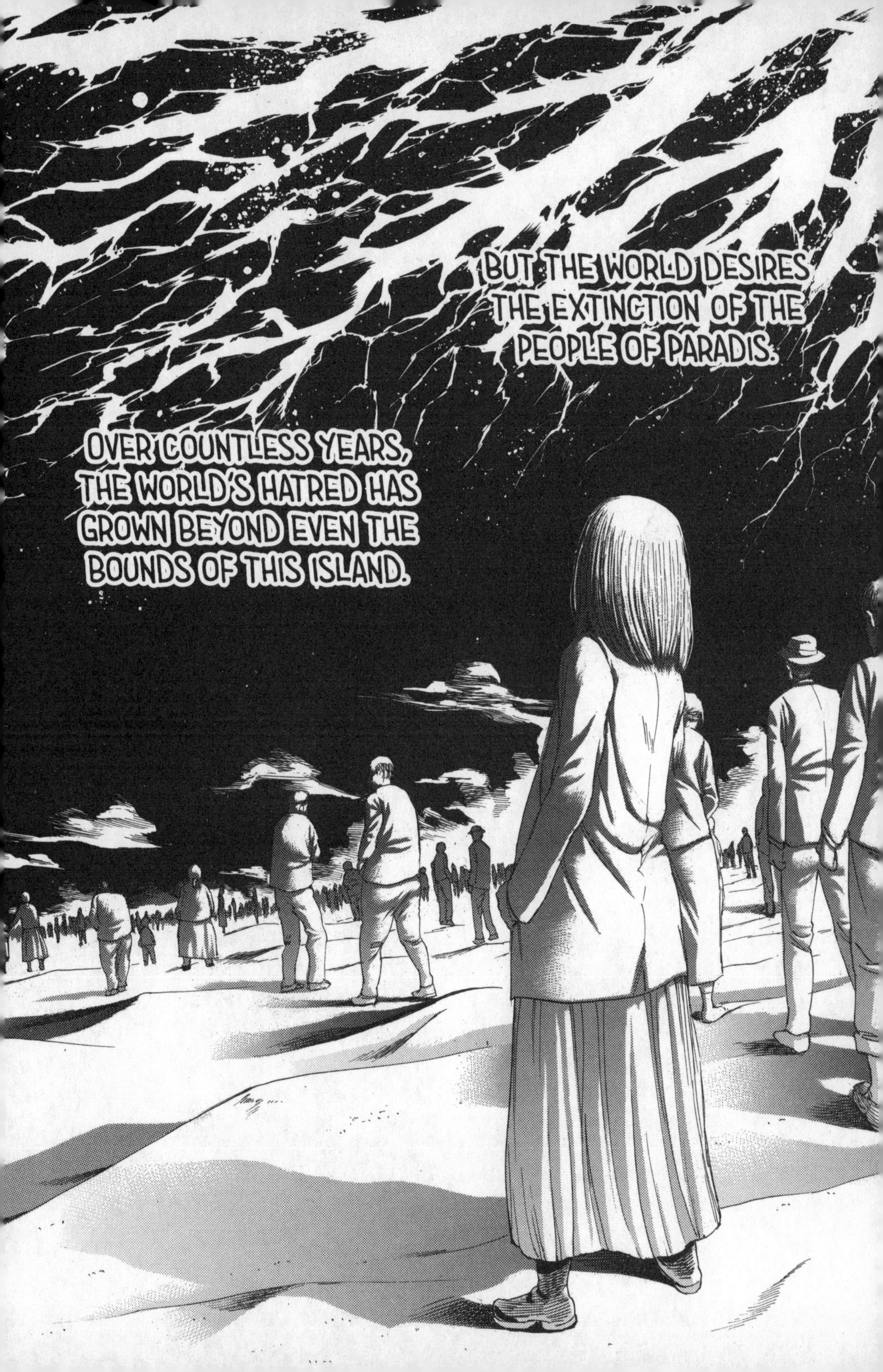
BUT THE WORLD DESIRES THE EXTINCTION OF THE PEOPLE OF PARADIS.
OVER COUNTLESS YEARS, THE WORLD'S HATRED HAS GROWN BEYOND EVEN THE BOUNDS OF THIS ISLAND.

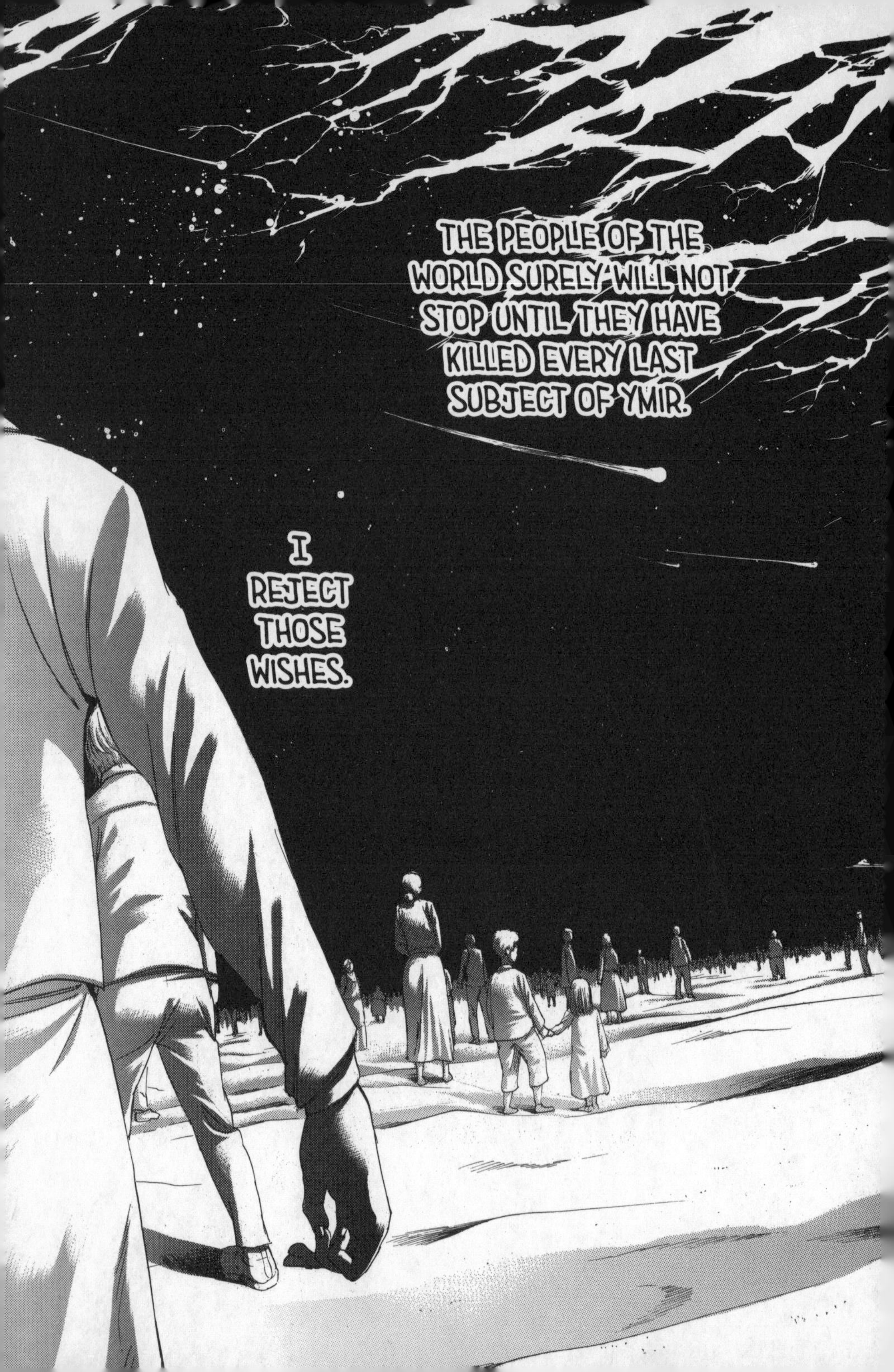
THE PEOPLE OF THE WORLD SURELY WILL NOT STOP UNTIL THEY HAVE KILLED EVERY LAST SUBJECT OF YMIR.
I REJECT THOSE WISHES.

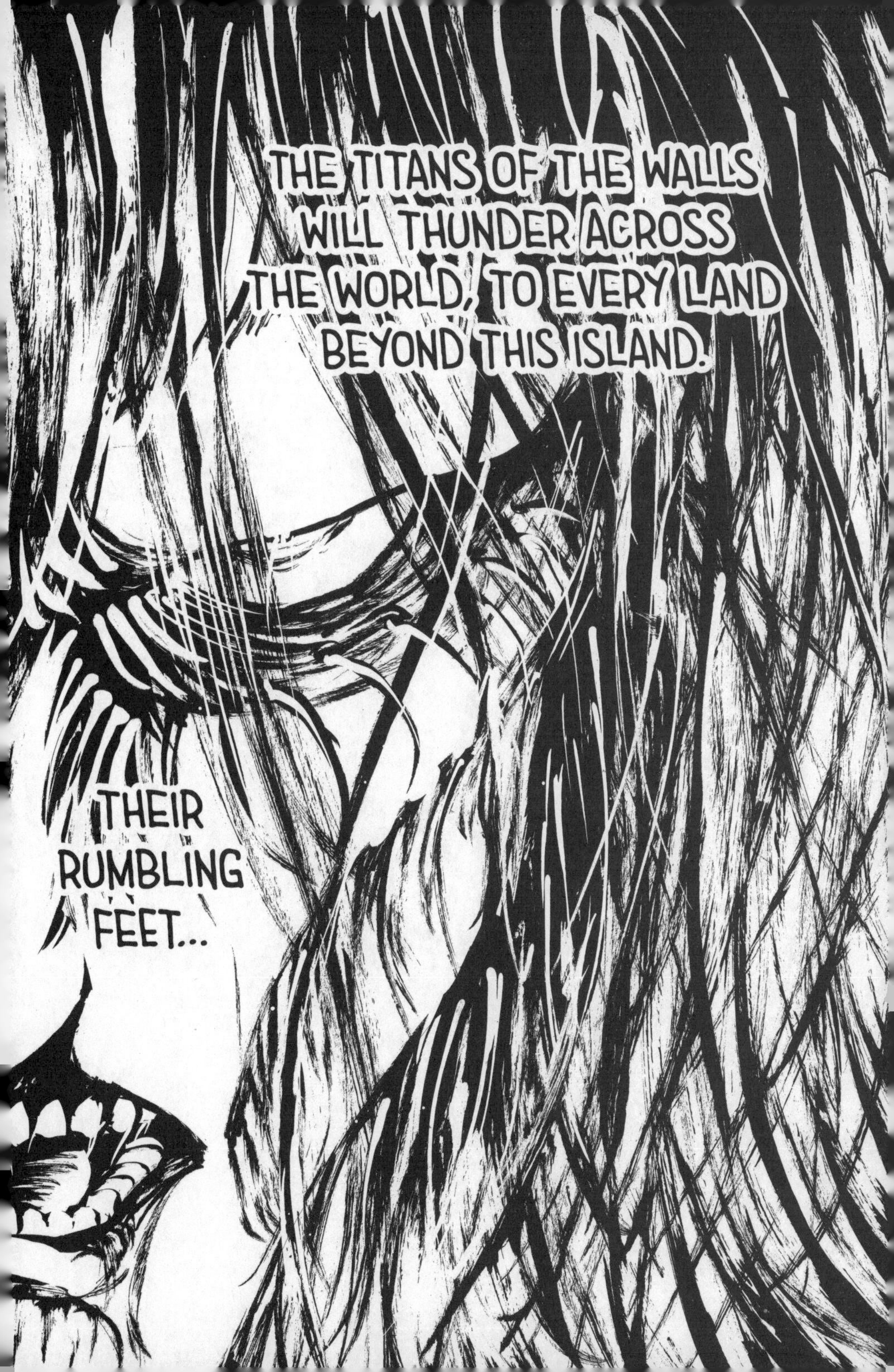
THE TITANS OF THE WALLS WILL THUNDER ACROSS THE WORLD, TO EVERY LAND BEYOND THIS ISLAND.
THEIR RUMBLING FEET...

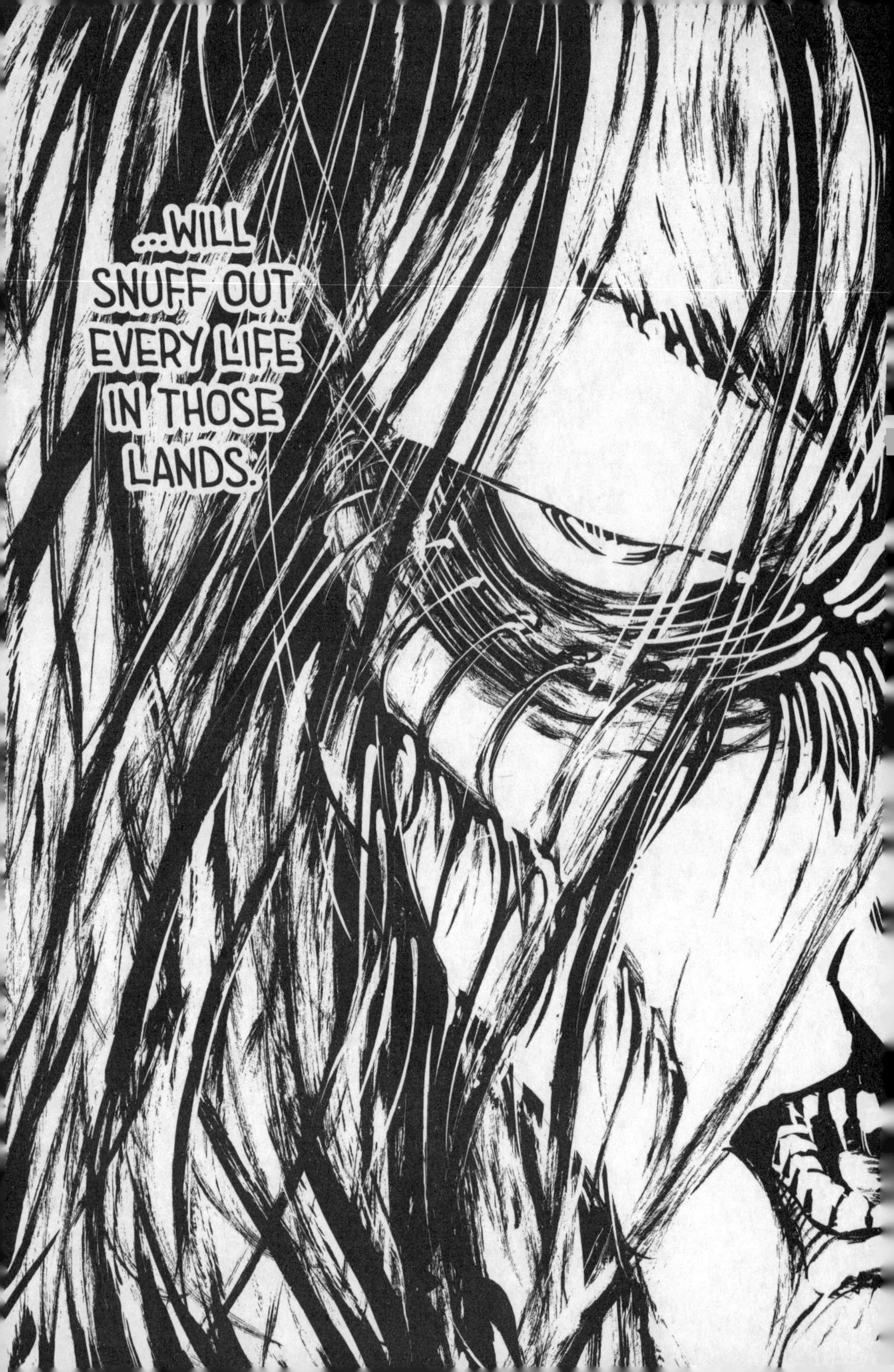
...WILL SNUFF OUT EVERY LIFE IN THOSE LANDS.

ATTACK on TITAN

Episode 124: Thaw

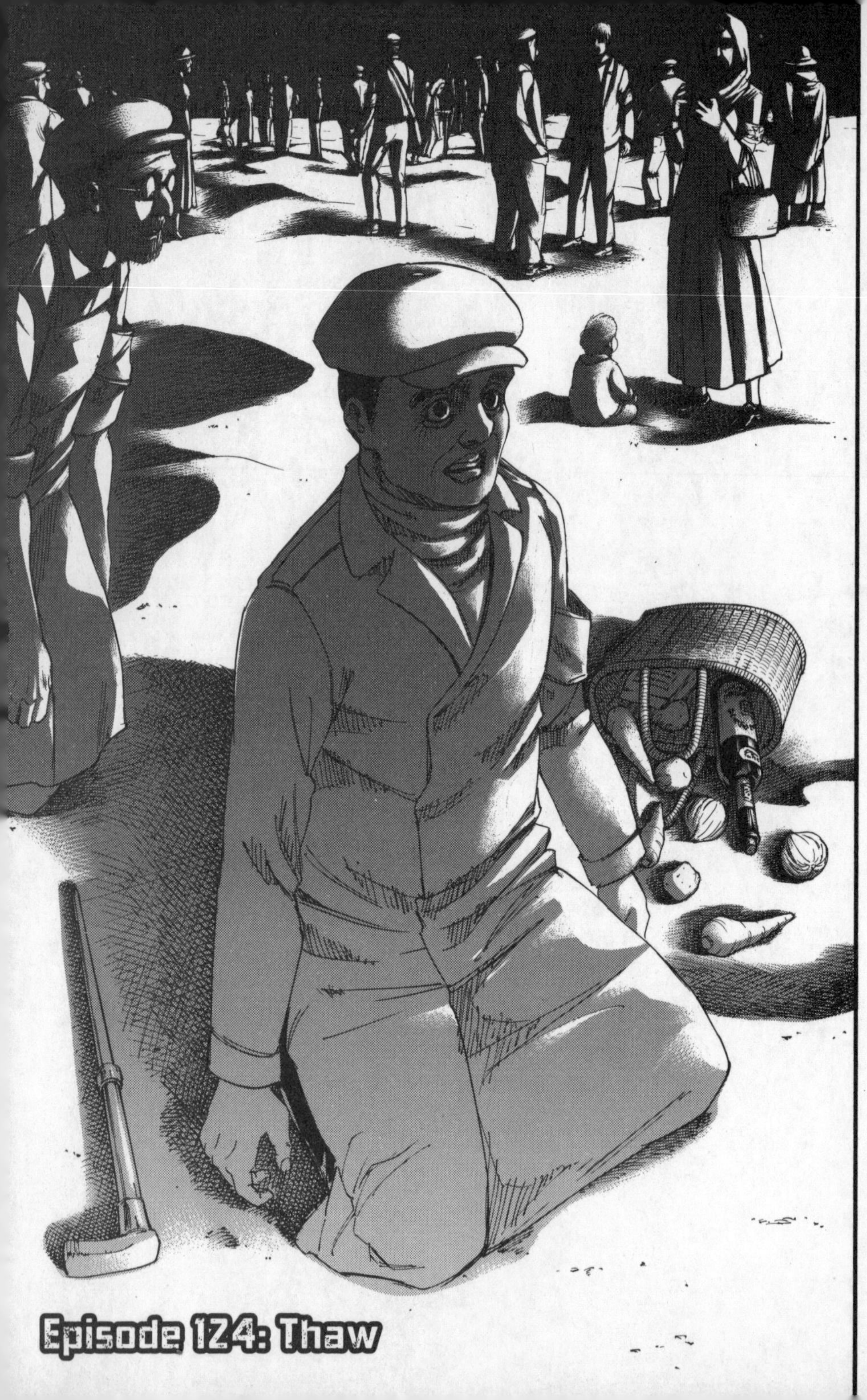

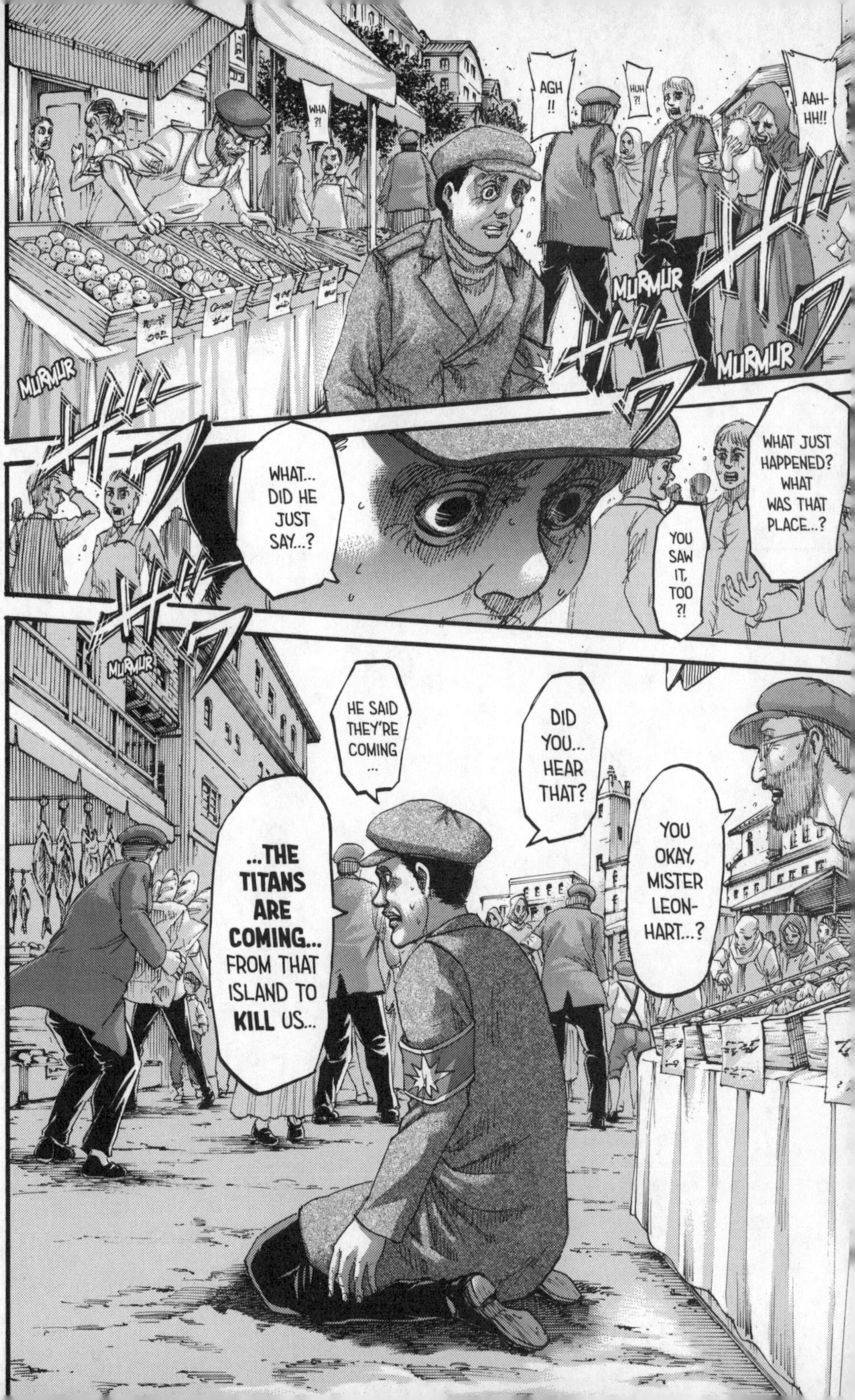
AAH-HH!!
HUH ?!
AGH !!
WHA ?!
MURMUR
MURMUR
MURMUR
WHAT JUST HAPPENED? WHAT WAS THAT PLACE...?
YOU SAW IT, TOO ?!
WHAT... DID HE JUST SAY...?
MURMUR
YOU OKAY, MISTER LEON-HART...?
DID YOU... HEAR THAT?
HE SAID THEY'RE COMING ...
...THE TITANS ARE COMING... FROM THAT ISLAND TO KILL US...

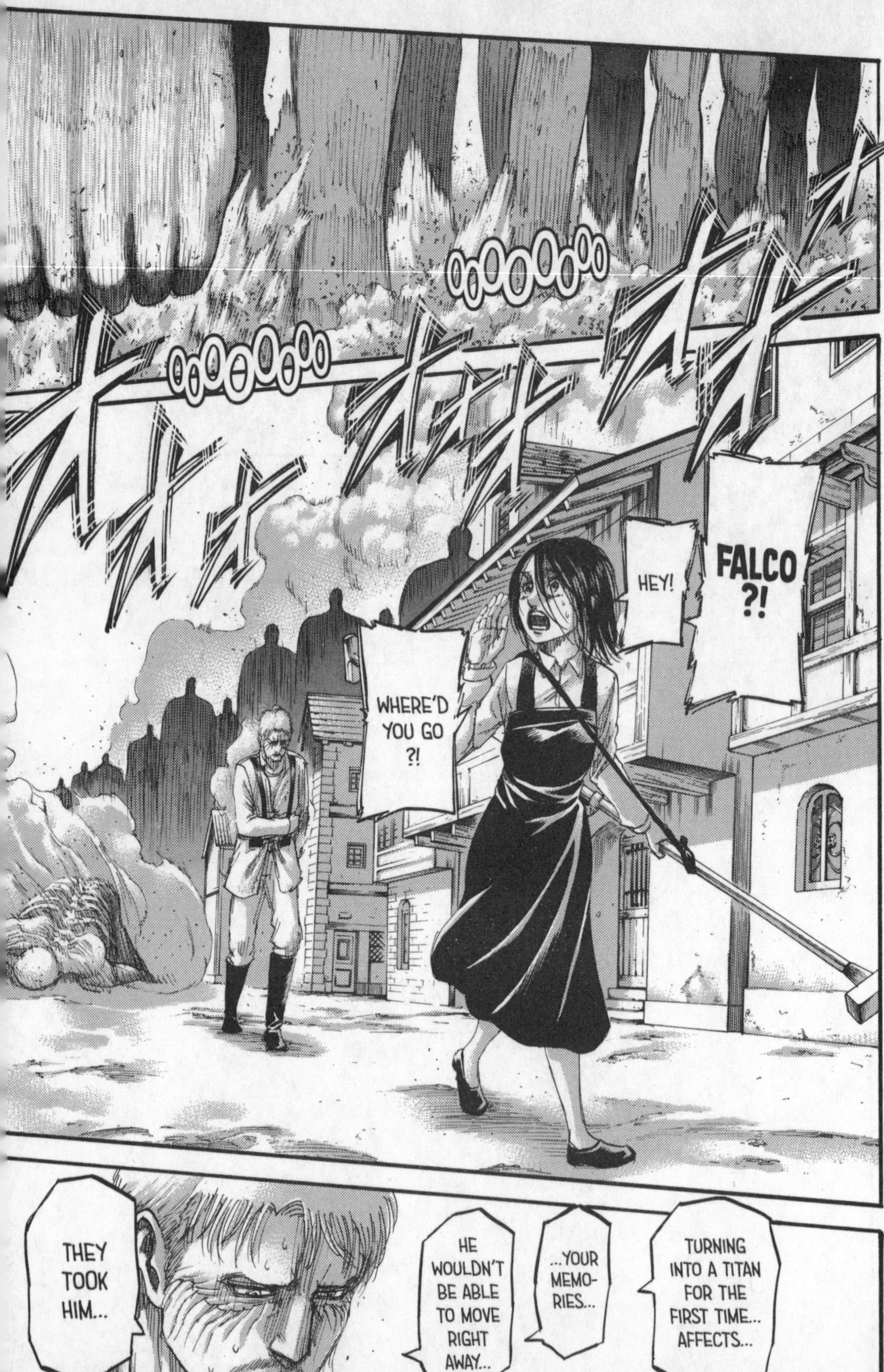
OOOOOOOOO
OOOOOOOOO
FALCO ?!
HEY!
WHERE'D YOU GO ?!
TURNING INTO A TITAN FOR THE FIRST TIME... AFFECTS...
...YOUR MEMO- RIES...
HE WOULDN'T BE ABLE TO MOVE RIGHT AWAY...
THEY TOOK HIM...

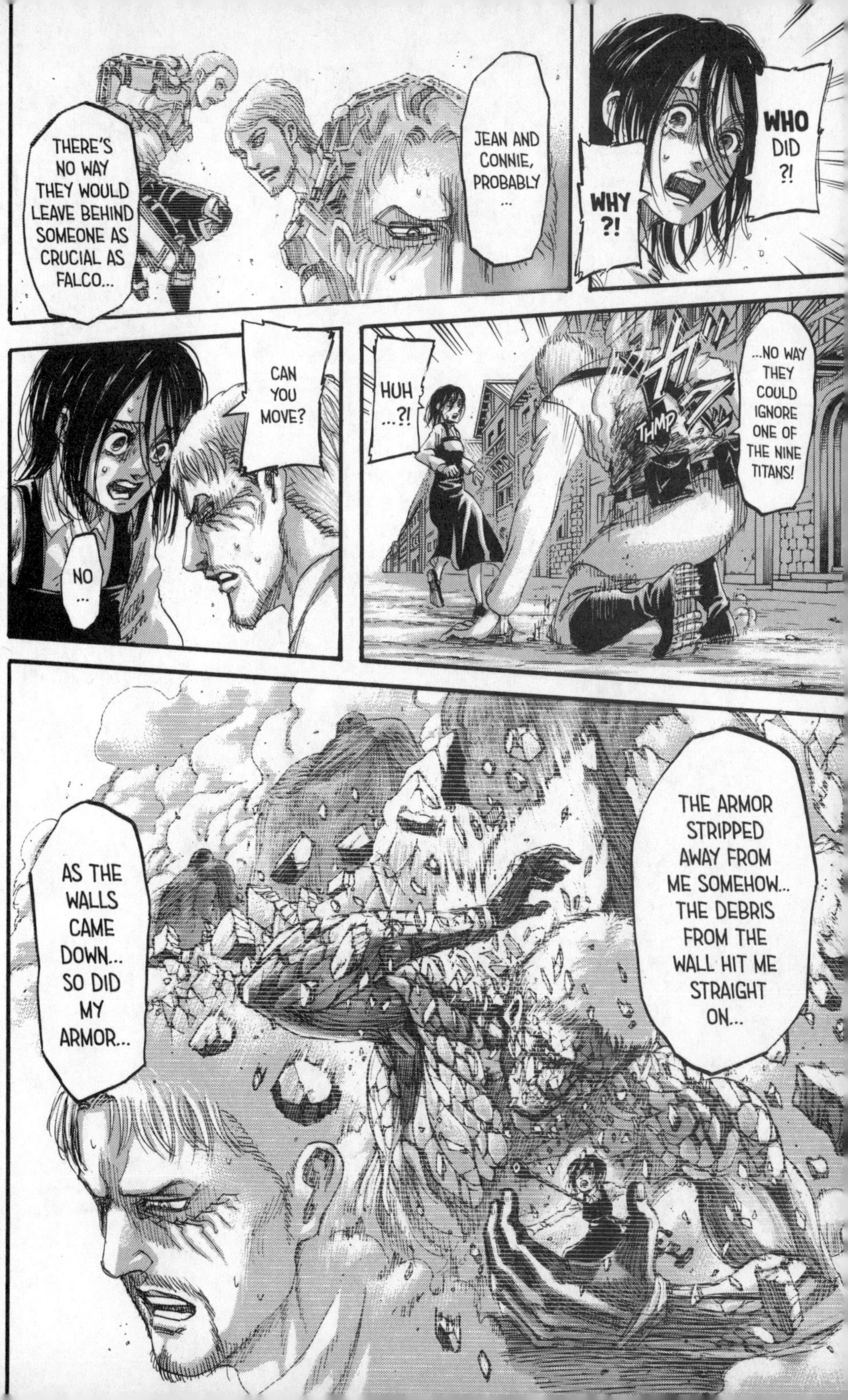
WHO DID ?!
WHY ?!
JEAN AND CONNIE, PROBABLY ...
THERE'S NO WAY THEY WOULD LEAVE BEHIND SOMEONE AS CRUCIAL AS FALCO...
...NO WAY THEY COULD IGNORE ONE OF THE NINE TITANS!
THMP
HUH ...?!
CAN YOU MOVE?
NO ...
THE ARMOR STRIPPED AWAY FROM ME SOMEHOW... THE DEBRIS FROM THE WALL HIT ME STRAIGHT ON...
AS THE WALLS CAME DOWN... SO DID MY ARMOR...

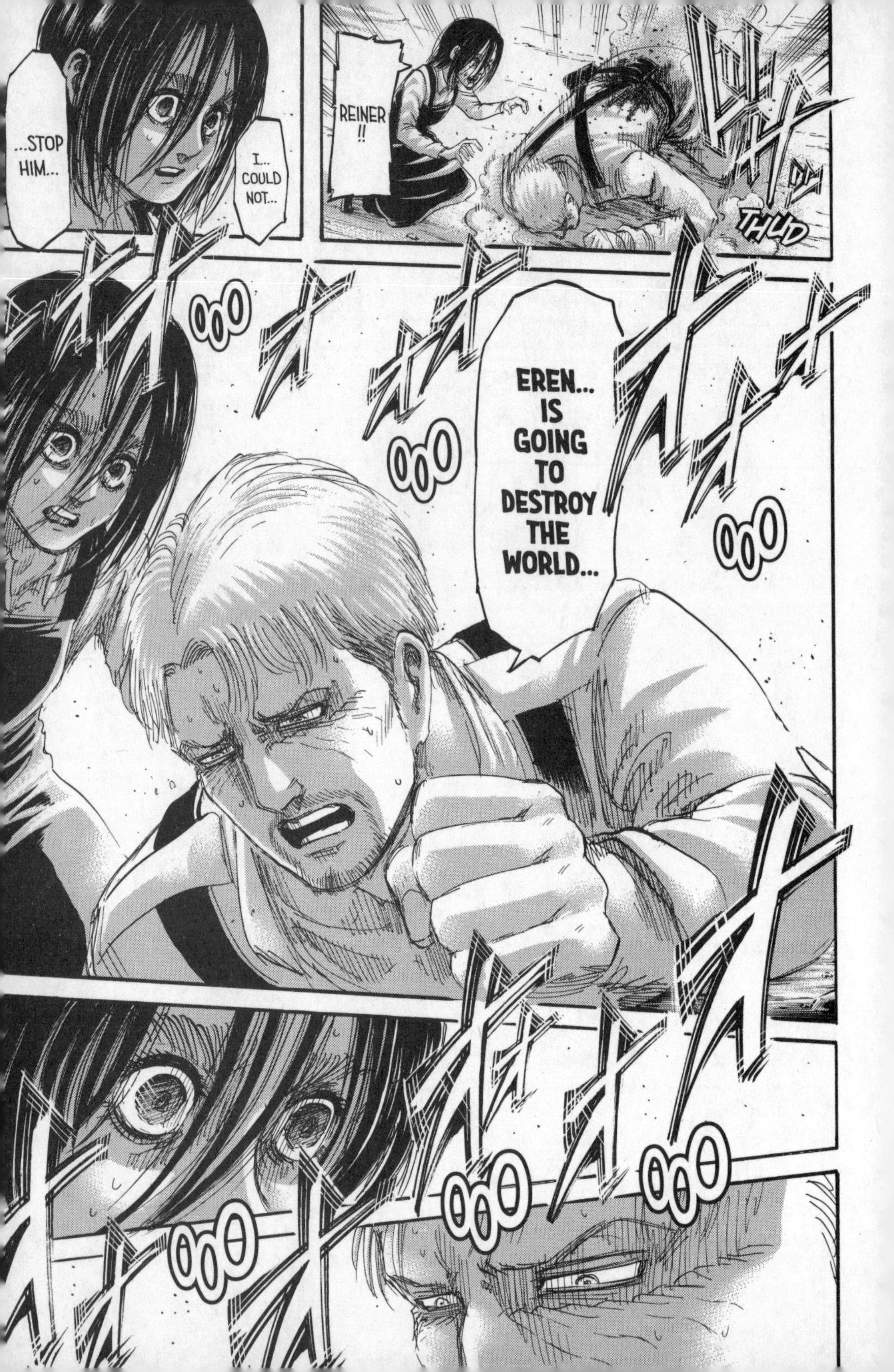
THUD
REINER !!
I... COULD NOT...
...STOP HIM...
OOO
OOO
EREN... IS GOING TO DESTROY THE WORLD...
OOO
OOO
OOO
OOO

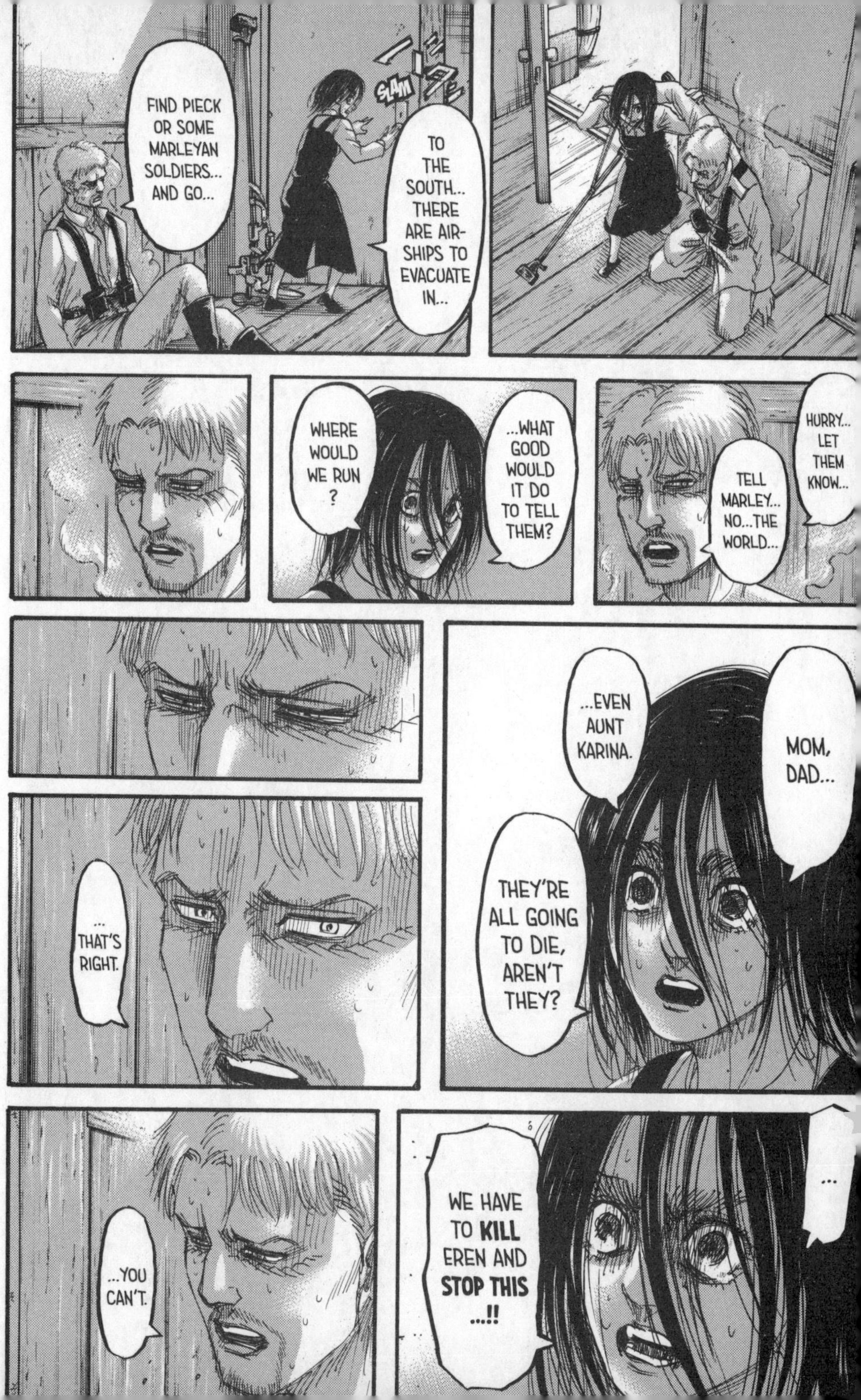

FIND PIECK OR SOME MARLEYAN SOLDIERS... AND GO...
SLAM
TO THE SOUTH... THERE ARE AIR-SHIPS TO EVACUATE IN...
HURRY... LET THEM KNOW...
TELL MARLEY... NO...THE WORLD...
...WHAT GOOD WOULD IT DO TO TELL THEM?
WHERE WOULD WE RUN?
MOM, DAD...
...EVEN AUNT KARINA.
THEY'RE ALL GOING TO DIE, AREN'T THEY?
... THAT'S RIGHT.
...
WE HAVE TO **KILL** EREN AND **STOP THIS** ...!!
...YOU CAN'T.

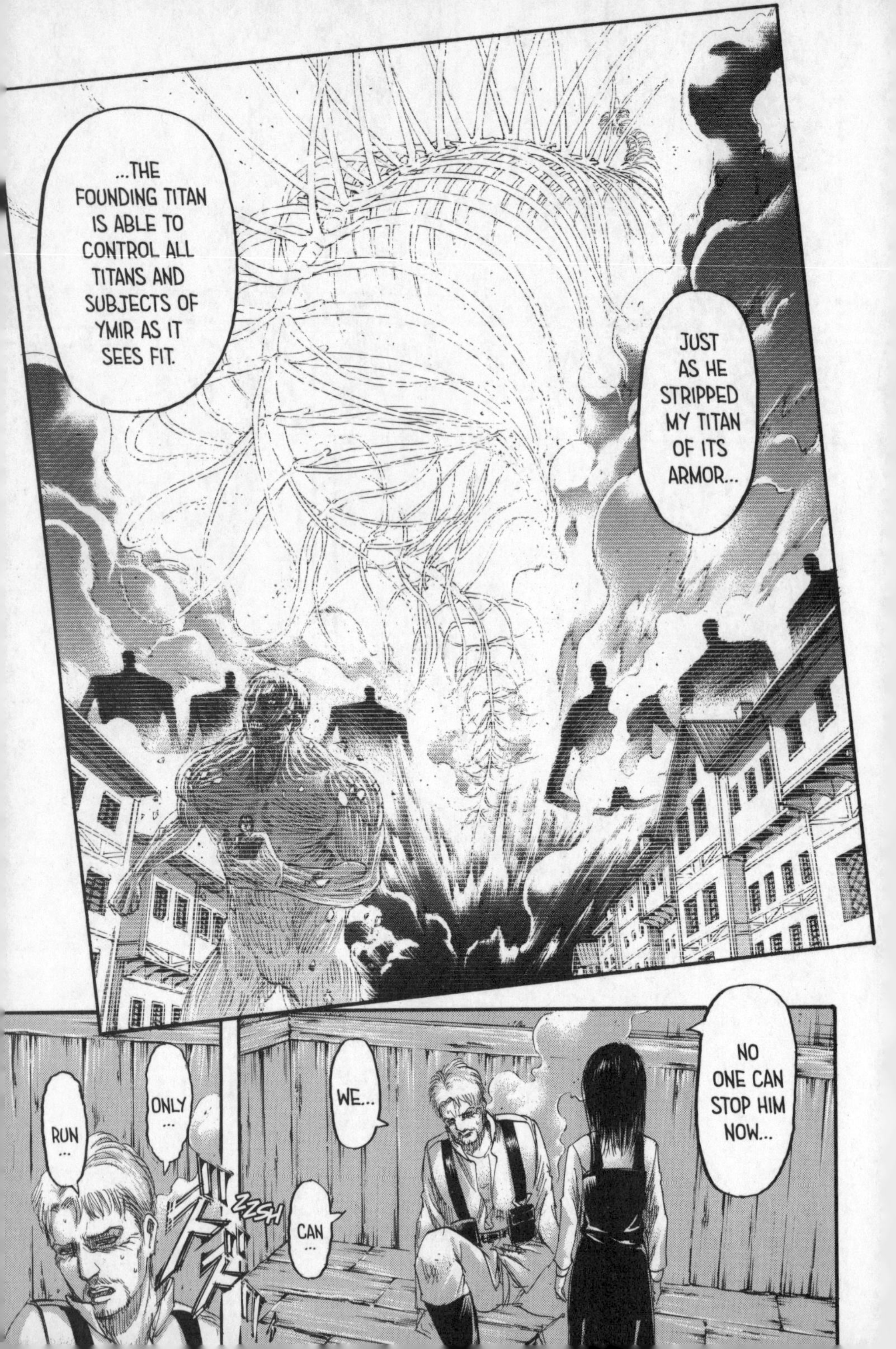
JUST AS HE STRIPPED MY TITAN OF ITS ARMOR...
...THE FOUNDING TITAN IS ABLE TO CONTROL ALL TITANS AND SUBJECTS OF YMIR AS IT SEES FIT.
NO ONE CAN STOP HIM NOW...
WE...
CAN...
ONLY...
RUN...
ZZSH

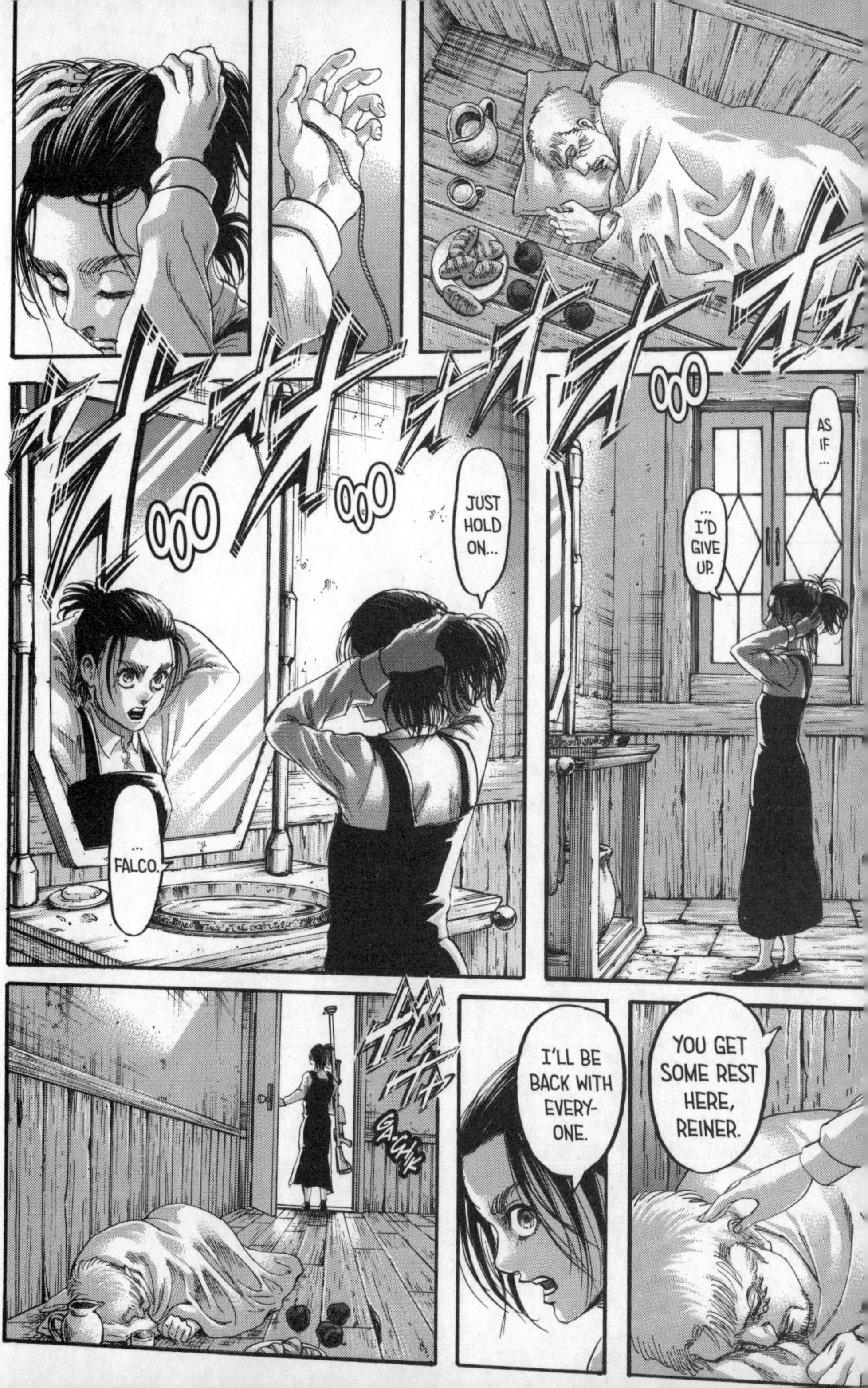
AS IF...
...I'D GIVE UP.
JUST HOLD ON...
...FALCO.
YOU GET SOME REST HERE, REINER.
I'LL BE BACK WITH EVERY-ONE.
GA-CHK

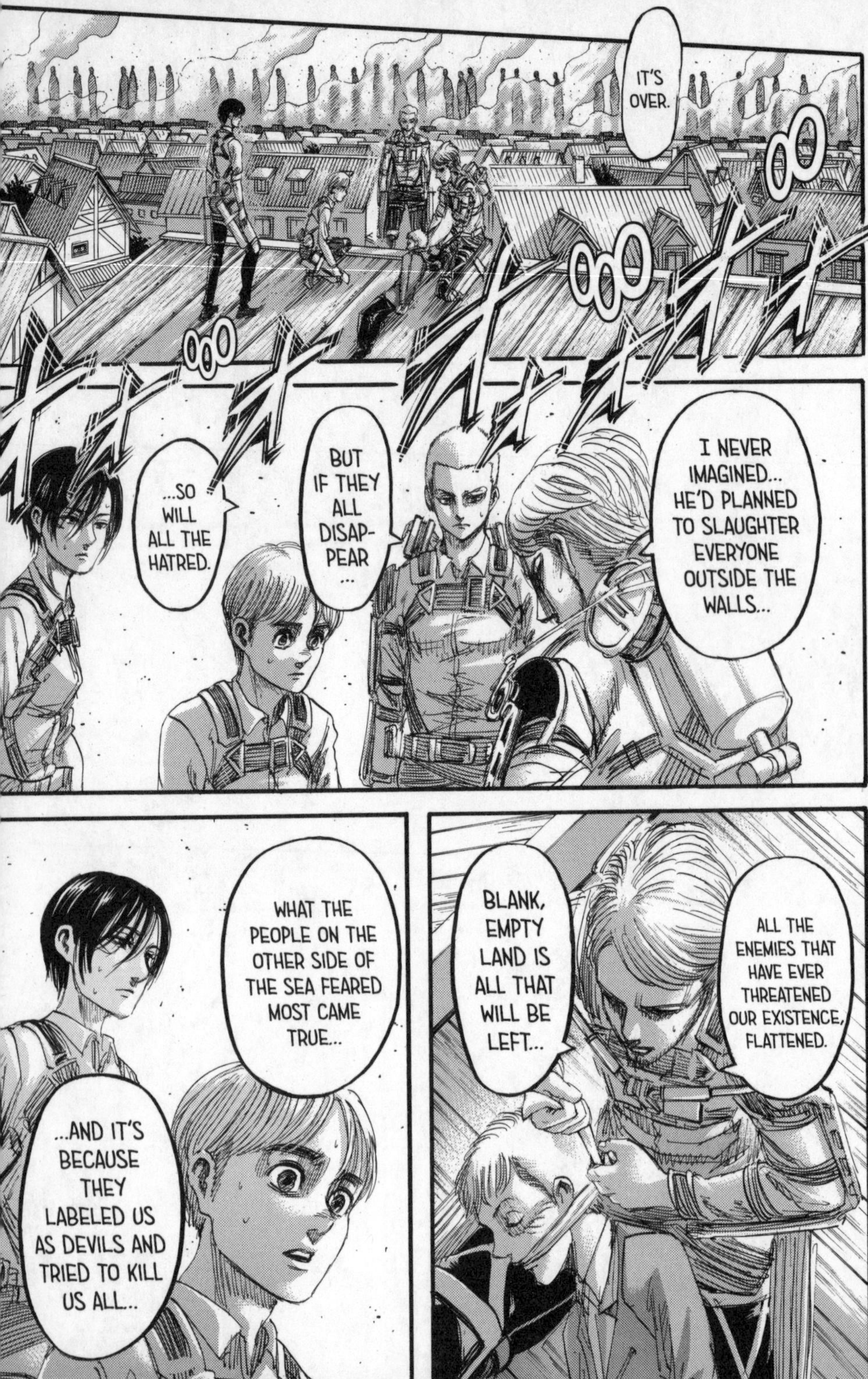
IT'S OVER.
I NEVER IMAGINED... HE'D PLANNED TO SLAUGHTER EVERYONE OUTSIDE THE WALLS...
BUT IF THEY ALL DISAPPEAR ...
...SO WILL ALL THE HATRED.
ALL THE ENEMIES THAT HAVE EVER THREATENED OUR EXISTENCE, FLATTENED.
BLANK, EMPTY LAND IS ALL THAT WILL BE LEFT...
WHAT THE PEOPLE ON THE OTHER SIDE OF THE SEA FEARED MOST CAME TRUE...
...AND IT'S BECAUSE THEY LABELED US AS DEVILS AND TRIED TO KILL US ALL..

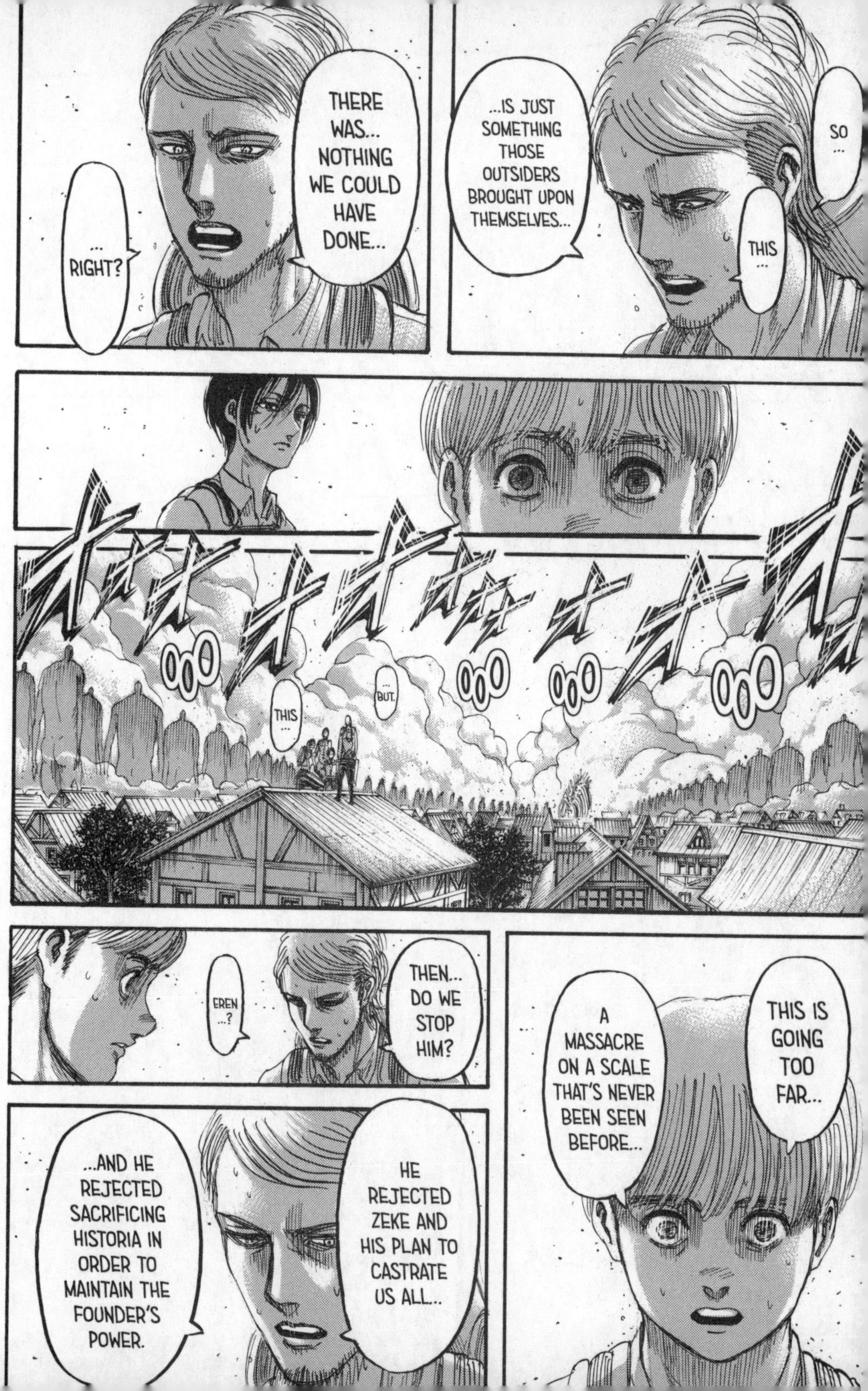
SO ...
THIS ...
...IS JUST SOMETHING THOSE OUTSIDERS BROUGHT UPON THEMSELVES...
THERE WAS... NOTHING WE COULD HAVE DONE...
... RIGHT?
OOO
OOO
OOO
OOO
... BUT.
THIS ...
OOO
THIS IS GOING TOO FAR...
A MASSACRE ON A SCALE THAT'S NEVER BEEN SEEN BEFORE...
THEN... DO WE STOP HIM?
EREN ...?
HE REJECTED ZEKE AND HIS PLAN TO CASTRATE US ALL..
...AND HE REJECTED SACRIFICING HISTORIA IN ORDER TO MAINTAIN THE FOUNDER'S POWER.

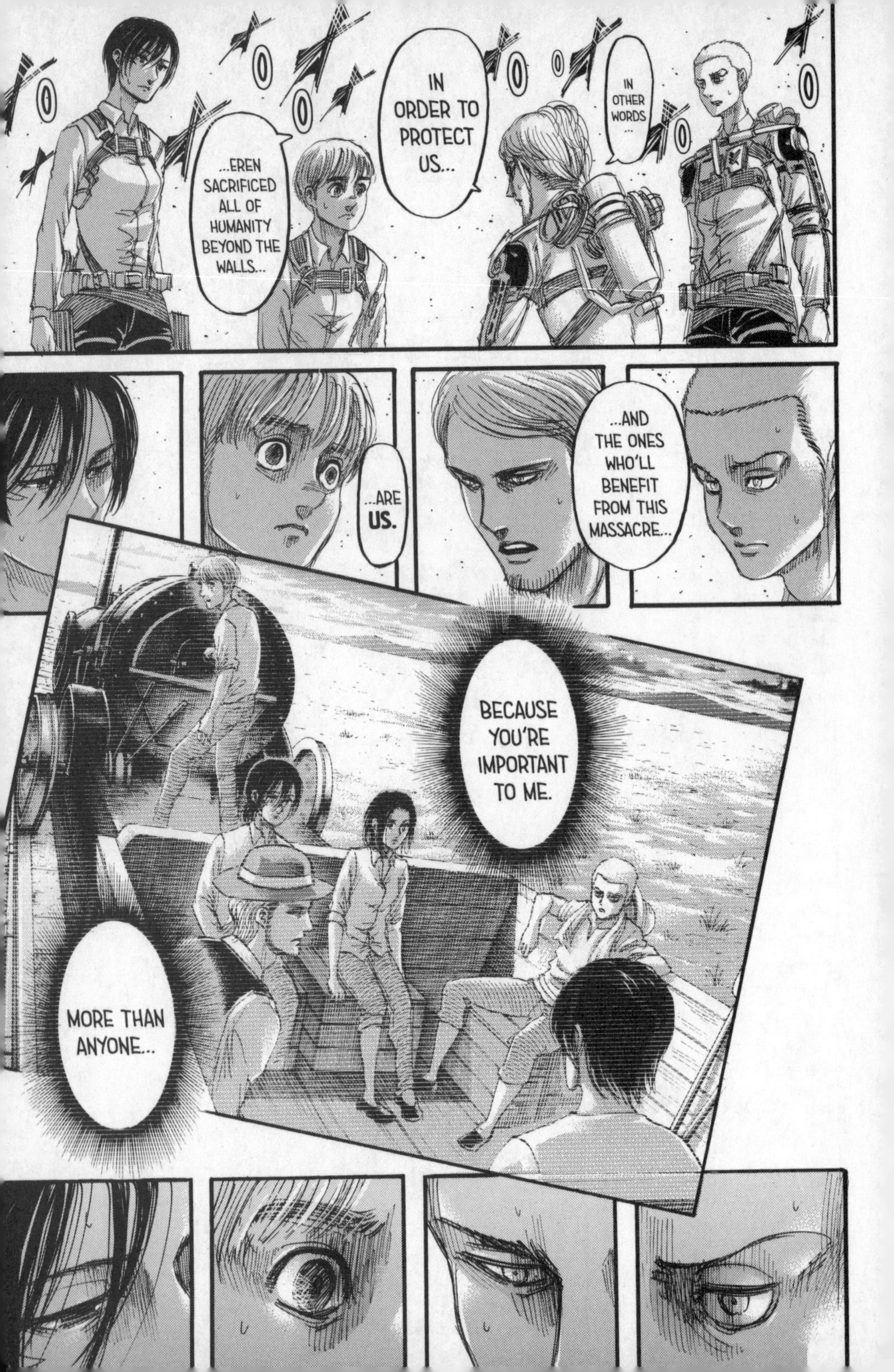
IN OTHER WORDS...
IN ORDER TO PROTECT US...
...EREN SACRIFICED ALL OF HUMANITY BEYOND THE WALLS...
...AND THE ONES WHO'LL BENEFIT FROM THIS MASSACRE...
...ARE **US.**
BECAUSE YOU'RE IMPORTANT TO ME.
MORE THAN ANYONE...

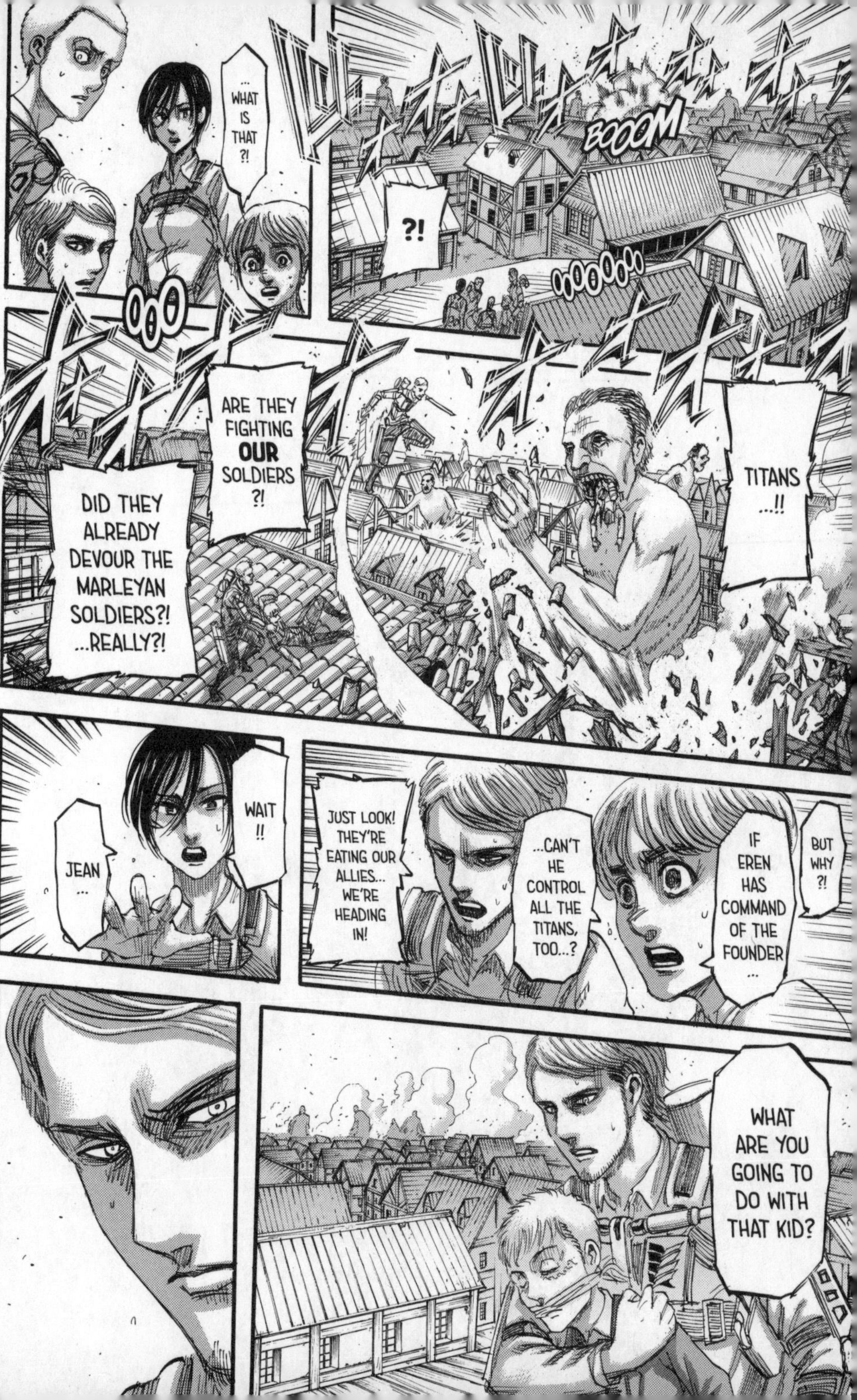
BOOOM
?!
OOOOOOOO
...WHAT IS THAT ?!
OOO
TITANS ...!!
ARE THEY FIGHTING **OUR** SOLDIERS ?!
DID THEY ALREADY DEVOUR THE MARLEYAN SOLDIERS?! ...REALLY?!
BUT WHY ?!
IF EREN HAS COMMAND OF THE FOUNDER ...
...CAN'T HE CONTROL ALL THE TITANS, TOO...?
JUST LOOK! THEY'RE EATING OUR ALLIES... WE'RE HEADING IN!
WAIT !!
JEAN ...
WHAT ARE YOU GOING TO DO WITH THAT KID?

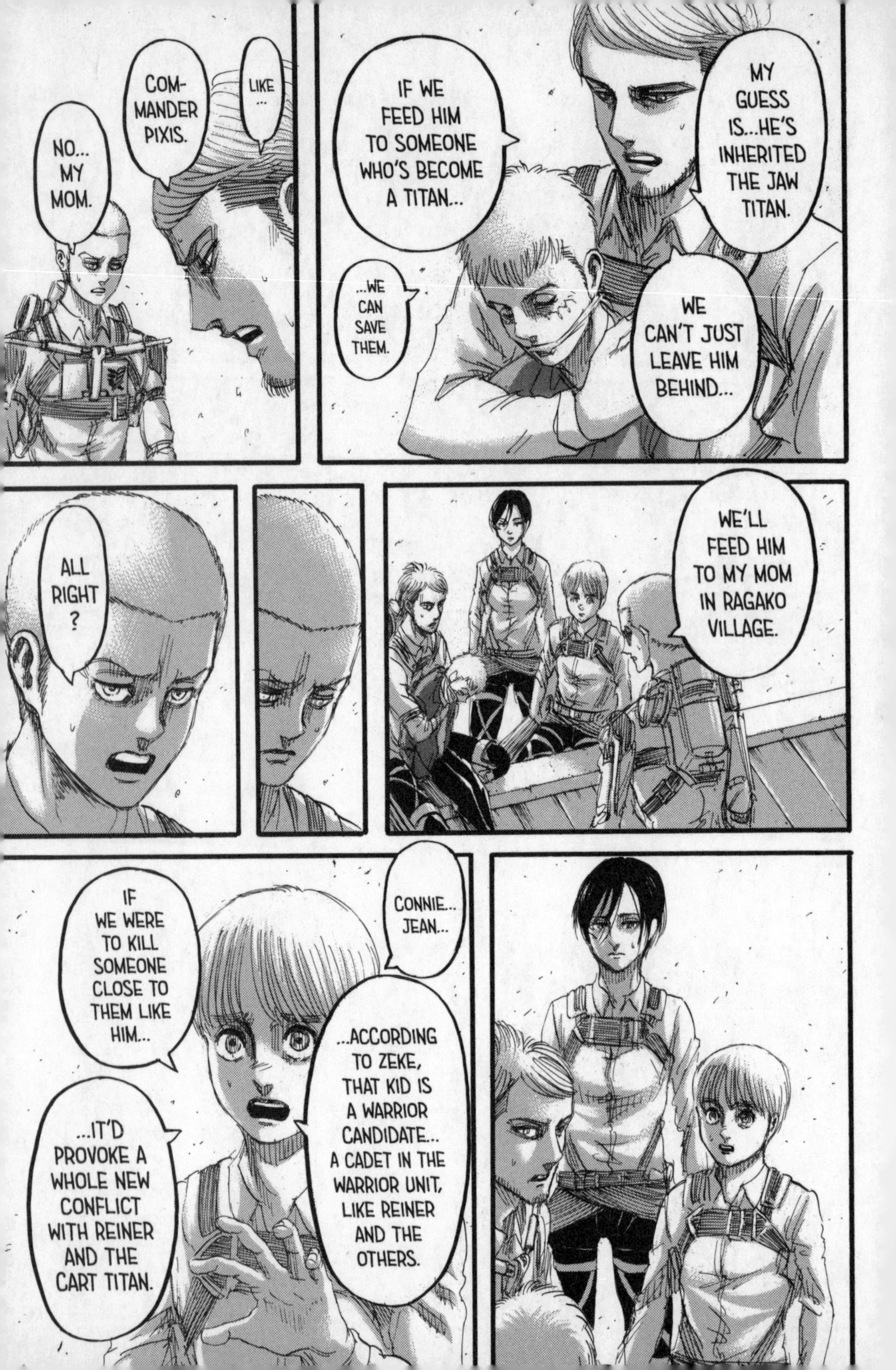
MY GUESS IS...HE'S INHERITED THE JAW TITAN.
IF WE FEED HIM TO SOMEONE WHO'S BECOME A TITAN...
...WE CAN SAVE THEM.
WE CAN'T JUST LEAVE HIM BEHIND...
LIKE...
COM-MANDER PIXIS.
NO... MY MOM.
WE'LL FEED HIM TO MY MOM IN RAGAKO VILLAGE.
ALL RIGHT?
CONNIE... JEAN...
...ACCORDING TO ZEKE, THAT KID IS A WARRIOR CANDIDATE... A CADET IN THE WARRIOR UNIT, LIKE REINER AND THE OTHERS.
IF WE WERE TO KILL SOMEONE CLOSE TO THEM LIKE HIM...
...IT'D PROVOKE A WHOLE NEW CONFLICT WITH REINER AND THE CART TITAN.

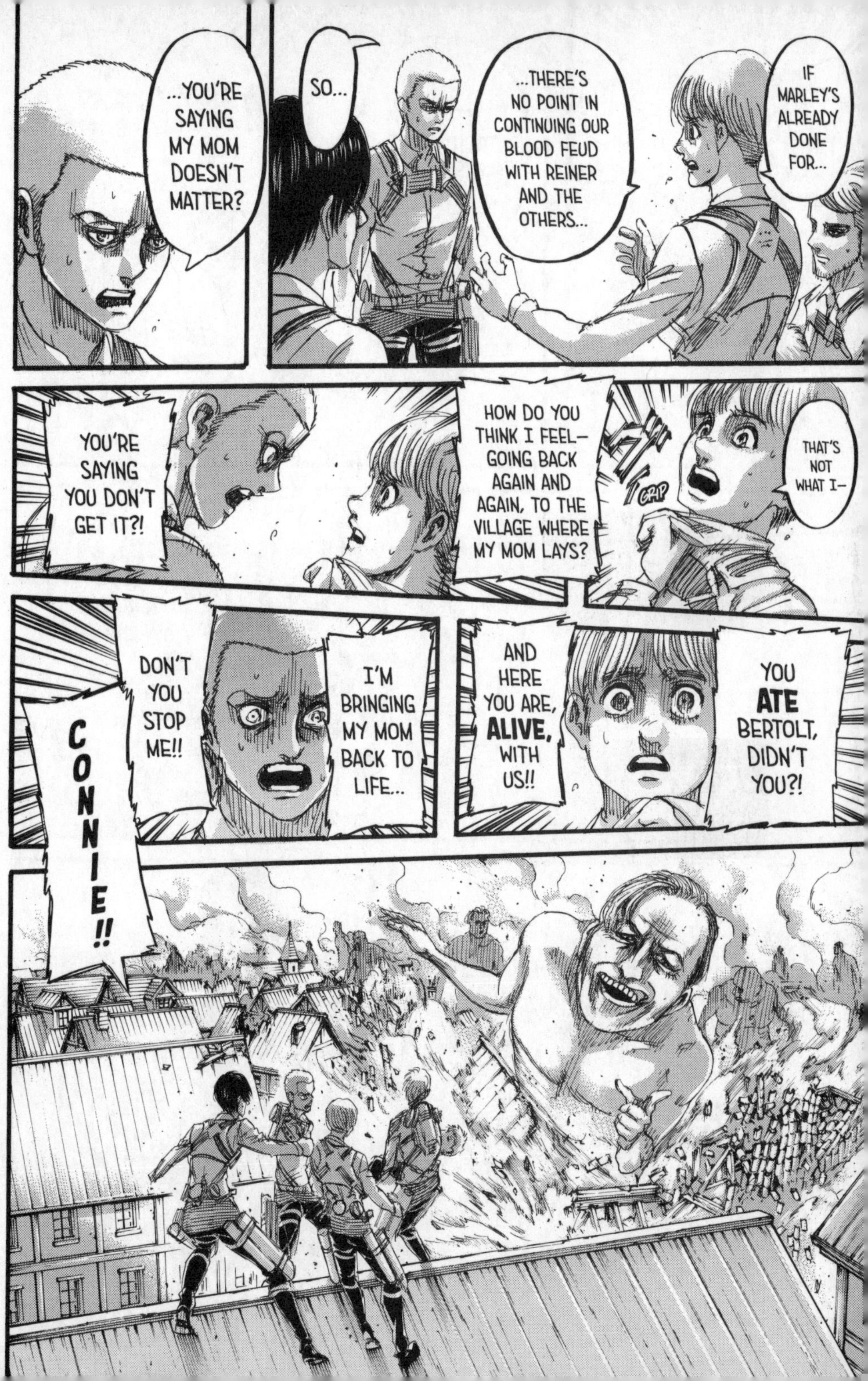
IF MARLEY'S ALREADY DONE FOR...
...THERE'S NO POINT IN CONTINUING OUR BLOOD FEUD WITH REINER AND THE OTHERS...
SO...
...YOU'RE SAYING MY MOM DOESN'T MATTER?
THAT'S NOT WHAT I—
GRIP
HOW DO YOU THINK I FEEL— GOING BACK AGAIN AND AGAIN, TO THE VILLAGE WHERE MY MOM LAYS?
YOU'RE SAYING YOU DON'T GET IT?!
YOU **ATE** BERTOLT, DIDN'T YOU?!
AND HERE YOU ARE, **ALIVE,** WITH US!!
I'M BRINGING MY MOM BACK TO LIFE...
DON'T YOU STOP ME!!
CONNIE!!

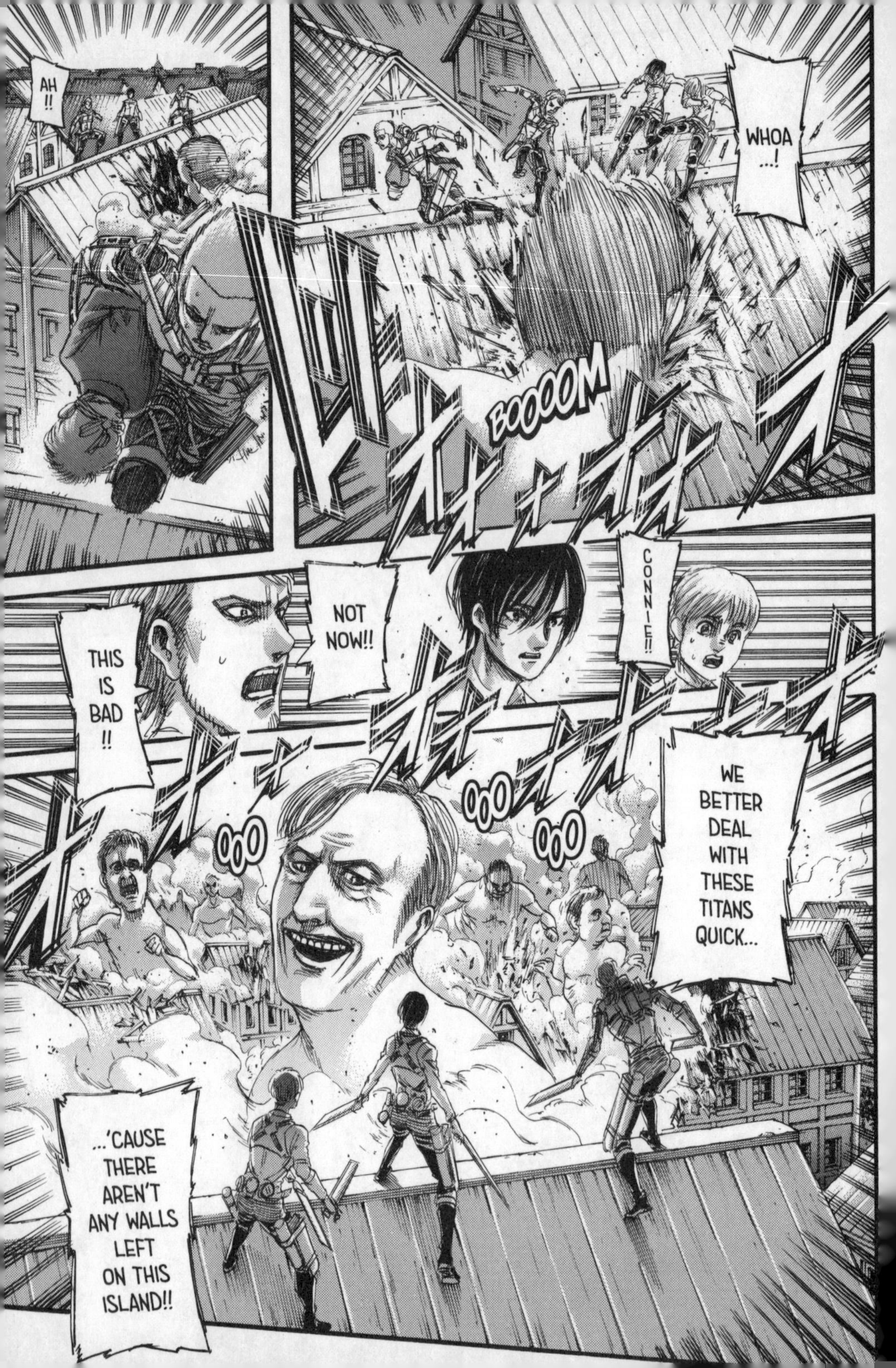

WHOA ...!
BOOOOM
AH !!
CONNIE!!
NOT NOW!!
THIS IS BAD !!
WE BETTER DEAL WITH THESE TITANS QUICK...
OOO
OOO
OOO
OOO
...'CAUSE THERE AREN'T ANY WALLS LEFT ON THIS ISLAND!!

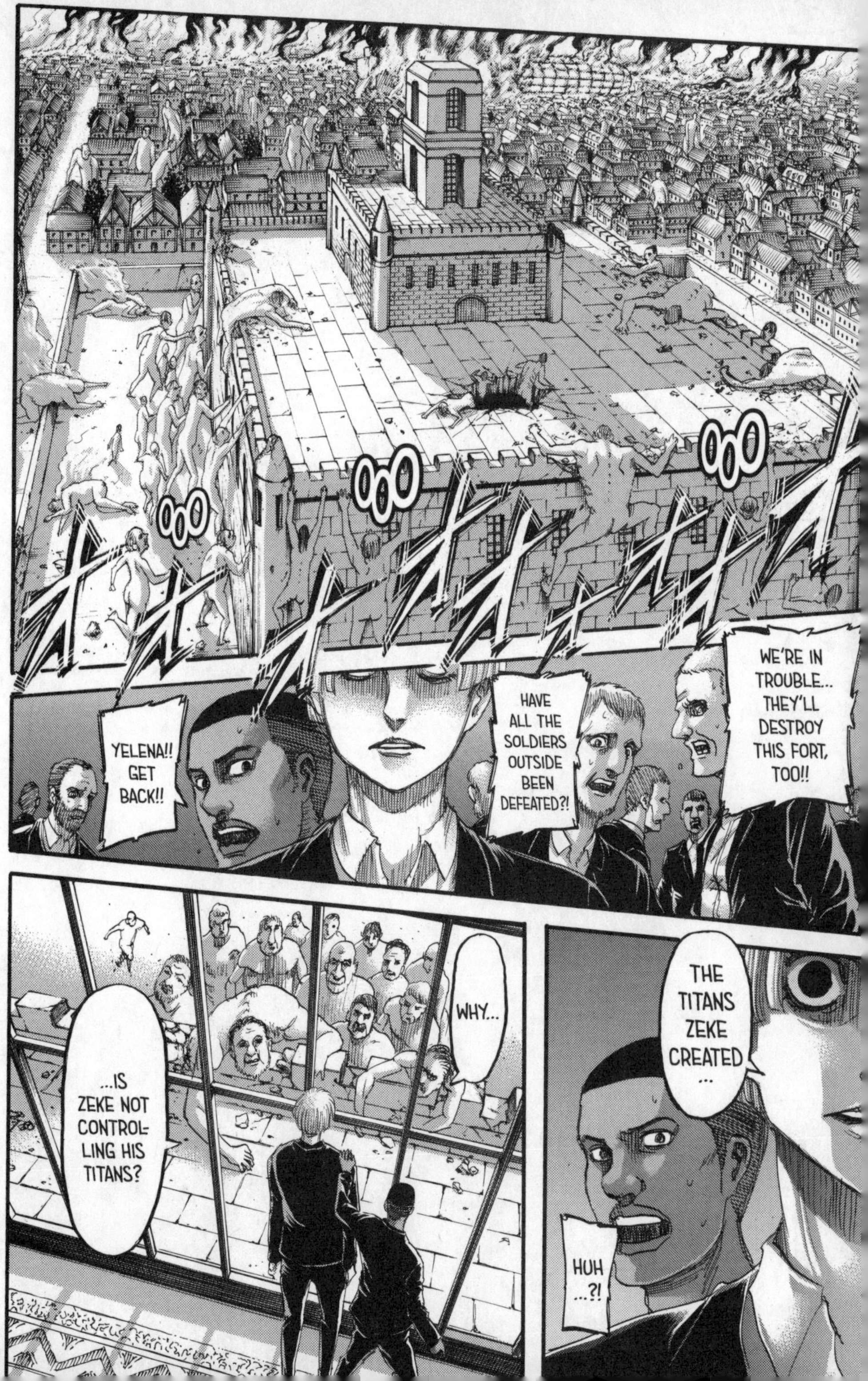

WE'RE IN TROUBLE... THEY'LL DESTROY THIS FORT, TOO!!
HAVE ALL THE SOLDIERS OUTSIDE BEEN DEFEATED?!
YELENA!! GET BACK!!
THE TITANS ZEKE CREATED ...
HUH ...?!
WHY...
...IS ZEKE NOT CONTROL-LING HIS TITANS?

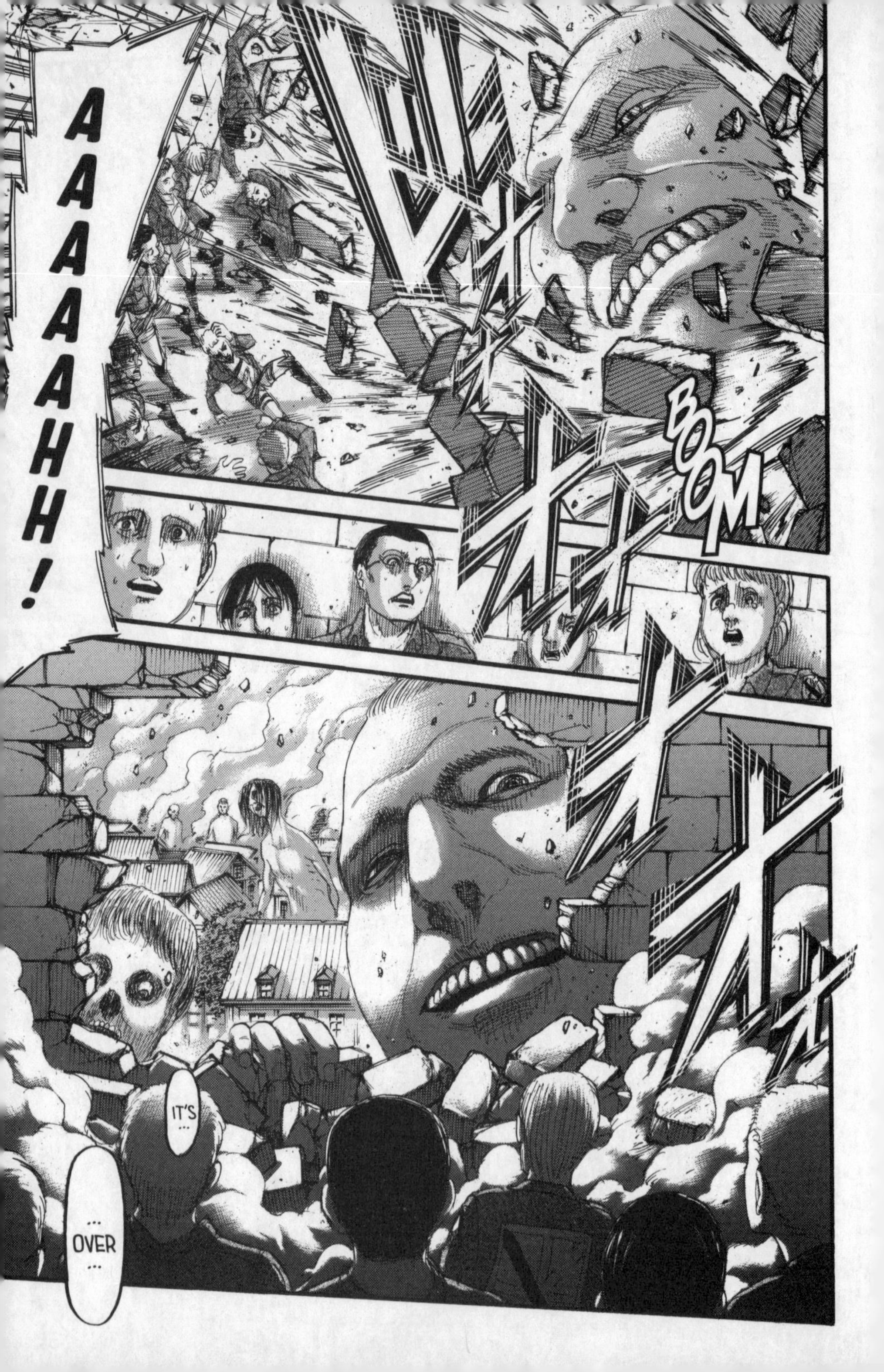
AAAAAAAHH!
BOOM
IT'S ...
... OVER ...

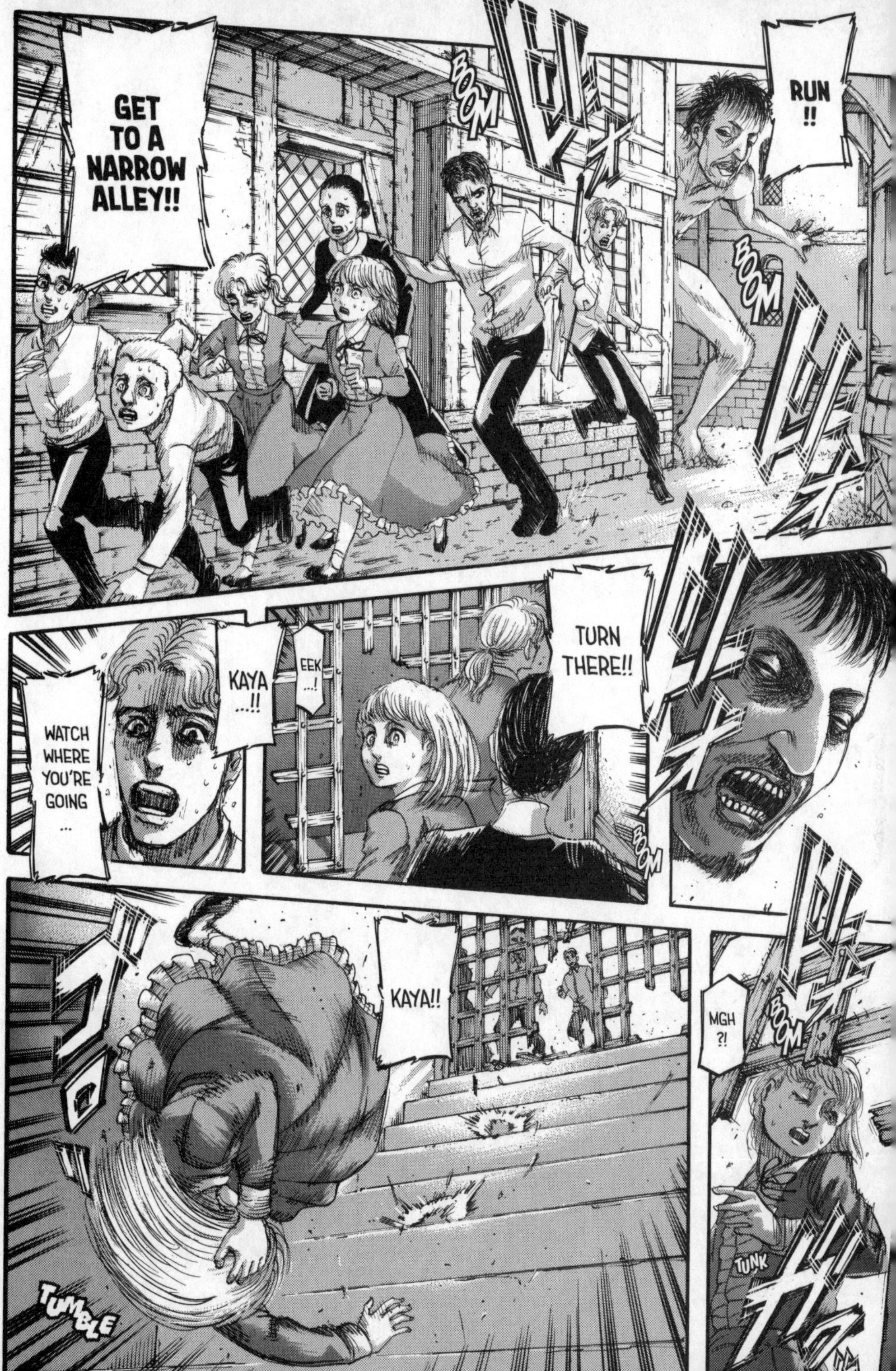
RUN!!
BOOM
BOOM
GET TO A NARROW ALLEY!!
BOOM
TURN THERE!!
EEK ...!
KAYA ...!!
WATCH WHERE YOU'RE GOING ...
BOOM
MGH ?!
TUNK
KAYA!!
TUMBLE

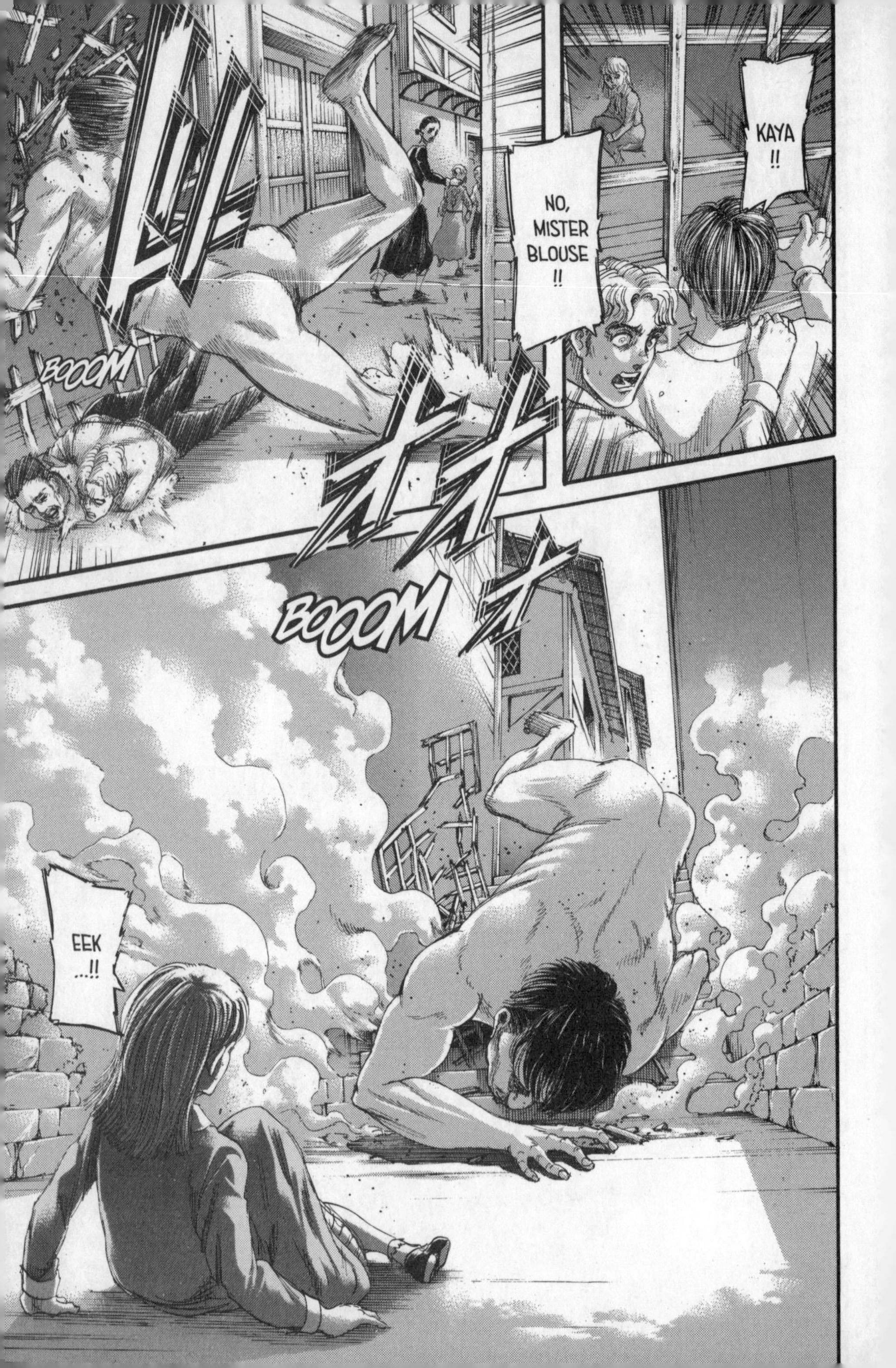
KAYA !!
NO, MISTER BLOUSE !!
BOOOM
BOOOM
EEK ...!!

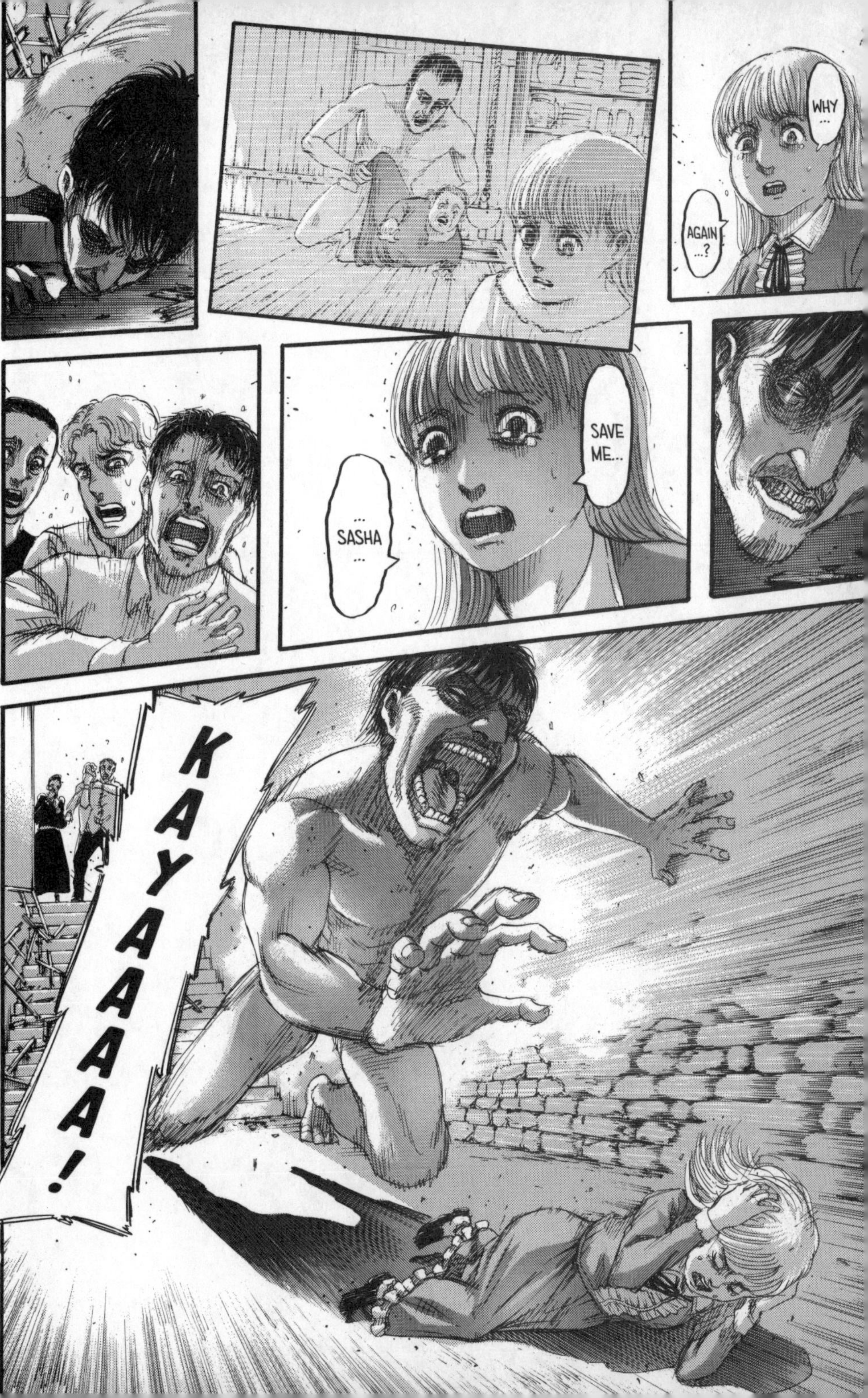
WHY ...
AGAIN ...?
SAVE ME...
... SASHA ...
KAYAAAAA!

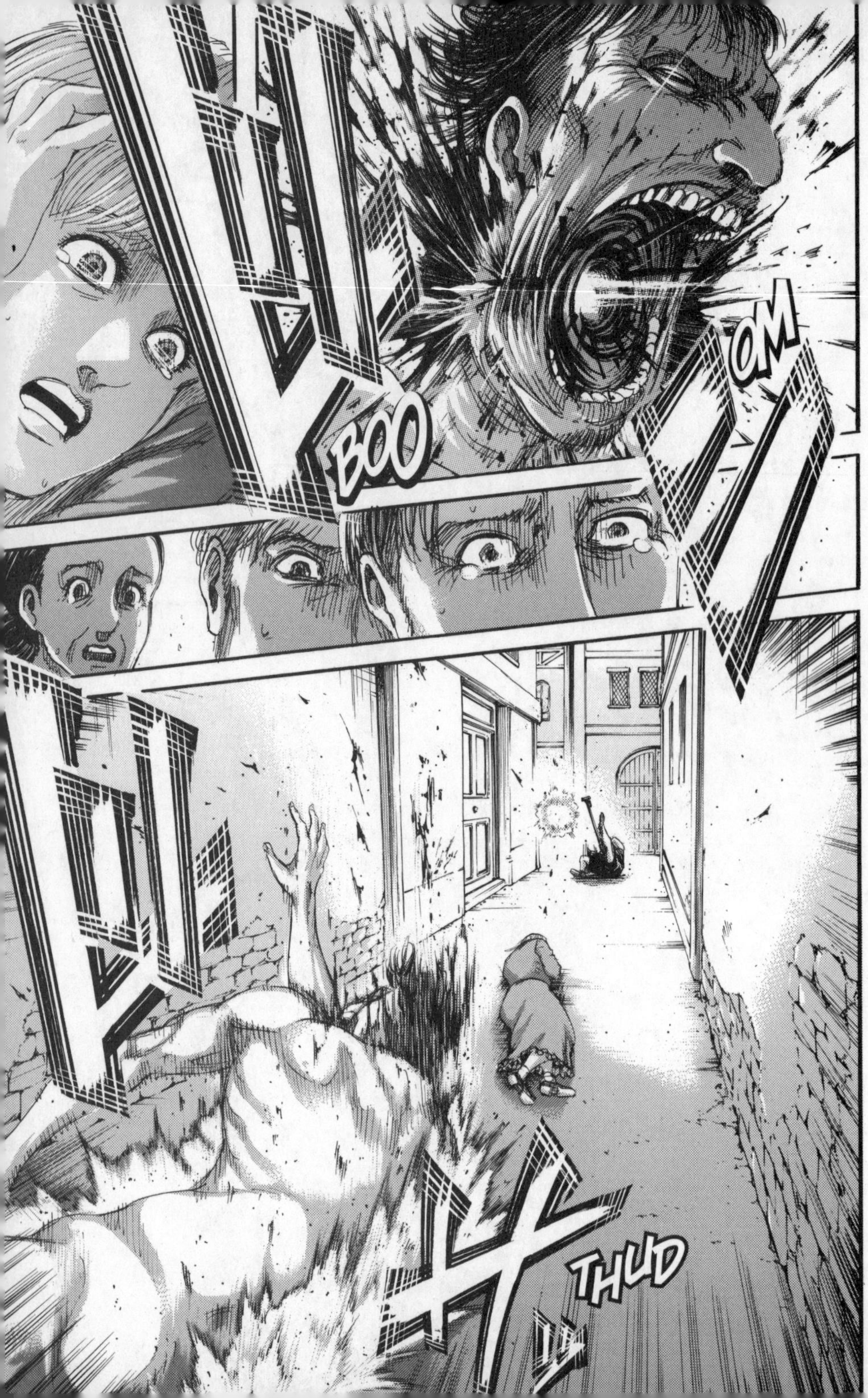

BOO
OM
THUD

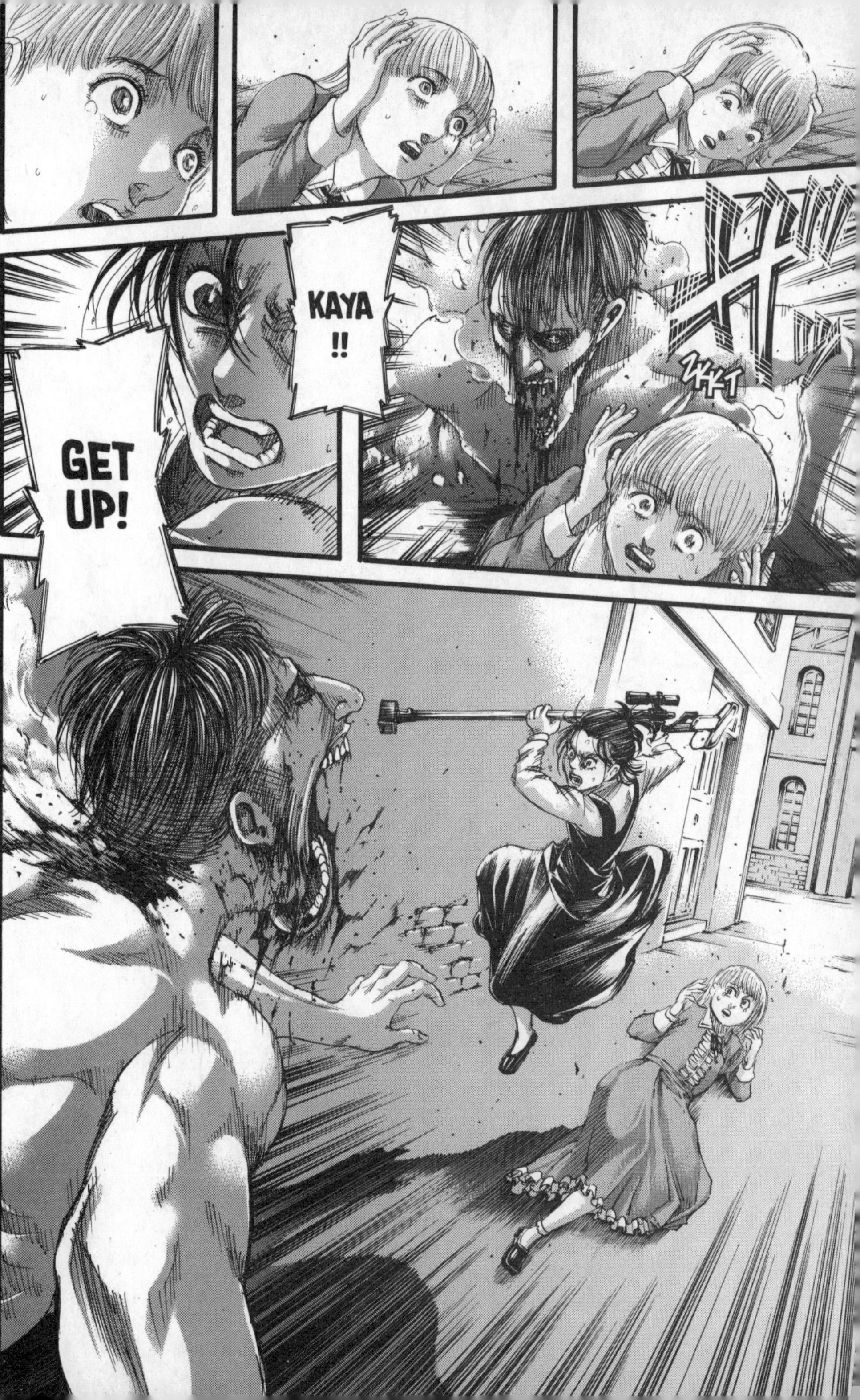
ZKKT
KAYA !!
GET UP!

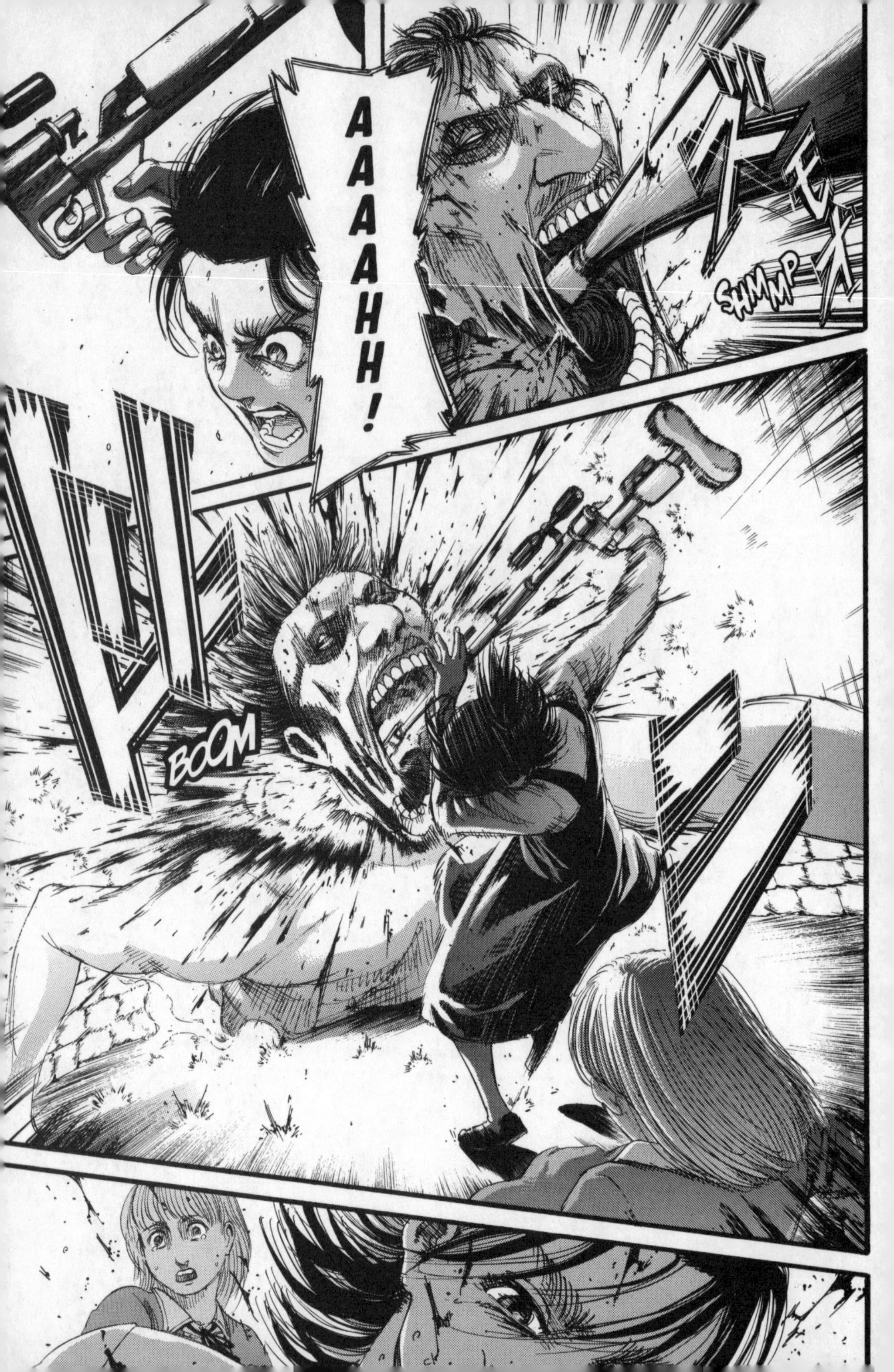
SHMMP
AAAAAHH!
BOOM

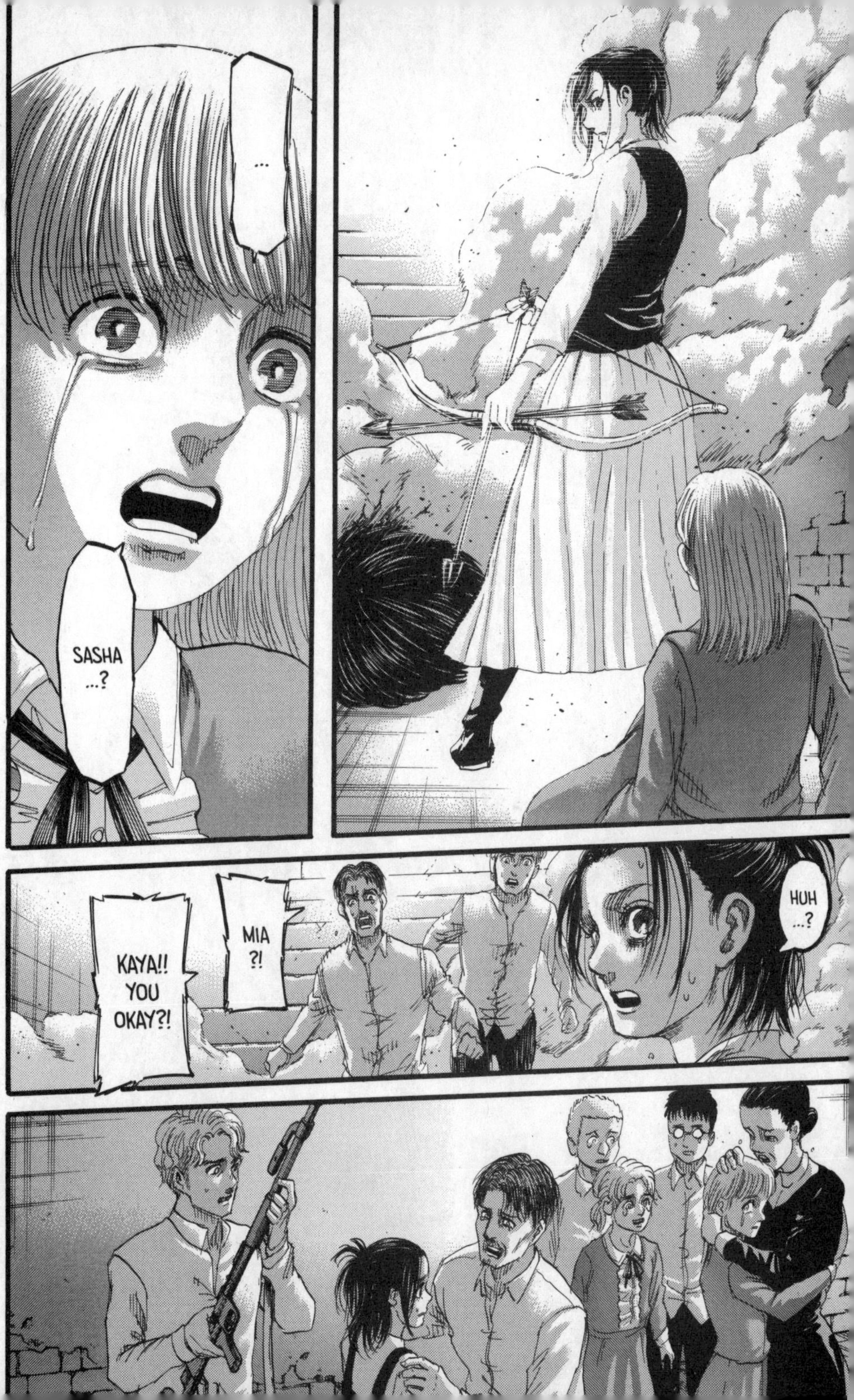
...
SASHA ...?
HUH ...?
MIA ?!
KAYA!! YOU OKAY?!

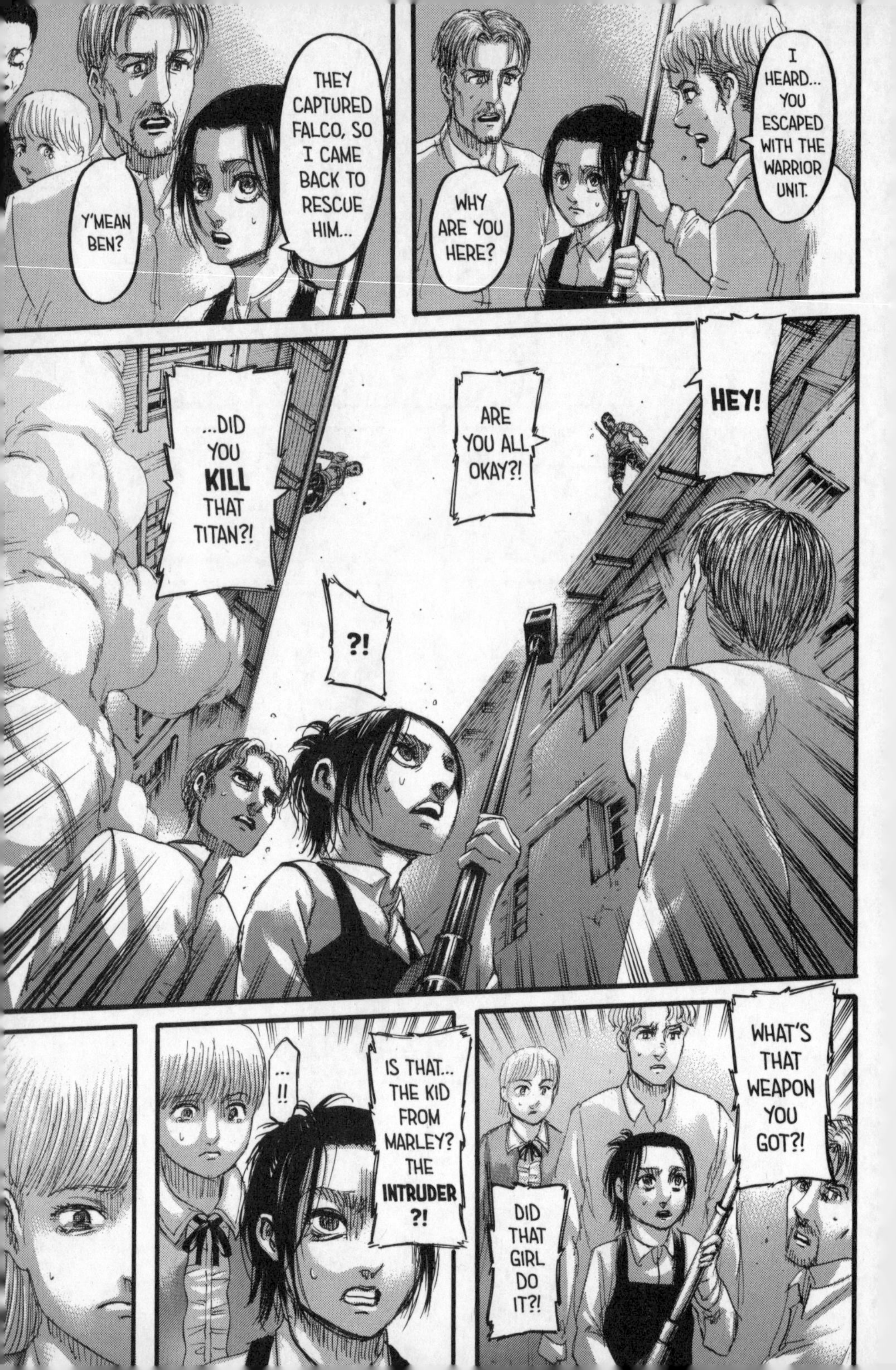
I HEARD... YOU ESCAPED WITH THE WARRIOR UNIT.
WHY ARE YOU HERE?
THEY CAPTURED FALCO, SO I CAME BACK TO RESCUE HIM...
Y'MEAN BEN?
HEY!
ARE YOU ALL OKAY?!
...DID YOU KILL THAT TITAN?!
?!
WHAT'S THAT WEAPON YOU GOT?!
DID THAT GIRL DO IT?!
IS THAT... THE KID FROM MARLEY? THE INTRUDER?!
...!!

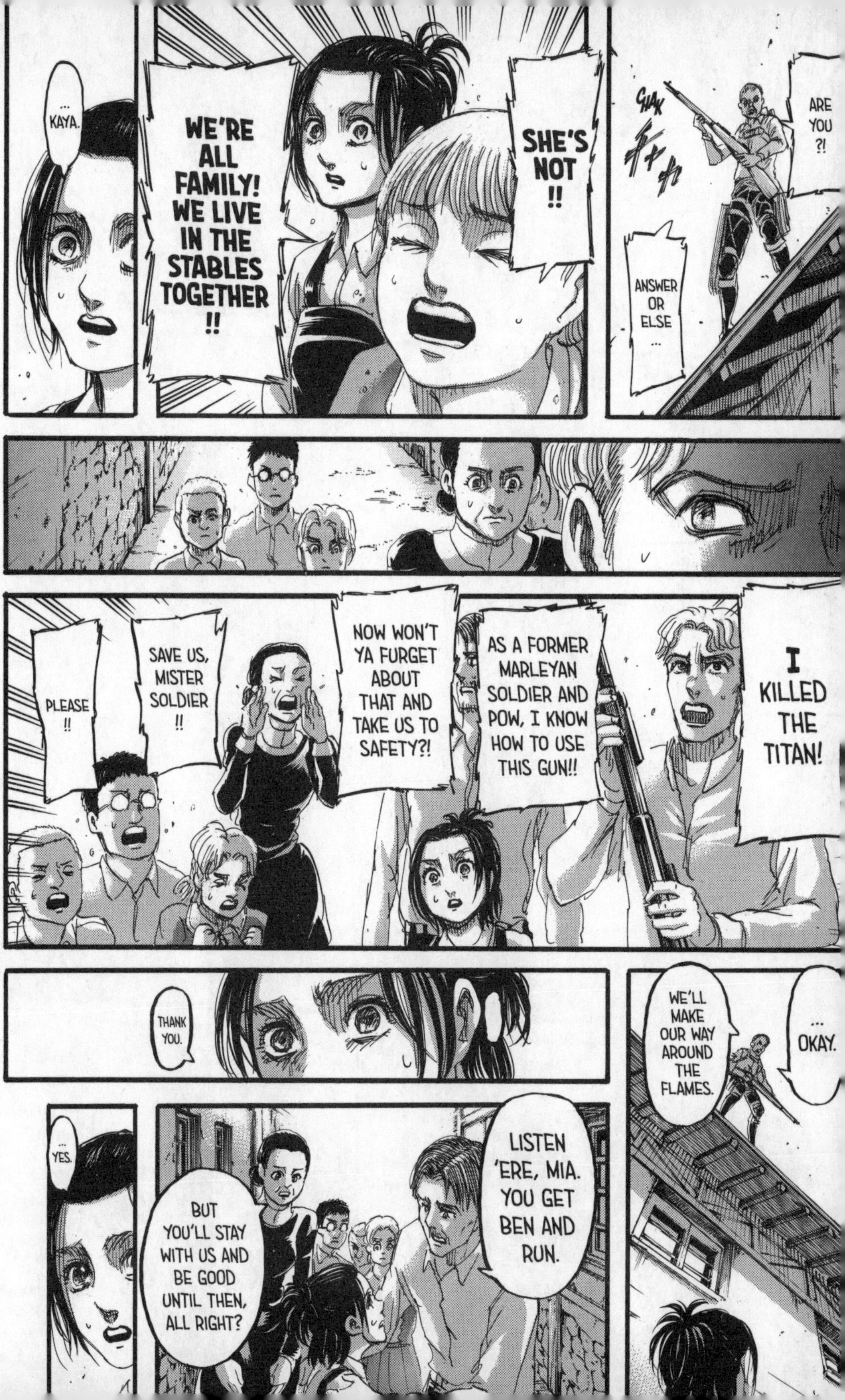
CHAK
チャキ
ARE YOU ?!
ANSWER OR ELSE ...
SHE'S NOT !!
WE'RE ALL FAMILY! WE LIVE IN THE STABLES TOGETHER !!
... KAYA.
I KILLED THE TITAN!
AS A FORMER MARLEYAN SOLDIER AND POW, I KNOW HOW TO USE THIS GUN!!
NOW WON'T YA FURGET ABOUT THAT AND TAKE US TO SAFETY?!
SAVE US, MISTER SOLDIER !!
PLEASE !!
... OKAY.
WE'LL MAKE OUR WAY AROUND THE FLAMES.
THANK YOU.
LISTEN 'ERE, MIA. YOU GET BEN AND RUN.
BUT YOU'LL STAY WITH US AND BE GOOD UNTIL THEN, ALL RIGHT?
... YES.

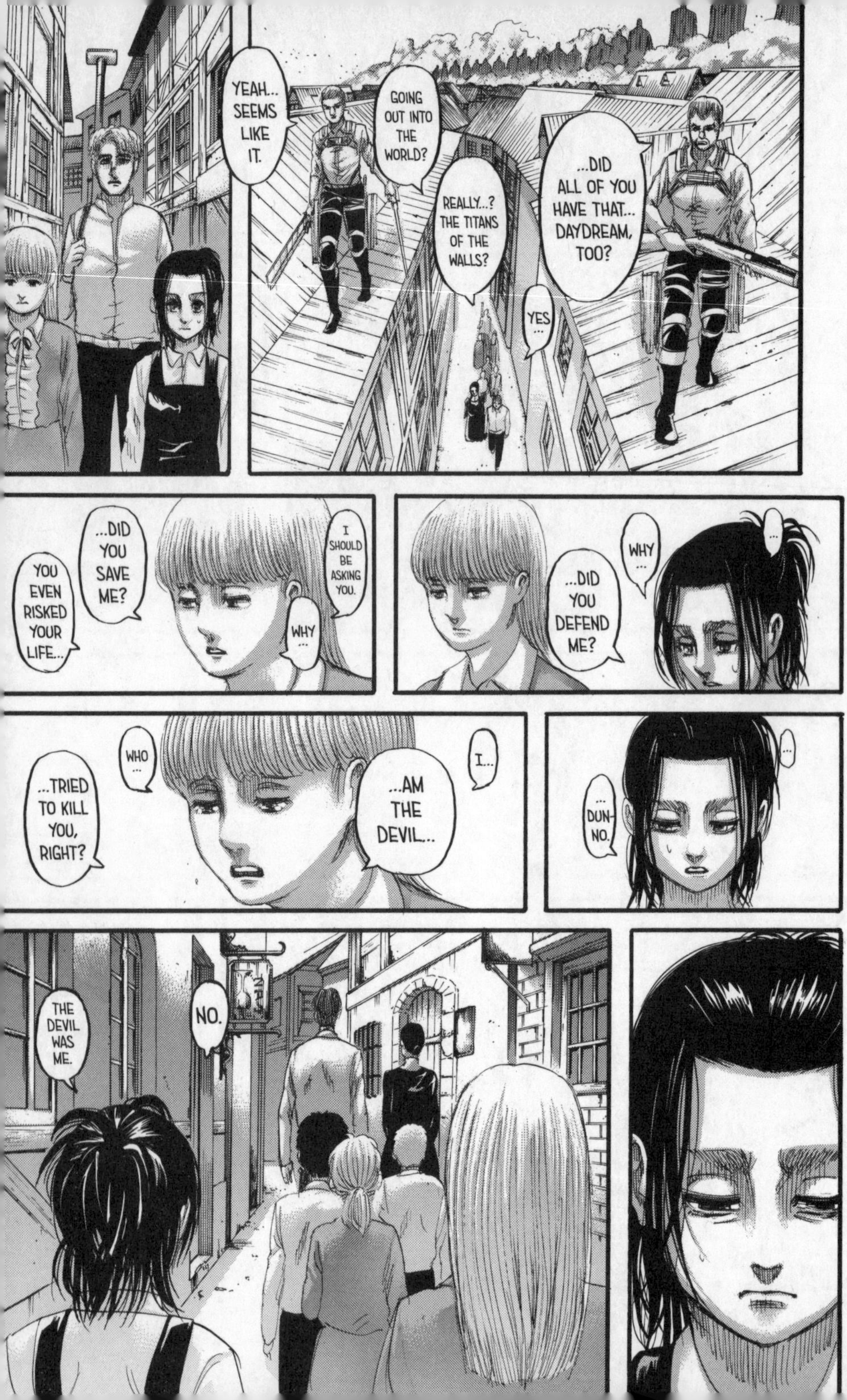
...DID ALL OF YOU HAVE THAT... DAYDREAM, TOO?
YES...
REALLY...? THE TITANS OF THE WALLS?
GOING OUT INTO THE WORLD?
YEAH... SEEMS LIKE IT.
WHY...
...DID YOU DEFEND ME?
I SHOULD BE ASKING YOU.
WHY...
...DID YOU SAVE ME?
YOU EVEN RISKED YOUR LIFE...
...
...DUN-NO.
I...
...AM THE DEVIL...
WHO...
...TRIED TO KILL YOU, RIGHT?
NO.
THE DEVIL WAS ME.

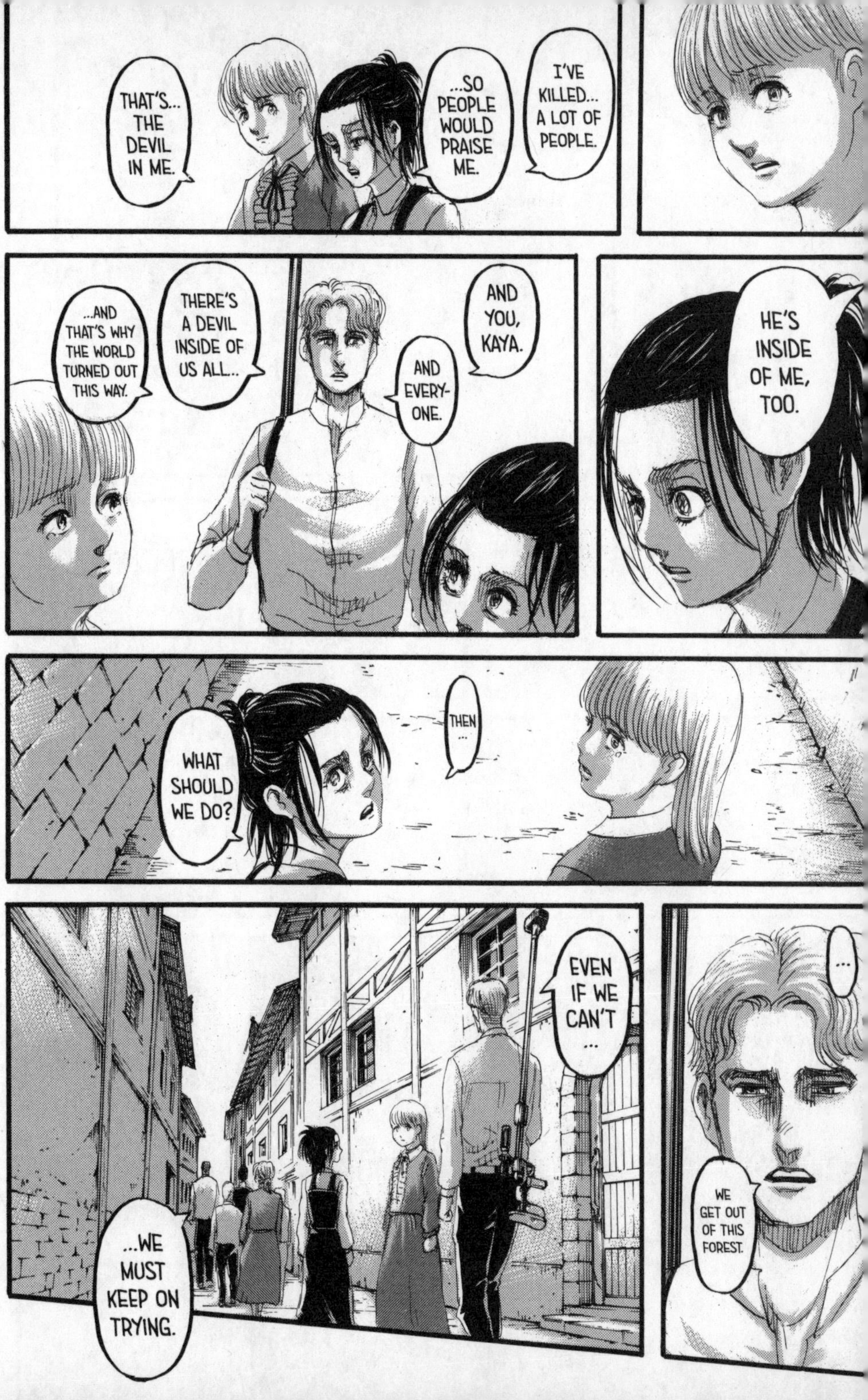

I'VE KILLED... A LOT OF PEOPLE.
...SO PEOPLE WOULD PRAISE ME.
THAT'S... THE DEVIL IN ME.
HE'S INSIDE OF ME, TOO.
AND YOU, KAYA.
AND EVERY-ONE.
THERE'S A DEVIL INSIDE OF US ALL...
...AND THAT'S WHY THE WORLD TURNED OUT THIS WAY.
THEN ...
WHAT SHOULD WE DO?
...
WE GET OUT OF THIS FOREST.
EVEN IF WE CAN'T ...
...WE MUST KEEP ON TRYING.

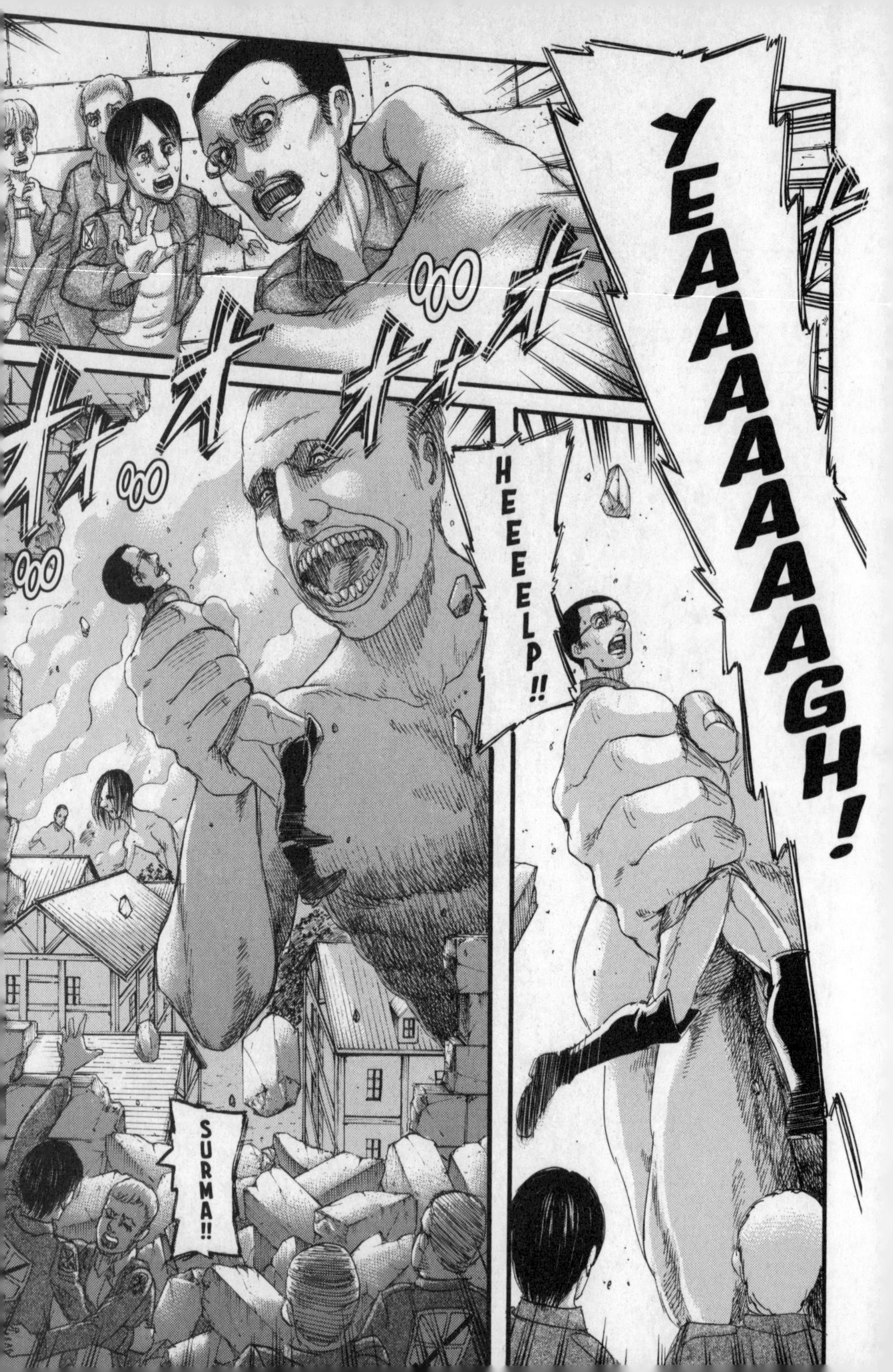
YEAAAAAAAGH!
HEEEEELP!!
SURMA!!

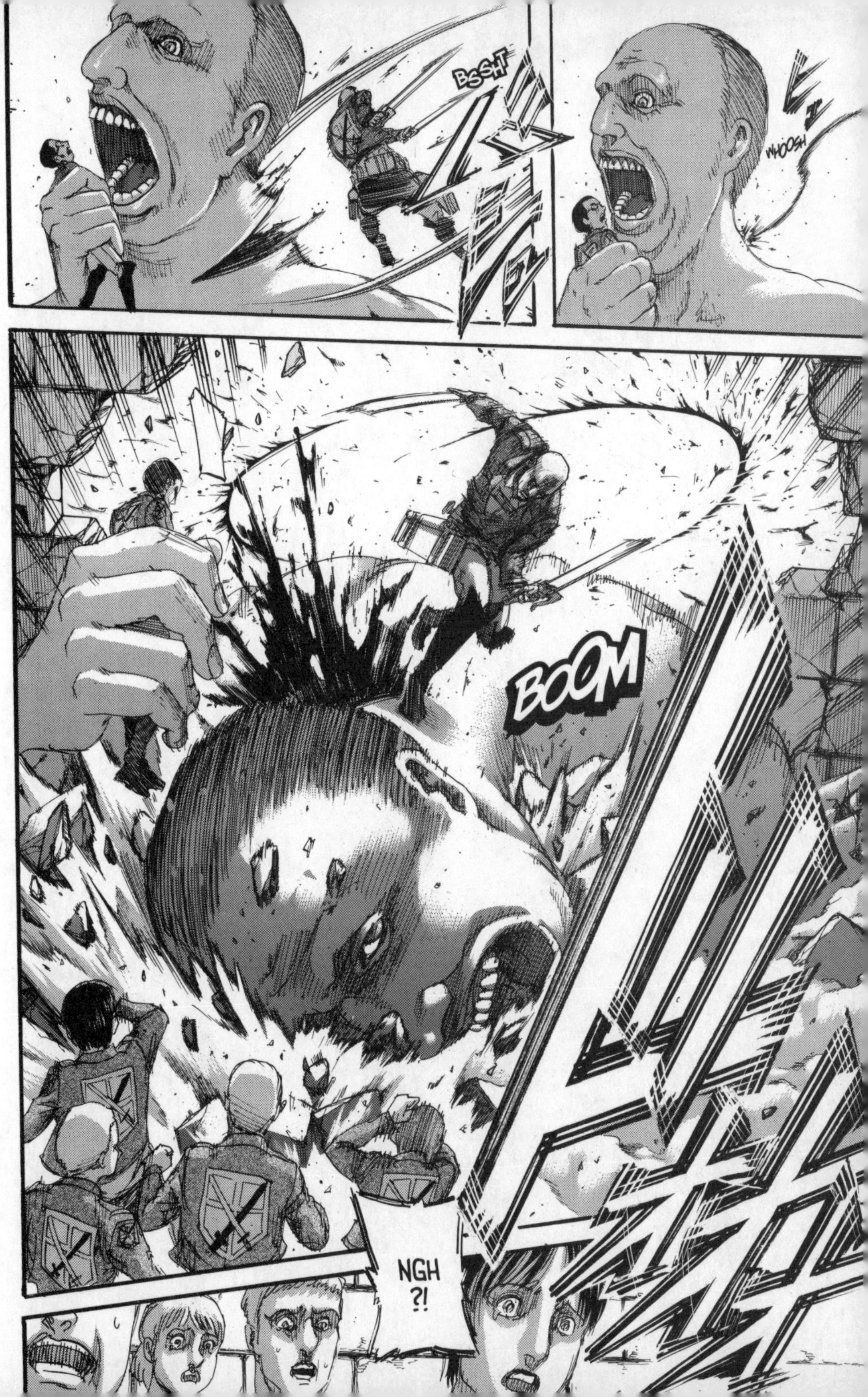
WHOOSH
BSSHT
BOOM
NGH ?!

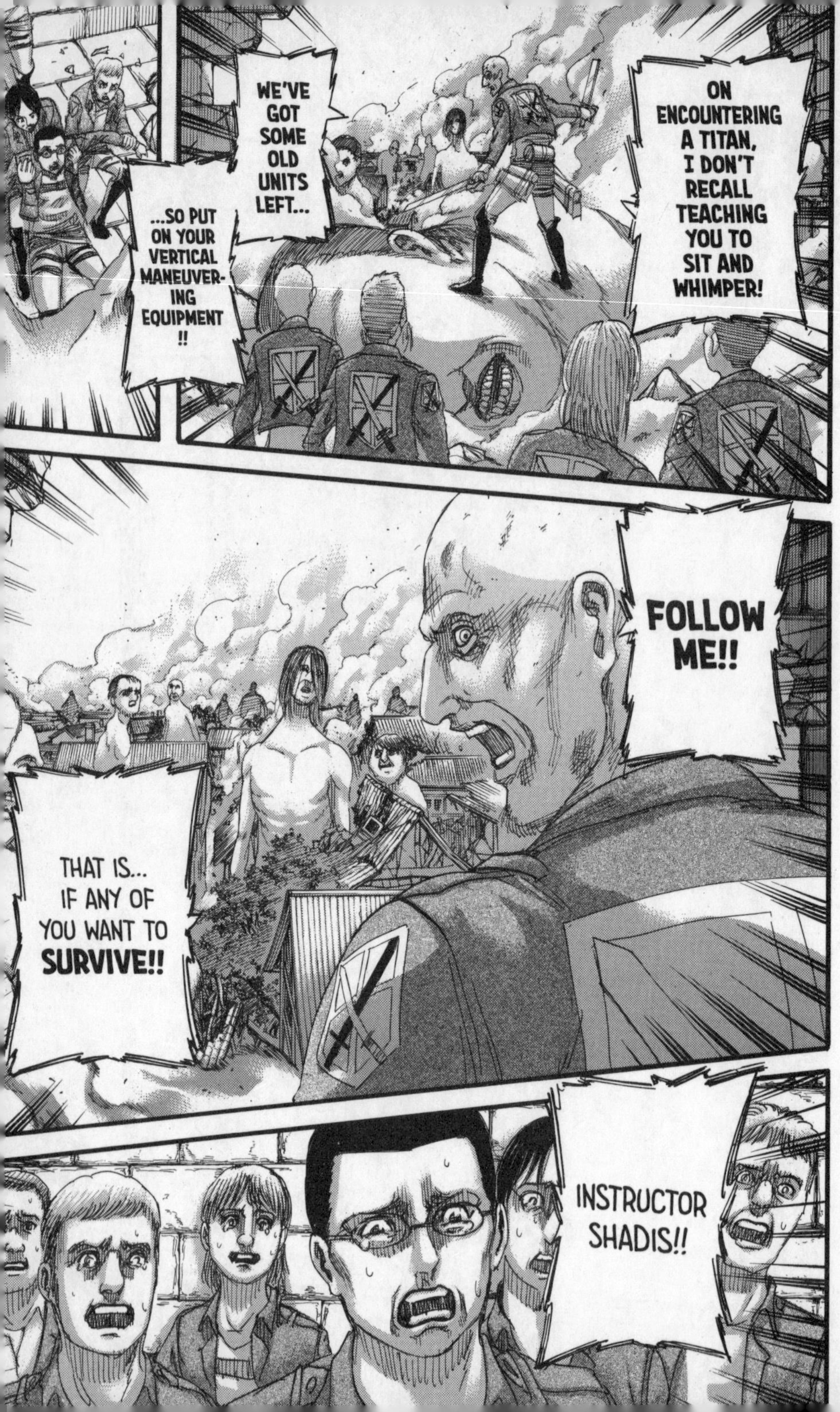
ON ENCOUNTERING A TITAN, I DON'T RECALL TEACHING YOU TO SIT AND WHIMPER!
WE'VE GOT SOME OLD UNITS LEFT...
...SO PUT ON YOUR VERTICAL MANEUVERING EQUIPMENT!!
FOLLOW ME!!
THAT IS... IF ANY OF YOU WANT TO SURVIVE!!
INSTRUCTOR SHADIS!!

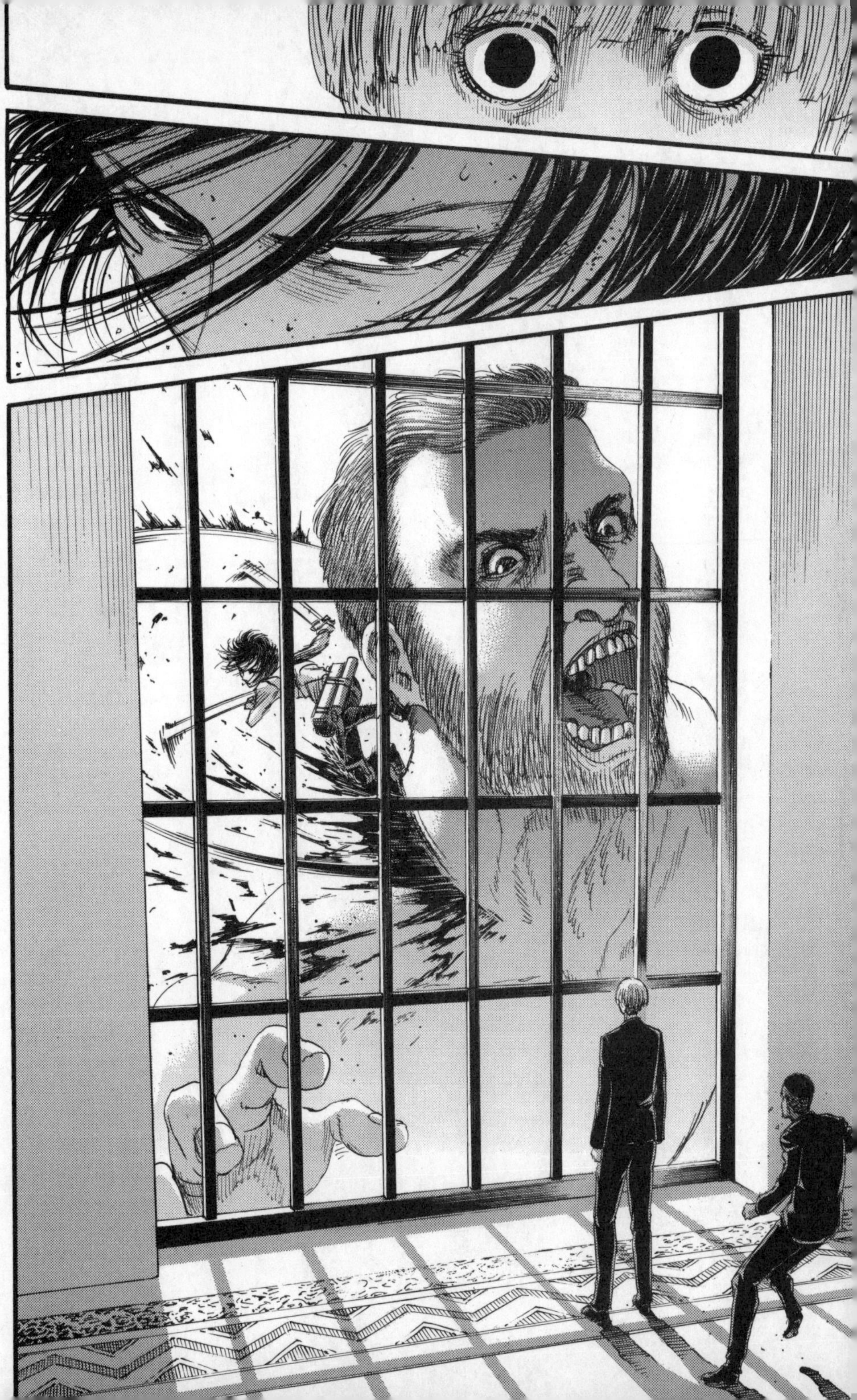

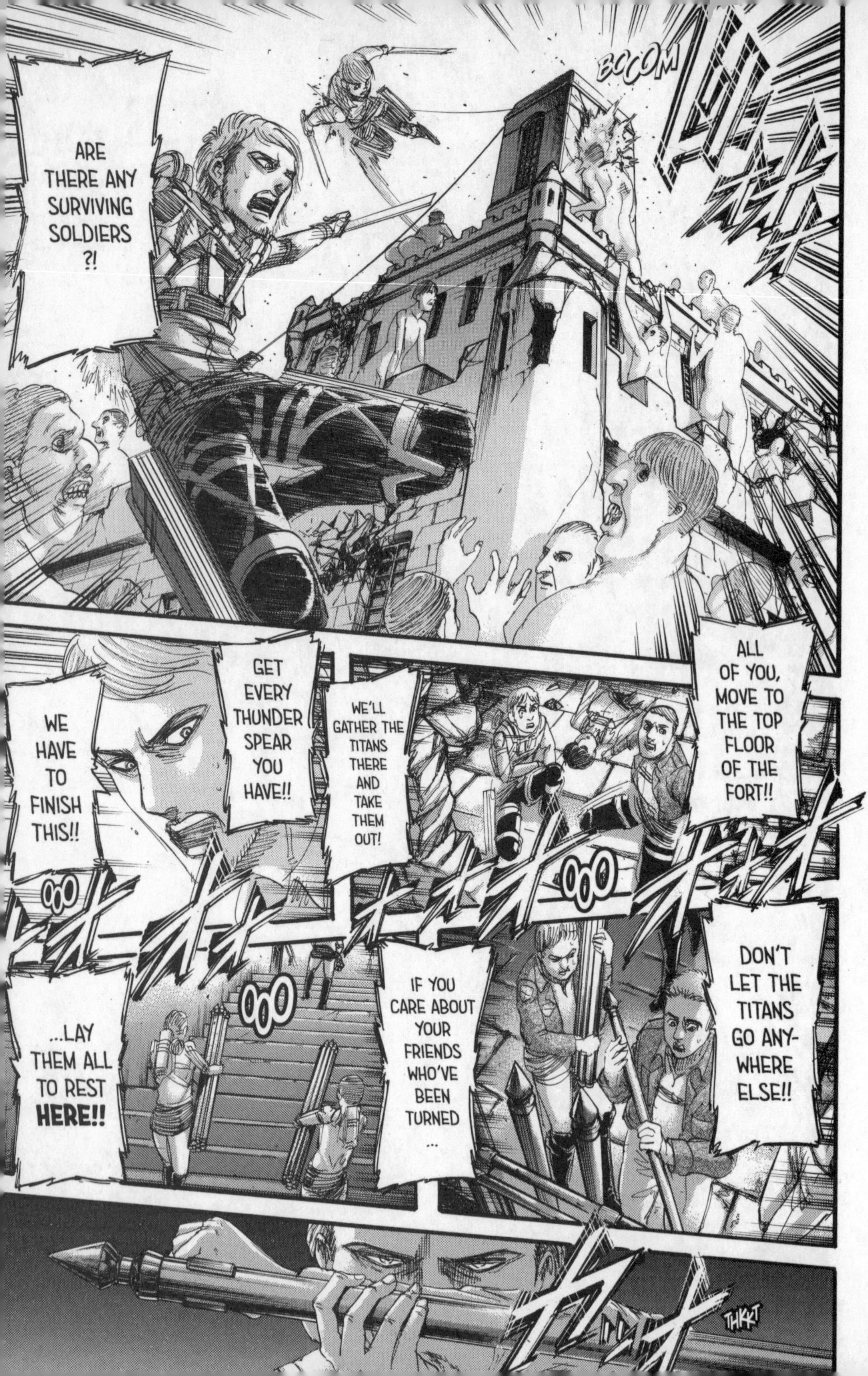
BOCOM
ARE THERE ANY SURVIVING SOLDIERS ?!
ALL OF YOU, MOVE TO THE TOP FLOOR OF THE FORT!!
WE'LL GATHER THE TITANS THERE AND TAKE THEM OUT!
GET EVERY THUNDER SPEAR YOU HAVE!!
WE HAVE TO FINISH THIS!!
DON'T LET THE TITANS GO ANY-WHERE ELSE!!
IF YOU CARE ABOUT YOUR FRIENDS WHO'VE BEEN TURNED ...
...LAY THEM ALL TO REST **HERE!!**
THKKT

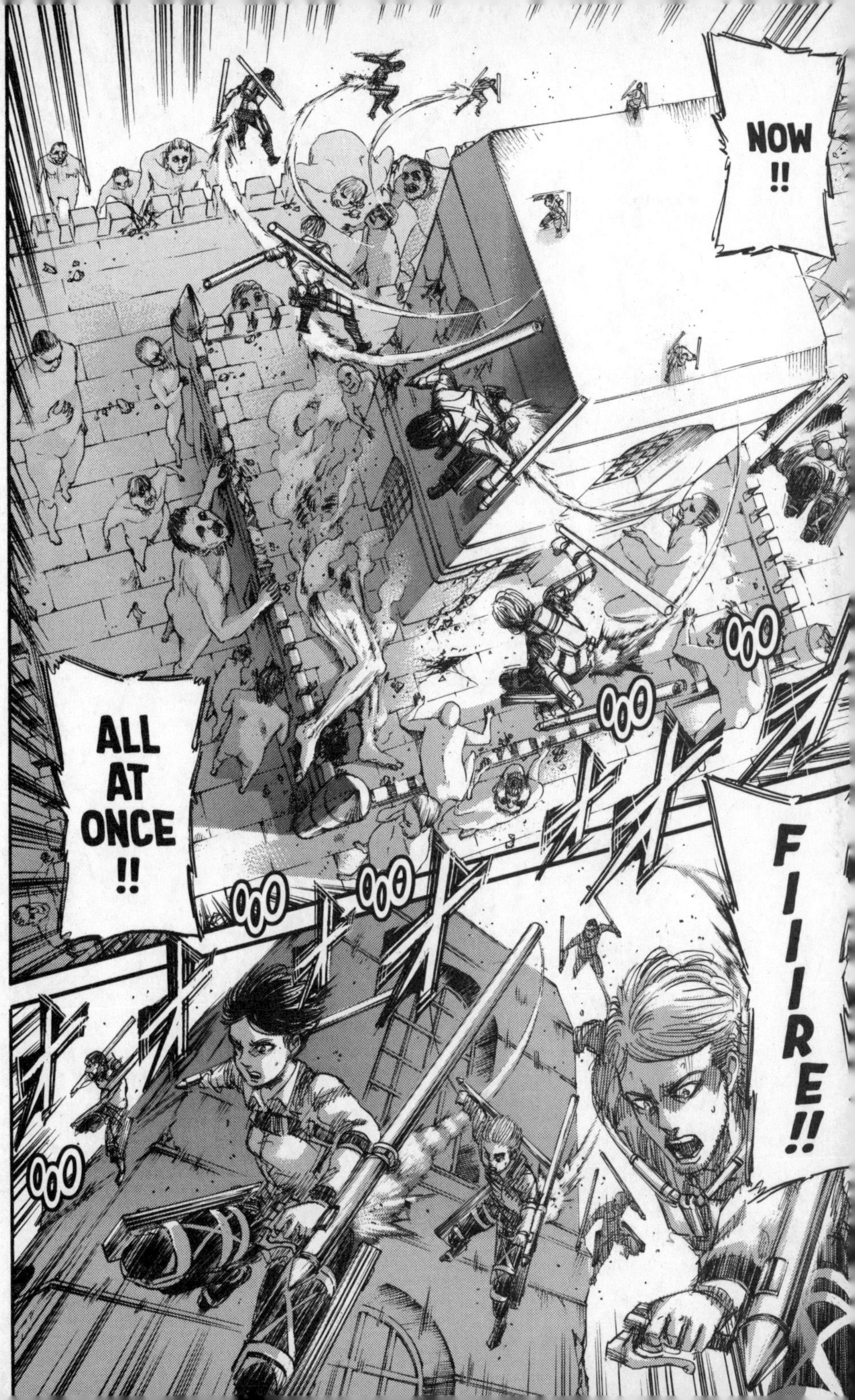
NOW!!
ALL AT ONCE!!
FIIIRE!!

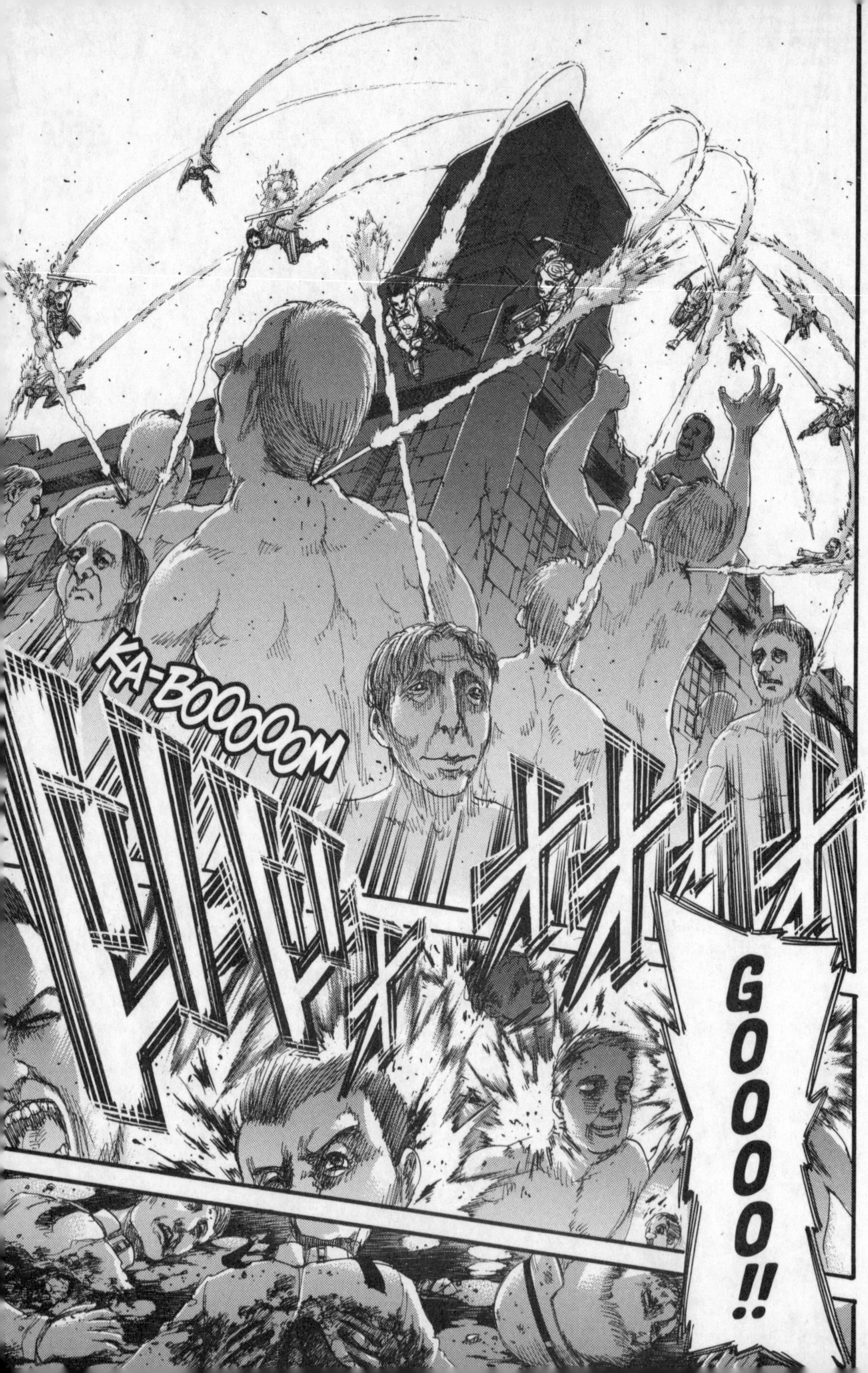
GOOOOO!!
KA-BOOOOOOM

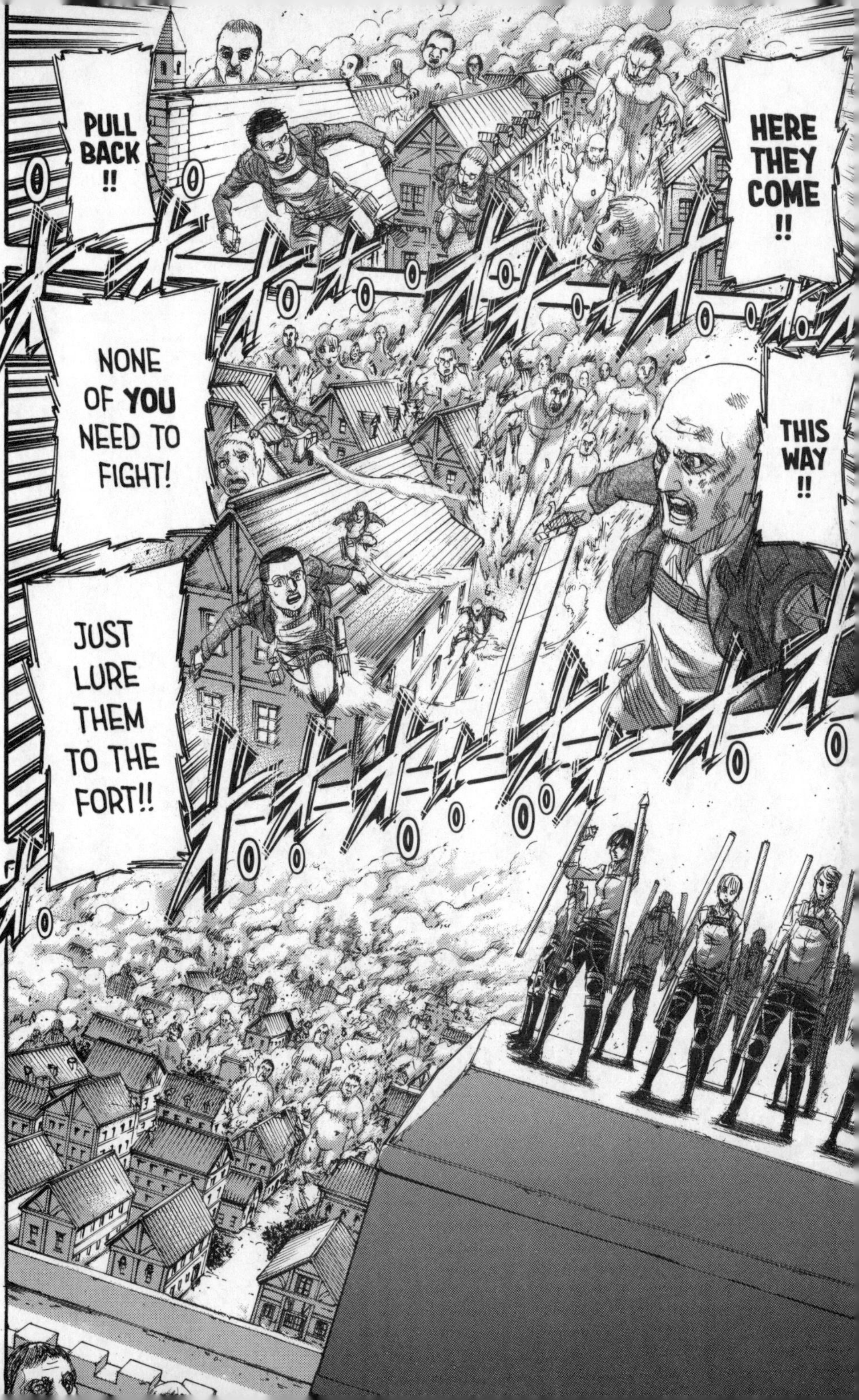

HERE THEY COME!!
PULL BACK!!
THIS WAY!!
NONE OF YOU NEED TO FIGHT!
JUST LURE THEM TO THE FORT!!

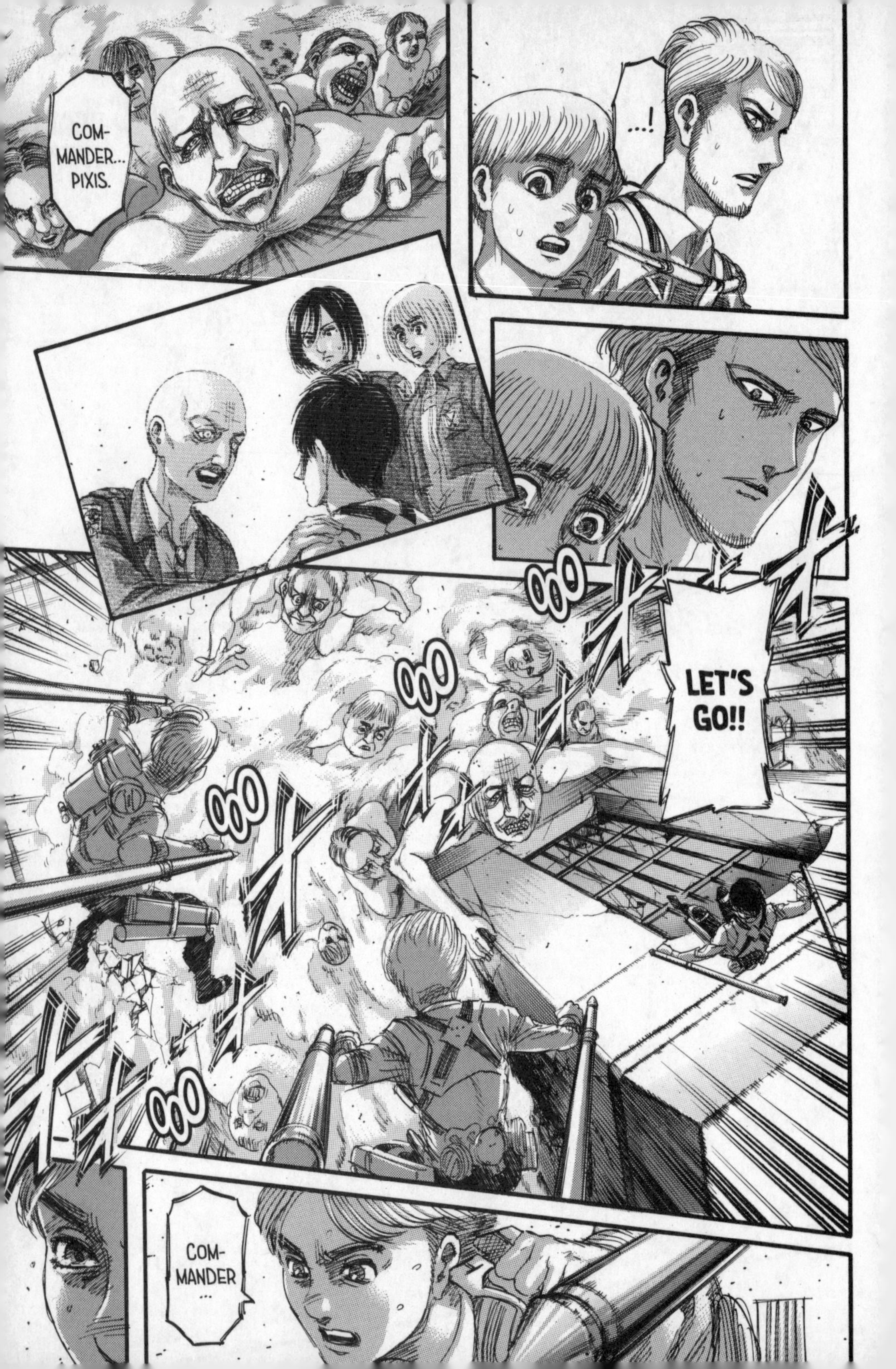
...!
COM-MANDER... PIXIS.
LET'S GO!!
COM-MANDER ...

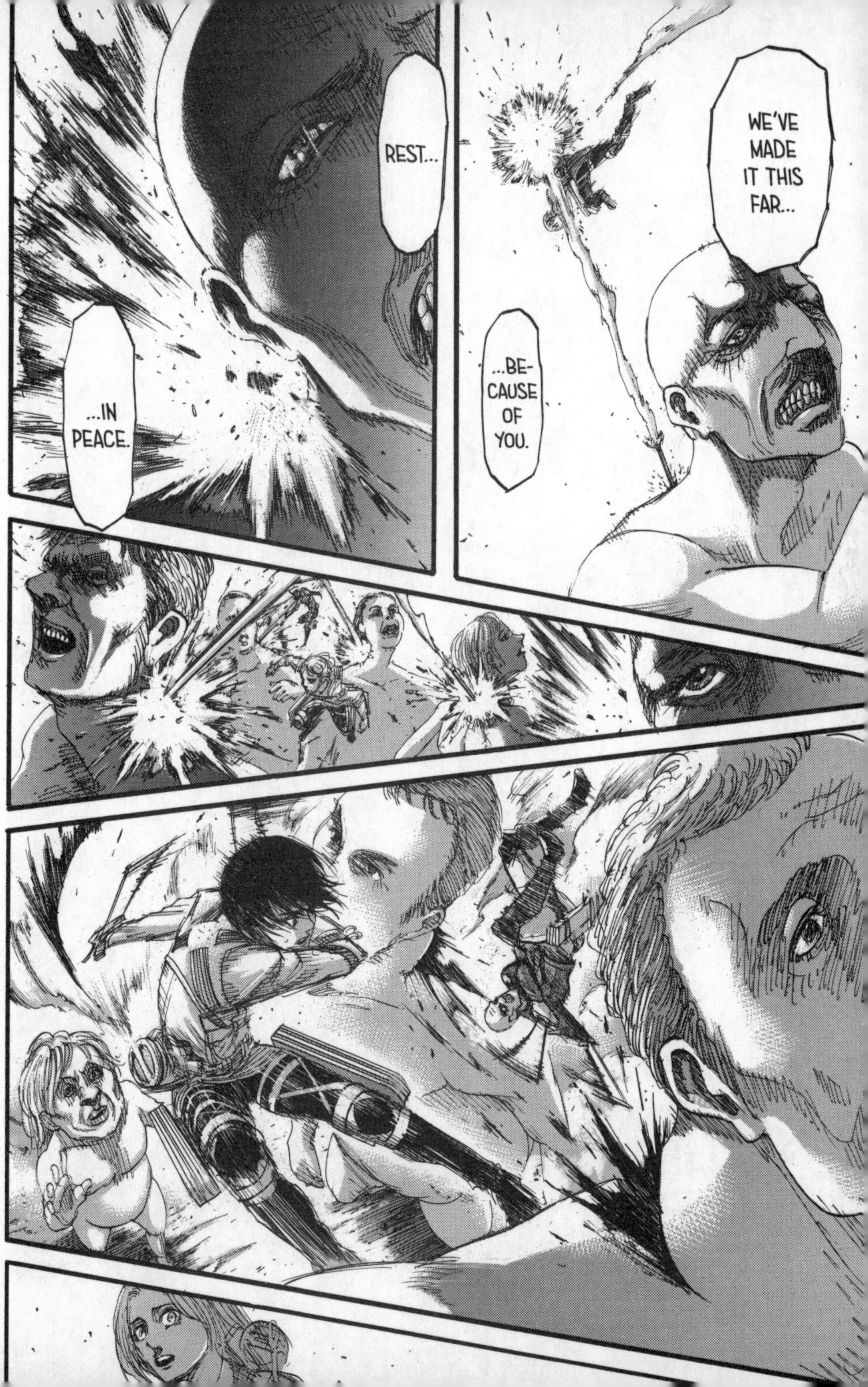
WE'VE MADE IT THIS FAR...
...BE-CAUSE OF YOU.
REST...
...IN PEACE.

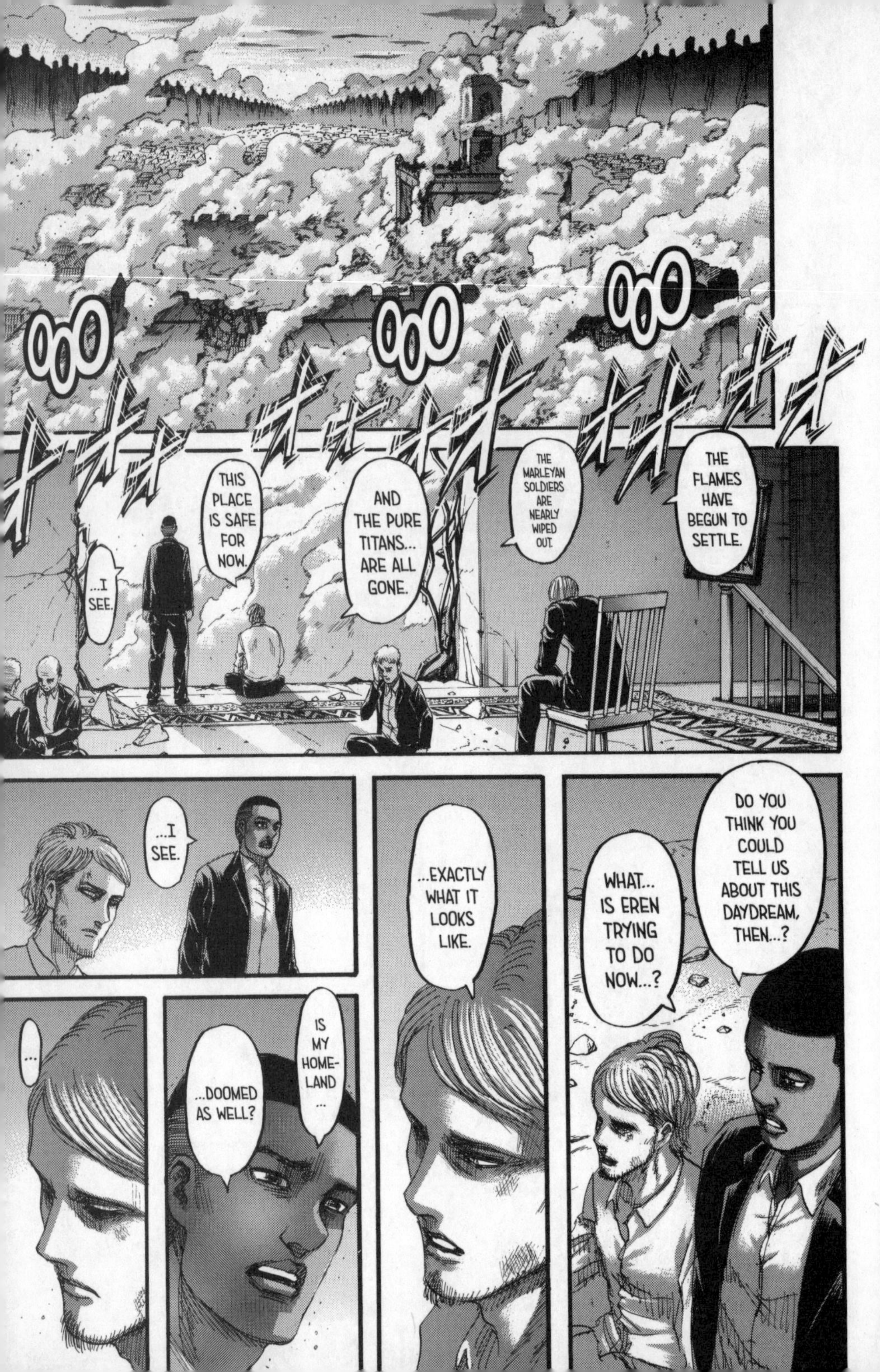
OOO
OOO
OOO
THE FLAMES HAVE BEGUN TO SETTLE.
THE MARLEYAN SOLDIERS ARE NEARLY WIPED OUT.
AND THE PURE TITANS... ARE ALL GONE.
THIS PLACE IS SAFE FOR NOW.
...I SEE.
DO YOU THINK YOU COULD TELL US ABOUT THIS DAYDREAM, THEN...?
WHAT... IS EREN TRYING TO DO NOW...?
...EXACTLY WHAT IT LOOKS LIKE.
...I SEE.
IS MY HOME-LAND ...
...DOOMED AS WELL?
...

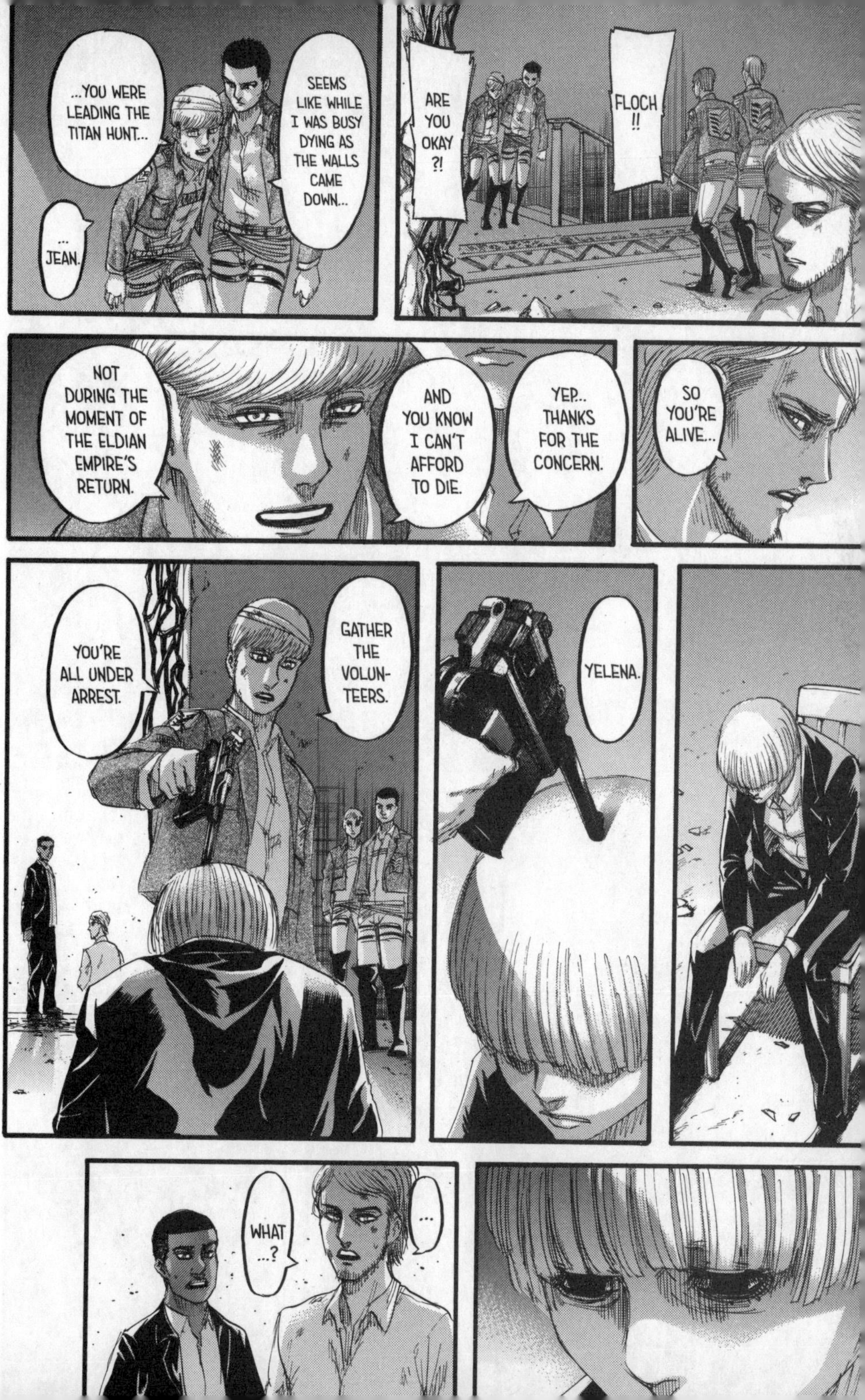
FLOCH !!
ARE YOU OKAY ?!
SEEMS LIKE WHILE I WAS BUSY DYING AS THE WALLS CAME DOWN...
...YOU WERE LEADING THE TITAN HUNT...
... JEAN.
SO YOU'RE ALIVE...
YEP.. THANKS FOR THE CONCERN.
AND YOU KNOW I CAN'T AFFORD TO DIE.
NOT DURING THE MOMENT OF THE ELDIAN EMPIRE'S RETURN.
YELENA.
GATHER THE VOLUN-TEERS.
YOU'RE ALL UNDER ARREST.
...
WHAT ...?

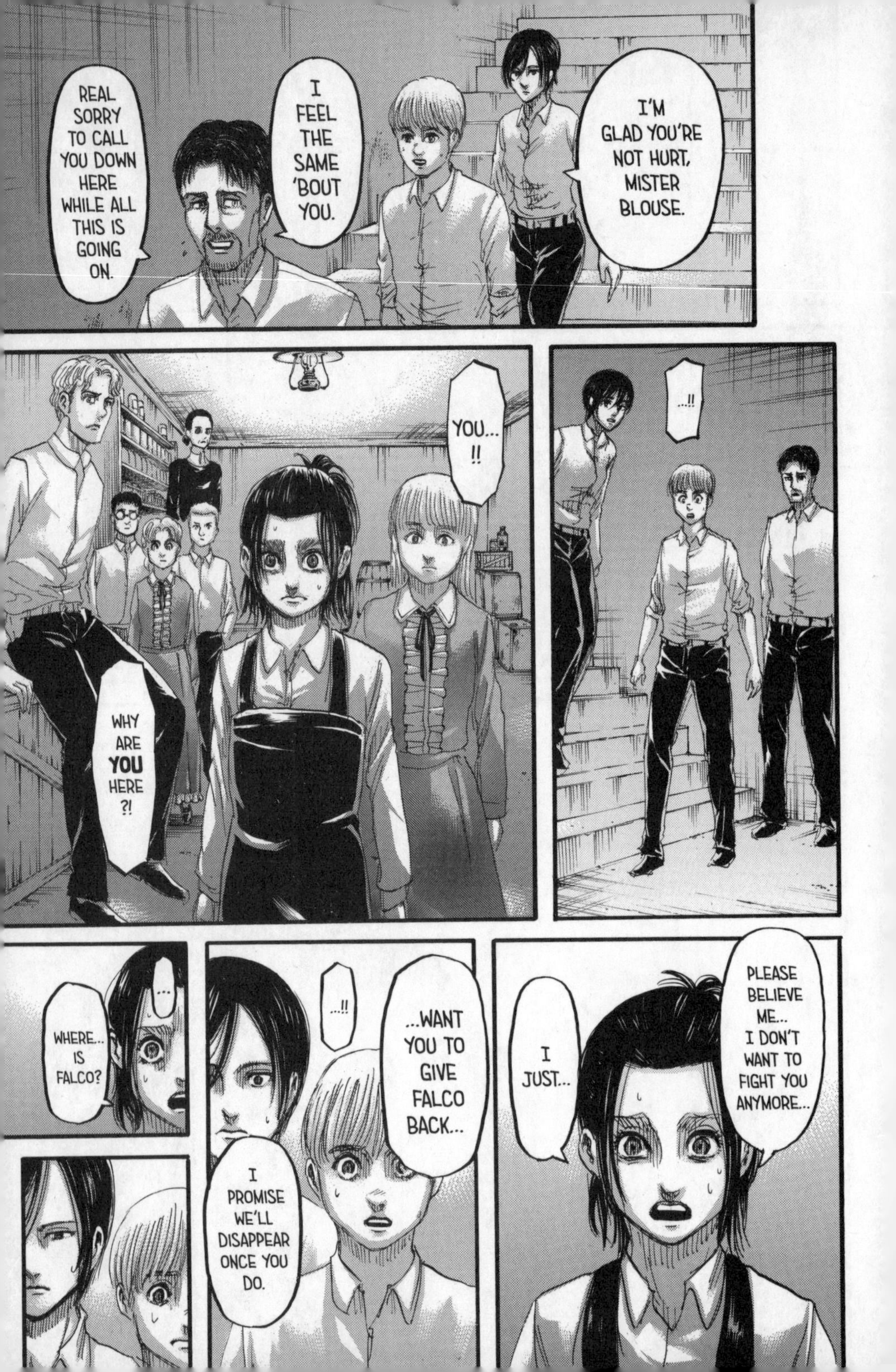
I'M GLAD YOU'RE NOT HURT, MISTER BLOUSE.
I FEEL THE SAME 'BOUT YOU.
REAL SORRY TO CALL YOU DOWN HERE WHILE ALL THIS IS GOING ON.
...!!
YOU... !!
WHY ARE **YOU** HERE ?!
PLEASE BELIEVE ME... I DON'T WANT TO FIGHT YOU ANYMORE...
I JUST...
...WANT YOU TO GIVE FALCO BACK...
...!!
I PROMISE WE'LL DISAPPEAR ONCE YOU DO.
...
WHERE... IS FALCO?

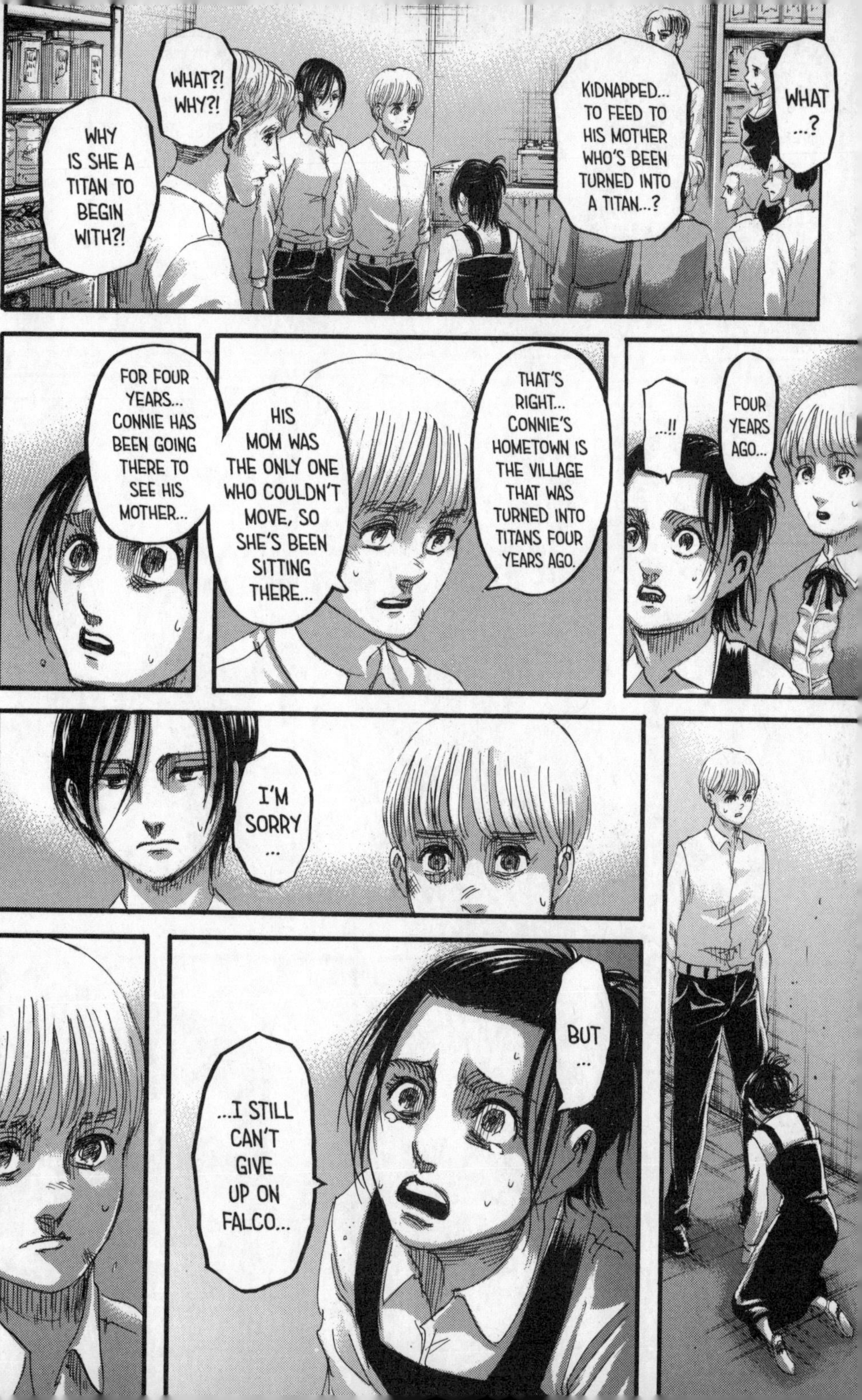
WHAT ...?
KIDNAPPED... TO FEED TO HIS MOTHER WHO'S BEEN TURNED INTO A TITAN...?
WHAT?! WHY?!
WHY IS SHE A TITAN TO BEGIN WITH?!
FOUR YEARS AGO...
...!!
THAT'S RIGHT... CONNIE'S HOMETOWN IS THE VILLAGE THAT WAS TURNED INTO TITANS FOUR YEARS AGO.
HIS MOM WAS THE ONLY ONE WHO COULDN'T MOVE, SO SHE'S BEEN SITTING THERE...
FOR FOUR YEARS... CONNIE HAS BEEN GOING THERE TO SEE HIS MOTHER...
I'M SORRY ...
BUT ...
...I STILL CAN'T GIVE UP ON FALCO...

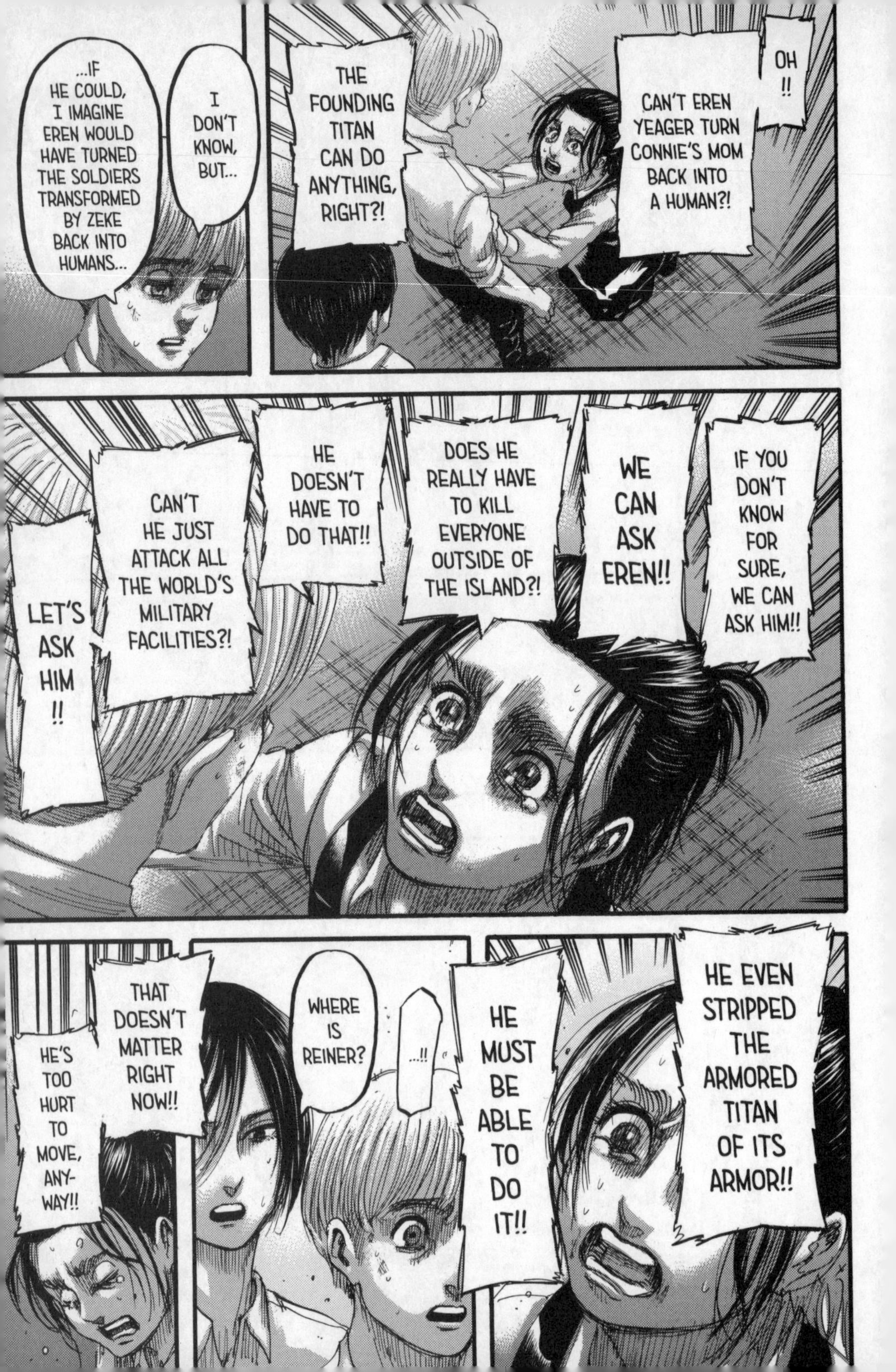
OH !!
CAN'T EREN YEAGER TURN CONNIE'S MOM BACK INTO A HUMAN?!
THE FOUNDING TITAN CAN DO ANYTHING, RIGHT?!
I DON'T KNOW, BUT...
...IF HE COULD, I IMAGINE EREN WOULD HAVE TURNED THE SOLDIERS TRANSFORMED BY ZEKE BACK INTO HUMANS...
IF YOU DON'T KNOW FOR SURE, WE CAN ASK HIM!!
WE CAN ASK EREN!!
DOES HE REALLY HAVE TO KILL EVERYONE OUTSIDE OF THE ISLAND?!
HE DOESN'T HAVE TO DO THAT!!
CAN'T HE JUST ATTACK ALL THE WORLD'S MILITARY FACILITIES?!
LET'S ASK HIM !!
HE EVEN STRIPPED THE ARMORED TITAN OF ITS ARMOR!!
HE MUST BE ABLE TO DO IT!!
...!!
WHERE IS REINER?
THAT DOESN'T MATTER RIGHT NOW!!
HE'S TOO HURT TO MOVE, ANY-WAY!!

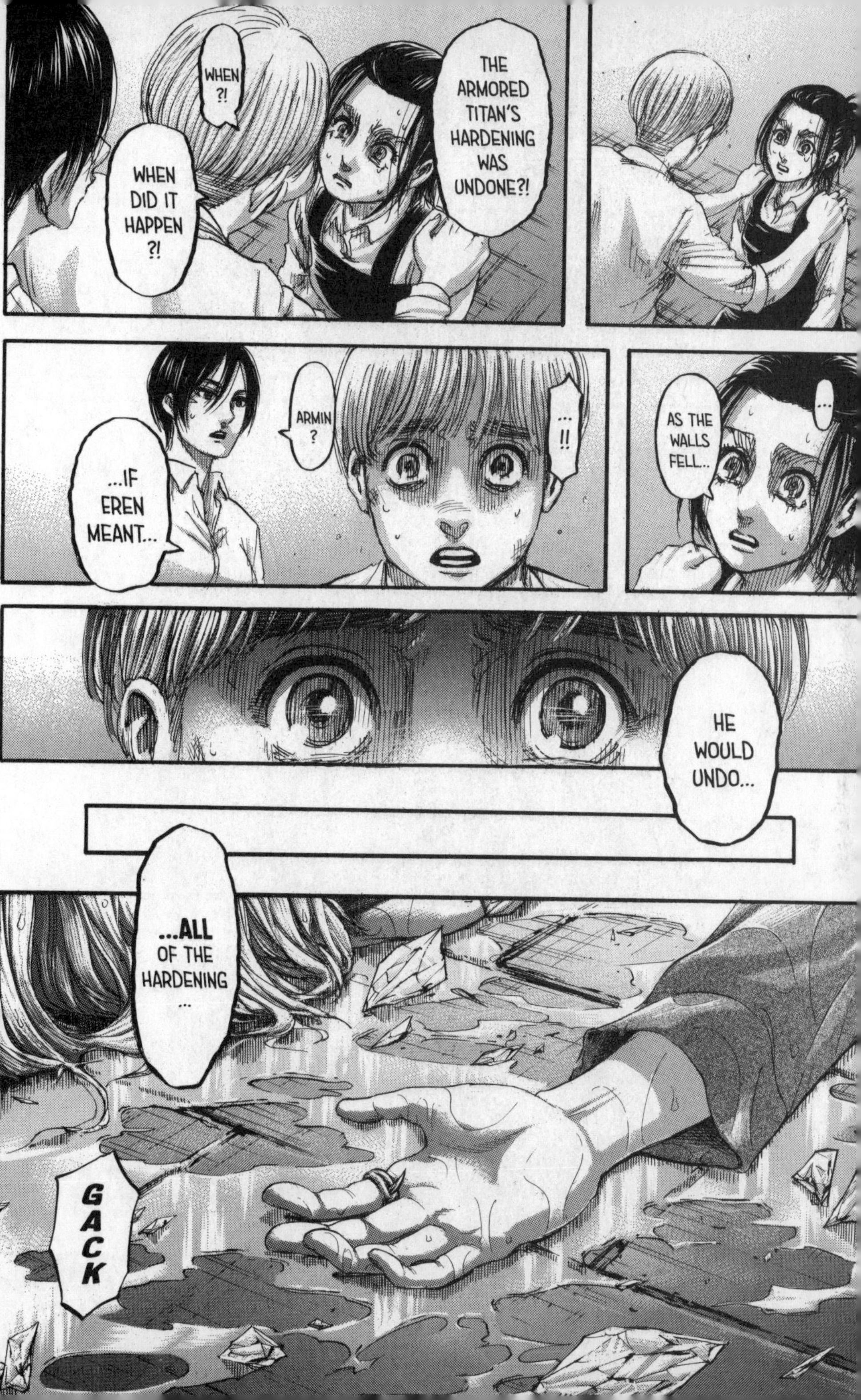
THE ARMORED TITAN'S HARDENING WAS UNDONE?!
WHEN ?!
WHEN DID IT HAPPEN ?!
...
AS THE WALLS FELL...
...!!
ARMIN ?
...IF EREN MEANT...
HE WOULD UNDO...
...ALL OF THE HARDENING ...
GACK

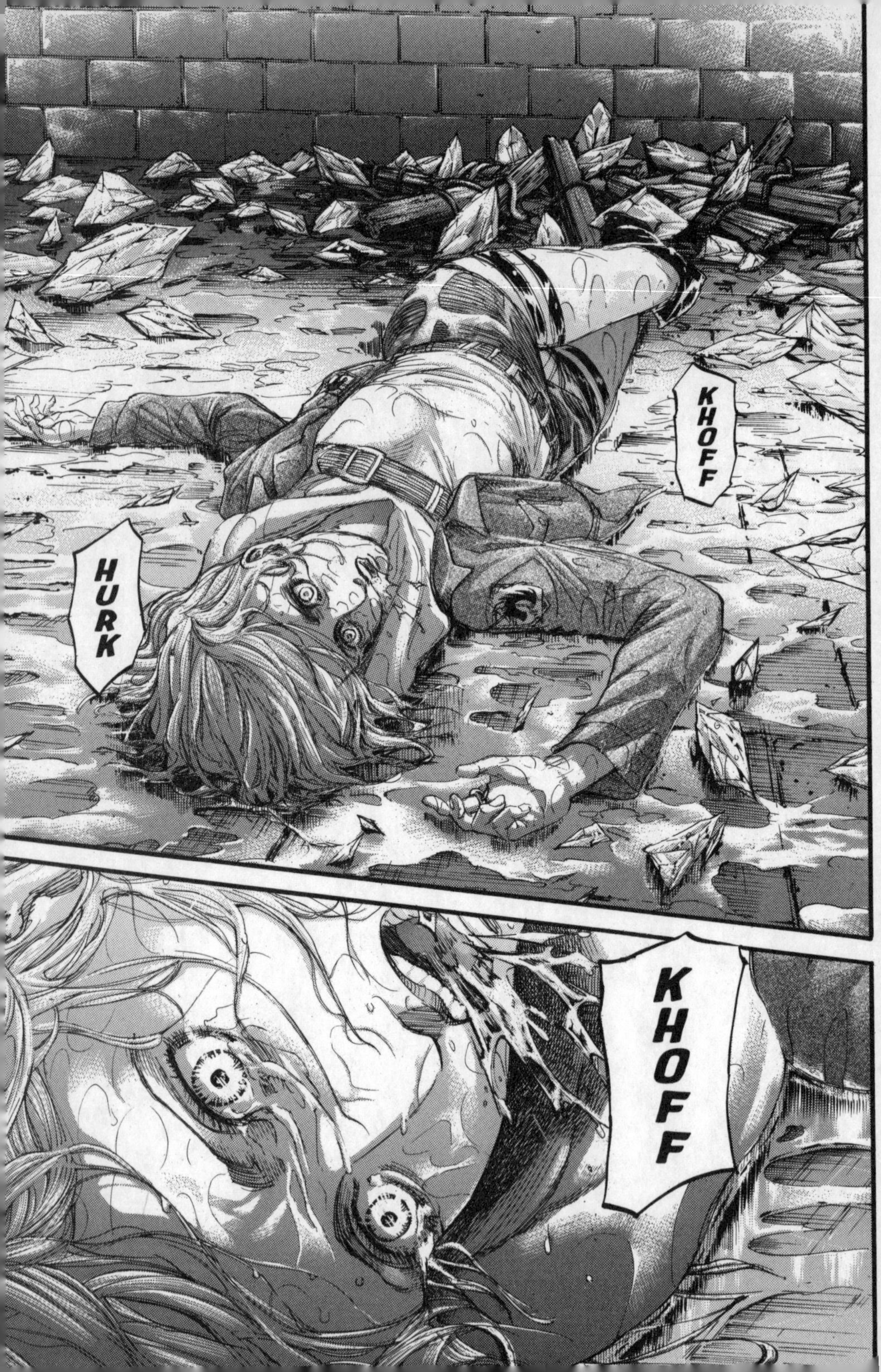
KHOFF
HURK
KHOFF

ATTACK on TITAN

Episode 125: Sunset

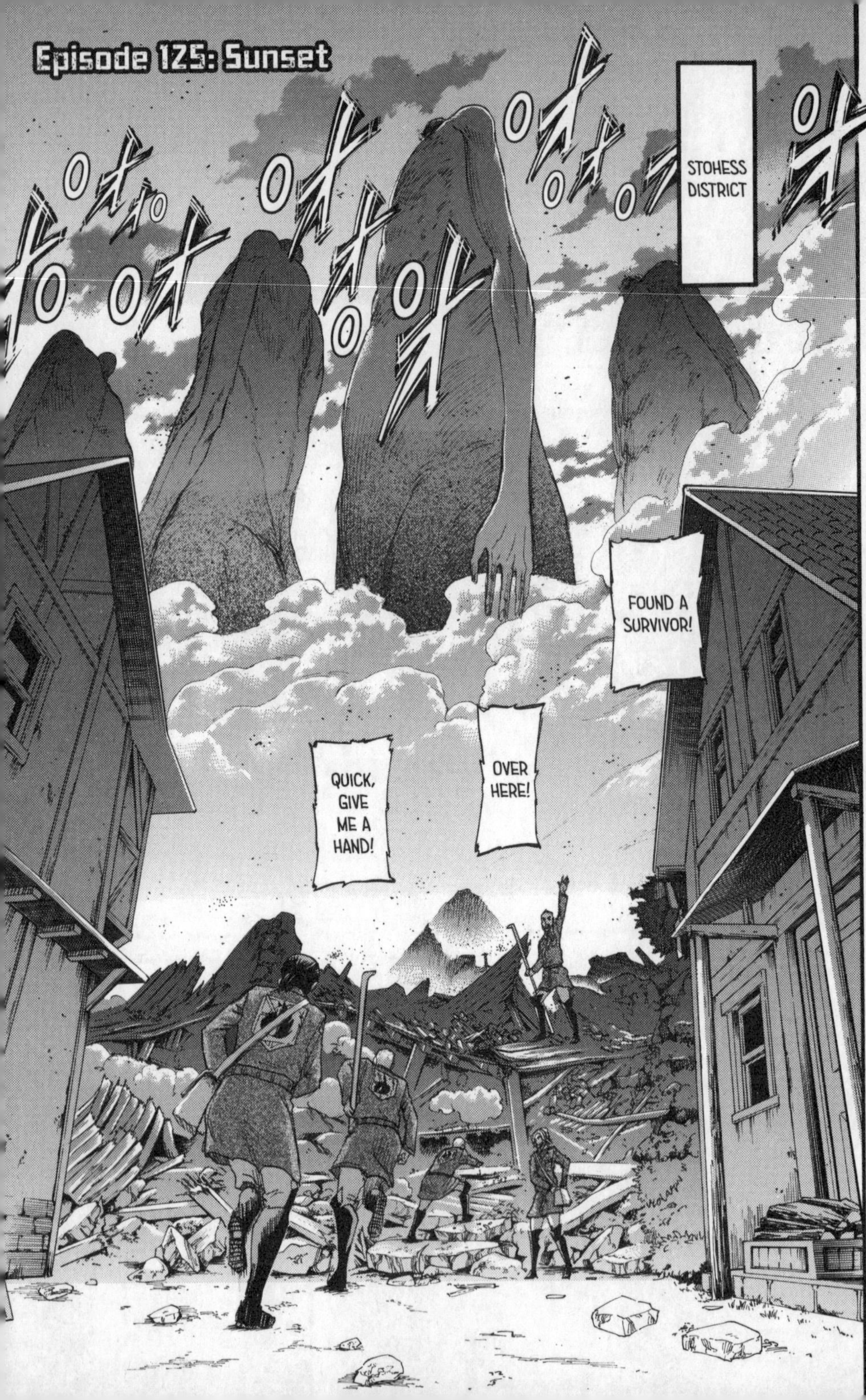
STOHESS DISTRICT
FOUND A SURVIVOR!
OVER HERE!
QUICK, GIVE ME A HAND!

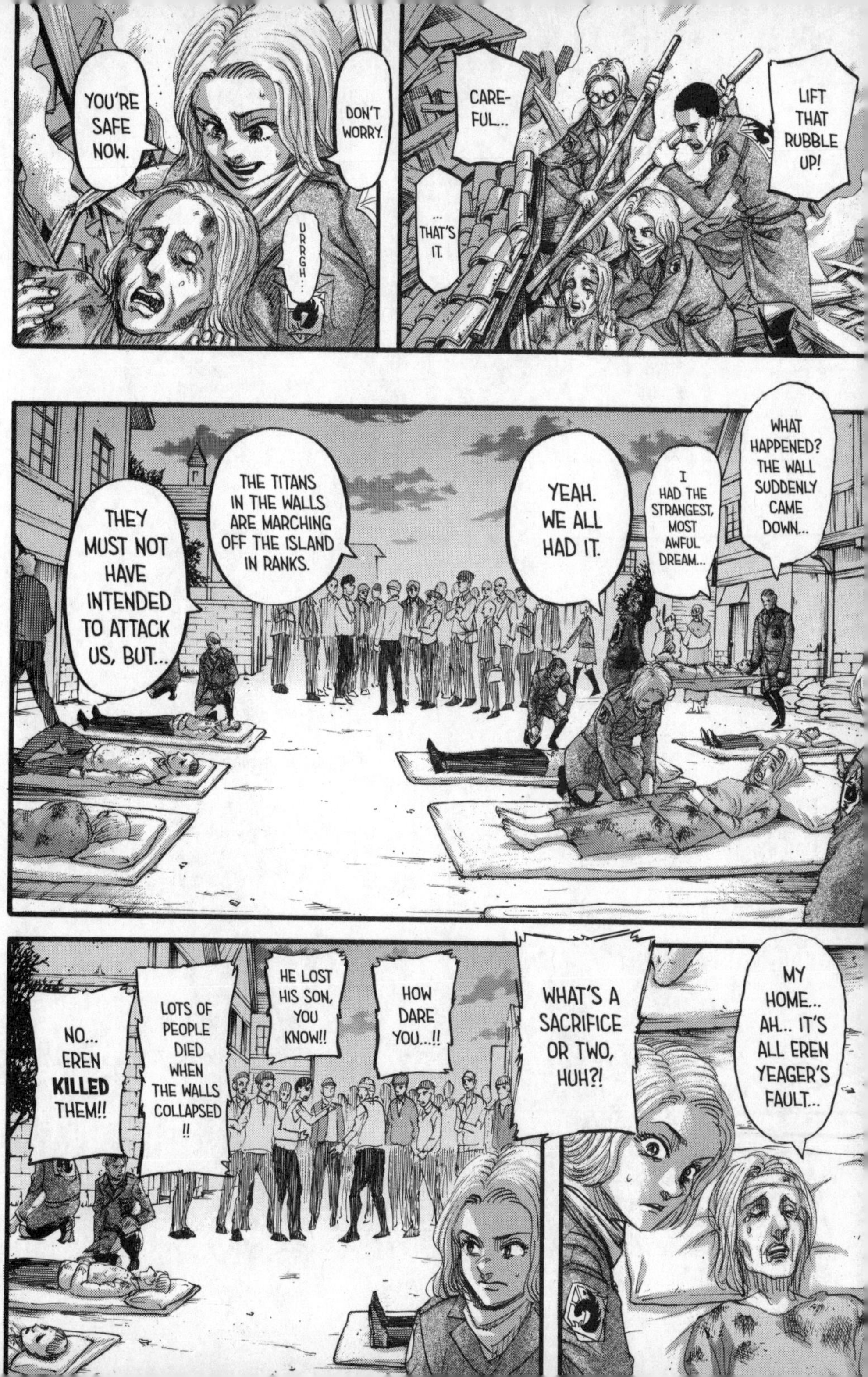
LIFT THAT RUBBLE UP!
CARE-FUL...
...THAT'S IT.
DON'T WORRY.
URRGH...
YOU'RE SAFE NOW.
WHAT HAPPENED? THE WALL SUDDENLY CAME DOWN...
I HAD THE STRANGEST, MOST AWFUL DREAM...
YEAH. WE ALL HAD IT.
THE TITANS IN THE WALLS ARE MARCHING OFF THE ISLAND IN RANKS.
THEY MUST NOT HAVE INTENDED TO ATTACK US, BUT...
MY HOME... AH... IT'S ALL EREN YEAGER'S FAULT...
WHAT'S A SACRIFICE OR TWO, HUH?!
HOW DARE YOU...!!
HE LOST HIS SON, YOU KNOW!!
LOTS OF PEOPLE DIED WHEN THE WALLS COLLAPSED!!
NO... EREN **KILLED** THEM!!

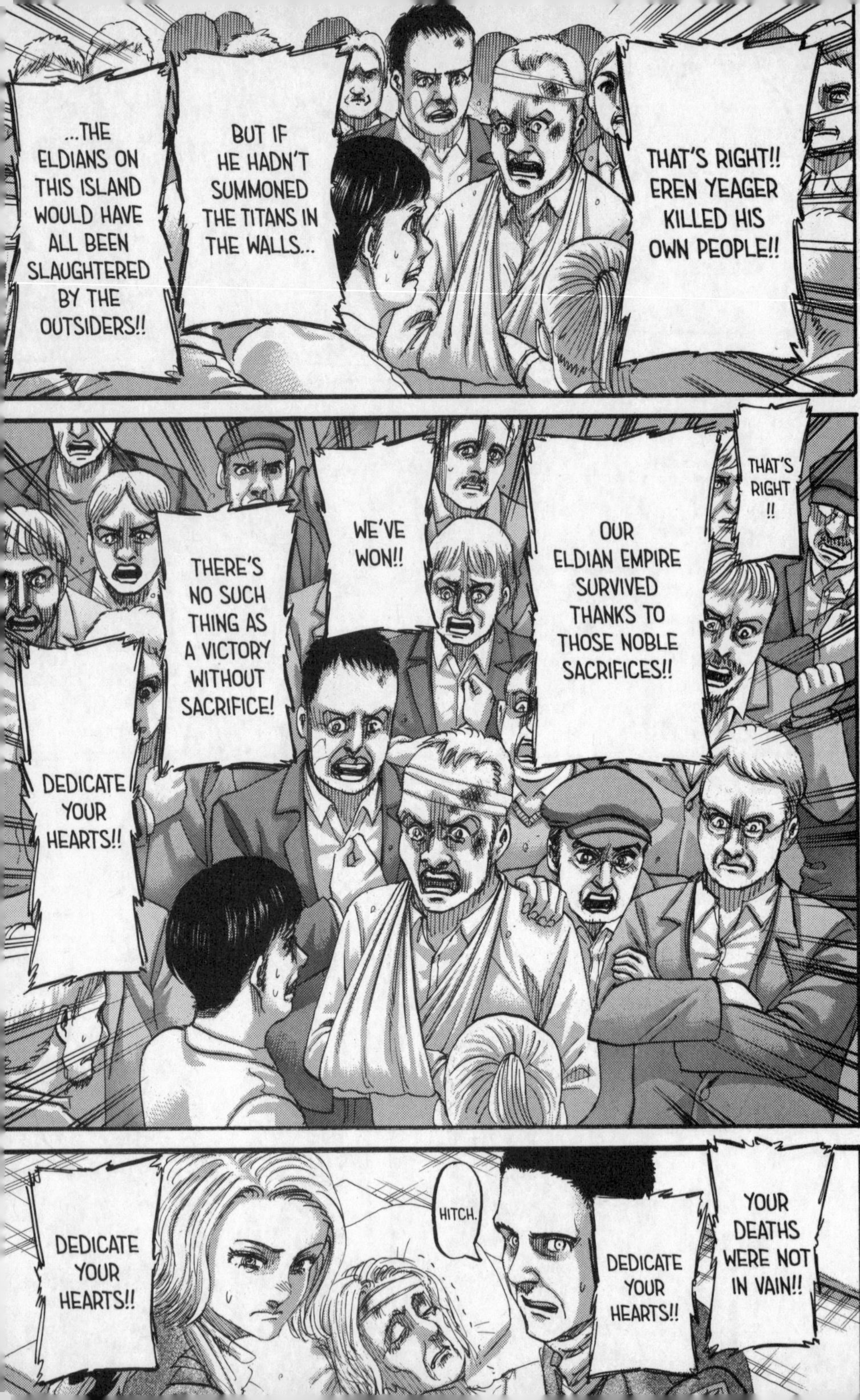
THAT'S RIGHT!! EREN YEAGER KILLED HIS OWN PEOPLE!!
BUT IF HE HADN'T SUMMONED THE TITANS IN THE WALLS...
...THE ELDIANS ON THIS ISLAND WOULD HAVE ALL BEEN SLAUGHTERED BY THE OUTSIDERS!!
THAT'S RIGHT!!
OUR ELDIAN EMPIRE SURVIVED THANKS TO THOSE NOBLE SACRIFICES!!
WE'VE WON!!
THERE'S NO SUCH THING AS A VICTORY WITHOUT SACRIFICE!
DEDICATE YOUR HEARTS!!
YOUR DEATHS WERE NOT IN VAIN!!
DEDICATE YOUR HEARTS!!
HITCH.
DEDICATE YOUR HEARTS!!

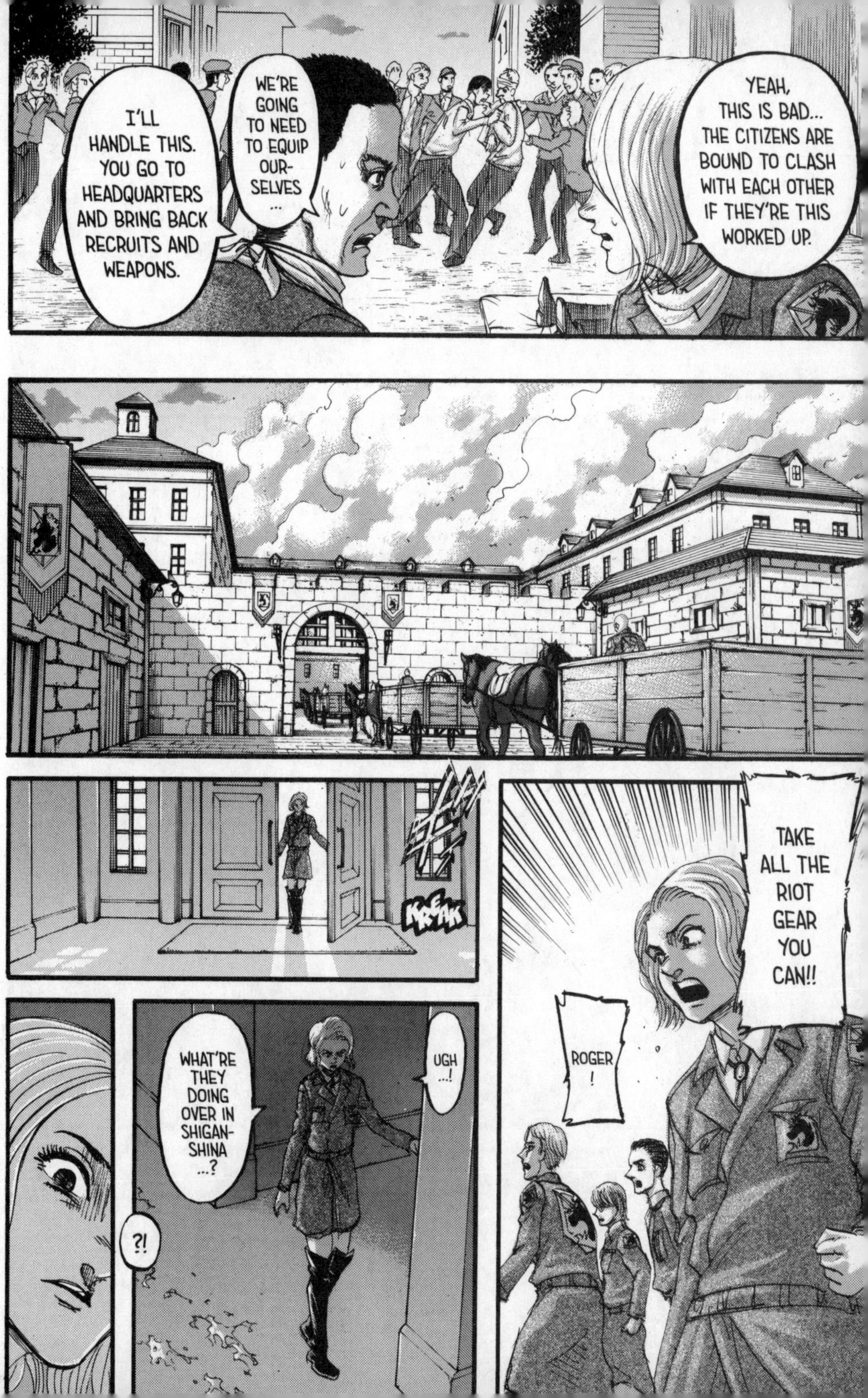
YEAH, THIS IS BAD... THE CITIZENS ARE BOUND TO CLASH WITH EACH OTHER IF THEY'RE THIS WORKED UP.
WE'RE GOING TO NEED TO EQUIP OUR-SELVES...
I'LL HANDLE THIS. YOU GO TO HEADQUARTERS AND BRING BACK RECRUITS AND WEAPONS.
TAKE ALL THE RIOT GEAR YOU CAN!!
ROGER!
KREAK
UGH...!
WHAT'RE THEY DOING OVER IN SHIGAN-SHINA...?
?!

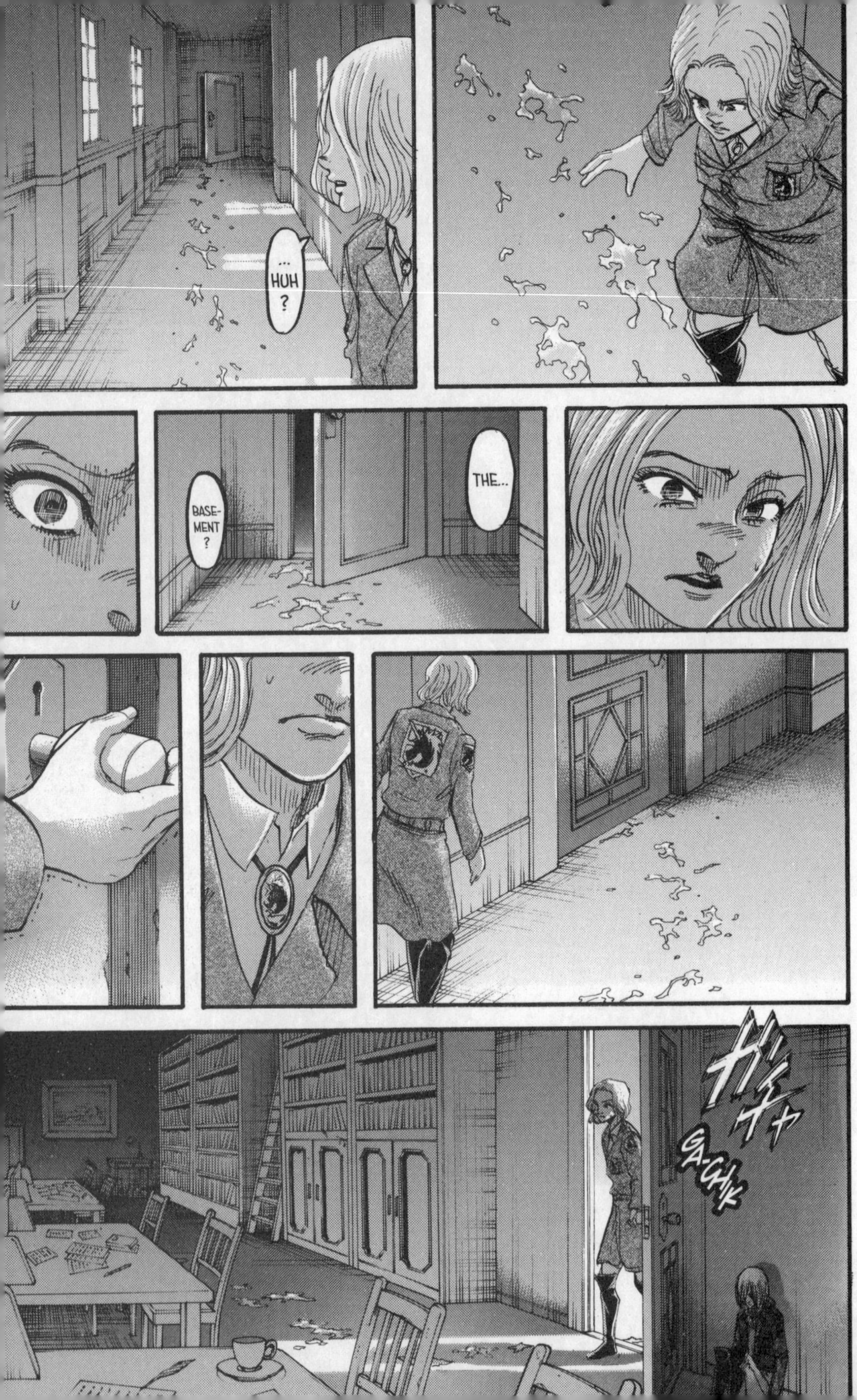
...HUH?
THE...
BASEMENT?
GA-CHIK

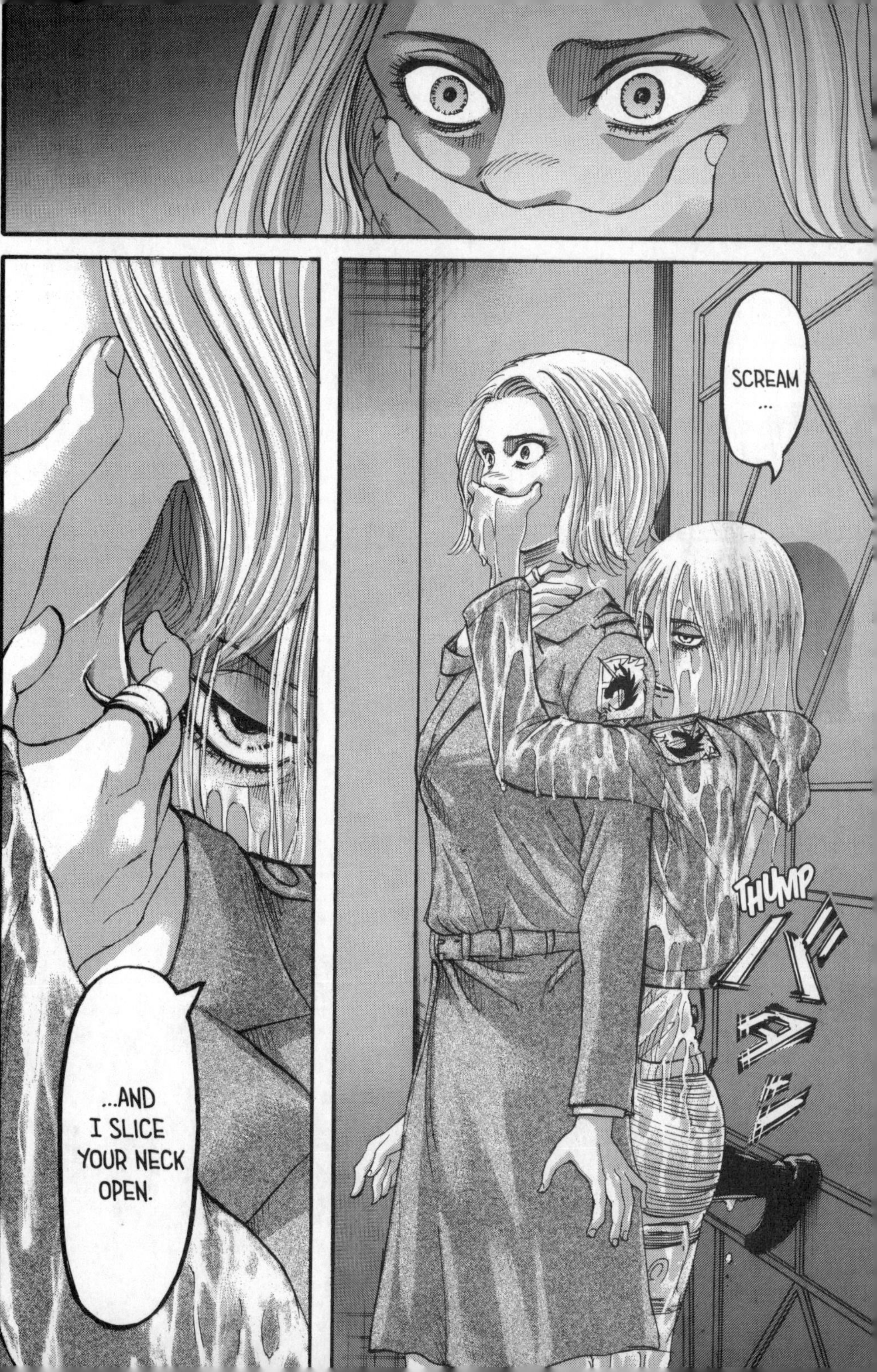
SCREAM ...
THUMP
...AND I SLICE YOUR NECK OPEN.

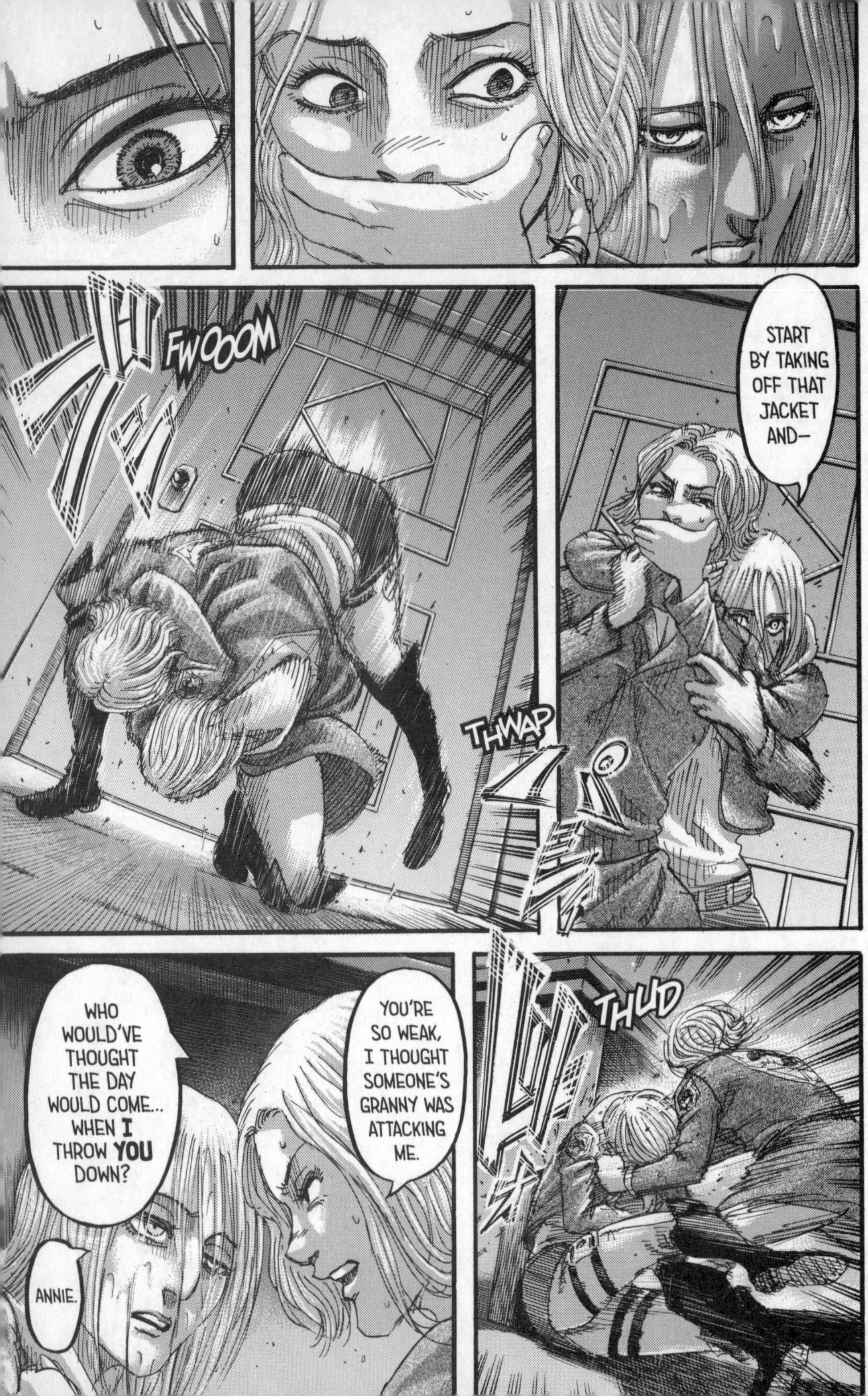
START BY TAKING OFF THAT JACKET AND—
THWAP
FWOOOM
THUD
YOU'RE SO WEAK, I THOUGHT SOMEONE'S GRANNY WAS ATTACKING ME.
WHO WOULD'VE THOUGHT THE DAY WOULD COME... WHEN **I** THROW **YOU** DOWN?
ANNIE.

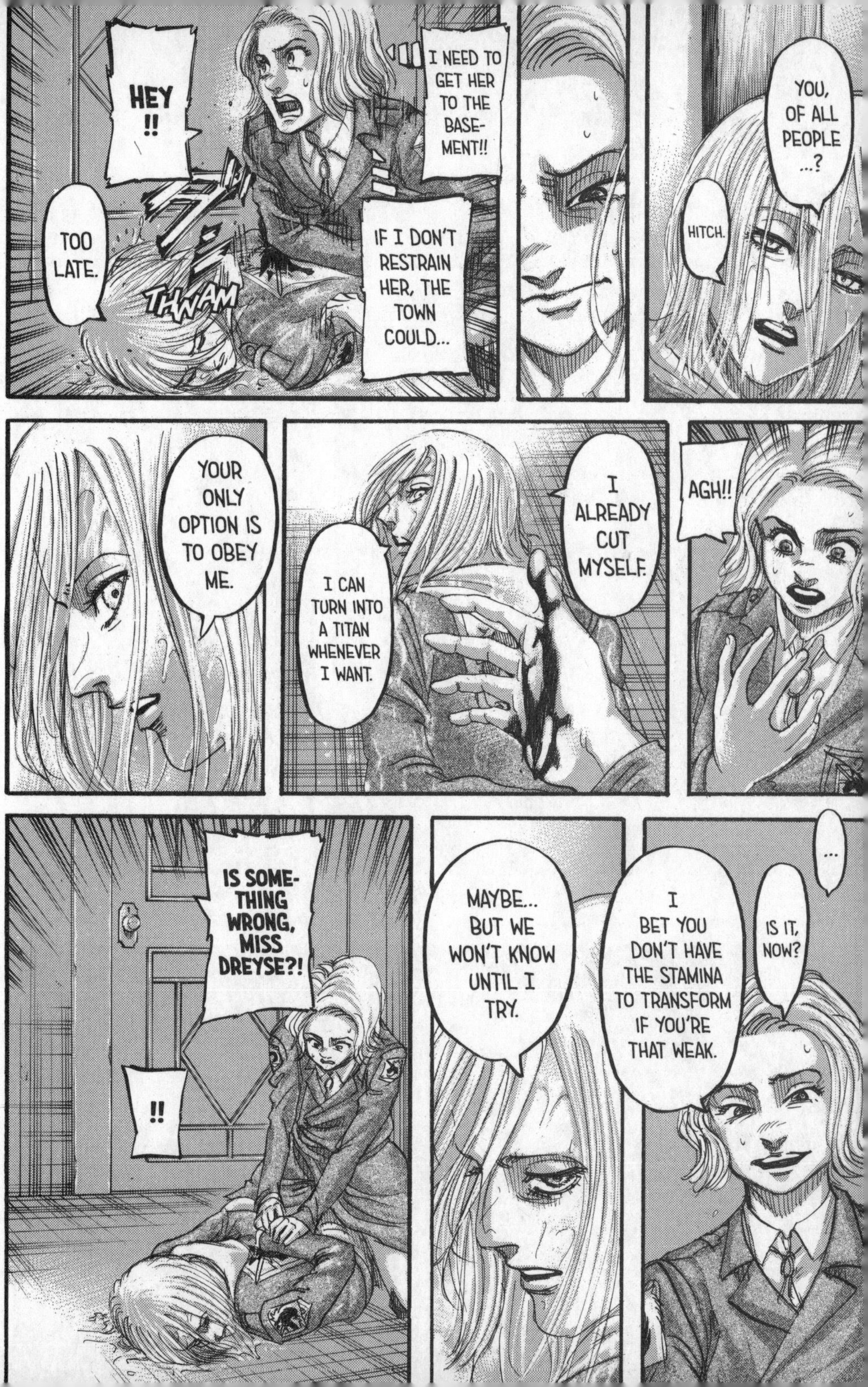
YOU, OF ALL PEOPLE ...?
HITCH.
I NEED TO GET HER TO THE BASEMENT!!
HEY !!
IF I DON'T RESTRAIN HER, THE TOWN COULD...
THWAM
TOO LATE.
AGH!!
I ALREADY CUT MYSELF.
I CAN TURN INTO A TITAN WHENEVER I WANT.
YOUR ONLY OPTION IS TO OBEY ME.
...
IS IT, NOW?
I BET YOU DON'T HAVE THE STAMINA TO TRANSFORM IF YOU'RE THAT WEAK.
MAYBE... BUT WE WON'T KNOW UNTIL I TRY.
IS SOMETHING WRONG, MISS DREYSE?!
!!

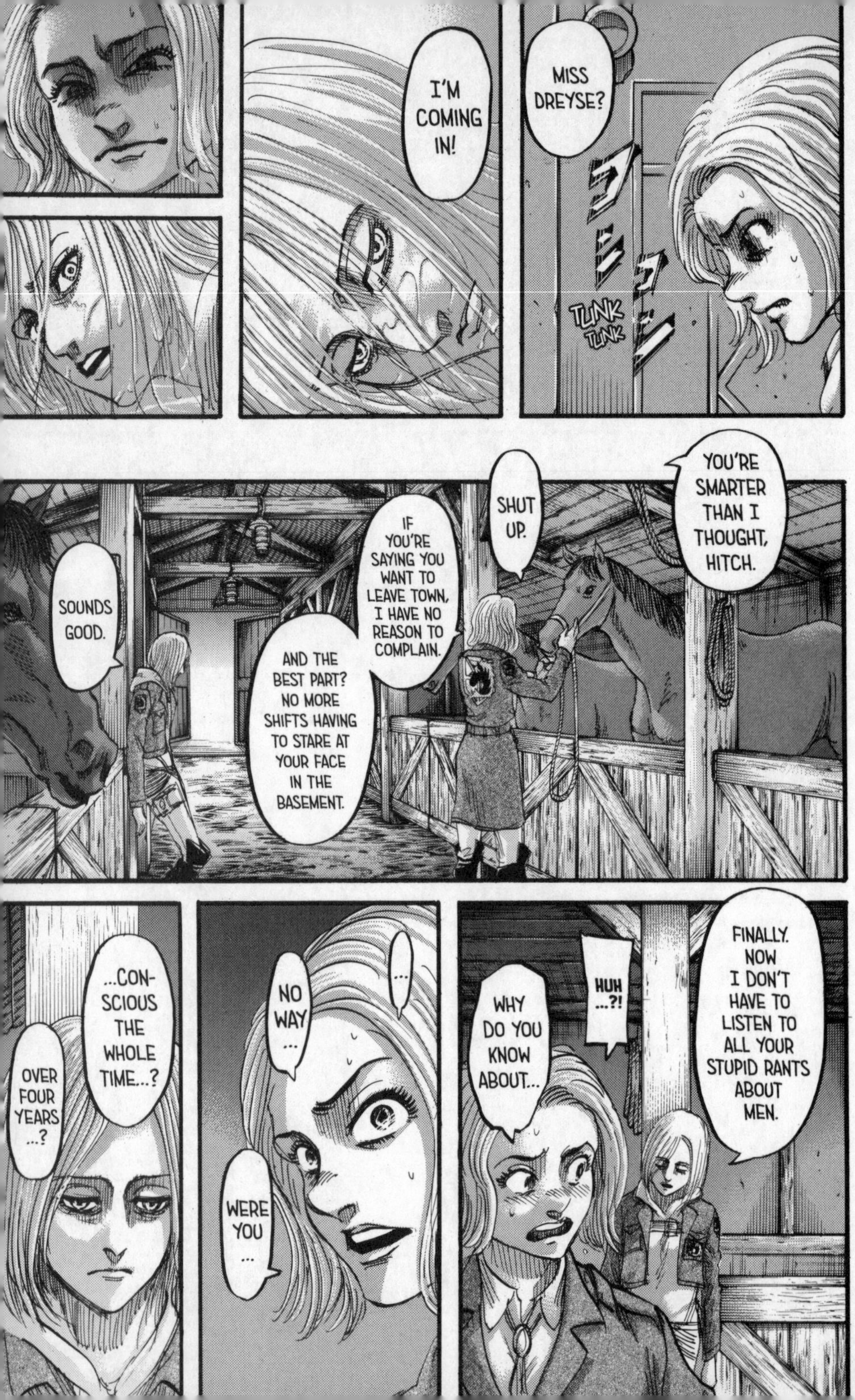
MISS DREYSE?
TUNK TUNK
I'M COMING IN!
YOU'RE SMARTER THAN I THOUGHT, HITCH.
SHUT UP.
IF YOU'RE SAYING YOU WANT TO LEAVE TOWN, I HAVE NO REASON TO COMPLAIN.
AND THE BEST PART? NO MORE SHIFTS HAVING TO STARE AT YOUR FACE IN THE BASEMENT.
SOUNDS GOOD.
FINALLY. NOW I DON'T HAVE TO LISTEN TO ALL YOUR STUPID RANTS ABOUT MEN.
HUH ...?!
WHY DO YOU KNOW ABOUT...
...
NO WAY ...
WERE YOU ...
...CON-SCIOUS THE WHOLE TIME...?
OVER FOUR YEARS ...?

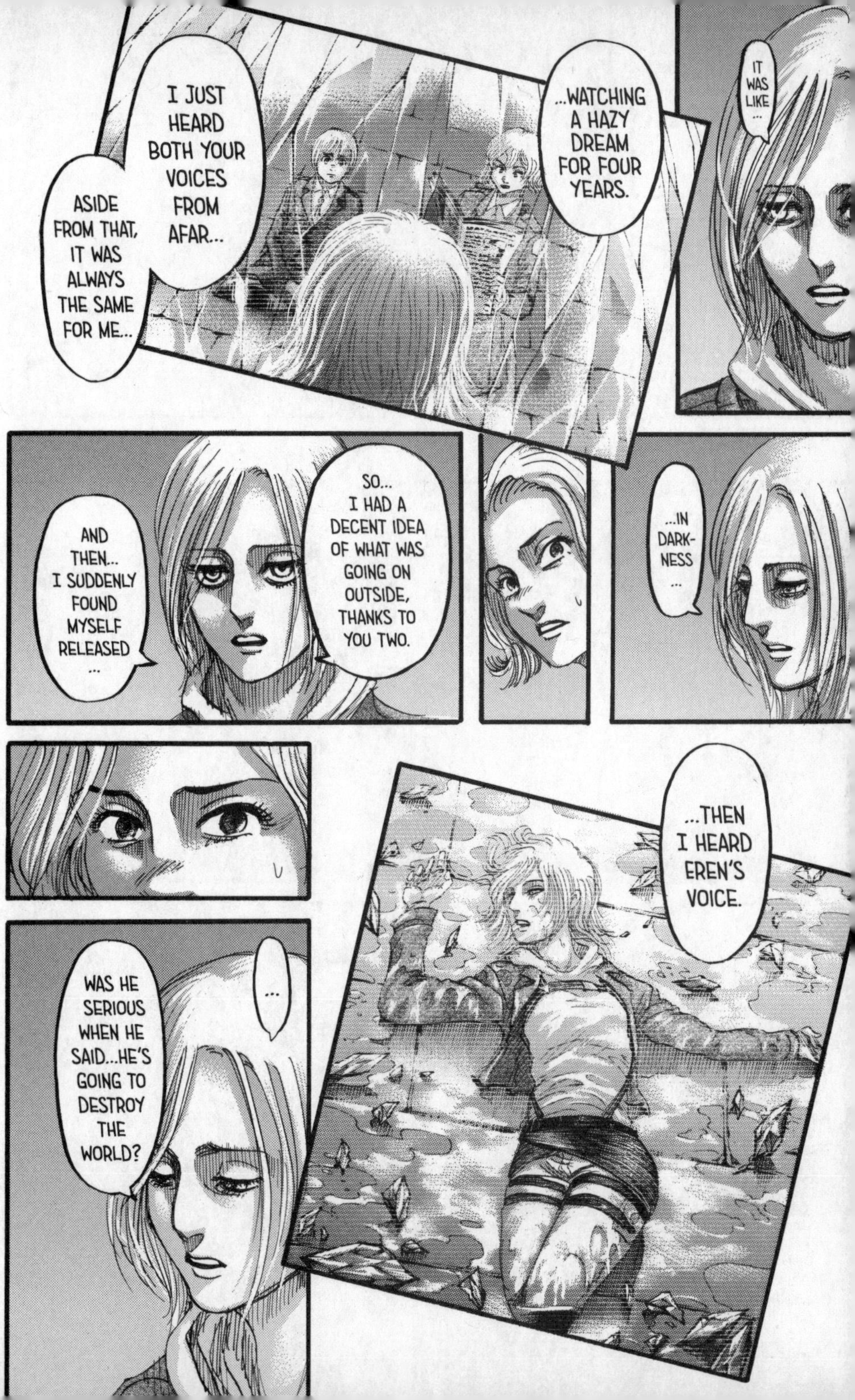
IT WAS LIKE ...
...WATCHING A HAZY DREAM FOR FOUR YEARS.
I JUST HEARD BOTH YOUR VOICES FROM AFAR...
ASIDE FROM THAT, IT WAS ALWAYS THE SAME FOR ME...
...IN DARKNESS ...
SO... I HAD A DECENT IDEA OF WHAT WAS GOING ON OUTSIDE, THANKS TO YOU TWO.
AND THEN... I SUDDENLY FOUND MYSELF RELEASED ...
...THEN I HEARD EREN'S VOICE.
...
WAS HE SERIOUS WHEN HE SAID...HE'S GOING TO DESTROY THE WORLD?

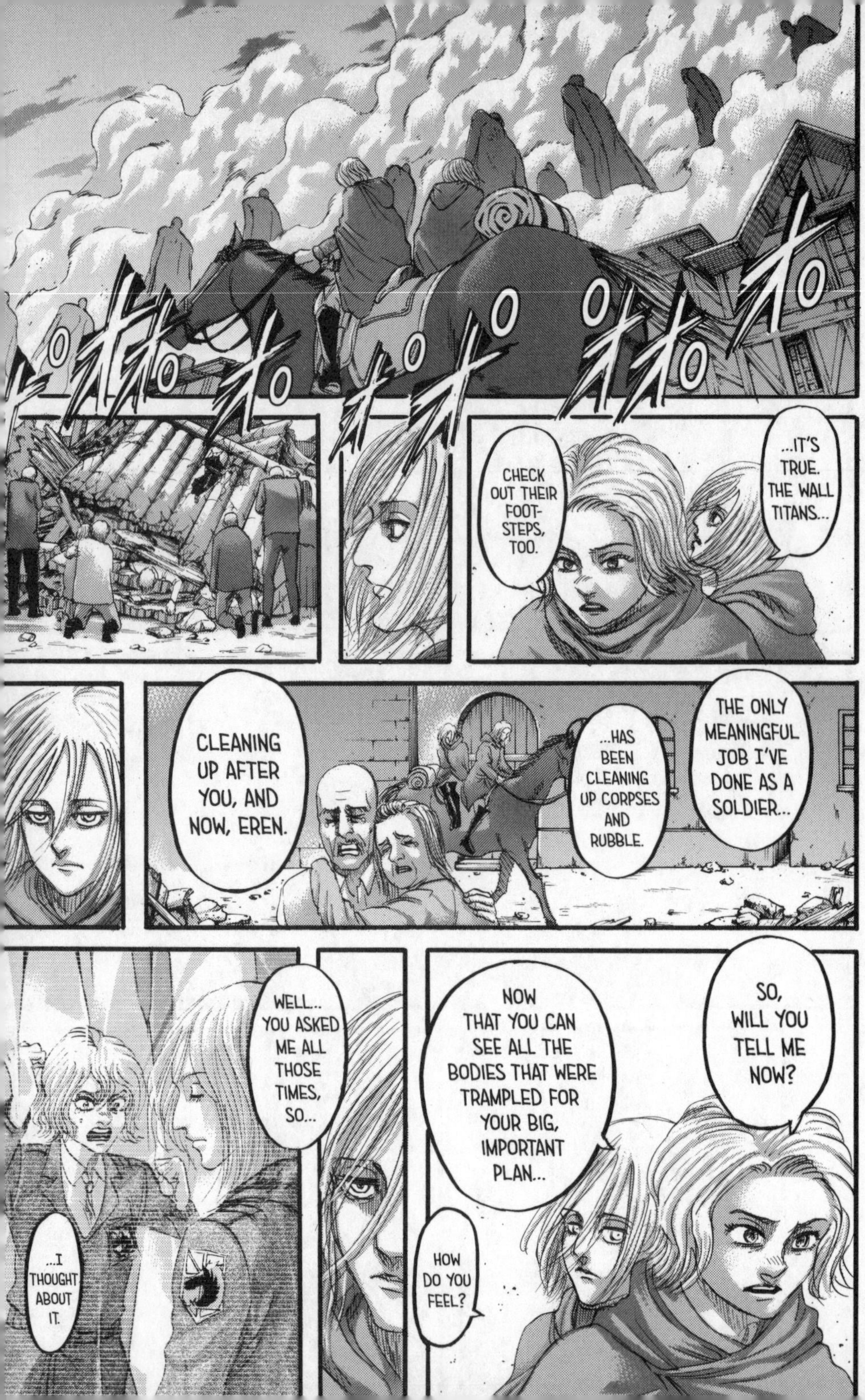
...IT'S TRUE. THE WALL TITANS...
CHECK OUT THEIR FOOT-STEPS, TOO.
THE ONLY MEANINGFUL JOB I'VE DONE AS A SOLDIER...
...HAS BEEN CLEANING UP CORPSES AND RUBBLE.
CLEANING UP AFTER YOU, AND NOW, EREN.
SO, WILL YOU TELL ME NOW?
NOW THAT YOU CAN SEE ALL THE BODIES THAT WERE TRAMPLED FOR YOUR BIG, IMPORTANT PLAN...
HOW DO YOU FEEL?
WELL... YOU ASKED ME ALL THOSE TIMES, SO...
...I THOUGHT ABOUT IT.

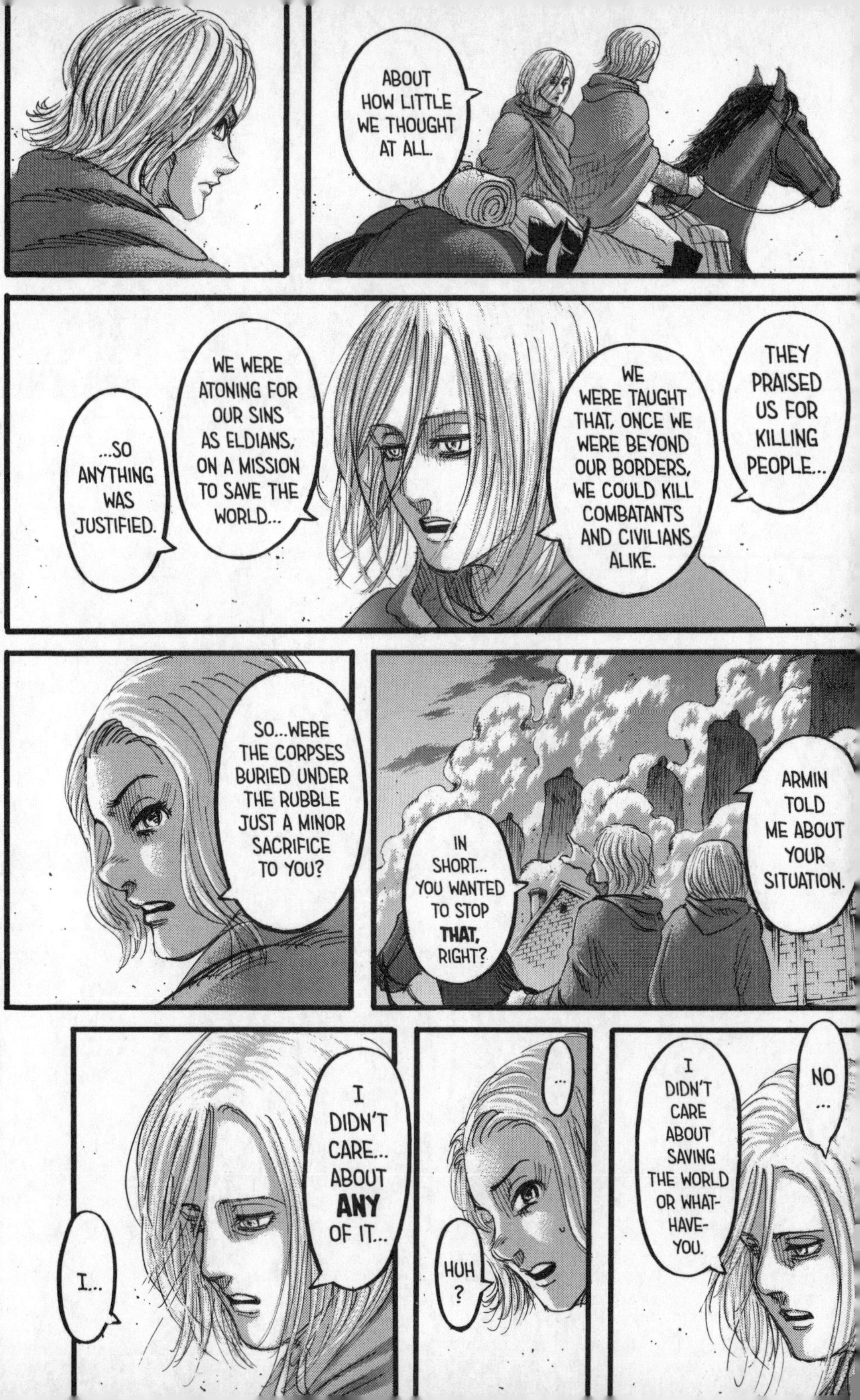
ABOUT HOW LITTLE WE THOUGHT AT ALL.
THEY PRAISED US FOR KILLING PEOPLE...
WE WERE TAUGHT THAT, ONCE WE WERE BEYOND OUR BORDERS, WE COULD KILL COMBATANTS AND CIVILIANS ALIKE.
WE WERE ATONING FOR OUR SINS AS ELDIANS, ON A MISSION TO SAVE THE WORLD...
...SO ANYTHING WAS JUSTIFIED.
ARMIN TOLD ME ABOUT YOUR SITUATION.
IN SHORT... YOU WANTED TO STOP **THAT,** RIGHT?
SO...WERE THE CORPSES BURIED UNDER THE RUBBLE JUST A MINOR SACRIFICE TO YOU?
NO...
I DIDN'T CARE ABOUT SAVING THE WORLD OR WHAT-HAVE-YOU.
...
HUH?
I DIDN'T CARE... ABOUT **ANY** OF IT...
I...

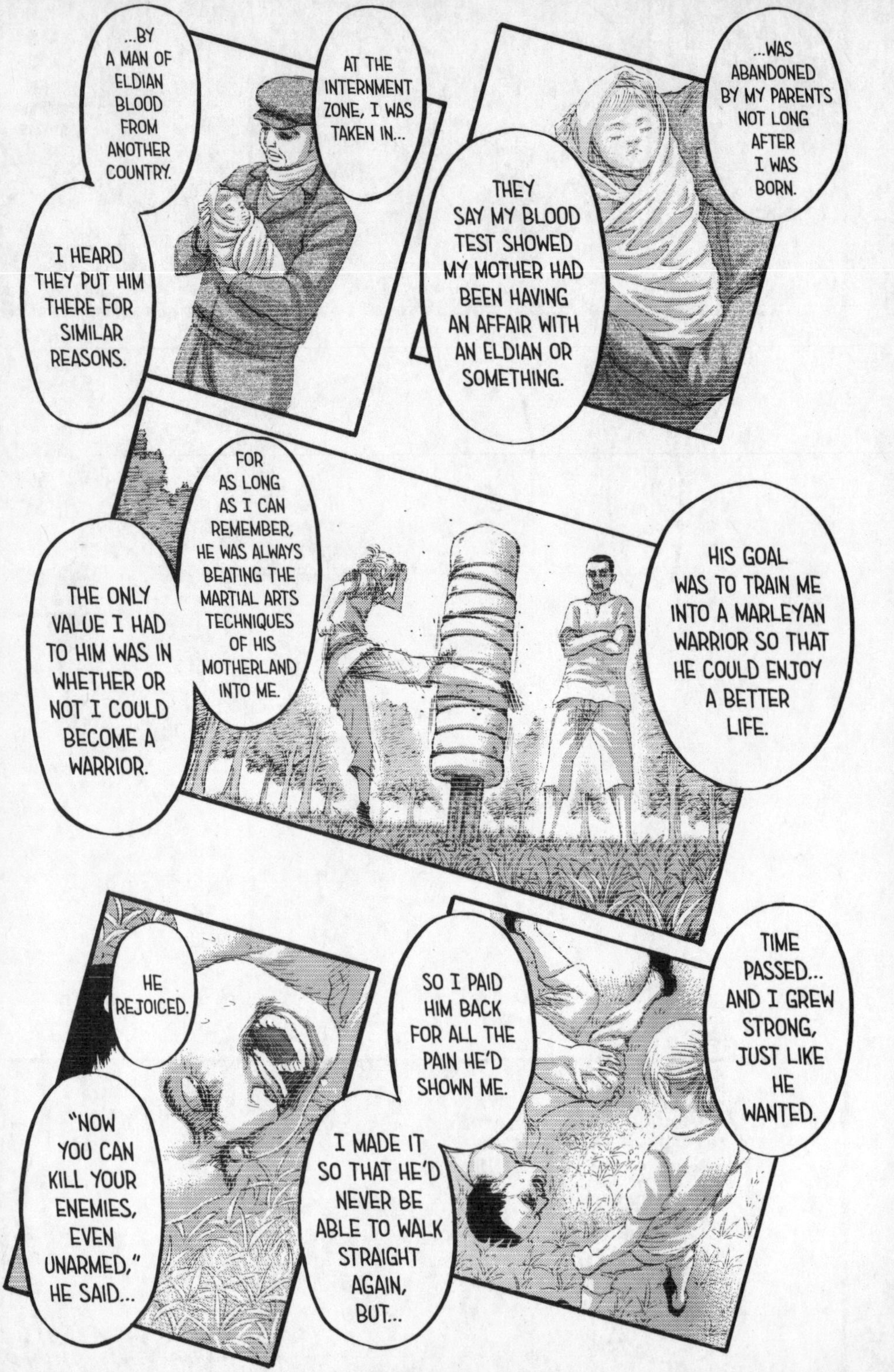
...WAS ABANDONED BY MY PARENTS NOT LONG AFTER I WAS BORN.
THEY SAY MY BLOOD TEST SHOWED MY MOTHER HAD BEEN HAVING AN AFFAIR WITH AN ELDIAN OR SOMETHING.
AT THE INTERNMENT ZONE, I WAS TAKEN IN...
...BY A MAN OF ELDIAN BLOOD FROM ANOTHER COUNTRY.
I HEARD THEY PUT HIM THERE FOR SIMILAR REASONS.
HIS GOAL WAS TO TRAIN ME INTO A MARLEYAN WARRIOR SO THAT HE COULD ENJOY A BETTER LIFE.
FOR AS LONG AS I CAN REMEMBER, HE WAS ALWAYS BEATING THE MARTIAL ARTS TECHNIQUES OF HIS MOTHERLAND INTO ME.
THE ONLY VALUE I HAD TO HIM WAS IN WHETHER OR NOT I COULD BECOME A WARRIOR.
TIME PASSED... AND I GREW STRONG, JUST LIKE HE WANTED.
SO I PAID HIM BACK FOR ALL THE PAIN HE'D SHOWN ME.
I MADE IT SO THAT HE'D NEVER BE ABLE TO WALK STRAIGHT AGAIN, BUT...
HE REJOICED.
"NOW YOU CAN KILL YOUR ENEMIES, EVEN UNARMED," HE SAID...

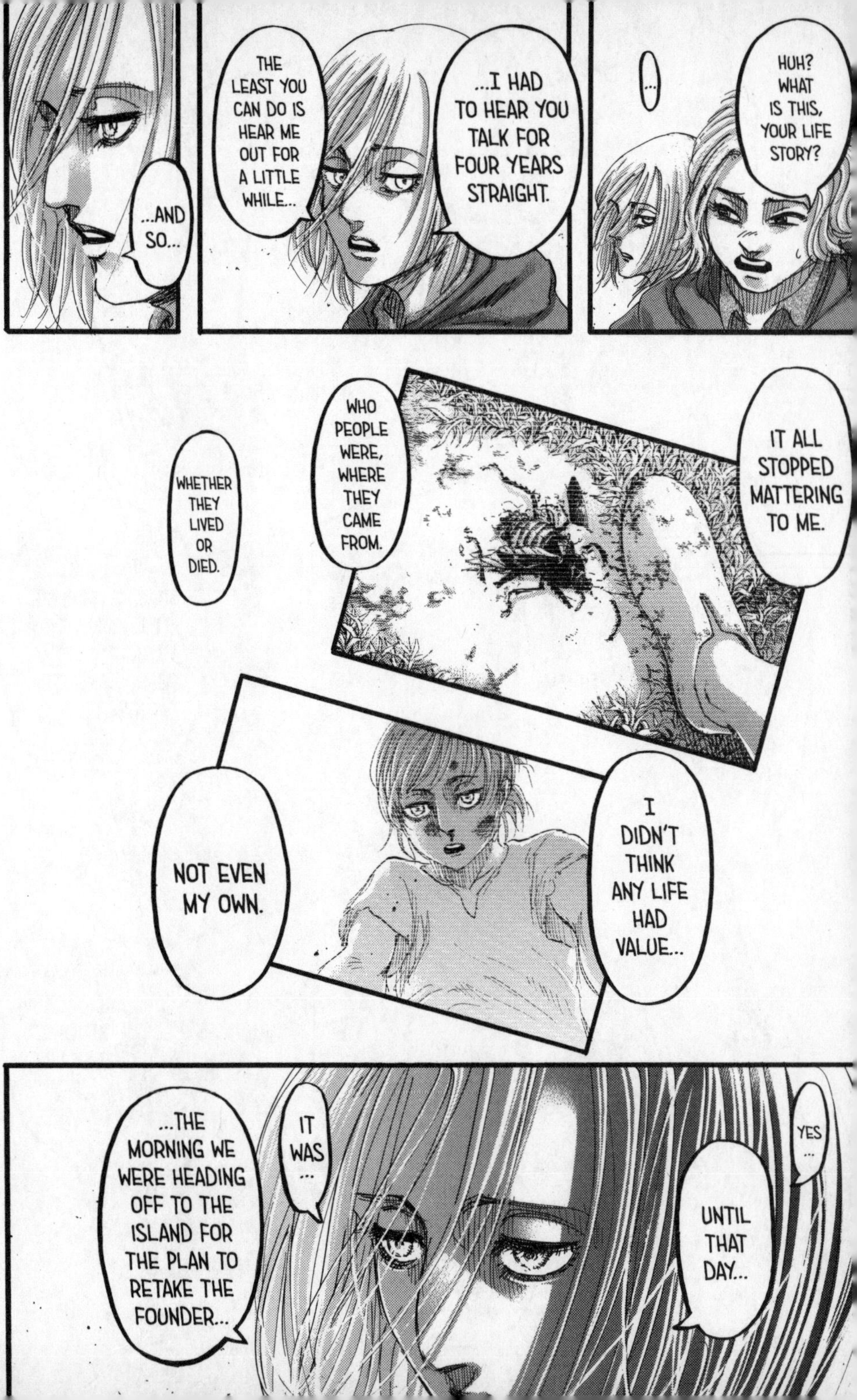
HUH? WHAT IS THIS, YOUR LIFE STORY?
...
...I HAD TO HEAR YOU TALK FOR FOUR YEARS STRAIGHT.
THE LEAST YOU CAN DO IS HEAR ME OUT FOR A LITTLE WHILE...
...AND SO...
IT ALL STOPPED MATTERING TO ME.
WHO PEOPLE WERE, WHERE THEY CAME FROM.
WHETHER THEY LIVED OR DIED.
I DIDN'T THINK ANY LIFE HAD VALUE...
NOT EVEN MY OWN.
YES...
UNTIL THAT DAY...
IT WAS...
...THE MORNING WE WERE HEADING OFF TO THE ISLAND FOR THE PLAN TO RETAKE THE FOUNDER...

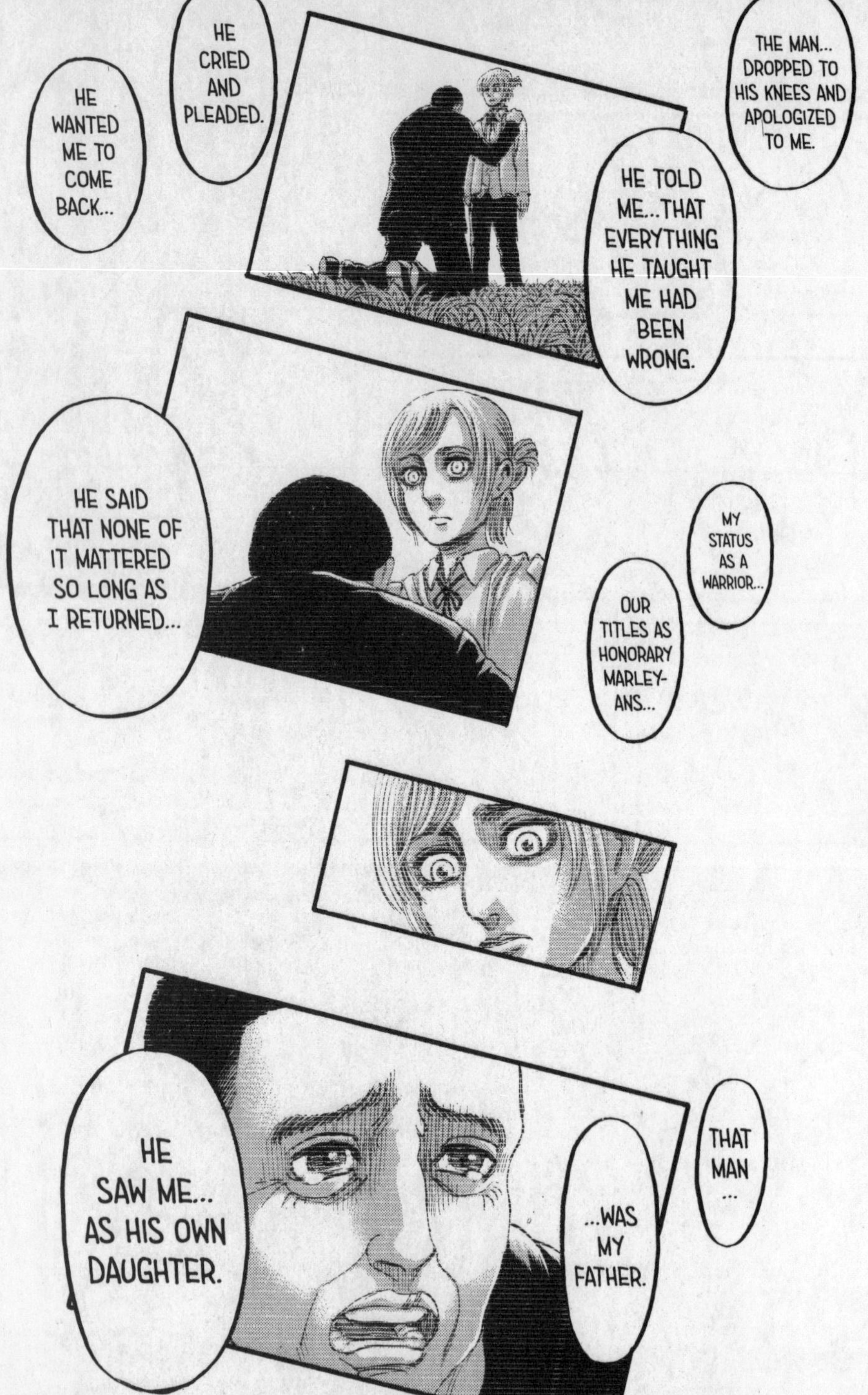
THE MAN... DROPPED TO HIS KNEES AND APOLOGIZED TO ME.
HE TOLD ME...THAT EVERYTHING HE TAUGHT ME HAD BEEN WRONG.
HE CRIED AND PLEADED.
HE WANTED ME TO COME BACK...
MY STATUS AS A WARRIOR...
OUR TITLES AS HONORARY MARLEY-ANS...
HE SAID THAT NONE OF IT MATTERED SO LONG AS I RETURNED...
THAT MAN...
...WAS MY FATHER.
HE SAW ME... AS HIS OWN DAUGHTER.

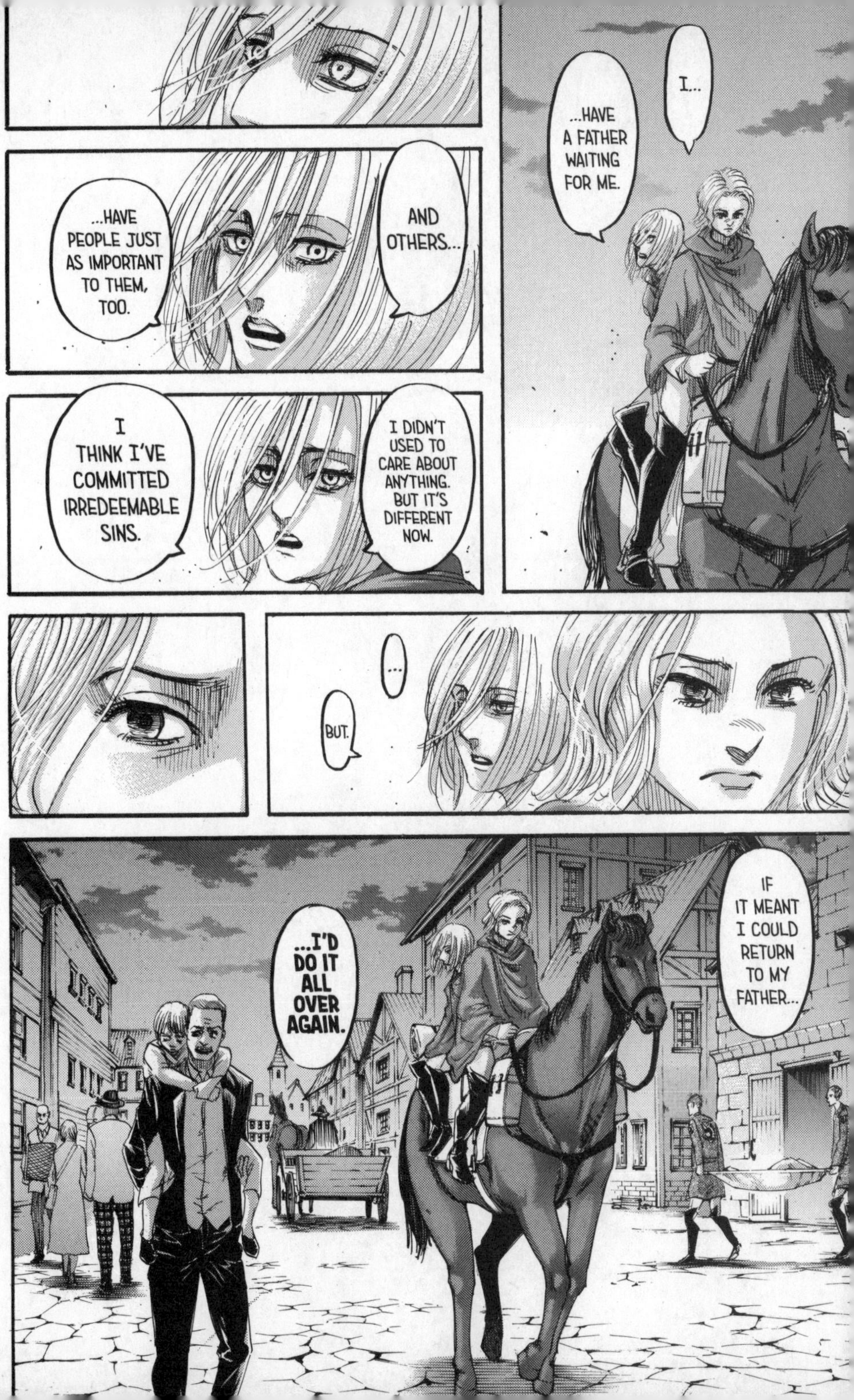
I...
...HAVE A FATHER WAITING FOR ME.
AND OTHERS...
...HAVE PEOPLE JUST AS IMPORTANT TO THEM, TOO.
I DIDN'T USED TO CARE ABOUT ANYTHING. BUT IT'S DIFFERENT NOW.
I THINK I'VE COMMITTED IRREDEEMABLE SINS.
...
BUT.
IF IT MEANT I COULD RETURN TO MY FATHER...
...I'D DO IT ALL OVER AGAIN.

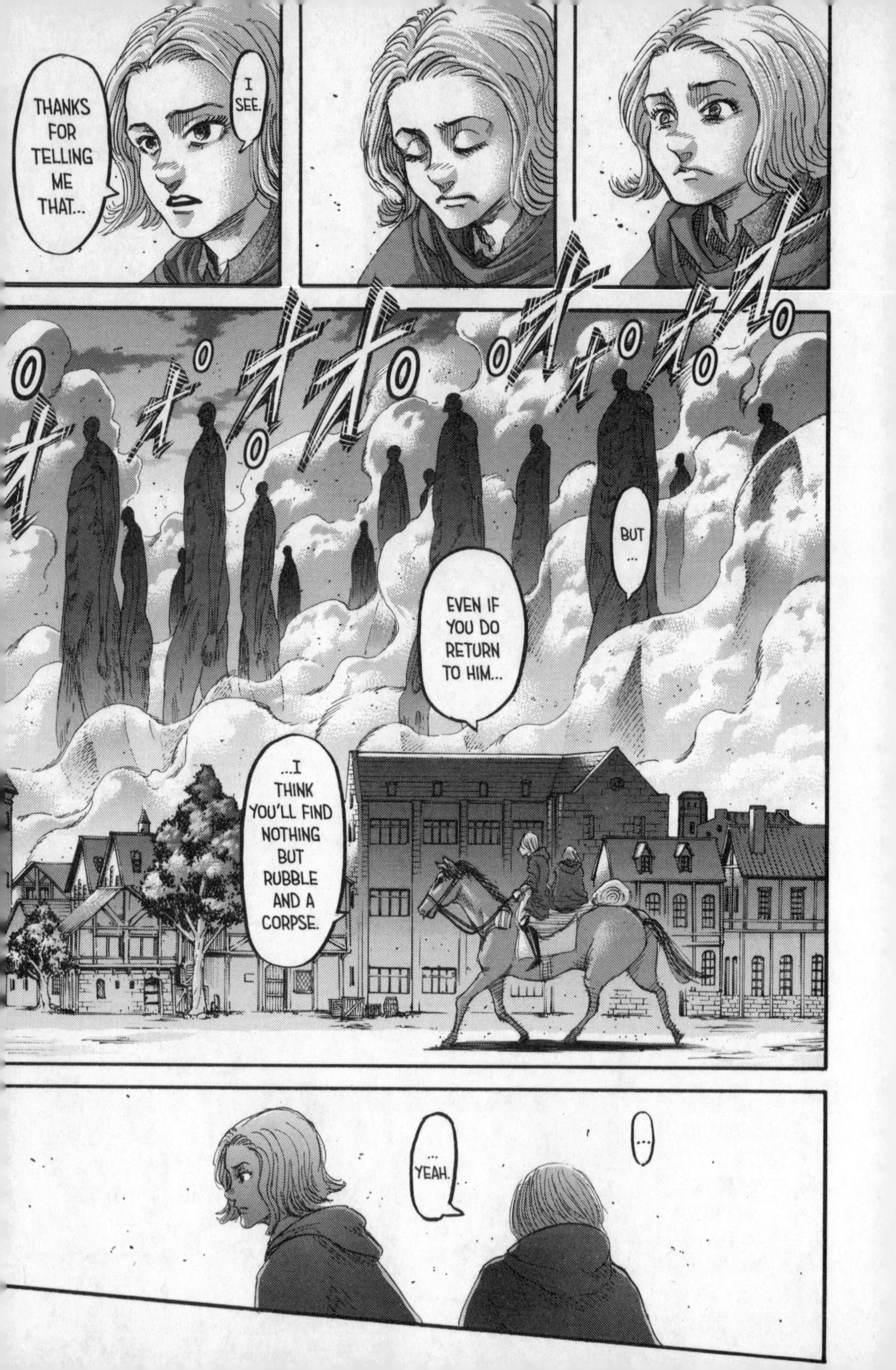
I SEE.
THANKS FOR TELLING ME THAT...
BUT...
EVEN IF YOU DO RETURN TO HIM...
...I THINK YOU'LL FIND NOTHING BUT RUBBLE AND A CORPSE.
...
... YEAH.

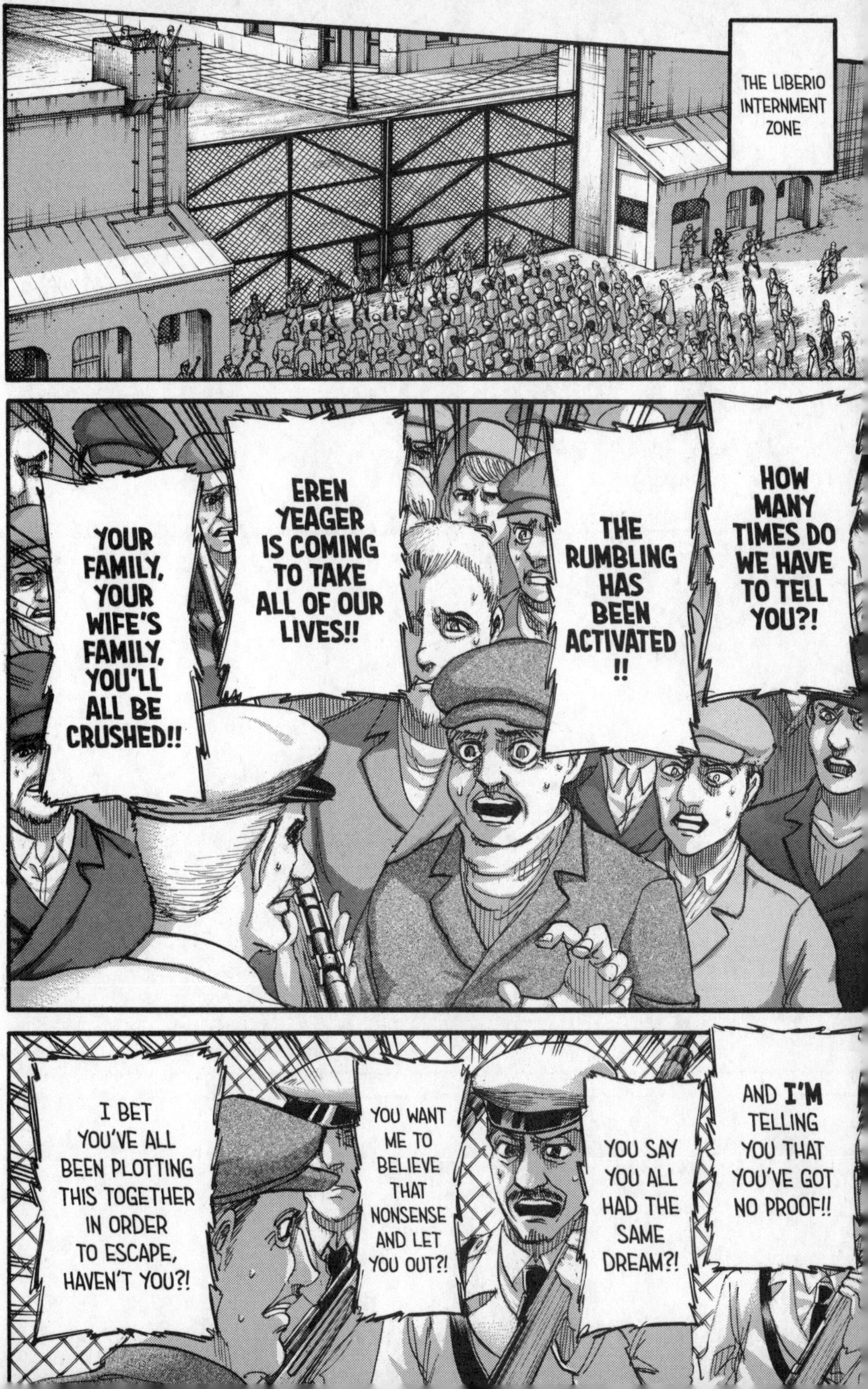
THE LIBERIO INTERNMENT ZONE
HOW MANY TIMES DO WE HAVE TO TELL YOU?!
THE RUMBLING HAS BEEN ACTIVATED!!
EREN YEAGER IS COMING TO TAKE ALL OF OUR LIVES!!
YOUR FAMILY, YOUR WIFE'S FAMILY, YOU'LL ALL BE CRUSHED!!
AND I'M TELLING YOU THAT YOU'VE GOT NO PROOF!!
YOU SAY YOU ALL HAD THE SAME DREAM?!
YOU WANT ME TO BELIEVE THAT NONSENSE AND LET YOU OUT?!
I BET YOU'VE ALL BEEN PLOTTING THIS TOGETHER IN ORDER TO ESCAPE, HAVEN'T YOU?!

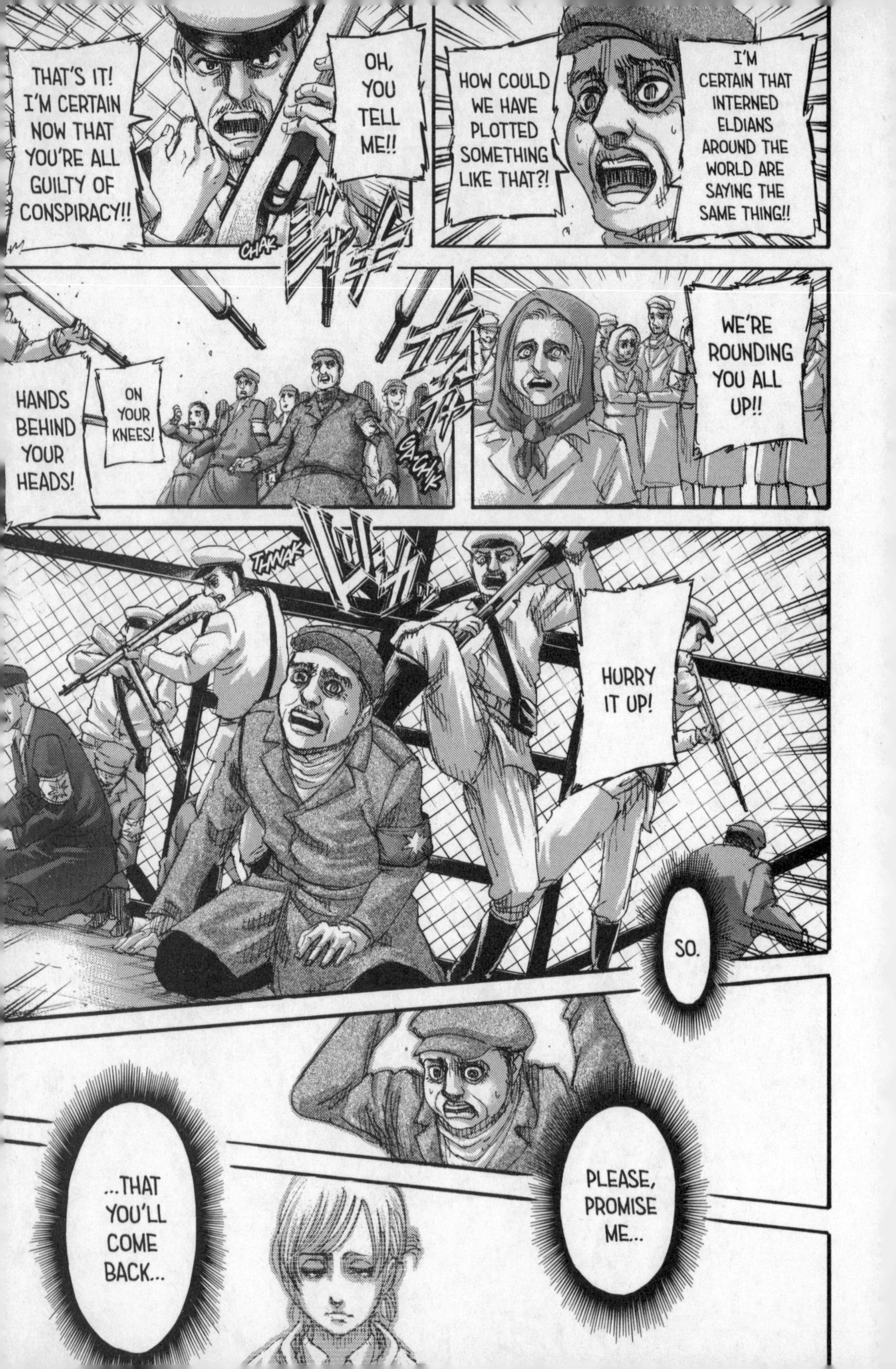
I'M CERTAIN THAT INTERNED ELDIANS AROUND THE WORLD ARE SAYING THE SAME THING!!
HOW COULD WE HAVE PLOTTED SOMETHING LIKE THAT?!
OH, YOU TELL ME!!
THAT'S IT! I'M CERTAIN NOW THAT YOU'RE ALL GUILTY OF CONSPIRACY!!
CHAK
WE'RE ROUNDING YOU ALL UP!!
GA-CHAK
ON YOUR KNEES!
HANDS BEHIND YOUR HEADS!
HURRY IT UP!
THWAK
SO.
PLEASE, PROMISE ME...
...THAT YOU'LL COME BACK...

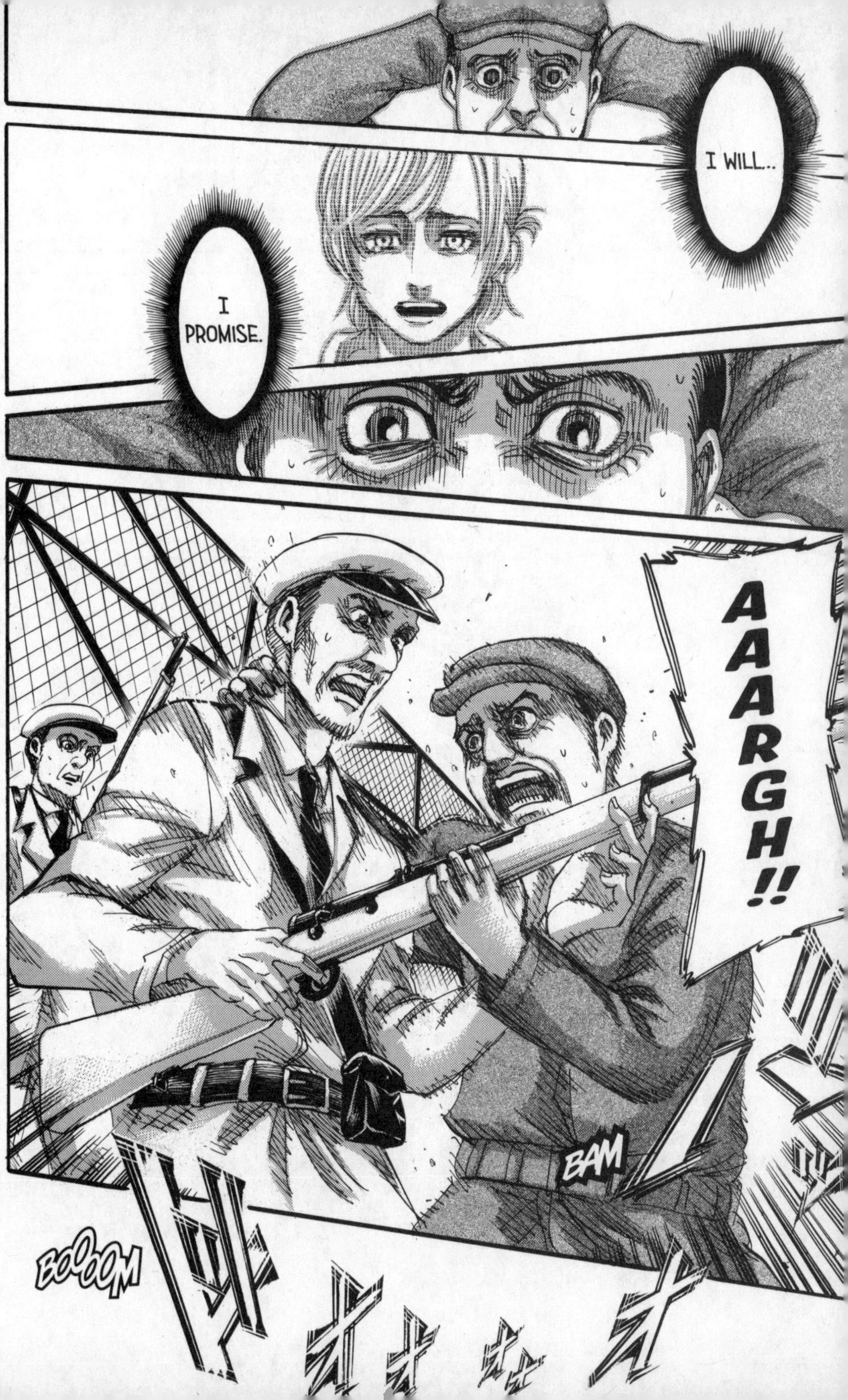
I WILL...
I PROMISE.
AAARGH!!
BAM
BOOOOM

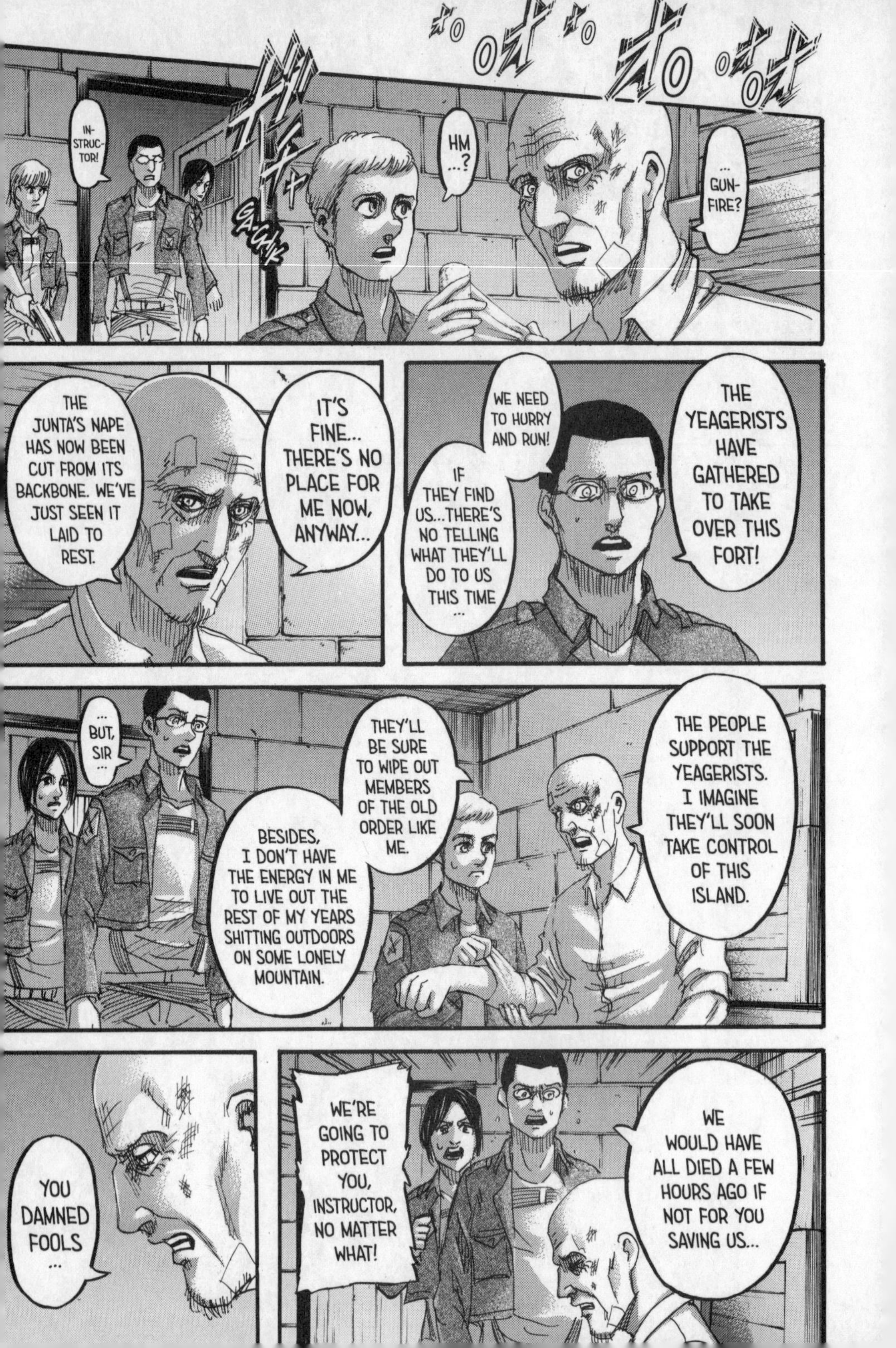

... GUN- FIRE?
HM ...?
GA-CHAK
IN- STRUC- TOR!
THE YEAGERISTS HAVE GATHERED TO TAKE OVER THIS FORT!
WE NEED TO HURRY AND RUN!
IF THEY FIND US...THERE'S NO TELLING WHAT THEY'LL DO TO US THIS TIME ...
IT'S FINE... THERE'S NO PLACE FOR ME NOW, ANYWAY...
THE JUNTA'S NAPE HAS NOW BEEN CUT FROM ITS BACKBONE. WE'VE JUST SEEN IT LAID TO REST.
THE PEOPLE SUPPORT THE YEAGERISTS. I IMAGINE THEY'LL SOON TAKE CONTROL OF THIS ISLAND.
THEY'LL BE SURE TO WIPE OUT MEMBERS OF THE OLD ORDER LIKE ME.
BESIDES, I DON'T HAVE THE ENERGY IN ME TO LIVE OUT THE REST OF MY YEARS SHITTING OUTDOORS ON SOME LONELY MOUNTAIN.
... BUT, SIR ...
WE WOULD HAVE ALL DIED A FEW HOURS AGO IF NOT FOR YOU SAVING US...
WE'RE GOING TO PROTECT YOU, INSTRUCTOR, NO MATTER WHAT!
YOU DAMNED FOOLS ...

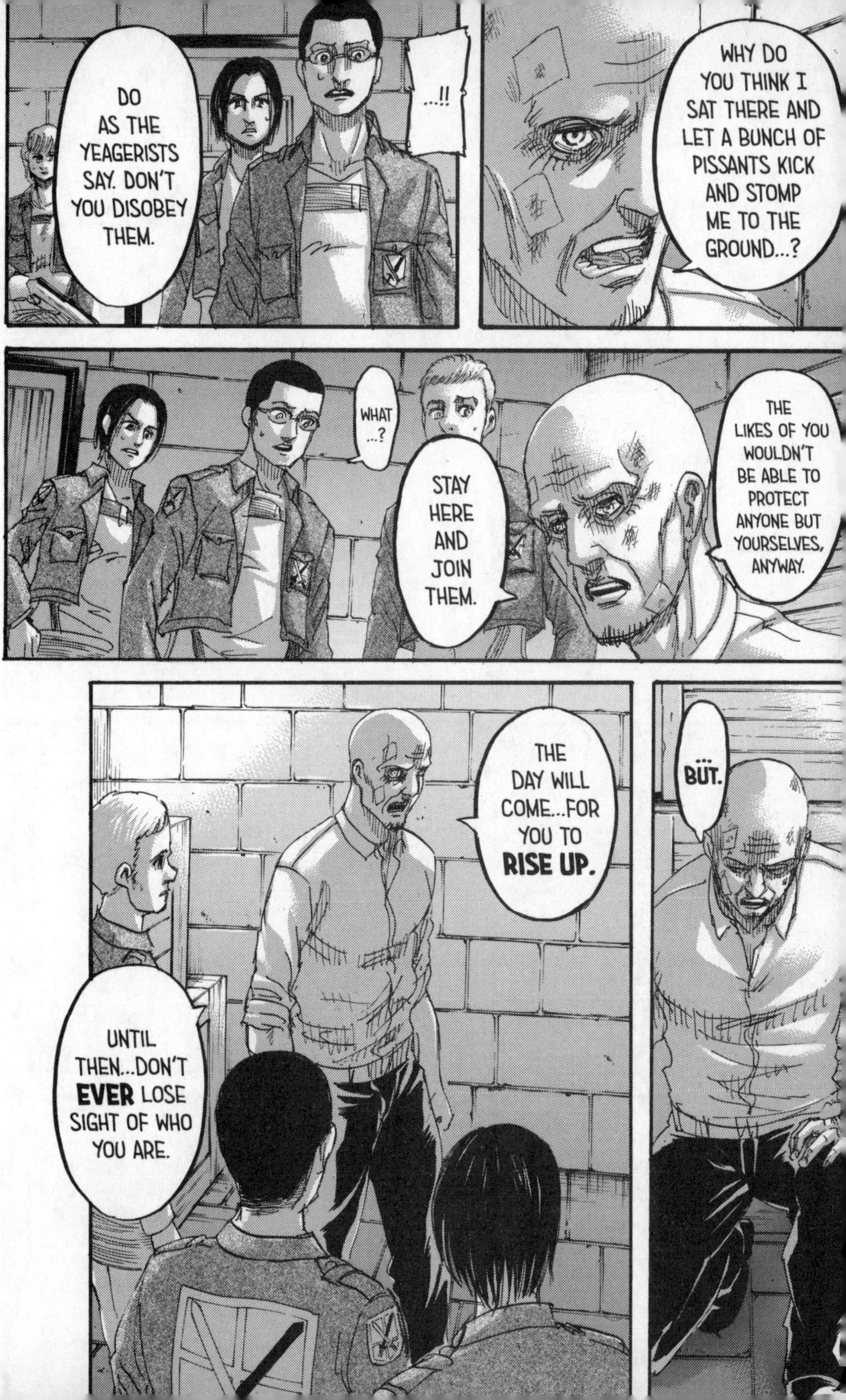

WHY DO YOU THINK I SAT THERE AND LET A BUNCH OF PISSANTS KICK AND STOMP ME TO THE GROUND...?
...!!
DO AS THE YEAGERISTS SAY. DON'T YOU DISOBEY THEM.
THE LIKES OF YOU WOULDN'T BE ABLE TO PROTECT ANYONE BUT YOURSELVES, ANYWAY.
STAY HERE AND JOIN THEM.
WHAT ...?
...BUT.
THE DAY WILL COME...FOR YOU TO **RISE UP.**
UNTIL THEN...DON'T **EVER** LOSE SIGHT OF WHO YOU ARE.

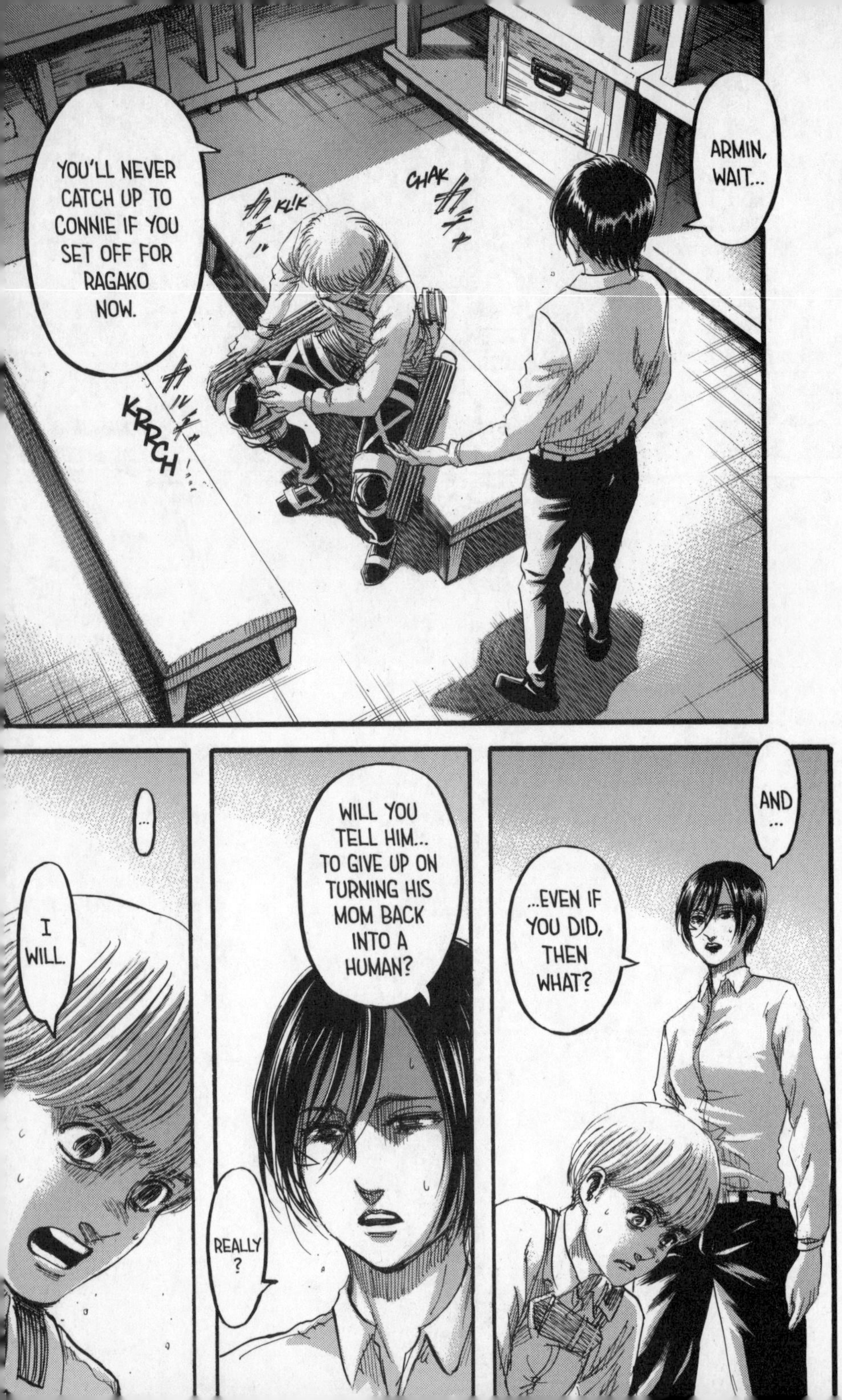
ARMIN, WAIT...
CHAK
KLIK
YOU'LL NEVER CATCH UP TO CONNIE IF YOU SET OFF FOR RAGAKO NOW.
KRRCH
AND ...
...EVEN IF YOU DID, THEN WHAT?
WILL YOU TELL HIM... TO GIVE UP ON TURNING HIS MOM BACK INTO A HUMAN?
REALLY ?
...
I WILL.

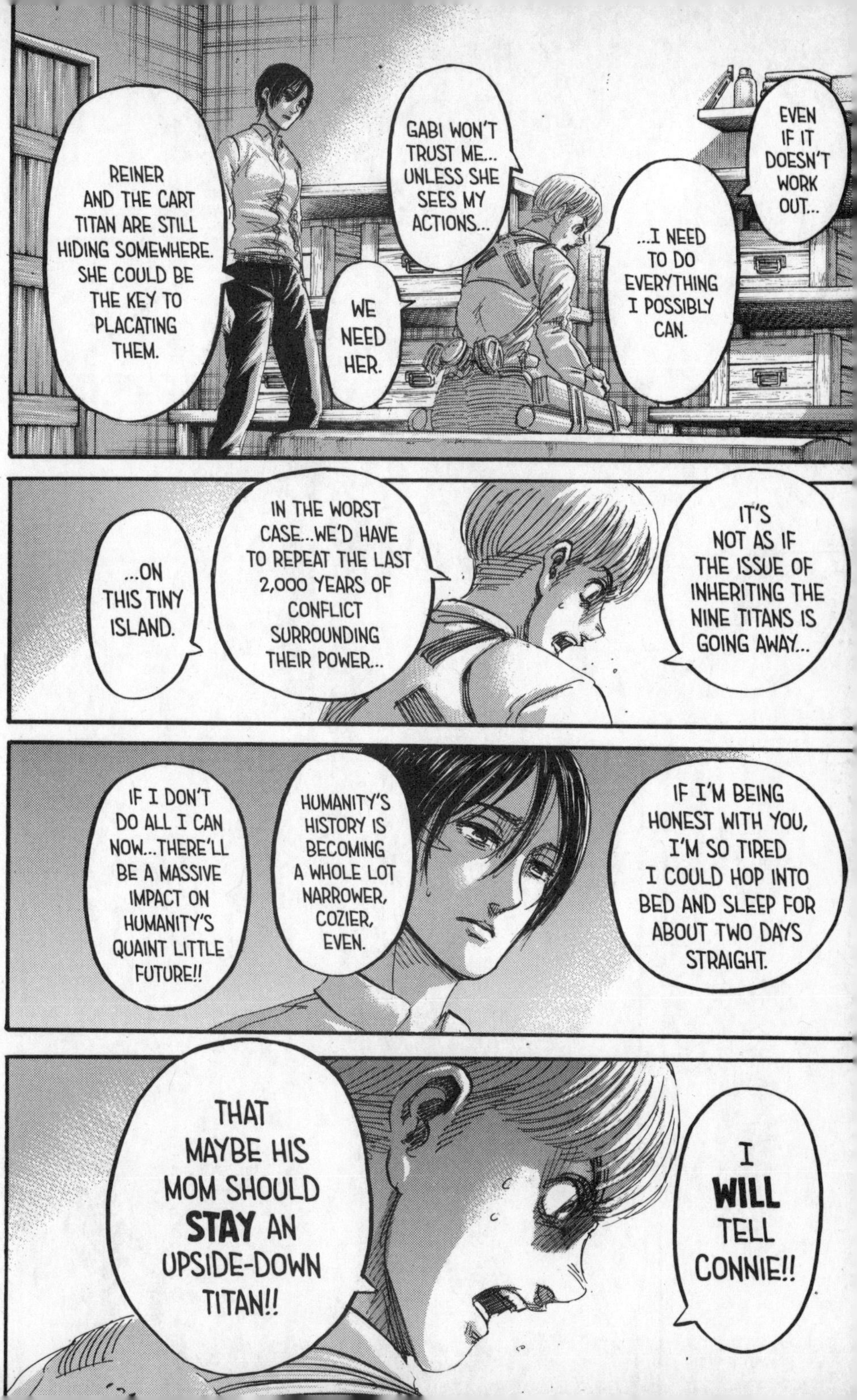
EVEN IF IT DOESN'T WORK OUT...
...I NEED TO DO EVERYTHING I POSSIBLY CAN.
GABI WON'T TRUST ME... UNLESS SHE SEES MY ACTIONS...
WE NEED HER.
REINER AND THE CART TITAN ARE STILL HIDING SOMEWHERE. SHE COULD BE THE KEY TO PLACATING THEM.
IT'S NOT AS IF THE ISSUE OF INHERITING THE NINE TITANS IS GOING AWAY...
IN THE WORST CASE...WE'D HAVE TO REPEAT THE LAST 2,000 YEARS OF CONFLICT SURROUNDING THEIR POWER...
...ON THIS TINY ISLAND.
IF I'M BEING HONEST WITH YOU, I'M SO TIRED I COULD HOP INTO BED AND SLEEP FOR ABOUT TWO DAYS STRAIGHT.
HUMANITY'S HISTORY IS BECOMING A WHOLE LOT NARROWER, COZIER, EVEN.
IF I DON'T DO ALL I CAN NOW...THERE'LL BE A MASSIVE IMPACT ON HUMANITY'S QUAINT LITTLE FUTURE!!
I **WILL** TELL CONNIE!!
THAT MAYBE HIS MOM SHOULD **STAY** AN UPSIDE-DOWN TITAN!!

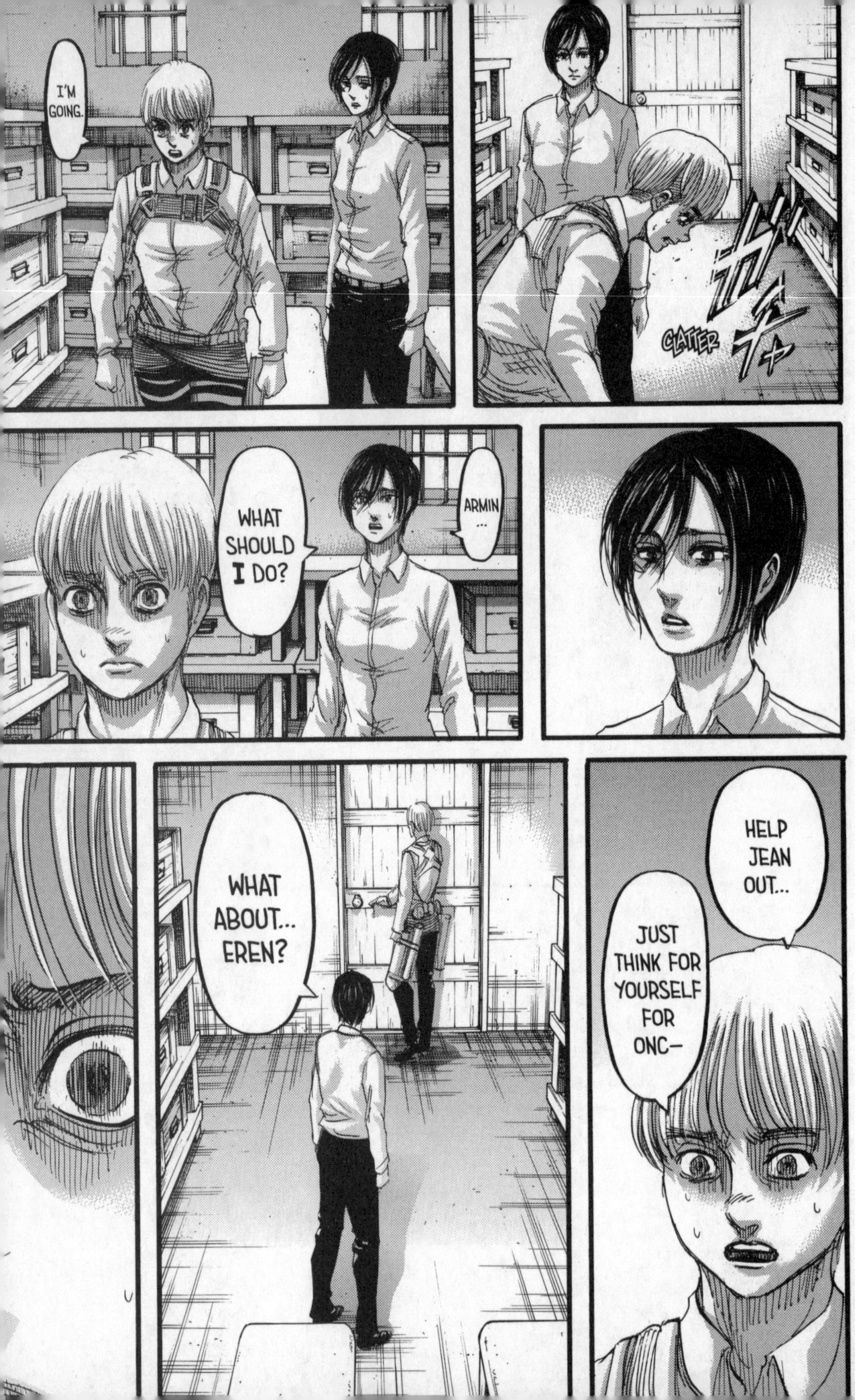
ガチャ
CLATTER
I'M GOING.
ARMIN...
WHAT SHOULD I DO?
HELP JEAN OUT...
JUST THINK FOR YOURSELF FOR ONC—
WHAT ABOUT... EREN?

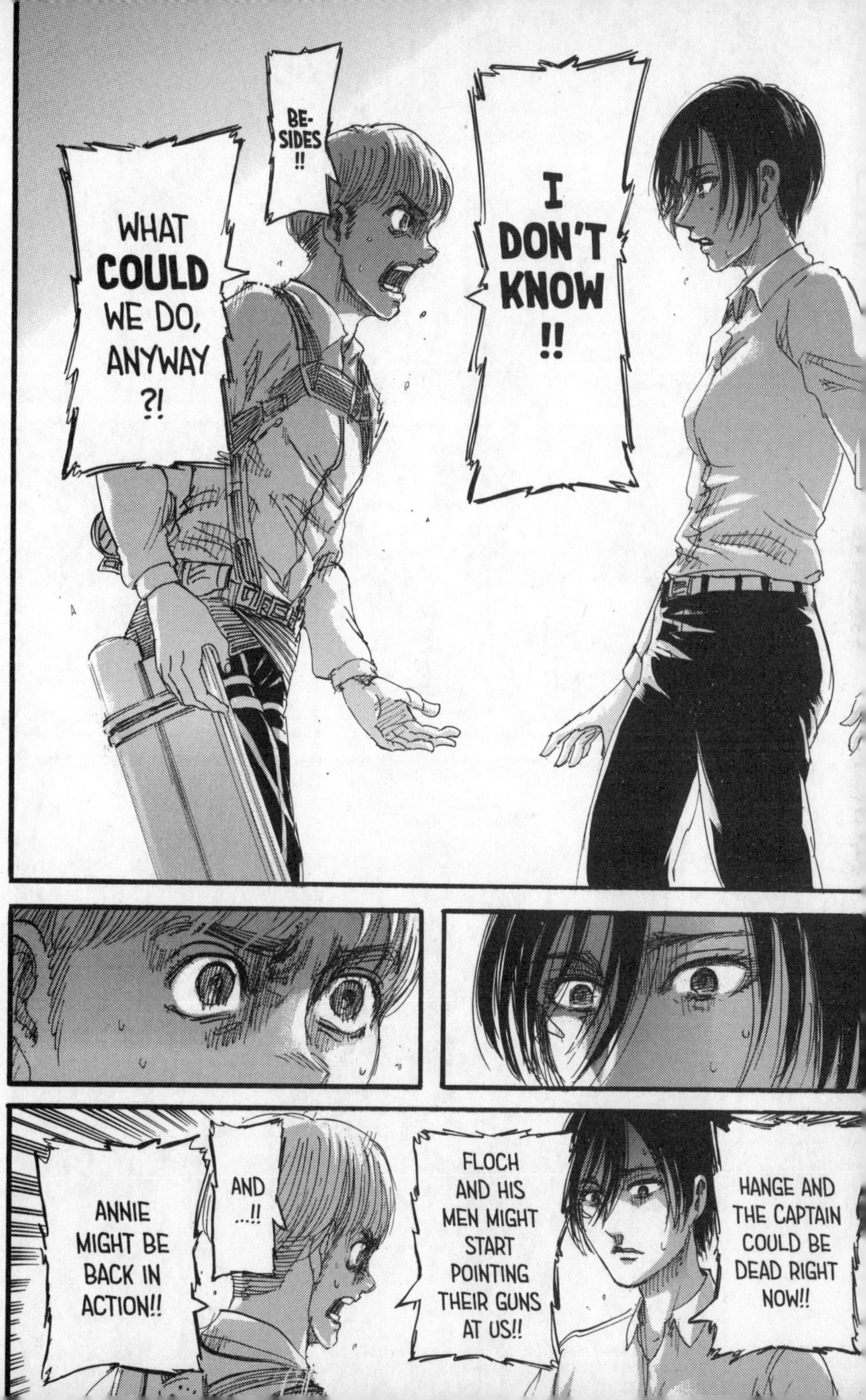
I DON'T KNOW!!
BE-SIDES!!
WHAT COULD WE DO, ANYWAY?!
HANGE AND THE CAPTAIN COULD BE DEAD RIGHT NOW!!
FLOCH AND HIS MEN MIGHT START POINTING THEIR GUNS AT US!!
AND...!!
ANNIE MIGHT BE BACK IN ACTION!!

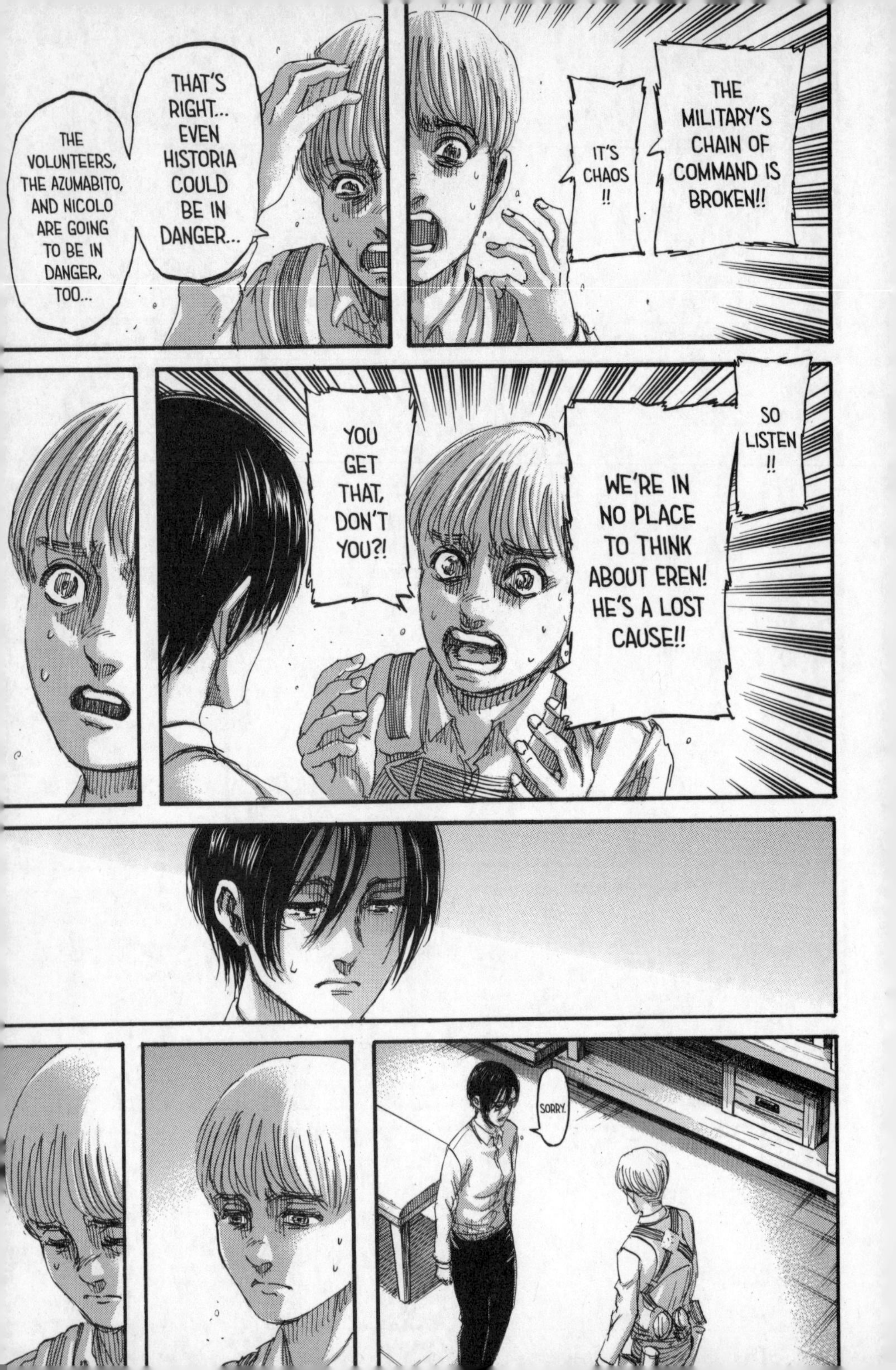
THE MILITARY'S CHAIN OF COMMAND IS BROKEN!!
IT'S CHAOS!!
THAT'S RIGHT... EVEN HISTORIA COULD BE IN DANGER...
THE VOLUNTEERS, THE AZUMABITO, AND NICOLO ARE GOING TO BE IN DANGER, TOO...
SO LISTEN!!
WE'RE IN NO PLACE TO THINK ABOUT EREN! HE'S A LOST CAUSE!!
YOU GET THAT, DON'T YOU?!
SORRY.

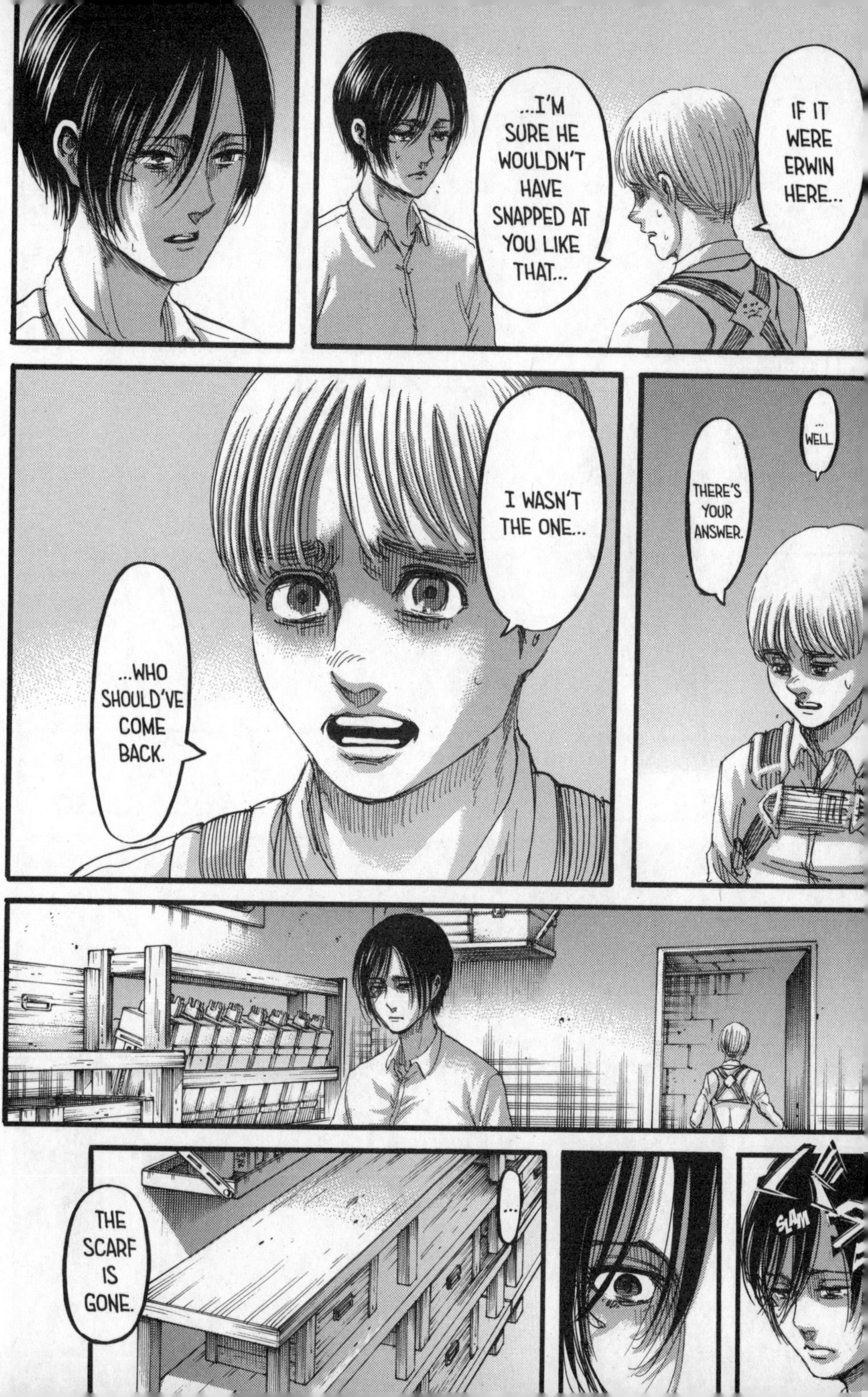
IF IT WERE ERWIN HERE...
...I'M SURE HE WOULDN'T HAVE SNAPPED AT YOU LIKE THAT...
... WELL.
THERE'S YOUR ANSWER.
I WASN'T THE ONE...
...WHO SHOULD'VE COME BACK.
SLAM
...
THE SCARF IS GONE.

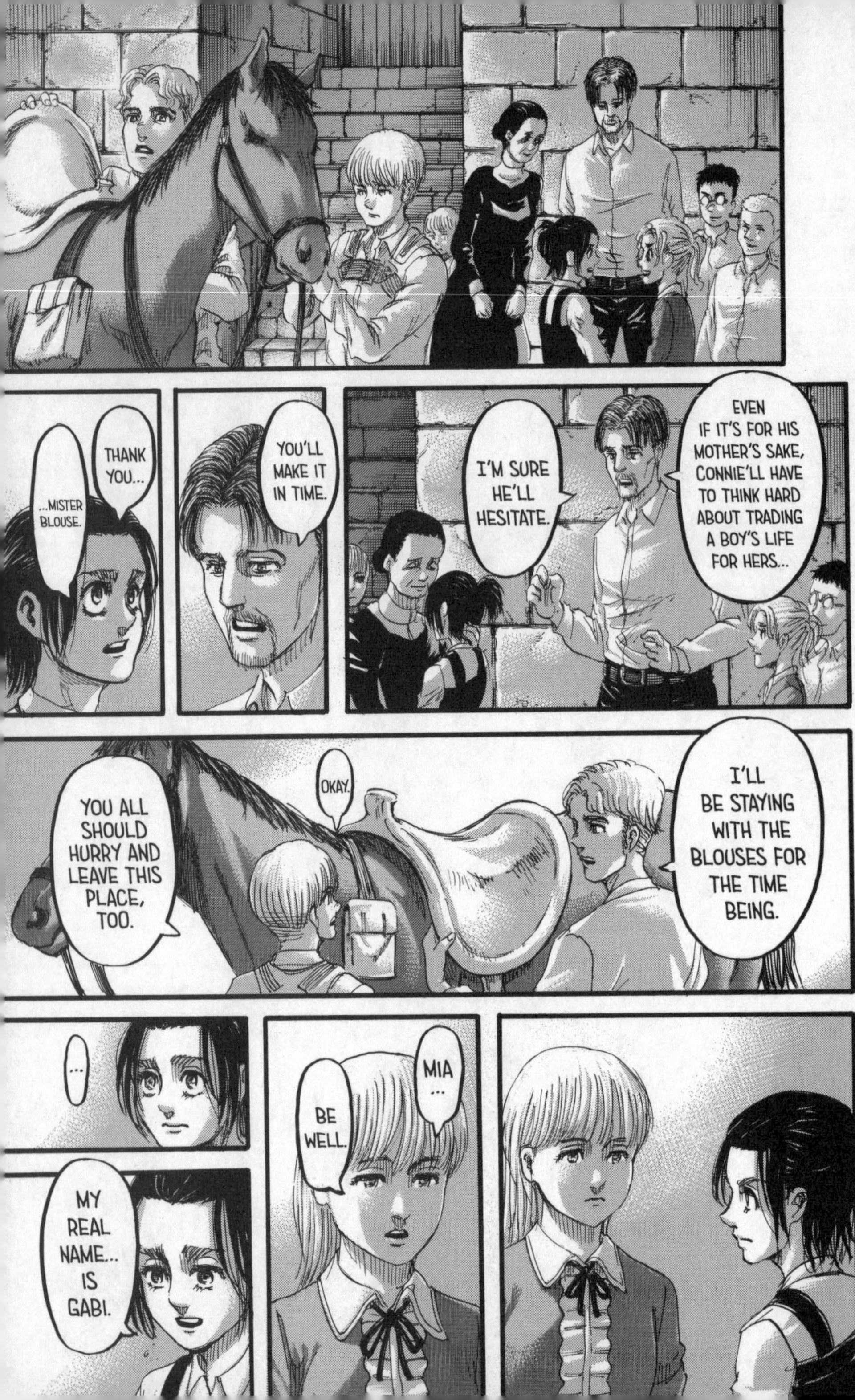
EVEN IF IT'S FOR HIS MOTHER'S SAKE, CONNIE'LL HAVE TO THINK HARD ABOUT TRADING A BOY'S LIFE FOR HERS...
I'M SURE HE'LL HESITATE.
YOU'LL MAKE IT IN TIME.
THANK YOU...
...MISTER BLOUSE.
I'LL BE STAYING WITH THE BLOUSES FOR THE TIME BEING.
OKAY.
YOU ALL SHOULD HURRY AND LEAVE THIS PLACE, TOO.
MIA ...
BE WELL.
...
MY REAL NAME... IS GABI.

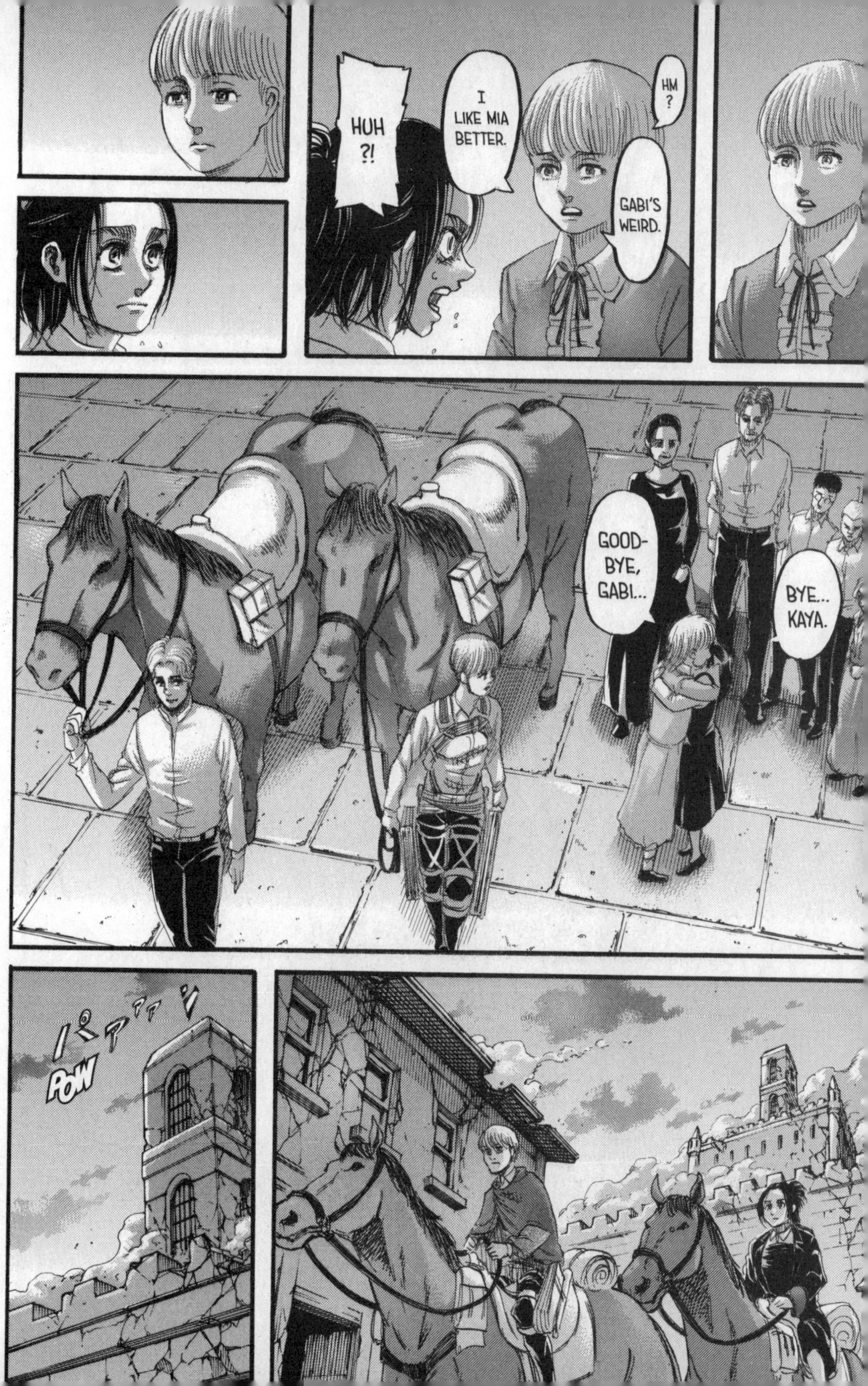
HM ?
GABI'S WEIRD.
I LIKE MIA BETTER.
HUH ?!
BYE... KAYA.
GOOD-BYE, GABI...
POW

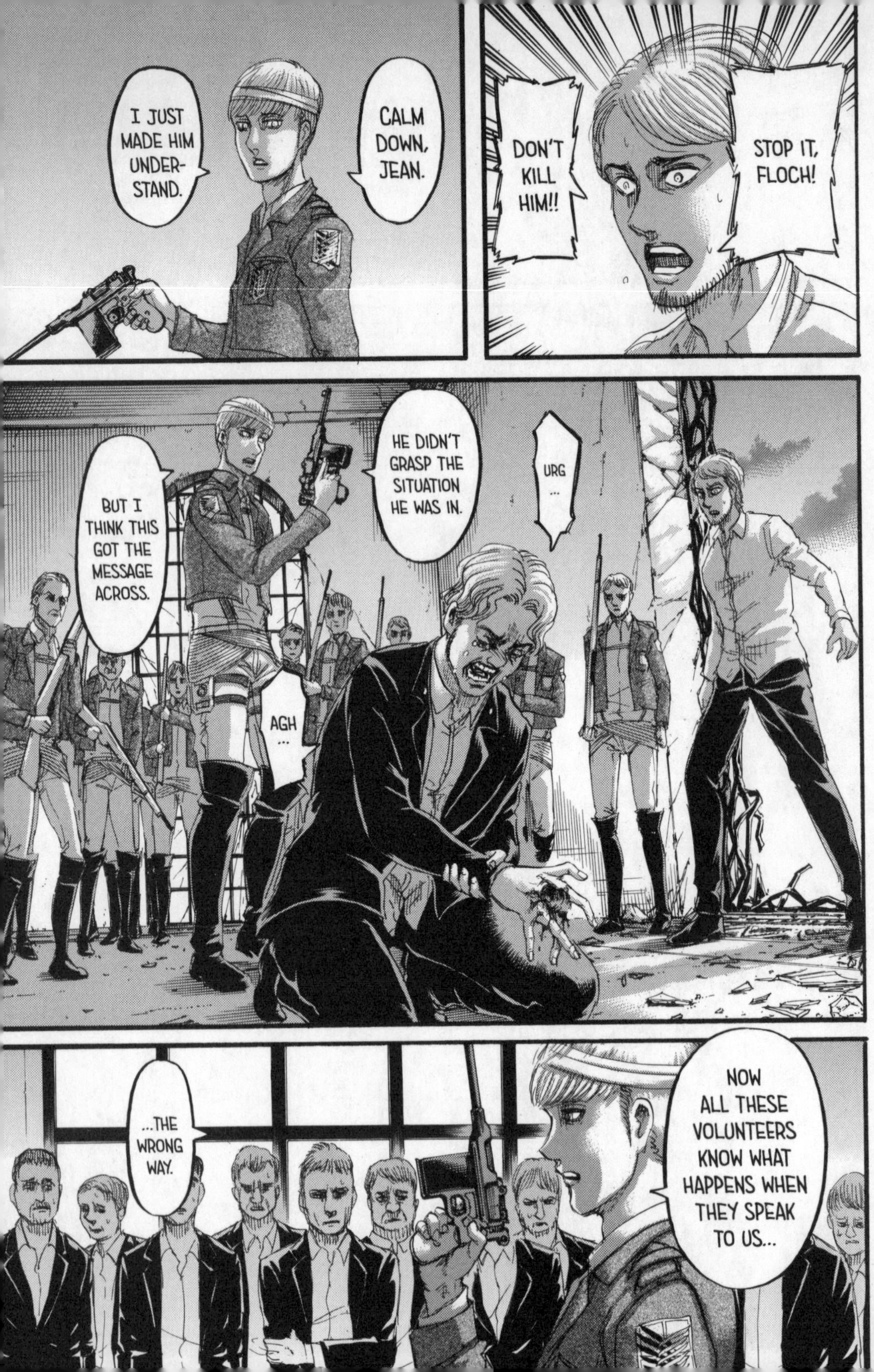

STOP IT, FLOCH!
DON'T KILL HIM!!
CALM DOWN, JEAN.
I JUST MADE HIM UNDER-STAND.
URG ...
HE DIDN'T GRASP THE SITUATION HE WAS IN.
BUT I THINK THIS GOT THE MESSAGE ACROSS.
AGH ...
NOW ALL THESE VOLUNTEERS KNOW WHAT HAPPENS WHEN THEY SPEAK TO US...
...THE WRONG WAY.

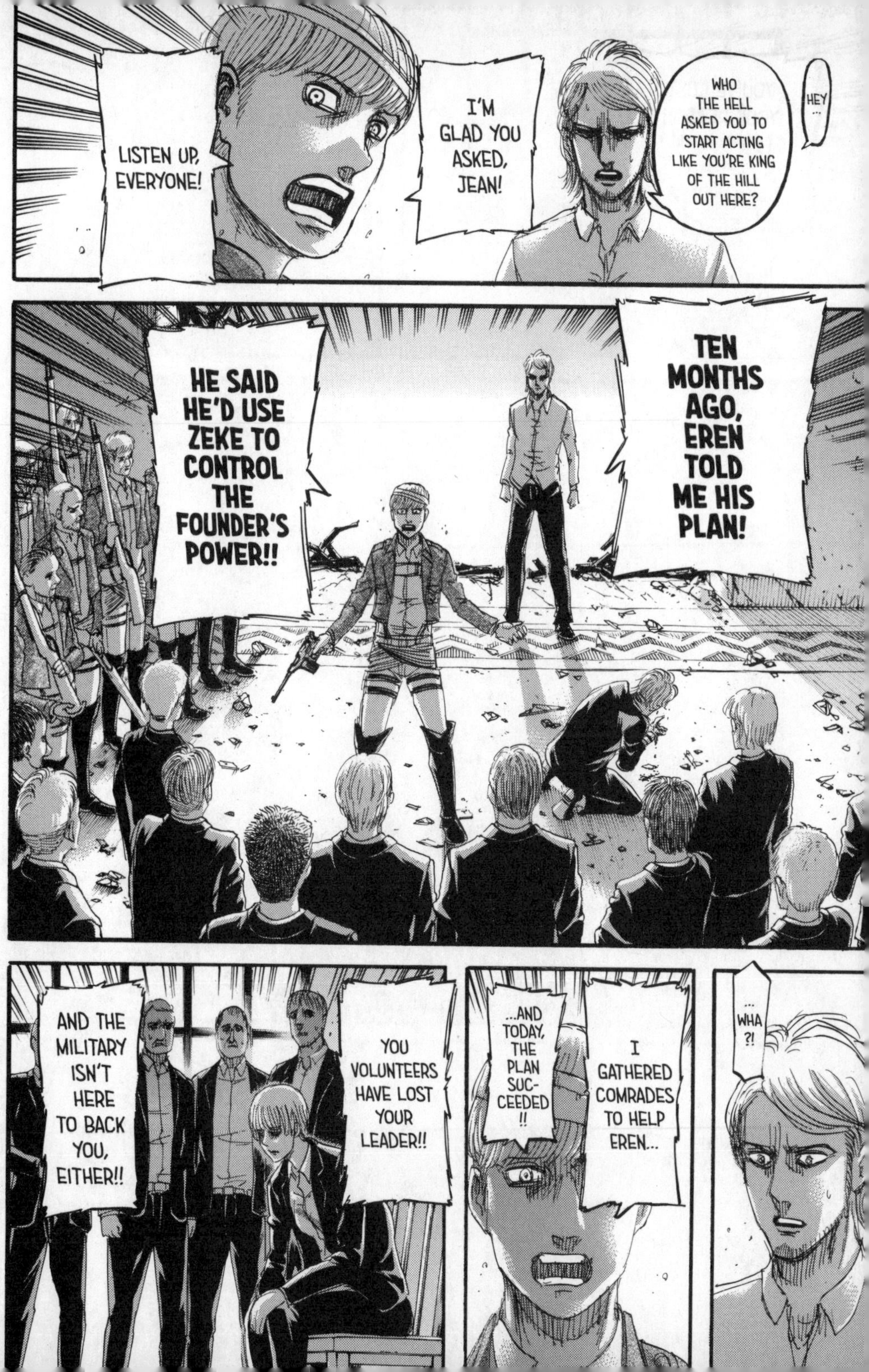
HEY ...
WHO THE HELL ASKED YOU TO START ACTING LIKE YOU'RE KING OF THE HILL OUT HERE?
I'M GLAD YOU ASKED, JEAN!
LISTEN UP, EVERYONE!
TEN MONTHS AGO, EREN TOLD ME HIS PLAN!
HE SAID HE'D USE ZEKE TO CONTROL THE FOUNDER'S POWER!!
... WHA ?!
I GATHERED COMRADES TO HELP EREN...
...AND TODAY, THE PLAN SUCCEEDED!!
YOU VOLUNTEERS HAVE LOST YOUR LEADER!!
AND THE MILITARY ISN'T HERE TO BACK YOU, EITHER!!

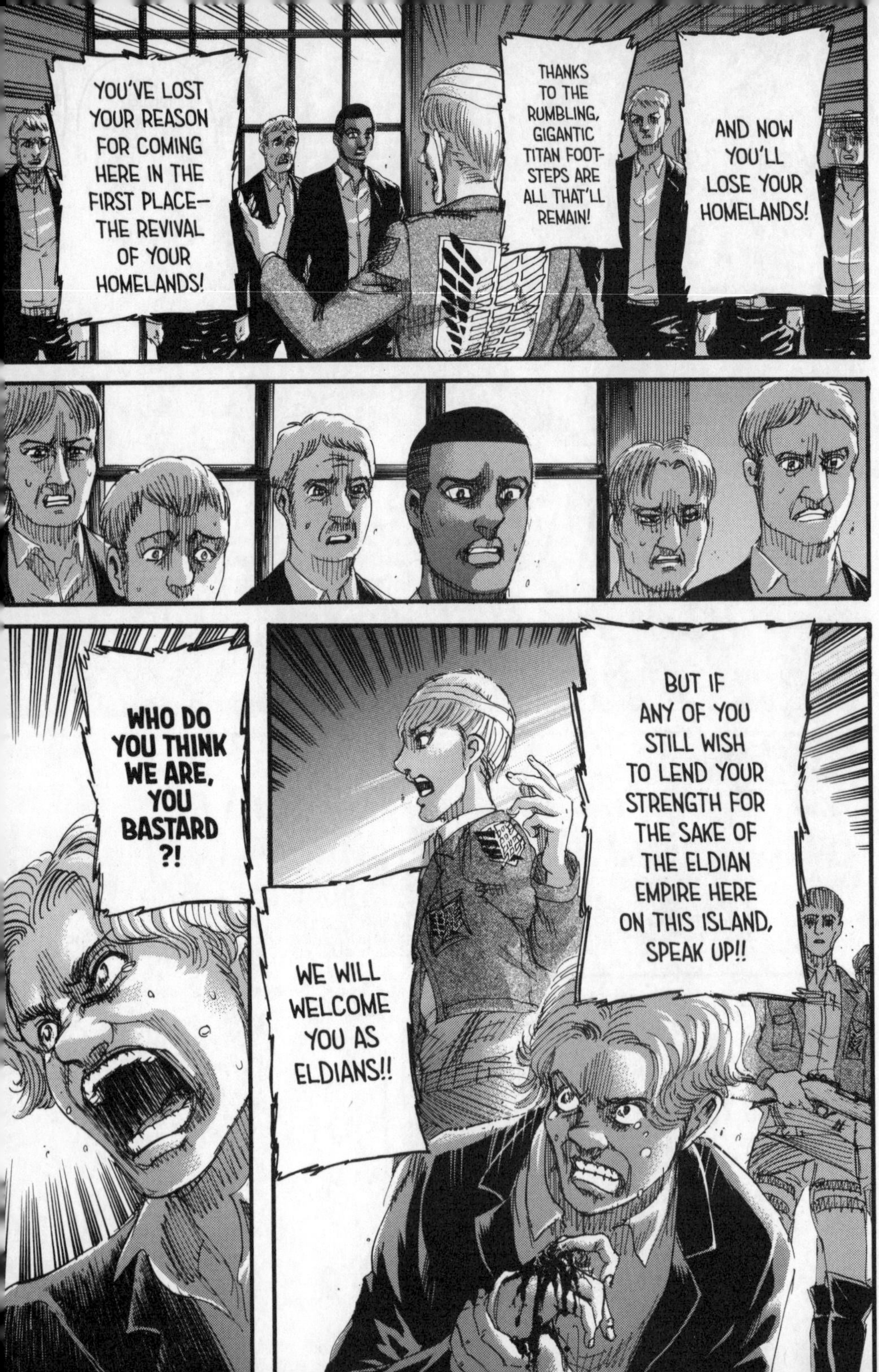
AND NOW YOU'LL LOSE YOUR HOMELANDS!
THANKS TO THE RUMBLING, GIGANTIC TITAN FOOT-STEPS ARE ALL THAT'LL REMAIN!
YOU'VE LOST YOUR REASON FOR COMING HERE IN THE FIRST PLACE— THE REVIVAL OF YOUR HOMELANDS!
BUT IF ANY OF YOU STILL WISH TO LEND YOUR STRENGTH FOR THE SAKE OF THE ELDIAN EMPIRE HERE ON THIS ISLAND, SPEAK UP!!
WE WILL WELCOME YOU AS ELDIANS!!
WHO DO YOU THINK WE ARE, YOU BASTARD ?!

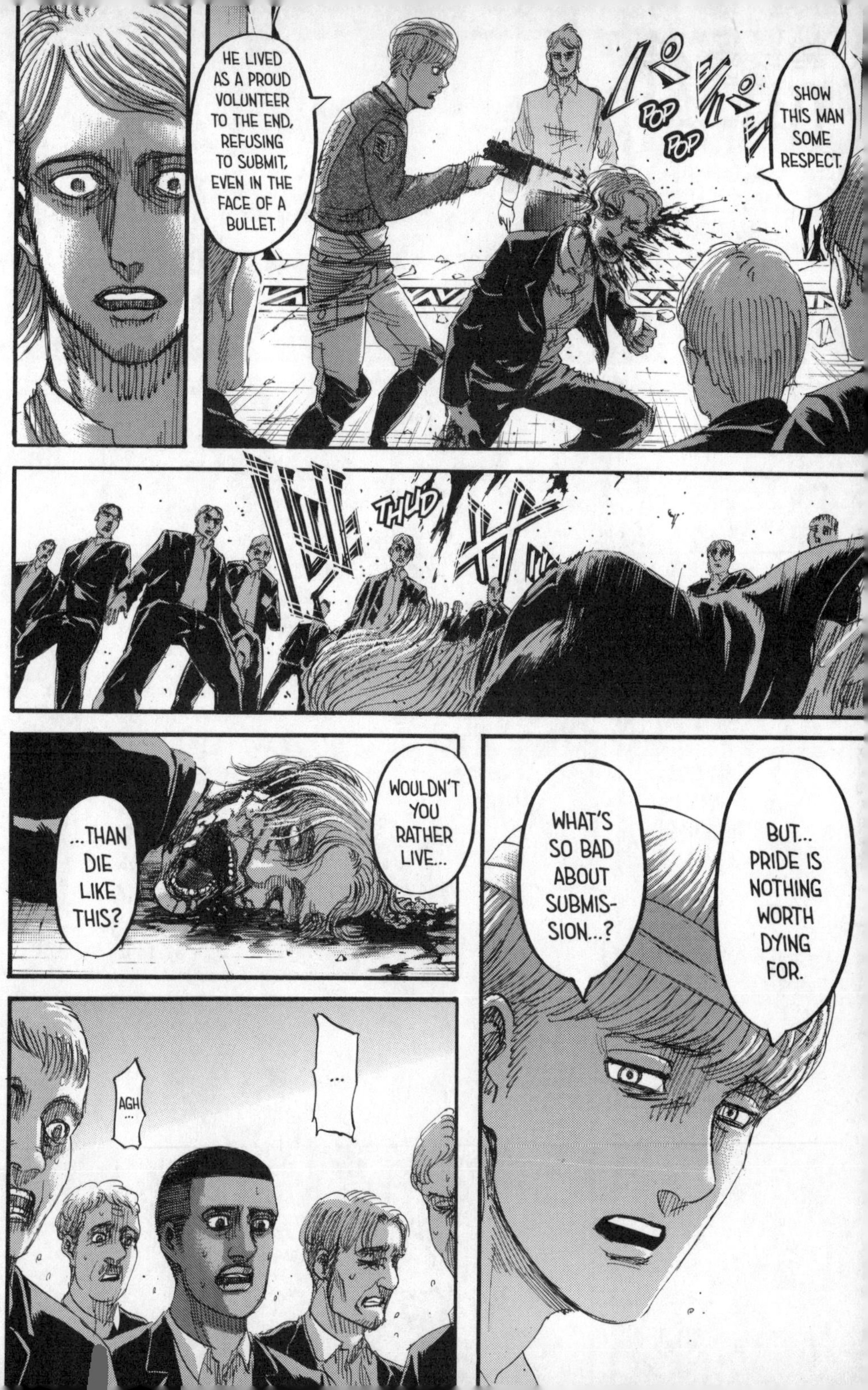
SHOW THIS MAN SOME RESPECT.
POP
POP
POP
HE LIVED AS A PROUD VOLUNTEER TO THE END, REFUSING TO SUBMIT, EVEN IN THE FACE OF A BULLET.
THUD
BUT... PRIDE IS NOTHING WORTH DYING FOR.
WHAT'S SO BAD ABOUT SUBMISSION...?
WOULDN'T YOU RATHER LIVE...
...THAN DIE LIKE THIS?
...
AGH...

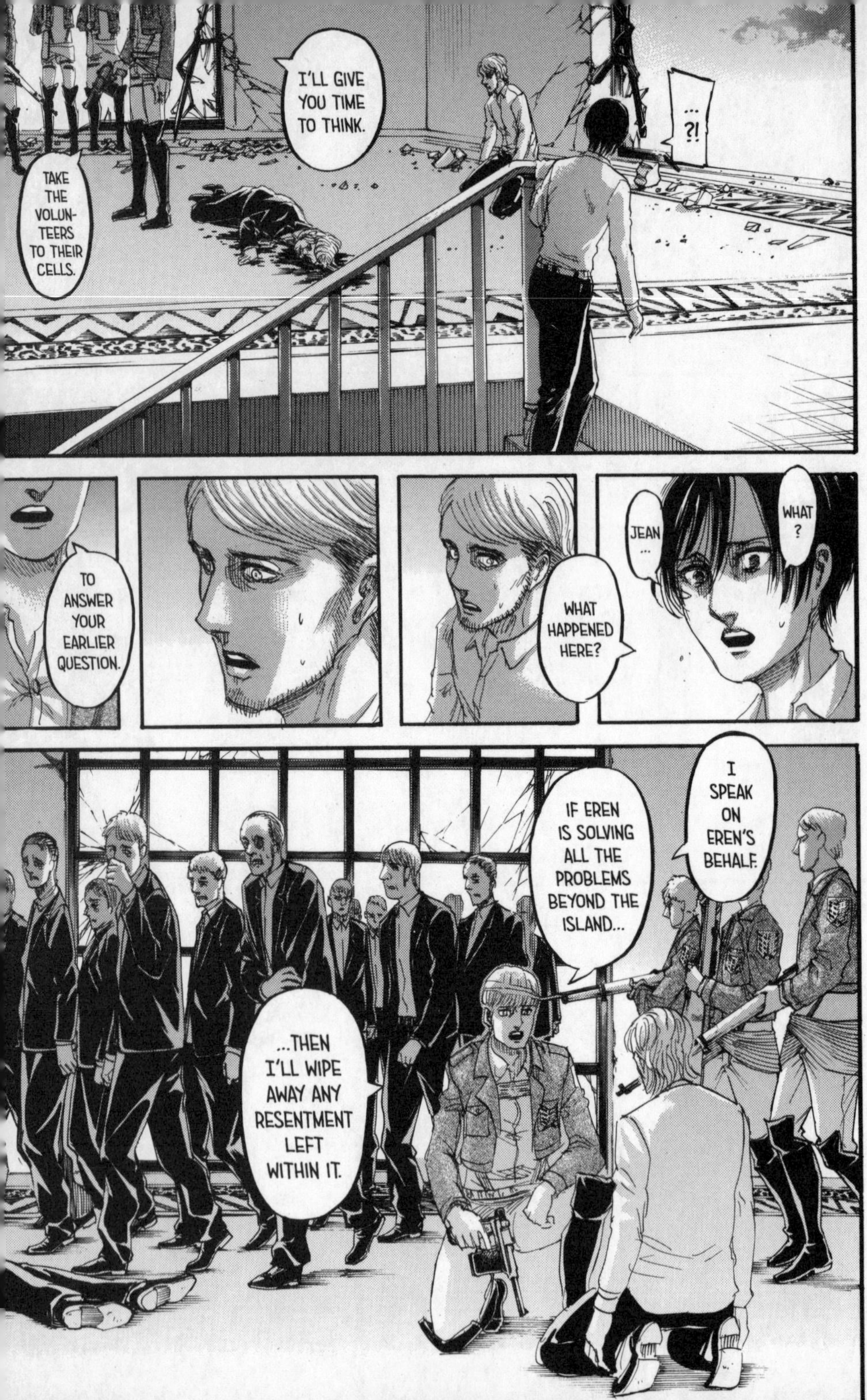
...
?!
I'LL GIVE YOU TIME TO THINK.
TAKE THE VOLUN-TEERS TO THEIR CELLS.
WHAT?
JEAN...
WHAT HAPPENED HERE?
TO ANSWER YOUR EARLIER QUESTION.
I SPEAK ON EREN'S BEHALF.
IF EREN IS SOLVING ALL THE PROBLEMS BEYOND THE ISLAND...
...THEN I'LL WIPE AWAY ANY RESENTMENT LEFT WITHIN IT.

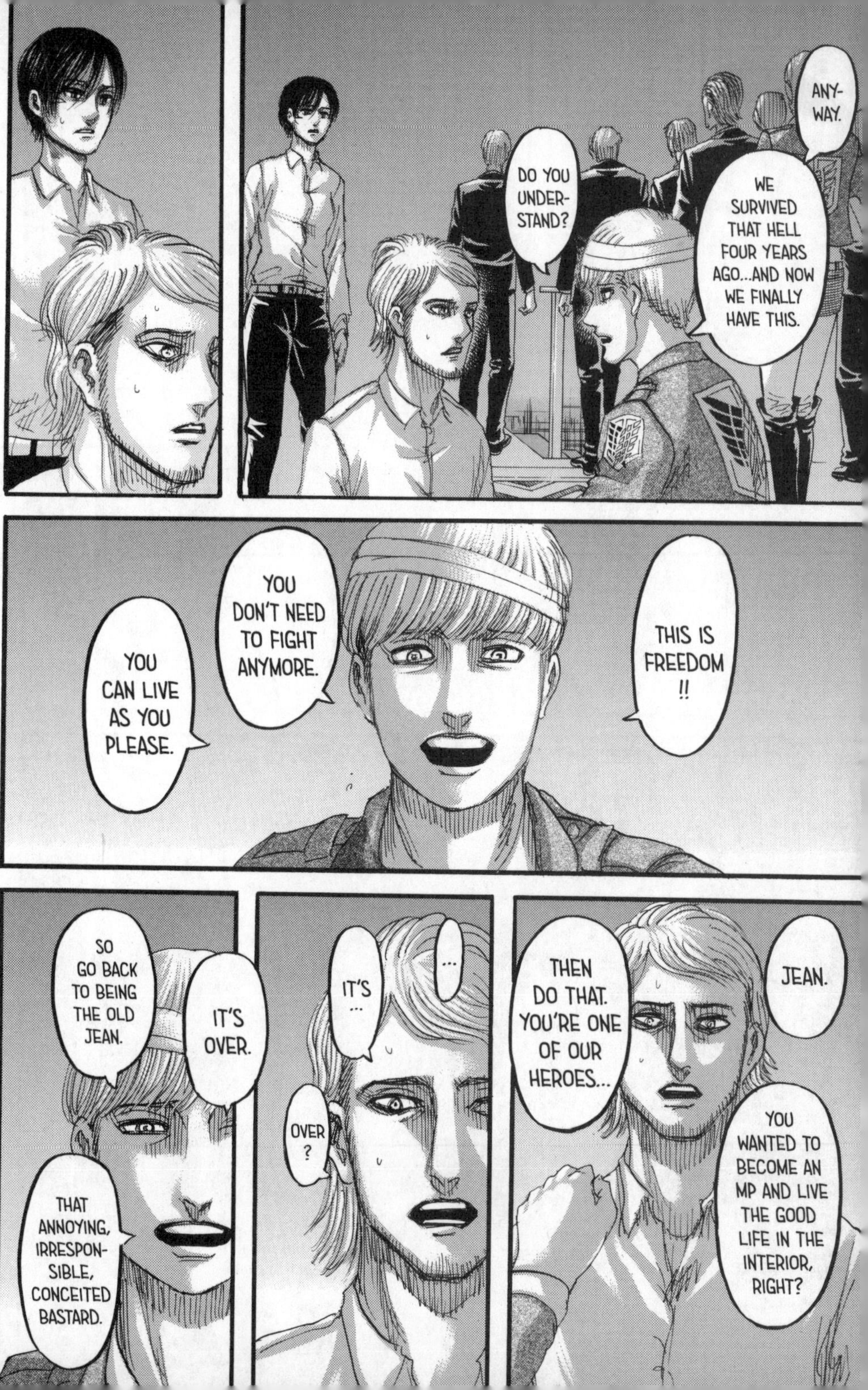
ANY-WAY.
WE SURVIVED THAT HELL FOUR YEARS AGO...AND NOW WE FINALLY HAVE THIS.
DO YOU UNDERSTAND?
THIS IS FREEDOM !!
YOU DON'T NEED TO FIGHT ANYMORE.
YOU CAN LIVE AS YOU PLEASE.
JEAN.
YOU WANTED TO BECOME AN MP AND LIVE THE GOOD LIFE IN THE INTERIOR, RIGHT?
THEN DO THAT. YOU'RE ONE OF OUR HEROES...
...
IT'S ...
OVER ?
IT'S OVER.
SO GO BACK TO BEING THE OLD JEAN.
THAT ANNOYING, IRRESPONSIBLE, CONCEITED BASTARD.

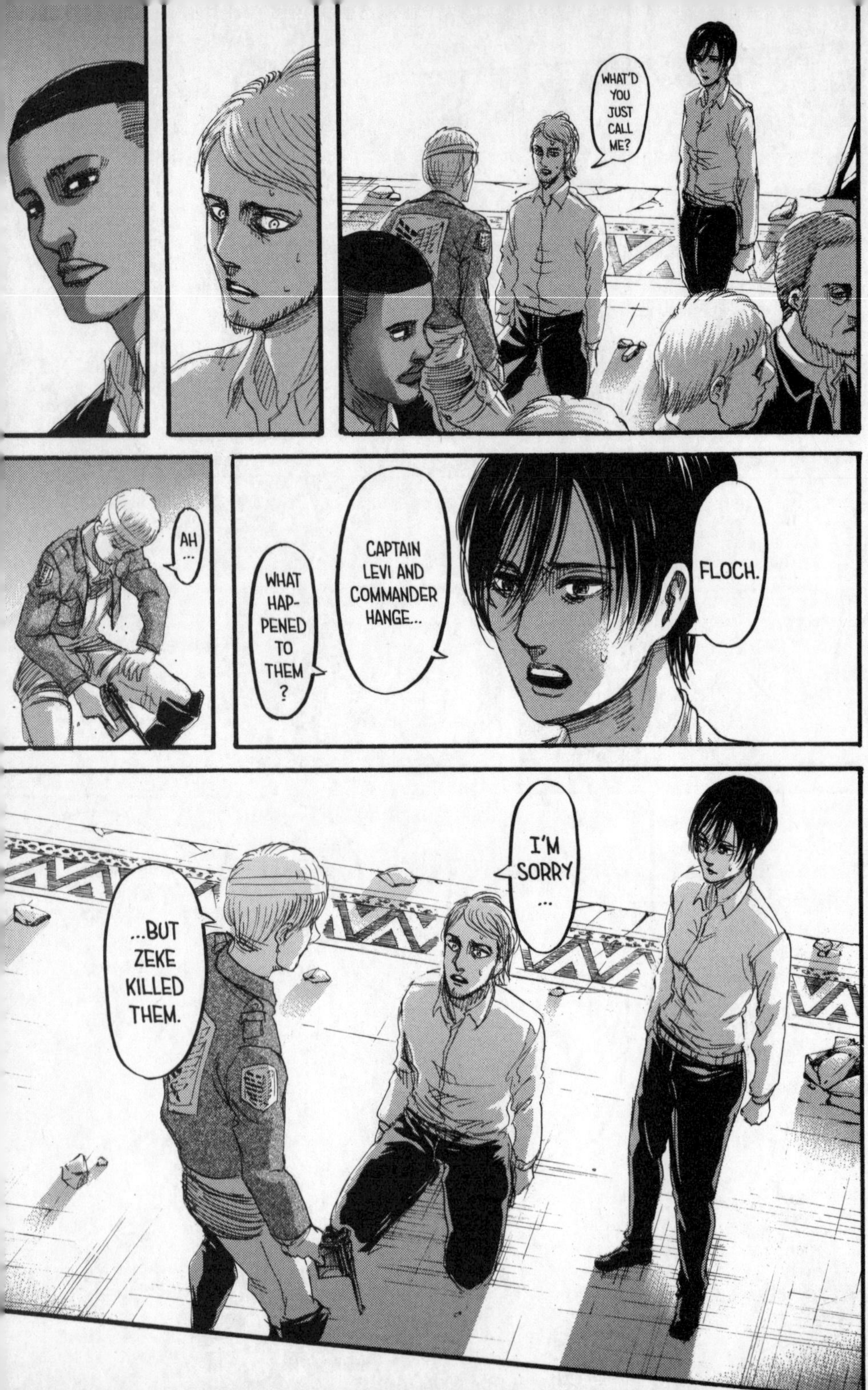
WHAT'D YOU JUST CALL ME?
FLOCH.
CAPTAIN LEVI AND COMMANDER HANGE...
WHAT HAP-PENED TO THEM?
AH...
I'M SORRY...
...BUT ZEKE KILLED THEM.

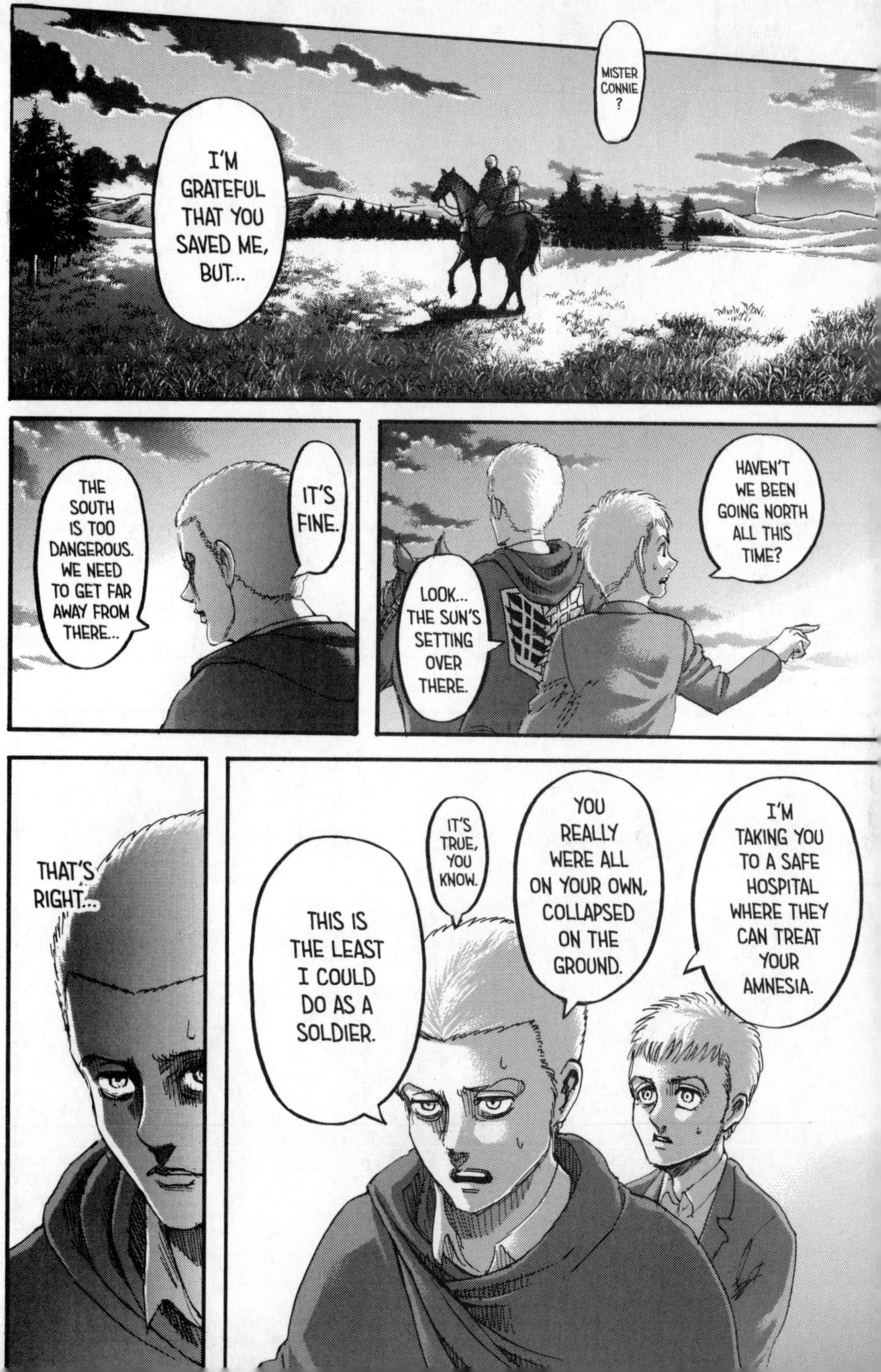
MISTER CONNIE?
I'M GRATEFUL THAT YOU SAVED ME, BUT...
HAVEN'T WE BEEN GOING NORTH ALL THIS TIME?
LOOK... THE SUN'S SETTING OVER THERE.
IT'S FINE.
THE SOUTH IS TOO DANGEROUS. WE NEED TO GET FAR AWAY FROM THERE...
I'M TAKING YOU TO A SAFE HOSPITAL WHERE THEY CAN TREAT YOUR AMNESIA.
YOU REALLY WERE ALL ON YOUR OWN, COLLAPSED ON THE GROUND.
IT'S TRUE, YOU KNOW.
THIS IS THE LEAST I COULD DO AS A SOLDIER.
THAT'S RIGHT...

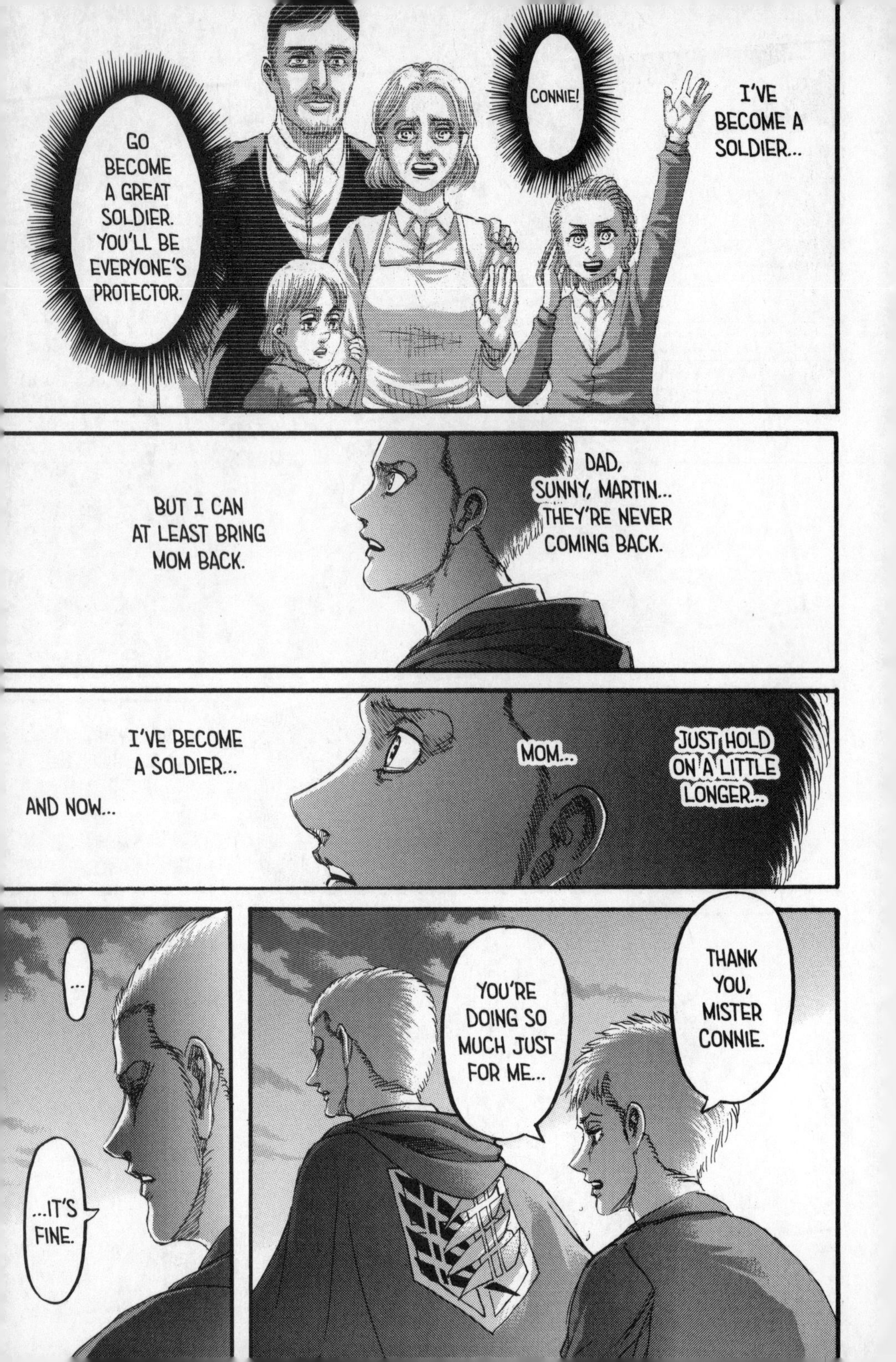
I'VE BECOME A SOLDIER...
CONNIE!
GO BECOME A GREAT SOLDIER. YOU'LL BE EVERYONE'S PROTECTOR.
DAD, SUNNY, MARTIN... THEY'RE NEVER COMING BACK.
BUT I CAN AT LEAST BRING MOM BACK.
JUST HOLD ON A LITTLE LONGER...
MOM...
I'VE BECOME A SOLDIER...
AND NOW...
THANK YOU, MISTER CONNIE.
YOU'RE DOING SO MUCH JUST FOR ME...
...
...IT'S FINE.

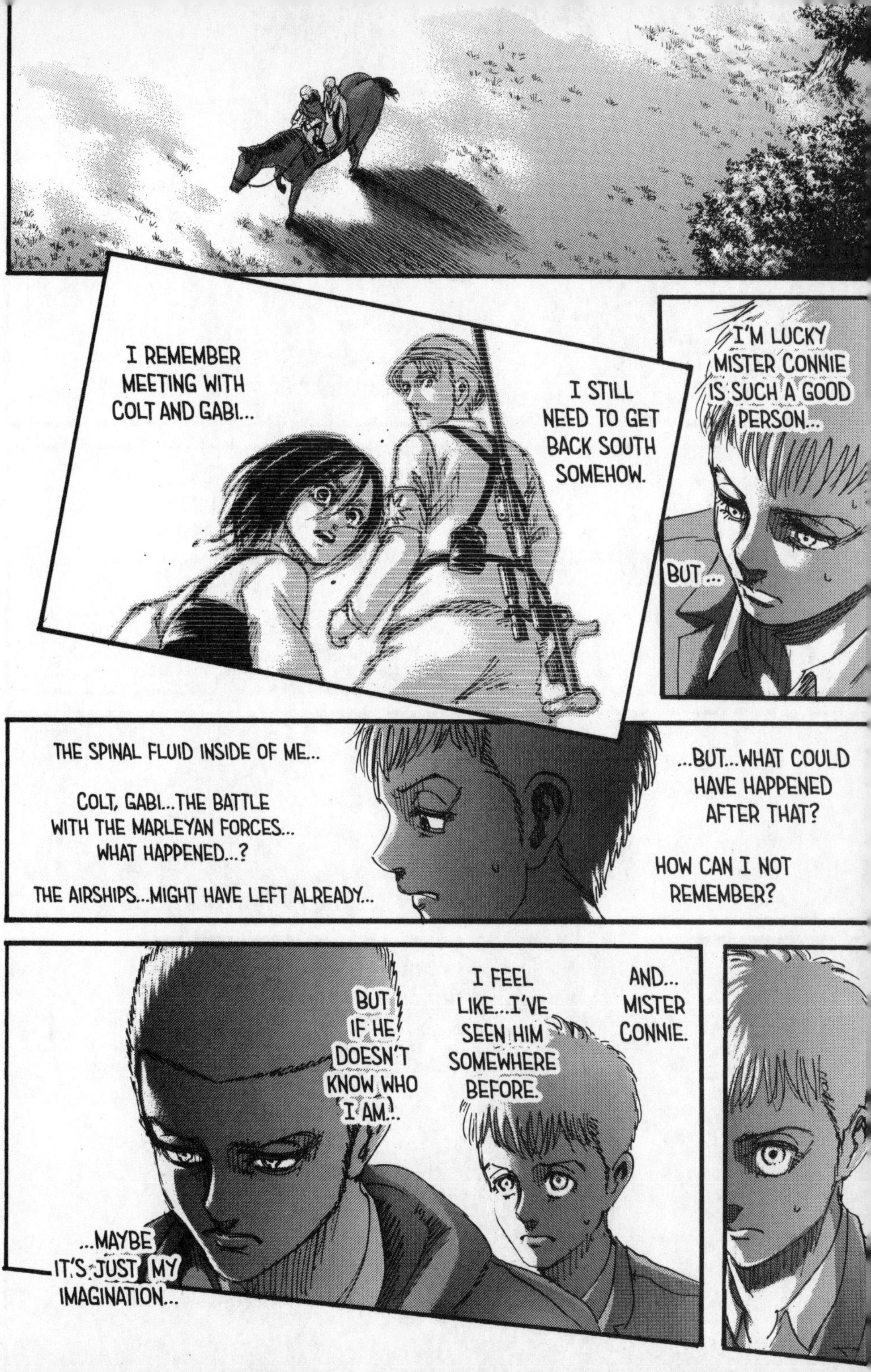
I'M LUCKY MISTER CONNIE IS SUCH A GOOD PERSON...
BUT...
I STILL NEED TO GET BACK SOUTH SOMEHOW.
I REMEMBER MEETING WITH COLT AND GABI...
...BUT...WHAT COULD HAVE HAPPENED AFTER THAT?
HOW CAN I NOT REMEMBER?
THE SPINAL FLUID INSIDE OF ME...
COLT, GABI...THE BATTLE WITH THE MARLEYAN FORCES... WHAT HAPPENED...?
THE AIRSHIPS...MIGHT HAVE LEFT ALREADY...
AND... MISTER CONNIE.
I FEEL LIKE...I'VE SEEN HIM SOMEWHERE BEFORE.
BUT IF HE DOESN'T KNOW WHO I AM...
...MAYBE IT'S JUST MY IMAGINATION...

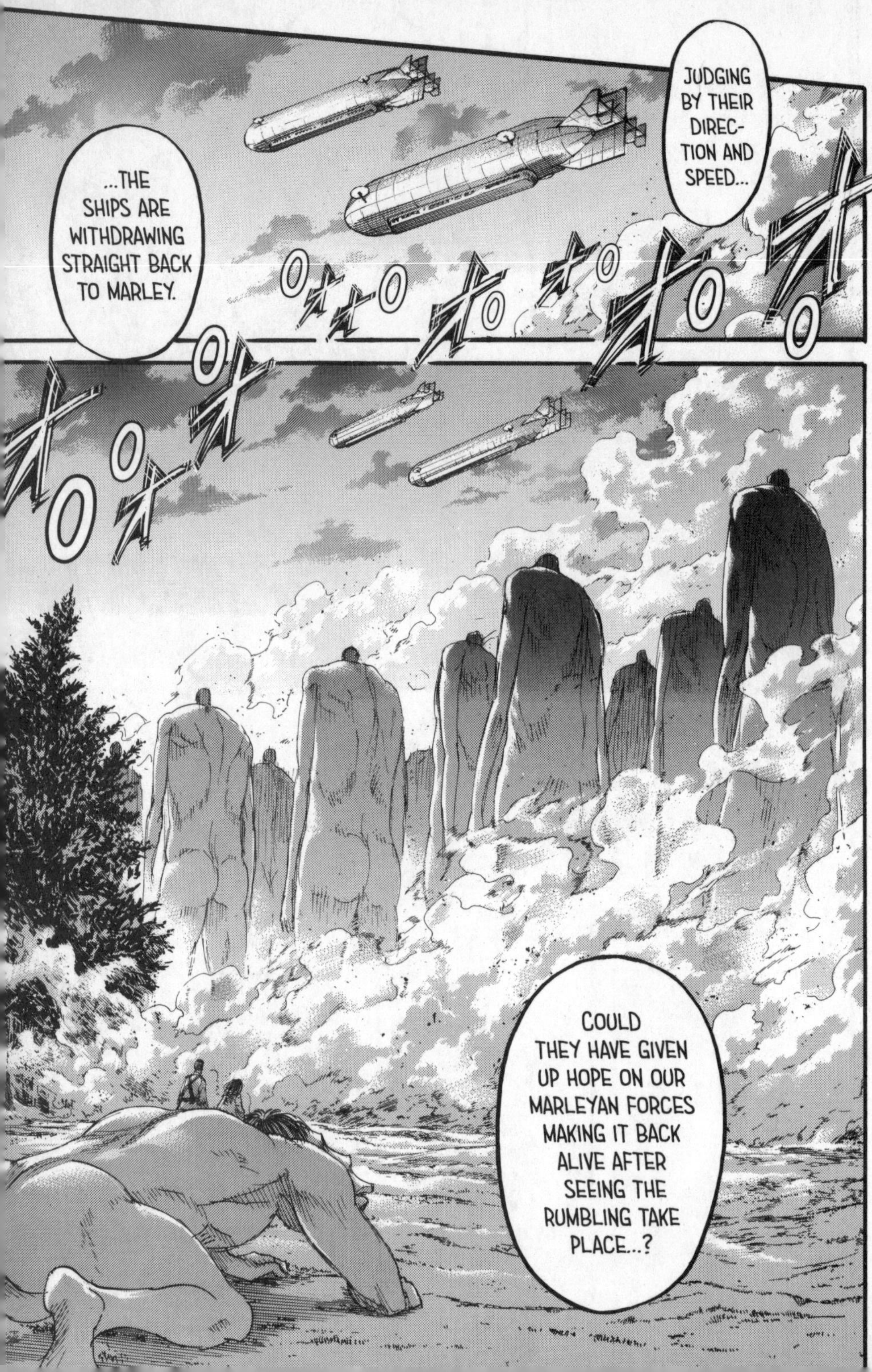
JUDGING BY THEIR DIRECTION AND SPEED...
...THE SHIPS ARE WITHDRAWING STRAIGHT BACK TO MARLEY.
COULD THEY HAVE GIVEN UP HOPE ON OUR MARLEYAN FORCES MAKING IT BACK ALIVE AFTER SEEING THE RUMBLING TAKE PLACE...?

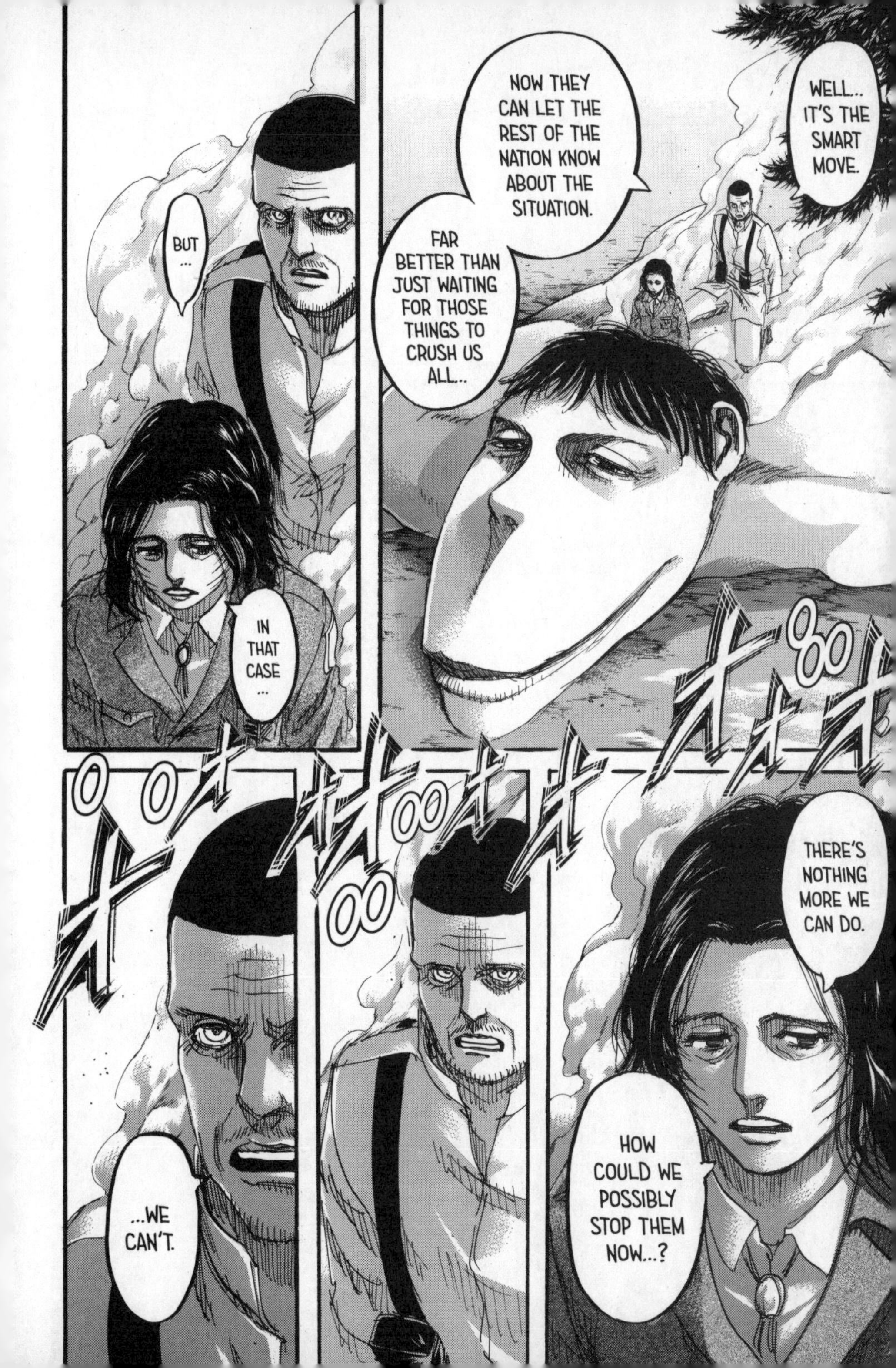
WELL.. IT'S THE SMART MOVE.
NOW THEY CAN LET THE REST OF THE NATION KNOW ABOUT THE SITUATION.
FAR BETTER THAN JUST WAITING FOR THOSE THINGS TO CRUSH US ALL..
BUT ...
IN THAT CASE ...
THERE'S NOTHING MORE WE CAN DO.
HOW COULD WE POSSIBLY STOP THEM NOW...?
...WE CAN'T.

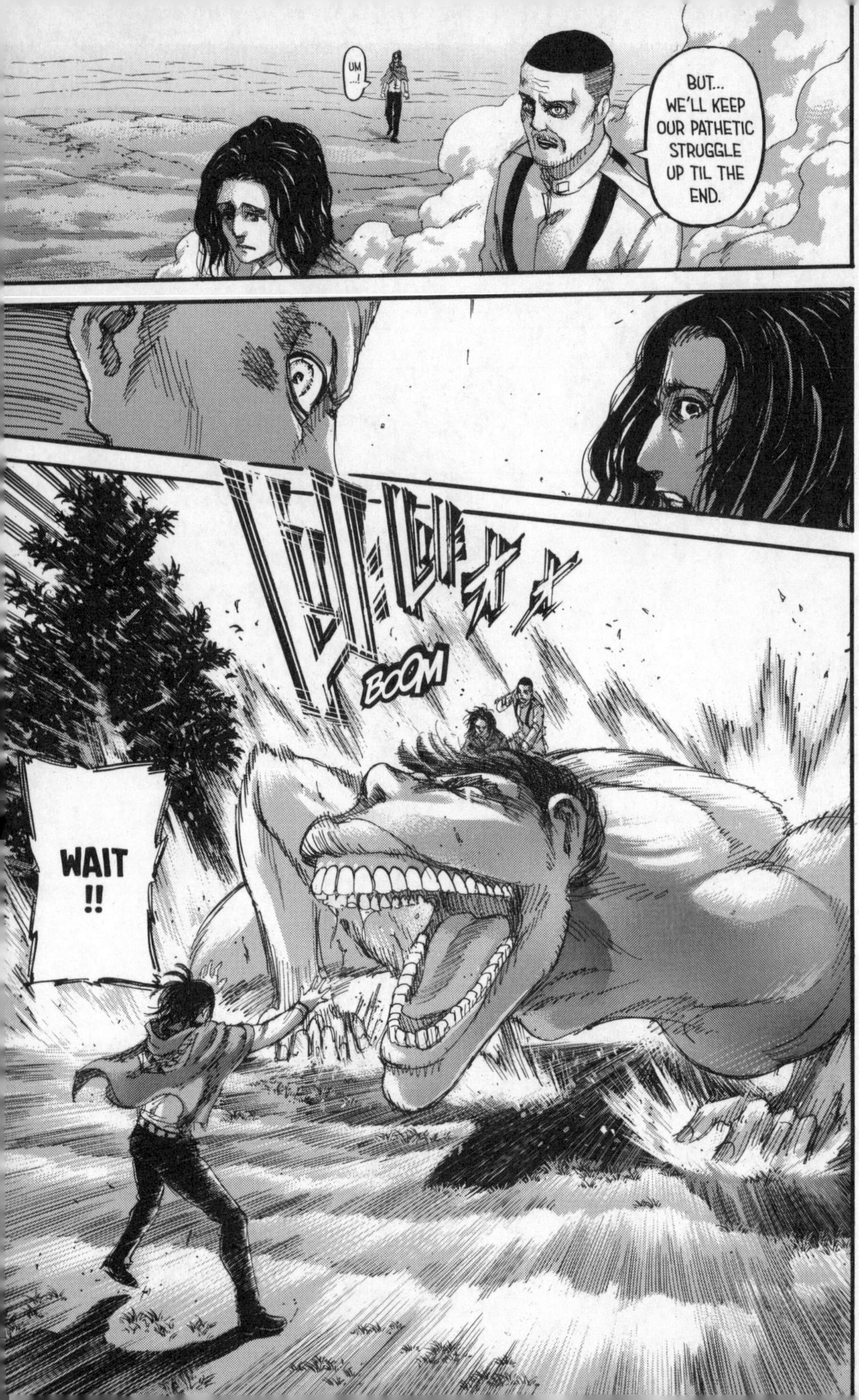
BUT... WE'LL KEEP OUR PATHETIC STRUGGLE UP TIL THE END.
UM ...!
BOOM
WAIT !!

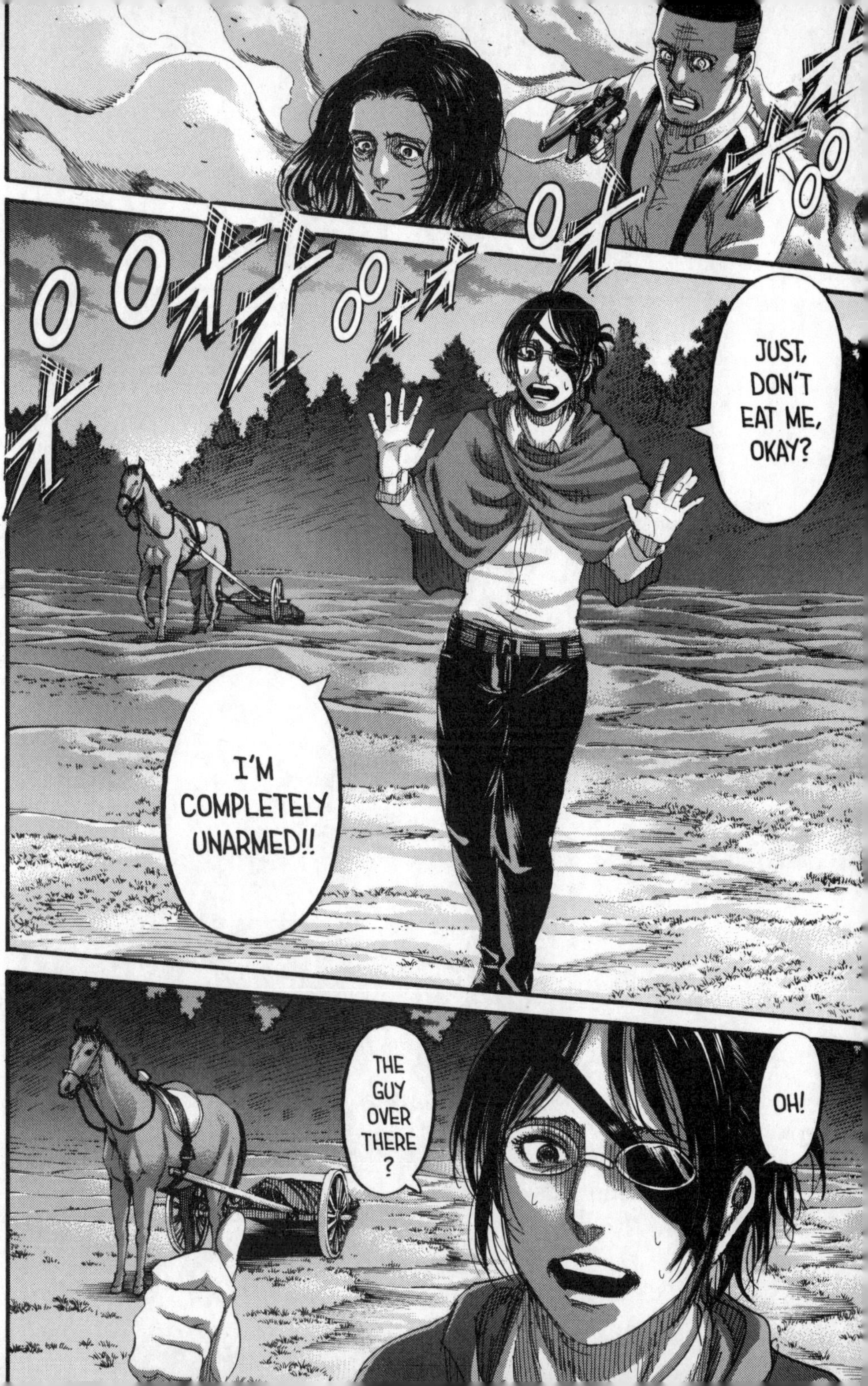
JUST, DON'T EAT ME, OKAY?
I'M COMPLETELY UNARMED!!
OH!
THE GUY OVER THERE?

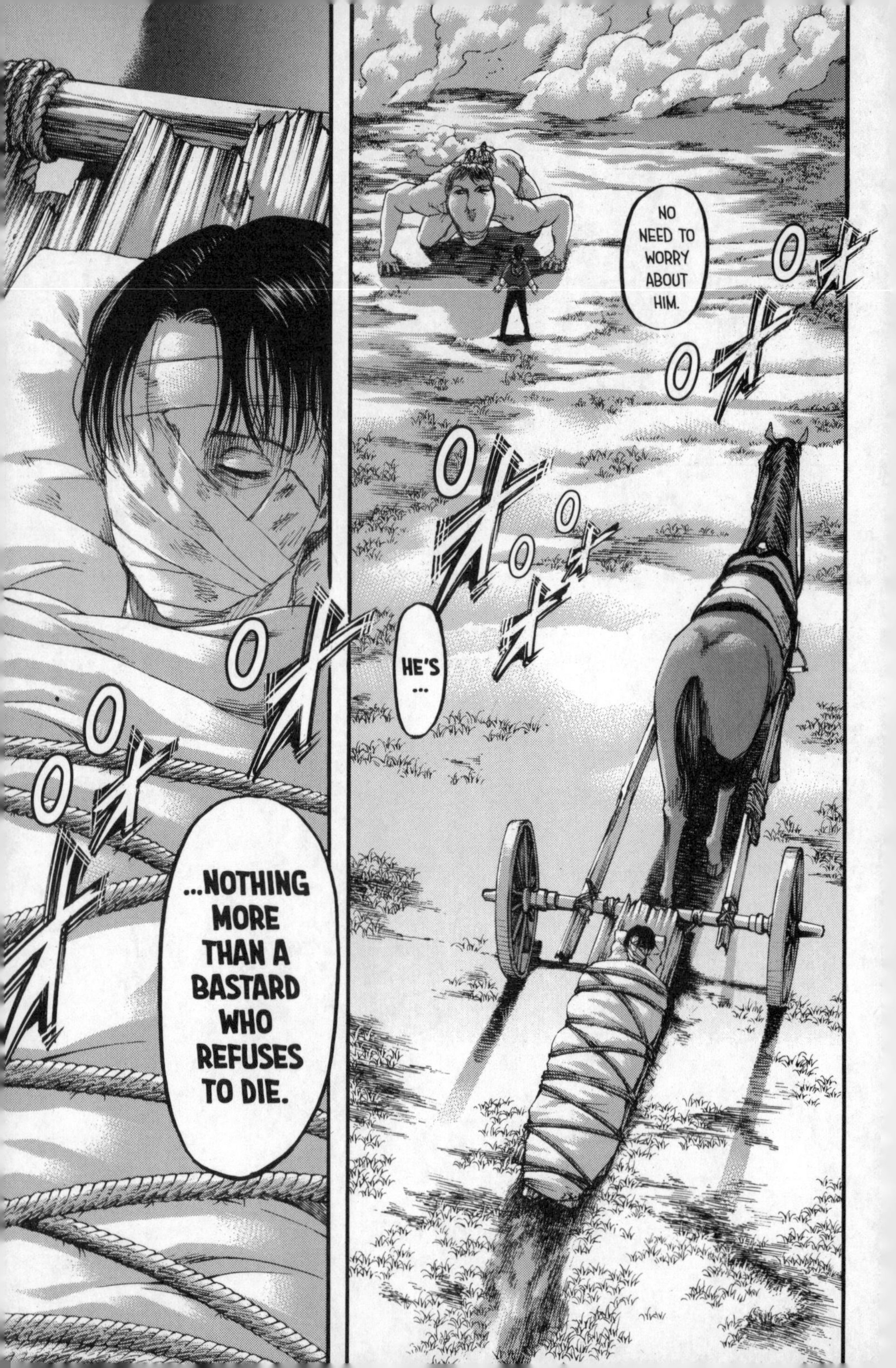
NO NEED TO WORRY ABOUT HIM.
HE'S ...
...NOTHING MORE THAN A BASTARD WHO REFUSES TO DIE.

ATTACK
on TITAN

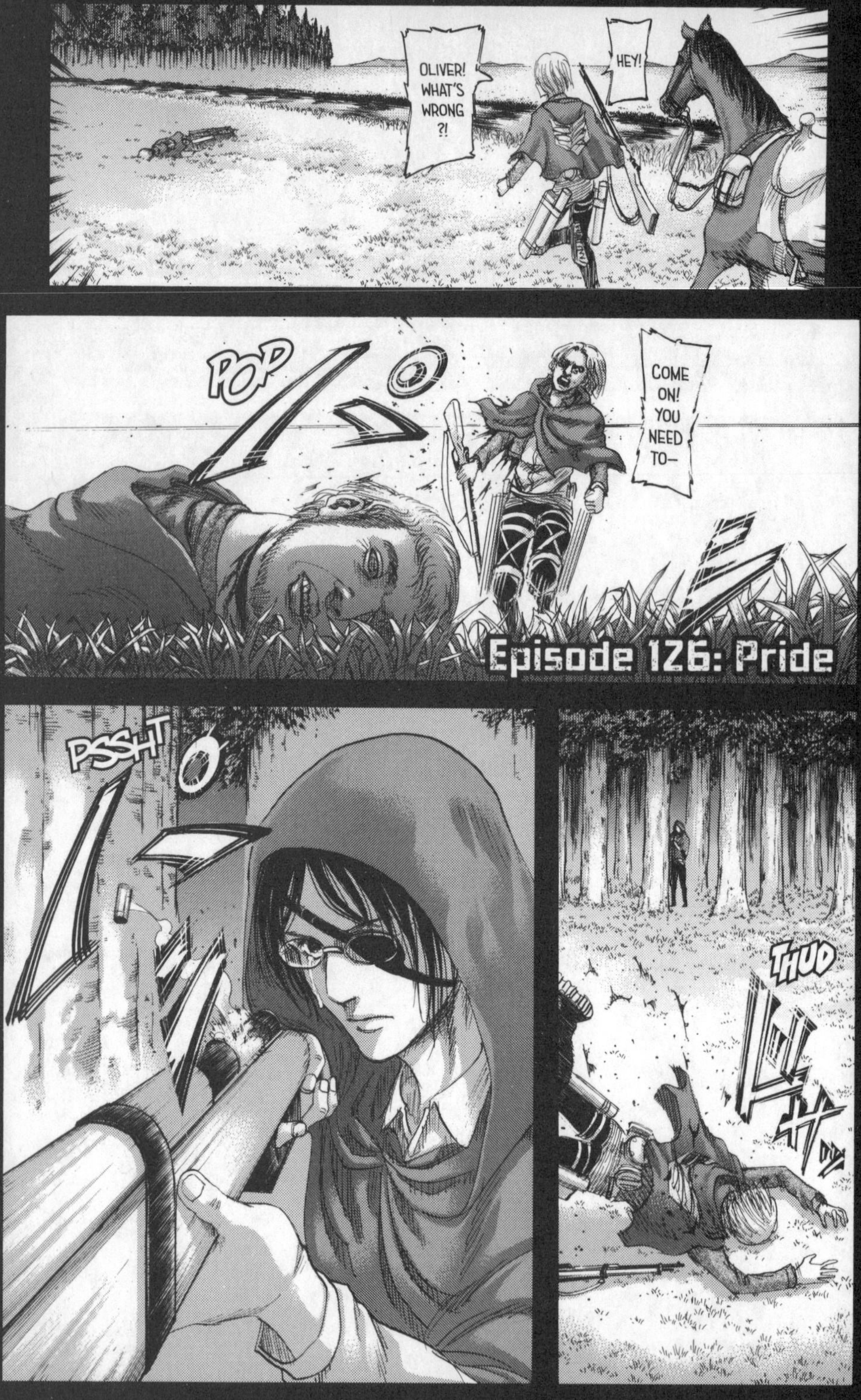
HEY!
OLIVER! WHAT'S WRONG ?!
COME ON! YOU NEED TO—
POP
Episode 126: Pride
THUD
PSSHT

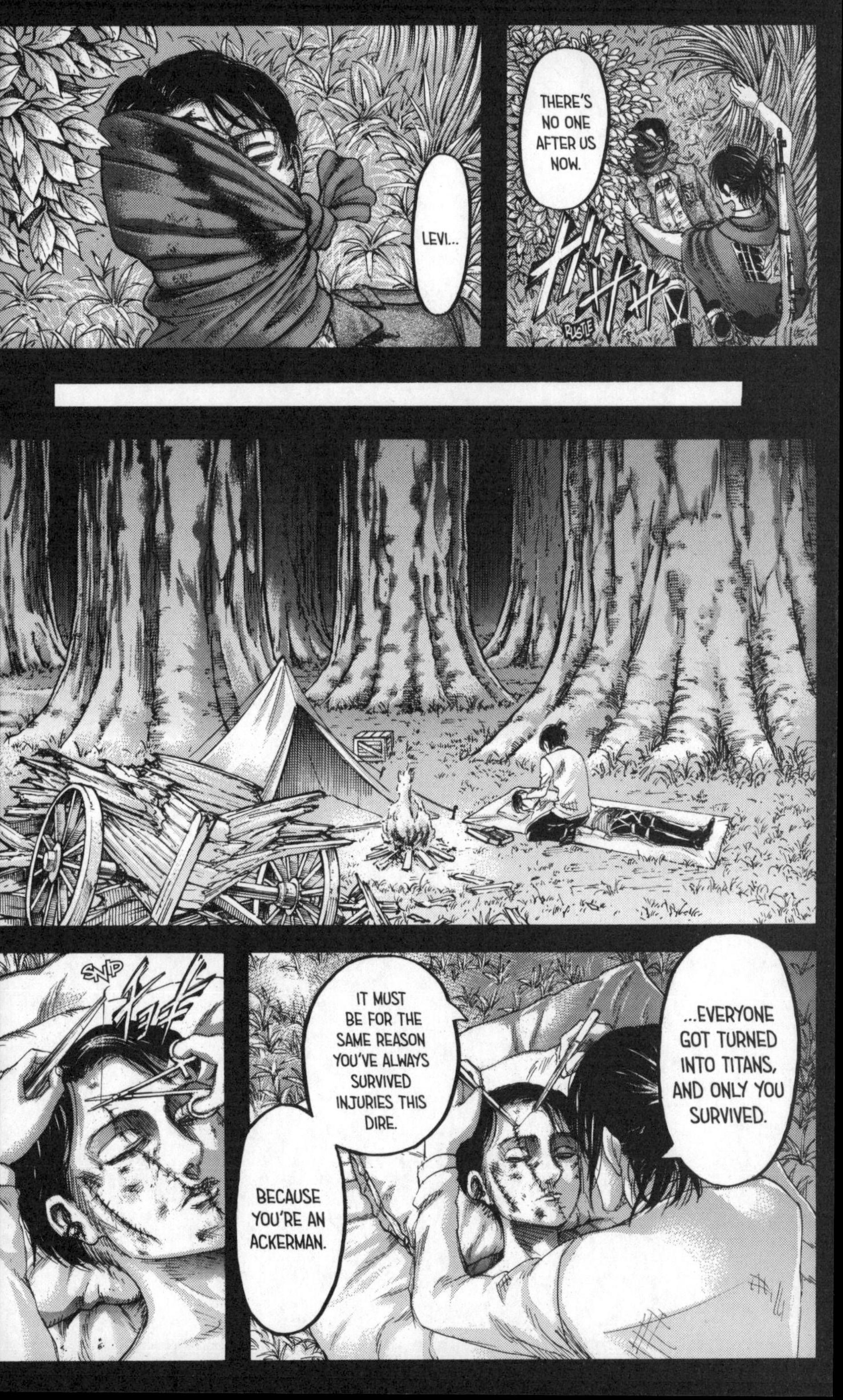
THERE'S NO ONE AFTER US NOW.
RUSTLE
LEVI...
...EVERYONE GOT TURNED INTO TITANS, AND ONLY YOU SURVIVED.
IT MUST BE FOR THE SAME REASON YOU'VE ALWAYS SURVIVED INJURIES THIS DIRE.
BECAUSE YOU'RE AN ACKERMAN.
SNIP

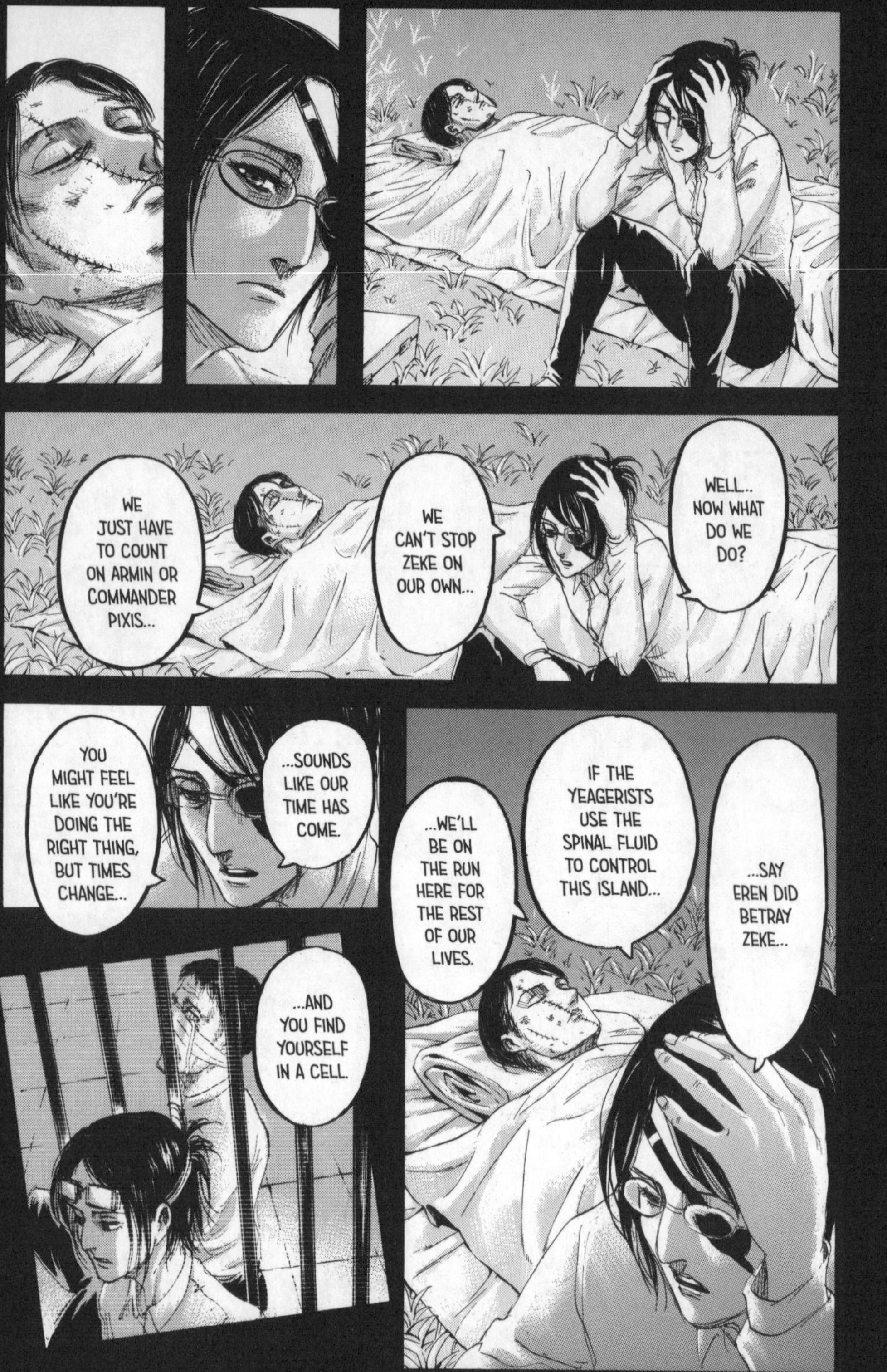
WELL.. NOW WHAT DO WE DO?
WE CAN'T STOP ZEKE ON OUR OWN...
WE JUST HAVE TO COUNT ON ARMIN OR COMMANDER PIXIS...
...SAY EREN DID BETRAY ZEKE...
IF THE YEAGERISTS USE THE SPINAL FLUID TO CONTROL THIS ISLAND...
...WE'LL BE ON THE RUN HERE FOR THE REST OF OUR LIVES.
...SOUNDS LIKE OUR TIME HAS COME.
YOU MIGHT FEEL LIKE YOU'RE DOING THE RIGHT THING, BUT TIMES CHANGE...
...AND YOU FIND YOURSELF IN A CELL.

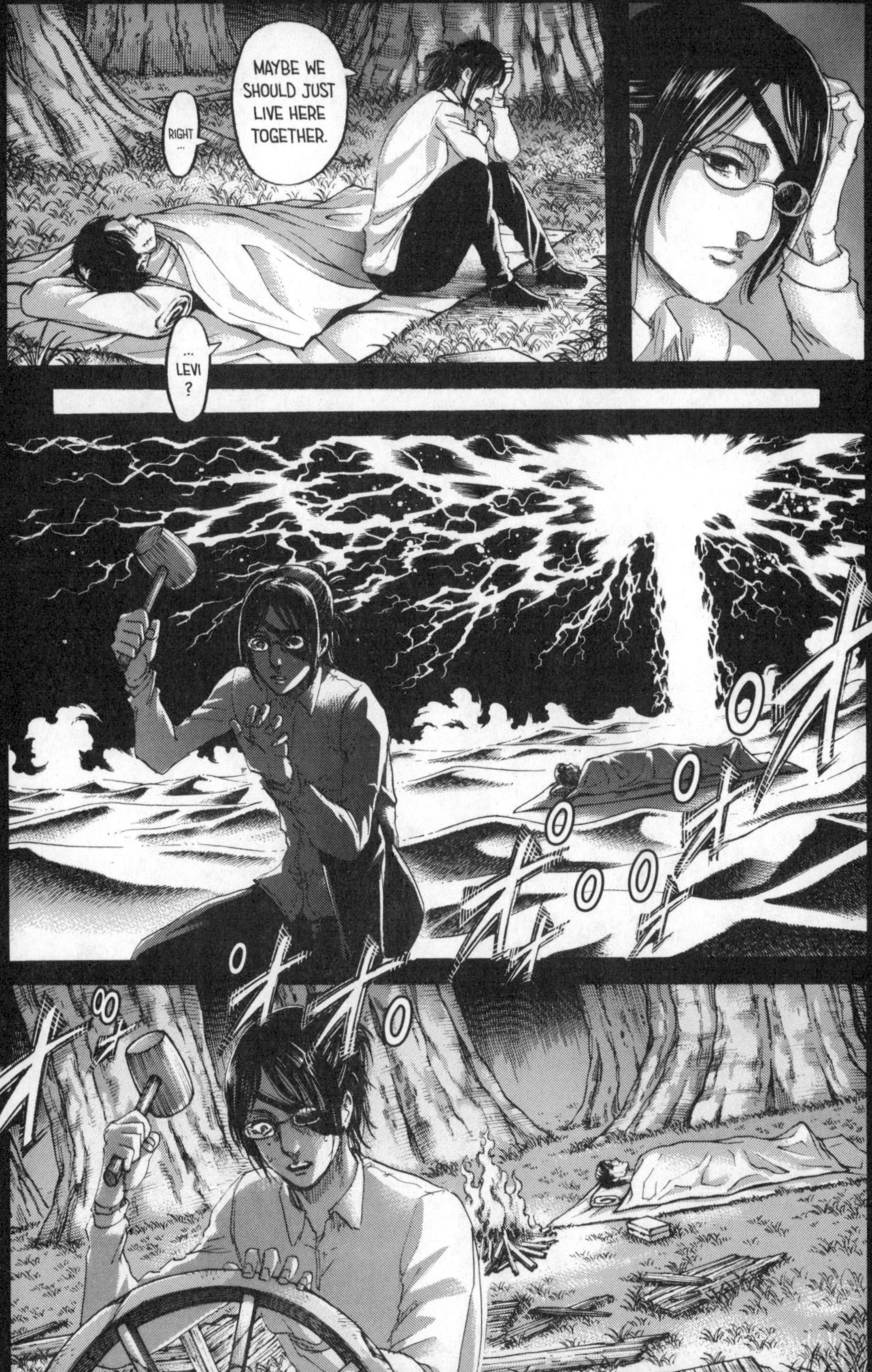
MAYBE WE SHOULD JUST LIVE HERE TOGETHER.
RIGHT ...
... LEVI ?

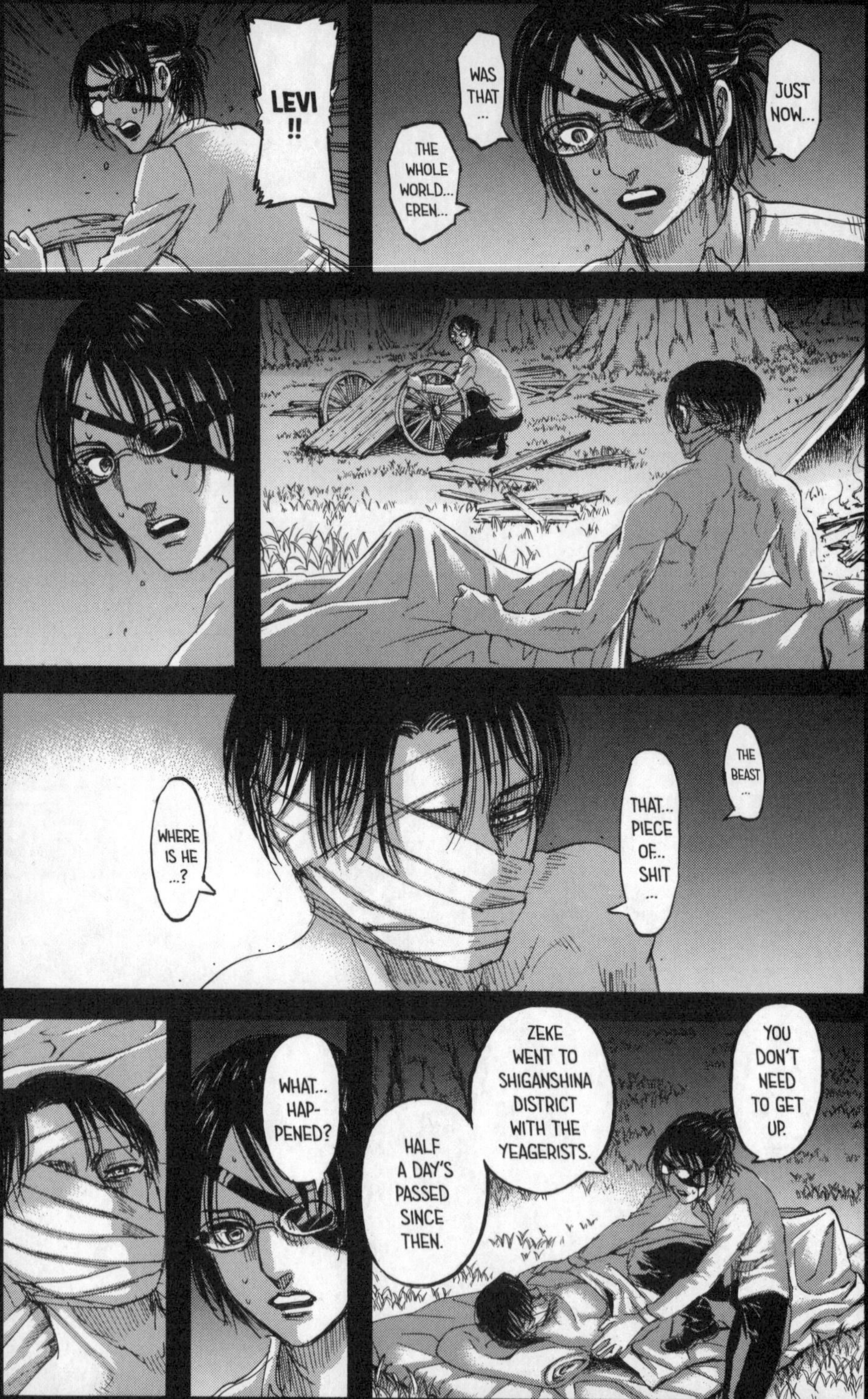
JUST NOW...
WAS THAT ...
THE WHOLE WORLD... EREN...
LEVI !!
THE BEAST ...
THAT... PIECE OF.. SHIT ...
WHERE IS HE ...?
YOU DON'T NEED TO GET UP.
ZEKE WENT TO SHIGANSHINA DISTRICT WITH THE YEAGERISTS.
HALF A DAY'S PASSED SINCE THEN.
WHAT... HAP-PENED?

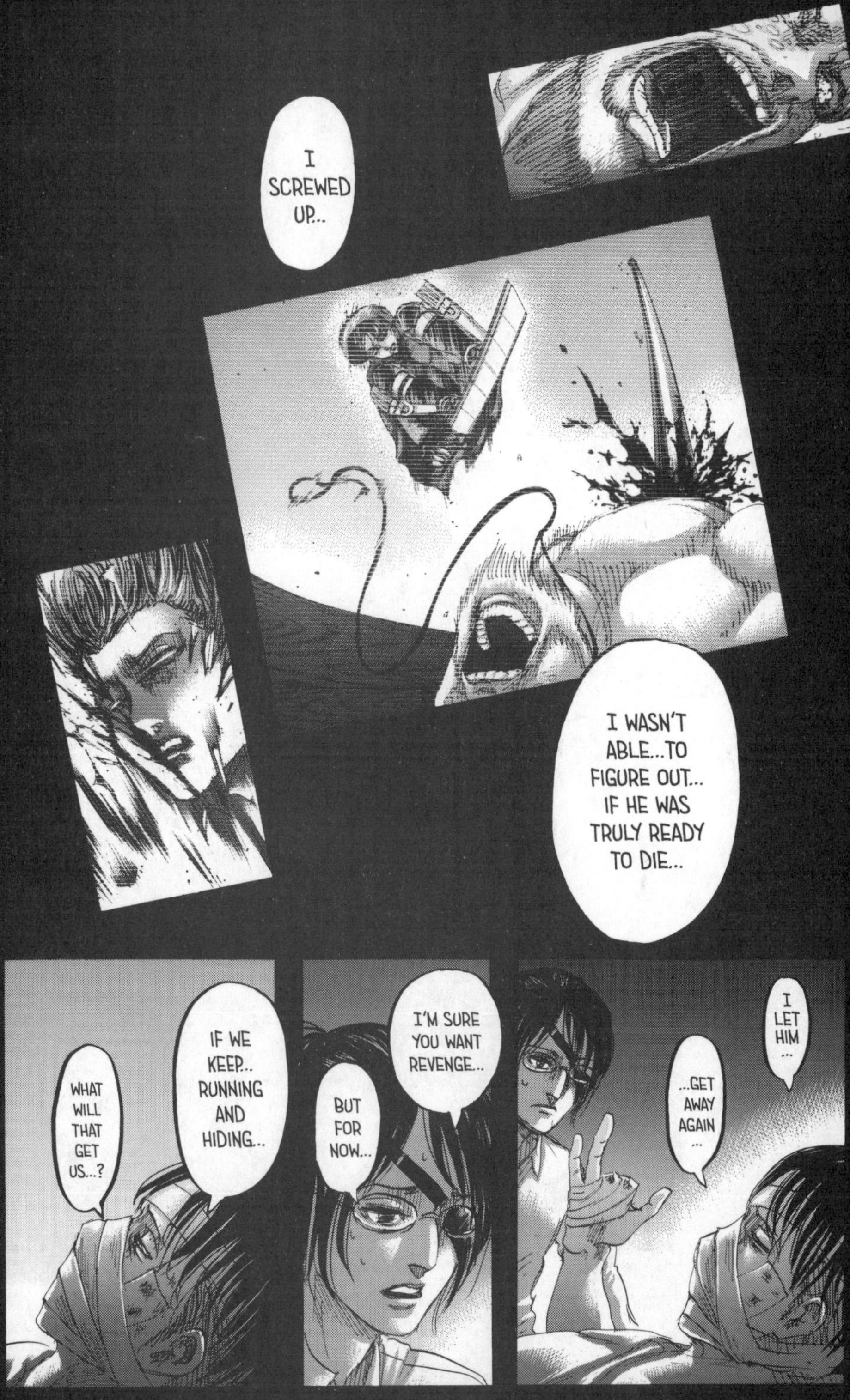
I SCREWED UP...
I WASN'T ABLE...TO FIGURE OUT... IF HE WAS TRULY READY TO DIE...
I LET HIM...
...GET AWAY AGAIN...
I'M SURE YOU WANT REVENGE...
BUT FOR NOW...
IF WE KEEP... RUNNING AND HIDING...
WHAT WILL THAT GET US...?

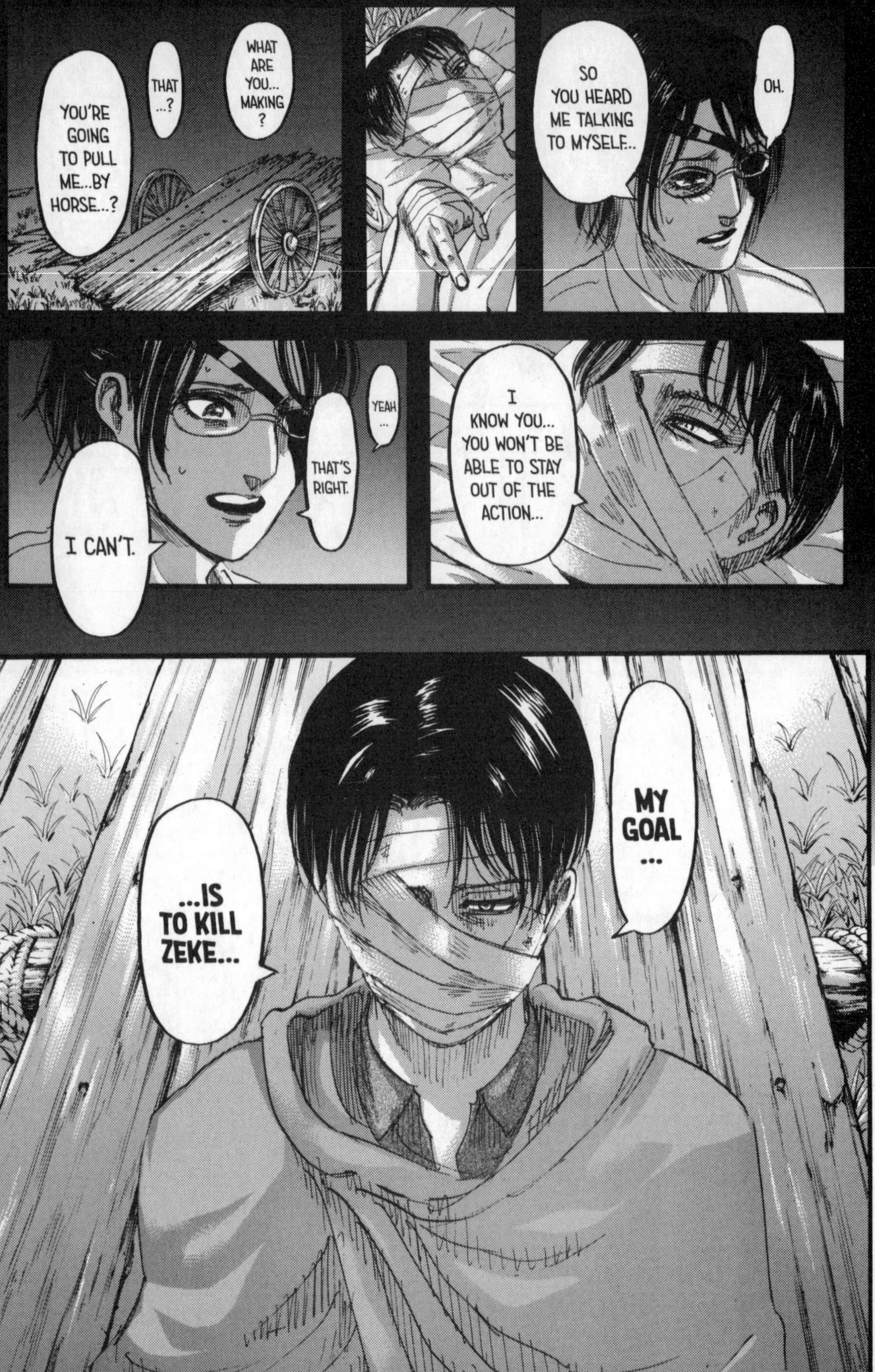
OH.
SO YOU HEARD ME TALKING TO MYSELF..
WHAT ARE YOU... MAKING?
THAT ...?
YOU'RE GOING TO PULL ME...BY HORSE...?
I KNOW YOU... YOU WON'T BE ABLE TO STAY OUT OF THE ACTION...
YEAH ...
THAT'S RIGHT.
I CAN'T.
MY GOAL ...
...IS TO KILL ZEKE...

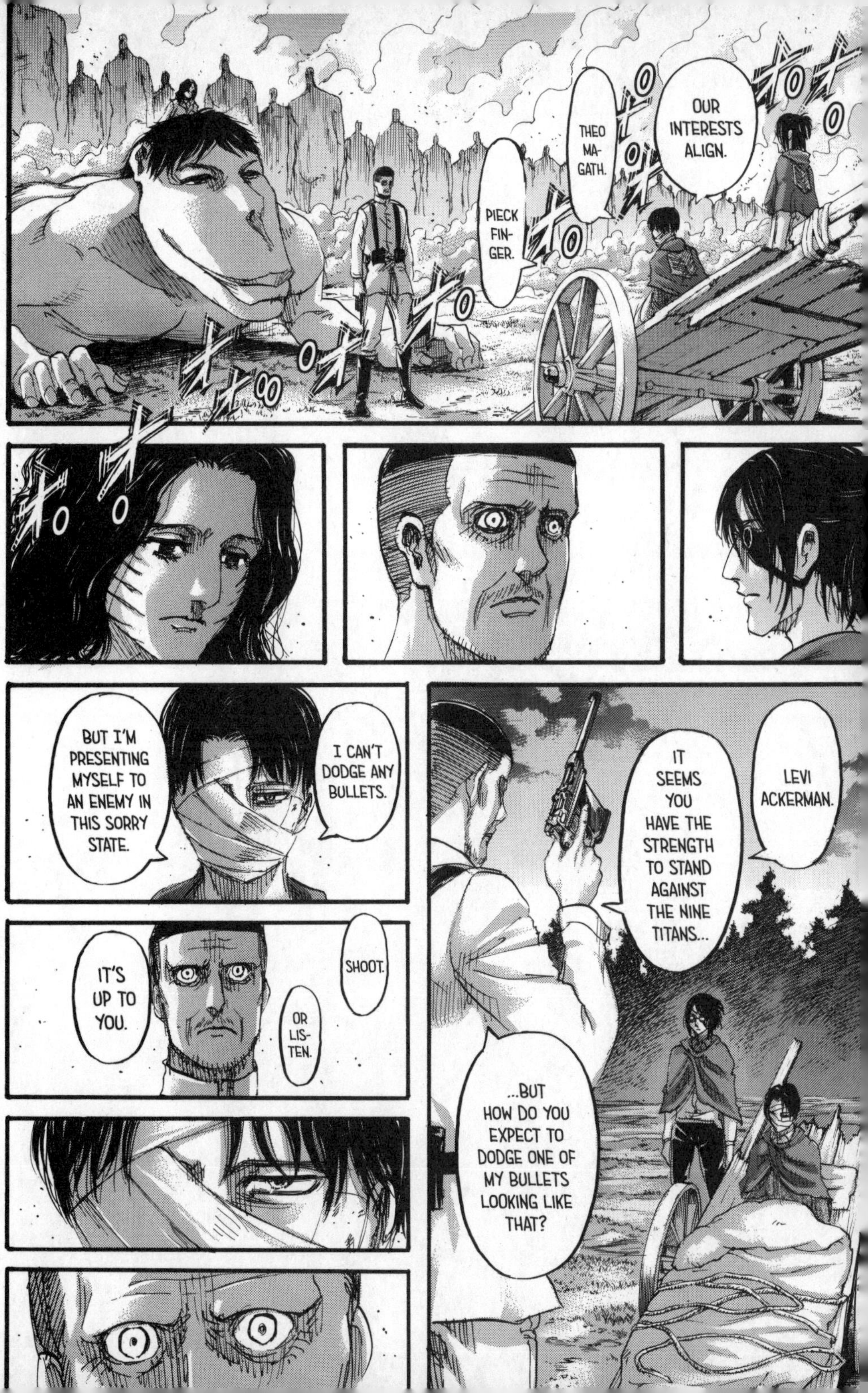
OUR INTERESTS ALIGN.
THEO MAGATH.
PIECK FINGER.
LEVI ACKERMAN.
IT SEEMS YOU HAVE THE STRENGTH TO STAND AGAINST THE NINE TITANS...
...BUT HOW DO YOU EXPECT TO DODGE ONE OF MY BULLETS LOOKING LIKE THAT?
I CAN'T DODGE ANY BULLETS.
BUT I'M PRESENTING MYSELF TO AN ENEMY IN THIS SORRY STATE.
SHOOT.
OR LISTEN.
IT'S UP TO YOU.

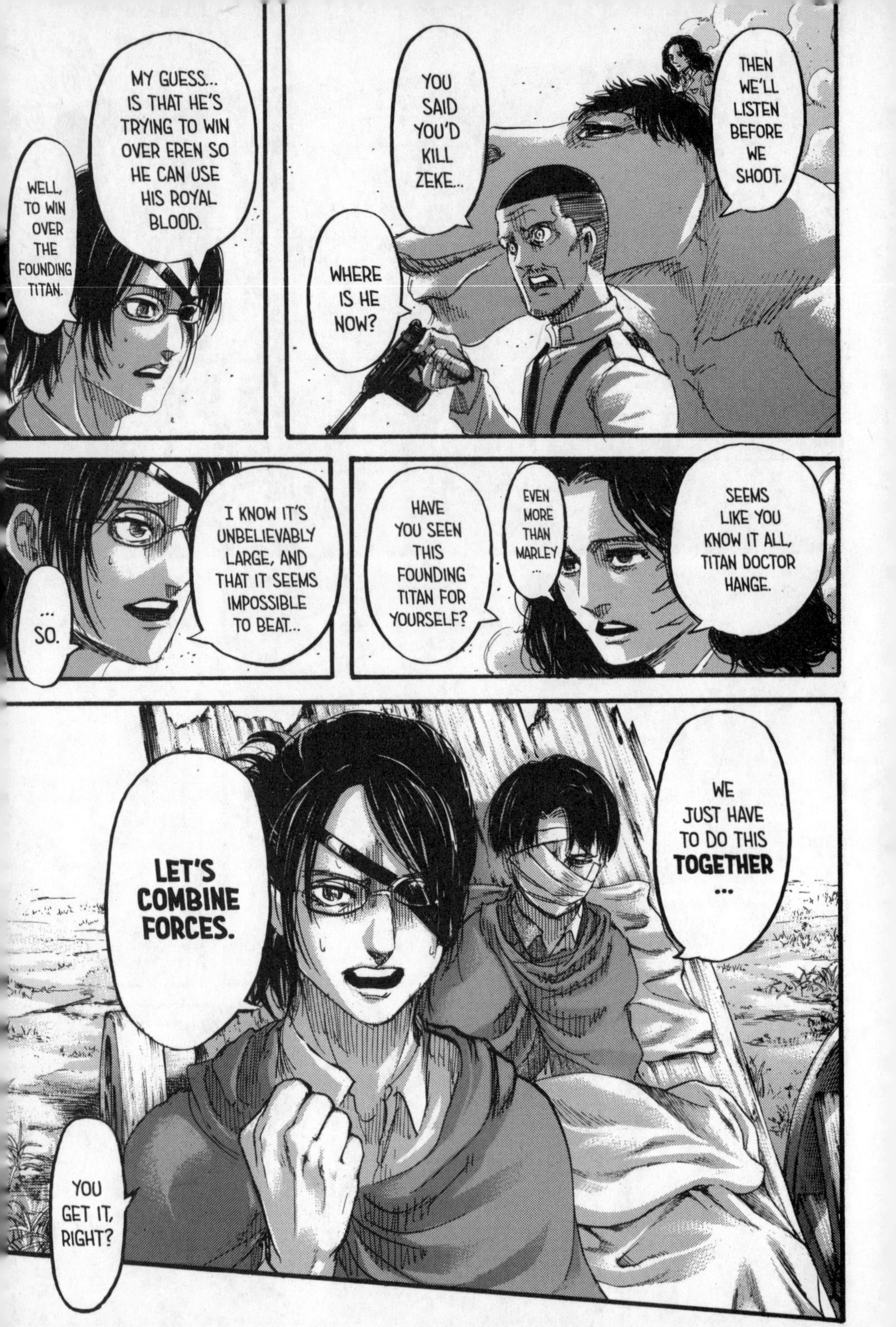
THEN WE'LL LISTEN BEFORE WE SHOOT.
YOU SAID YOU'D KILL ZEKE...
WHERE IS HE NOW?
MY GUESS... IS THAT HE'S TRYING TO WIN OVER EREN SO HE CAN USE HIS ROYAL BLOOD.
WELL, TO WIN OVER THE FOUNDING TITAN.
SEEMS LIKE YOU KNOW IT ALL, TITAN DOCTOR HANGE.
EVEN MORE THAN MARLEY...
HAVE YOU SEEN THIS FOUNDING TITAN FOR YOURSELF?
I KNOW IT'S UNBELIEVABLY LARGE, AND THAT IT SEEMS IMPOSSIBLE TO BEAT...
... SO.
WE JUST HAVE TO DO THIS **TOGETHER**...
LET'S COMBINE FORCES.
YOU GET IT, RIGHT?

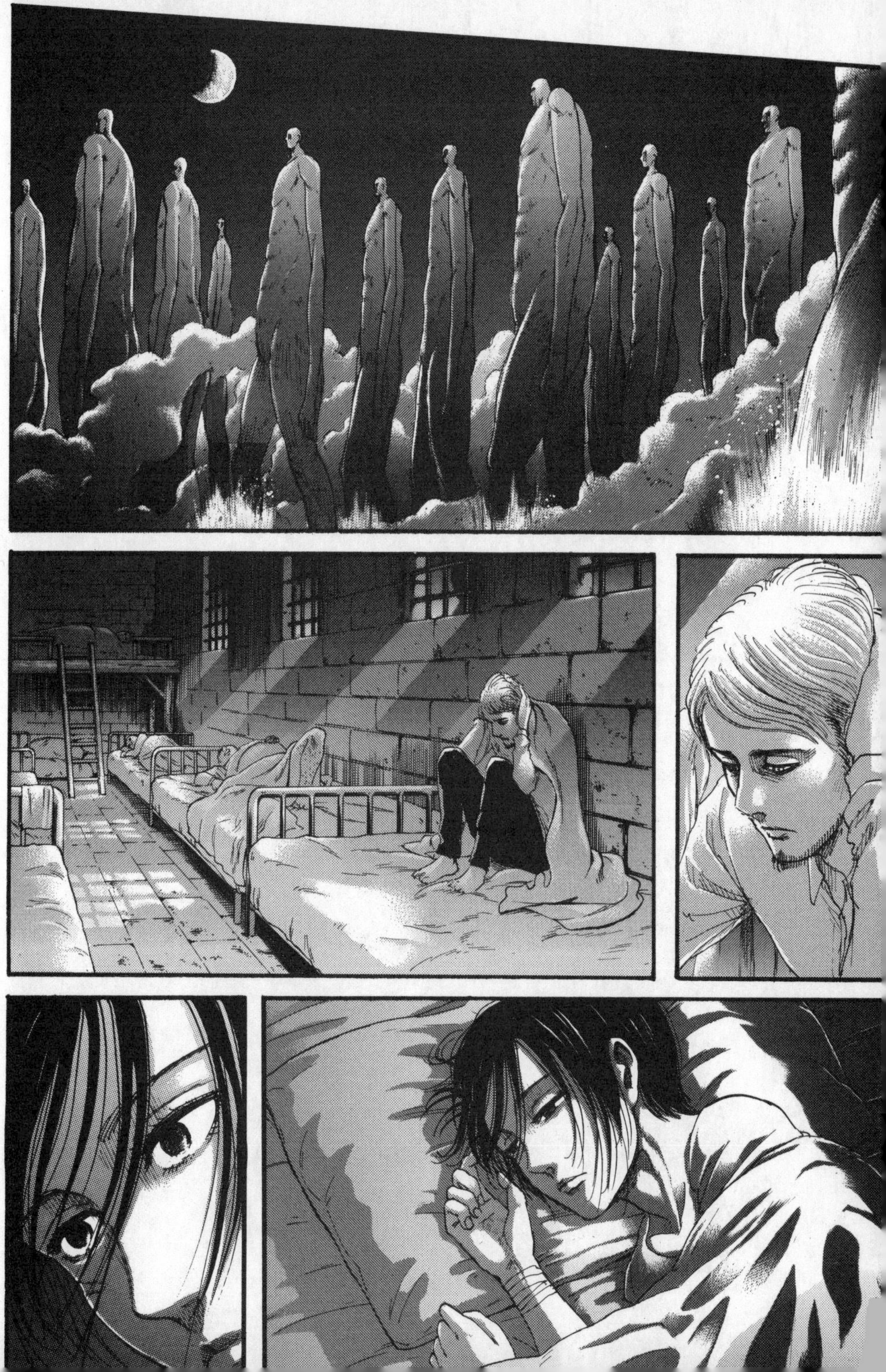

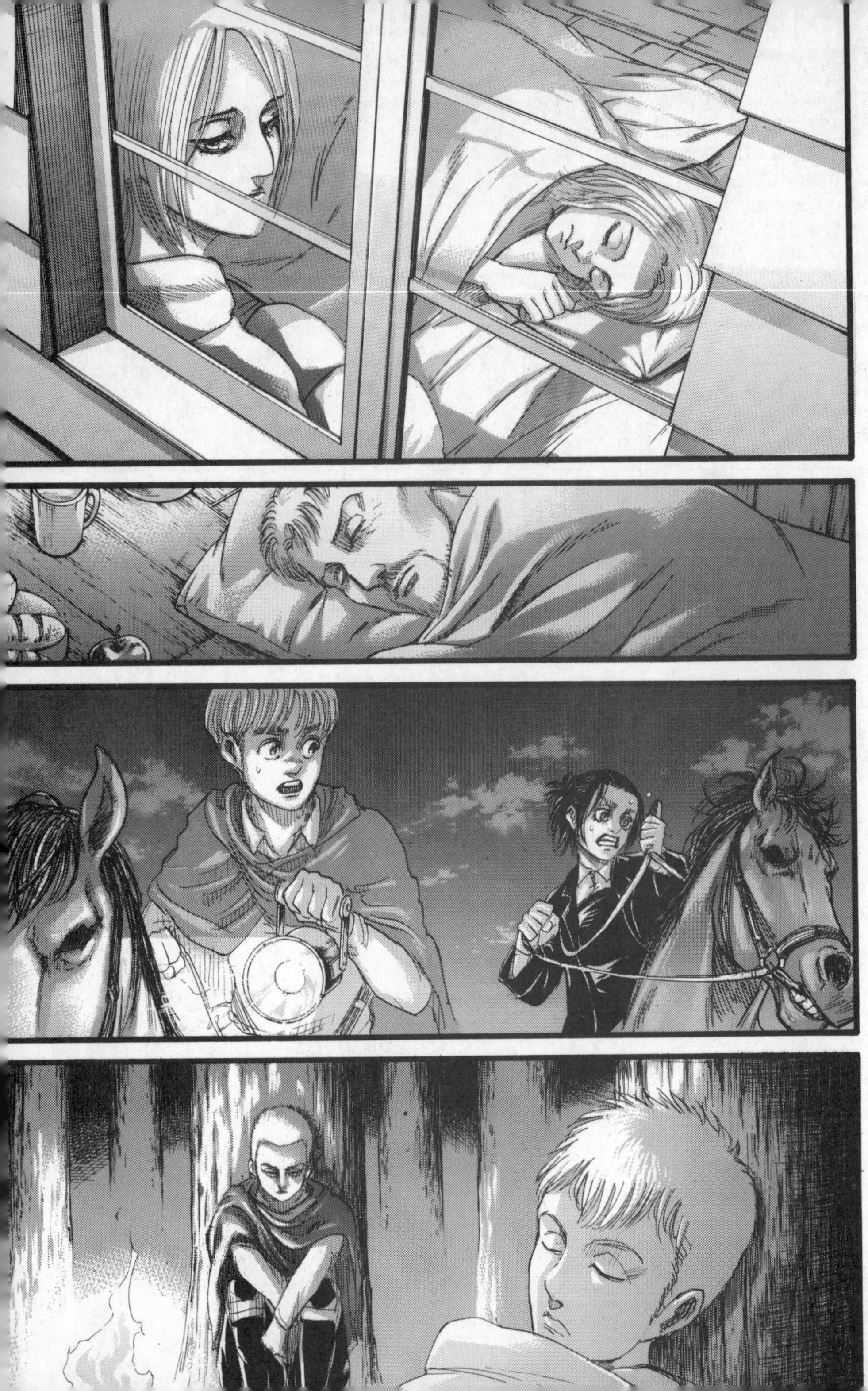

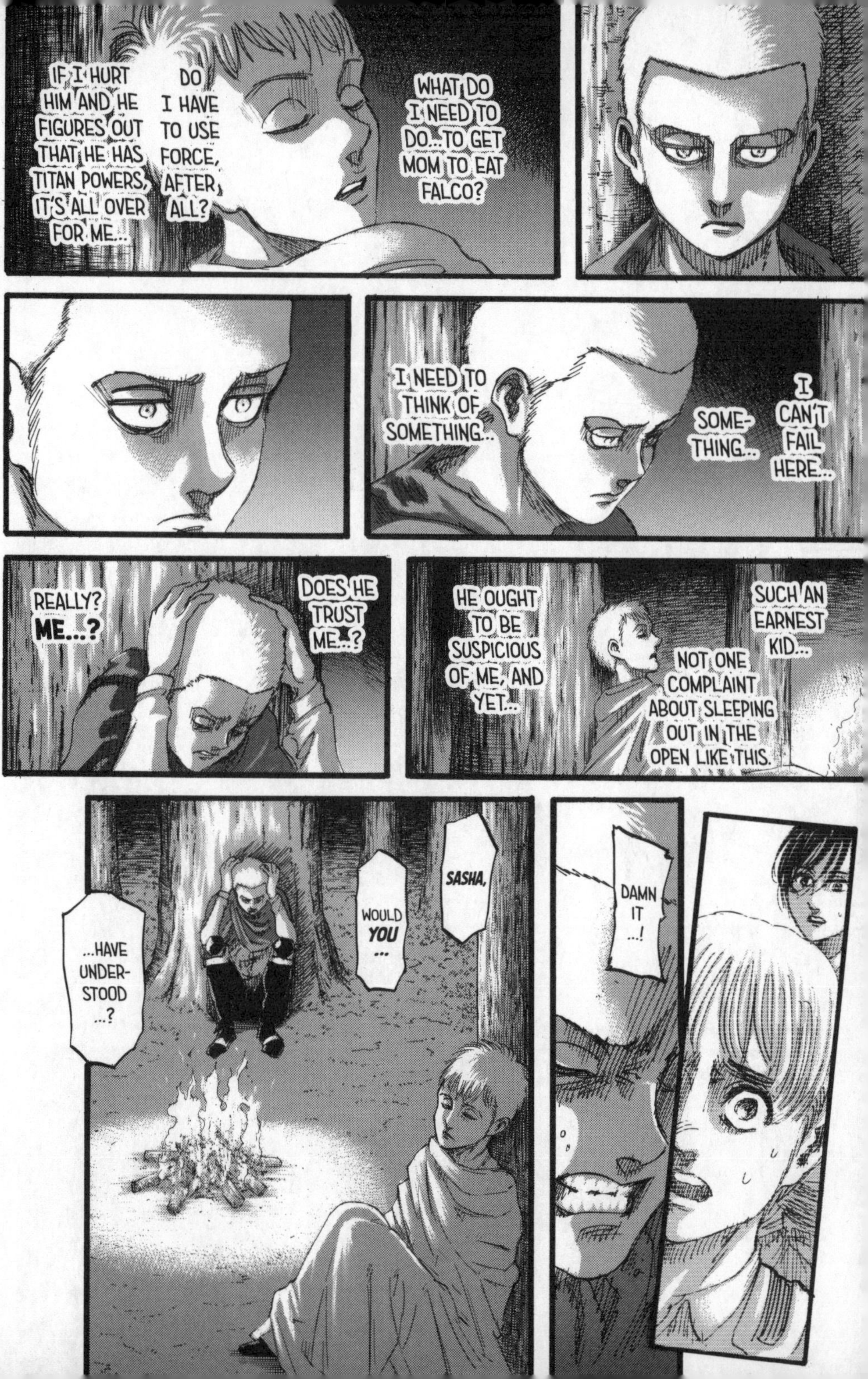
WHAT DO I NEED TO DO...TO GET MOM TO EAT FALCO?
DO I HAVE TO USE FORCE, AFTER ALL?
IF I HURT HIM AND HE FIGURES OUT THAT HE HAS TITAN POWERS, IT'S ALL OVER FOR ME...
I CAN'T FAIL HERE...
SOME-THING...
I NEED TO THINK OF SOMETHING...
SUCH AN EARNEST KID...
NOT ONE COMPLAINT ABOUT SLEEPING OUT IN THE OPEN LIKE THIS.
HE OUGHT TO BE SUSPICIOUS OF ME, AND YET...
DOES HE TRUST ME...?
REALLY? **ME...?**
DAMN IT ...!
SASHA,
WOULD *YOU* ...
...HAVE UNDER-STOOD ...?

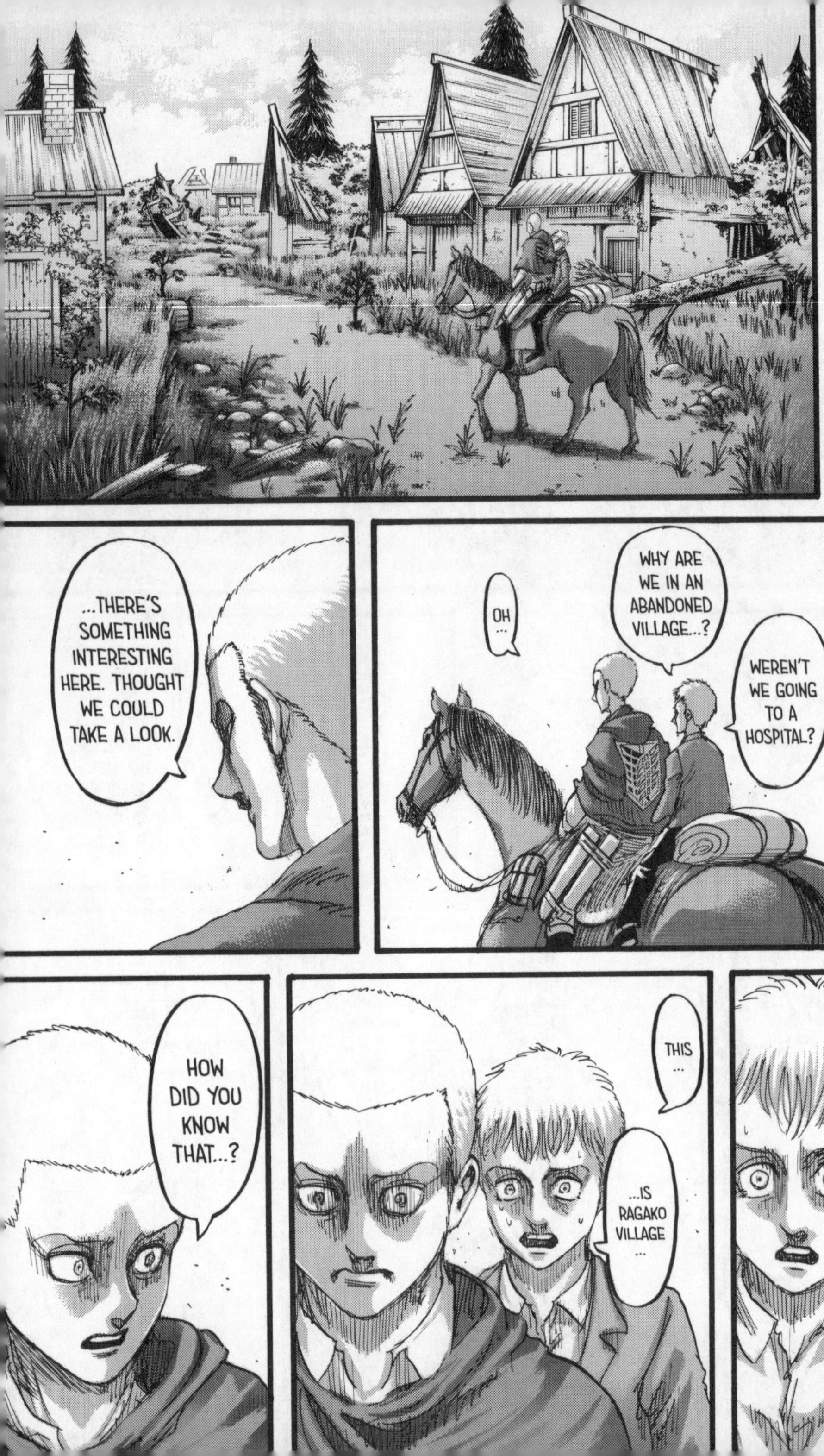
UM...
WEREN'T WE GOING TO A HOSPITAL?
WHY ARE WE IN AN ABANDONED VILLAGE...?
OH...
...THERE'S SOMETHING INTERESTING HERE. THOUGHT WE COULD TAKE A LOOK.
THIS...
...IS RAGAKO VILLAGE...
HOW DID YOU KNOW THAT...?

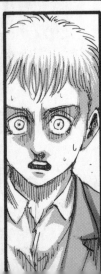

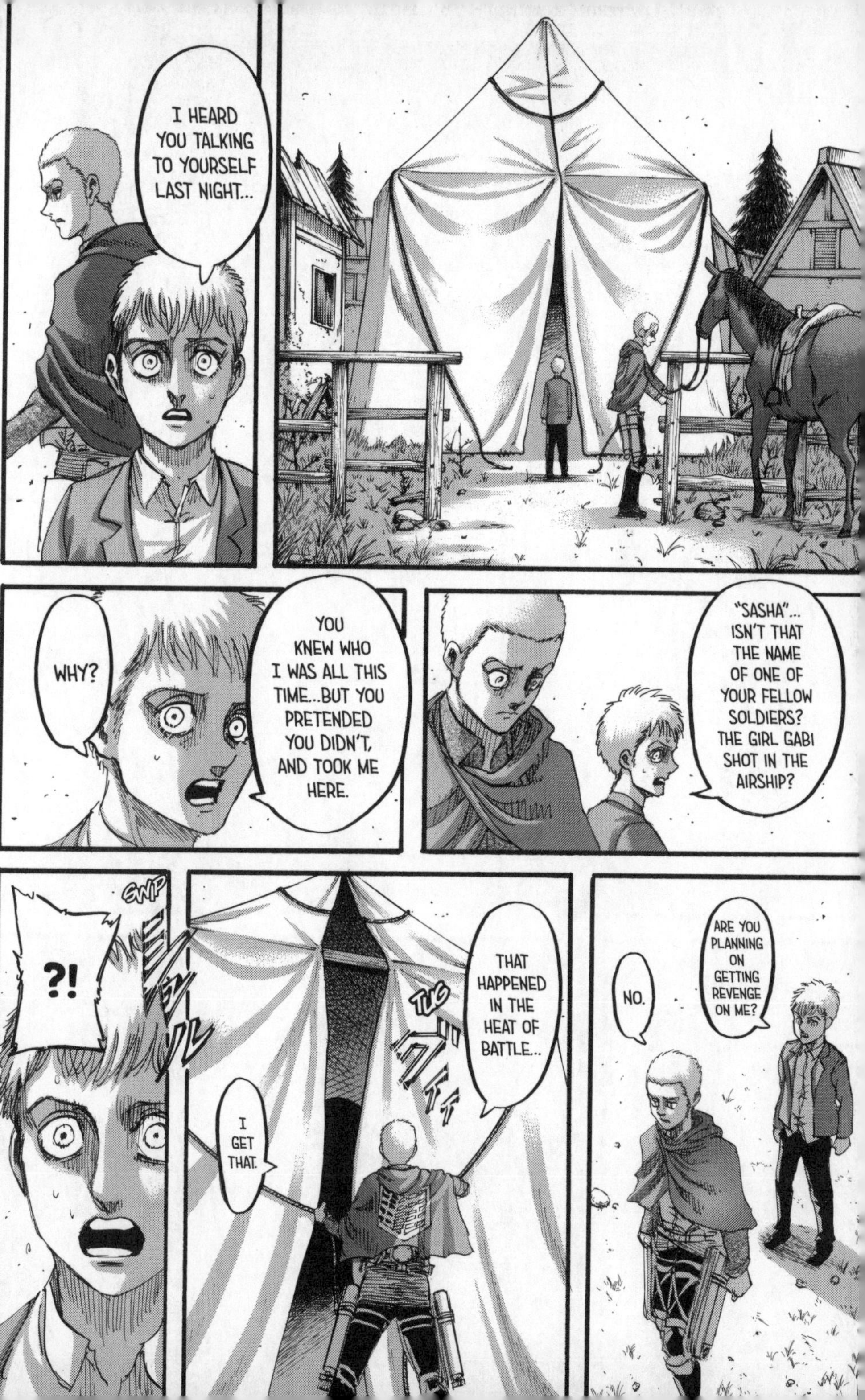
I HEARD YOU TALKING TO YOURSELF LAST NIGHT...
"SASHA"... ISN'T THAT THE NAME OF ONE OF YOUR FELLOW SOLDIERS? THE GIRL GABI SHOT IN THE AIRSHIP?
YOU KNEW WHO I WAS ALL THIS TIME...BUT YOU PRETENDED YOU DIDN'T, AND TOOK ME HERE.
WHY?
ARE YOU PLANNING ON GETTING REVENGE ON ME?
NO.
THAT HAPPENED IN THE HEAT OF BATTLE...
TUG
I GET THAT.
SWIP
?!

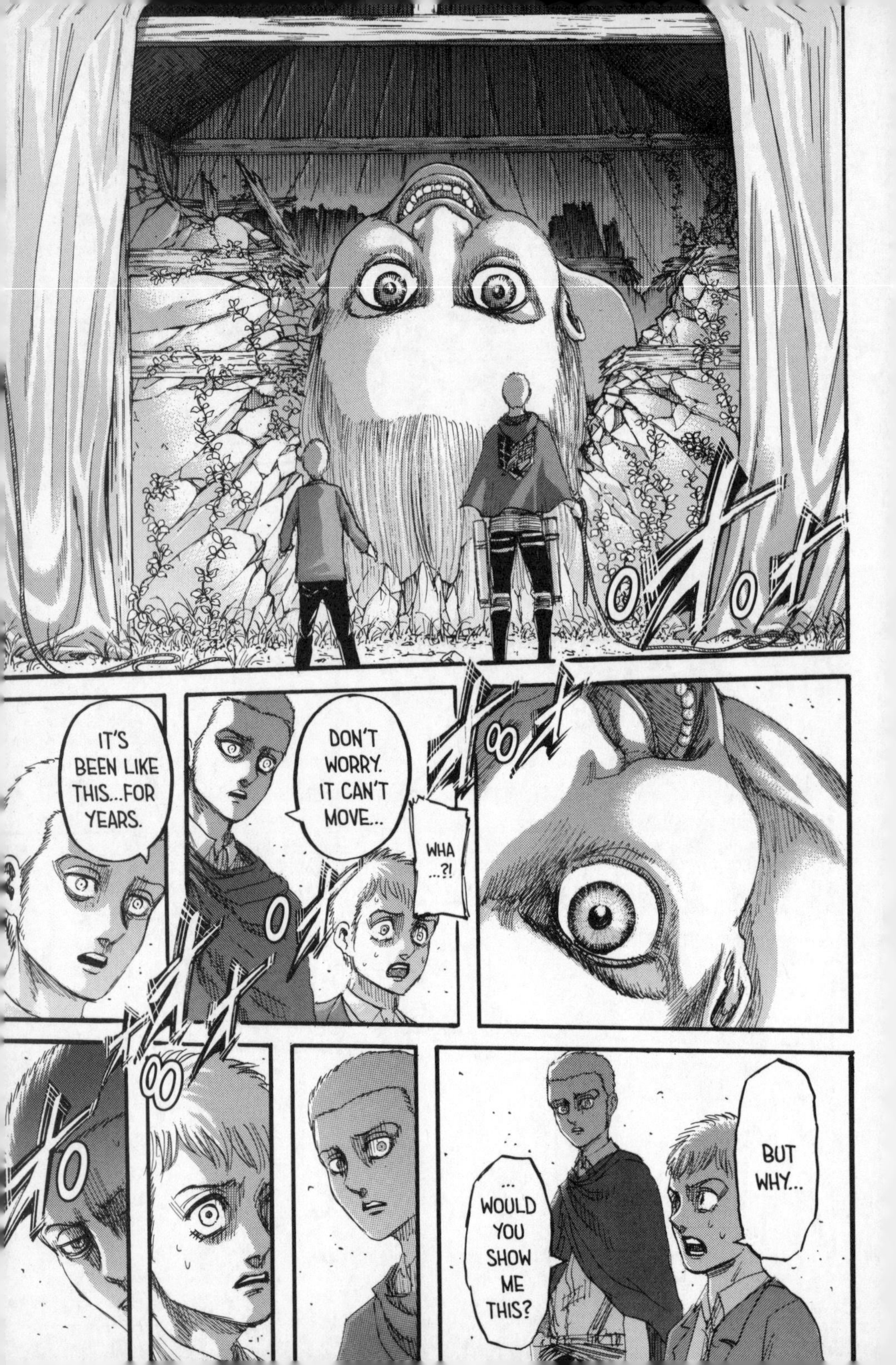
DON'T WORRY. IT CAN'T MOVE...
WHA ...?!
IT'S BEEN LIKE THIS...FOR YEARS.
BUT WHY...
...WOULD YOU SHOW ME THIS?

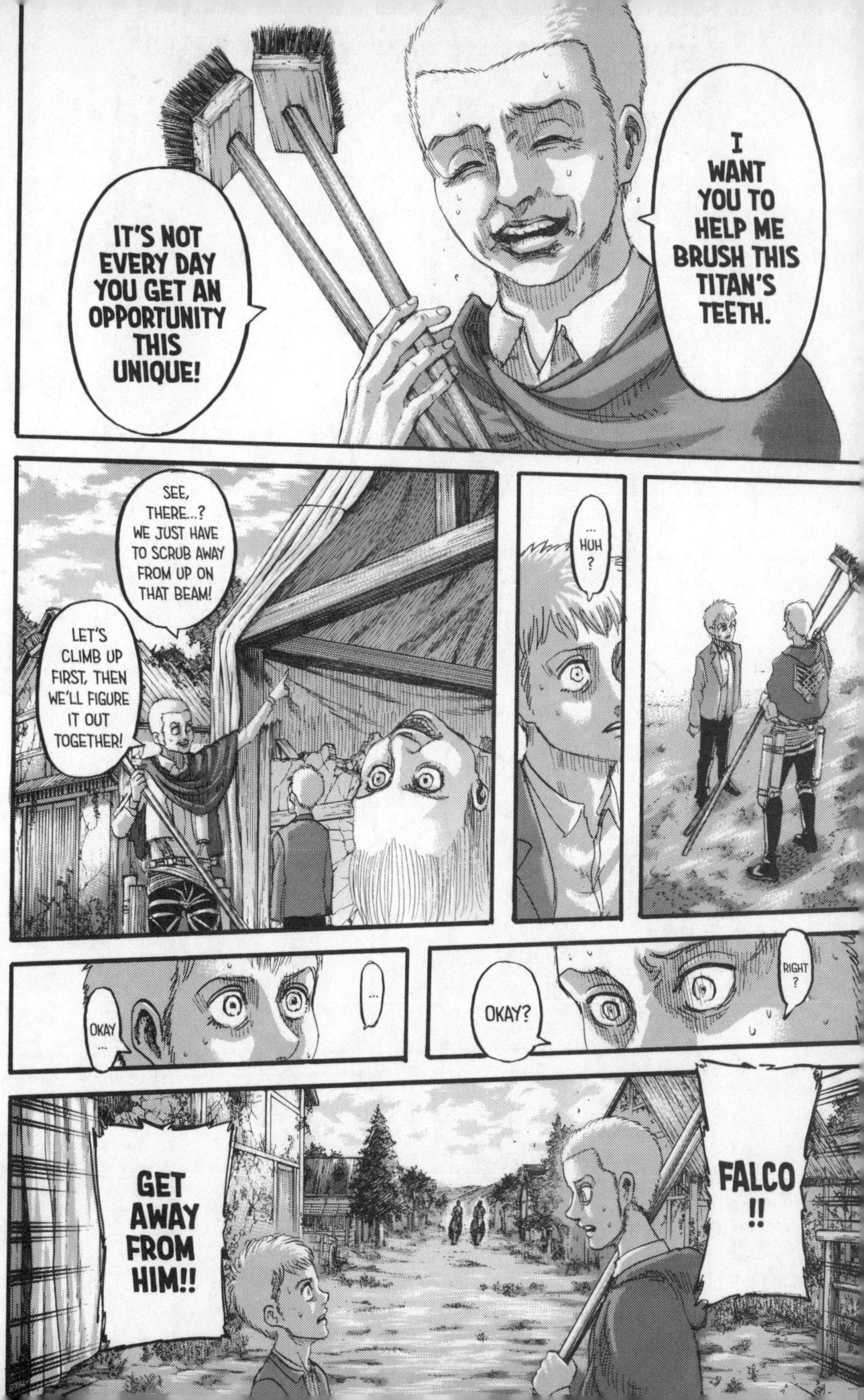
I WANT YOU TO HELP ME BRUSH THIS TITAN'S TEETH.
IT'S NOT EVERY DAY YOU GET AN OPPORTUNITY THIS UNIQUE!
... HUH?
SEE, THERE...? WE JUST HAVE TO SCRUB AWAY FROM UP ON THAT BEAM!
LET'S CLIMB UP FIRST, THEN WE'LL FIGURE IT OUT TOGETHER!
RIGHT?
OKAY?
...
OKAY ...
FALCO!!
GET AWAY FROM HIM!!

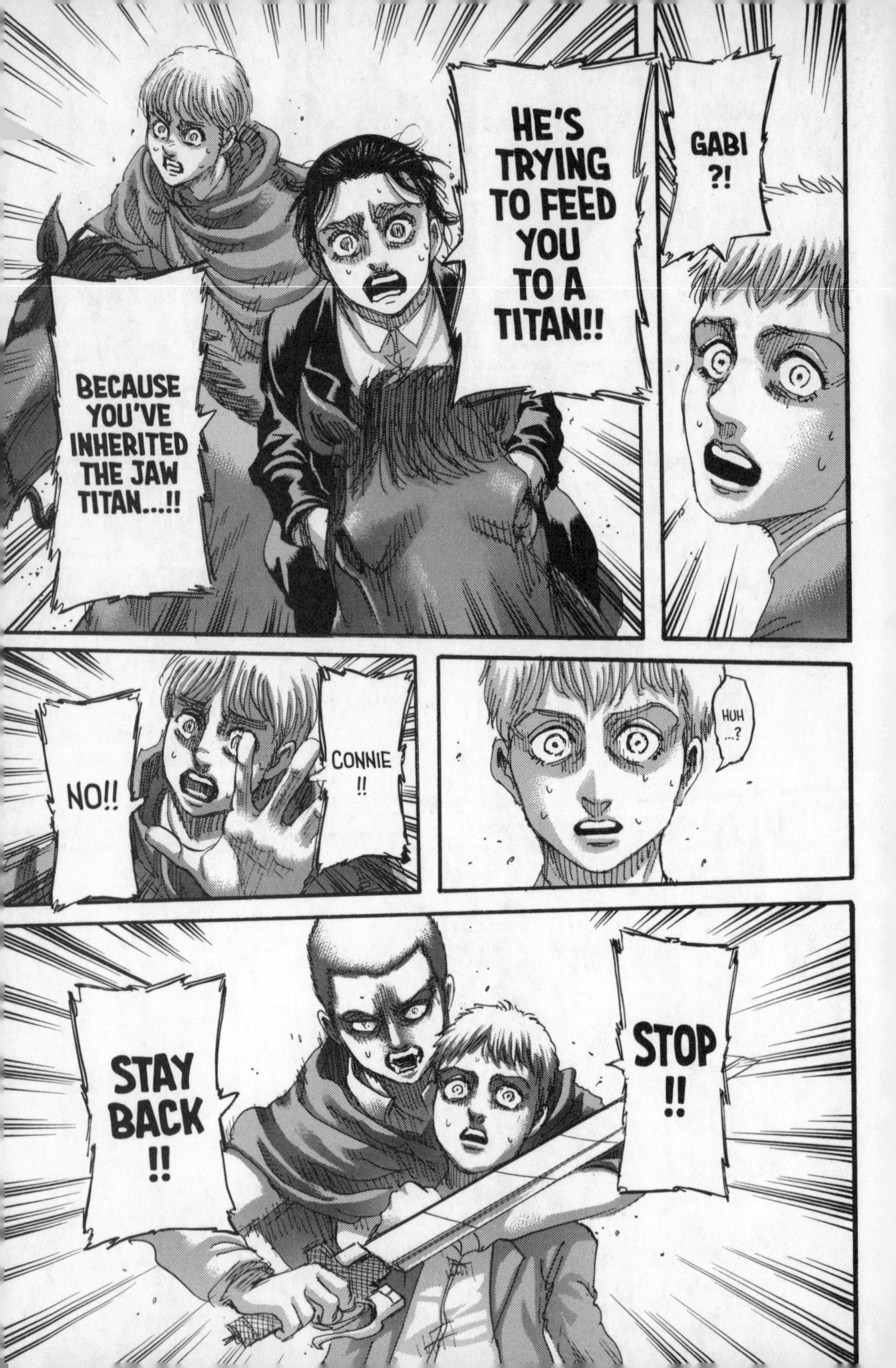
GABI ?!
HE'S TRYING TO FEED YOU TO A TITAN!!
BECAUSE YOU'VE INHERITED THE JAW TITAN...!!
HUH ...?
CONNIE !!
NO!!
STOP !!
STAY BACK !!

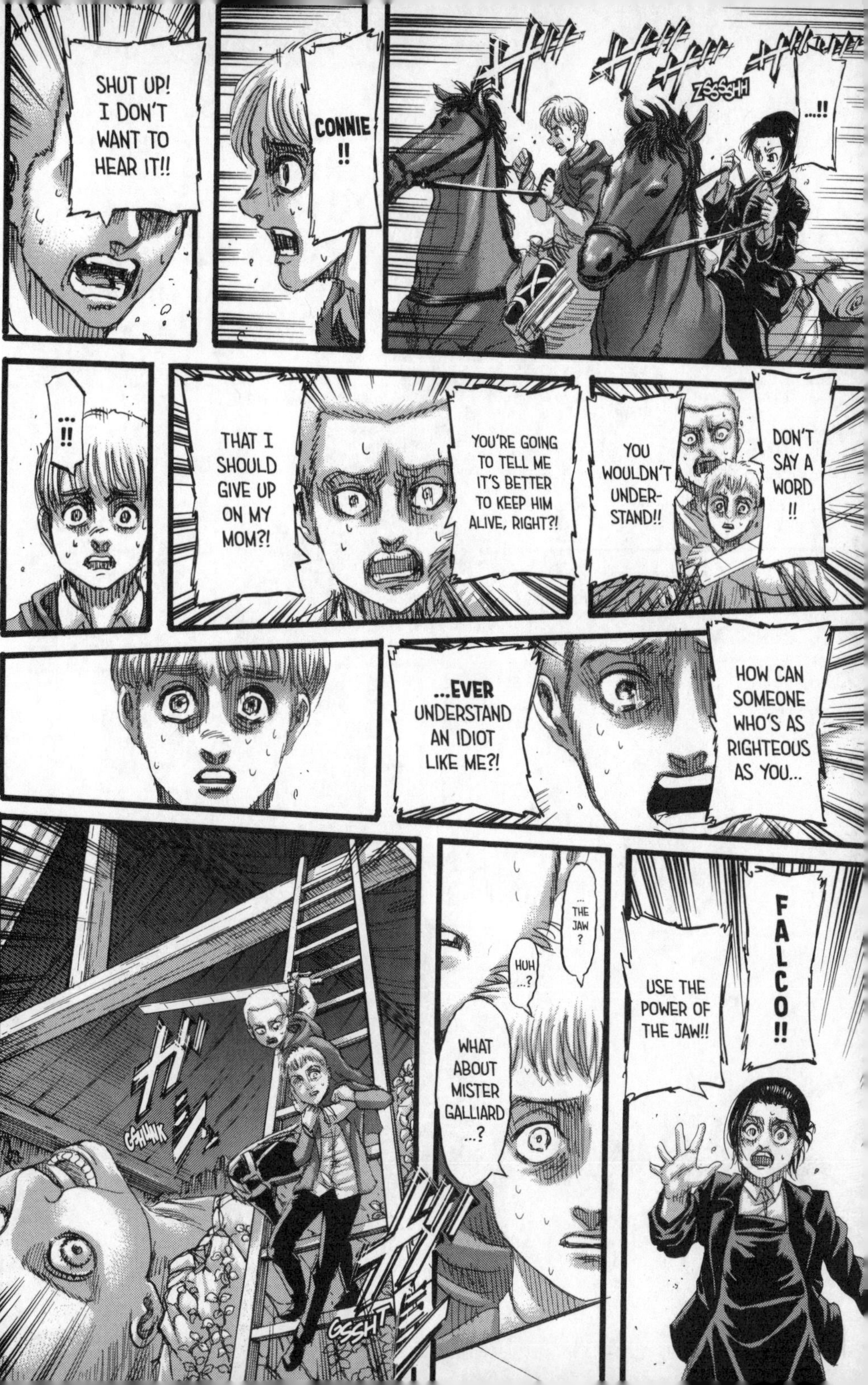
ZSSSSHH
...!!
CONNIE !!
SHUT UP! I DON'T WANT TO HEAR IT!!
DON'T SAY A WORD !!
YOU WOULDN'T UNDER-STAND!!
YOU'RE GOING TO TELL ME IT'S BETTER TO KEEP HIM ALIVE, RIGHT?!
THAT I SHOULD GIVE UP ON MY MOM?!
...!!
HOW CAN SOMEONE WHO'S AS RIGHTEOUS AS YOU...
...EVER UNDERSTAND AN IDIOT LIKE ME?!
FALCO!!
USE THE POWER OF THE JAW!!
...THE JAW?
HUH...?
WHAT ABOUT MISTER GALLIARD...?
GSHUNK
GSSHT

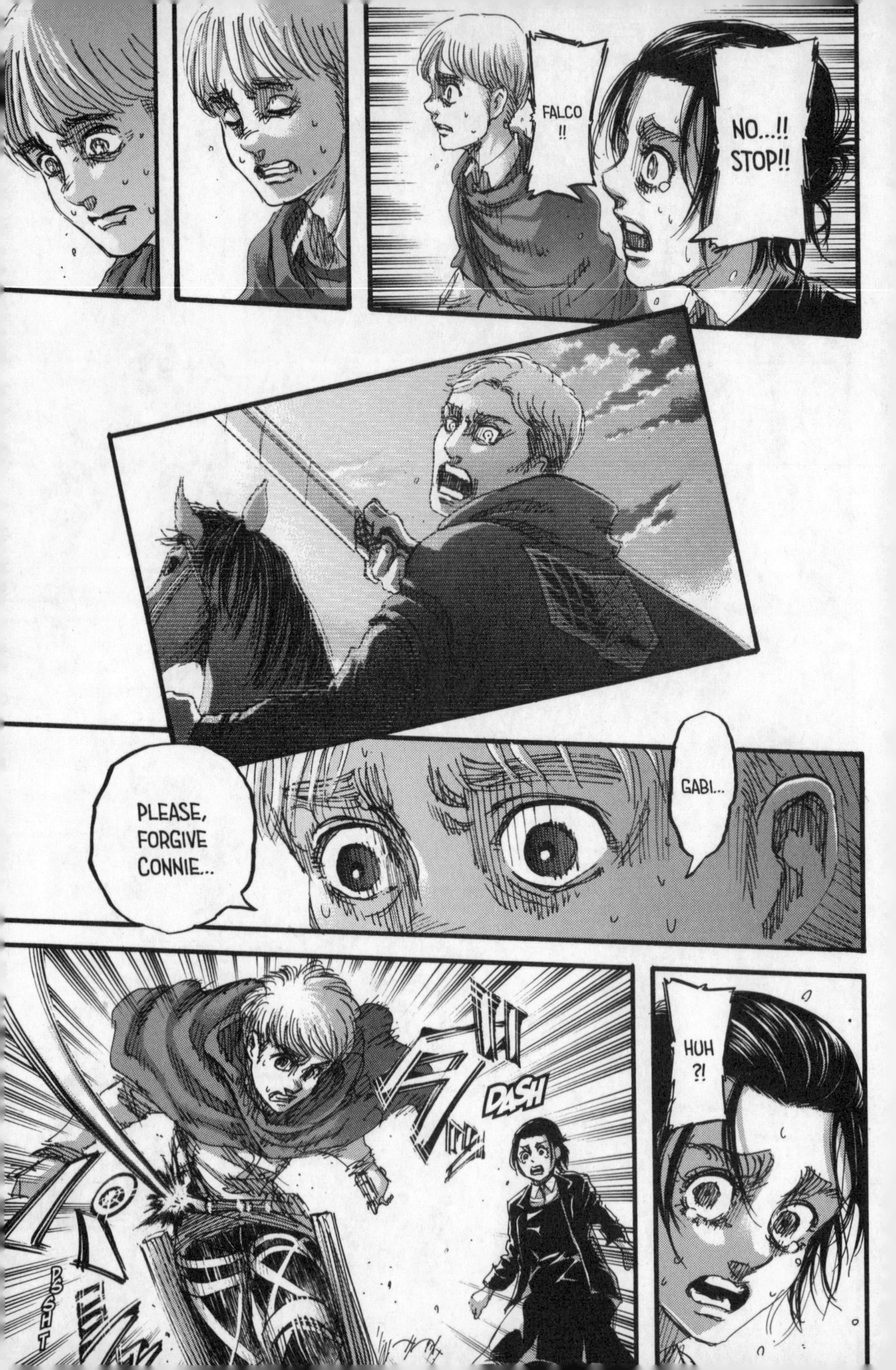
NO...!! STOP!!
FALCO !!
GABI...
PLEASE, FORGIVE CONNIE...
HUH ?!
DASH
PSSHT

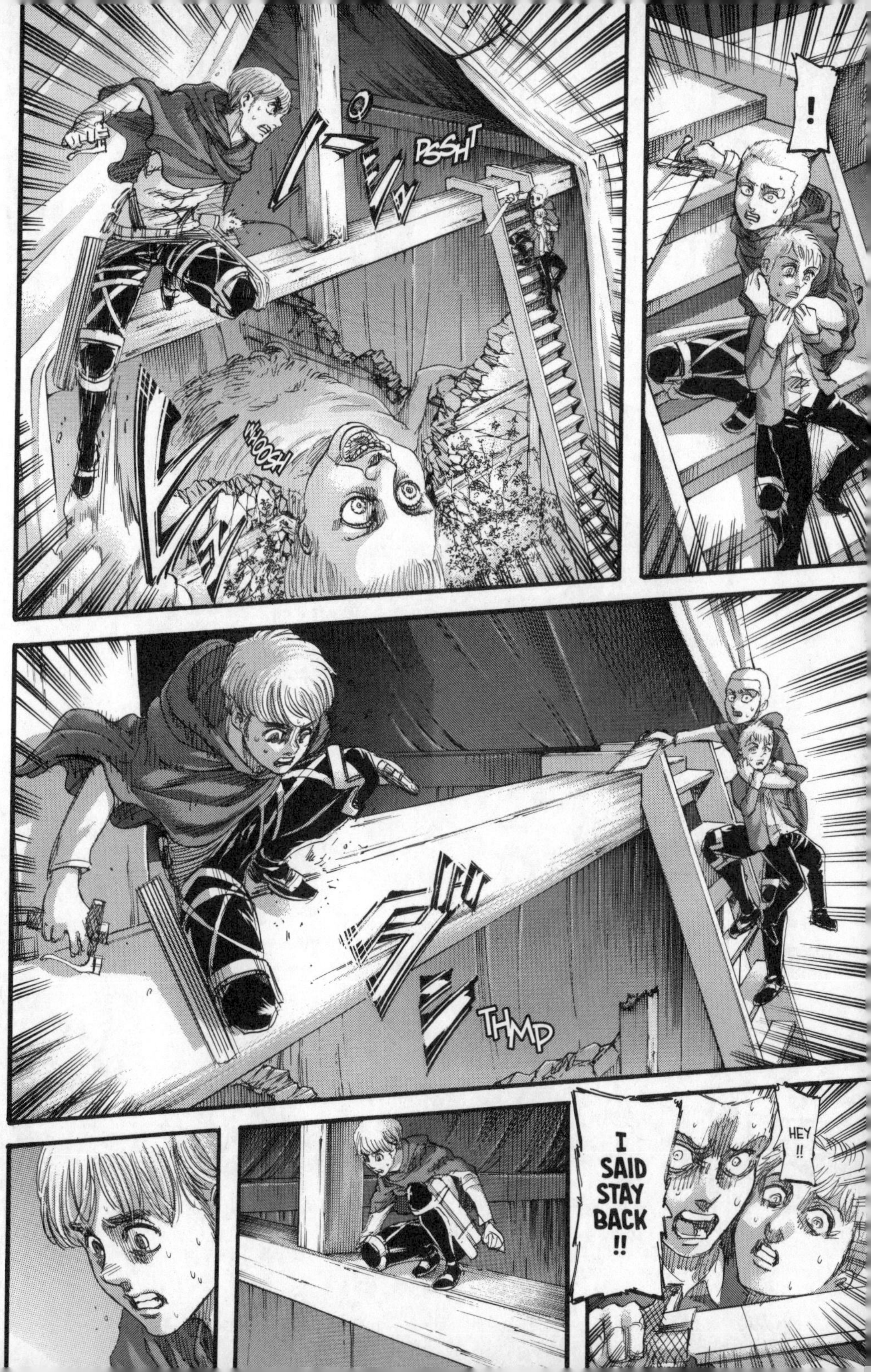
!
PSSHT
WHOOSH
THMP
HEY !!
I SAID STAY BACK !!

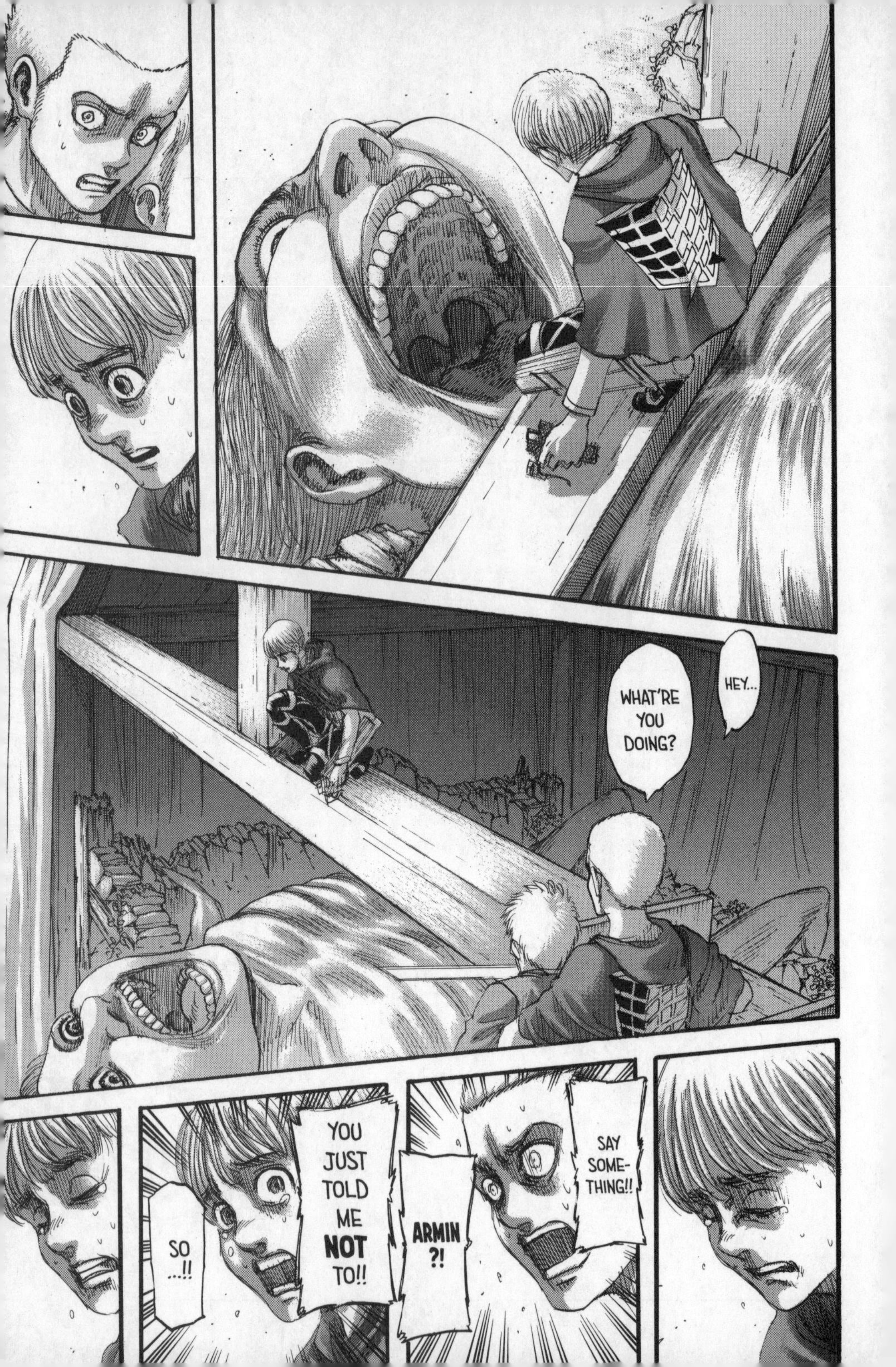
HEY...
WHAT'RE YOU DOING?
SAY SOME-THING!!
ARMIN?!
YOU JUST TOLD ME **NOT** TO!!
SO ...!!

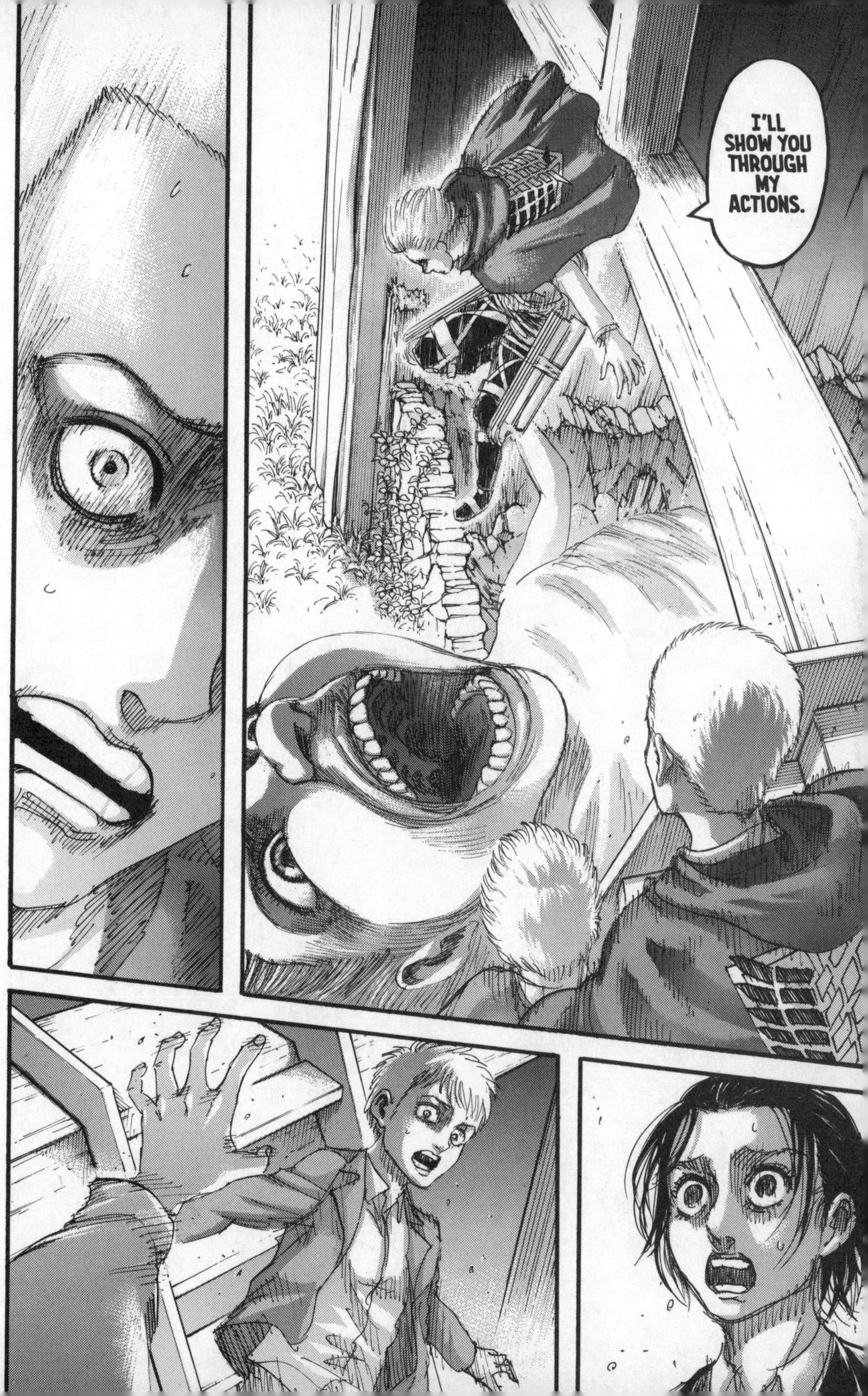
I'LL SHOW YOU THROUGH MY ACTIONS.

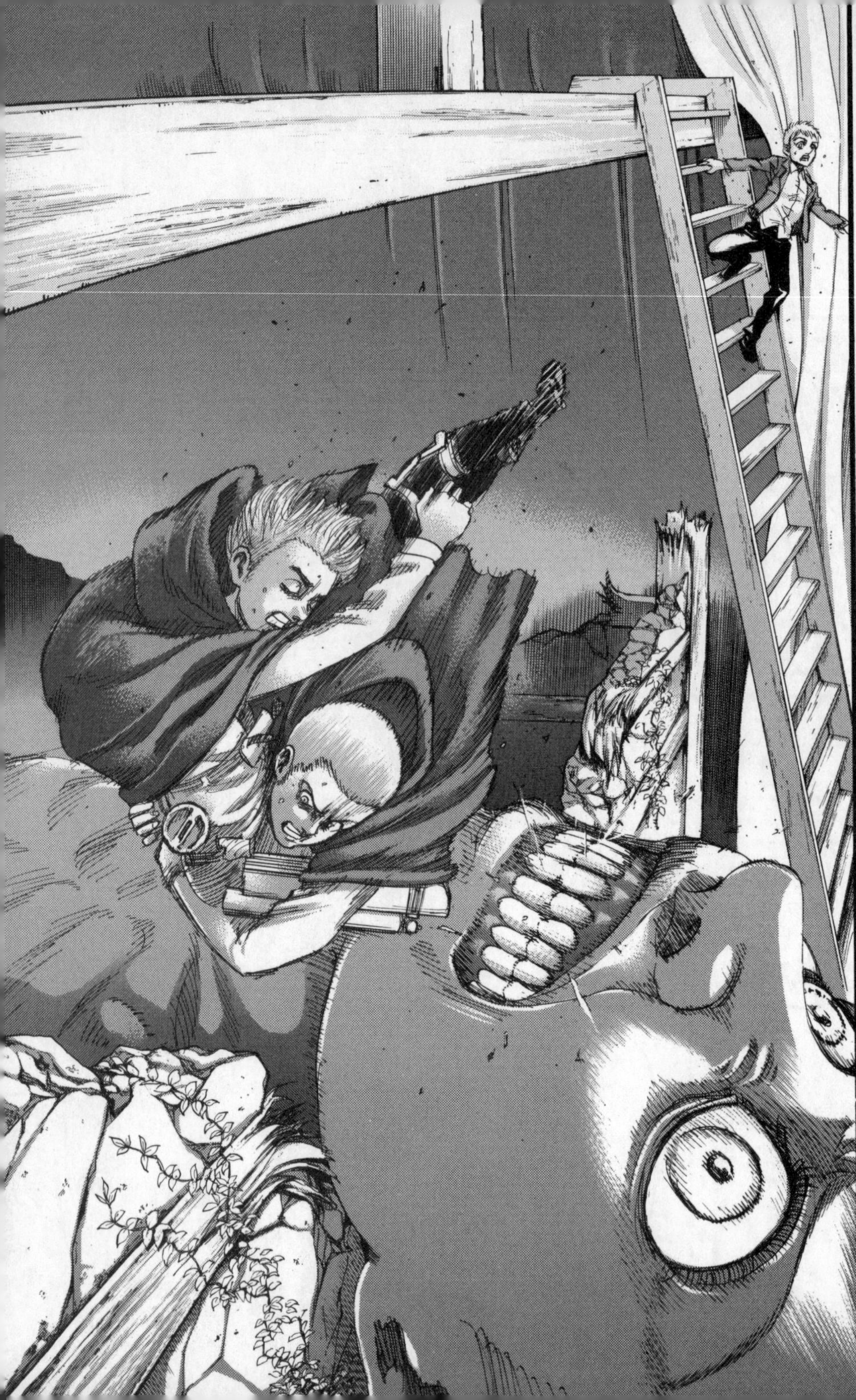

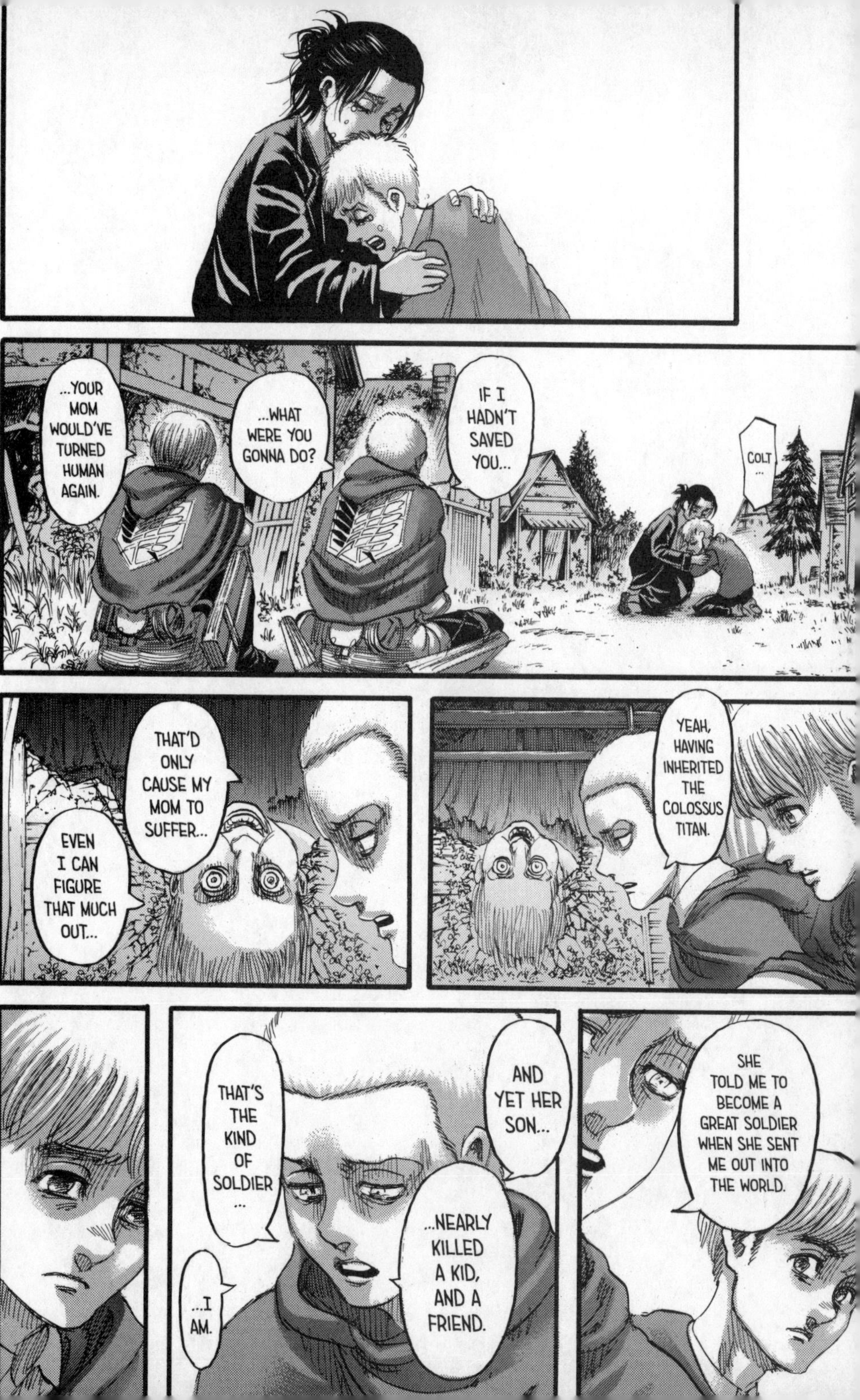
COLT...
IF I HADN'T SAVED YOU...
...WHAT WERE YOU GONNA DO?
...YOUR MOM WOULD'VE TURNED HUMAN AGAIN.
YEAH, HAVING INHERITED THE COLOSSUS TITAN.
THAT'D ONLY CAUSE MY MOM TO SUFFER...
EVEN I CAN FIGURE THAT MUCH OUT...
SHE TOLD ME TO BECOME A GREAT SOLDIER WHEN SHE SENT ME OUT INTO THE WORLD.
AND YET HER SON...
...NEARLY KILLED A KID, AND A FRIEND.
THAT'S THE KIND OF SOLDIER...
...I AM.

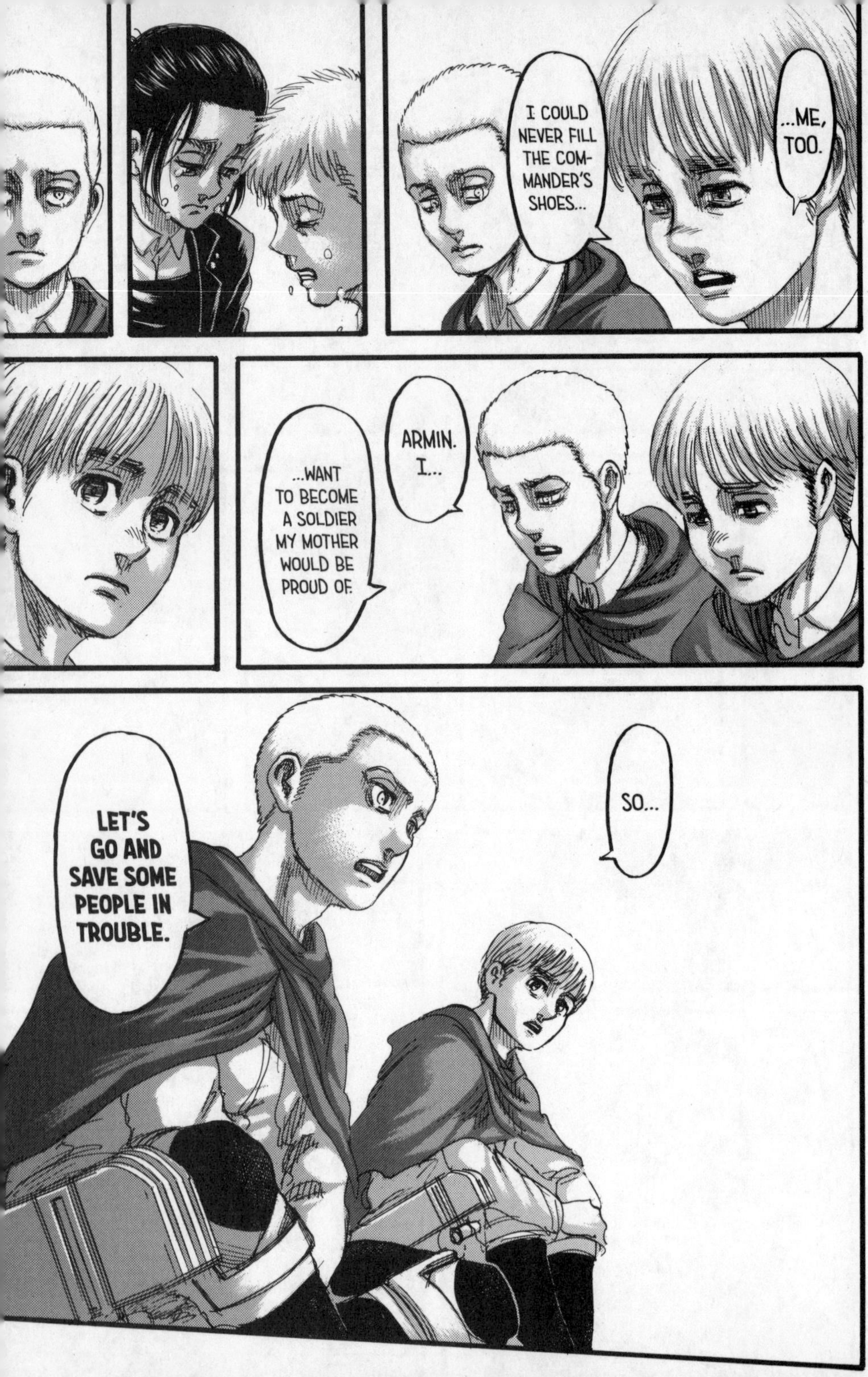
I COULD NEVER FILL THE COMMANDER'S SHOES...
...ME, TOO.
ARMIN. I...
...WANT TO BECOME A SOLDIER MY MOTHER WOULD BE PROUD OF.
SO...
LET'S GO AND SAVE SOME PEOPLE IN TROUBLE.

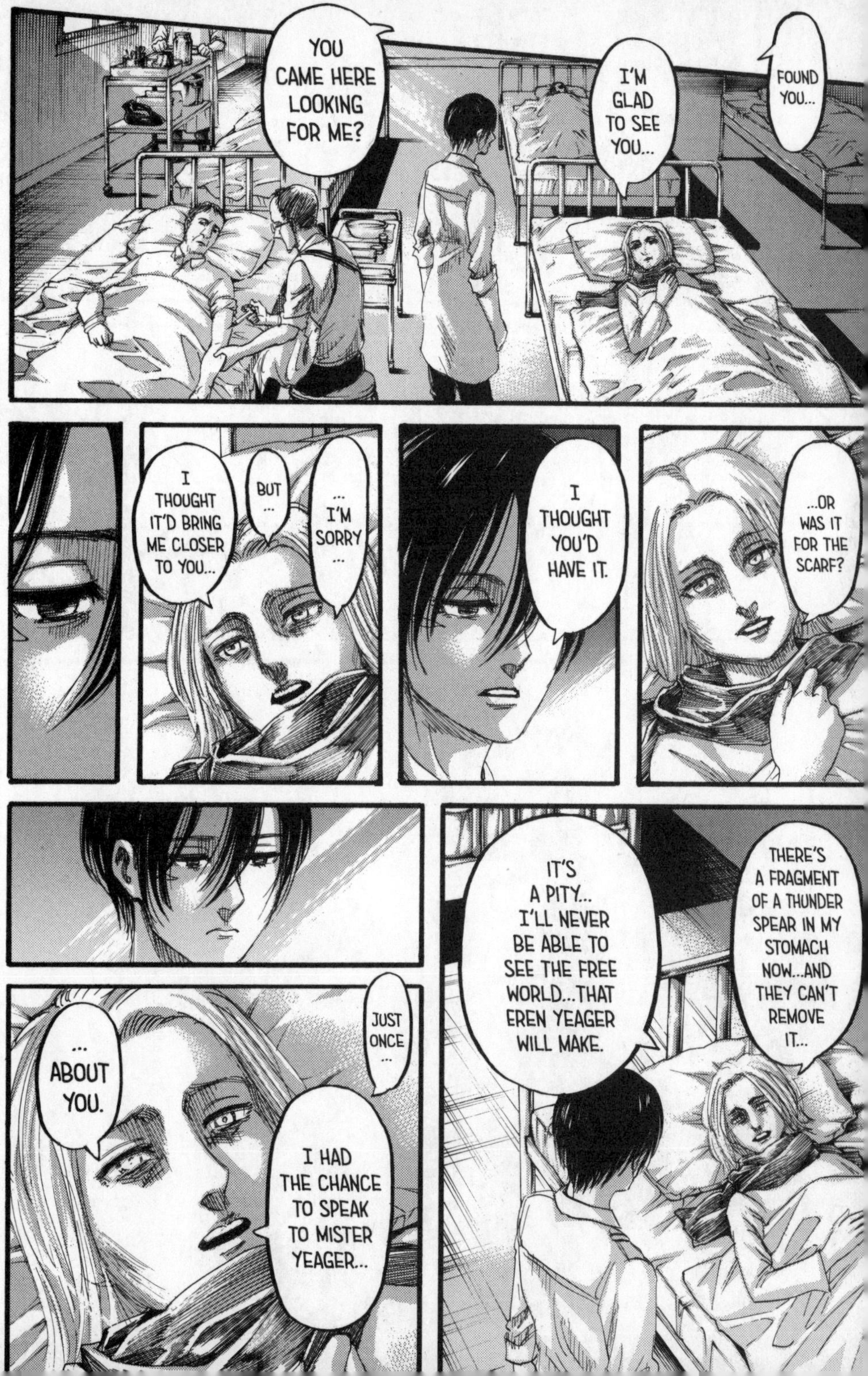
FOUND YOU...
I'M GLAD TO SEE YOU...
YOU CAME HERE LOOKING FOR ME?
...OR WAS IT FOR THE SCARF?
I THOUGHT YOU'D HAVE IT.
... I'M SORRY ...
BUT ...
I THOUGHT IT'D BRING ME CLOSER TO YOU...
THERE'S A FRAGMENT OF A THUNDER SPEAR IN MY STOMACH NOW...AND THEY CAN'T REMOVE IT...
IT'S A PITY... I'LL NEVER BE ABLE TO SEE THE FREE WORLD...THAT EREN YEAGER WILL MAKE.
JUST ONCE ...
I HAD THE CHANCE TO SPEAK TO MISTER YEAGER...
... ABOUT YOU.

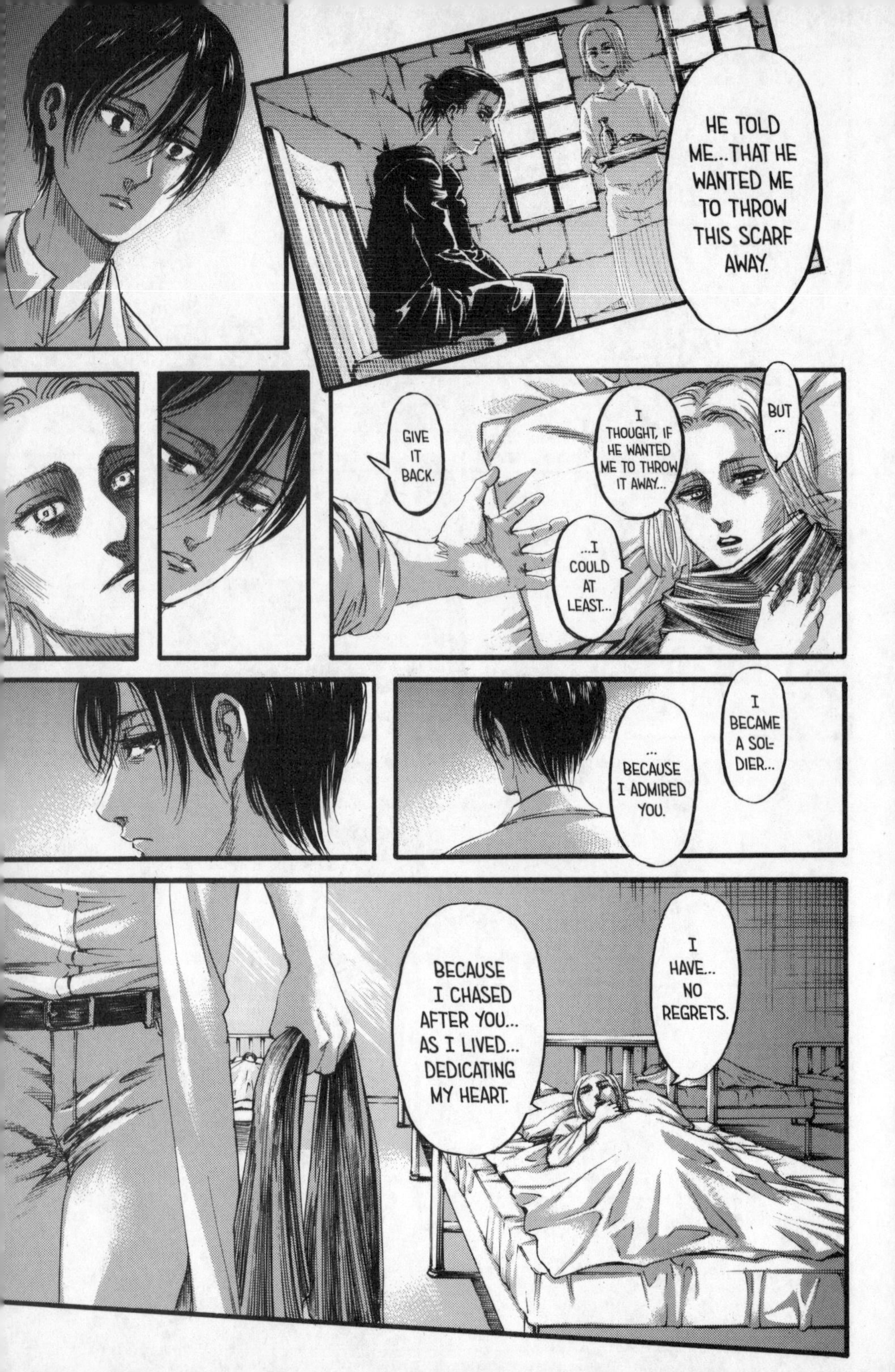
HE TOLD ME...THAT HE WANTED ME TO THROW THIS SCARF AWAY.
BUT ...
I THOUGHT, IF HE WANTED ME TO THROW IT AWAY...
...I COULD AT LEAST...
GIVE IT BACK.
I BECAME A SOL-DIER...
... BECAUSE I ADMIRED YOU.
I HAVE... NO REGRETS.
BECAUSE I CHASED AFTER YOU... AS I LIVED... DEDICATING MY HEART.

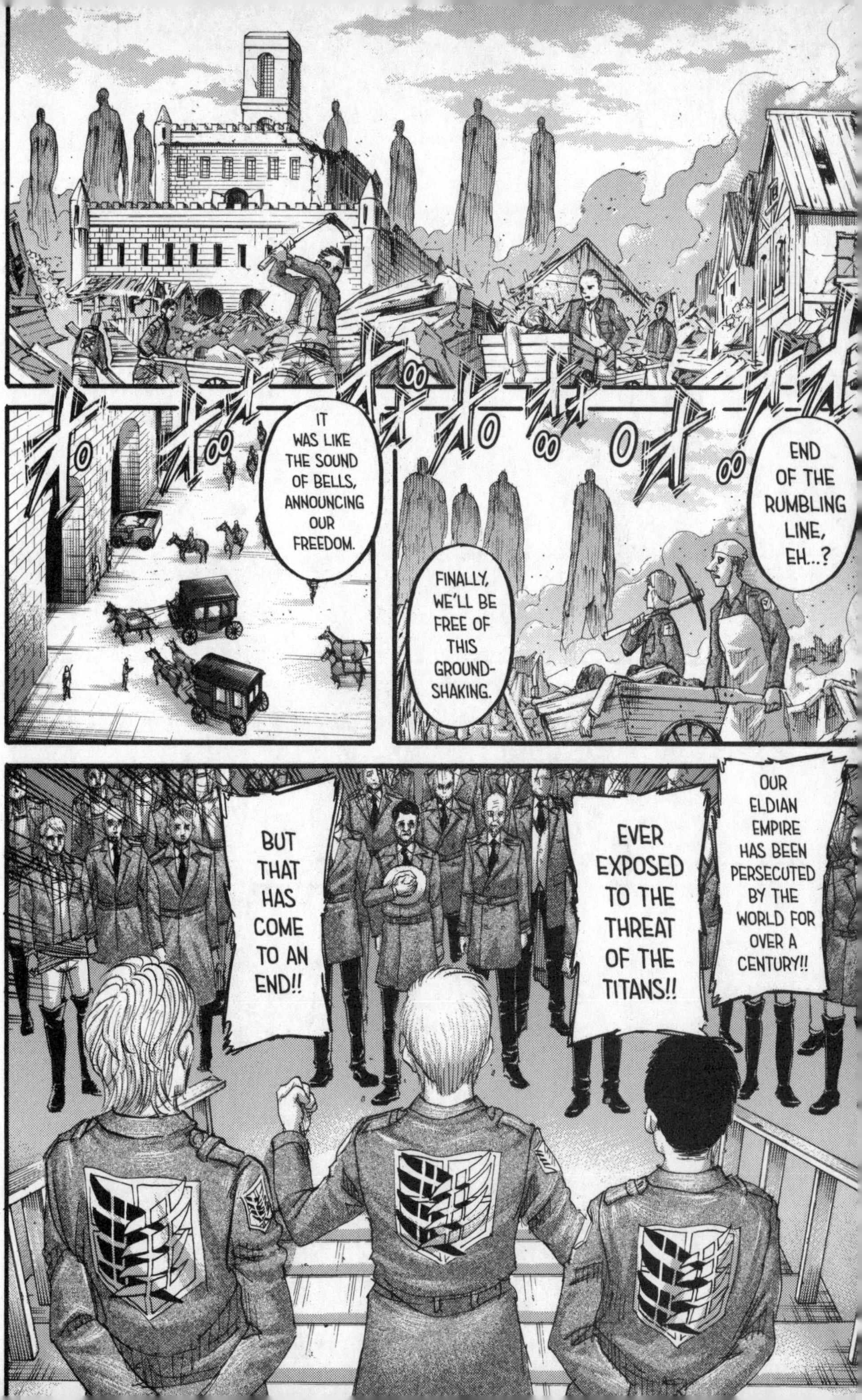
END OF THE RUMBLING LINE, EH...?
FINALLY, WE'LL BE FREE OF THIS GROUND-SHAKING.
IT WAS LIKE THE SOUND OF BELLS, ANNOUNCING OUR FREEDOM.
OUR ELDIAN EMPIRE HAS BEEN PERSECUTED BY THE WORLD FOR OVER A CENTURY!!
EVER EXPOSED TO THE THREAT OF THE TITANS!!
BUT THAT HAS COME TO AN END!!

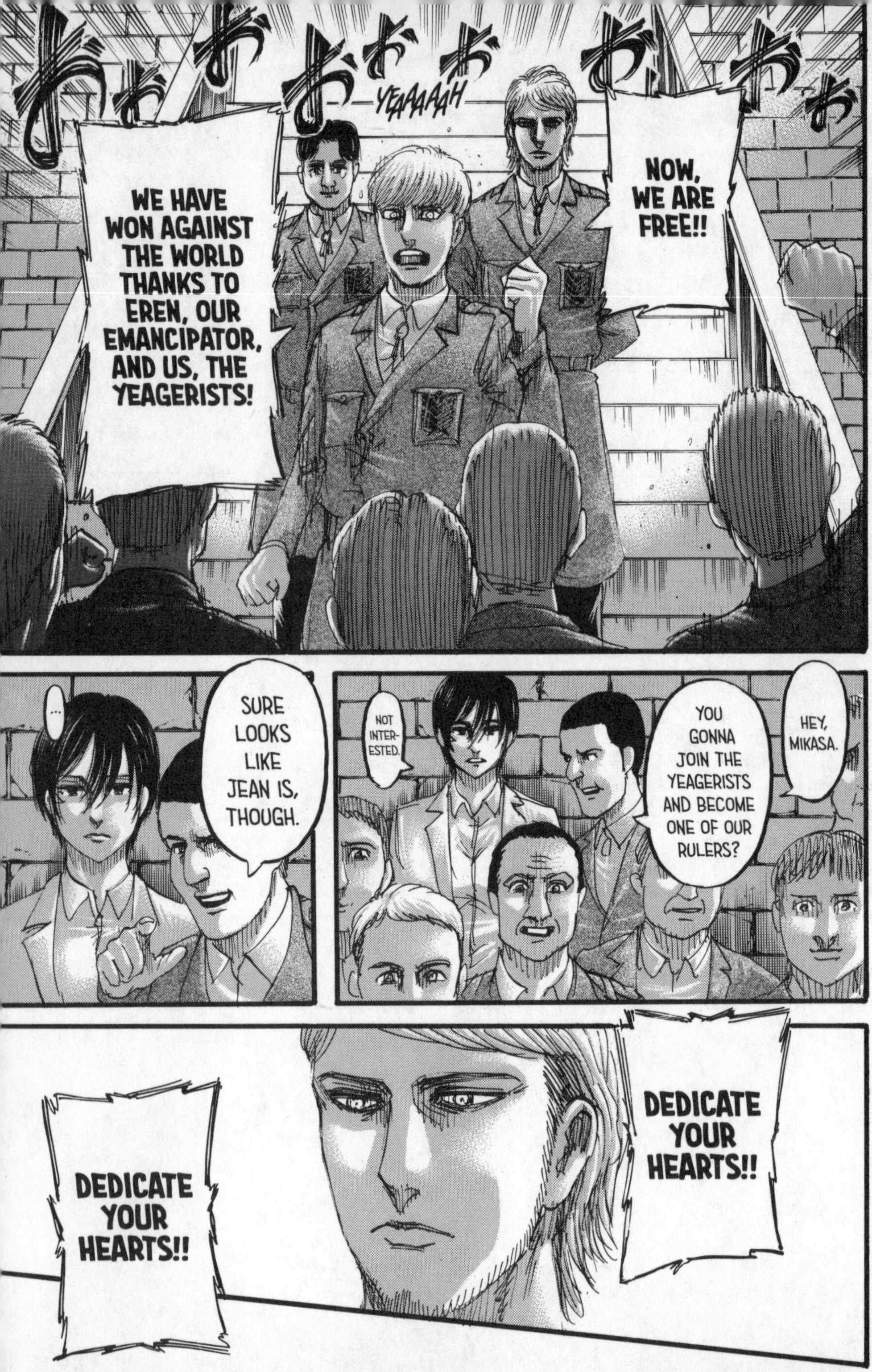
YEAAAAAH
NOW, WE ARE FREE!!
WE HAVE WON AGAINST THE WORLD THANKS TO EREN, OUR EMANCIPATOR, AND US, THE YEAGERISTS!
HEY, MIKASA.
YOU GONNA JOIN THE YEAGERISTS AND BECOME ONE OF OUR RULERS?
NOT INTERESTED.
SURE LOOKS LIKE JEAN IS, THOUGH.
...
DEDICATE YOUR HEARTS!!
DEDICATE YOUR HEARTS!!

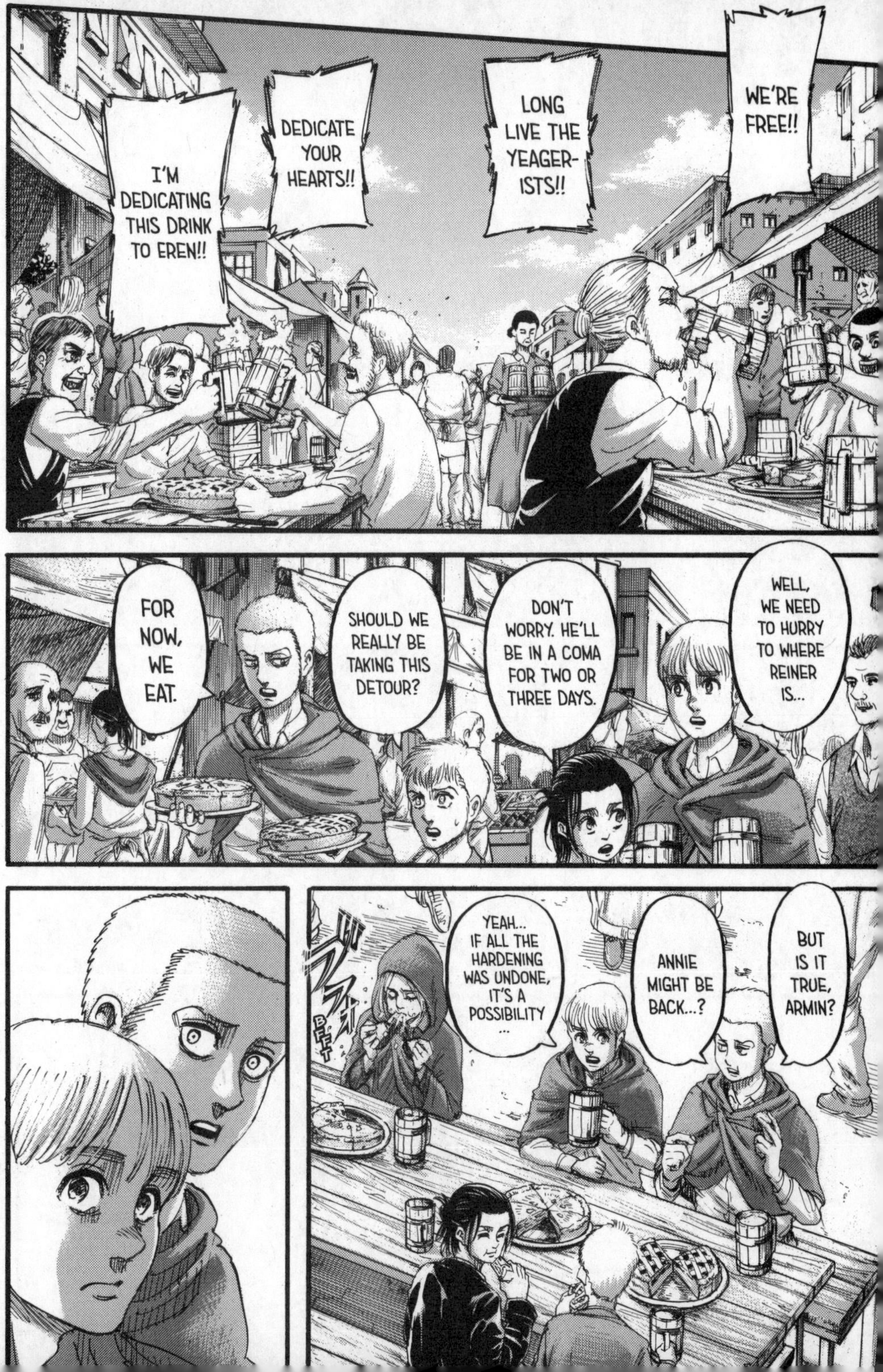

WE'RE FREE!!
LONG LIVE THE YEAGER-ISTS!!
DEDICATE YOUR HEARTS!!
I'M DEDICATING THIS DRINK TO EREN!!
WELL, WE NEED TO HURRY TO WHERE REINER IS...
DON'T WORRY. HE'LL BE IN A COMA FOR TWO OR THREE DAYS.
SHOULD WE REALLY BE TAKING THIS DETOUR?
FOR NOW, WE EAT.
BUT IS IT TRUE, ARMIN?
ANNIE MIGHT BE BACK...?
YEAH... IF ALL THE HARDENING WAS UNDONE, IT'S A POSSIBILITY...
BFFT

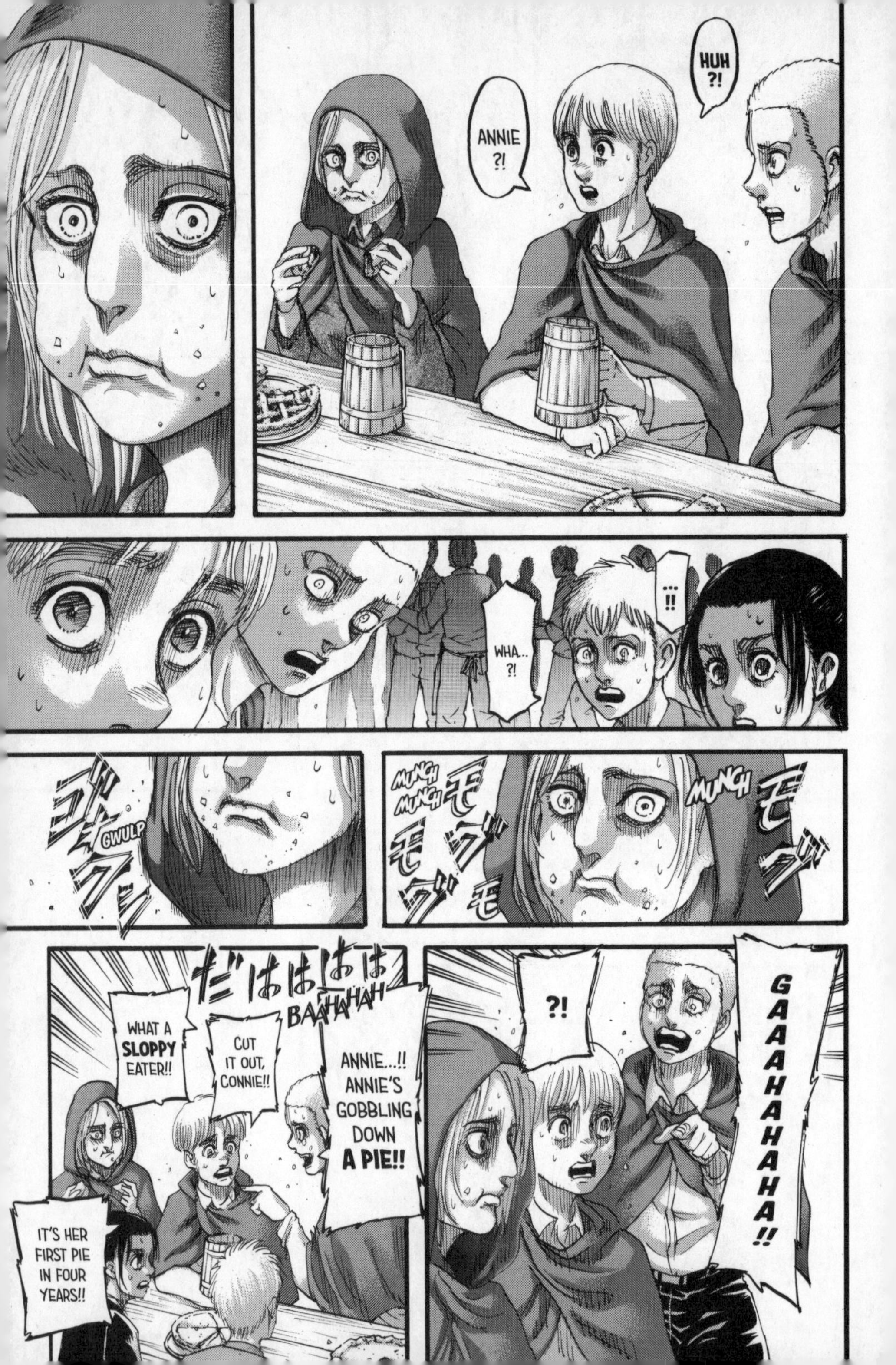
HUH ?!
ANNIE ?!
...!!
WHA... ?!
MUNCH
MUNCH MUNCH
GWULP
GAAAAHAHAHAHA!!
?!
だはははは
BAAHAHAH
ANNIE...!! ANNIE'S GOBBLING DOWN A PIE!!
CUT IT OUT, CONNIE!!
WHAT A SLOPPY EATER!!
IT'S HER FIRST PIE IN FOUR YEARS!!

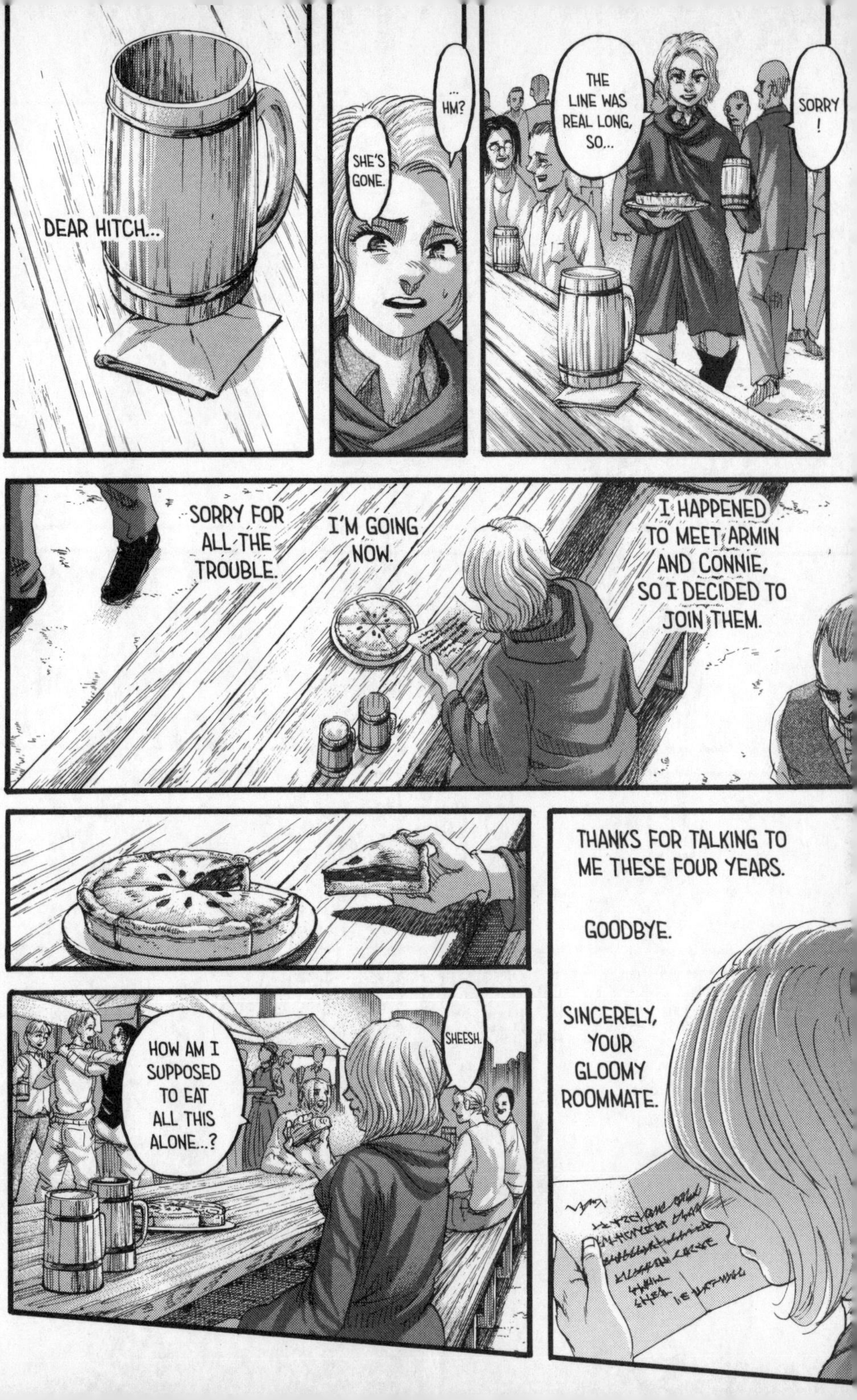
SORRY !
THE LINE WAS REAL LONG, SO...
... HM?
SHE'S GONE.
DEAR HITCH...
I HAPPENED TO MEET ARMIN AND CONNIE, SO I DECIDED TO JOIN THEM.
I'M GOING NOW.
SORRY FOR ALL THE TROUBLE.
THANKS FOR TALKING TO ME THESE FOUR YEARS.
GOODBYE.
SINCERELY, YOUR GLOOMY ROOMMATE.
SHEESH.
HOW AM I SUPPOSED TO EAT ALL THIS ALONE...?

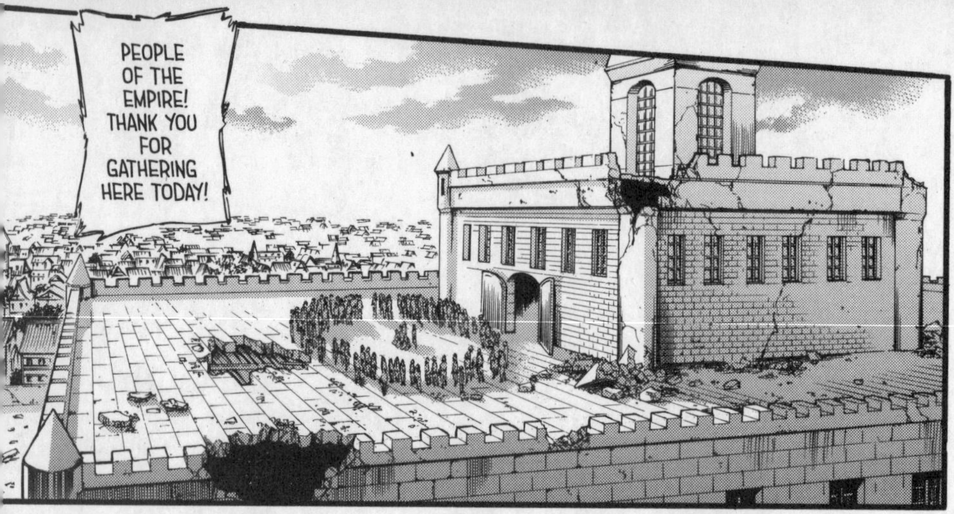
PEOPLE OF THE EMPIRE! THANK YOU FOR GATHERING HERE TODAY!

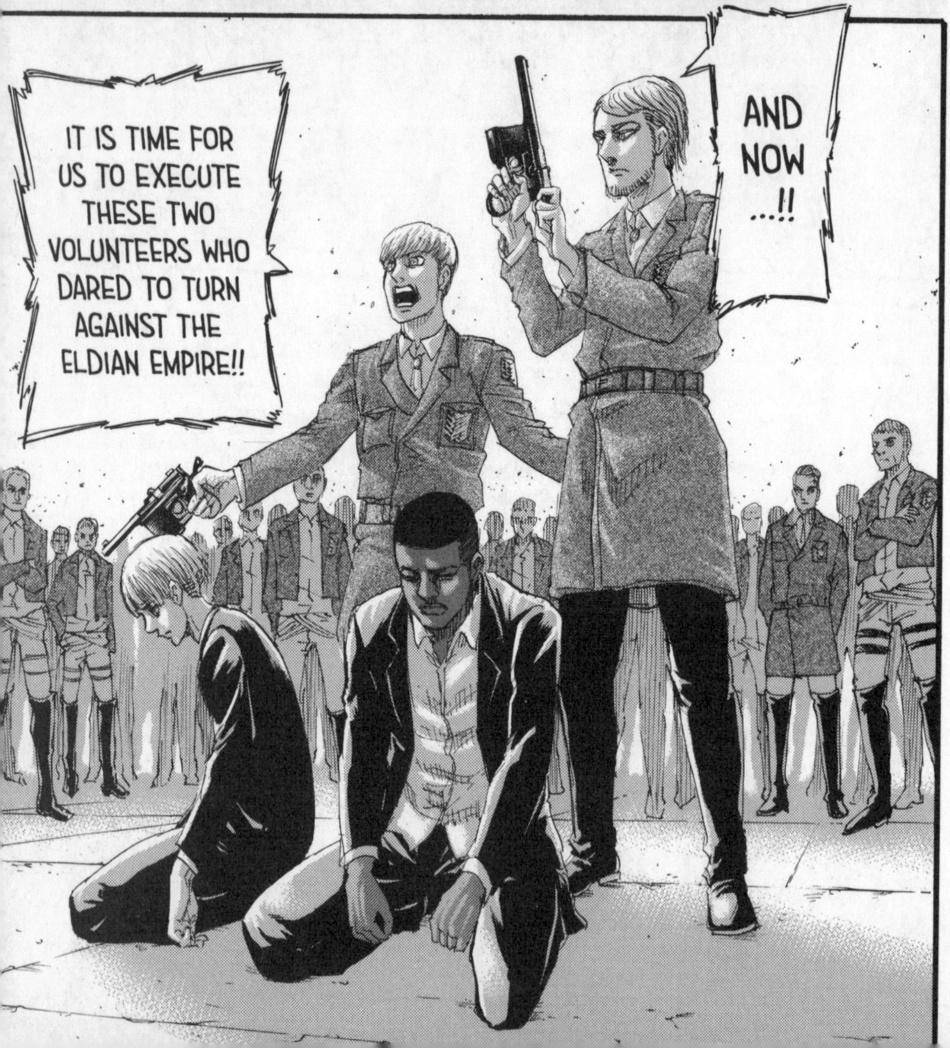
AND NOW ...!!
IT IS TIME FOR US TO EXECUTE THESE TWO VOLUNTEERS WHO DARED TO TURN AGAINST THE ELDIAN EMPIRE!!

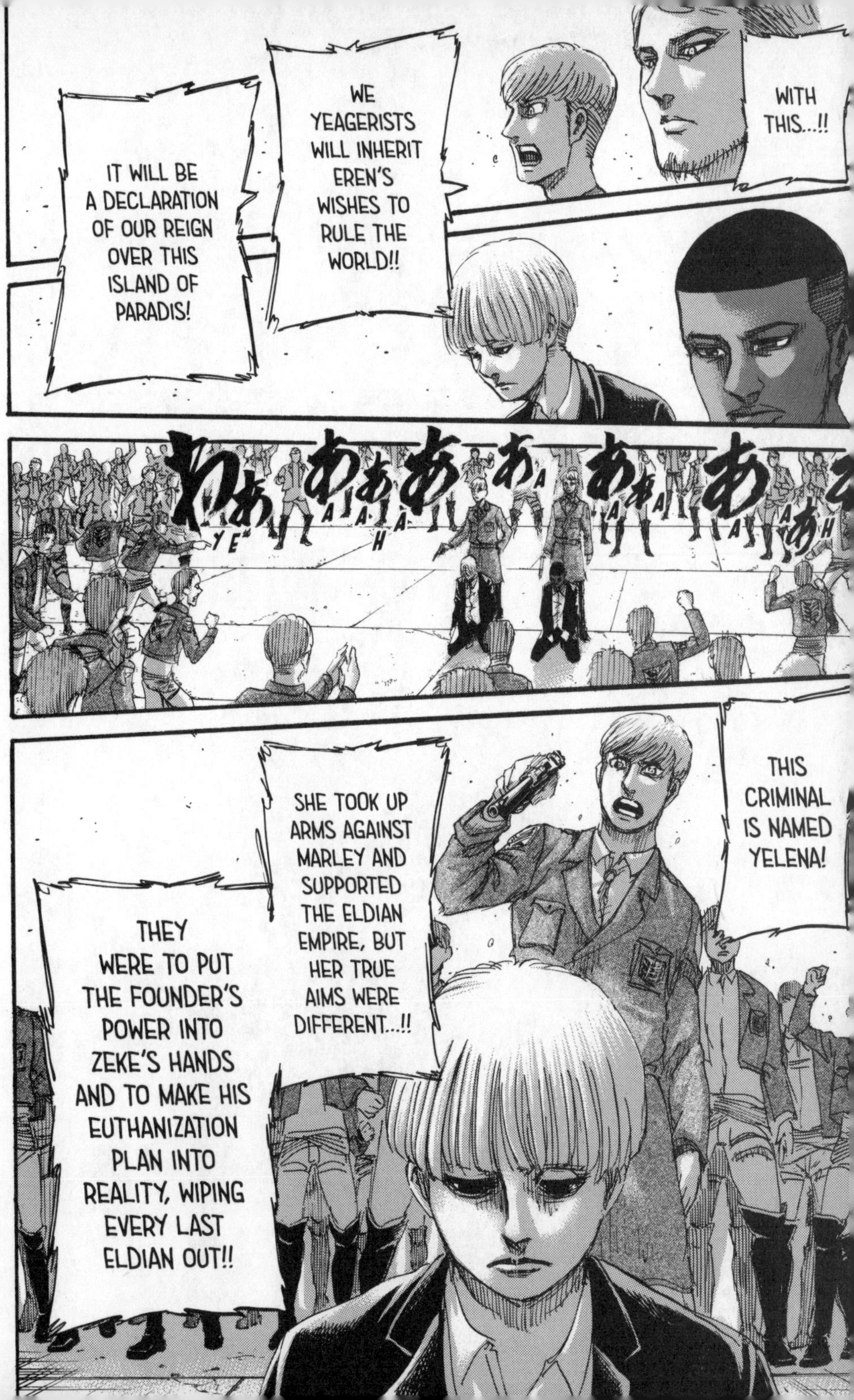

WITH THIS...!!
WE YEAGERISTS WILL INHERIT EREN'S WISHES TO RULE THE WORLD!!
IT WILL BE A DECLARATION OF OUR REIGN OVER THIS ISLAND OF PARADIS!
THIS CRIMINAL IS NAMED YELENA!
SHE TOOK UP ARMS AGAINST MARLEY AND SUPPORTED THE ELDIAN EMPIRE, BUT HER TRUE AIMS WERE DIFFERENT...!!
THEY WERE TO PUT THE FOUNDER'S POWER INTO ZEKE'S HANDS AND TO MAKE HIS EUTHANIZATION PLAN INTO REALITY, WIPING EVERY LAST ELDIAN OUT!!

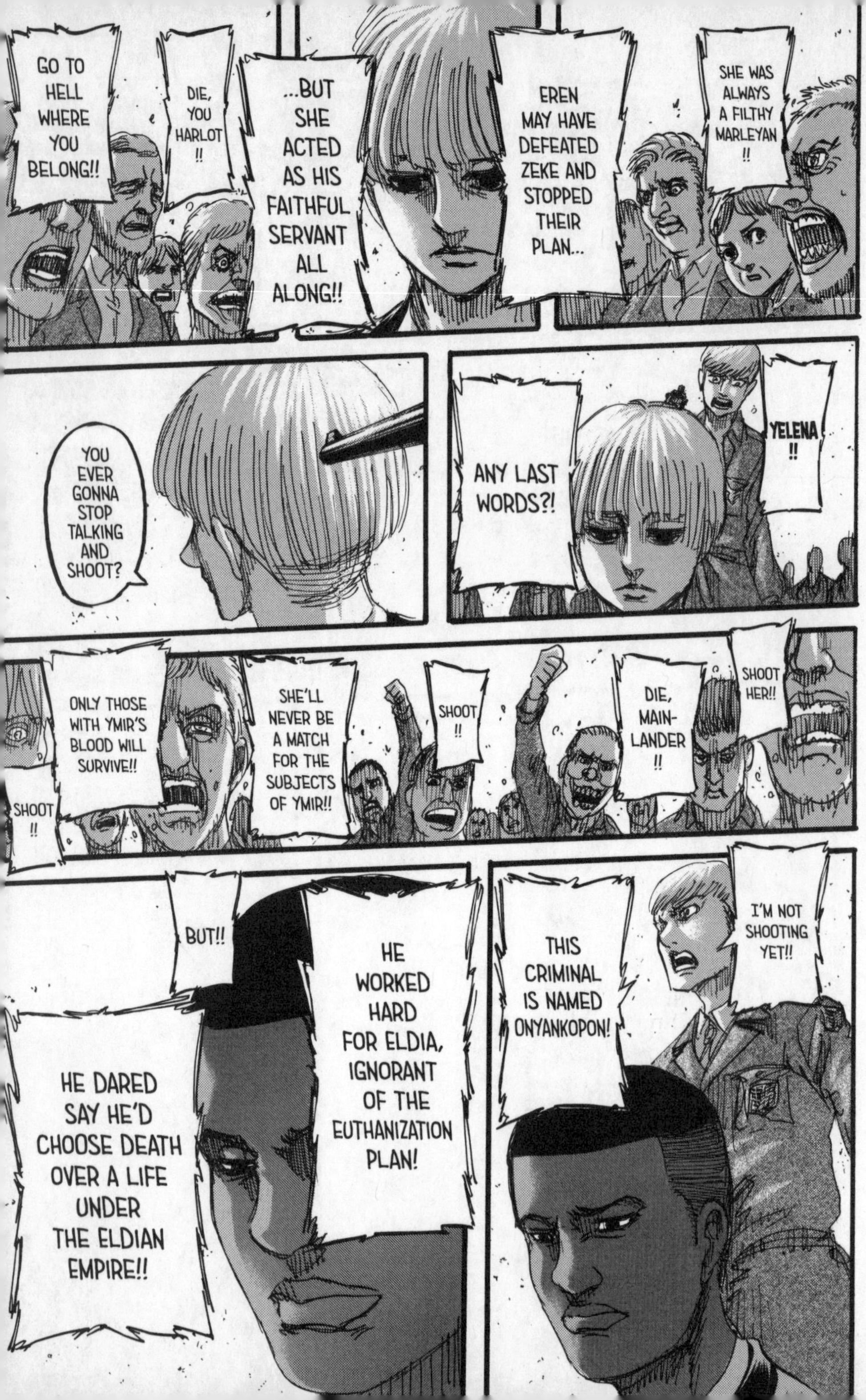
SHE WAS ALWAYS A FILTHY MARLEYAN!!
EREN MAY HAVE DEFEATED ZEKE AND STOPPED THEIR PLAN...
...BUT SHE ACTED AS HIS FAITHFUL SERVANT ALL ALONG!!
DIE, YOU HARLOT!!
GO TO HELL WHERE YOU BELONG!!
YELENA!!
ANY LAST WORDS?!
YOU EVER GONNA STOP TALKING AND SHOOT?
SHOOT HER!!
DIE, MAIN-LANDER!!
SHOOT!!
SHE'LL NEVER BE A MATCH FOR THE SUBJECTS OF YMIR!!
ONLY THOSE WITH YMIR'S BLOOD WILL SURVIVE!!
SHOOT!!
I'M NOT SHOOTING YET!!
THIS CRIMINAL IS NAMED ONYANKOPON!
HE WORKED HARD FOR ELDIA, IGNORANT OF THE EUTHANIZATION PLAN!
BUT!!
HE DARED SAY HE'D CHOOSE DEATH OVER A LIFE UNDER THE ELDIAN EMPIRE!!

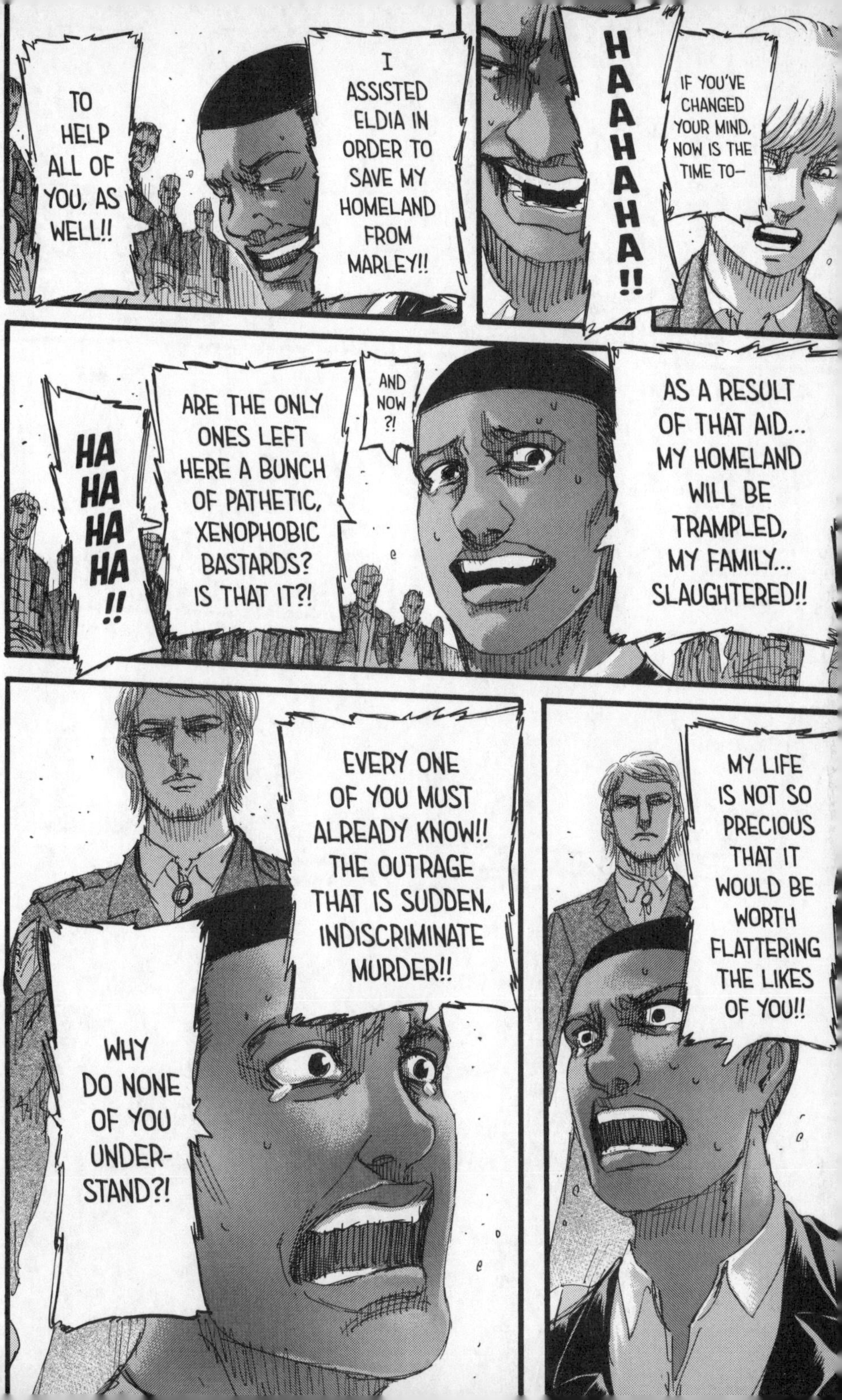
IF YOU'VE CHANGED YOUR MIND, NOW IS THE TIME TO—
HAHAHAHA!!
I ASSISTED ELDIA IN ORDER TO SAVE MY HOMELAND FROM MARLEY!!
TO HELP ALL OF YOU, AS WELL!!
AS A RESULT OF THAT AID... MY HOMELAND WILL BE TRAMPLED, MY FAMILY... SLAUGHTERED!!
AND NOW?!
ARE THE ONLY ONES LEFT HERE A BUNCH OF PATHETIC, XENOPHOBIC BASTARDS? IS THAT IT?!
HA HA HA HA!!
MY LIFE IS NOT SO PRECIOUS THAT IT WOULD BE WORTH FLATTERING THE LIKES OF YOU!!
EVERY ONE OF YOU MUST ALREADY KNOW!! THE OUTRAGE THAT IS SUDDEN, INDISCRIMINATE MURDER!!
WHY DO NONE OF YOU UNDERSTAND?!

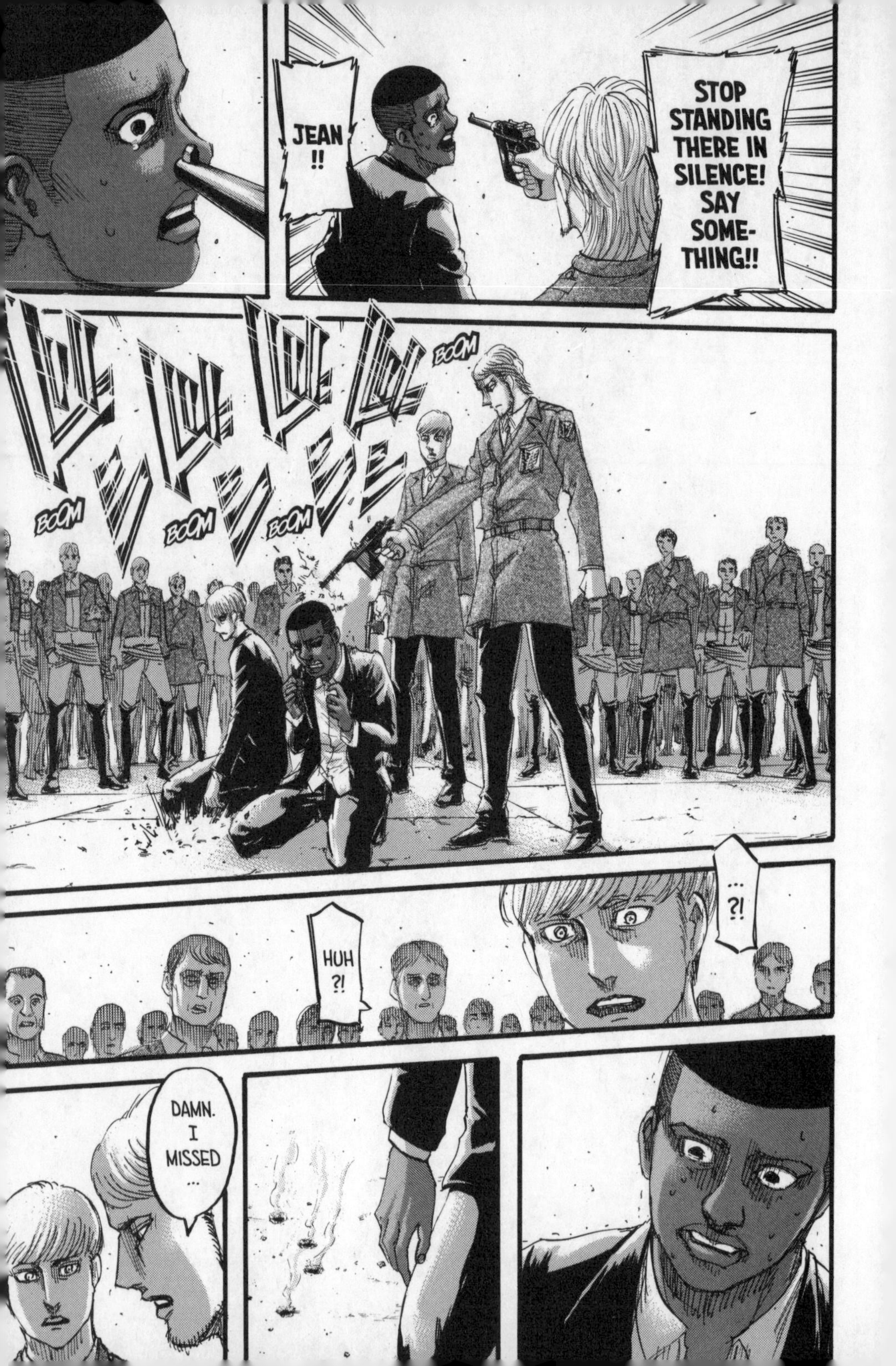
STOP STANDING THERE IN SILENCE! SAY SOME-THING!!
JEAN !!
BOOM
BOOM
BOOM
BOOM
...?!
HUH ?!
DAMN. I MISSED ...

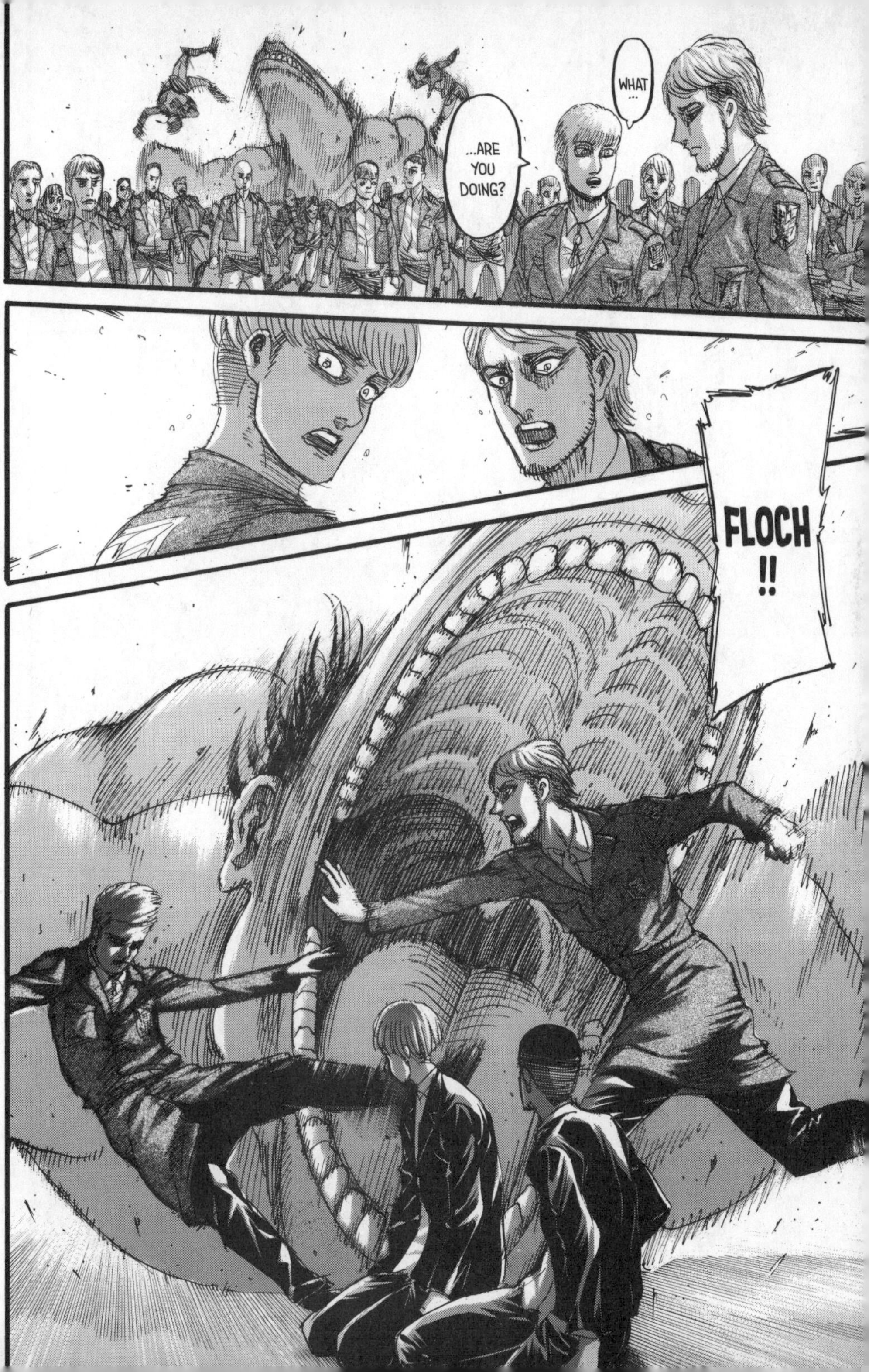
WHAT ...
...ARE YOU DOING?
FLOCH !!

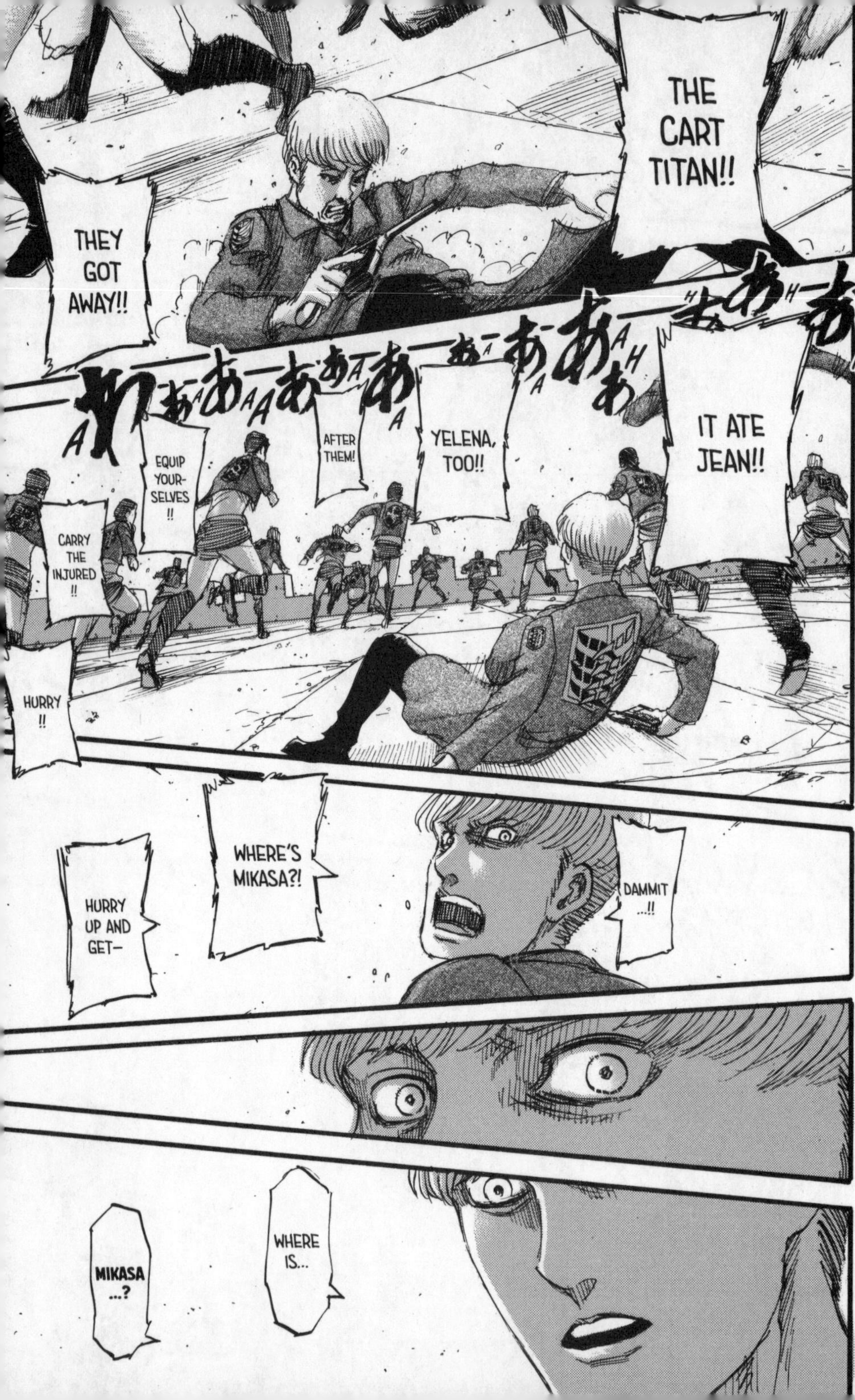
THE CART TITAN!!
THEY GOT AWAY!!
IT ATE JEAN!!
YELENA, TOO!!
AFTER THEM!
EQUIP YOURSELVES!!
CARRY THE INJURED!!
HURRY!!
DAMMIT...!!
WHERE'S MIKASA?!
HURRY UP AND GET–
WHERE IS...
MIKASA...?

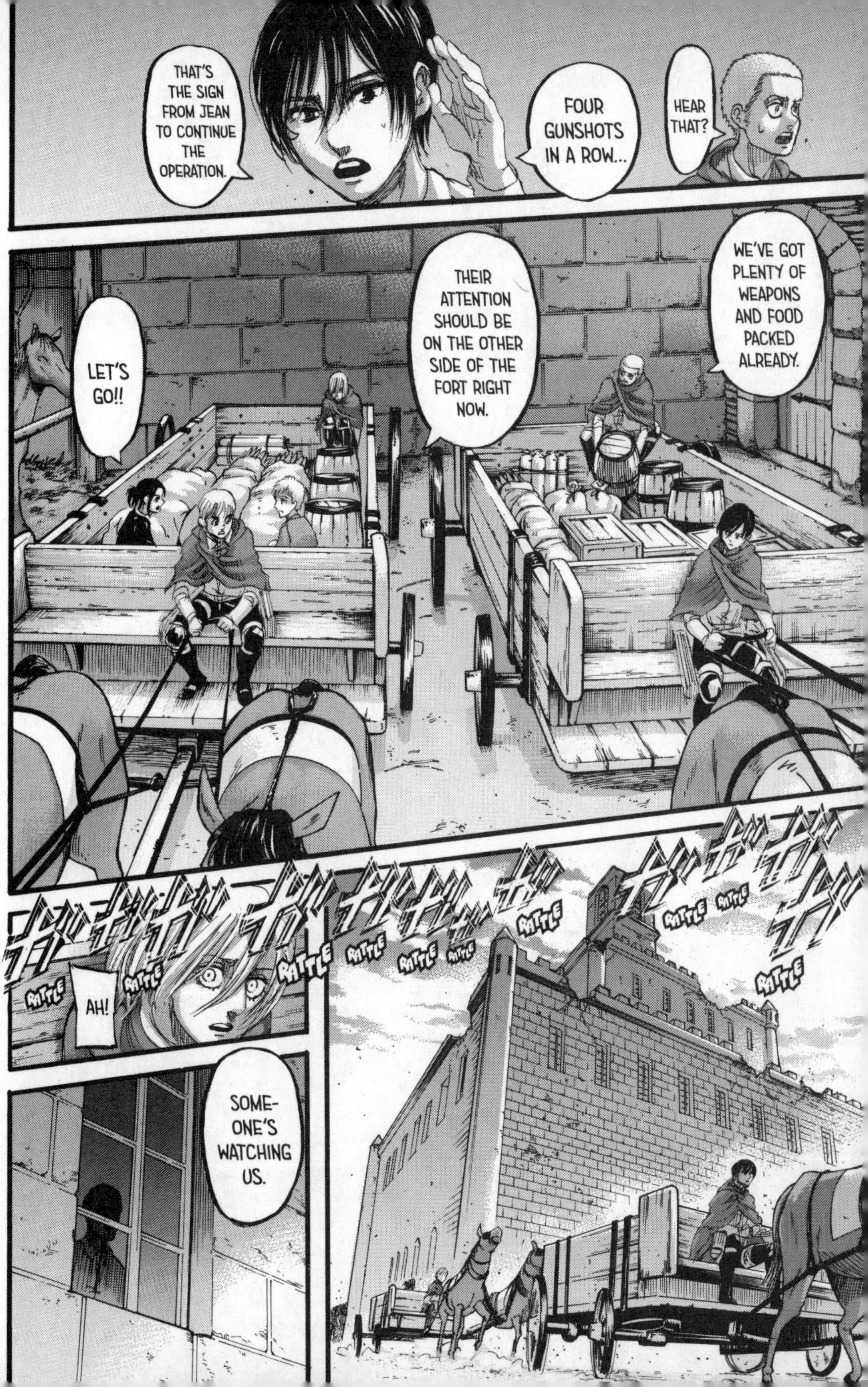
HEAR THAT?
FOUR GUNSHOTS IN A ROW...
THAT'S THE SIGN FROM JEAN TO CONTINUE THE OPERATION.
WE'VE GOT PLENTY OF WEAPONS AND FOOD PACKED ALREADY.
THEIR ATTENTION SHOULD BE ON THE OTHER SIDE OF THE FORT RIGHT NOW.
LET'S GO!!
RATTLE
RATTLE
RATTLE
RATTLE
RATTLE
RATTLE
RATTLE
RATTLE
RATTLE
RATTLE
AH!
SOME-ONE'S WATCHING US.

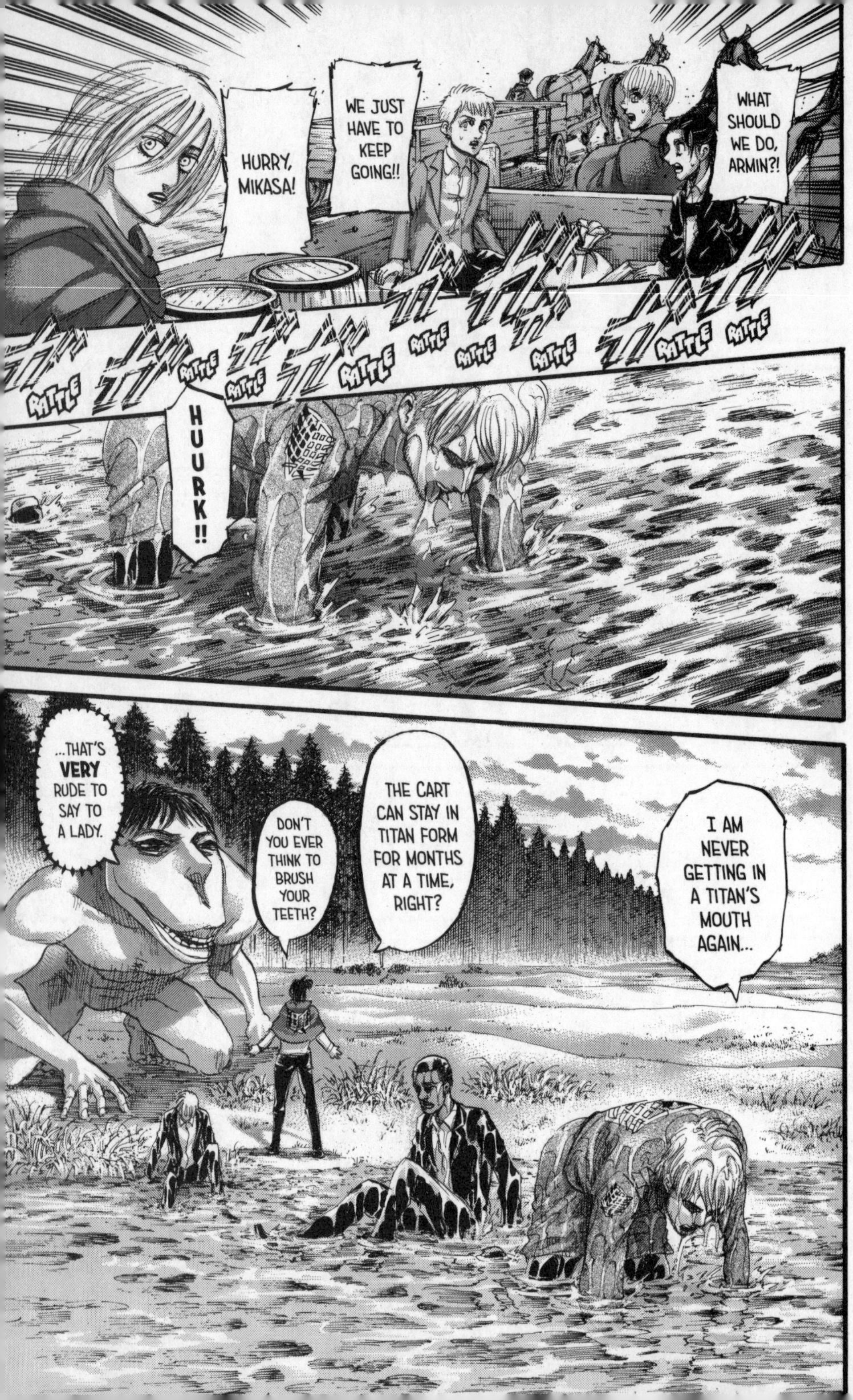
WHAT SHOULD WE DO, ARMIN?!
WE JUST HAVE TO KEEP GOING!!
HURRY, MIKASA!
RATTLE
RATTLE
RATTLE
RATTLE
RATTLE
RATTLE
RATTLE
RATTLE
RATTLE
HUURK!!
I AM NEVER GETTING IN A TITAN'S MOUTH AGAIN...
THE CART CAN STAY IN TITAN FORM FOR MONTHS AT A TIME, RIGHT?
DON'T YOU EVER THINK TO BRUSH YOUR TEETH?
...THAT'S VERY RUDE TO SAY TO A LADY.

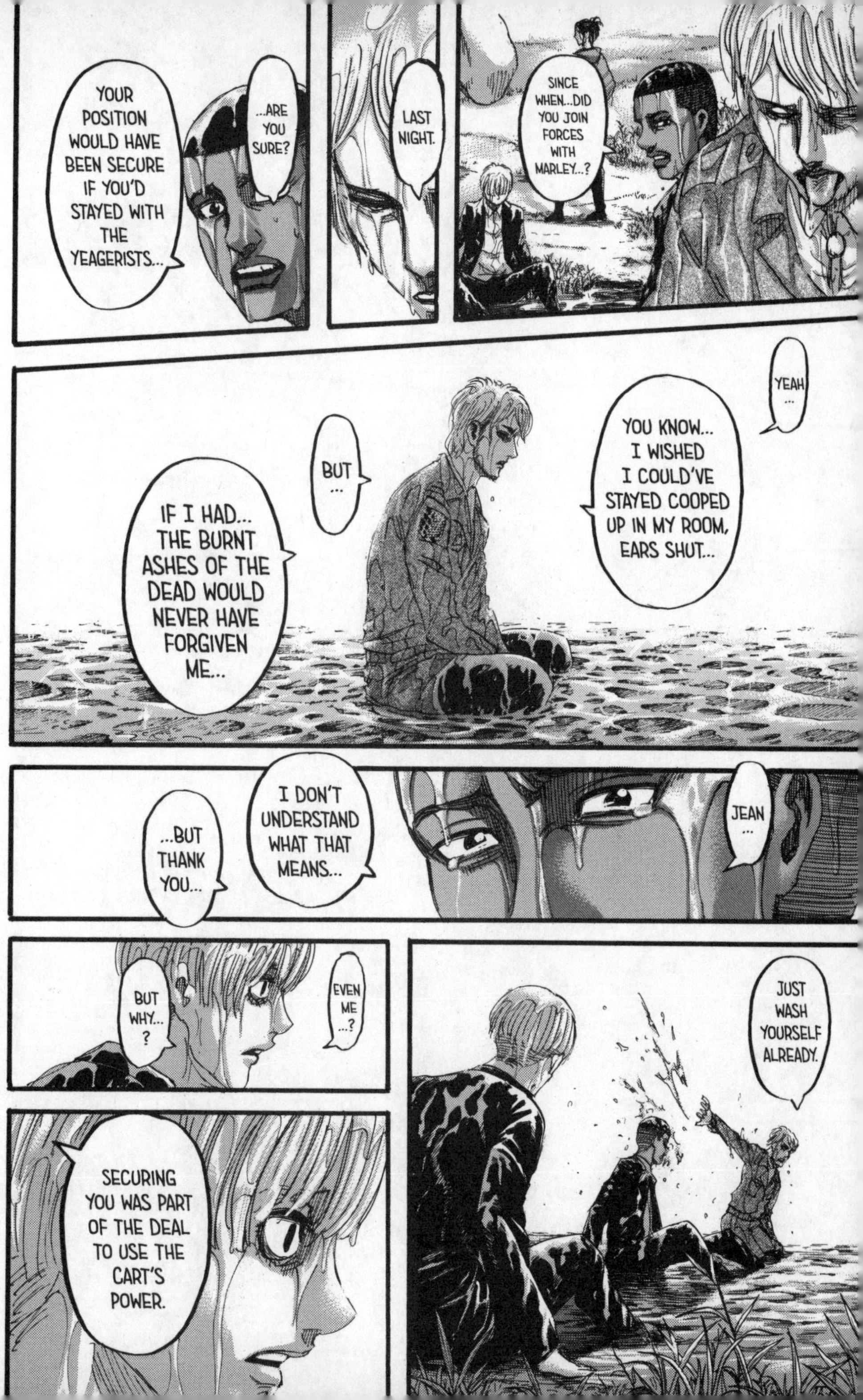

SINCE WHEN...DID YOU JOIN FORCES WITH MARLEY...?
LAST NIGHT.
...ARE YOU SURE?
YOUR POSITION WOULD HAVE BEEN SECURE IF YOU'D STAYED WITH THE YEAGERISTS...
YEAH...
YOU KNOW... I WISHED I COULD'VE STAYED COOPED UP IN MY ROOM, EARS SHUT...
BUT...
IF I HAD... THE BURNT ASHES OF THE DEAD WOULD NEVER HAVE FORGIVEN ME...
JEAN...
I DON'T UNDERSTAND WHAT THAT MEANS...
...BUT THANK YOU...
JUST WASH YOURSELF ALREADY.
EVEN ME...?
BUT WHY...?
SECURING YOU WAS PART OF THE DEAL TO USE THE CART'S POWER.

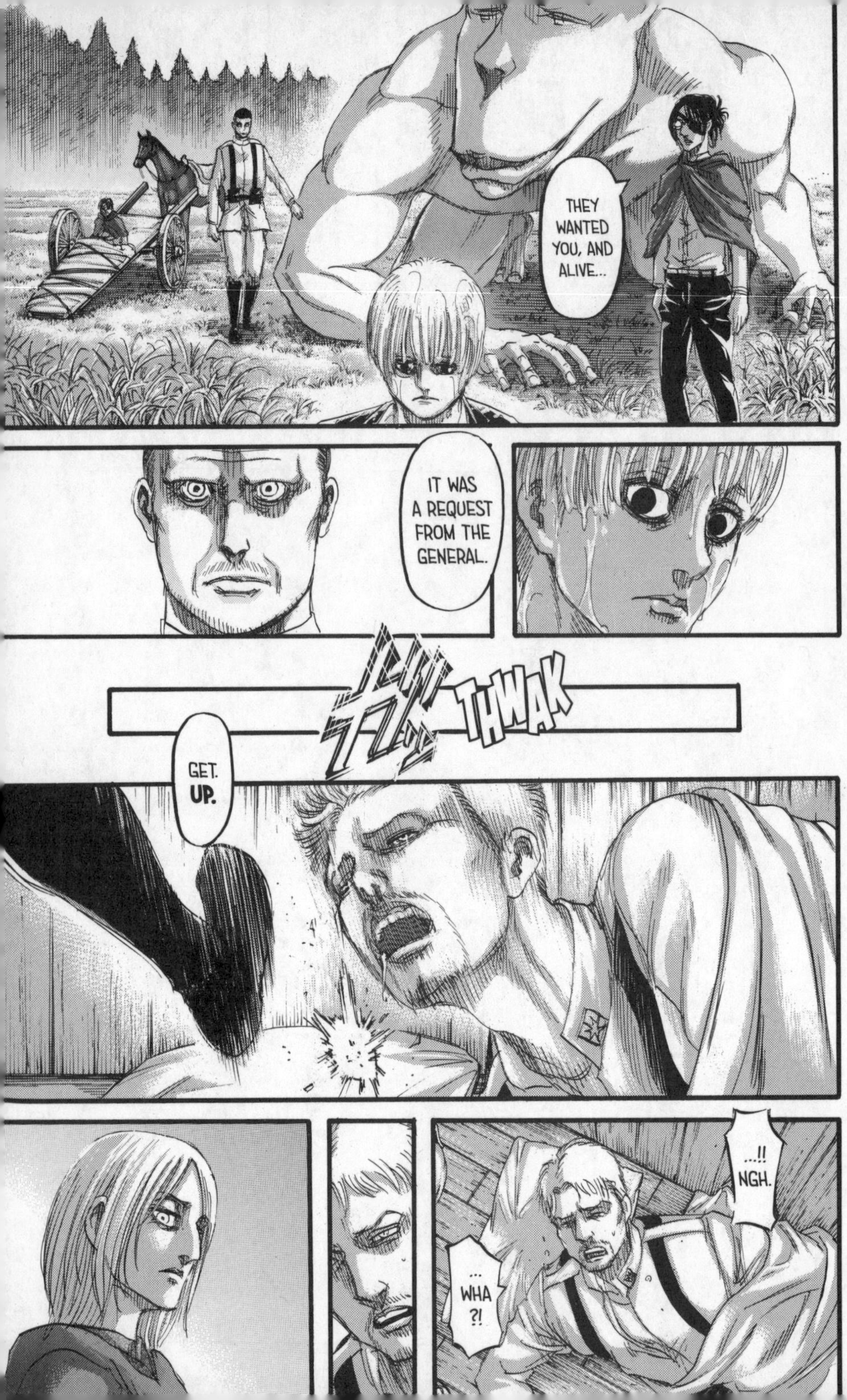
THEY WANTED YOU, AND ALIVE...
IT WAS A REQUEST FROM THE GENERAL.
THWAK
GET. UP.
...!! NGH.
... WHA ?!

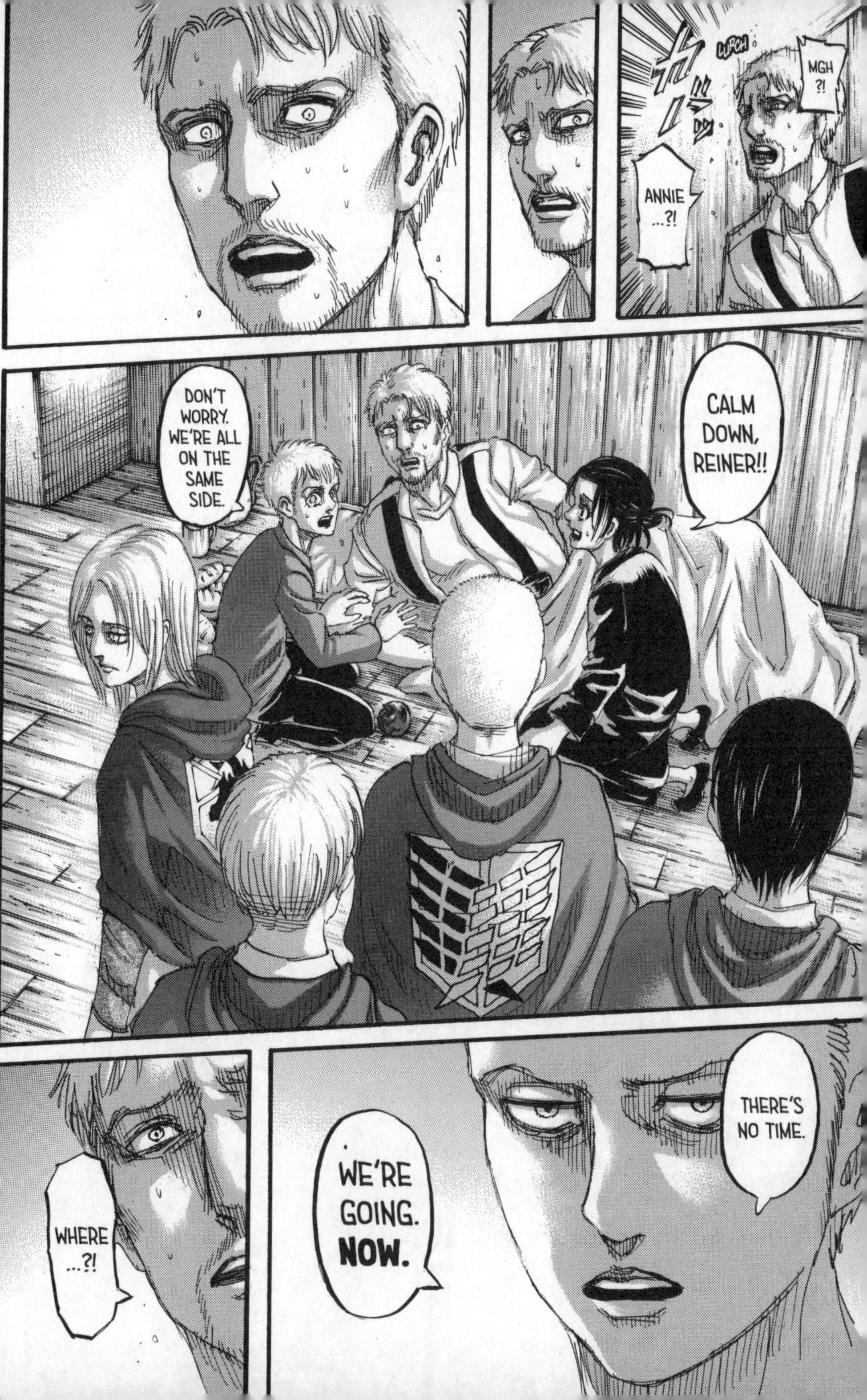
MGH ?!
LURCH
ANNIE ...?!
CALM DOWN, REINER!!
DON'T WORRY. WE'RE ALL ON THE SAME SIDE.
THERE'S NO TIME.
WE'RE GOING. **NOW.**
WHERE ...?!

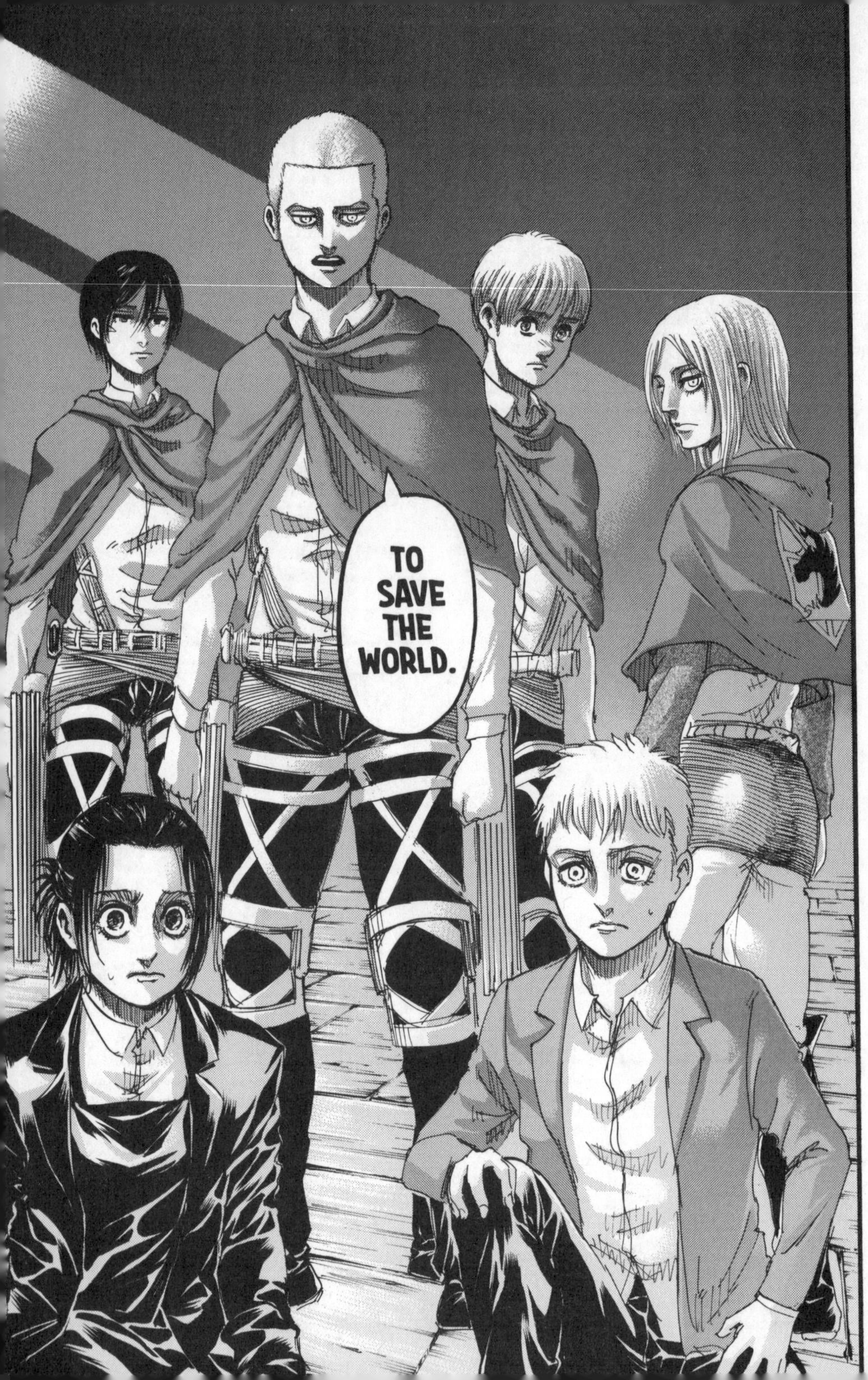
TO SAVE THE WORLD.

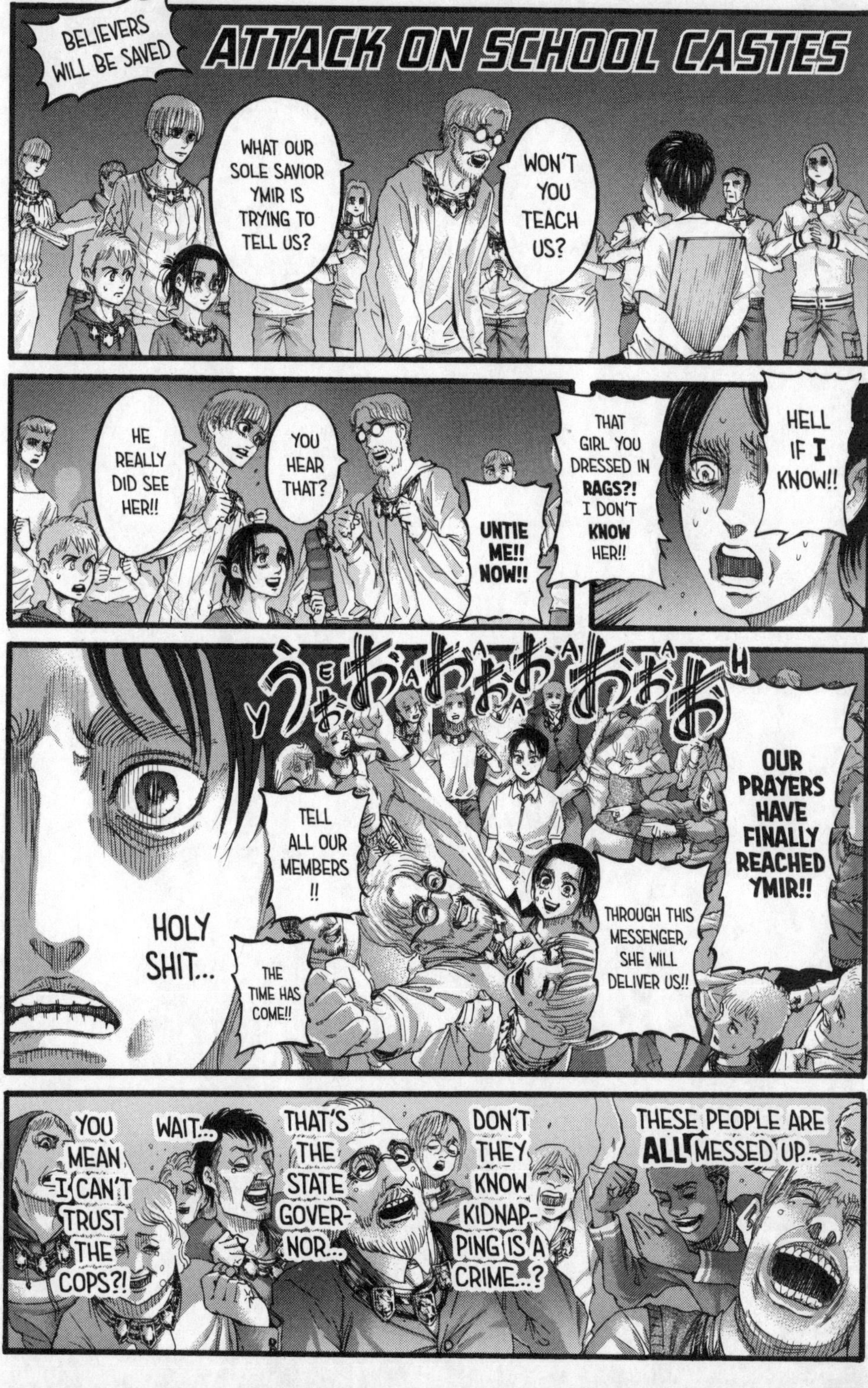
ATTACK ON SCHOOL CASTES
BELIEVERS WILL BE SAVED
WON'T YOU TEACH US?
WHAT OUR SOLE SAVIOR YMIR IS TRYING TO TELL US?
HELL IF I KNOW!!
THAT GIRL YOU DRESSED IN RAGS?! I DON'T KNOW HER!!
UNTIE ME!! NOW!!
YOU HEAR THAT?
HE REALLY DID SEE HER!!
OUR PRAYERS HAVE FINALLY REACHED YMIR!!
THROUGH THIS MESSENGER, SHE WILL DELIVER US!!
TELL ALL OUR MEMBERS !!
THE TIME HAS COME!!
HOLY SHIT...
THESE PEOPLE ARE ALL MESSED UP...
DON'T THEY KNOW KIDNAP-PING IS A CRIME...?
THAT'S THE STATE GOVER-NOR...
WAIT...
YOU MEAN I CAN'T TRUST THE COPS?!

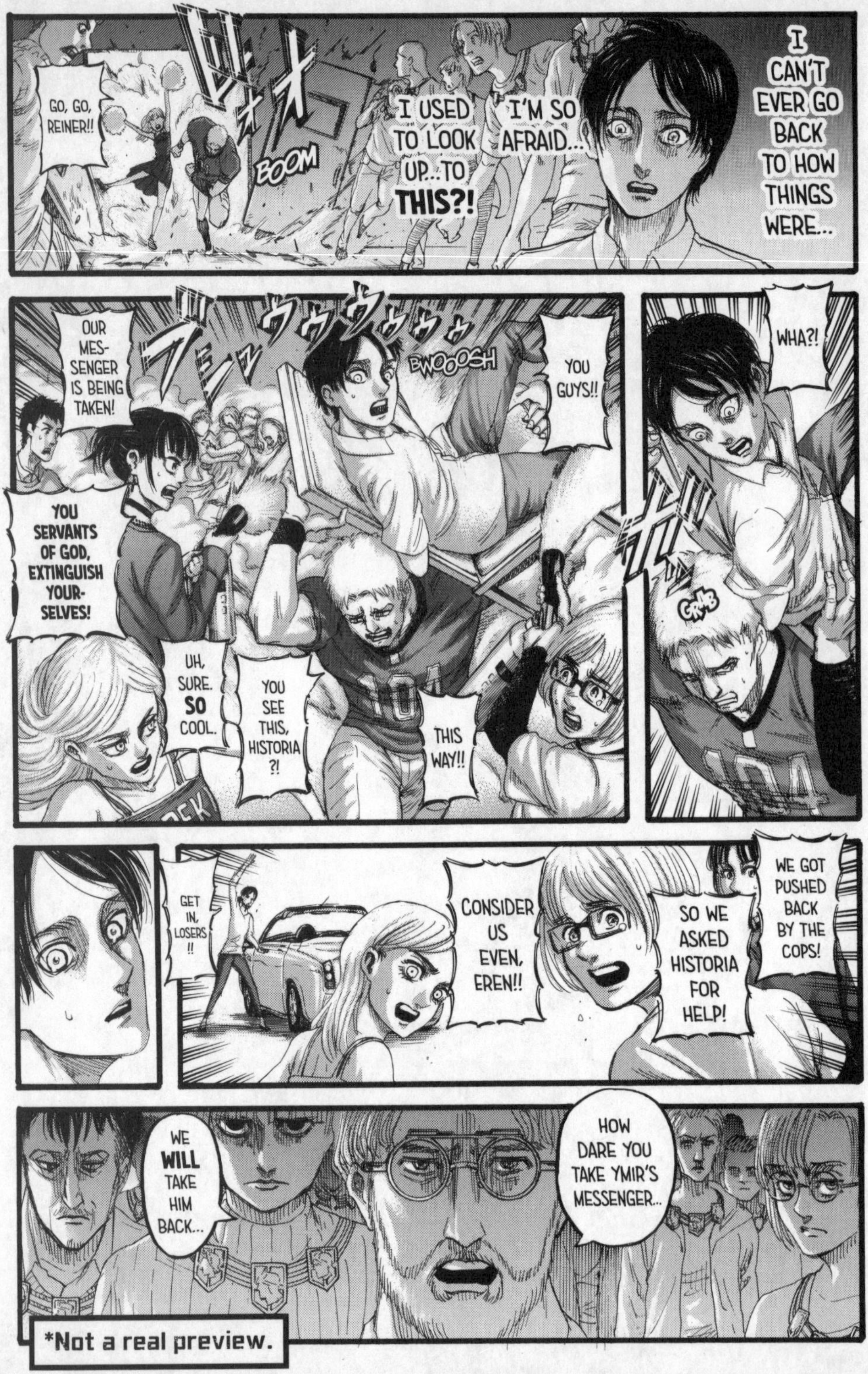
I CAN'T EVER GO BACK TO HOW THINGS WERE...
I'M SO AFRAID...
I USED TO LOOK UP... TO THIS?!
BOOM
GO, GO, REINER!!
WHA?!
GRAB
YOU GUYS!!
BWOOOSH
OUR MESSENGER IS BEING TAKEN!
YOU SERVANTS OF GOD, EXTINGUISH YOURSELVES!
THIS WAY!!
YOU SEE THIS, HISTORIA?!
UH, SURE. SO COOL.
WE GOT PUSHED BACK BY THE COPS!
SO WE ASKED HISTORIA FOR HELP!
CONSIDER US EVEN, EREN!!
GET IN, LOSERS!!
HOW DARE YOU TAKE YMIR'S MESSENGER...
WE WILL TAKE HIM BACK...

*Not a real preview.

ATTACK on TITAN

ATTACK ON TITAN 32

HAJIME ISAYAMA

THE CHARACTERS OF ATTACK ON TITAN

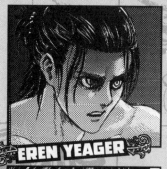

EREN YEAGER

FROM THE 104TH TRAINING CORPS; NOW IN THE SURVEY CORPS. HOLDS THE POWER OF THE ATTACK TITAN AND THE FOUNDING TITAN. BOLDLY INFILTRATED MARLEY ON HIS OWN.

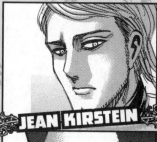

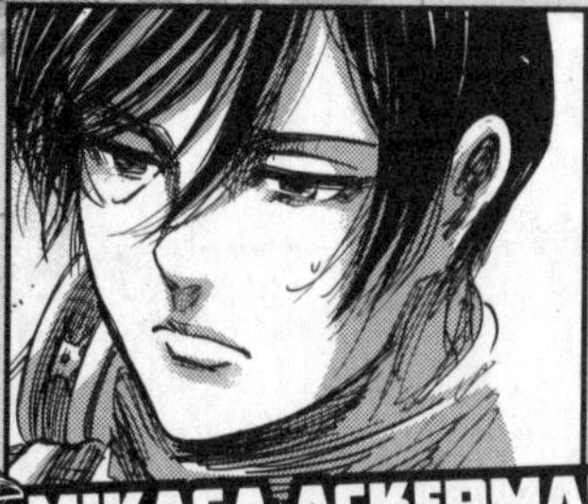

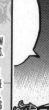

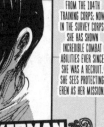

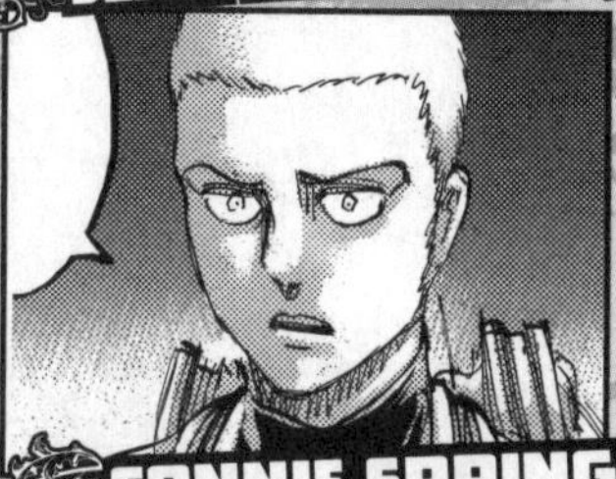

MIKASA ACKERMAN

FROM THE 104TH TRAINING CORPS; NOW IN THE SURVEY CORPS. SHE HAS SHOWN INCREDIBLE COMBAT ABILITIES EVER SINCE SHE WAS A RECRUIT. SHE SEES PROTECTING EREN AS HER MISSION.

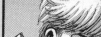

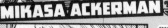

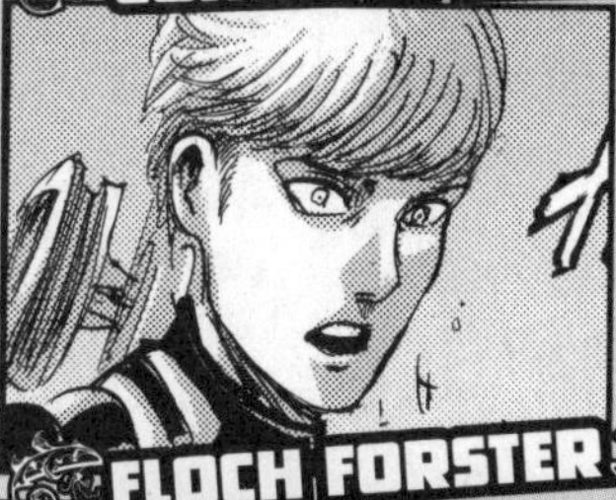

ARMIN ARLERT

FROM THE 104TH TRAINING CORPS; NOW IN THE SURVEY CORPS. HOLDS THE POWER OF THE COLOSSUS TITAN. HE HAS SAVED HIS COMRADES COUNTLESS TIMES WITH HIS SHARP INTELLECT AND BRAVERY.

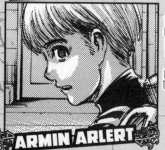

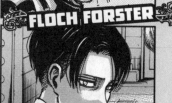

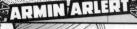

HISTORIA REISS

A DESCENDANT OF THE REISS FAMILY, THE TRUE ROYAL BLOODLINE. HISTORIA HAS NOW ASCENDED TO THE THRONE AS QUEEN. SHE ONCE BELONGED TO THE SURVEY CORPS UNDER THE NAME KRISTA LENZ.

THE NATION OF ELDIA [THE ISLAND OF PARADIS]

JEAN KIRSTEIN

FROM THE 104TH TRAINING CORPS; NOW IN THE SURVEY CORPS. ONCE KNOWN FOR HIS SARCASTIC PERSONALITY, HE HAS NOW GROWN INTO A LEADER FIGURE.

CONNIE SPRINGER

FROM THE 104TH TRAINING CORPS; NOW IN THE SURVEY CORPS. HE IS CHEERFUL IN PERSONALITY, BUT FINDS HIMSELF LOSING EVERYONE IMPORTANT TO HIM... ORIGINALLY FROM RAGAKO VILLAGE.

FLOCH FORSTER

A MEMBER OF THE SURVEY CORPS. A SURVIVOR OF THE DECISIVE BATTLE FOR SHIGANSHINA DISTRICT, WHICH CLAIMED MANY LIVES, INCLUDING ERWIN'S.

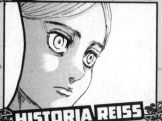

LEVI ACKERMAN

CAPTAIN OF THE SURVEY CORPS. KNOWN AS "HUMANITY'S STRONGEST SOLDIER." HE FIGHTS THROUGH HIS STRUGGLES IN ORDER TO CARRY ON HIS GOOD FRIEND ERWIN'S DYING WISHES.

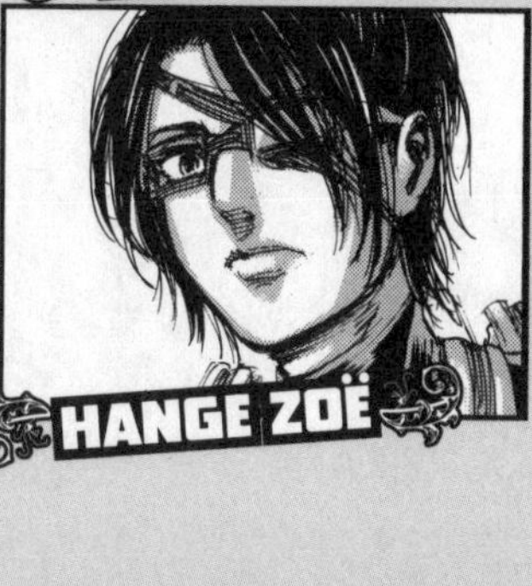

HANGE ZOË

COMMANDER OF THE SURVEY CORPS. DESPITE THE STRANGE WAY HANGE MAY ACT, THEIR KEEN POWERS OF OBSERVATION LED ERWIN TO NAME HANGE HIS SUCCESSOR.

THE ELDIAN WARRIORS OF THE MARLEYAN ARMY

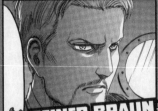

REINER BRAUN

HOLDS THE ARMORED TITAN WITHIN HIM. SINCE HE WAS THE ONLY ONE TO MAKE IT BACK FROM THE MISSION ON PARADIS, HE SUFFERS FROM A GUILTY CONSCIENCE.

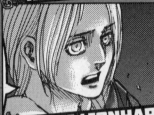

ANNIE LEONHART

HOLDS THE FEMALE TITAN WITHIN HER. HER HARDENED STATE WAS UNDONE BY THE POWER OF THE FOUNDING TITAN, WAKING HER FROM HER FOUR YEARS OF SLEEP.

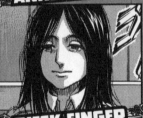

PIECK FINGER

HOLDS THE CART TITAN WITHIN HER, CARRYING THE PANZER UNIT ON THE BACK OF THE "CARTMAN" TO FIGHT. HIGHLY PERCEPTIVE.

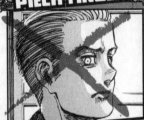

PORCO GALLIARD

HOLDS THE JAW TITAN WITHIN HIM. THERE IS STRIFE BETWEEN HIM AND REINER OVER BOTH THE INHERITANCE OF THE ARMORED TITAN AND THE DEATH OF HIS OLDER BROTHER, MARCEL.

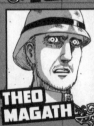

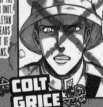

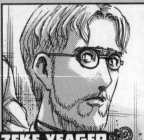

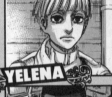

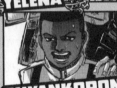

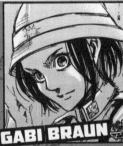

GABI BRAUN

BOLD DESPITE HER SMALL SIZE, GABI IS A DYNAMIC WARRIOR CANDIDATE. HER GOAL IS TO EVENTUALLY INHERIT THE ARMORED TITAN. REINER'S COUSIN.

THEO MAGATH

LEADER OF THE WARRIOR UNIT. A MARLEYAN WHO LEADS A UNIT OF ELDIANS.

COLT GRICE

FALCO'S OLDER BROTHER. THE OLDEST OF THE WARRIOR CANDIDATES, AND, IN EFFECT, THEIR LEADER.

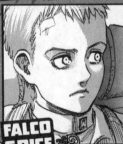

FALCO GRICE

A WARRIOR CANDIDATE. HE HAS AFFECTION FOR GABI AND WANTS TO PROTECT HER. DURING EREN'S TIME INFILTRATING MARLEY, FALCO COMES IN CONTACT WITH EREN WITHOUT REALIZING HIS TRUE IDENTITY.

THE ANTI-MARLEYAN VOLUNTEERS

ZEKE YEAGER

HOLDS THE POWER OF THE BEAST TITAN. A LEADER OF THE WARRIORS, HE WAS ONCE KNOWN AS THE "WONDER CHILD." HIS MOTHER IS A DESCENDANT OF THE ROYAL BLOODLINE. HE IS ALSO EREN'S HALF-BROTHER.

YELENA

YELENA COMMANDS THE VOLUNTEERS AND FOLLOWS ZEKE. SHE DRESSED AS A MAN DURING THE EXPEDITION TO MARLEY IN ORDER TO WORK IN SECRET.

ONYANKOPON

AFTER TRAVELING TO PARADIS WITH YELENA, HE TELLS ITS INHABITANTS OF MARLEY'S ADVANCED CULTURE.

ATTACK on TITAN

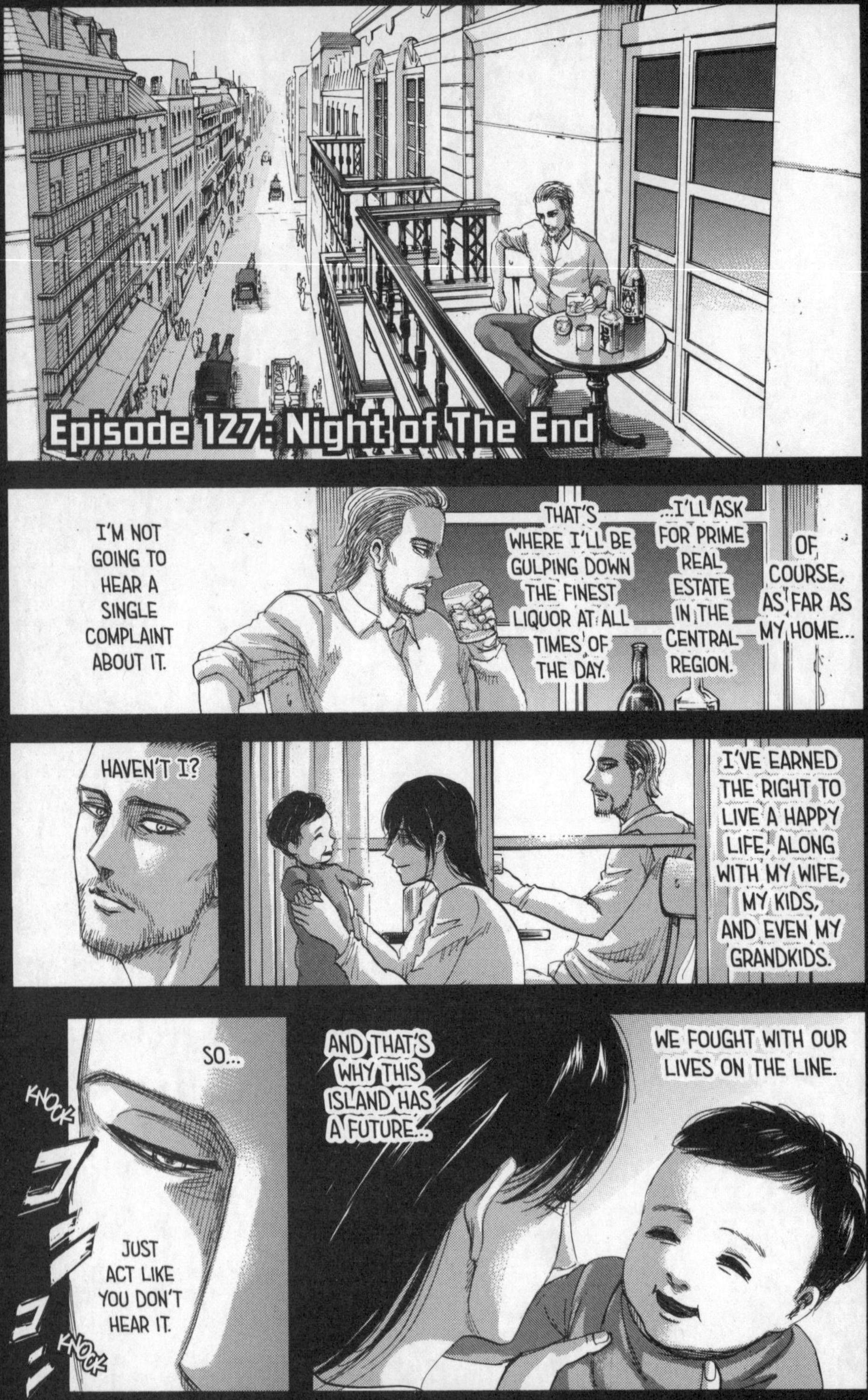
Episode 127: Night of The End
OF COURSE, AS FAR AS MY HOME...
...I'LL ASK FOR PRIME REAL ESTATE IN THE CENTRAL REGION.
THAT'S WHERE I'LL BE GULPING DOWN THE FINEST LIQUOR AT ALL TIMES OF THE DAY.
I'M NOT GOING TO HEAR A SINGLE COMPLAINT ABOUT IT.
I'VE EARNED THE RIGHT TO LIVE A HAPPY LIFE, ALONG WITH MY WIFE, MY KIDS, AND EVEN MY GRANDKIDS.
HAVEN'T I?
WE FOUGHT WITH OUR LIVES ON THE LINE.
AND THAT'S WHY THIS ISLAND HAS A FUTURE...
SO...
KNOCK
JUST ACT LIKE YOU DON'T HEAR IT.
KNOCK

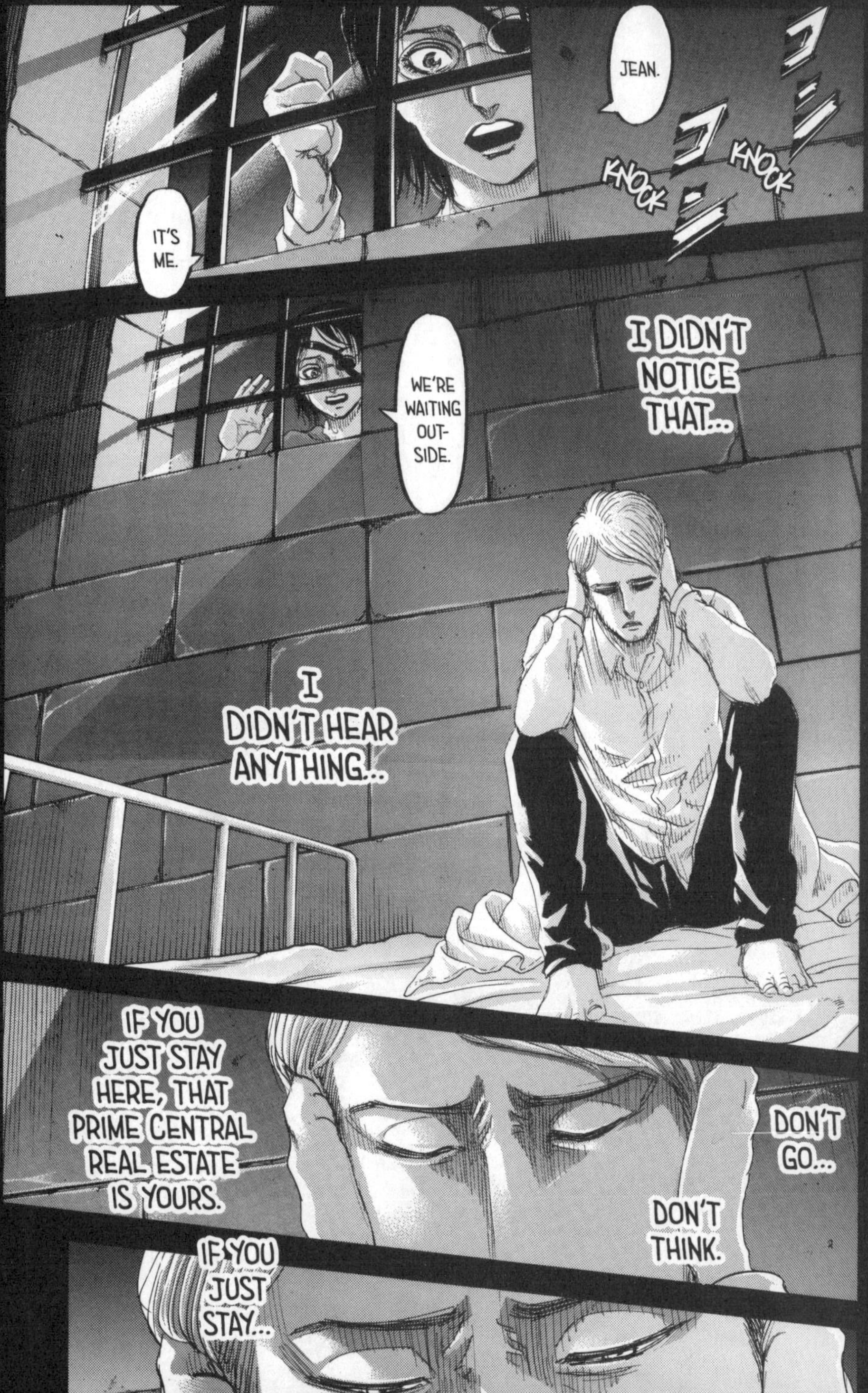
JEAN.
KNOCK
KNOCK
IT'S ME.
WE'RE WAITING OUT-SIDE.
I DIDN'T NOTICE THAT...
I DIDN'T HEAR ANYTHING...
DON'T GO...
IF YOU JUST STAY HERE, THAT PRIME CENTRAL REAL ESTATE IS YOURS.
DON'T THINK.
IF YOU JUST STAY...

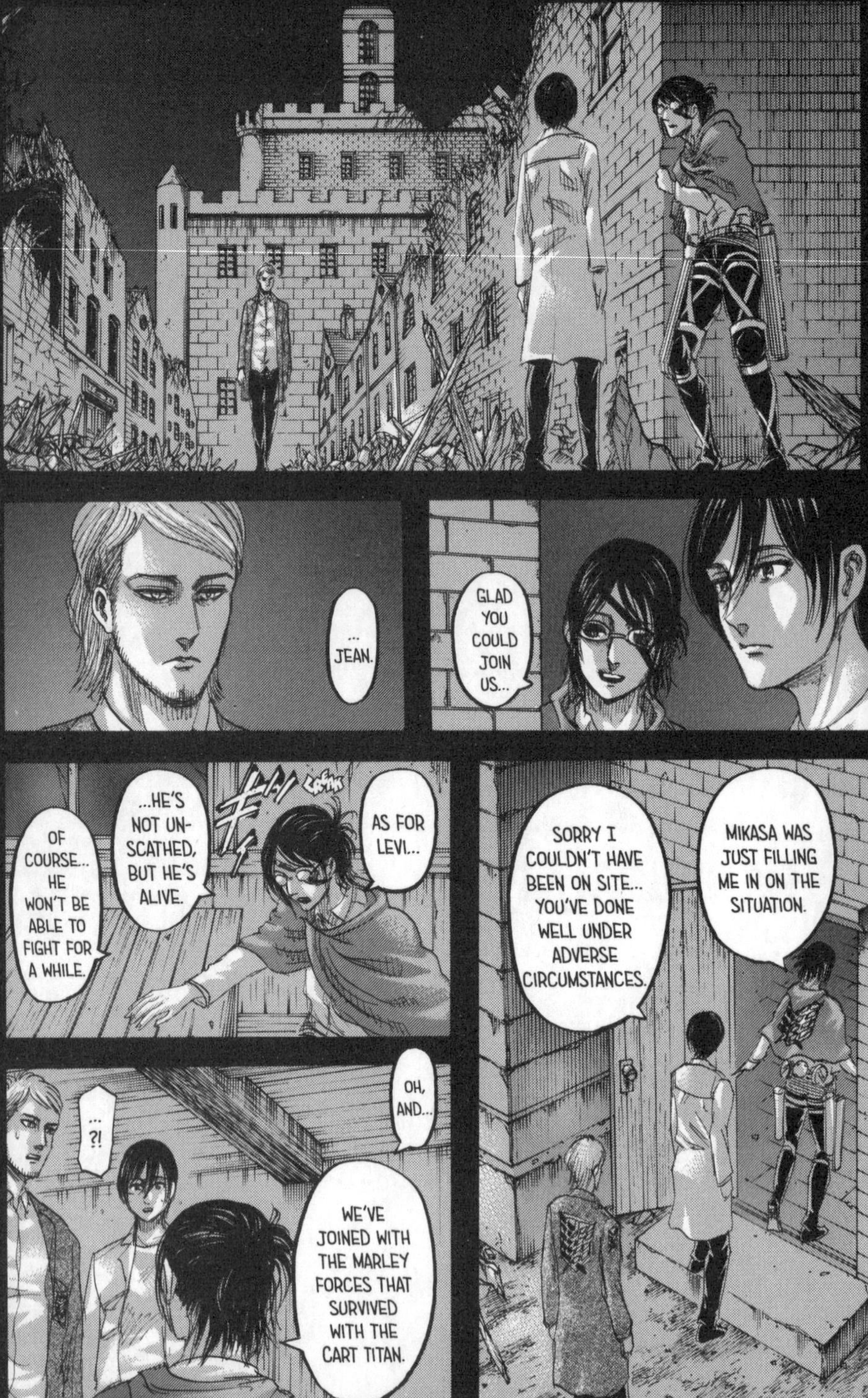
GLAD YOU COULD JOIN US...
... JEAN.
MIKASA WAS JUST FILLING ME IN ON THE SITUATION.
SORRY I COULDN'T HAVE BEEN ON SITE... YOU'VE DONE WELL UNDER ADVERSE CIRCUMSTANCES.
AS FOR LEVI...
...HE'S NOT UNSCATHED, BUT HE'S ALIVE.
OF COURSE... HE WON'T BE ABLE TO FIGHT FOR A WHILE.
OH, AND...
WE'VE JOINED WITH THE MARLEY FORCES THAT SURVIVED WITH THE CART TITAN.
... ?!

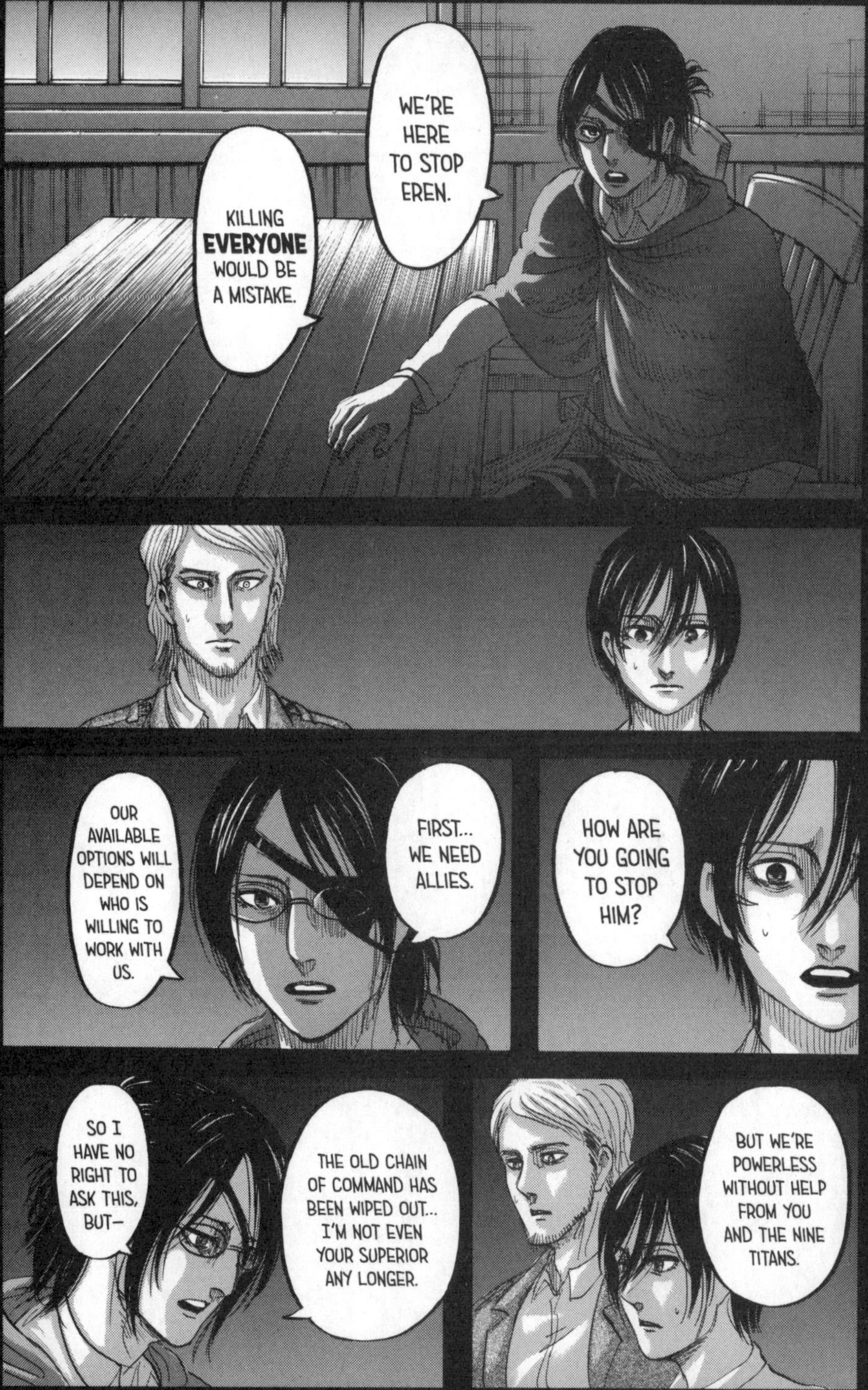
WE'RE HERE TO STOP EREN.
KILLING **EVERYONE** WOULD BE A MISTAKE.
HOW ARE YOU GOING TO STOP HIM?
FIRST... WE NEED ALLIES.
OUR AVAILABLE OPTIONS WILL DEPEND ON WHO IS WILLING TO WORK WITH US.
BUT WE'RE POWERLESS WITHOUT HELP FROM YOU AND THE NINE TITANS.
THE OLD CHAIN OF COMMAND HAS BEEN WIPED OUT... I'M NOT EVEN YOUR SUPERIOR ANY LONGER.
SO I HAVE NO RIGHT TO ASK THIS, BUT—

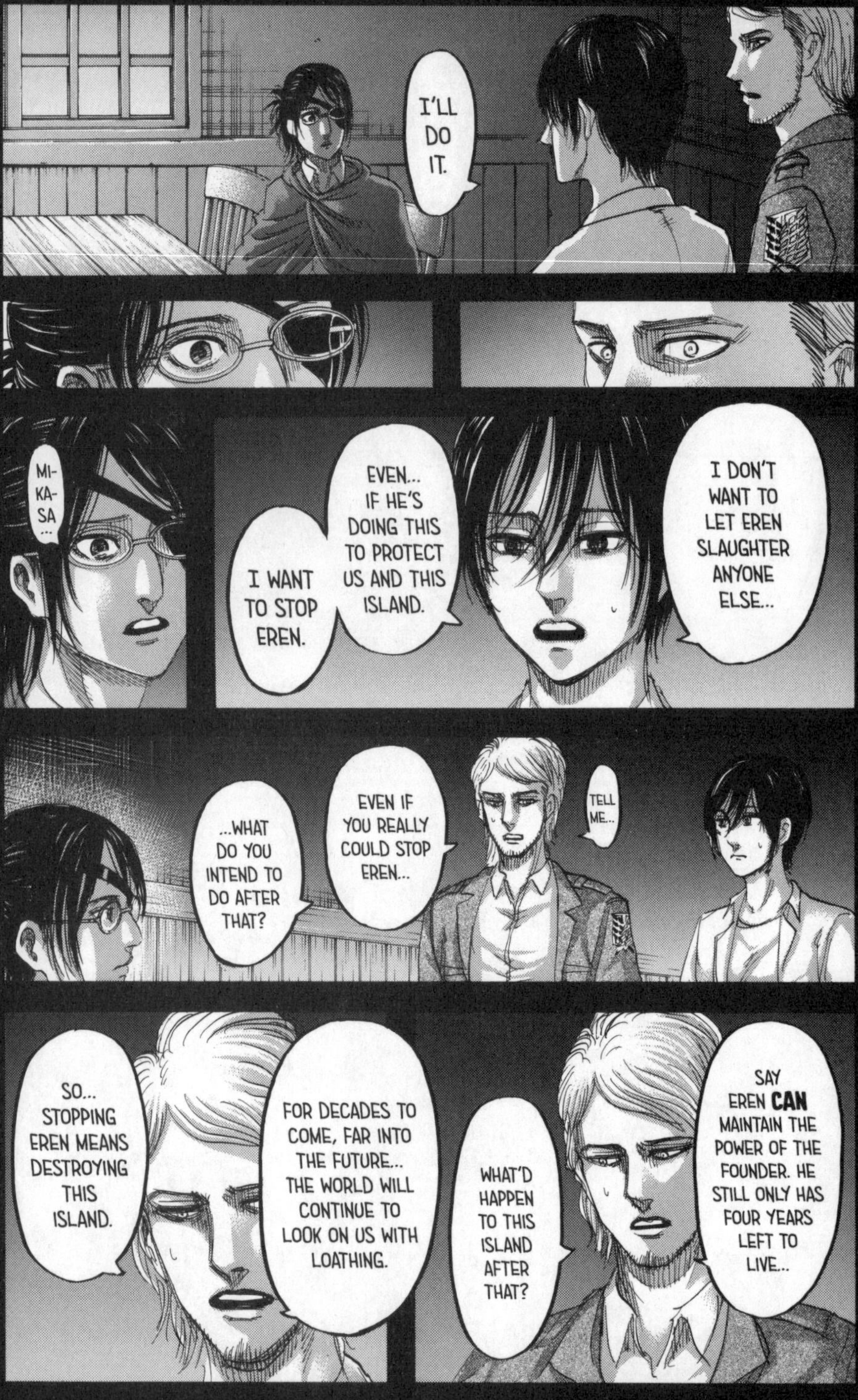
I'LL DO IT.
I DON'T WANT TO LET EREN SLAUGHTER ANYONE ELSE...
EVEN... IF HE'S DOING THIS TO PROTECT US AND THIS ISLAND.
I WANT TO STOP EREN.
MI-KA-SA...
TELL ME...
EVEN IF YOU REALLY COULD STOP EREN...
...WHAT DO YOU INTEND TO DO AFTER THAT?
SAY EREN **CAN** MAINTAIN THE POWER OF THE FOUNDER. HE STILL ONLY HAS FOUR YEARS LEFT TO LIVE...
WHAT'D HAPPEN TO THIS ISLAND AFTER THAT?
FOR DECADES TO COME, FAR INTO THE FUTURE... THE WORLD WILL CONTINUE TO LOOK ON US WITH LOATHING.
SO... STOPPING EREN MEANS DESTROYING THIS ISLAND.

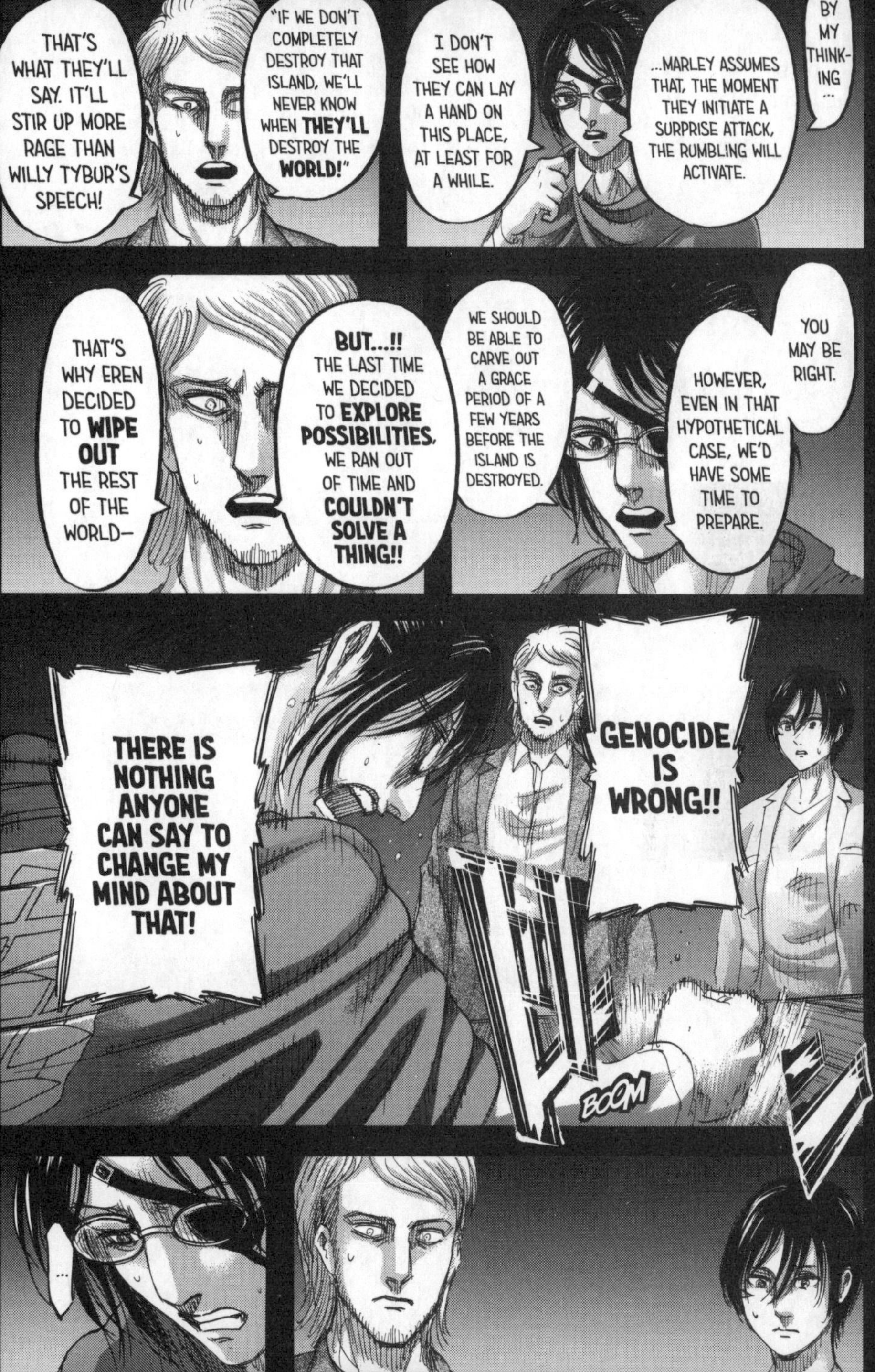
BY MY THINK-ING ...
...MARLEY ASSUMES THAT, THE MOMENT THEY INITIATE A SURPRISE ATTACK, THE RUMBLING WILL ACTIVATE.
I DON'T SEE HOW THEY CAN LAY A HAND ON THIS PLACE, AT LEAST FOR A WHILE.
"IF WE DON'T COMPLETELY DESTROY THAT ISLAND, WE'LL NEVER KNOW WHEN **THEY'LL** DESTROY THE **WORLD!**"
THAT'S WHAT THEY'LL SAY. IT'LL STIR UP MORE RAGE THAN WILLY TYBUR'S SPEECH!
YOU MAY BE RIGHT.
HOWEVER, EVEN IN THAT HYPOTHETICAL CASE, WE'D HAVE SOME TIME TO PREPARE.
WE SHOULD BE ABLE TO CARVE OUT A GRACE PERIOD OF A FEW YEARS BEFORE THE ISLAND IS DESTROYED.
BUT...!! THE LAST TIME WE DECIDED TO **EXPLORE POSSIBILITIES**, WE RAN OUT OF TIME AND **COULDN'T SOLVE A THING!!**
THAT'S WHY EREN DECIDED TO **WIPE OUT** THE REST OF THE WORLD—
GENOCIDE IS WRONG!!
THERE IS NOTHING ANYONE CAN SAY TO CHANGE MY MIND ABOUT THAT!
BOOM
...

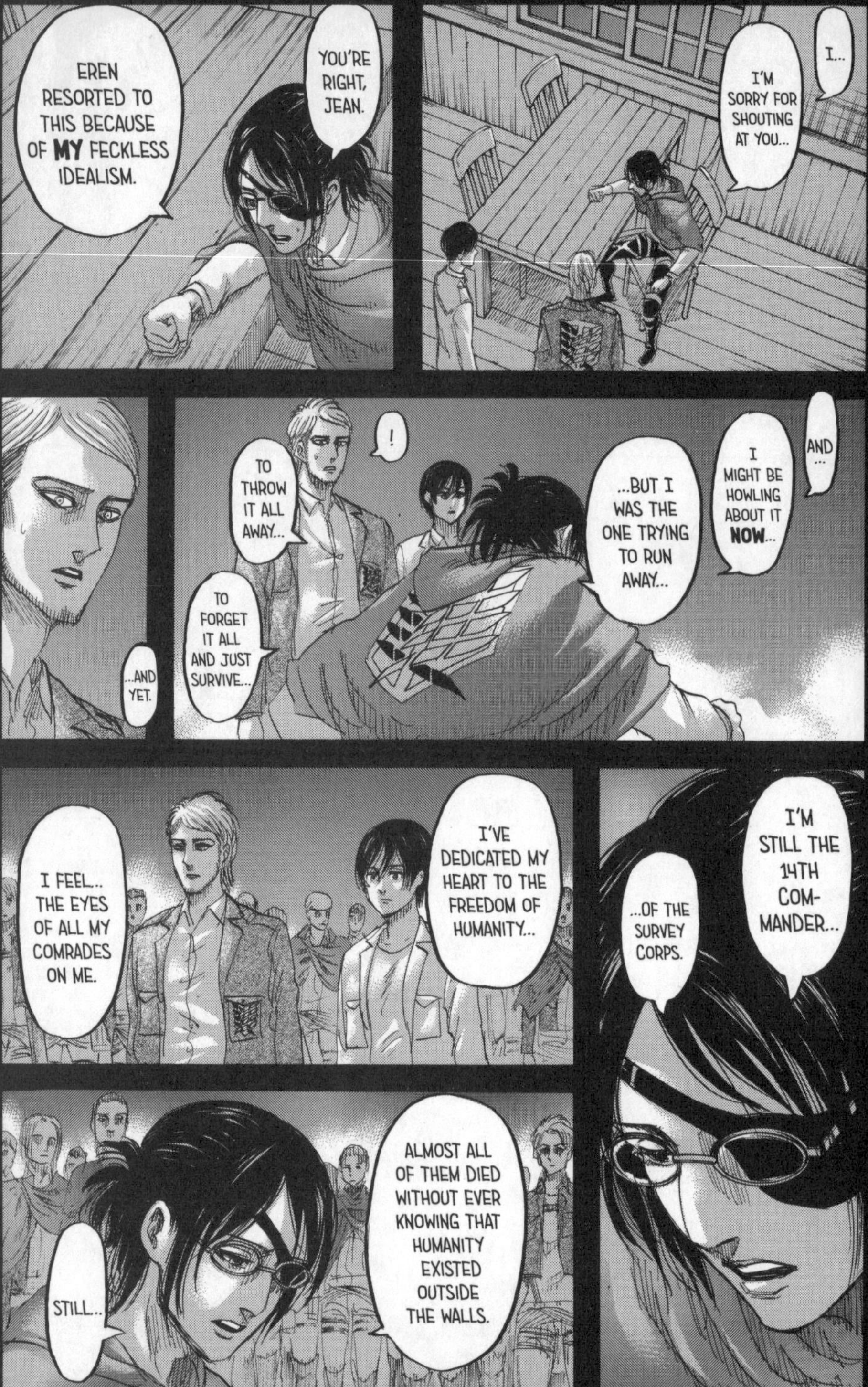
I...
I'M SORRY FOR SHOUTING AT YOU...
YOU'RE RIGHT, JEAN.
EREN RESORTED TO THIS BECAUSE OF **MY** FECKLESS IDEALISM.
AND...
I MIGHT BE HOWLING ABOUT IT **NOW**...
...BUT I WAS THE ONE TRYING TO RUN AWAY...
!
TO THROW IT ALL AWAY...
TO FORGET IT ALL AND JUST SURVIVE...
...AND YET.
I'M STILL THE 14TH COM-MANDER...
...OF THE SURVEY CORPS.
I'VE DEDICATED MY HEART TO THE FREEDOM OF HUMANITY...
I FEEL... THE EYES OF ALL MY COMRADES ON ME.
ALMOST ALL OF THEM DIED WITHOUT EVER KNOWING THAT HUMANITY EXISTED OUTSIDE THE WALLS.
STILL...

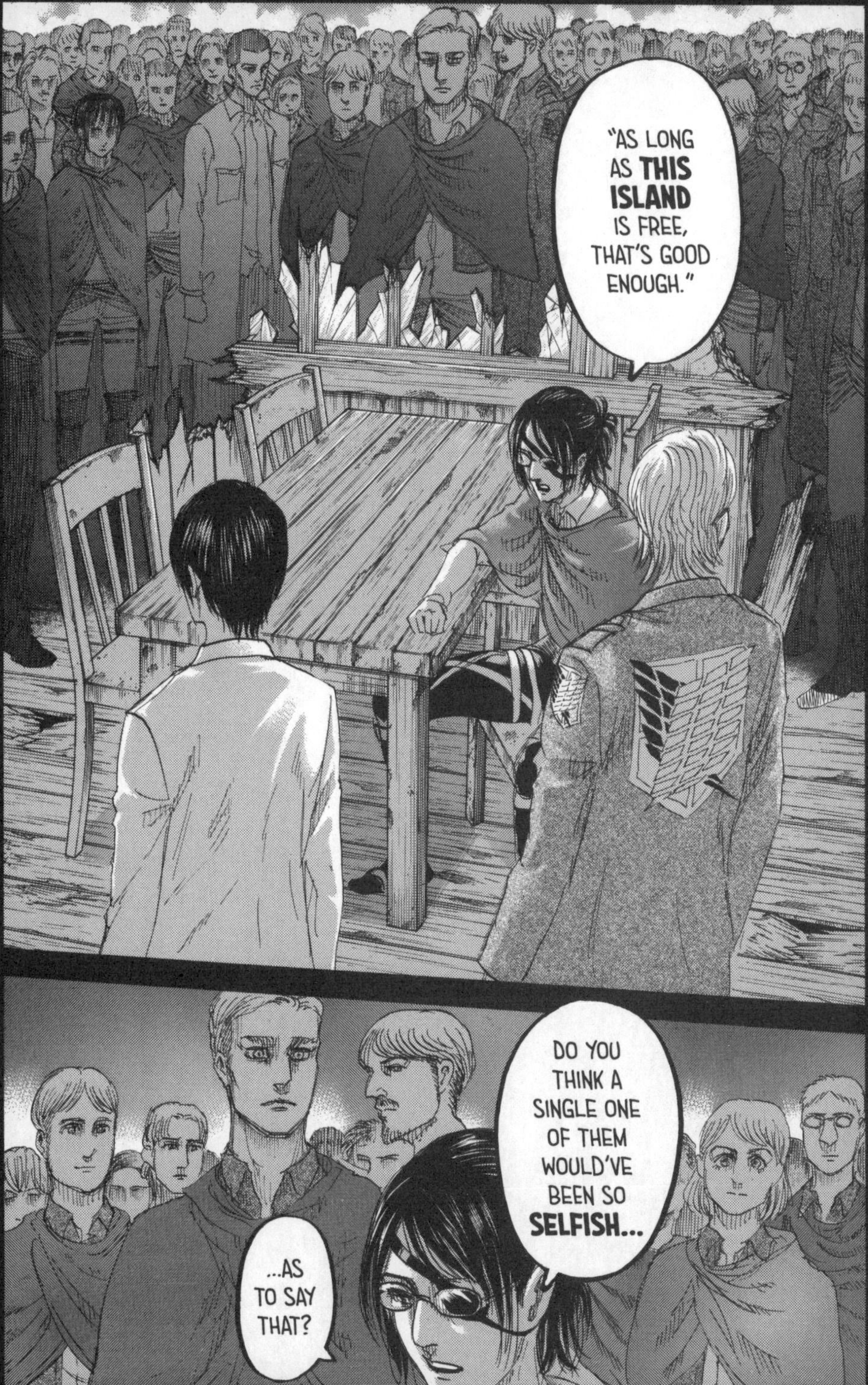
"AS LONG AS **THIS ISLAND** IS FREE, THAT'S GOOD ENOUGH."
DO YOU THINK A SINGLE ONE OF THEM WOULD'VE BEEN SO **SELFISH...**
...AS TO SAY THAT?

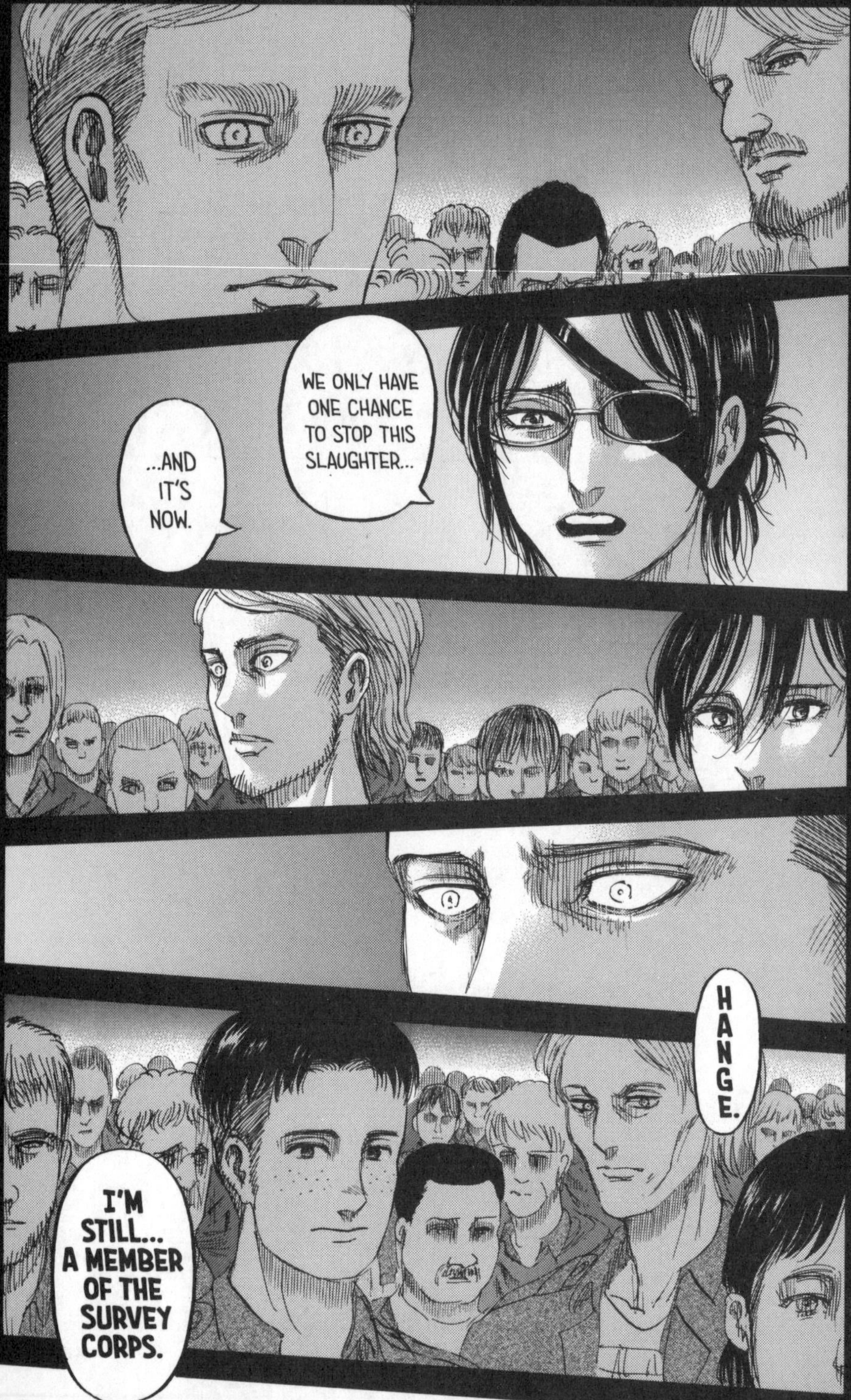
WE ONLY HAVE ONE CHANCE TO STOP THIS SLAUGHTER...
...AND IT'S NOW.
HANGE.
I'M STILL... A MEMBER OF THE SURVEY CORPS.

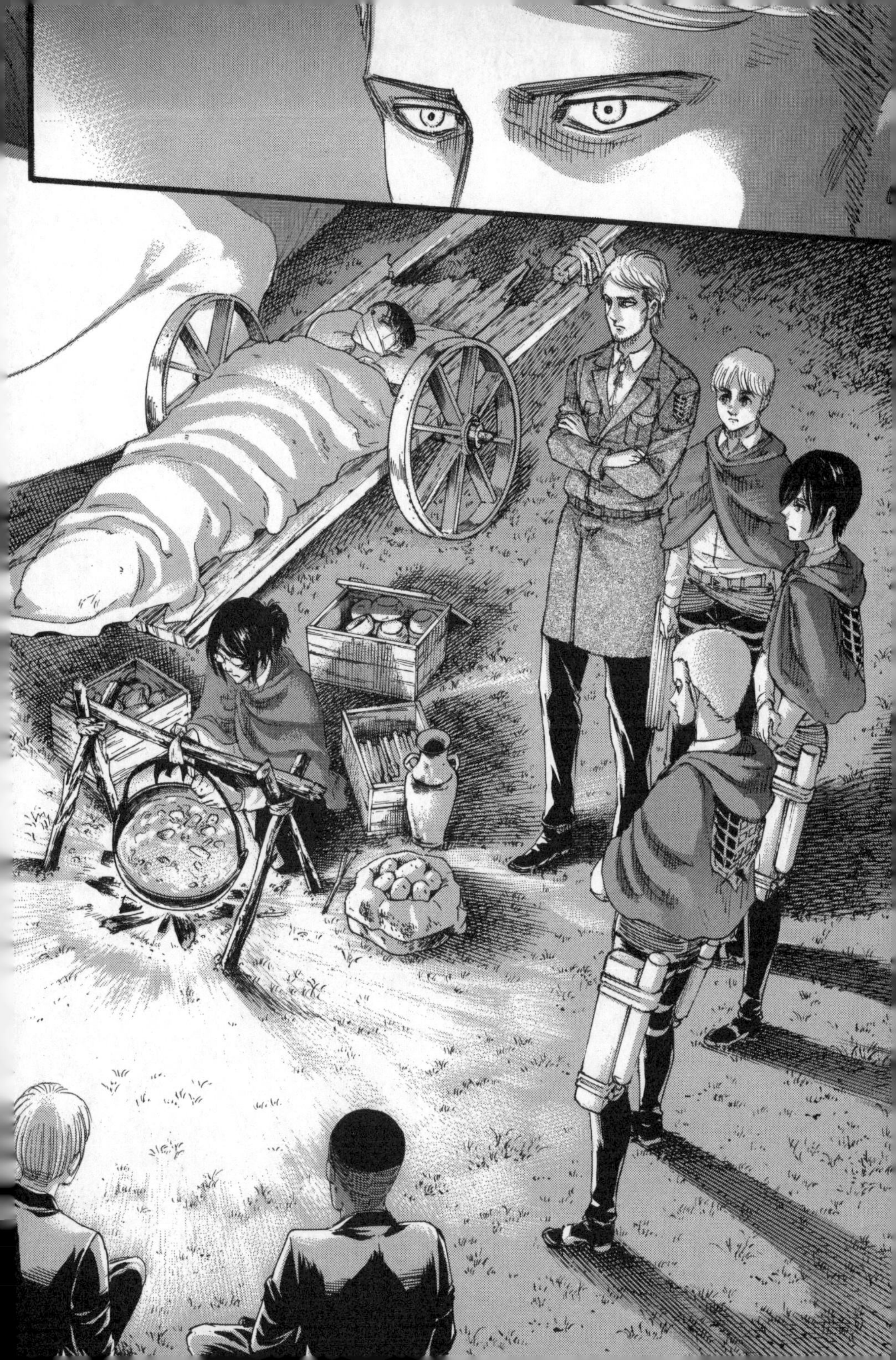

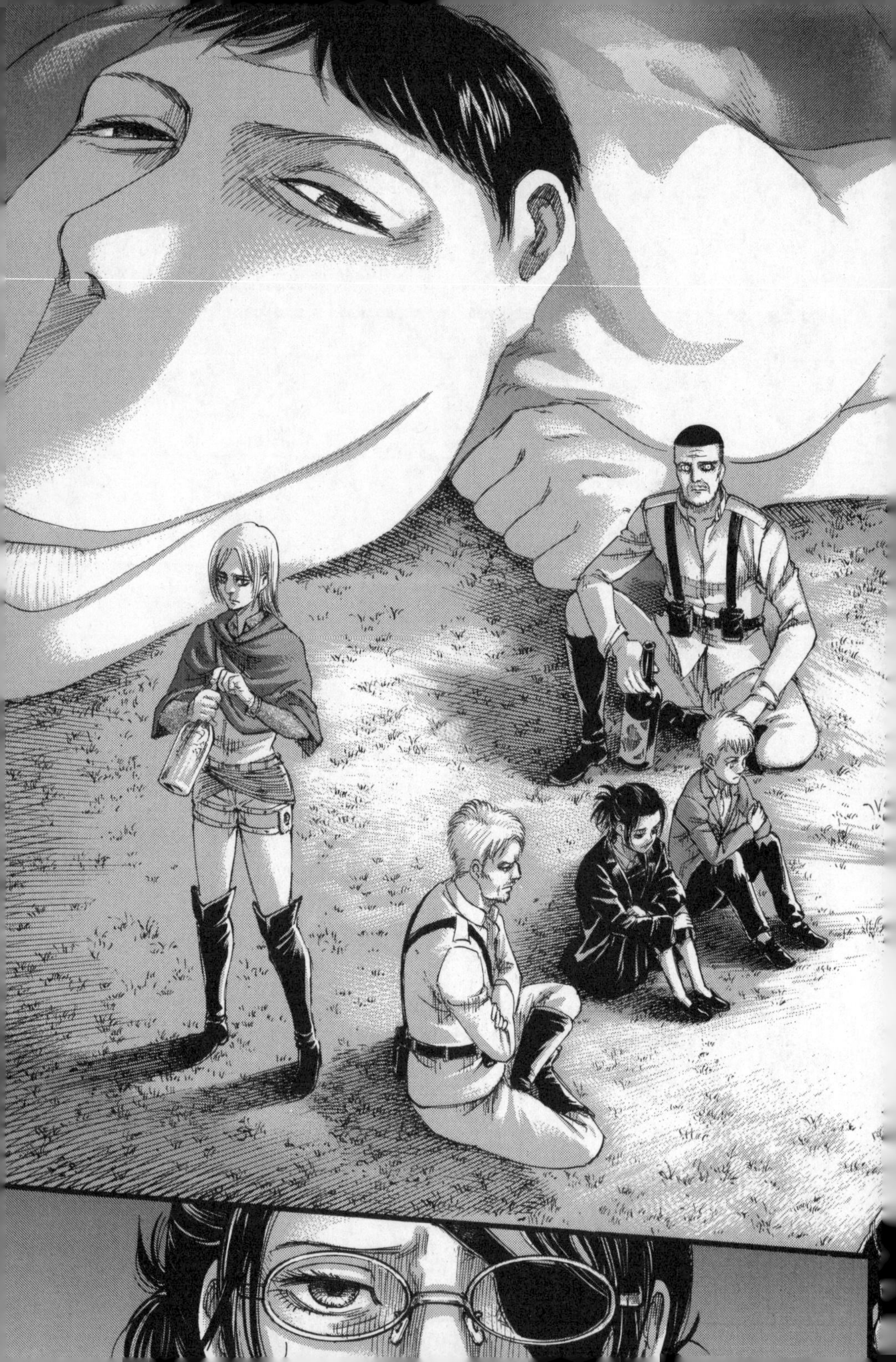

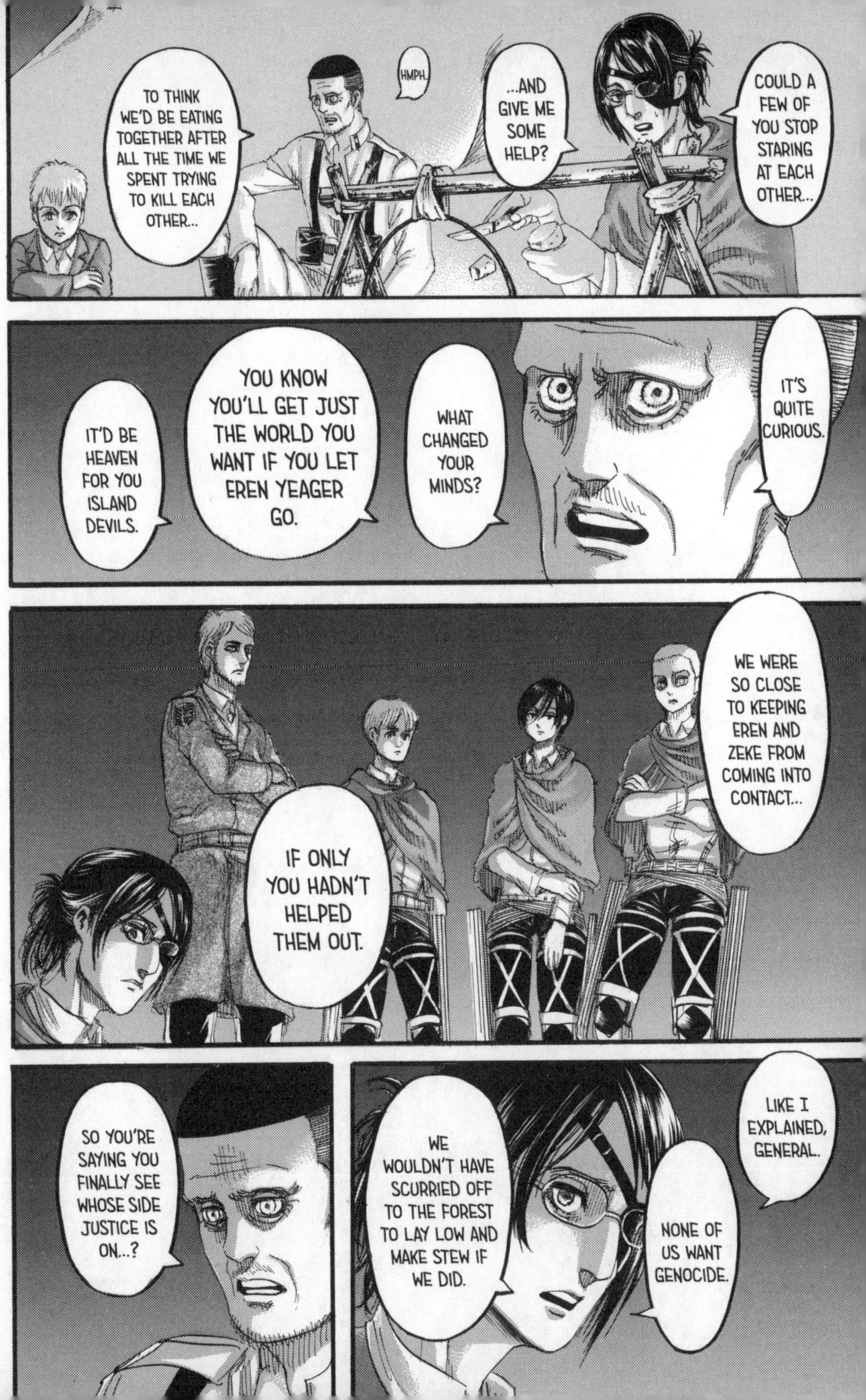
COULD A FEW OF YOU STOP STARING AT EACH OTHER...
...AND GIVE ME SOME HELP?
HMPH.
TO THINK WE'D BE EATING TOGETHER AFTER ALL THE TIME WE SPENT TRYING TO KILL EACH OTHER...
IT'S QUITE CURIOUS.
WHAT CHANGED YOUR MINDS?
YOU KNOW YOU'LL GET JUST THE WORLD YOU WANT IF YOU LET EREN YEAGER GO.
IT'D BE HEAVEN FOR YOU ISLAND DEVILS.
WE WERE SO CLOSE TO KEEPING EREN AND ZEKE FROM COMING INTO CONTACT...
IF ONLY YOU HADN'T HELPED THEM OUT.
LIKE I EXPLAINED, GENERAL.
NONE OF US WANT GENOCIDE.
WE WOULDN'T HAVE SCURRIED OFF TO THE FOREST TO LAY LOW AND MAKE STEW IF WE DID.
SO YOU'RE SAYING YOU FINALLY SEE WHOSE SIDE JUSTICE IS ON...?

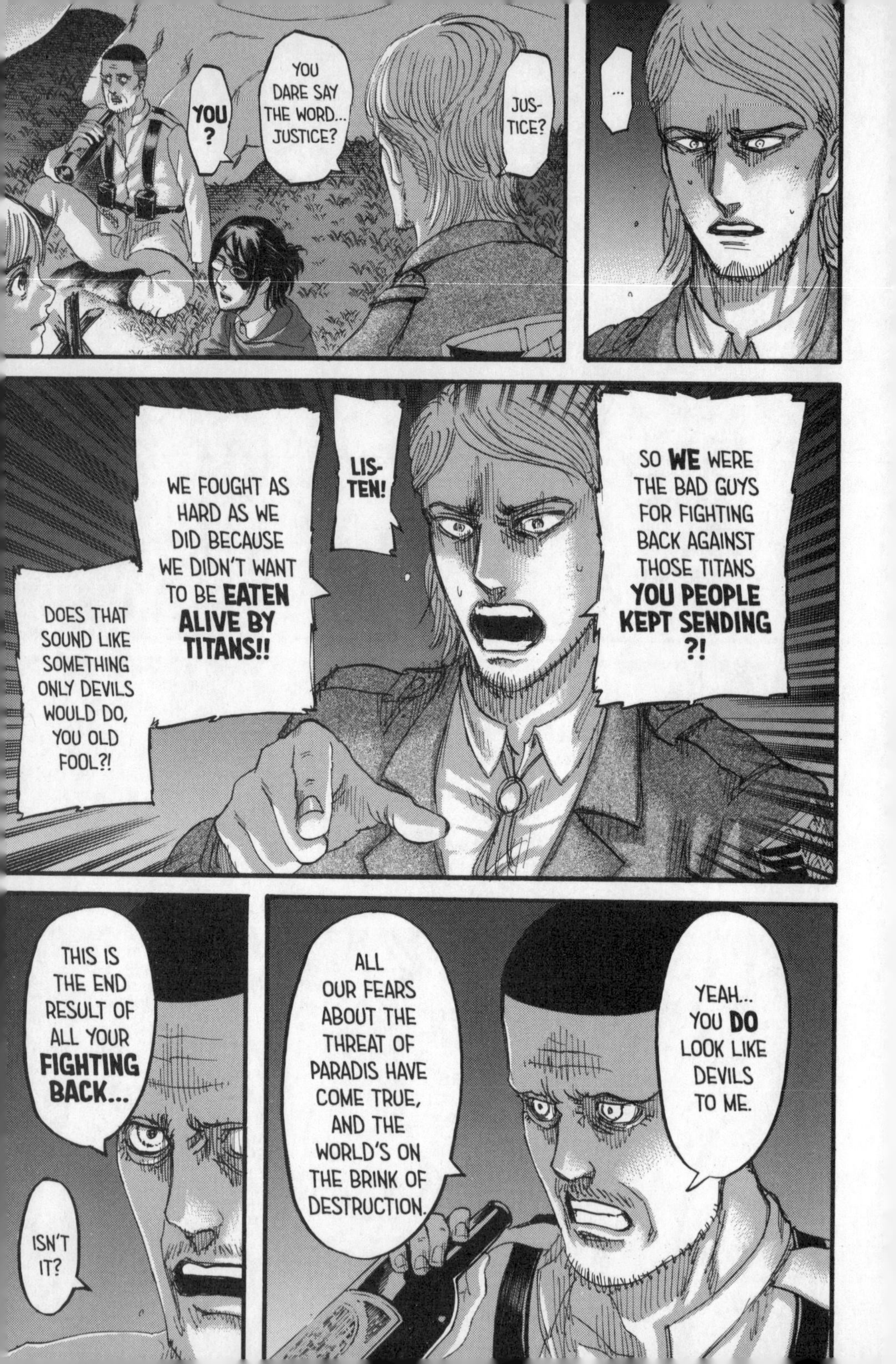

...
JUSTICE?
YOU DARE SAY THE WORD... JUSTICE?
YOU?
SO WE WERE THE BAD GUYS FOR FIGHTING BACK AGAINST THOSE TITANS YOU PEOPLE KEPT SENDING?!
LISTEN!
WE FOUGHT AS HARD AS WE DID BECAUSE WE DIDN'T WANT TO BE EATEN ALIVE BY TITANS!!
DOES THAT SOUND LIKE SOMETHING ONLY DEVILS WOULD DO, YOU OLD FOOL?!
YEAH... YOU DO LOOK LIKE DEVILS TO ME.
ALL OUR FEARS ABOUT THE THREAT OF PARADIS HAVE COME TRUE, AND THE WORLD'S ON THE BRINK OF DESTRUCTION.
THIS IS THE END RESULT OF ALL YOUR FIGHTING BACK...
ISN'T IT?

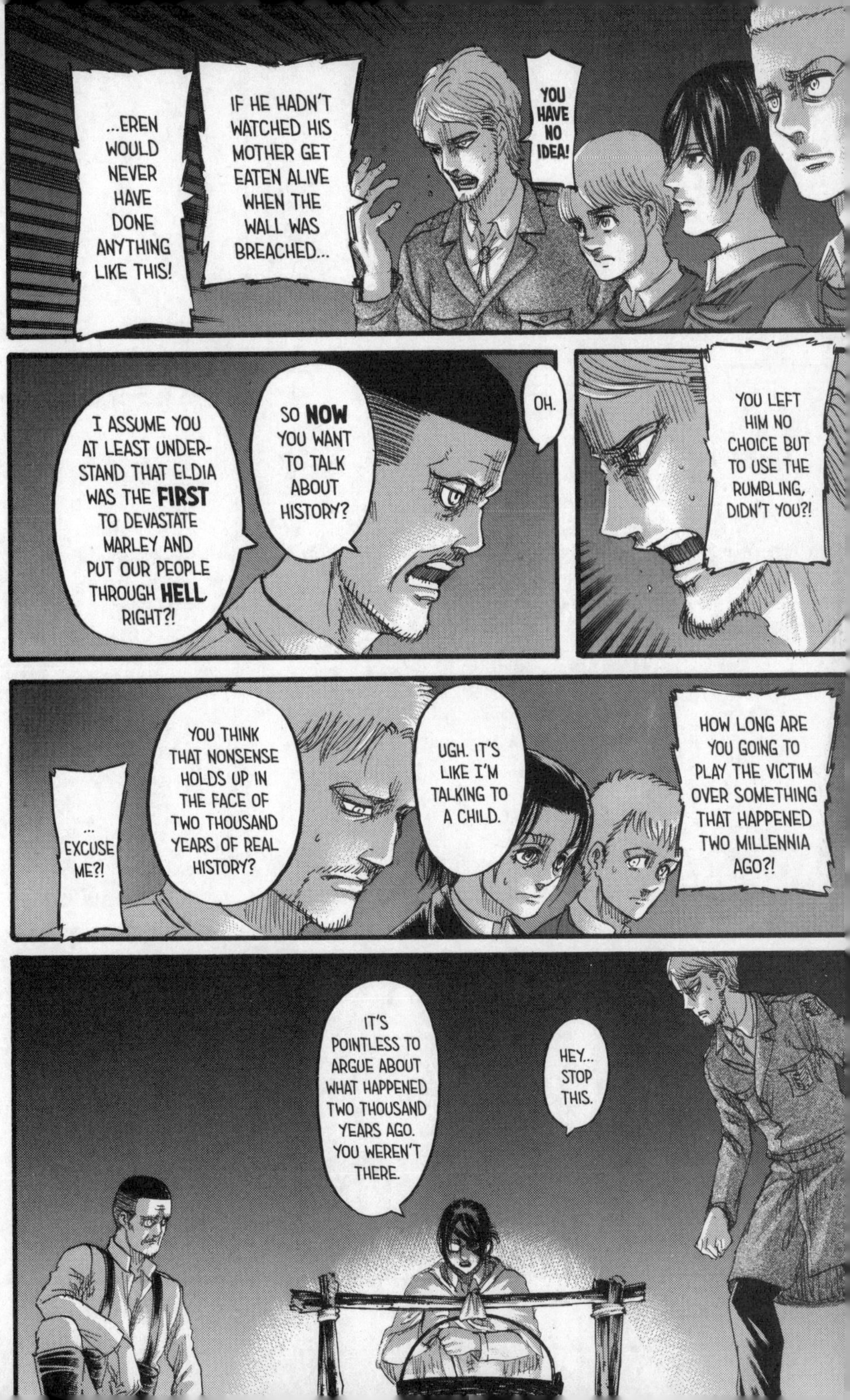
YOU HAVE NO IDEA!
IF HE HADN'T WATCHED HIS MOTHER GET EATEN ALIVE WHEN THE WALL WAS BREACHED...
...EREN WOULD NEVER HAVE DONE ANYTHING LIKE THIS!
YOU LEFT HIM NO CHOICE BUT TO USE THE RUMBLING, DIDN'T YOU?!
OH.
SO NOW YOU WANT TO TALK ABOUT HISTORY?
I ASSUME YOU AT LEAST UNDER-STAND THAT ELDIA WAS THE FIRST TO DEVASTATE MARLEY AND PUT OUR PEOPLE THROUGH HELL, RIGHT?!
HOW LONG ARE YOU GOING TO PLAY THE VICTIM OVER SOMETHING THAT HAPPENED TWO MILLENNIA AGO?!
UGH. IT'S LIKE I'M TALKING TO A CHILD.
YOU THINK THAT NONSENSE HOLDS UP IN THE FACE OF TWO THOUSAND YEARS OF REAL HISTORY?
...EXCUSE ME?!
HEY... STOP THIS.
IT'S POINTLESS TO ARGUE ABOUT WHAT HAPPENED TWO THOUSAND YEARS AGO. YOU WEREN'T THERE.

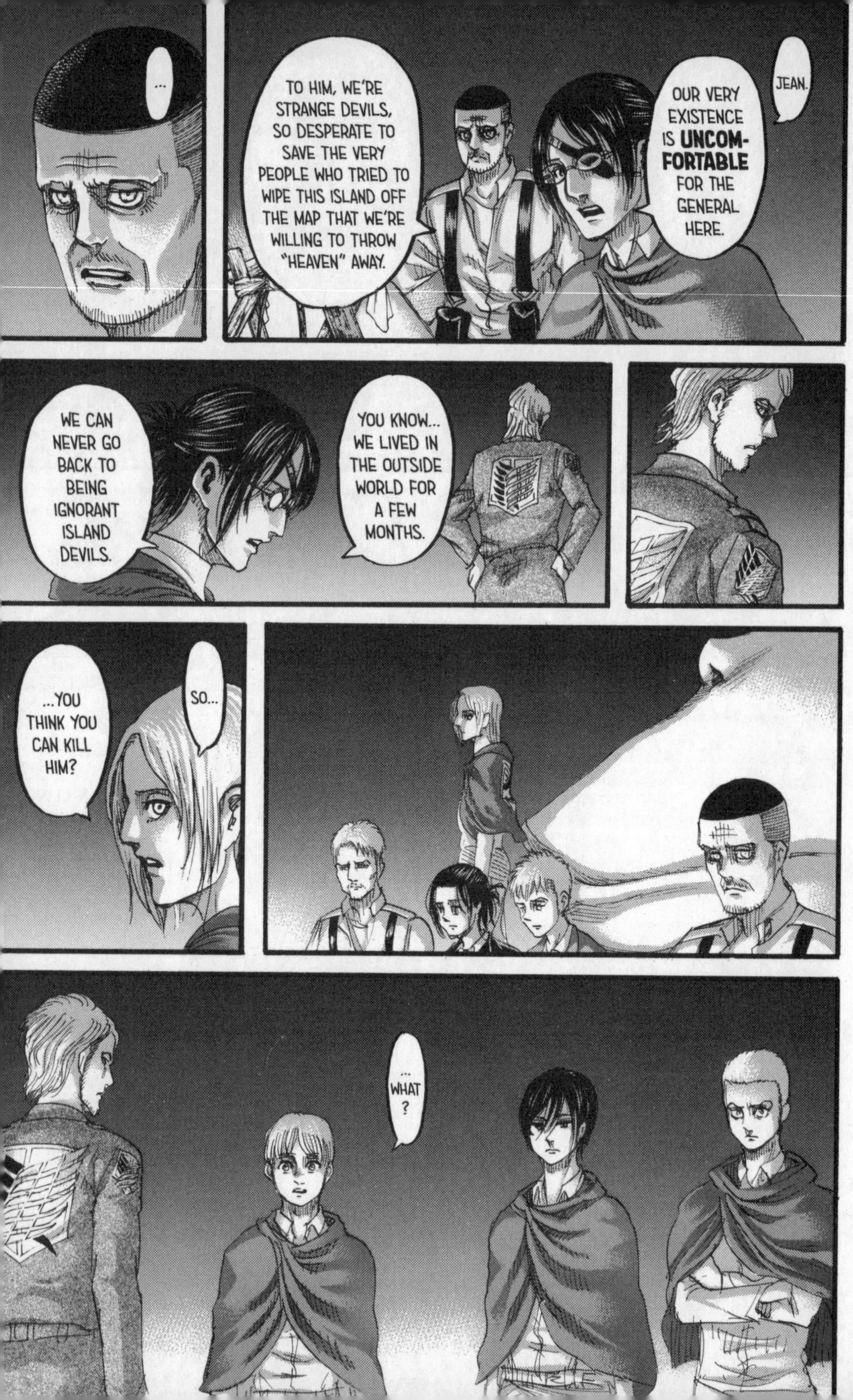
JEAN.
OUR VERY EXISTENCE IS **UNCOMFORTABLE** FOR THE GENERAL HERE.
TO HIM, WE'RE STRANGE DEVILS, SO DESPERATE TO SAVE THE VERY PEOPLE WHO TRIED TO WIPE THIS ISLAND OFF THE MAP THAT WE'RE WILLING TO THROW "HEAVEN" AWAY.
...
YOU KNOW... WE LIVED IN THE OUTSIDE WORLD FOR A FEW MONTHS.
WE CAN NEVER GO BACK TO BEING IGNORANT ISLAND DEVILS.
SO...
...YOU THINK YOU CAN KILL HIM?
... WHAT ?

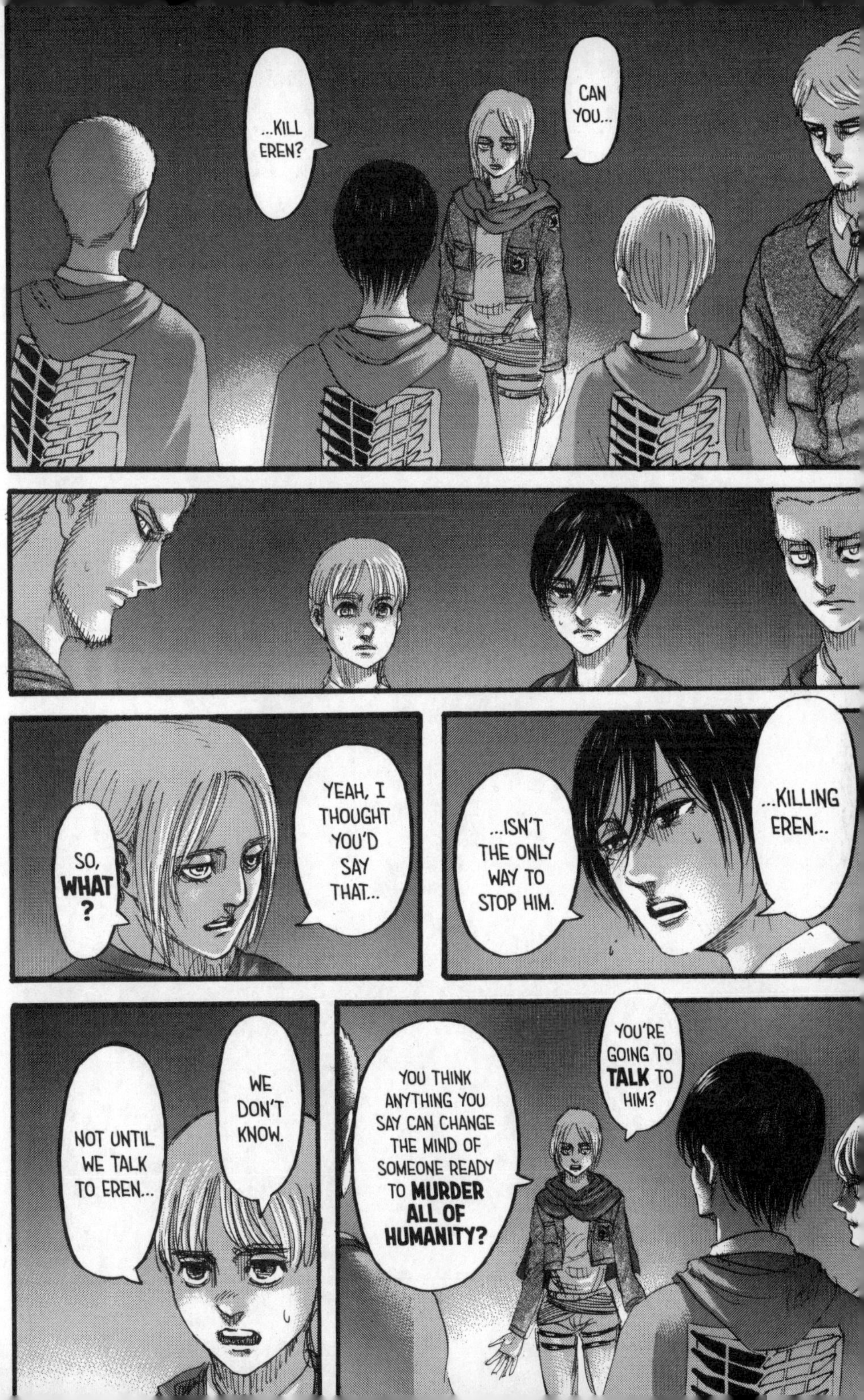
CAN YOU...
...KILL EREN?
...KILLING EREN...
...ISN'T THE ONLY WAY TO STOP HIM.
YEAH, I THOUGHT YOU'D SAY THAT...
SO, **WHAT**?
YOU'RE GOING TO **TALK** TO HIM?
YOU THINK ANYTHING YOU SAY CAN CHANGE THE MIND OF SOMEONE READY TO **MURDER ALL OF HUMANITY?**
WE DON'T KNOW.
NOT UNTIL WE TALK TO EREN...

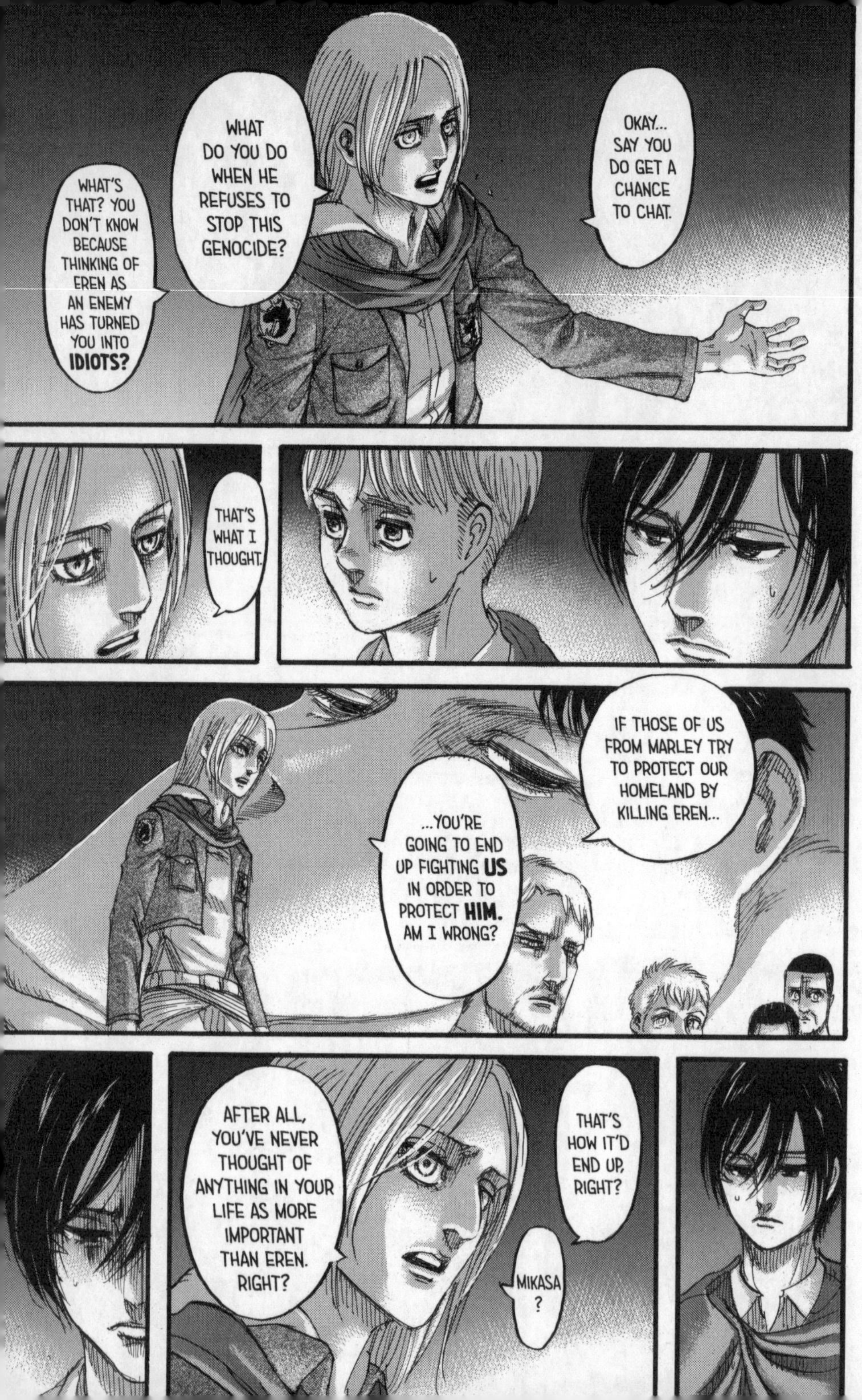
OKAY... SAY YOU DO GET A CHANCE TO CHAT.
WHAT DO YOU DO WHEN HE REFUSES TO STOP THIS GENOCIDE?
WHAT'S THAT? YOU DON'T KNOW BECAUSE THINKING OF EREN AS AN ENEMY HAS TURNED YOU INTO **IDIOTS?**
THAT'S WHAT I THOUGHT.
IF THOSE OF US FROM MARLEY TRY TO PROTECT OUR HOMELAND BY KILLING EREN...
...YOU'RE GOING TO END UP FIGHTING **US** IN ORDER TO PROTECT **HIM.** AM I WRONG?
THAT'S HOW IT'D END UP, RIGHT?
AFTER ALL, YOU'VE NEVER THOUGHT OF ANYTHING IN YOUR LIFE AS MORE IMPORTANT THAN EREN. RIGHT?
MIKASA?

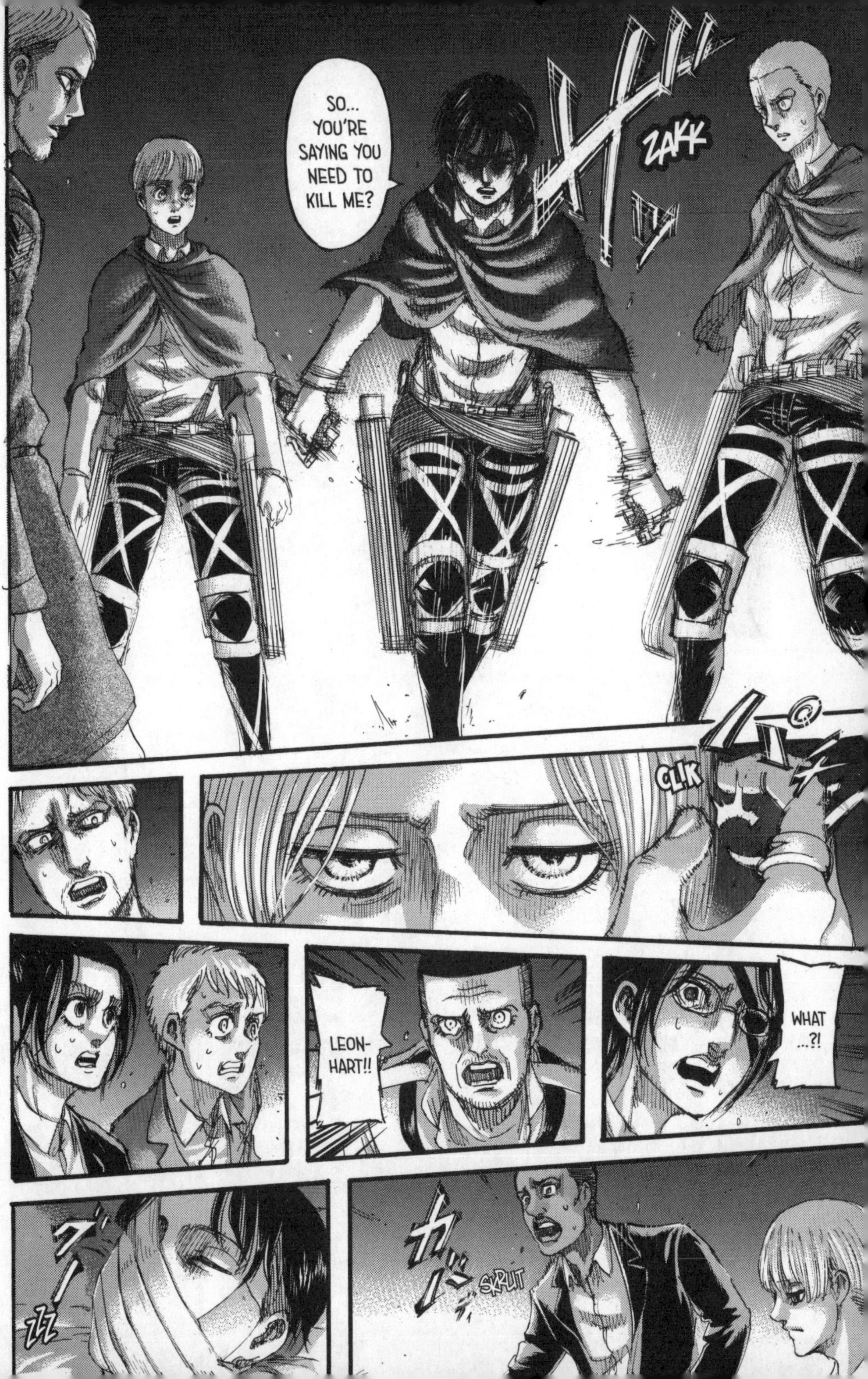
ZAKK
SO... YOU'RE SAYING YOU NEED TO KILL ME?
CLIK
WHAT ...?!
LEON-HART!!
SKRUT

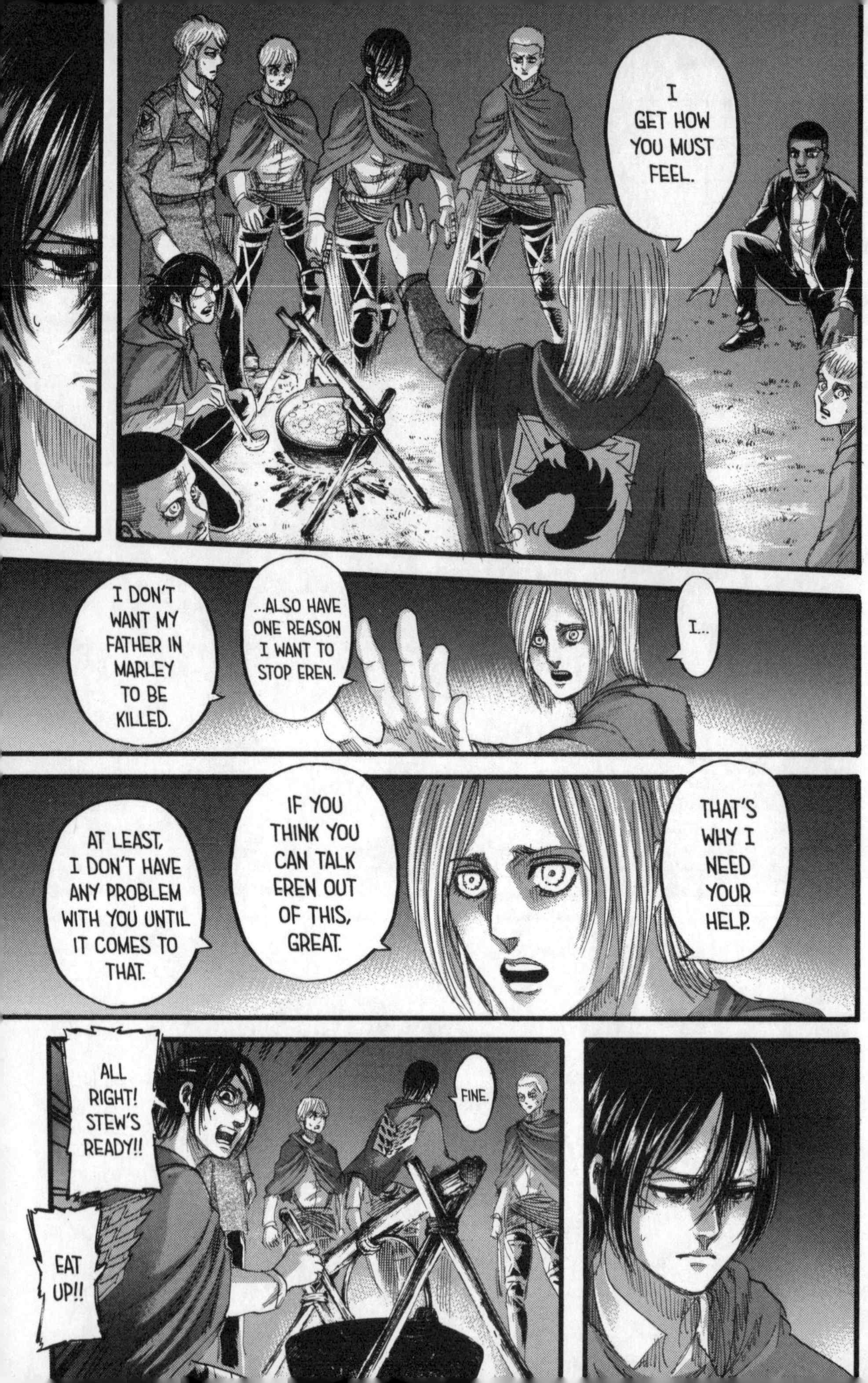
I GET HOW YOU MUST FEEL.
I...
...ALSO HAVE ONE REASON I WANT TO STOP EREN.
I DON'T WANT MY FATHER IN MARLEY TO BE KILLED.
THAT'S WHY I NEED YOUR HELP.
IF YOU THINK YOU CAN TALK EREN OUT OF THIS, GREAT.
AT LEAST, I DON'T HAVE ANY PROBLEM WITH YOU UNTIL IT COMES TO THAT.
FINE.
ALL RIGHT! STEW'S READY!!
EAT UP!!

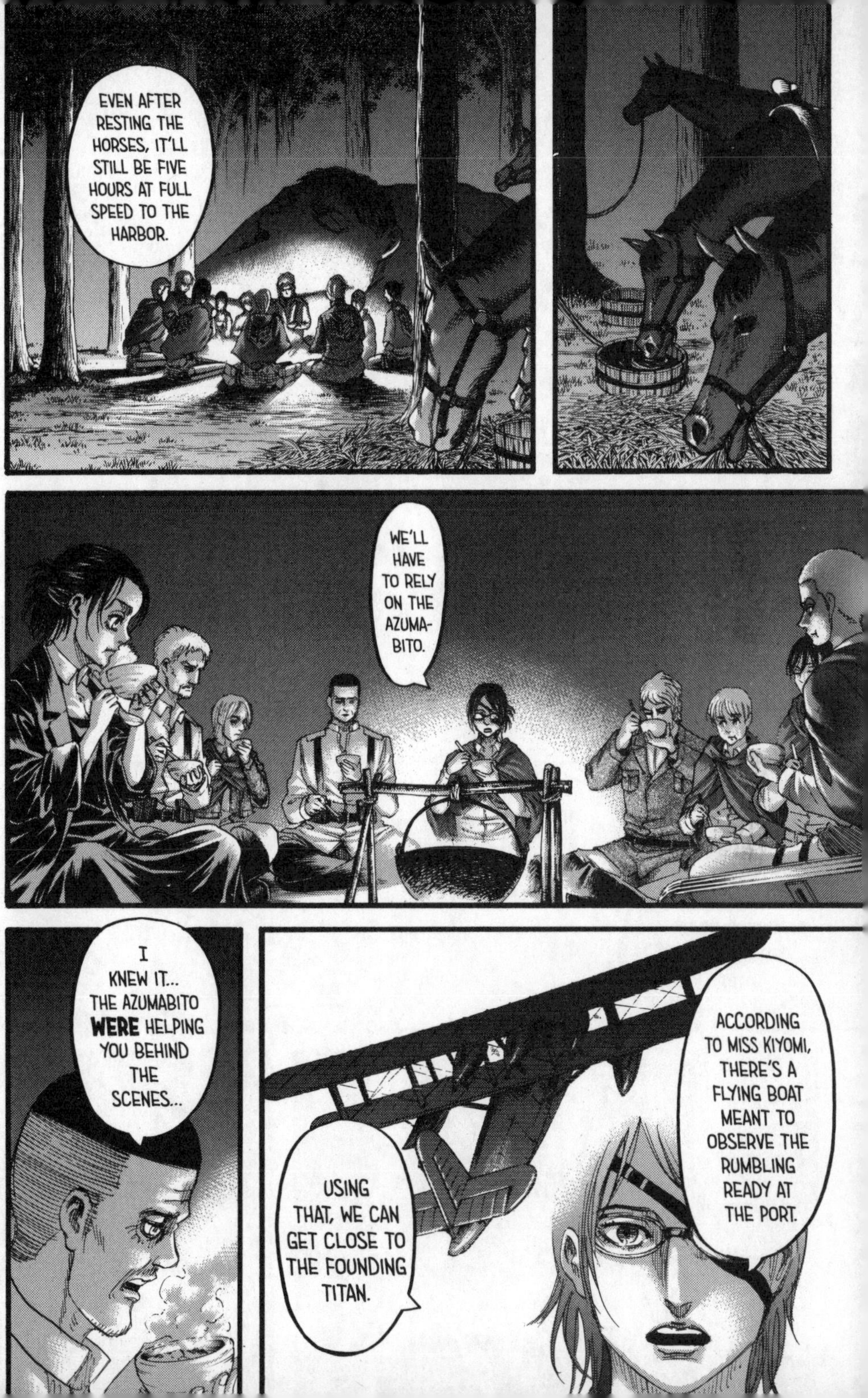
EVEN AFTER RESTING THE HORSES, IT'LL STILL BE FIVE HOURS AT FULL SPEED TO THE HARBOR.
WE'LL HAVE TO RELY ON THE AZUMABITO.
ACCORDING TO MISS KIYOMI, THERE'S A FLYING BOAT MEANT TO OBSERVE THE RUMBLING READY AT THE PORT.
USING THAT, WE CAN GET CLOSE TO THE FOUNDING TITAN.
I KNEW IT... THE AZUMABITO **WERE** HELPING YOU BEHIND THE SCENES...

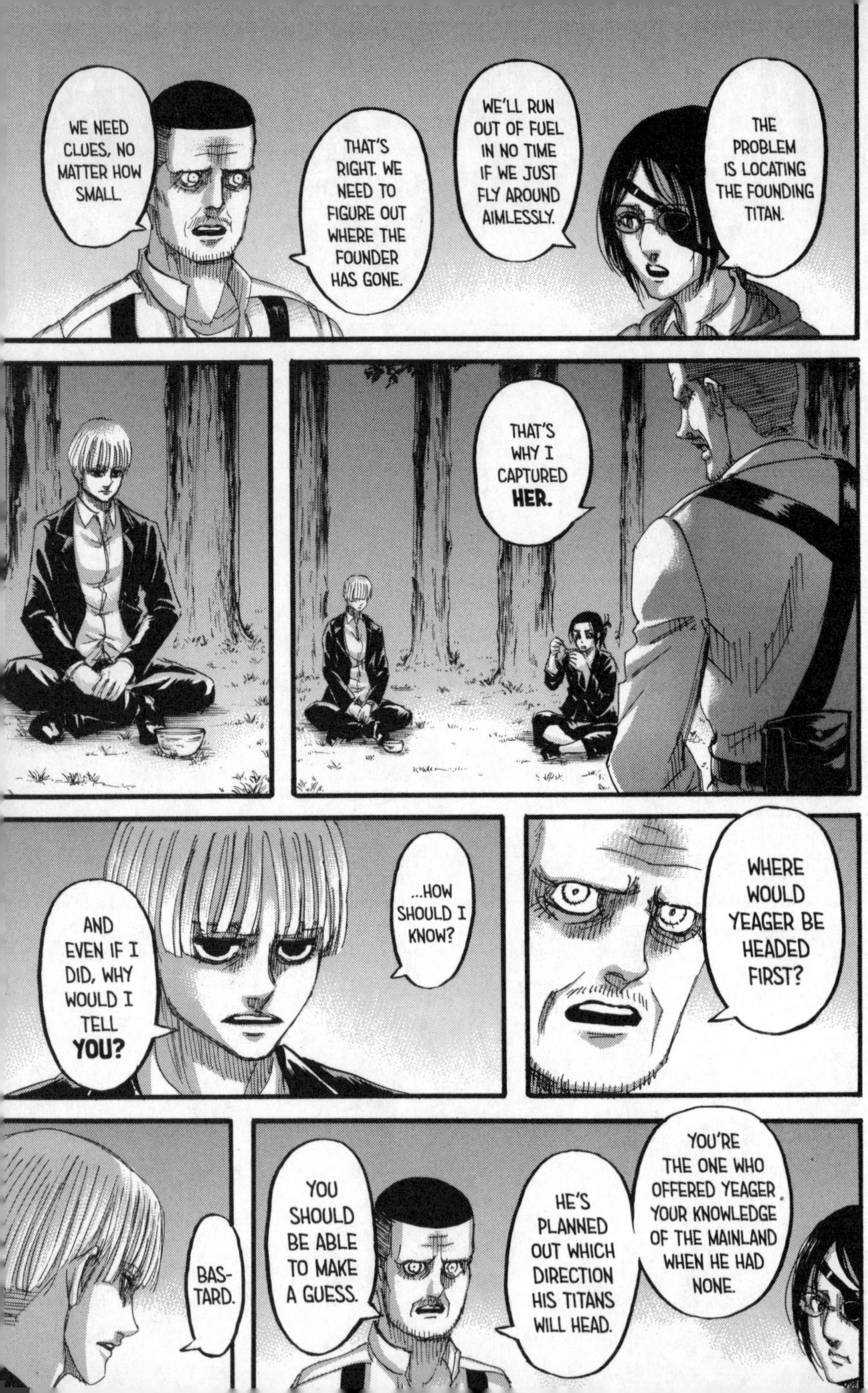
THE PROBLEM IS LOCATING THE FOUNDING TITAN.
WE'LL RUN OUT OF FUEL IN NO TIME IF WE JUST FLY AROUND AIMLESSLY.
THAT'S RIGHT. WE NEED TO FIGURE OUT WHERE THE FOUNDER HAS GONE.
WE NEED CLUES, NO MATTER HOW SMALL.
THAT'S WHY I CAPTURED **HER.**
WHERE WOULD YEAGER BE HEADED FIRST?
...HOW SHOULD I KNOW?
AND EVEN IF I DID, WHY WOULD I TELL **YOU?**
YOU'RE THE ONE WHO OFFERED YEAGER YOUR KNOWLEDGE OF THE MAINLAND WHEN HE HAD NONE.
HE'S PLANNED OUT WHICH DIRECTION HIS TITANS WILL HEAD.
YOU SHOULD BE ABLE TO MAKE A GUESS.
BAS-TARD.

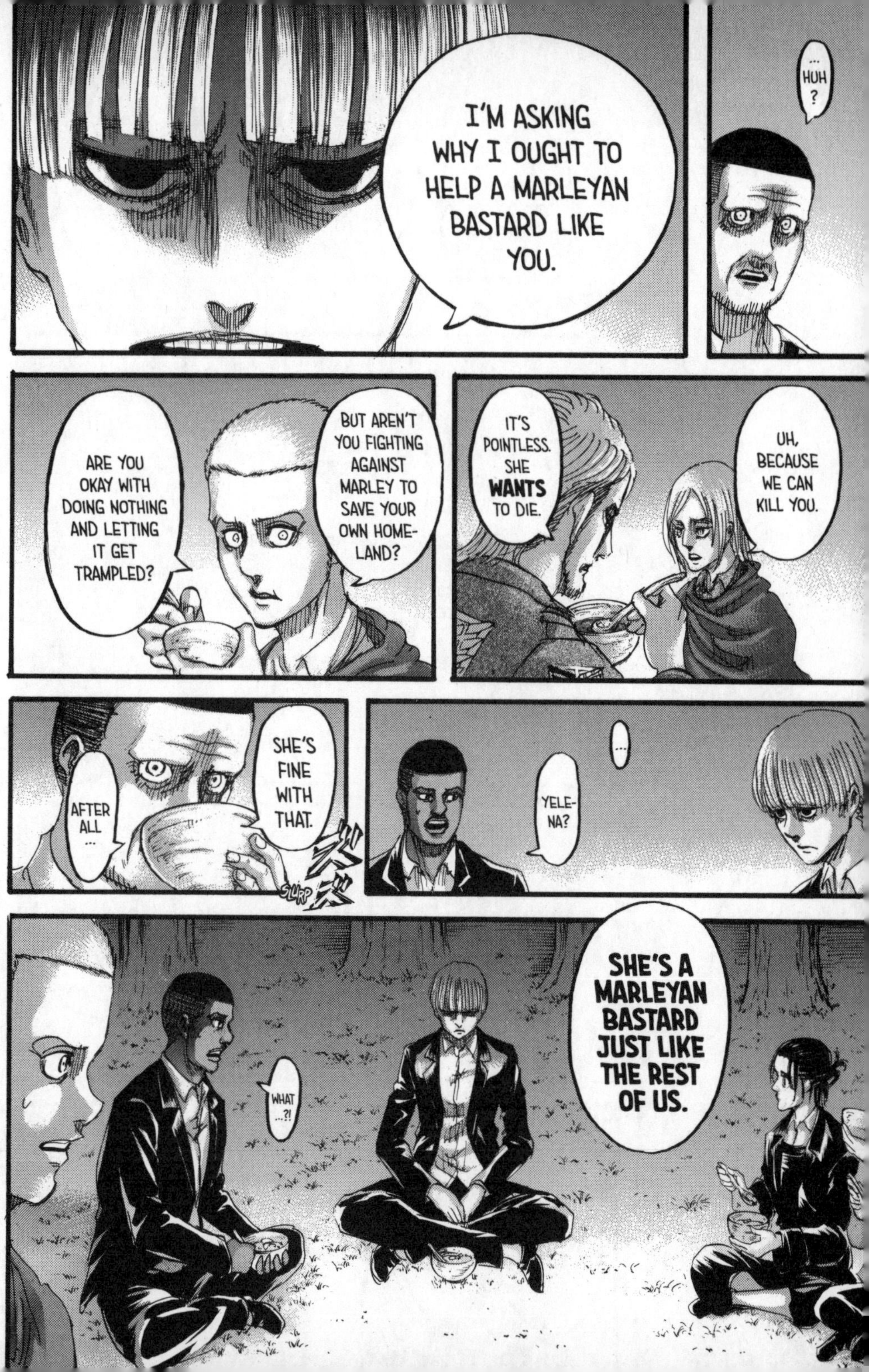

... HUH?
I'M ASKING WHY I OUGHT TO HELP A MARLEYAN BASTARD LIKE YOU.
UH, BECAUSE WE CAN KILL YOU.
IT'S POINTLESS. SHE **WANTS** TO DIE.
BUT AREN'T YOU FIGHTING AGAINST MARLEY TO SAVE YOUR OWN HOME-LAND?
ARE YOU OKAY WITH DOING NOTHING AND LETTING IT GET TRAMPLED?
...
YELE-NA?
SHE'S FINE WITH THAT.
SLURP
AFTER ALL ...
SHE'S A MARLEYAN BASTARD JUST LIKE THE REST OF US.
WHAT ...?!

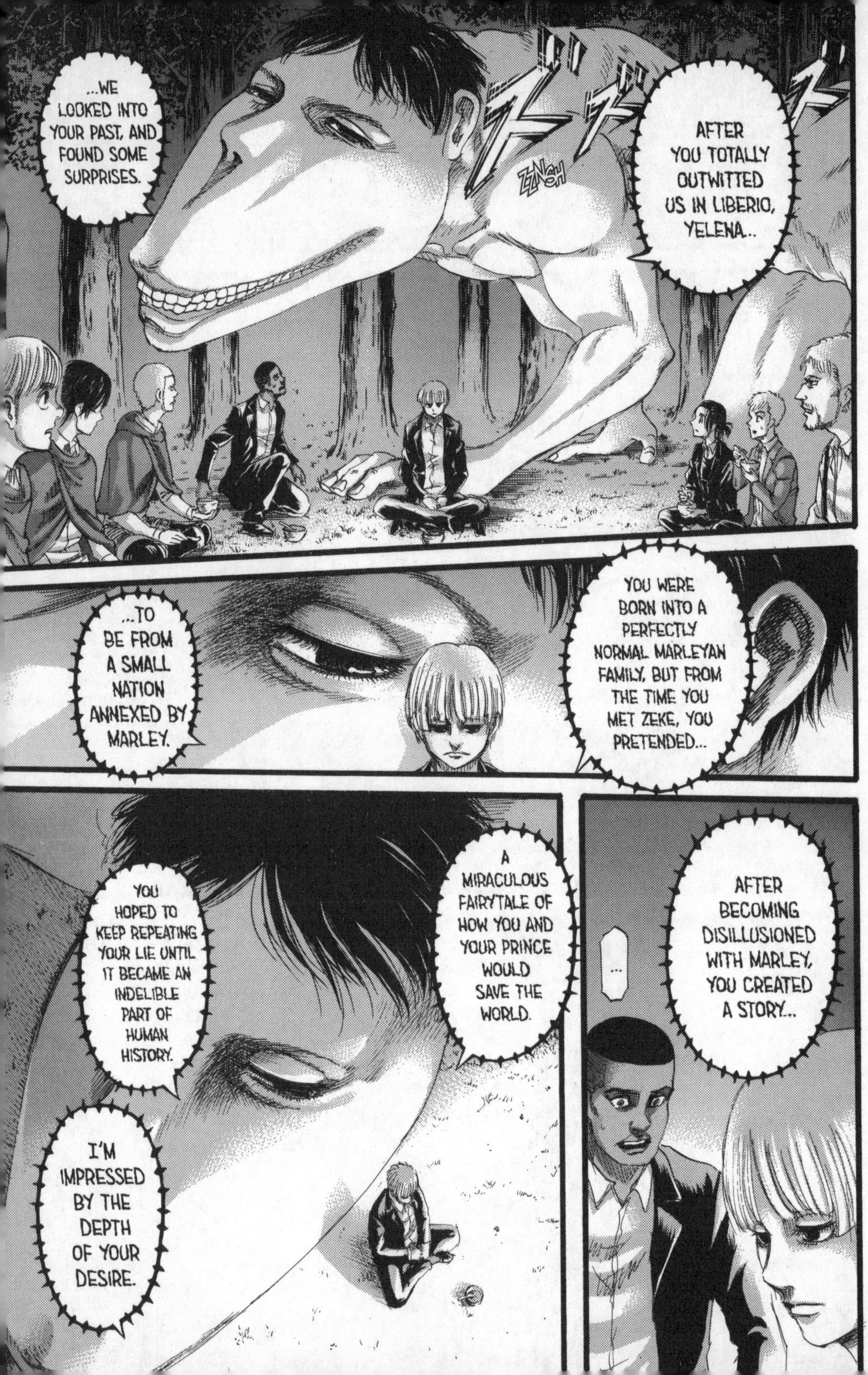
AFTER YOU TOTALLY OUTWITTED US IN LIBERIO, YELENA...
ZZNGH
...WE LOOKED INTO YOUR PAST, AND FOUND SOME SURPRISES.
YOU WERE BORN INTO A PERFECTLY NORMAL MARLEYAN FAMILY, BUT FROM THE TIME YOU MET ZEKE, YOU PRETENDED...
...TO BE FROM A SMALL NATION ANNEXED BY MARLEY.
AFTER BECOMING DISILLUSIONED WITH MARLEY, YOU CREATED A STORY...
...
A MIRACULOUS FAIRYTALE OF HOW YOU AND YOUR PRINCE WOULD SAVE THE WORLD.
YOU HOPED TO KEEP REPEATING YOUR LIE UNTIL IT BECAME AN INDELIBLE PART OF HUMAN HISTORY.
I'M IMPRESSED BY THE DEPTH OF YOUR DESIRE.

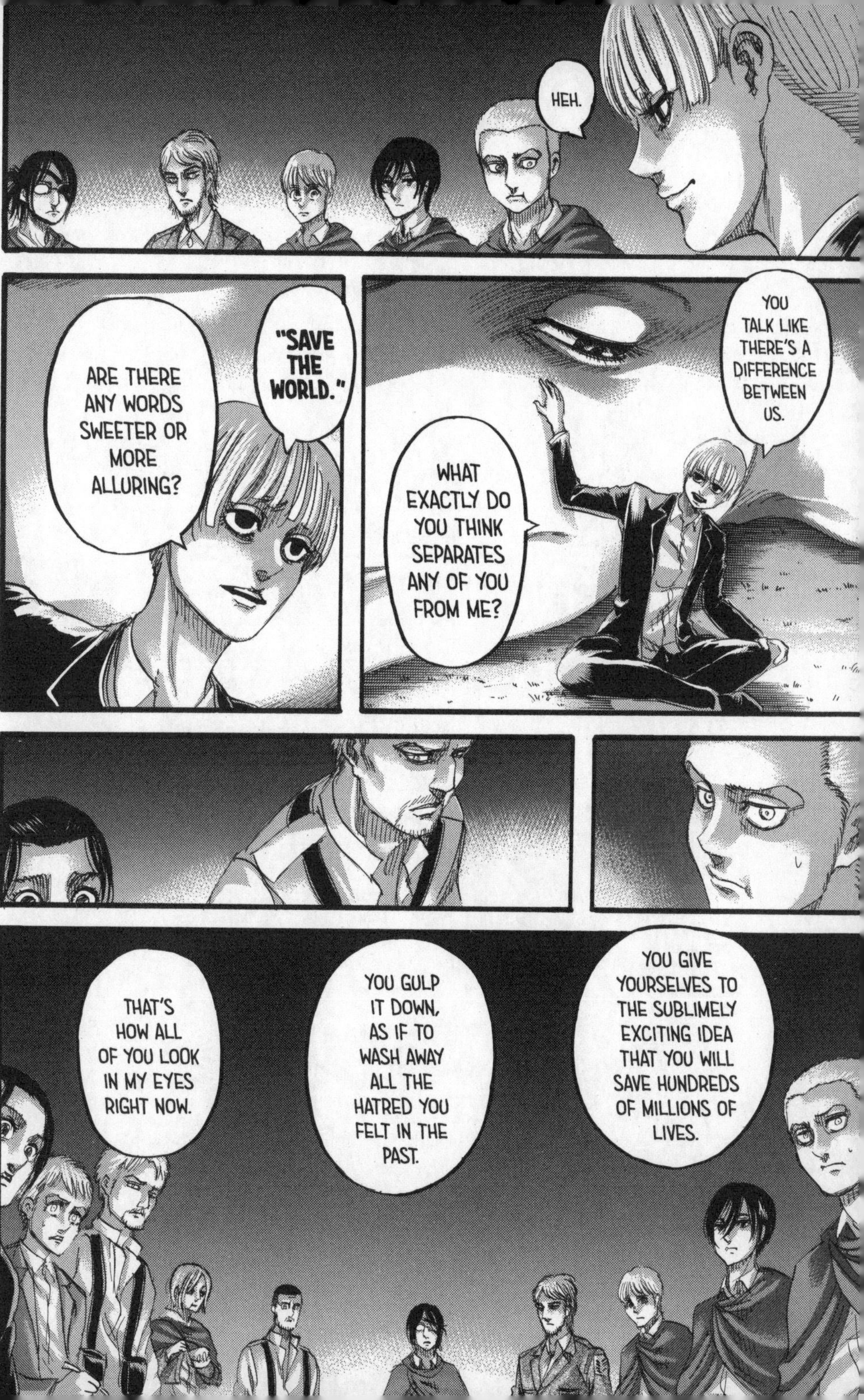
HEH.
YOU TALK LIKE THERE'S A DIFFERENCE BETWEEN US.
WHAT EXACTLY DO YOU THINK SEPARATES ANY OF YOU FROM ME?
"SAVE THE WORLD."
ARE THERE ANY WORDS SWEETER OR MORE ALLURING?
YOU GIVE YOURSELVES TO THE SUBLIMELY EXCITING IDEA THAT YOU WILL SAVE HUNDREDS OF MILLIONS OF LIVES.
YOU GULP IT DOWN, AS IF TO WASH AWAY ALL THE HATRED YOU FELT IN THE PAST.
THAT'S HOW ALL OF YOU LOOK IN MY EYES RIGHT NOW.

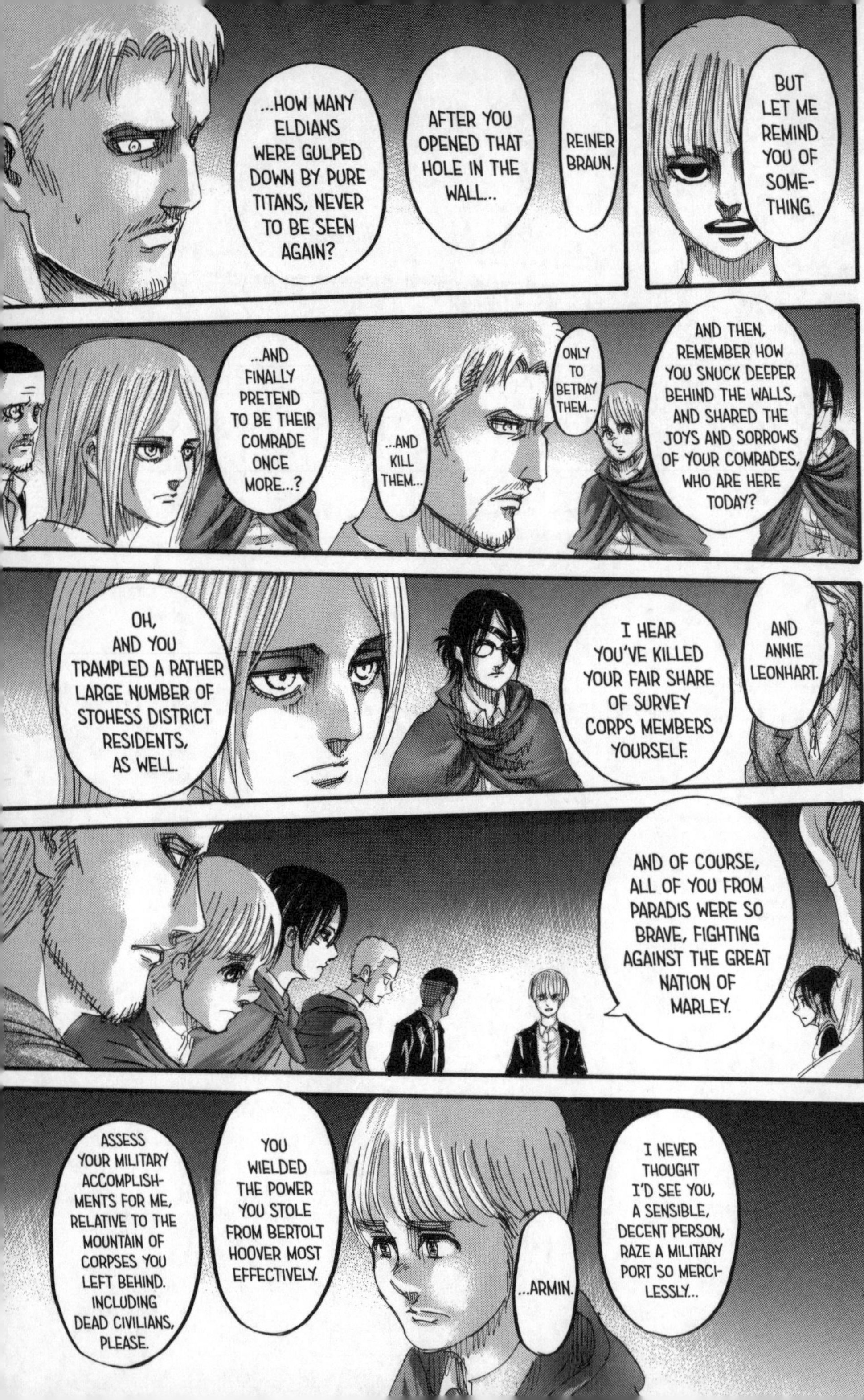
BUT LET ME REMIND YOU OF SOME-THING.
REINER BRAUN.
AFTER YOU OPENED THAT HOLE IN THE WALL...
...HOW MANY ELDIANS WERE GULPED DOWN BY PURE TITANS, NEVER TO BE SEEN AGAIN?
AND THEN, REMEMBER HOW YOU SNUCK DEEPER BEHIND THE WALLS, AND SHARED THE JOYS AND SORROWS OF YOUR COMRADES, WHO ARE HERE TODAY?
ONLY TO BETRAY THEM...
...AND KILL THEM...
...AND FINALLY PRETEND TO BE THEIR COMRADE ONCE MORE...?
AND ANNIE LEONHART.
I HEAR YOU'VE KILLED YOUR FAIR SHARE OF SURVEY CORPS MEMBERS YOURSELF.
OH, AND YOU TRAMPLED A RATHER LARGE NUMBER OF STOHESS DISTRICT RESIDENTS, AS WELL.
AND OF COURSE, ALL OF YOU FROM PARADIS WERE SO BRAVE, FIGHTING AGAINST THE GREAT NATION OF MARLEY.
I NEVER THOUGHT I'D SEE YOU, A SENSIBLE, DECENT PERSON, RAZE A MILITARY PORT SO MERCI-LESSLY...
...ARMIN.
YOU WIELDED THE POWER YOU STOLE FROM BERTOLT HOOVER MOST EFFECTIVELY.
ASSESS YOUR MILITARY ACCOMPLISH-MENTS FOR ME, RELATIVE TO THE MOUNTAIN OF CORPSES YOU LEFT BEHIND. INCLUDING DEAD CIVILIANS, PLEASE.

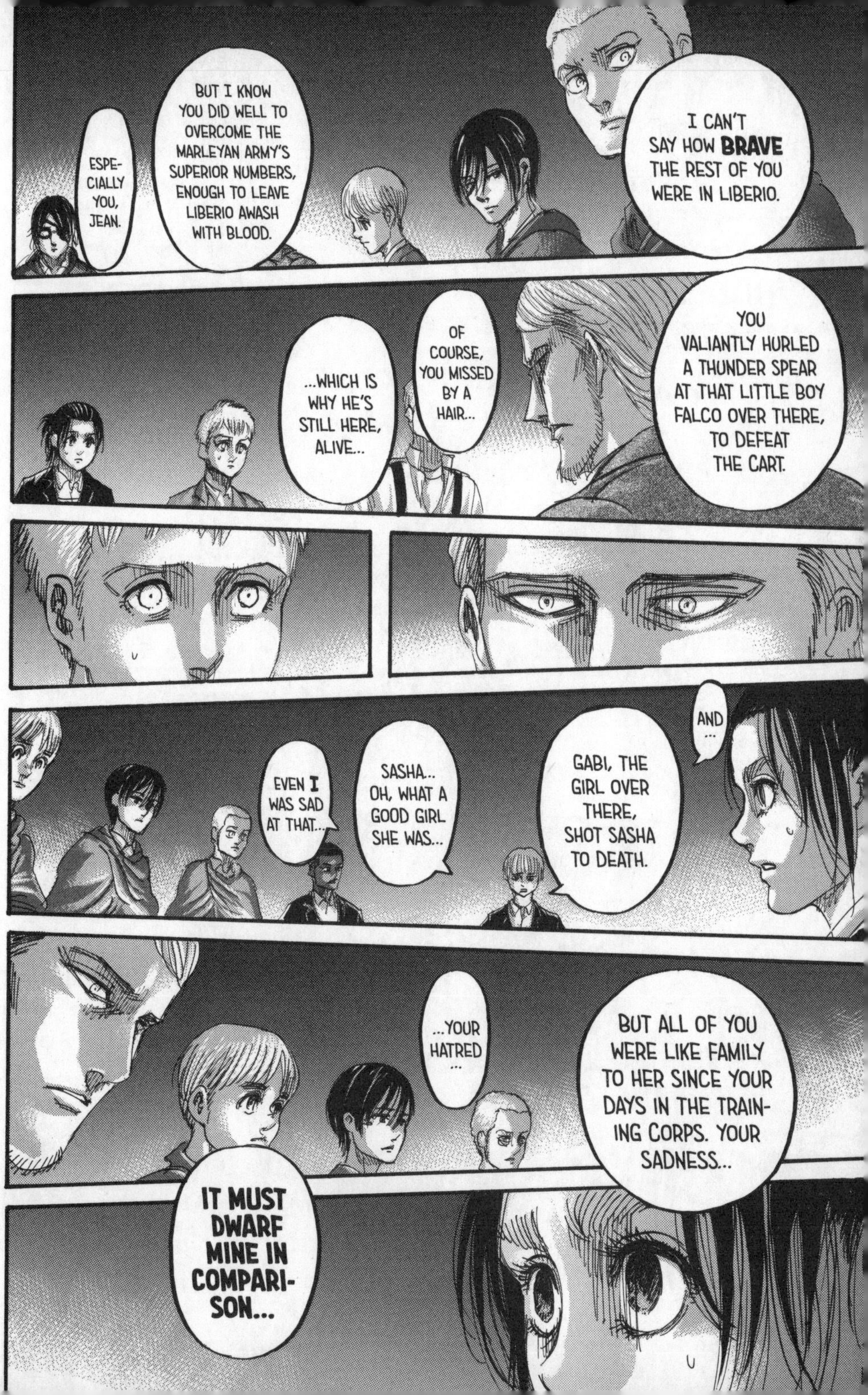
I CAN'T SAY HOW BRAVE THE REST OF YOU WERE IN LIBERIO.
BUT I KNOW YOU DID WELL TO OVERCOME THE MARLEYAN ARMY'S SUPERIOR NUMBERS, ENOUGH TO LEAVE LIBERIO AWASH WITH BLOOD.
ESPECIALLY YOU, JEAN.
YOU VALIANTLY HURLED A THUNDER SPEAR AT THAT LITTLE BOY FALCO OVER THERE, TO DEFEAT THE CART.
OF COURSE, YOU MISSED BY A HAIR...
...WHICH IS WHY HE'S STILL HERE, ALIVE...
AND...
GABI, THE GIRL OVER THERE, SHOT SASHA TO DEATH.
SASHA... OH, WHAT A GOOD GIRL SHE WAS...
EVEN I WAS SAD AT THAT...
BUT ALL OF YOU WERE LIKE FAMILY TO HER SINCE YOUR DAYS IN THE TRAINING CORPS. YOUR SADNESS...
...YOUR HATRED...
IT MUST DWARF MINE IN COMPARISON...

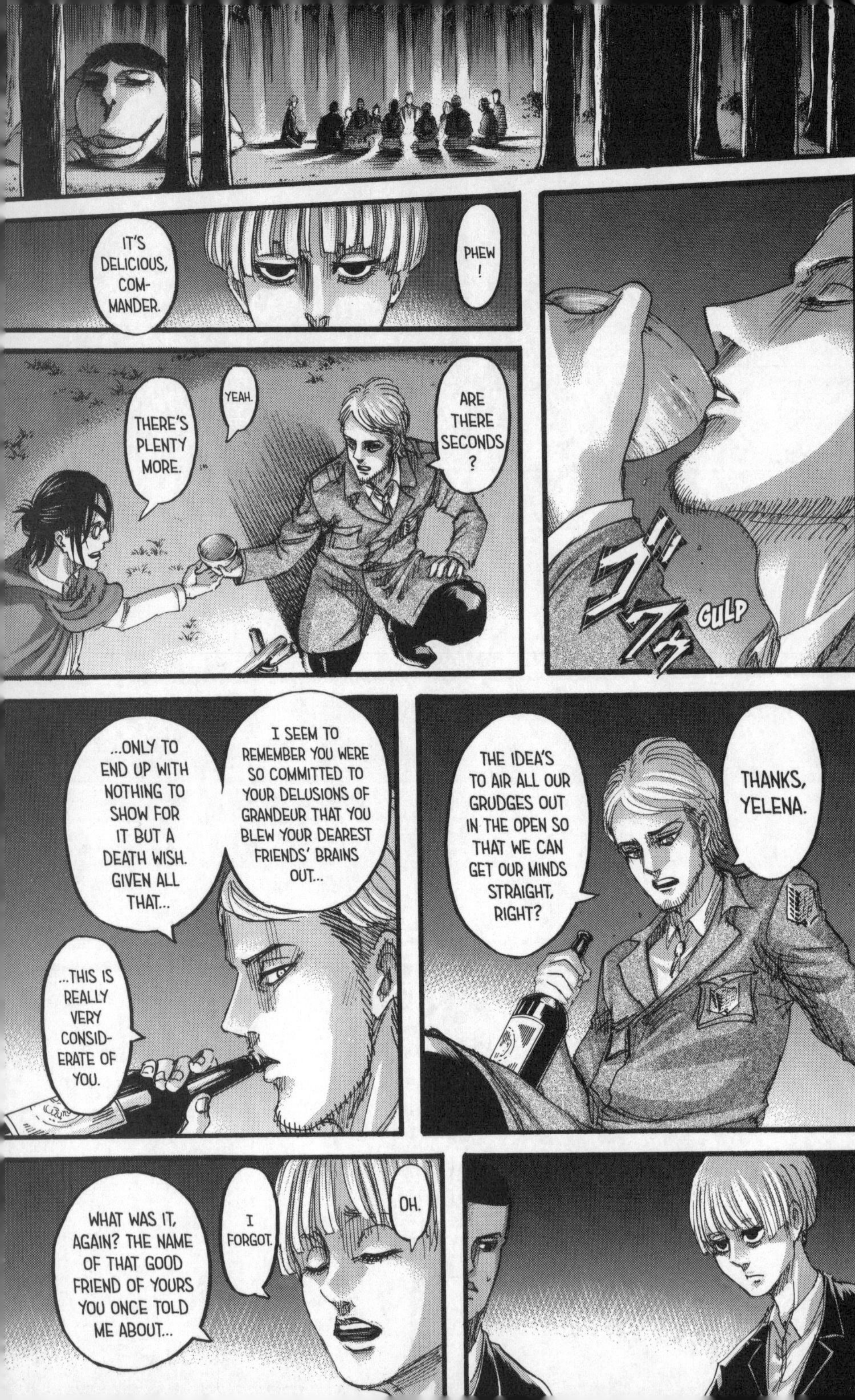
ゴクッ
GULP
PHEW!
IT'S DELICIOUS, COM-MANDER.
ARE THERE SECONDS?
YEAH.
THERE'S PLENTY MORE.
THANKS, YELENA.
THE IDEA'S TO AIR ALL OUR GRUDGES OUT IN THE OPEN SO THAT WE CAN GET OUR MINDS STRAIGHT, RIGHT?
I SEEM TO REMEMBER YOU WERE SO COMMITTED TO YOUR DELUSIONS OF GRANDEUR THAT YOU BLEW YOUR DEAREST FRIENDS' BRAINS OUT...
...ONLY TO END UP WITH NOTHING TO SHOW FOR IT BUT A DEATH WISH. GIVEN ALL THAT...
...THIS IS REALLY VERY CONSID-ERATE OF YOU.
OH.
I FORGOT.
WHAT WAS IT, AGAIN? THE NAME OF THAT GOOD FRIEND OF YOURS YOU ONCE TOLD ME ABOUT...

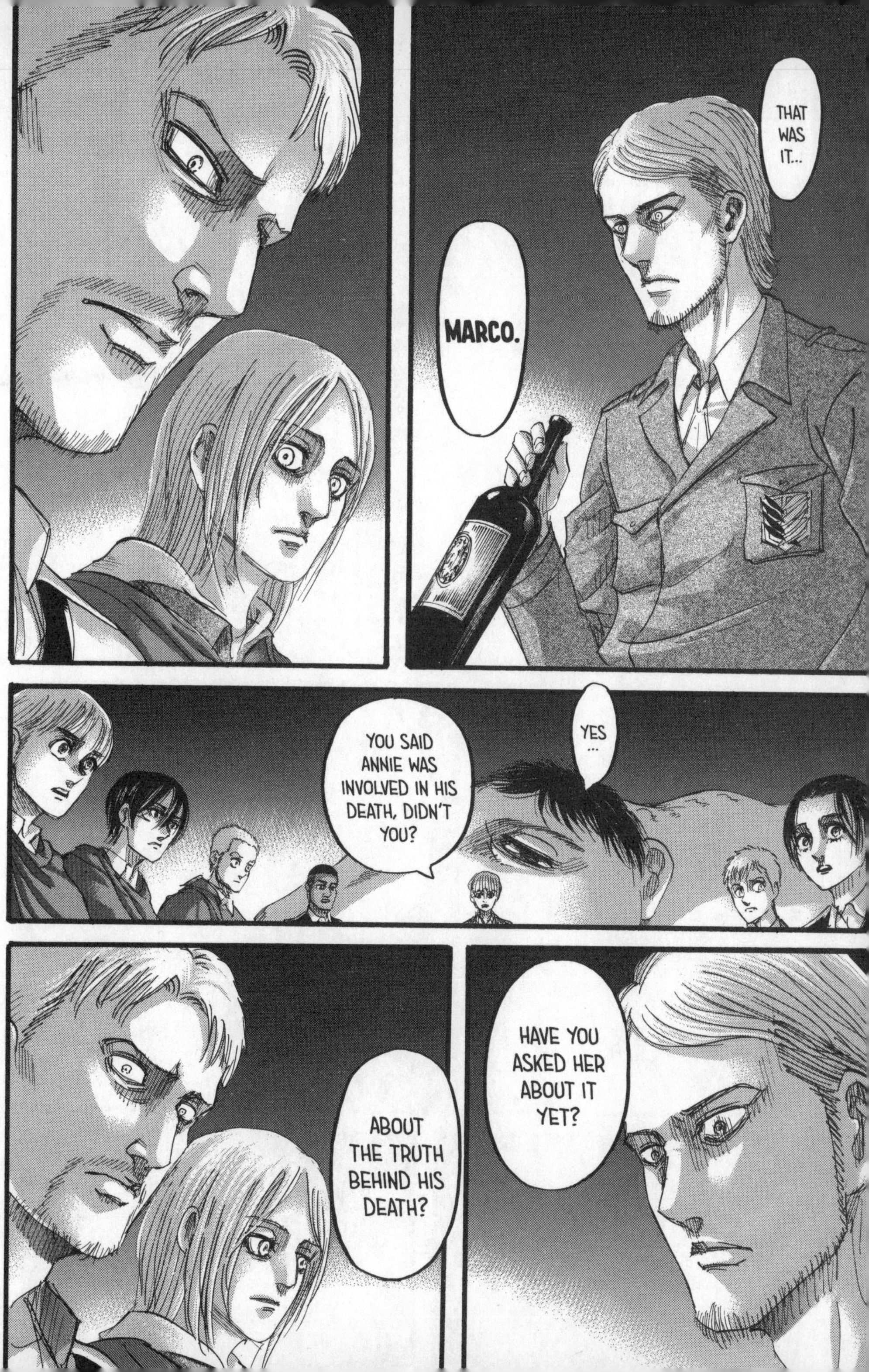
THAT WAS IT...
MARCO.
YES ...
YOU SAID ANNIE WAS INVOLVED IN HIS DEATH, DIDN'T YOU?
HAVE YOU ASKED HER ABOUT IT YET?
ABOUT THE TRUTH BEHIND HIS DEATH?

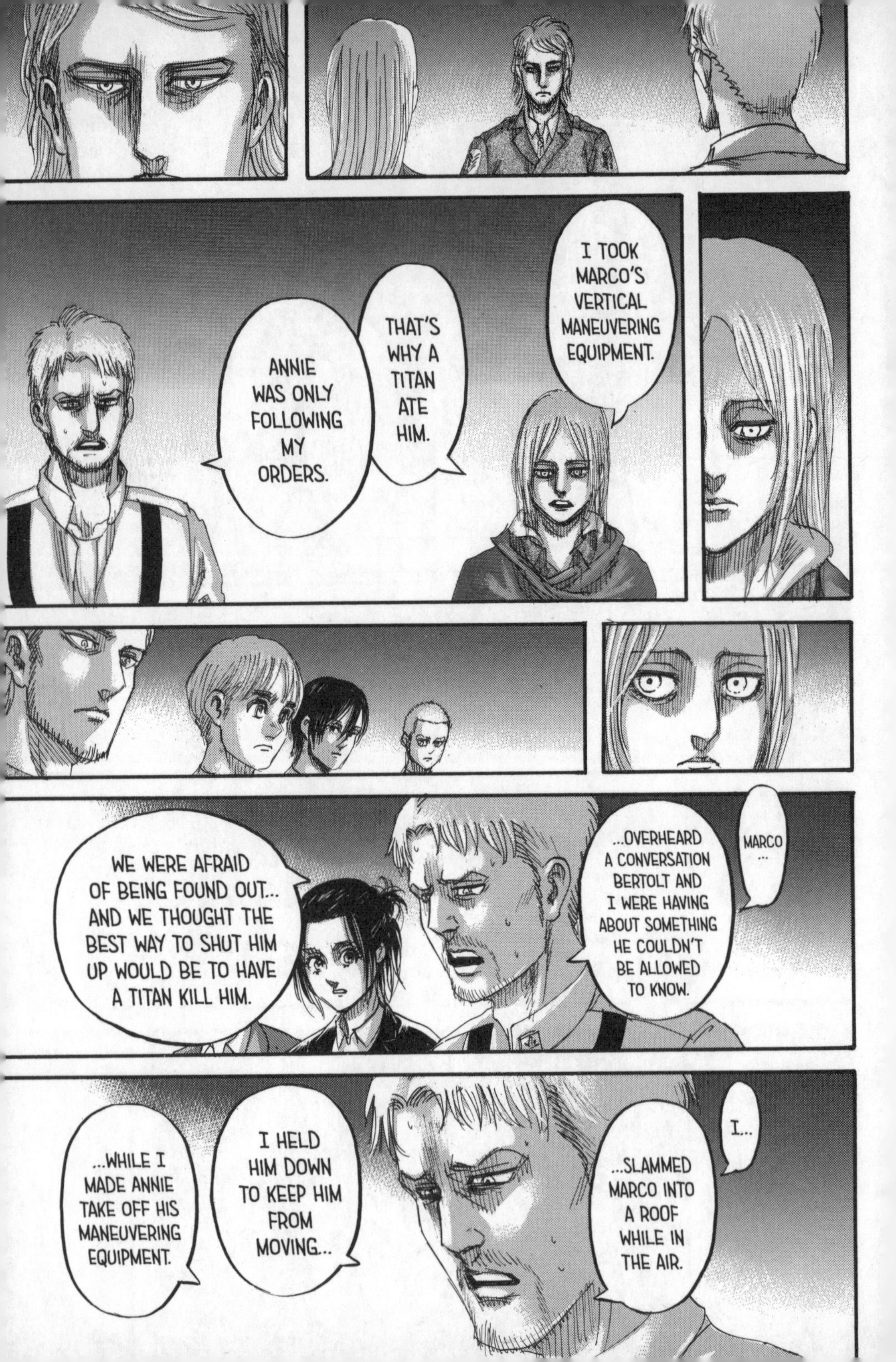
I TOOK MARCO'S VERTICAL MANEUVERING EQUIPMENT.
THAT'S WHY A TITAN ATE HIM.
ANNIE WAS ONLY FOLLOWING MY ORDERS.
MARCO...
...OVERHEARD A CONVERSATION BERTOLT AND I WERE HAVING ABOUT SOMETHING HE COULDN'T BE ALLOWED TO KNOW.
WE WERE AFRAID OF BEING FOUND OUT... AND WE THOUGHT THE BEST WAY TO SHUT HIM UP WOULD BE TO HAVE A TITAN KILL HIM.
I...
...SLAMMED MARCO INTO A ROOF WHILE IN THE AIR.
I HELD HIM DOWN TO KEEP HIM FROM MOVING...
...WHILE I MADE ANNIE TAKE OFF HIS MANEUVERING EQUIPMENT.

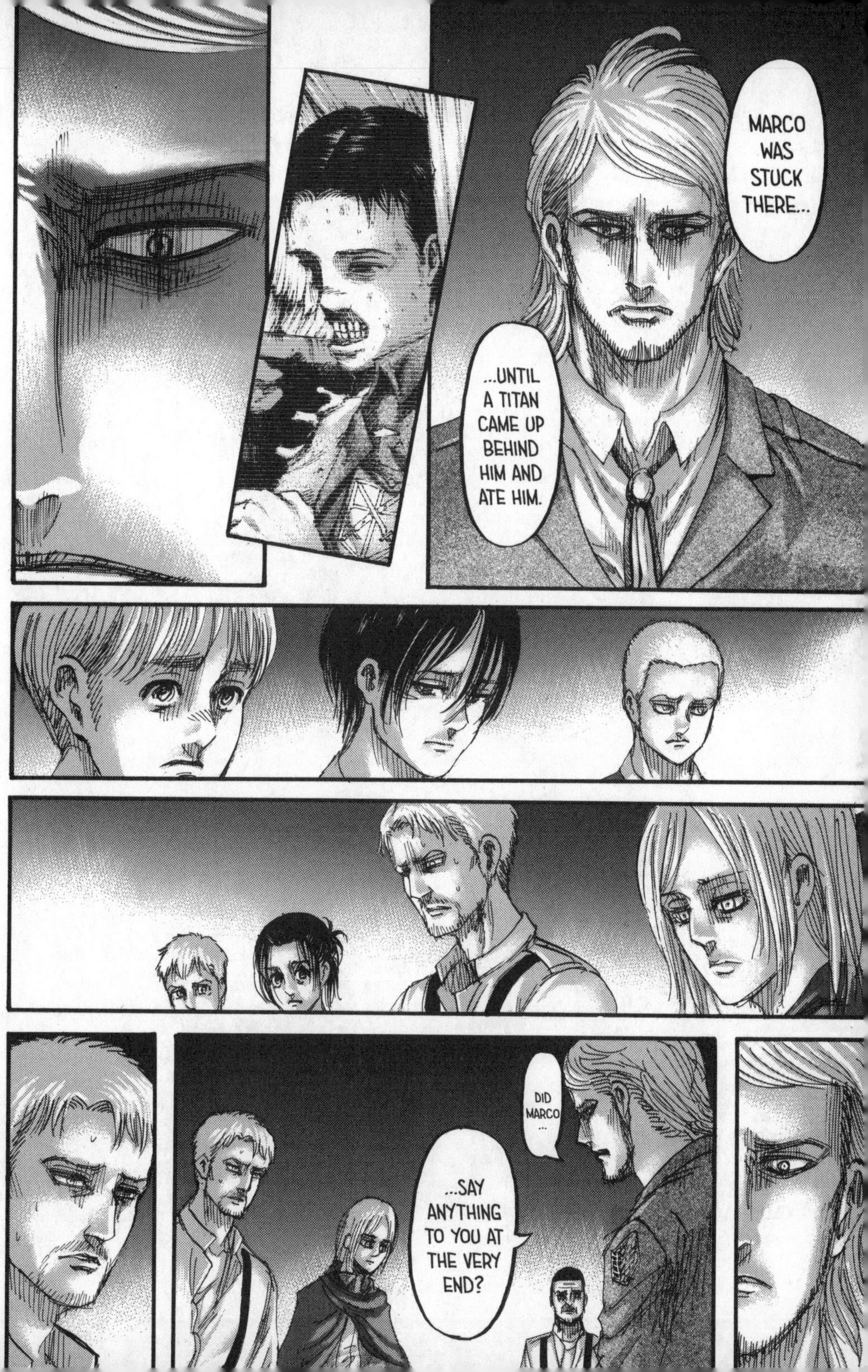
MARCO WAS STUCK THERE...
...UNTIL A TITAN CAME UP BEHIND HIM AND ATE HIM.
DID MARCO...
...SAY ANYTHING TO YOU AT THE VERY END?

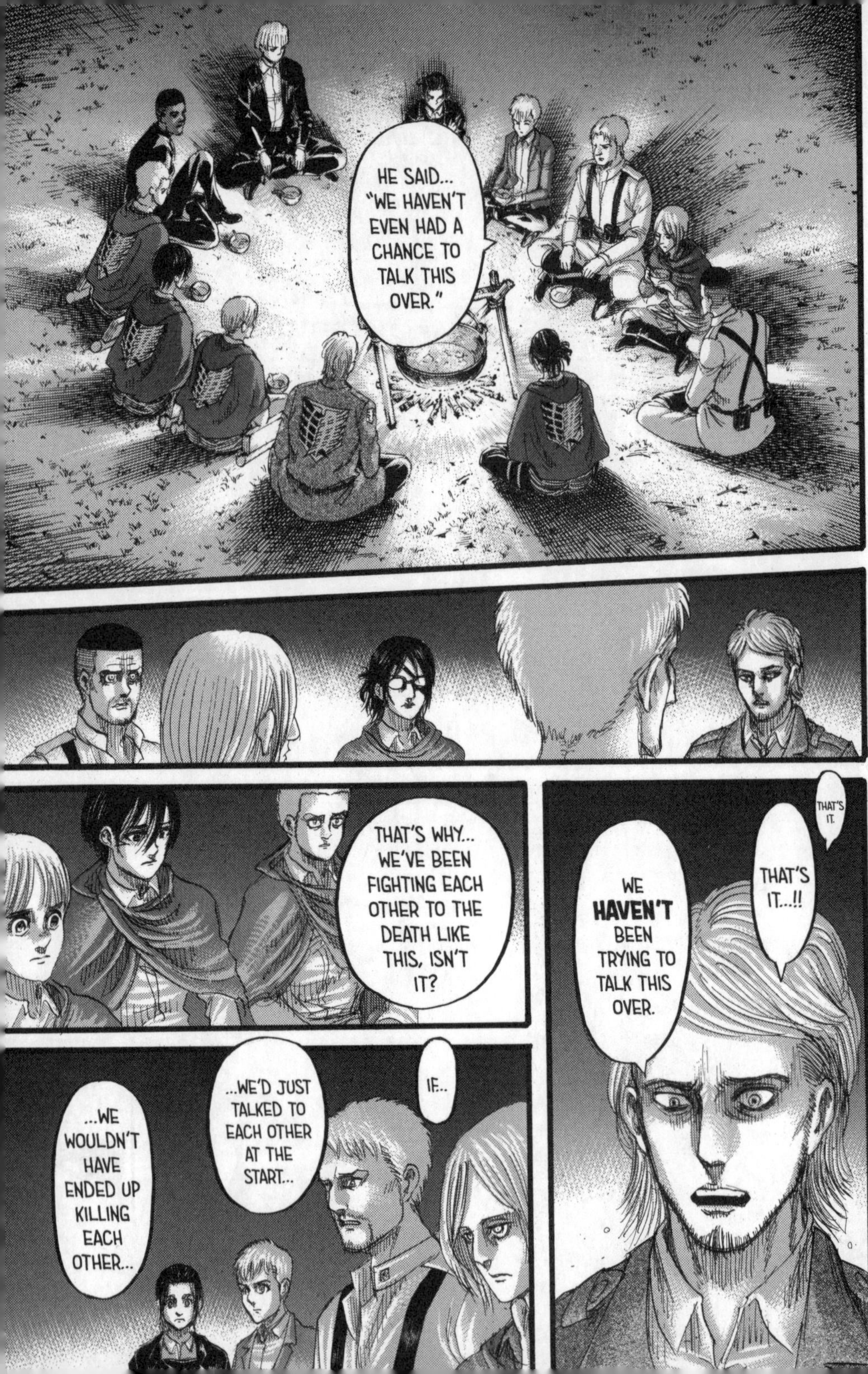
HE SAID... "WE HAVEN'T EVEN HAD A CHANCE TO TALK THIS OVER."
THAT'S IT.
THAT'S IT...!!
WE HAVEN'T BEEN TRYING TO TALK THIS OVER.
THAT'S WHY... WE'VE BEEN FIGHTING EACH OTHER TO THE DEATH LIKE THIS, ISN'T IT?
IF...
...WE'D JUST TALKED TO EACH OTHER AT THE START...
...WE WOULDN'T HAVE ENDED UP KILLING EACH OTHER...

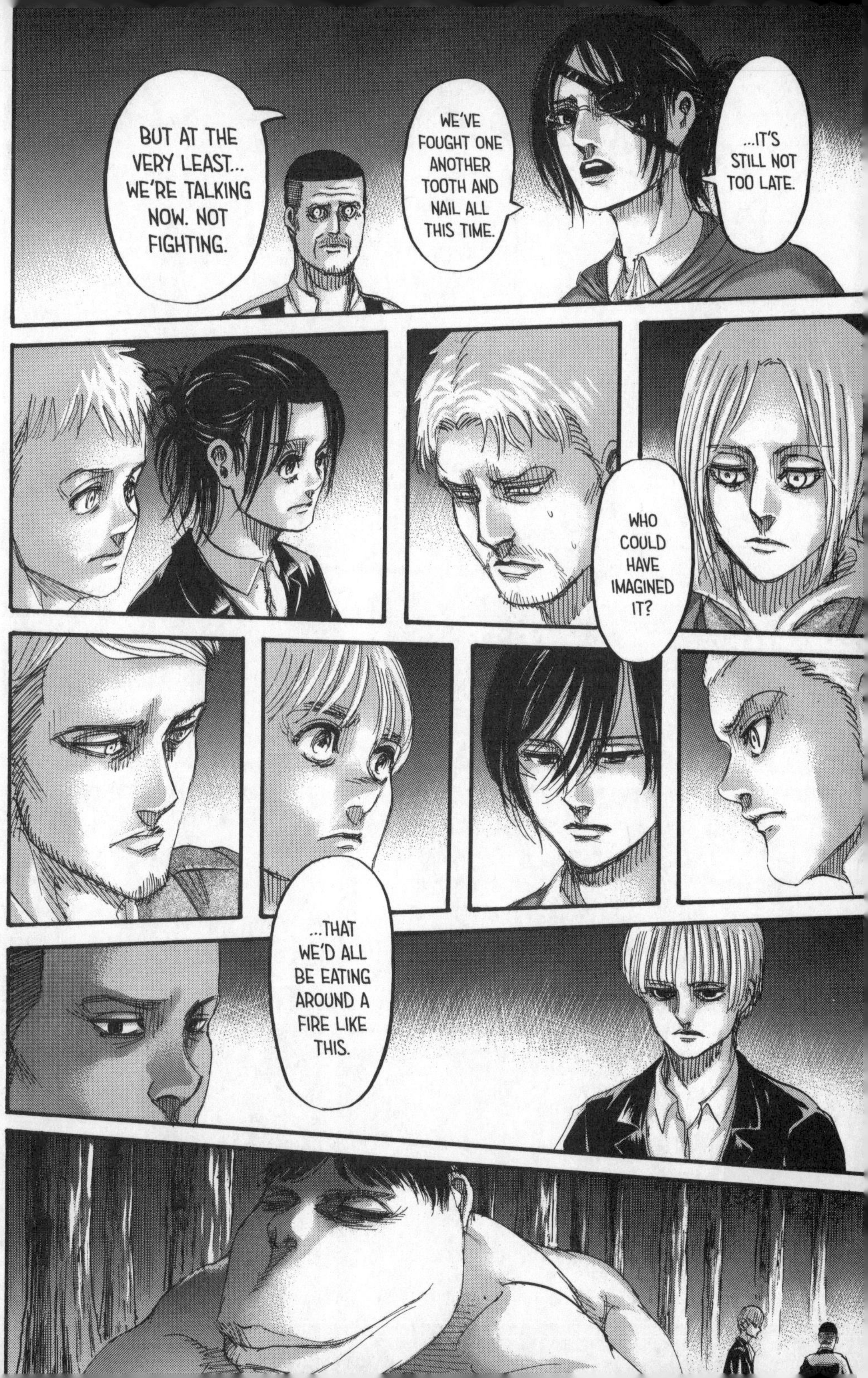
...IT'S STILL NOT TOO LATE.
WE'VE FOUGHT ONE ANOTHER TOOTH AND NAIL ALL THIS TIME.
BUT AT THE VERY LEAST... WE'RE TALKING NOW. NOT FIGHTING.
WHO COULD HAVE IMAGINED IT?
...THAT WE'D ALL BE EATING AROUND A FIRE LIKE THIS.

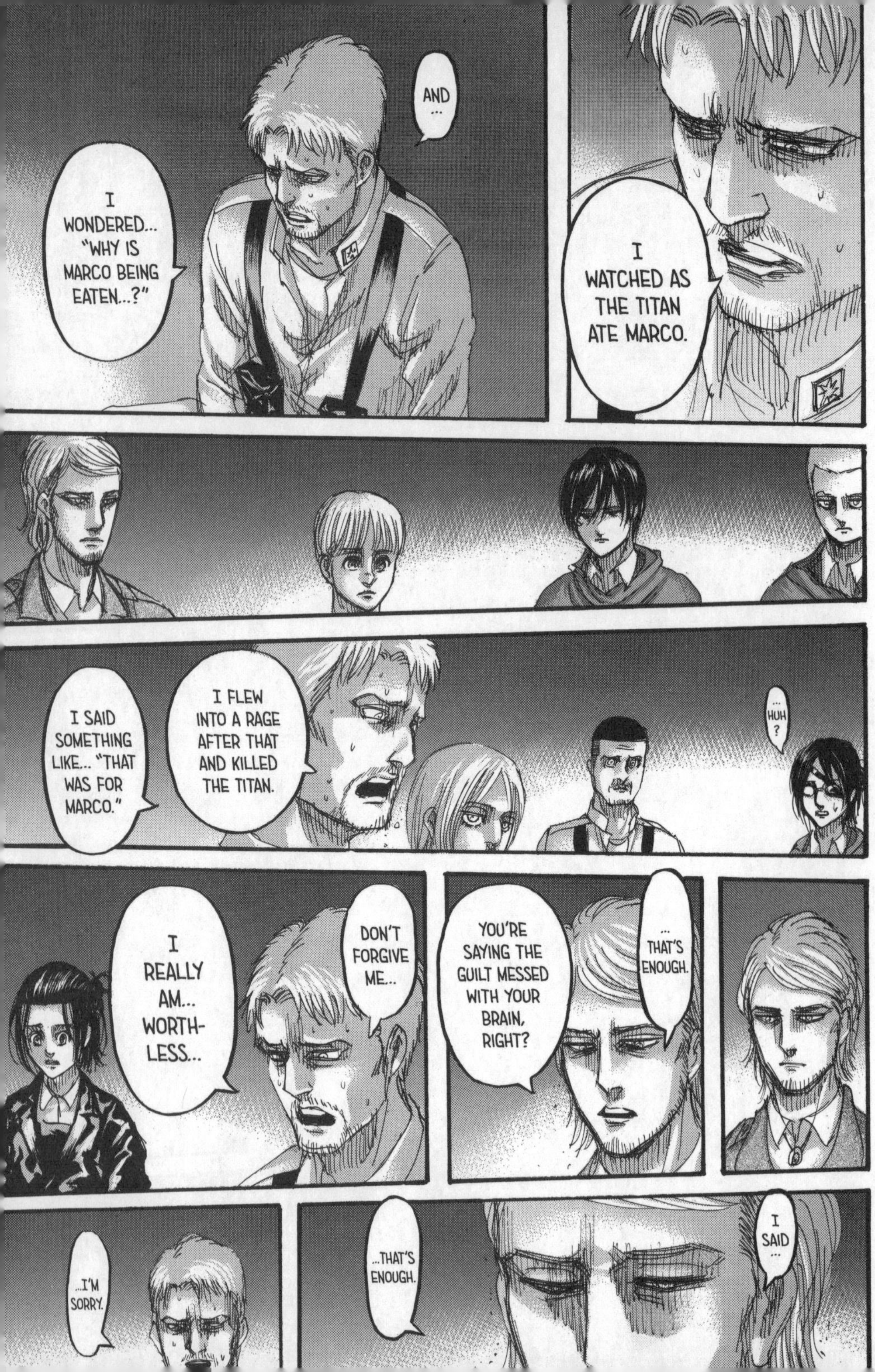
I WATCHED AS THE TITAN ATE MARCO.
AND ...
I WONDERED... "WHY IS MARCO BEING EATEN...?"
... HUH ?
I FLEW INTO A RAGE AFTER THAT AND KILLED THE TITAN.
I SAID SOMETHING LIKE... "THAT WAS FOR MARCO."
... THAT'S ENOUGH.
YOU'RE SAYING THE GUILT MESSED WITH YOUR BRAIN, RIGHT?
DON'T FORGIVE ME...
I REALLY AM... WORTH-LESS...
I SAID ...
...THAT'S ENOUGH.
...I'M SORRY.

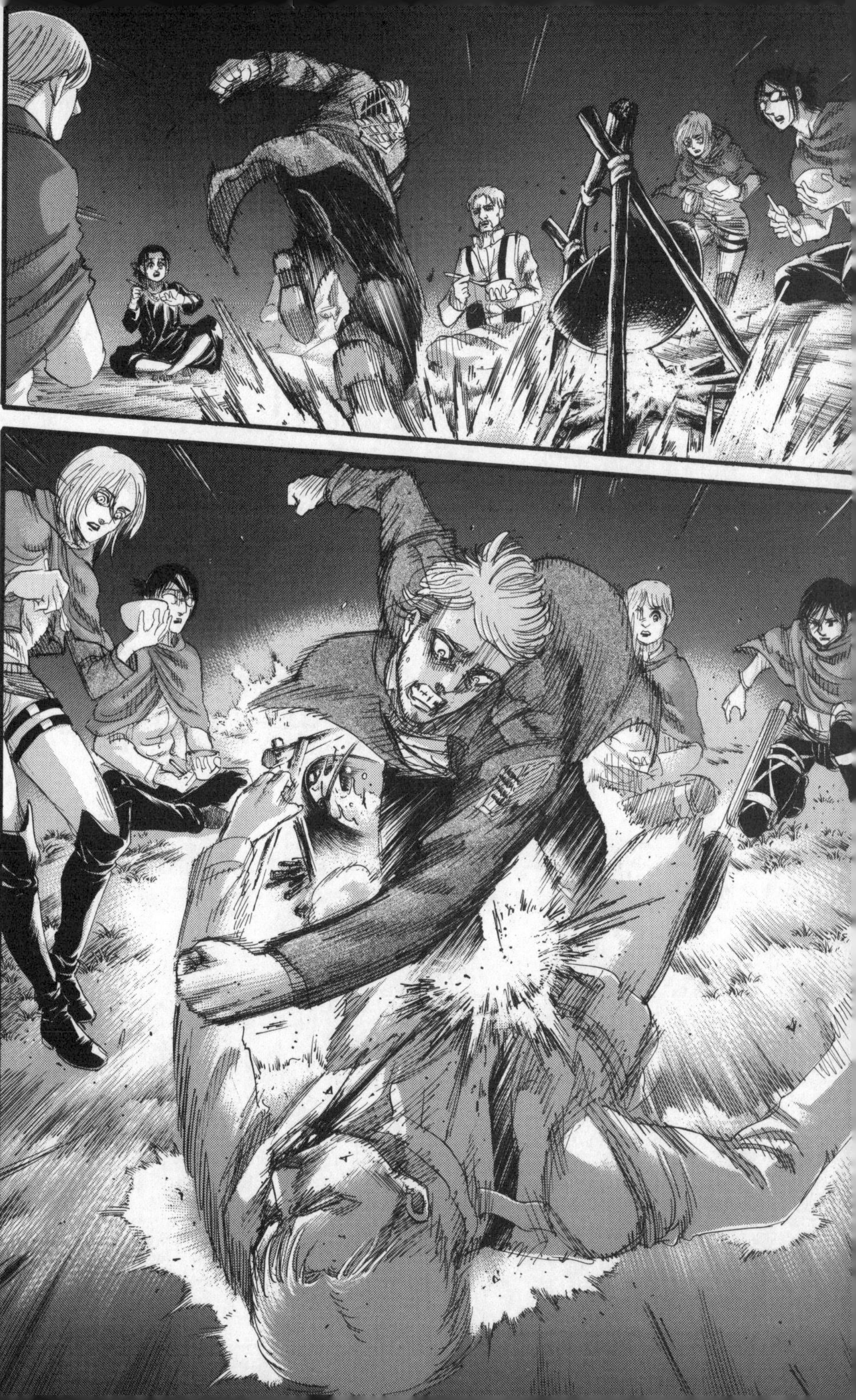

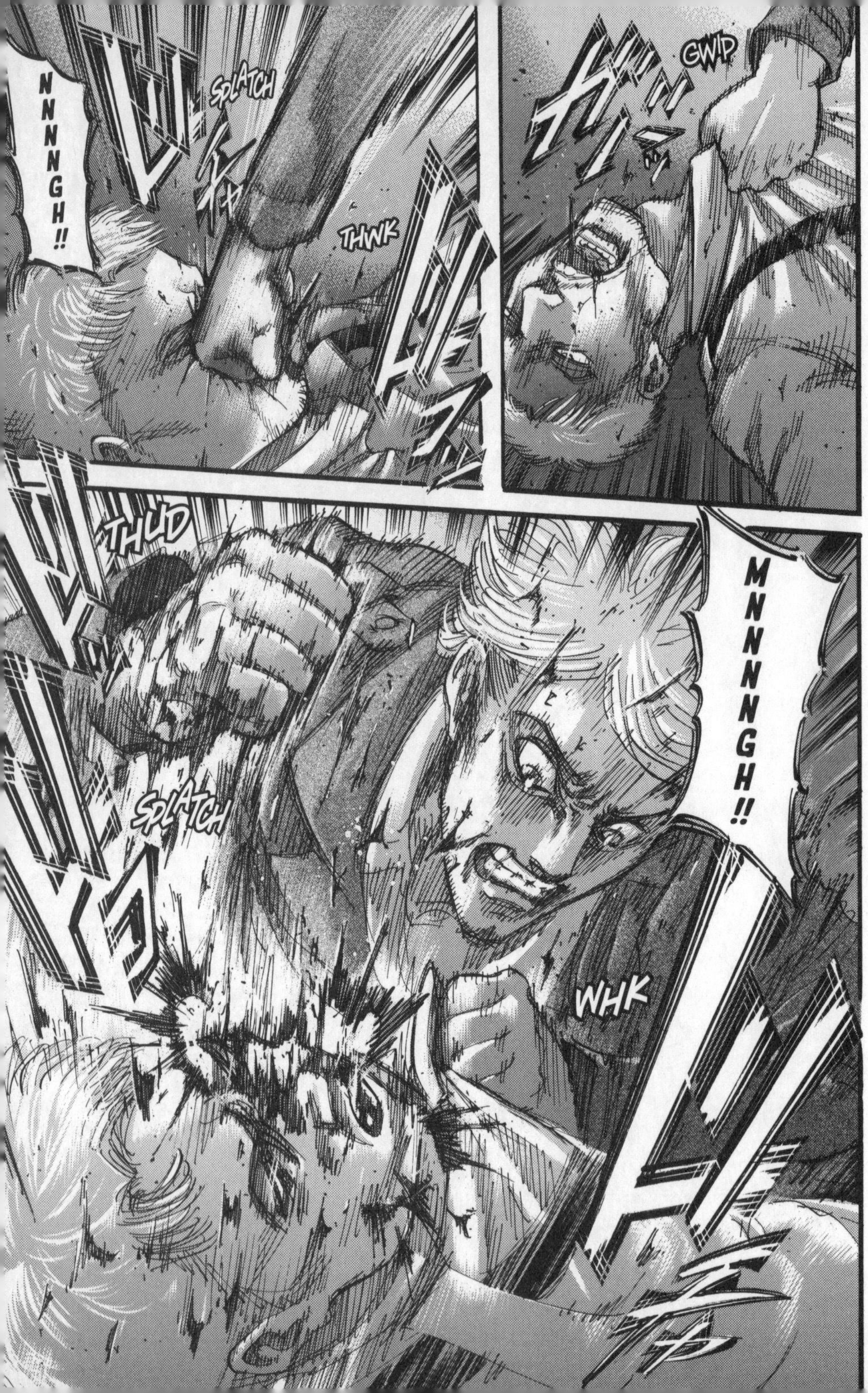
GWIP
NNNNGH!!
SPLATCH
THWK
MNNNNNGH!!
THUD
SPLATCH
WHK

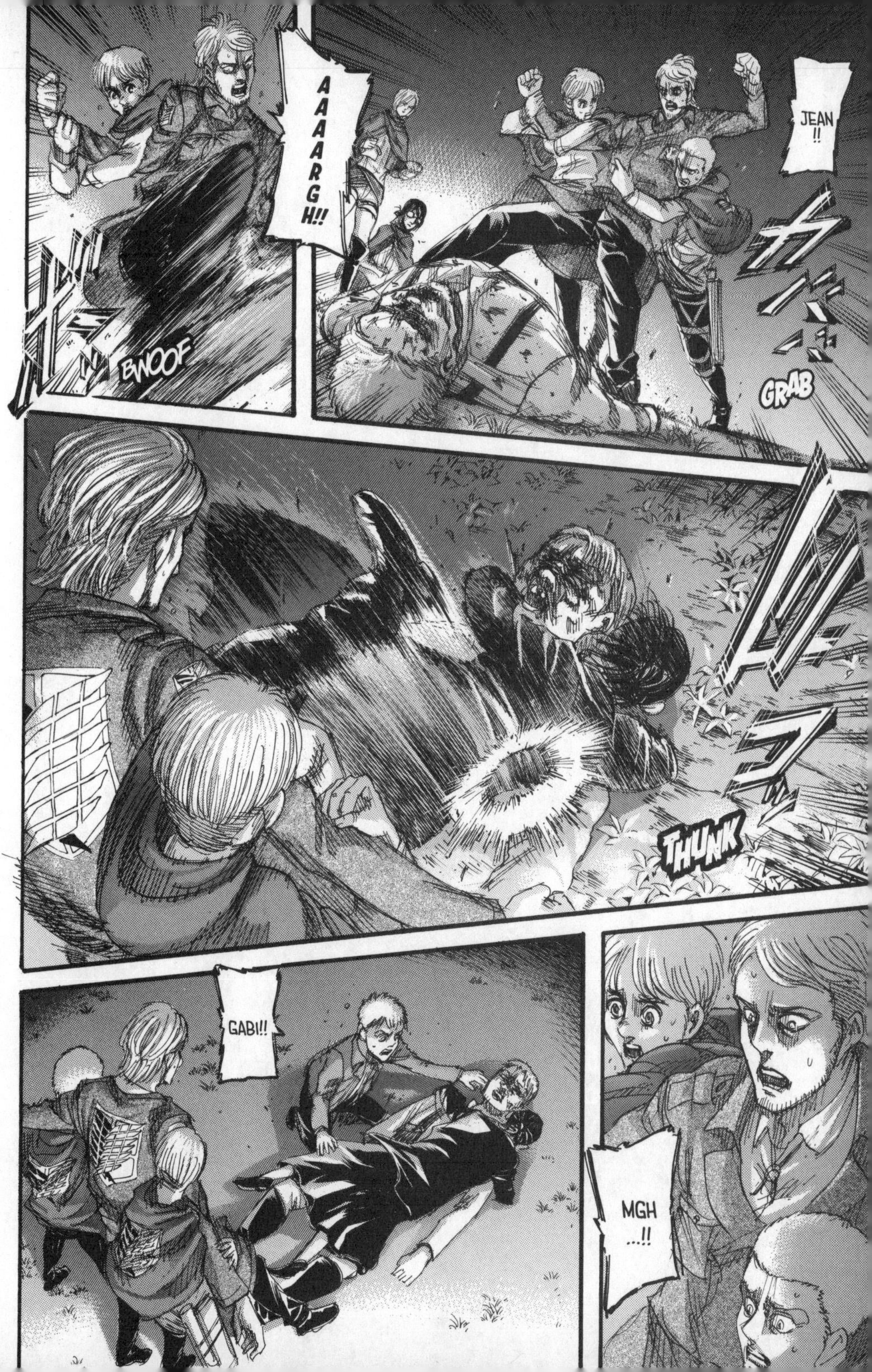
JEAN!!
GRAB
AAAAARGH!!
BWOOF
THUNK
MGH...!!
GABI!!

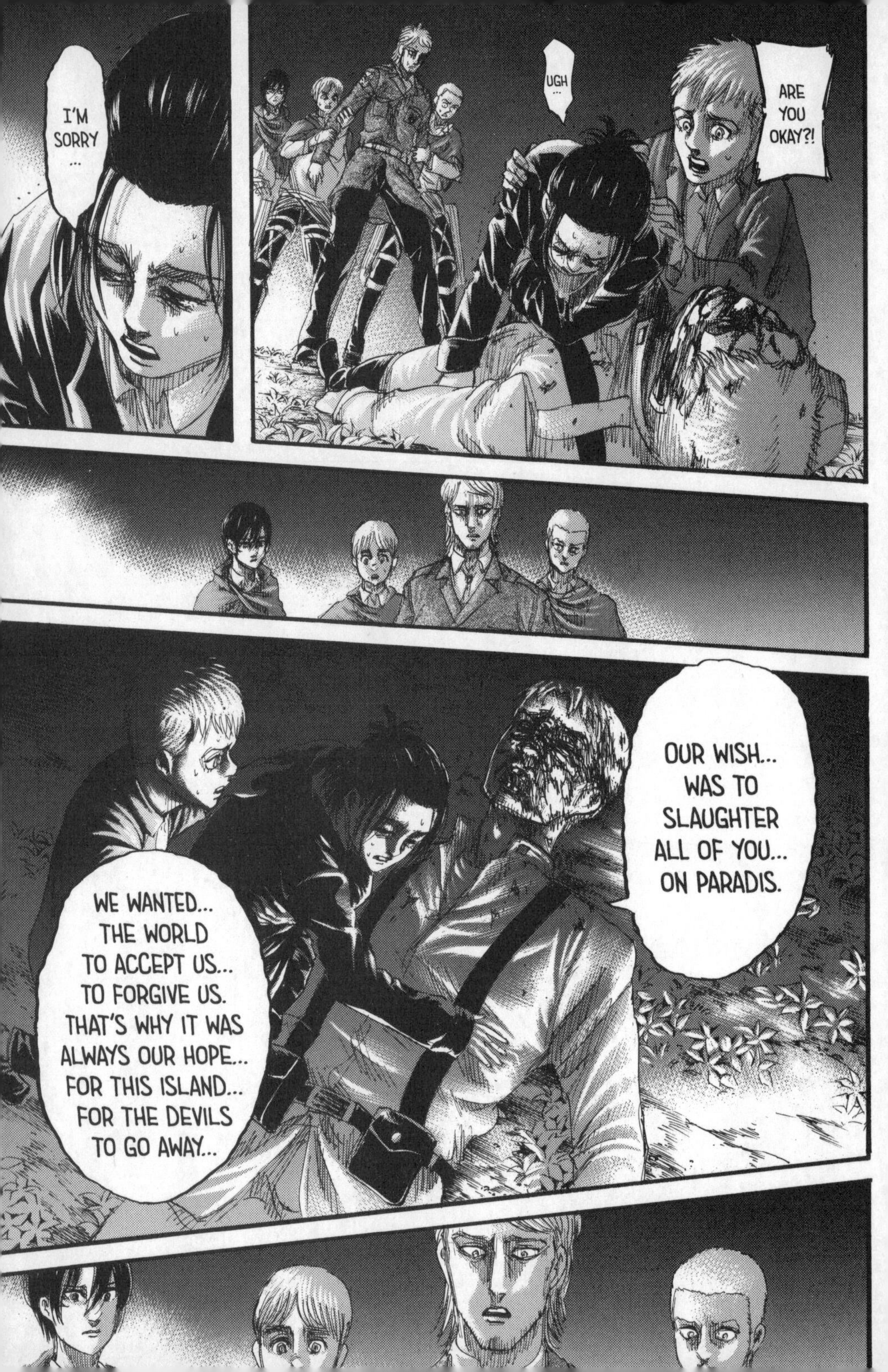
ARE YOU OKAY?!
UGH...
I'M SORRY...
OUR WISH... WAS TO SLAUGHTER ALL OF YOU... ON PARADIS.
WE WANTED... THE WORLD TO ACCEPT US... TO FORGIVE US. THAT'S WHY IT WAS ALWAYS OUR HOPE... FOR THIS ISLAND... FOR THE DEVILS TO GO AWAY...

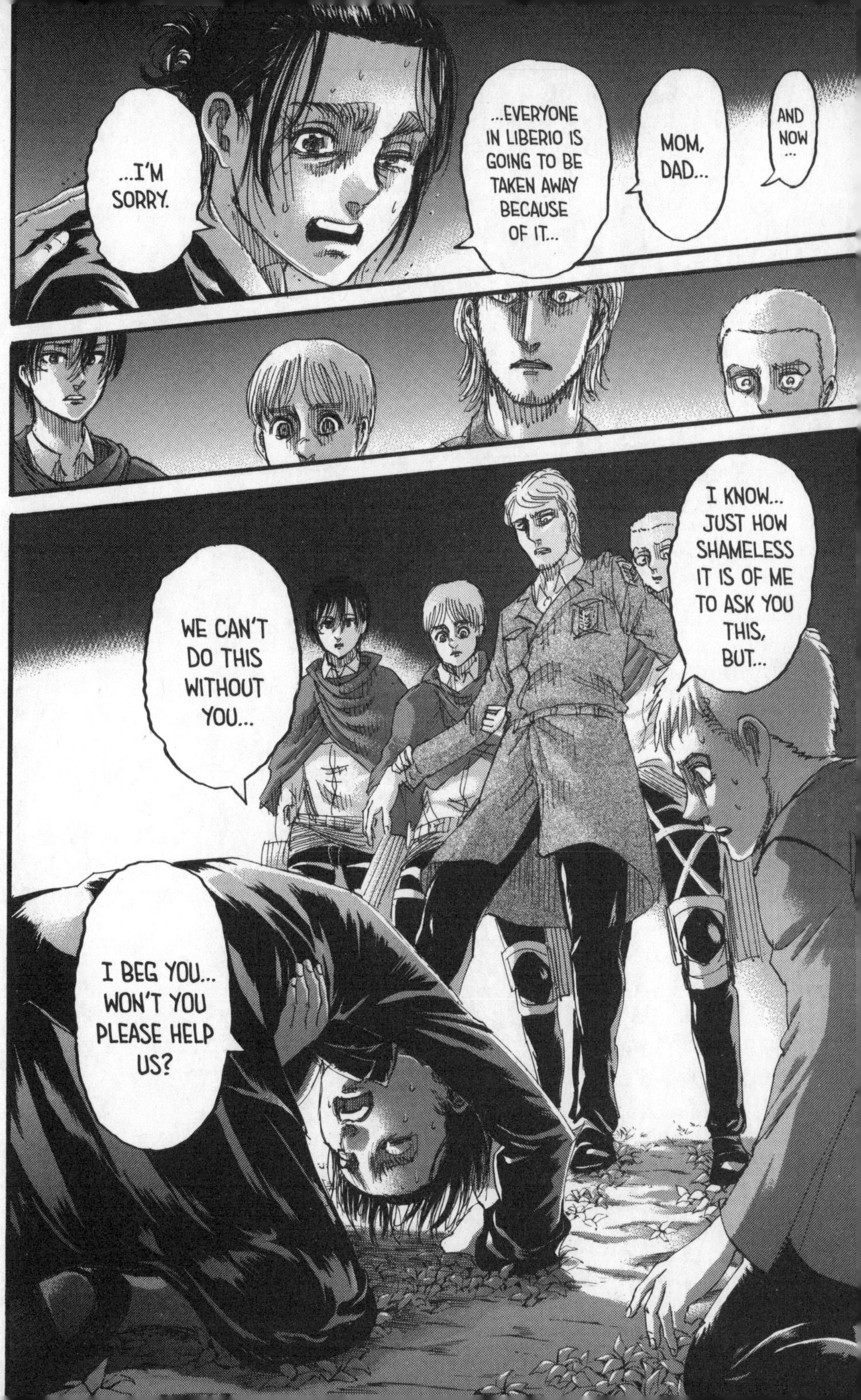
AND NOW...
MOM, DAD...
...EVERYONE IN LIBERIO IS GOING TO BE TAKEN AWAY BECAUSE OF IT...
...I'M SORRY.
I KNOW... JUST HOW SHAMELESS IT IS OF ME TO ASK YOU THIS, BUT...
WE CAN'T DO THIS WITHOUT YOU...
I BEG YOU... WON'T YOU PLEASE HELP US?

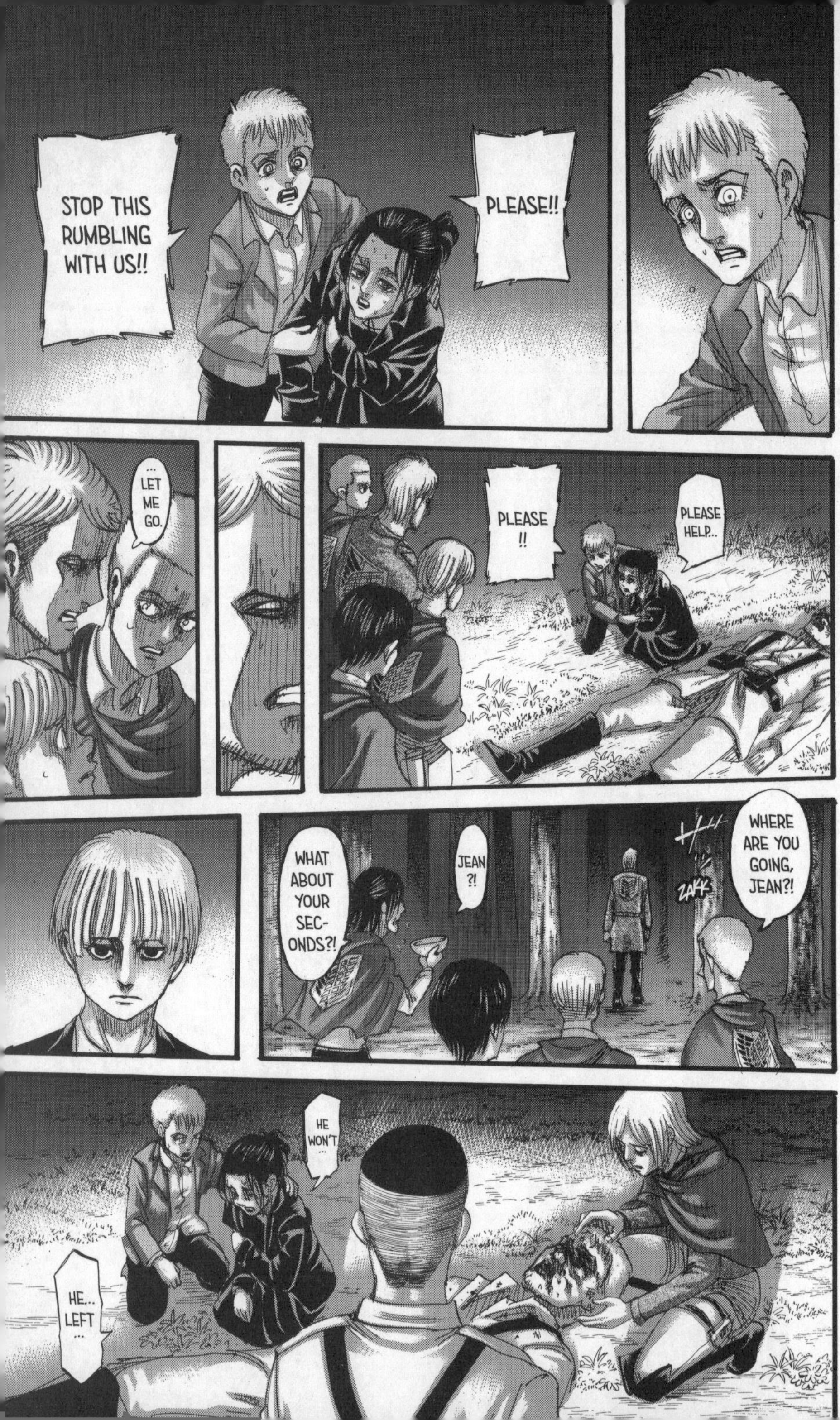
PLEASE!!
STOP THIS RUMBLING WITH US!!
PLEASE HELP...
PLEASE !!
... LET ME GO.
WHERE ARE YOU GOING, JEAN?!
ZAKK
JEAN ?!
WHAT ABOUT YOUR SEC-ONDS?!
HE WON'T ...
HE... LEFT ...

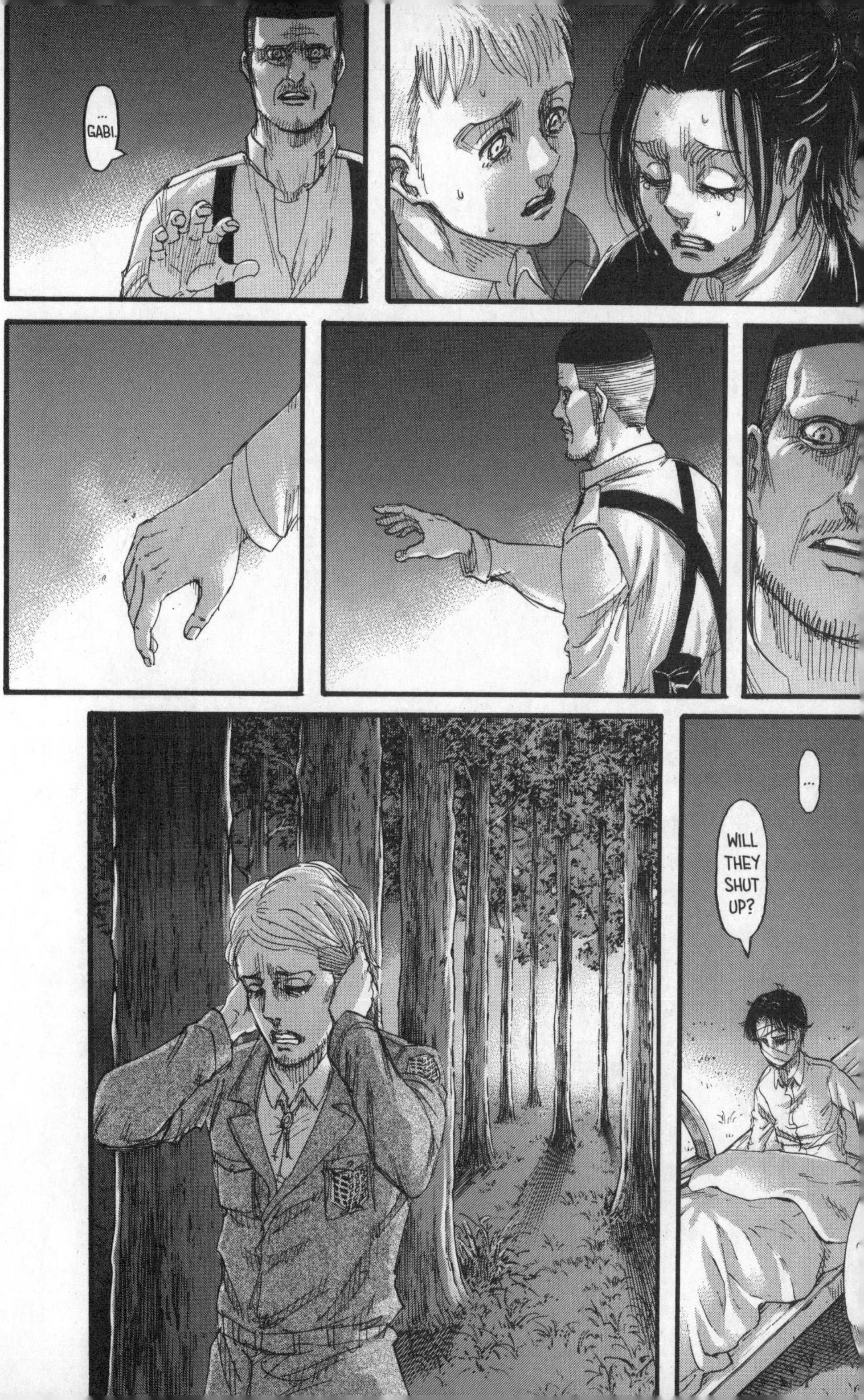
... GABI.
...
WILL THEY SHUT UP?

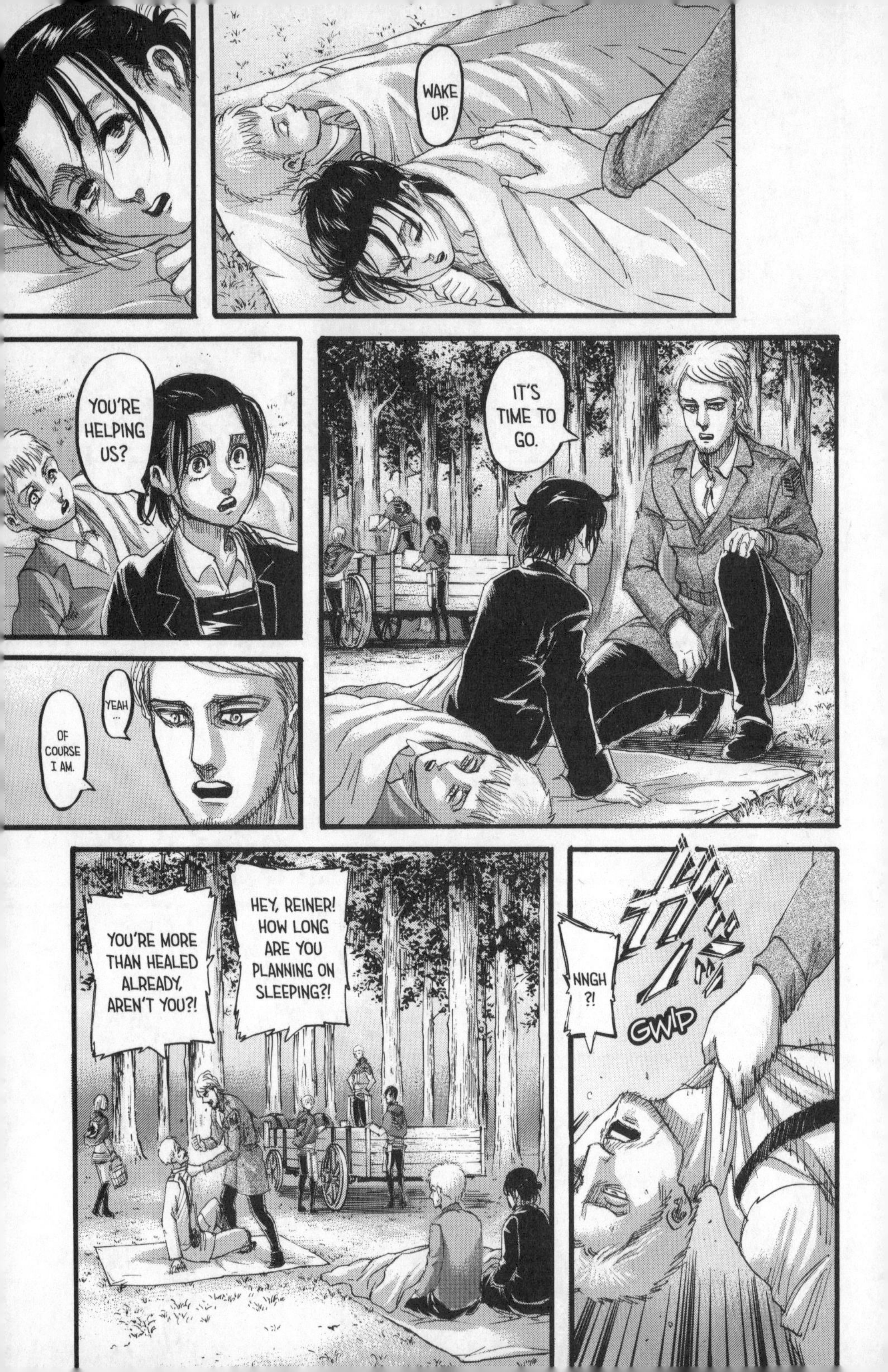
WAKE UP.
IT'S TIME TO GO.
YOU'RE HELPING US?
YEAH...
OF COURSE I AM.
NNGH ?!
GWIP
HEY, REINER! HOW LONG ARE YOU PLANNING ON SLEEPING?!
YOU'RE MORE THAN HEALED ALREADY, AREN'T YOU?!

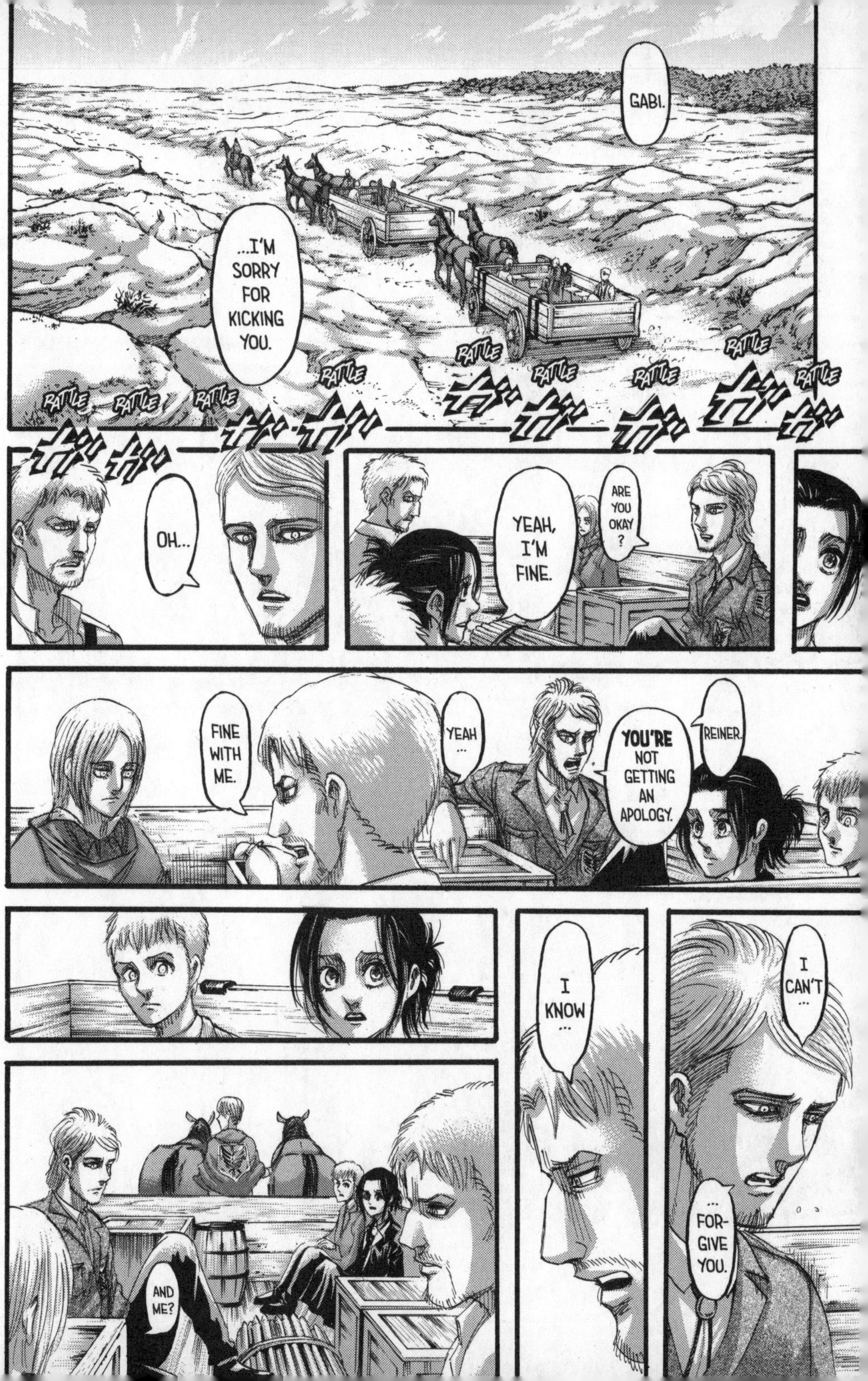
GABI.
RATTLE
RATTLE
RATTLE
RATTLE
RATTLE
RATTLE
...I'M SORRY FOR KICKING YOU.
RATTLE
RATTLE
RATTLE
ARE YOU OKAY?
YEAH, I'M FINE.
OH...
REINER.
YOU'RE NOT GETTING AN APOLOGY.
YEAH ...
FINE WITH ME.
I CAN'T ...
... FORGIVE YOU.
I KNOW ...
AND ME?

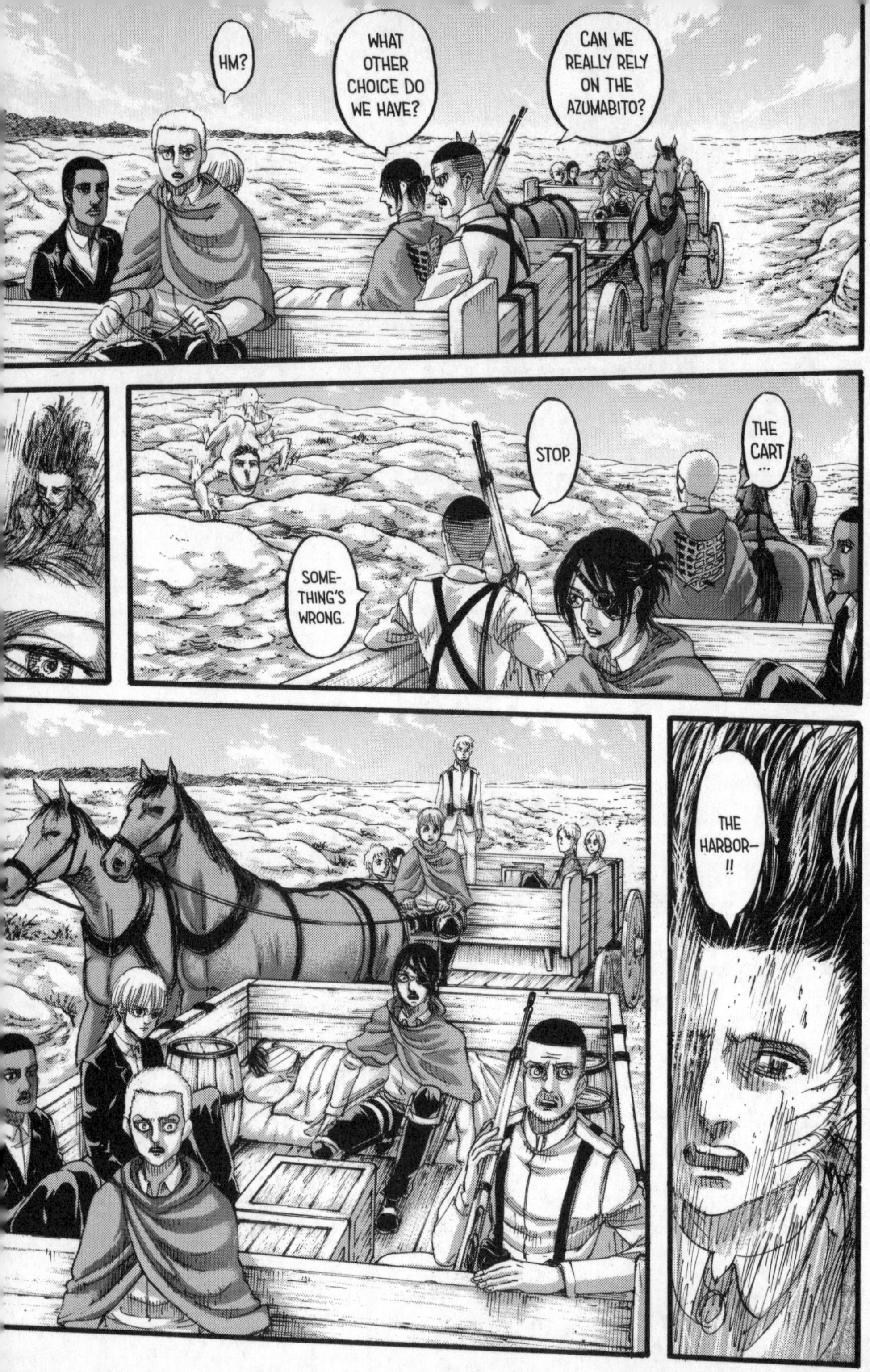
CAN WE REALLY RELY ON THE AZUMABITO?
WHAT OTHER CHOICE DO WE HAVE?
HM?
THE CART ...
STOP.
SOMETHING'S WRONG.
THE HARBOR— !!

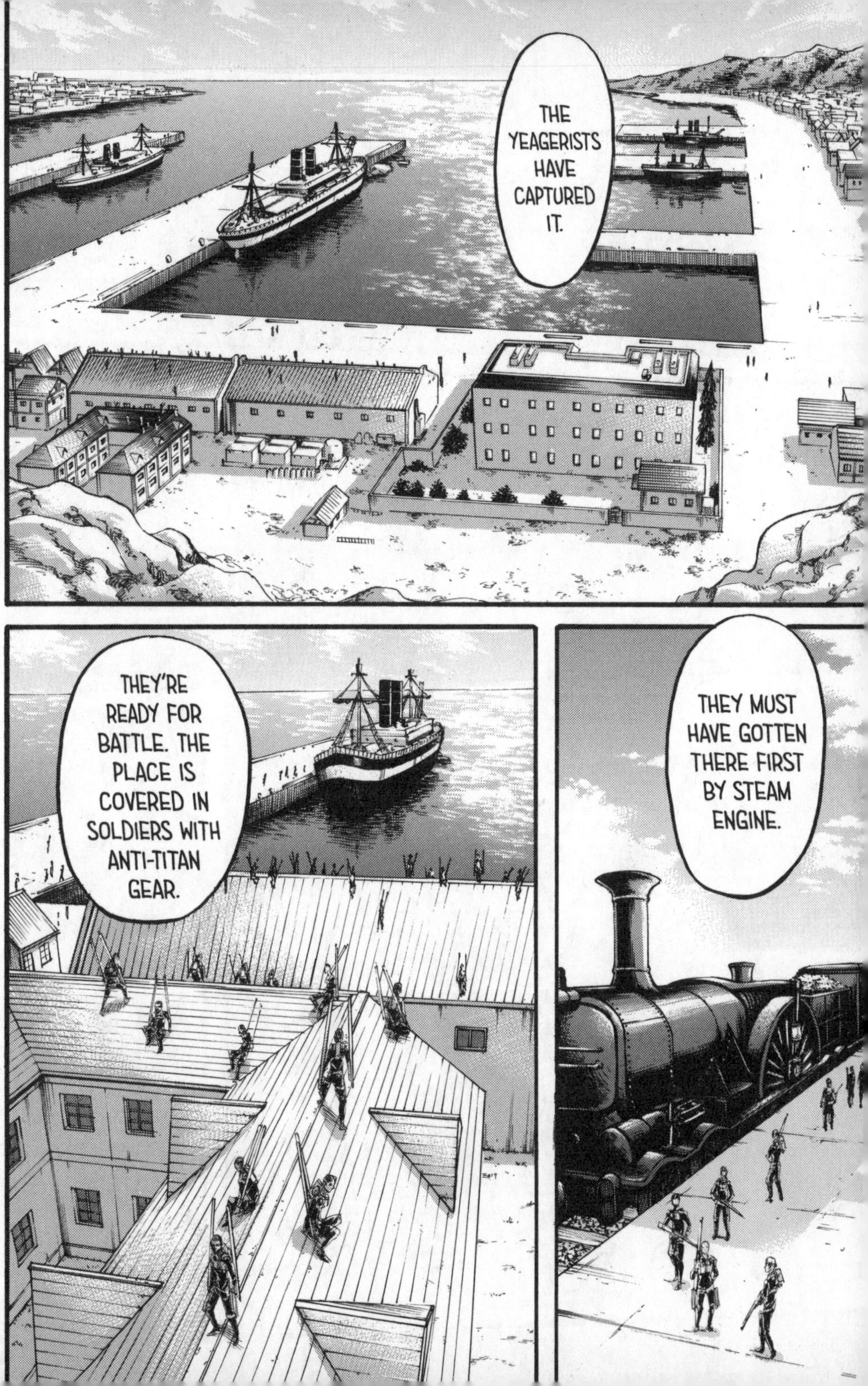
THE YEAGERISTS HAVE CAPTURED IT.
THEY MUST HAVE GOTTEN THERE FIRST BY STEAM ENGINE.
THEY'RE READY FOR BATTLE. THE PLACE IS COVERED IN SOLDIERS WITH ANTI-TITAN GEAR.

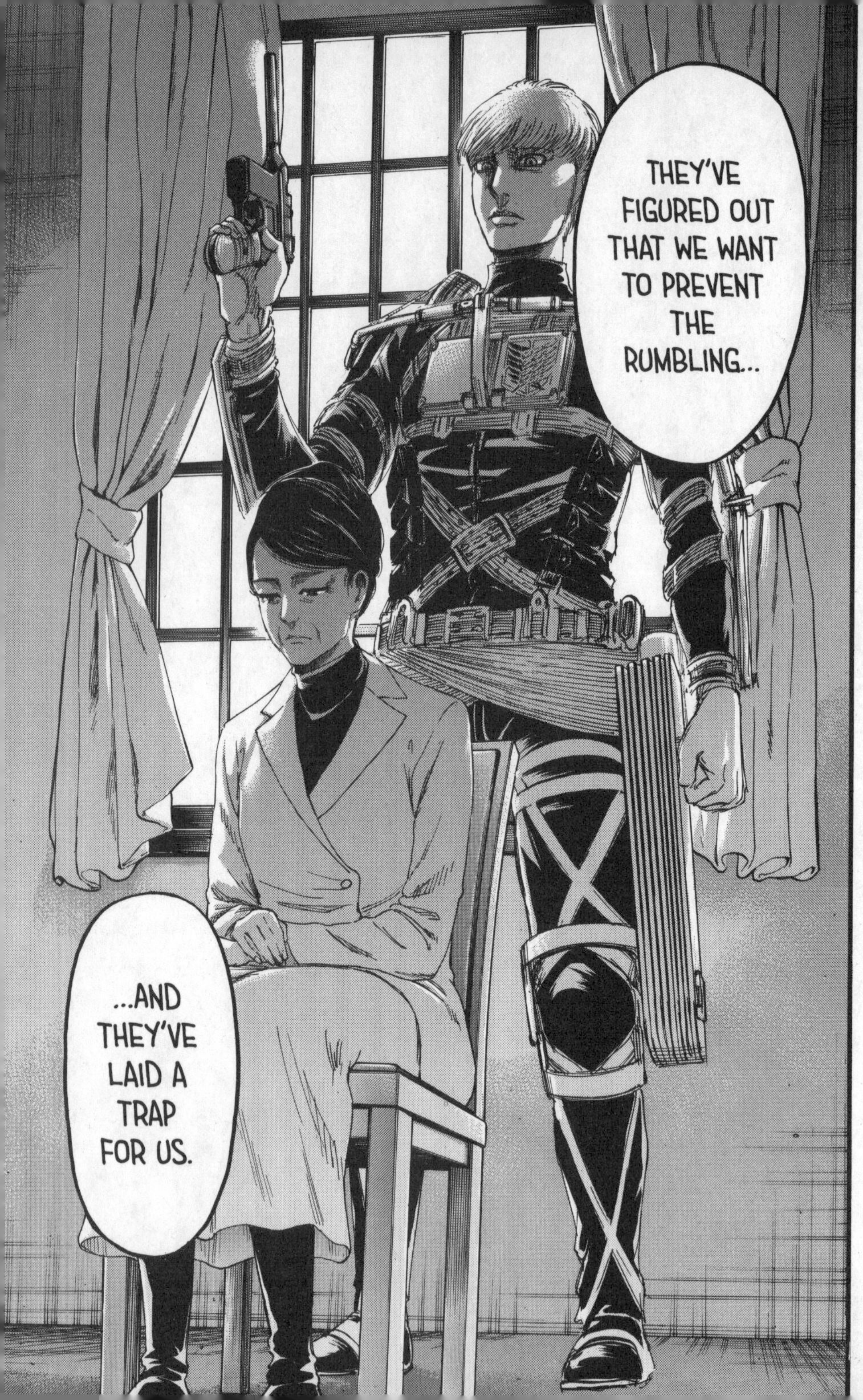
THEY'VE FIGURED OUT THAT WE WANT TO PREVENT THE RUMBLING...
...AND THEY'VE LAID A TRAP FOR US.

ATTACK on TITAN

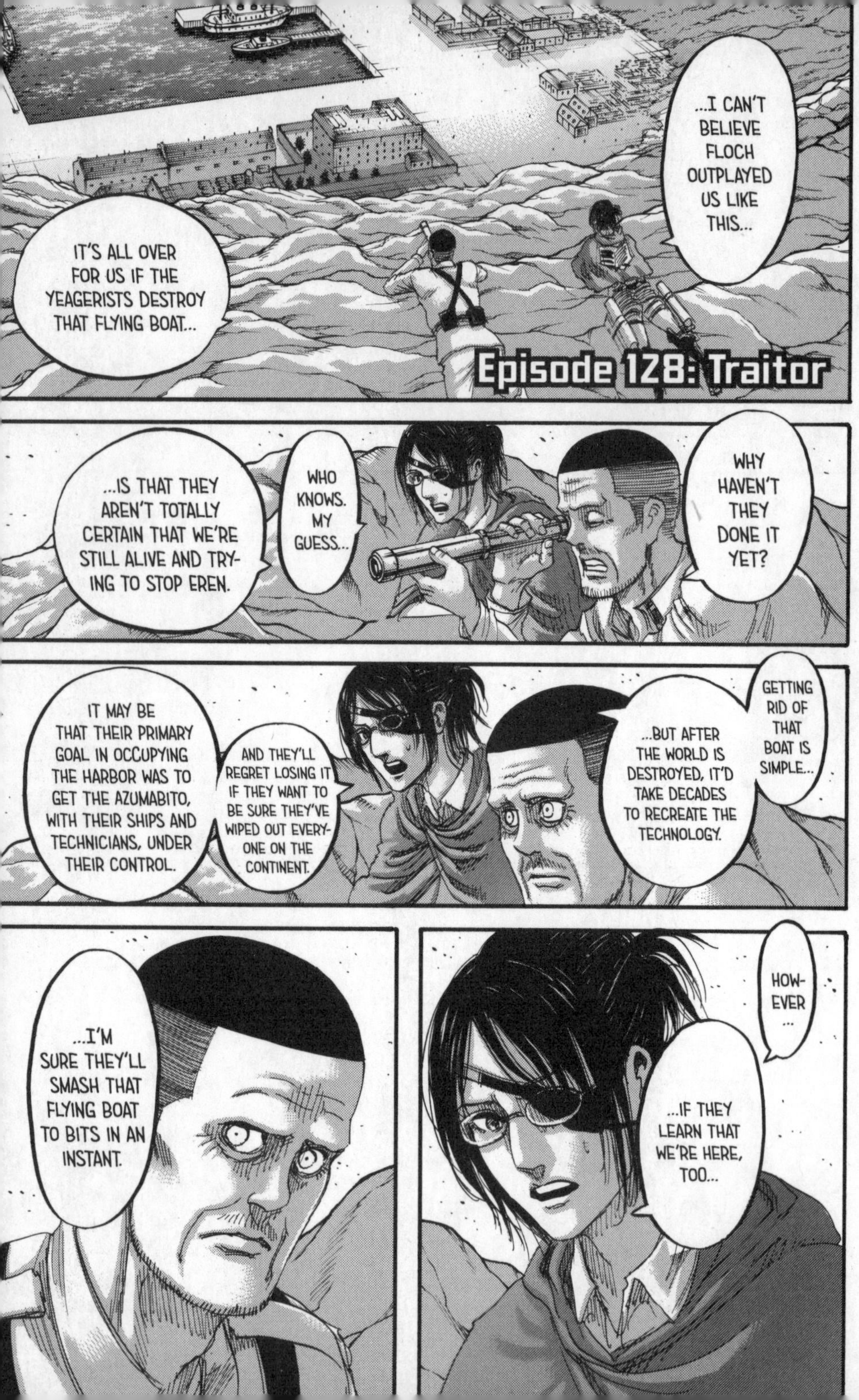
...I CAN'T BELIEVE FLOCH OUTPLAYED US LIKE THIS...
IT'S ALL OVER FOR US IF THE YEAGERISTS DESTROY THAT FLYING BOAT...
Episode 128: Traitor
WHY HAVEN'T THEY DONE IT YET?
WHO KNOWS. MY GUESS...
...IS THAT THEY AREN'T TOTALLY CERTAIN THAT WE'RE STILL ALIVE AND TRYING TO STOP EREN.
GETTING RID OF THAT BOAT IS SIMPLE...
...BUT AFTER THE WORLD IS DESTROYED, IT'D TAKE DECADES TO RECREATE THE TECHNOLOGY.
AND THEY'LL REGRET LOSING IT IF THEY WANT TO BE SURE THEY'VE WIPED OUT EVERYONE ON THE CONTINENT.
IT MAY BE THAT THEIR PRIMARY GOAL IN OCCUPYING THE HARBOR WAS TO GET THE AZUMABITO, WITH THEIR SHIPS AND TECHNICIANS, UNDER THEIR CONTROL.
HOWEVER...
...IF THEY LEARN THAT WE'RE HERE, TOO...
...I'M SURE THEY'LL SMASH THAT FLYING BOAT TO BITS IN AN INSTANT.

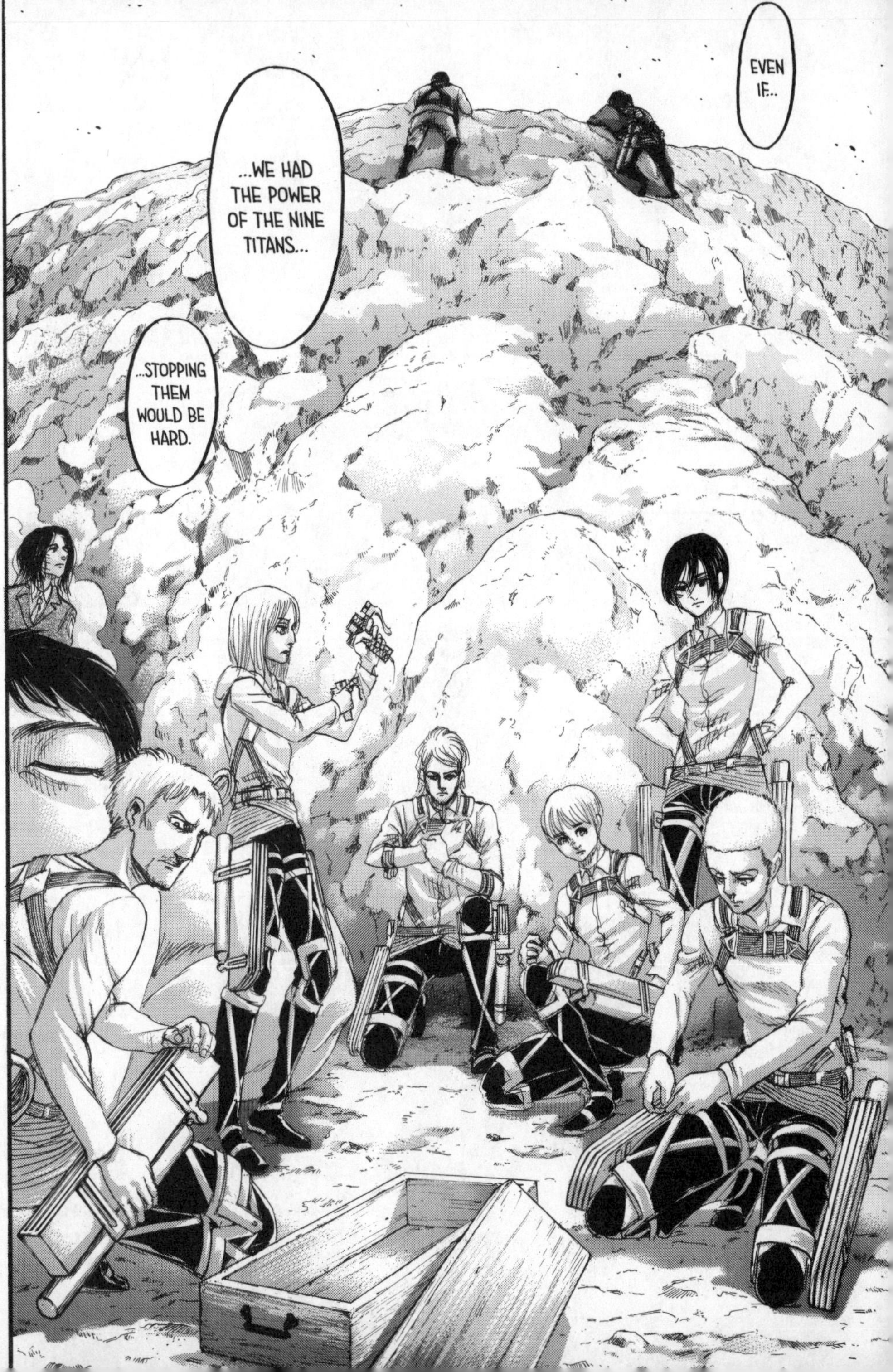
EVEN IF...
...WE HAD THE POWER OF THE NINE TITANS...
...STOPPING THEM WOULD BE HARD.

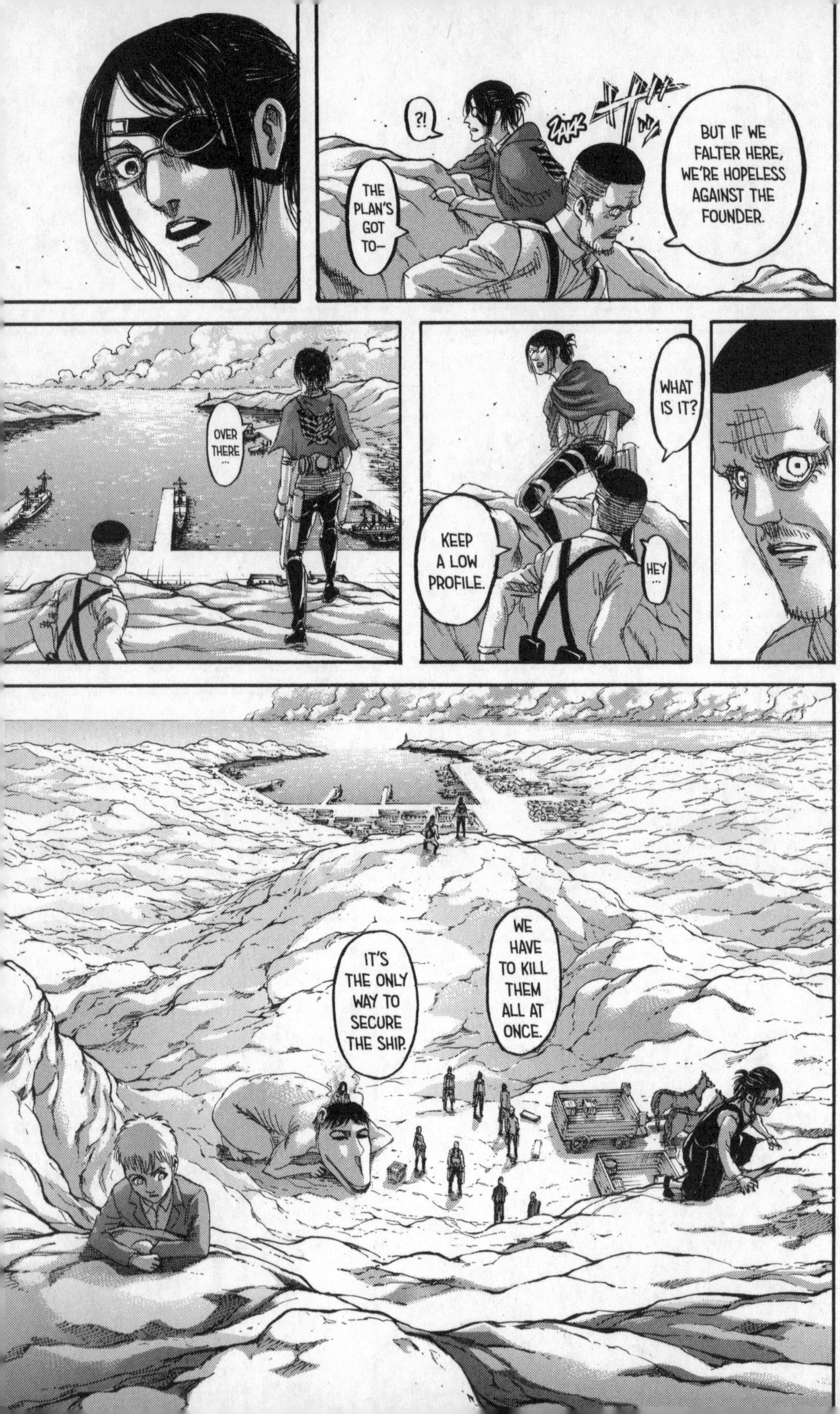
BUT IF WE FALTER HERE, WE'RE HOPELESS AGAINST THE FOUNDER.
ZAKK
?!
THE PLAN'S GOT TO—
WHAT IS IT?
HEY ...
KEEP A LOW PROFILE.
OVER THERE ...
WE HAVE TO KILL THEM ALL AT ONCE.
IT'S THE ONLY WAY TO SECURE THE SHIP.

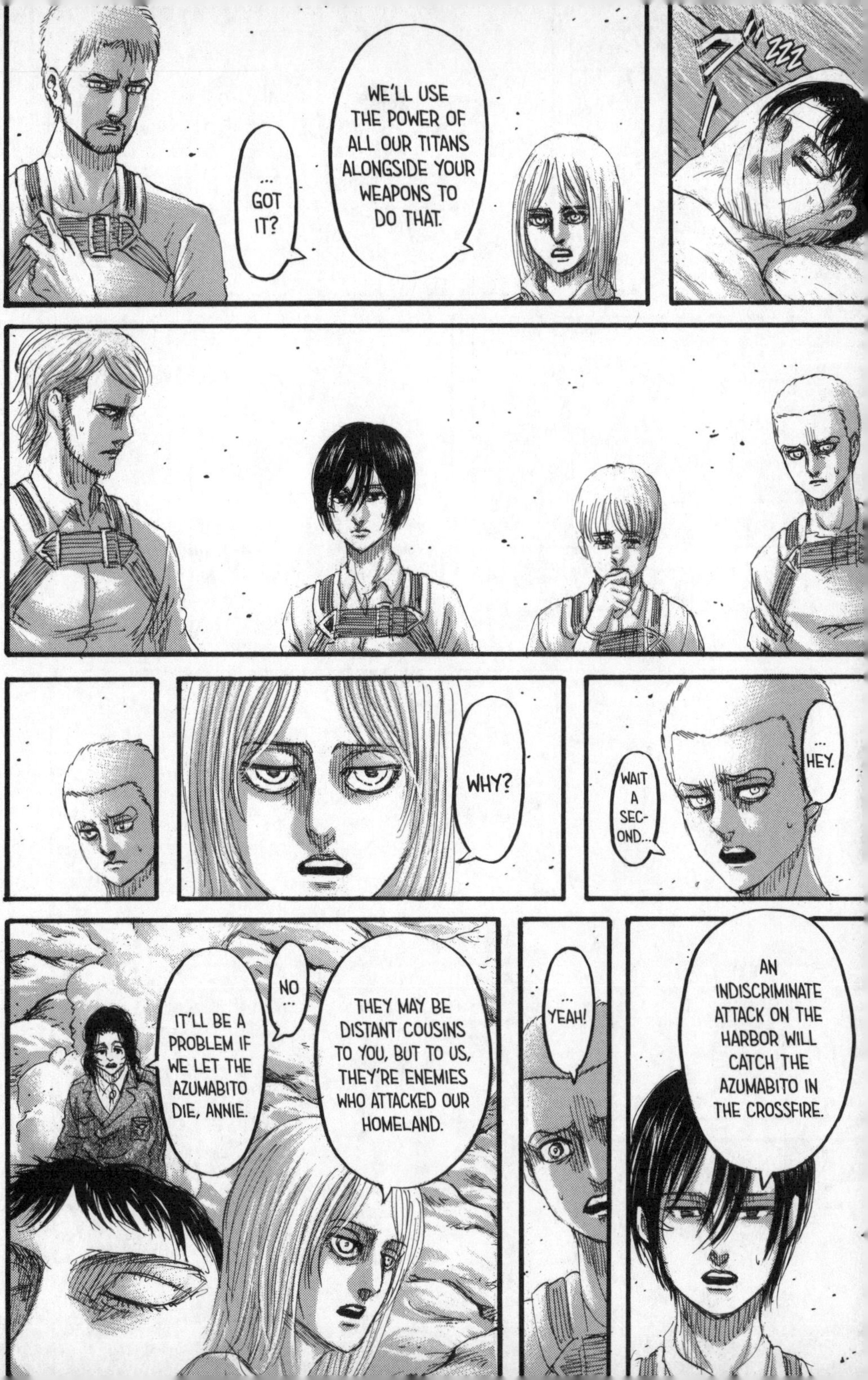
WE'LL USE THE POWER OF ALL OUR TITANS ALONGSIDE YOUR WEAPONS TO DO THAT.
... GOT IT?
... HEY.
WAIT A SEC-OND...
WHY?
AN INDISCRIMINATE ATTACK ON THE HARBOR WILL CATCH THE AZUMABITO IN THE CROSSFIRE.
... YEAH!
THEY MAY BE DISTANT COUSINS TO YOU, BUT TO US, THEY'RE ENEMIES WHO ATTACKED OUR HOMELAND.
NO ...
IT'LL BE A PROBLEM IF WE LET THE AZUMABITO DIE, ANNIE.

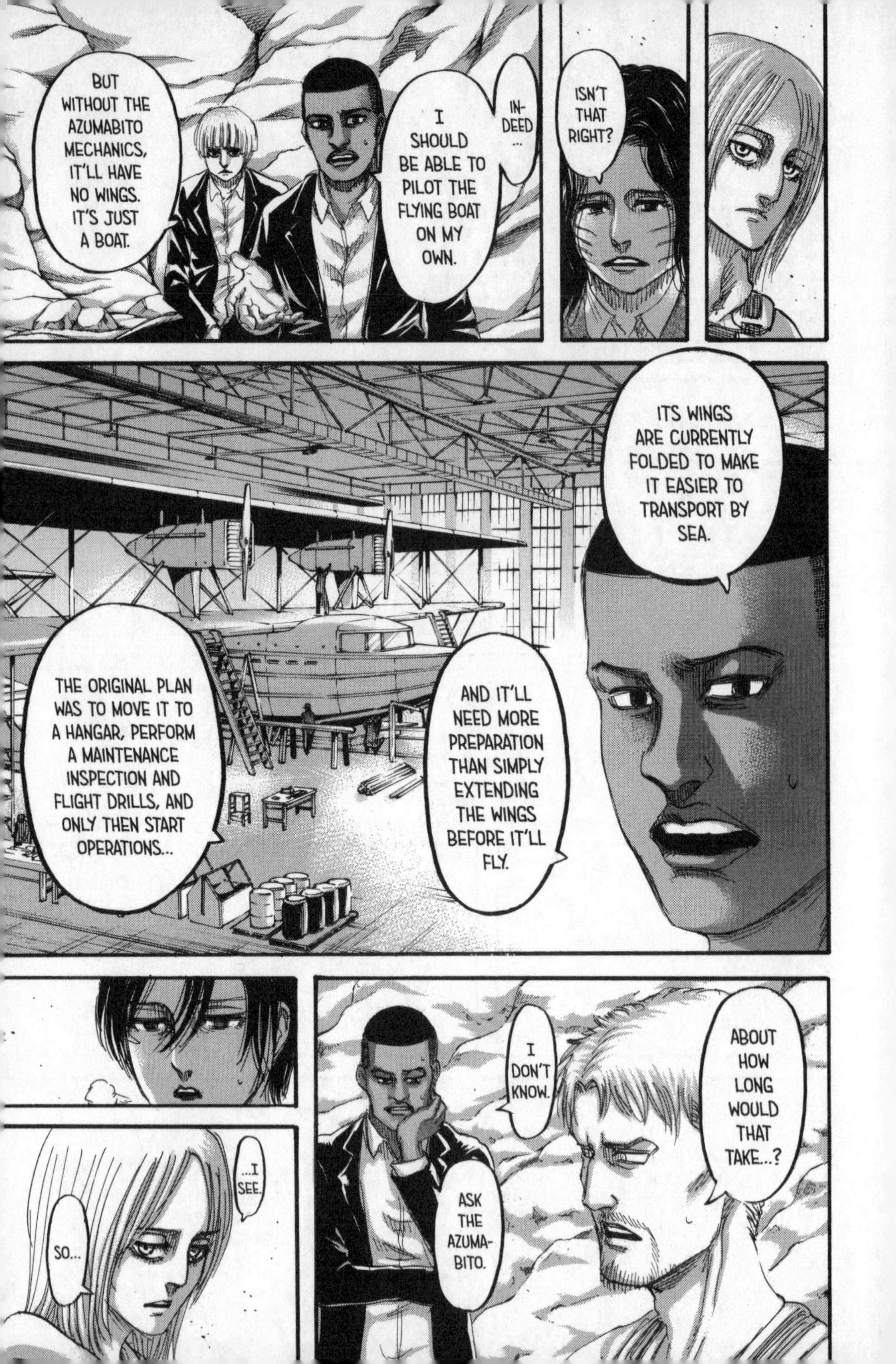
ISN'T THAT RIGHT?
IN-DEED...
I SHOULD BE ABLE TO PILOT THE FLYING BOAT ON MY OWN.
BUT WITHOUT THE AZUMABITO MECHANICS, IT'LL HAVE NO WINGS. IT'S JUST A BOAT.
ITS WINGS ARE CURRENTLY FOLDED TO MAKE IT EASIER TO TRANSPORT BY SEA.
AND IT'LL NEED MORE PREPARATION THAN SIMPLY EXTENDING THE WINGS BEFORE IT'LL FLY.
THE ORIGINAL PLAN WAS TO MOVE IT TO A HANGAR, PERFORM A MAINTENANCE INSPECTION AND FLIGHT DRILLS, AND ONLY THEN START OPERATIONS...
ABOUT HOW LONG WOULD THAT TAKE...?
I DON'T KNOW.
ASK THE AZUMA-BITO.
...I SEE.
SO...

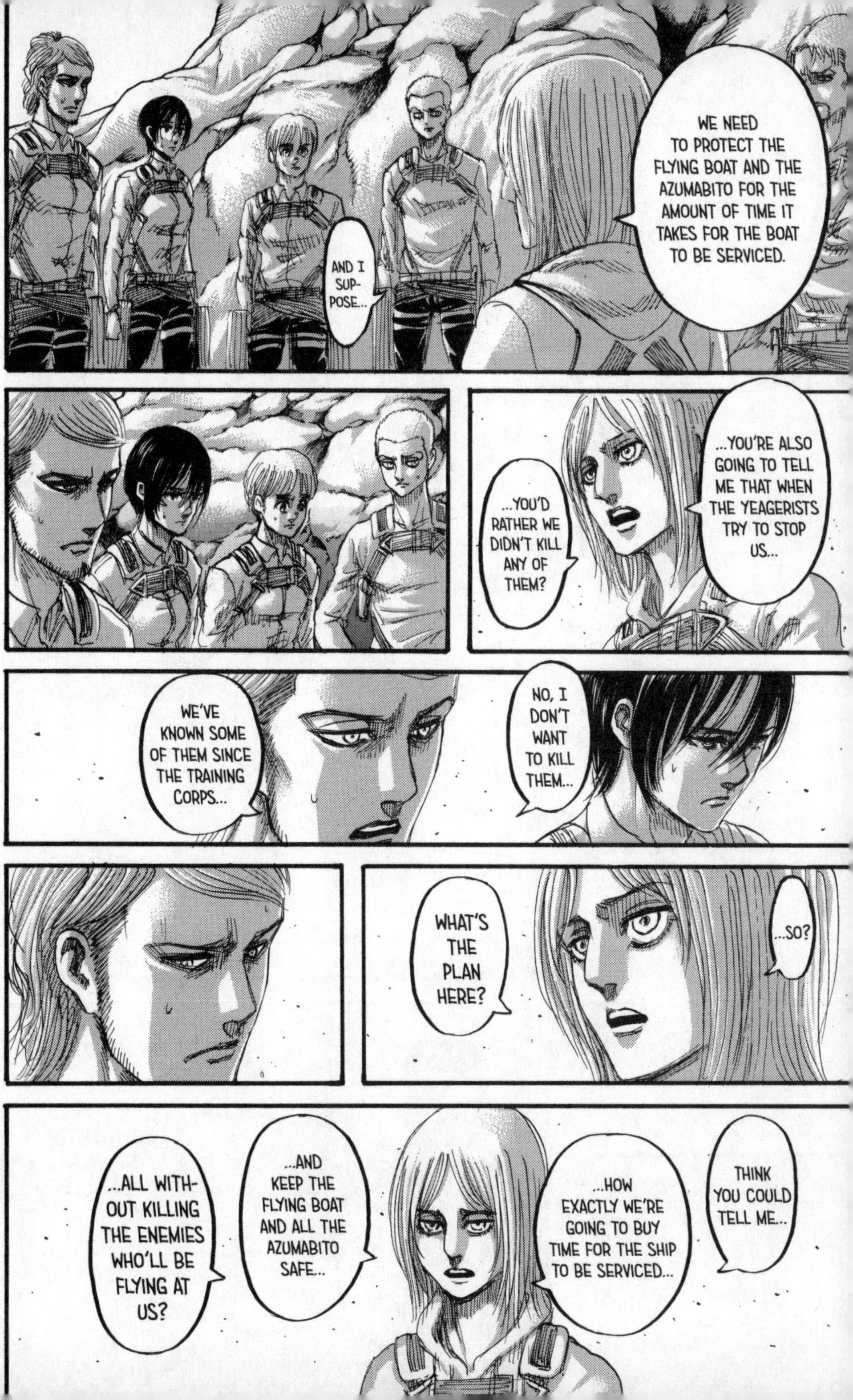
WE NEED TO PROTECT THE FLYING BOAT AND THE AZUMABITO FOR THE AMOUNT OF TIME IT TAKES FOR THE BOAT TO BE SERVICED.
AND I SUPPOSE...
...YOU'RE ALSO GOING TO TELL ME THAT WHEN THE YEAGERISTS TRY TO STOP US...
...YOU'D RATHER WE DIDN'T KILL ANY OF THEM?
NO, I DON'T WANT TO KILL THEM...
WE'VE KNOWN SOME OF THEM SINCE THE TRAINING CORPS...
...SO?
WHAT'S THE PLAN HERE?
THINK YOU COULD TELL ME...
...HOW EXACTLY WE'RE GOING TO BUY TIME FOR THE SHIP TO BE SERVICED...
...AND KEEP THE FLYING BOAT AND ALL THE AZUMABITO SAFE...
...ALL WITHOUT KILLING THE ENEMIES WHO'LL BE FLYING AT US?

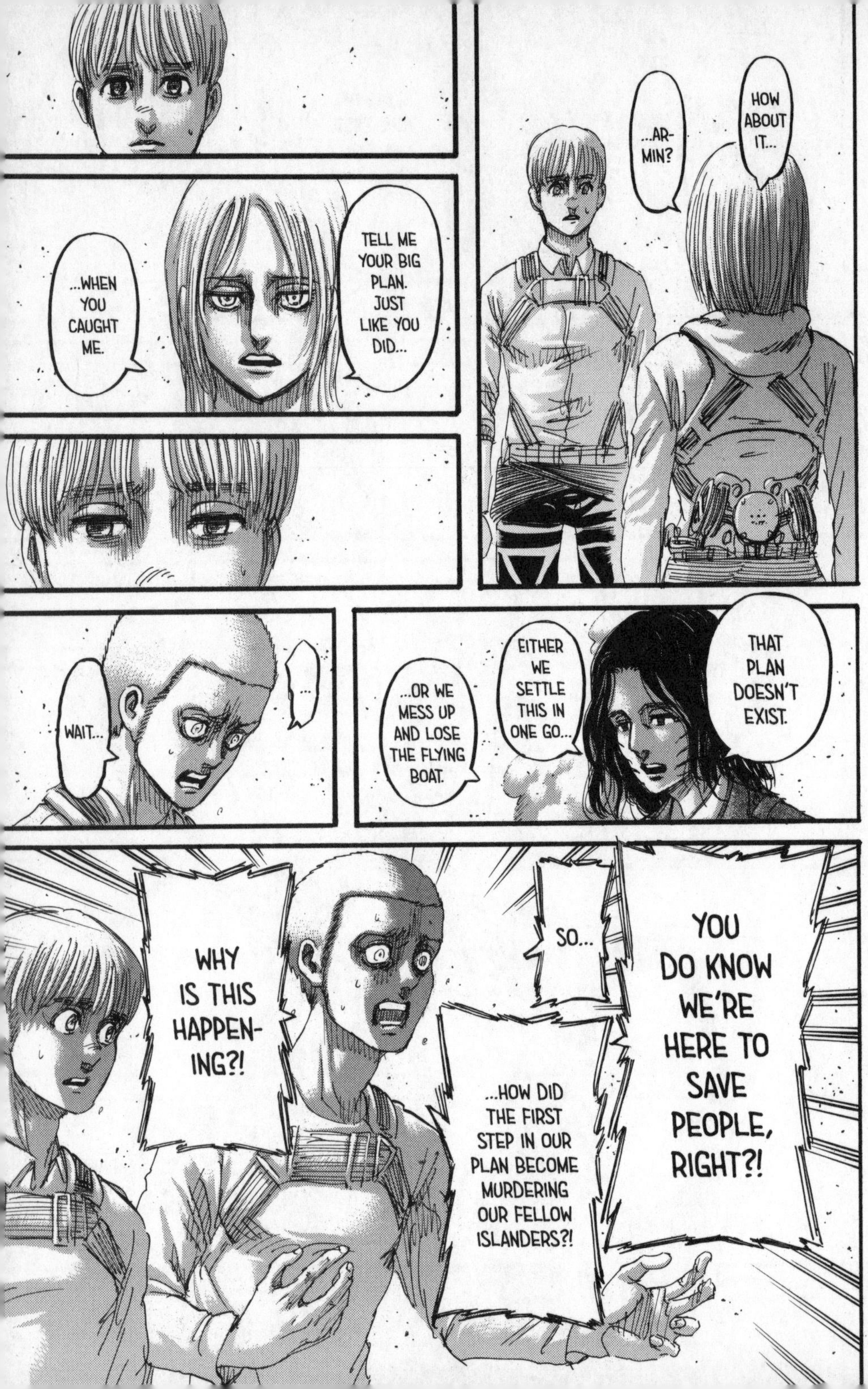
HOW ABOUT IT...
...ARMIN?
TELL ME YOUR BIG PLAN. JUST LIKE YOU DID...
...WHEN YOU CAUGHT ME.
THAT PLAN DOESN'T EXIST.
EITHER WE SETTLE THIS IN ONE GO...
...OR WE MESS UP AND LOSE THE FLYING BOAT.
...
WAIT...
YOU DO KNOW WE'RE HERE TO SAVE PEOPLE, RIGHT?!
SO...
...HOW DID THE FIRST STEP IN OUR PLAN BECOME MURDERING OUR FELLOW ISLANDERS?!
WHY IS THIS HAPPENING?!

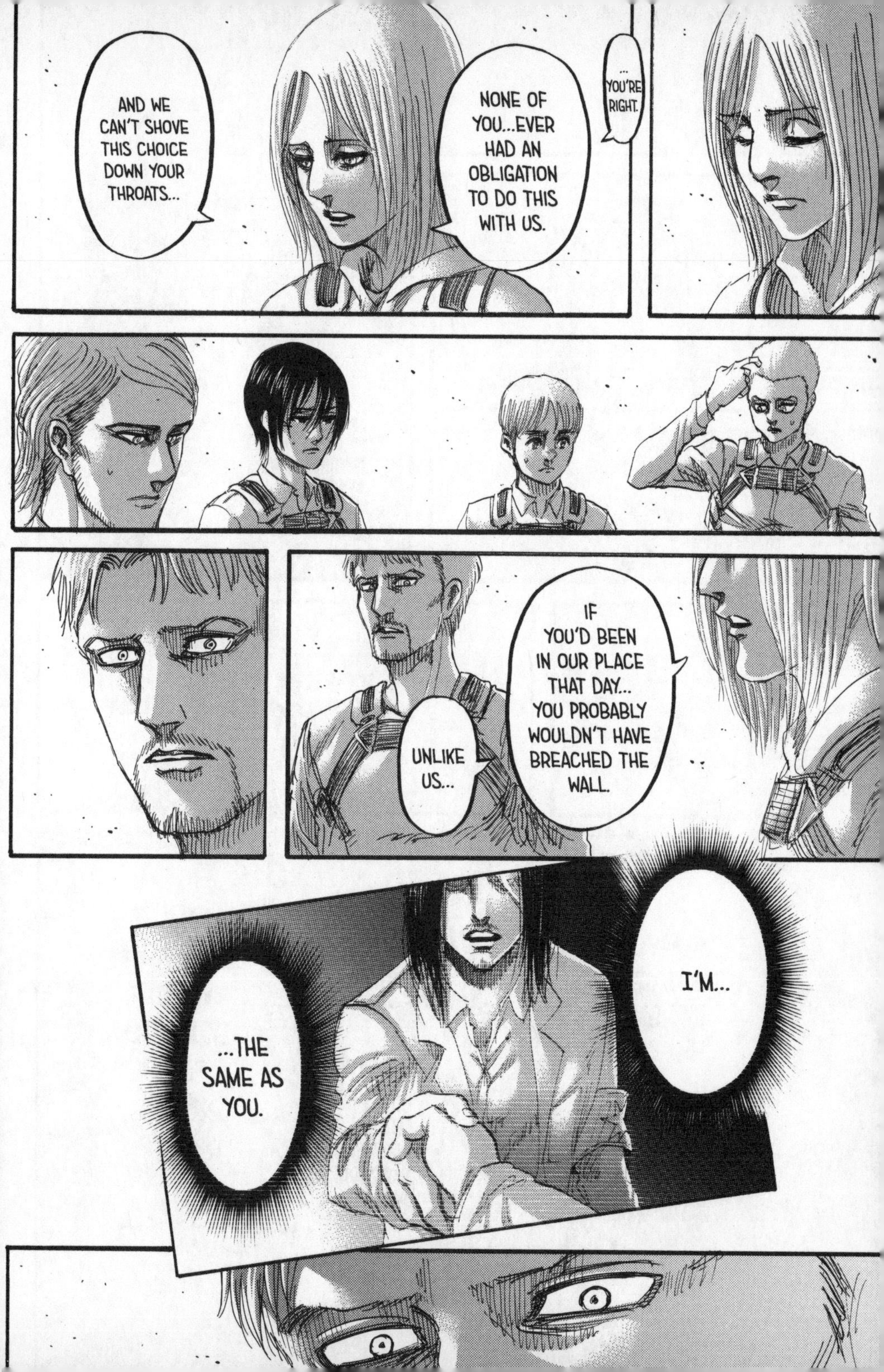
...YOU'RE RIGHT.
NONE OF YOU...EVER HAD AN OBLIGATION TO DO THIS WITH US.
AND WE CAN'T SHOVE THIS CHOICE DOWN YOUR THROATS...
IF YOU'D BEEN IN OUR PLACE THAT DAY... YOU PROBABLY WOULDN'T HAVE BREACHED THE WALL.
UNLIKE US...
I'M...
...THE SAME AS YOU.

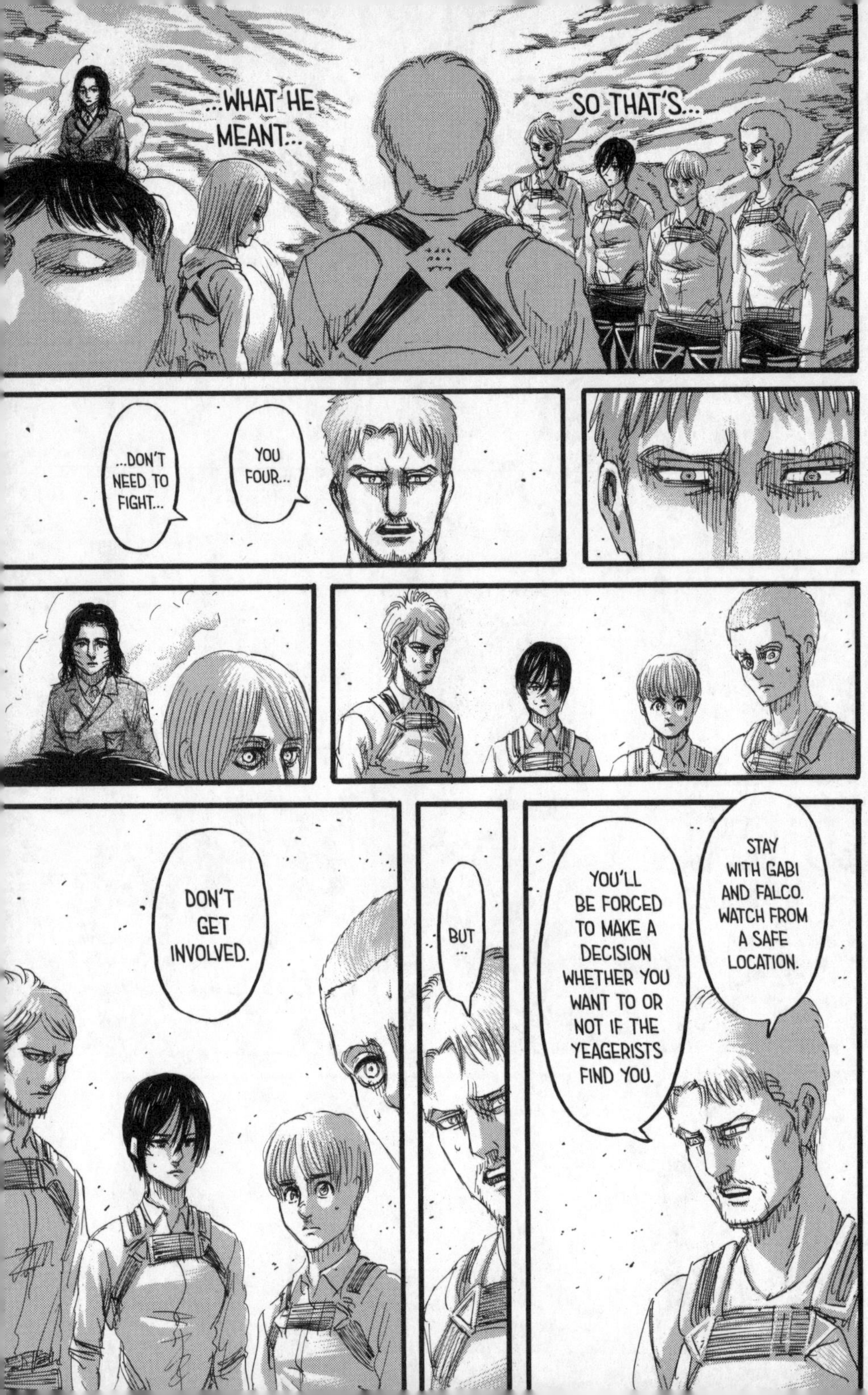
SO THAT'S...
...WHAT HE MEANT...
YOU FOUR...
...DON'T NEED TO FIGHT...
STAY WITH GABI AND FALCO. WATCH FROM A SAFE LOCATION.
YOU'LL BE FORCED TO MAKE A DECISION WHETHER YOU WANT TO OR NOT IF THE YEAGERISTS FIND YOU.
BUT ...
DON'T GET INVOLVED.

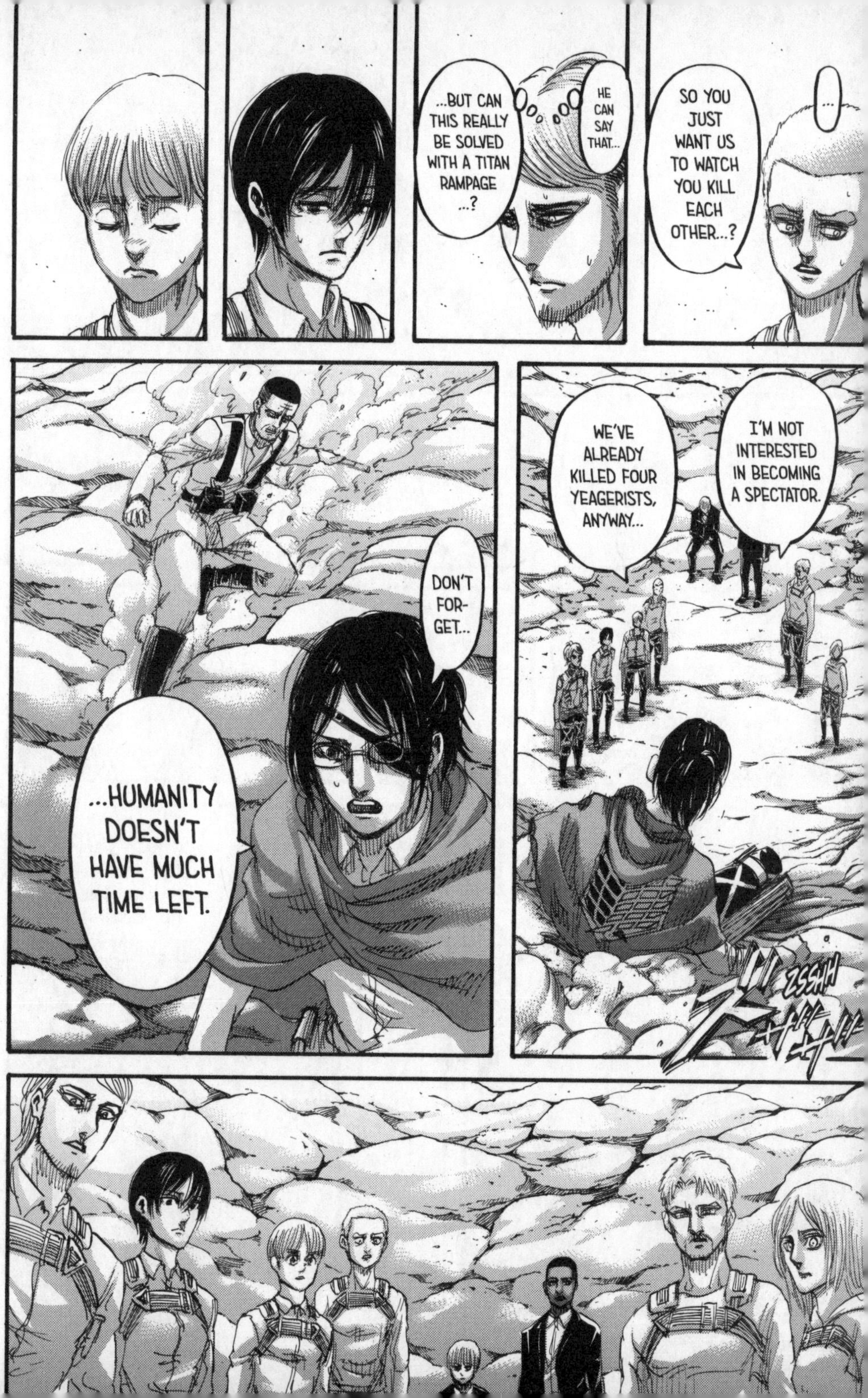
...
SO YOU JUST WANT US TO WATCH YOU KILL EACH OTHER...?
HE CAN SAY THAT...
...BUT CAN THIS REALLY BE SOLVED WITH A TITAN RAMPAGE ...?
I'M NOT INTERESTED IN BECOMING A SPECTATOR.
WE'VE ALREADY KILLED FOUR YEAGERISTS, ANYWAY...
HISSS
DON'T FOR-GET...
...HUMANITY DOESN'T HAVE MUCH TIME LEFT.

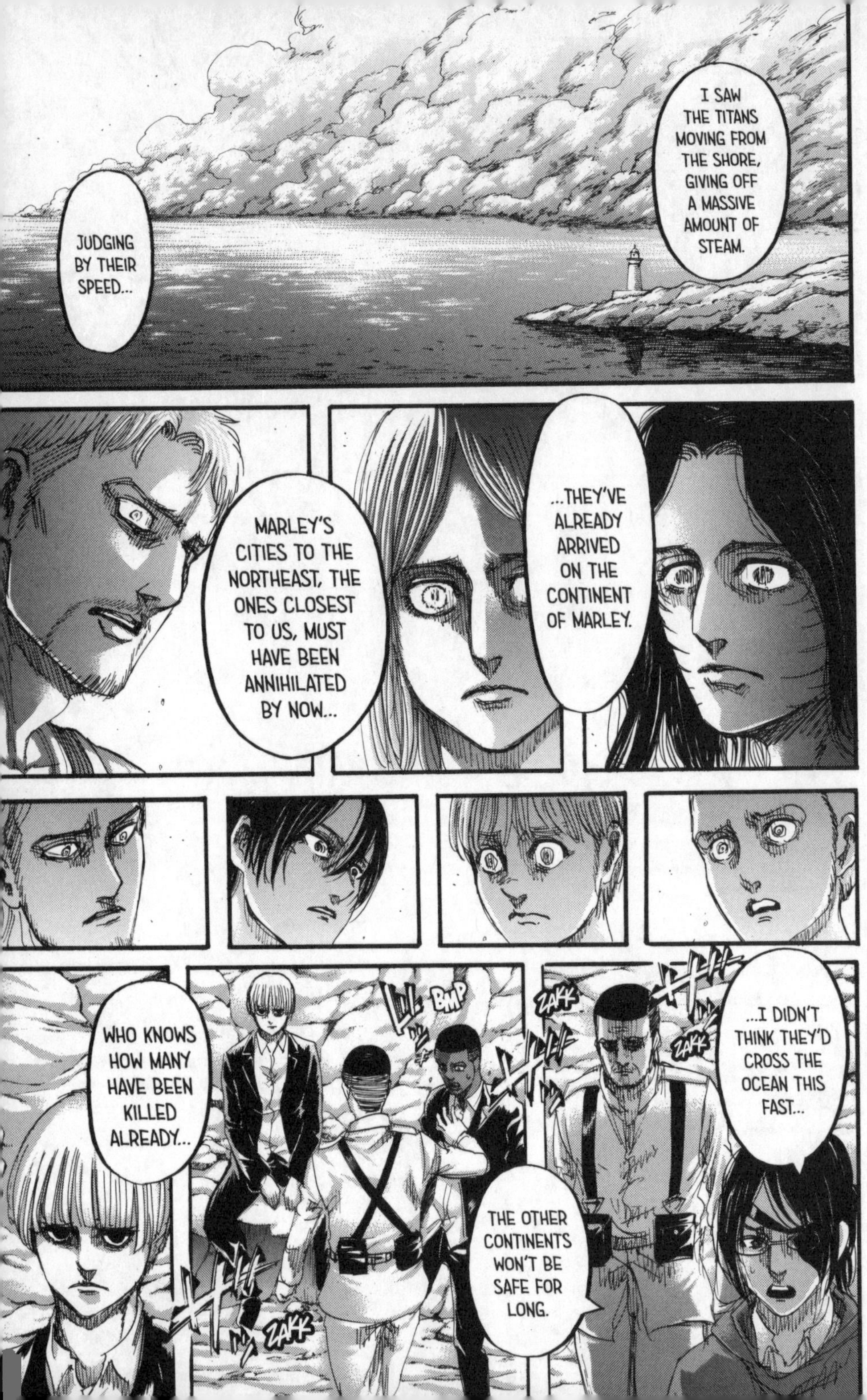
I SAW THE TITANS MOVING FROM THE SHORE, GIVING OFF A MASSIVE AMOUNT OF STEAM.
JUDGING BY THEIR SPEED...
...THEY'VE ALREADY ARRIVED ON THE CONTINENT OF MARLEY.
MARLEY'S CITIES TO THE NORTHEAST, THE ONES CLOSEST TO US, MUST HAVE BEEN ANNIHILATED BY NOW...
...I DIDN'T THINK THEY'D CROSS THE OCEAN THIS FAST...
ZAKK
ZAKK
THE OTHER CONTINENTS WON'T BE SAFE FOR LONG.
BMP
WHO KNOWS HOW MANY HAVE BEEN KILLED ALREADY...
ZAKK

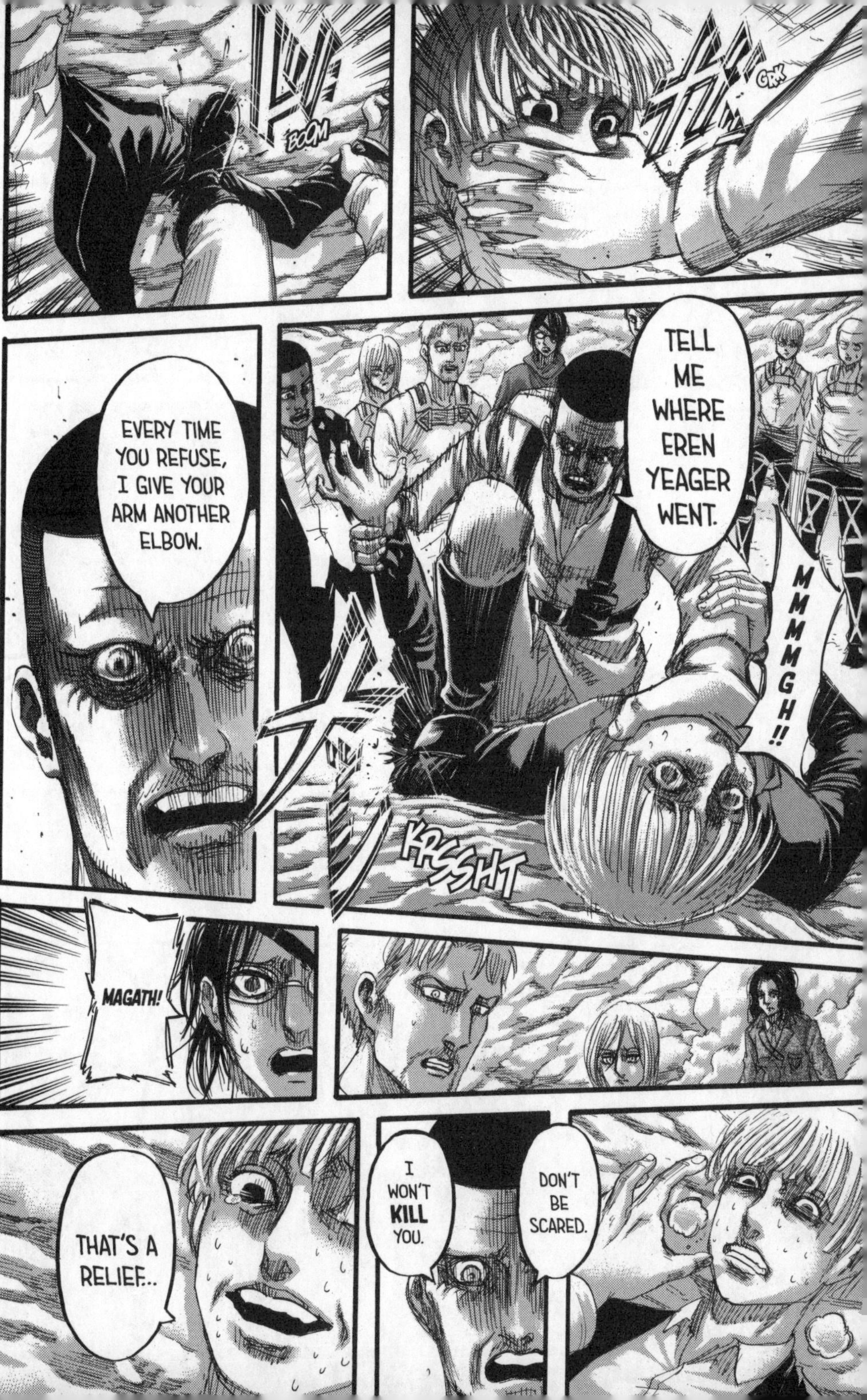
GRK
BOOM
TELL ME WHERE EREN YEAGER WENT.
MMMMGH!!
KRSSHT
EVERY TIME YOU REFUSE, I GIVE YOUR ARM ANOTHER ELBOW.
MAGATH!
DON'T BE SCARED.
I WON'T **KILL** YOU.
THAT'S A RELIEF...

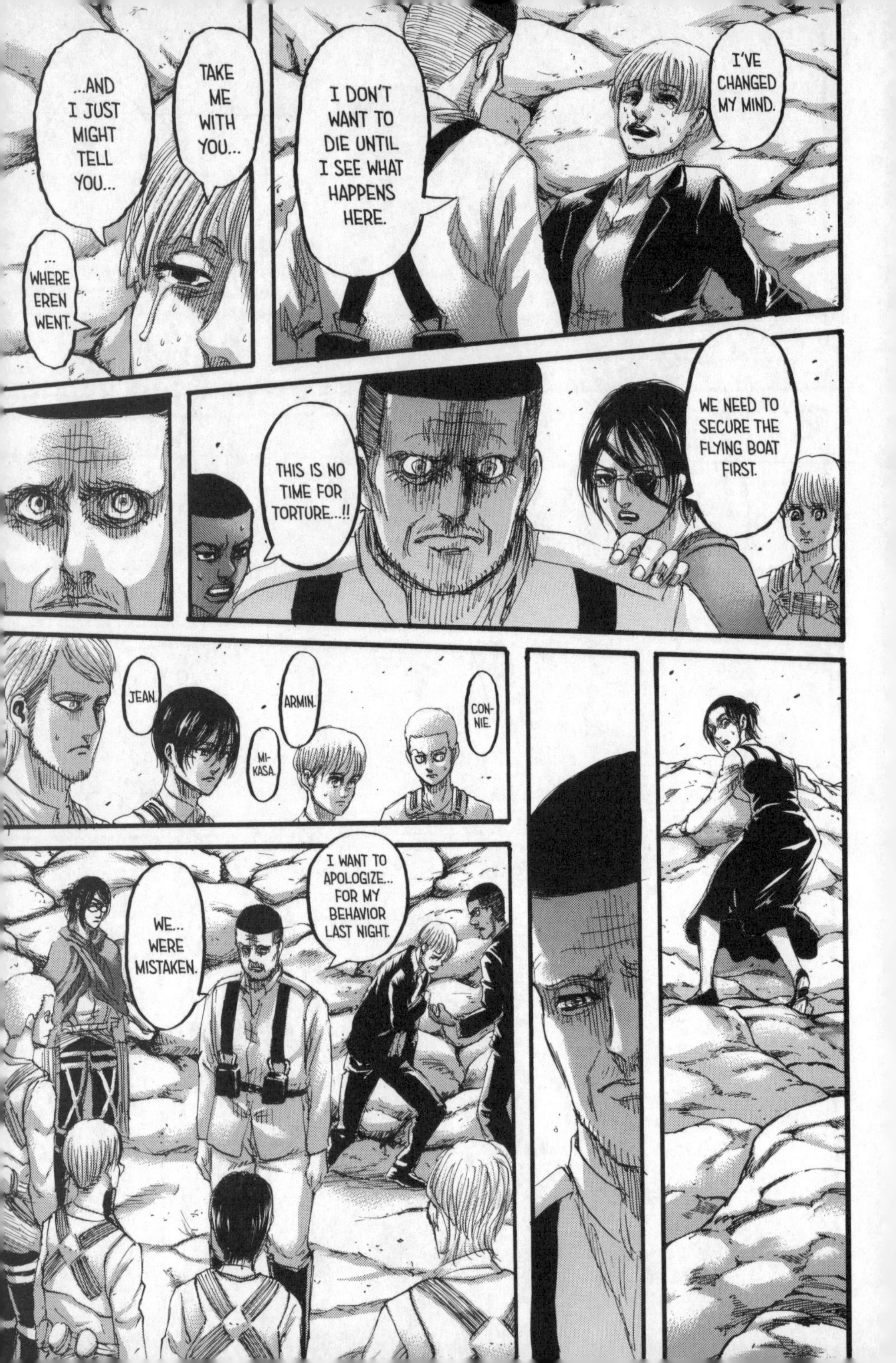
I'VE CHANGED MY MIND.
I DON'T WANT TO DIE UNTIL I SEE WHAT HAPPENS HERE.
TAKE ME WITH YOU...
...AND I JUST MIGHT TELL YOU...
... WHERE EREN WENT.
WE NEED TO SECURE THE FLYING BOAT FIRST.
THIS IS NO TIME FOR TORTURE...!!
CON-NIE.
ARMIN.
MI-KASA.
JEAN.
I WANT TO APOLOGIZE... FOR MY BEHAVIOR LAST NIGHT.
WE... WERE MISTAKEN.

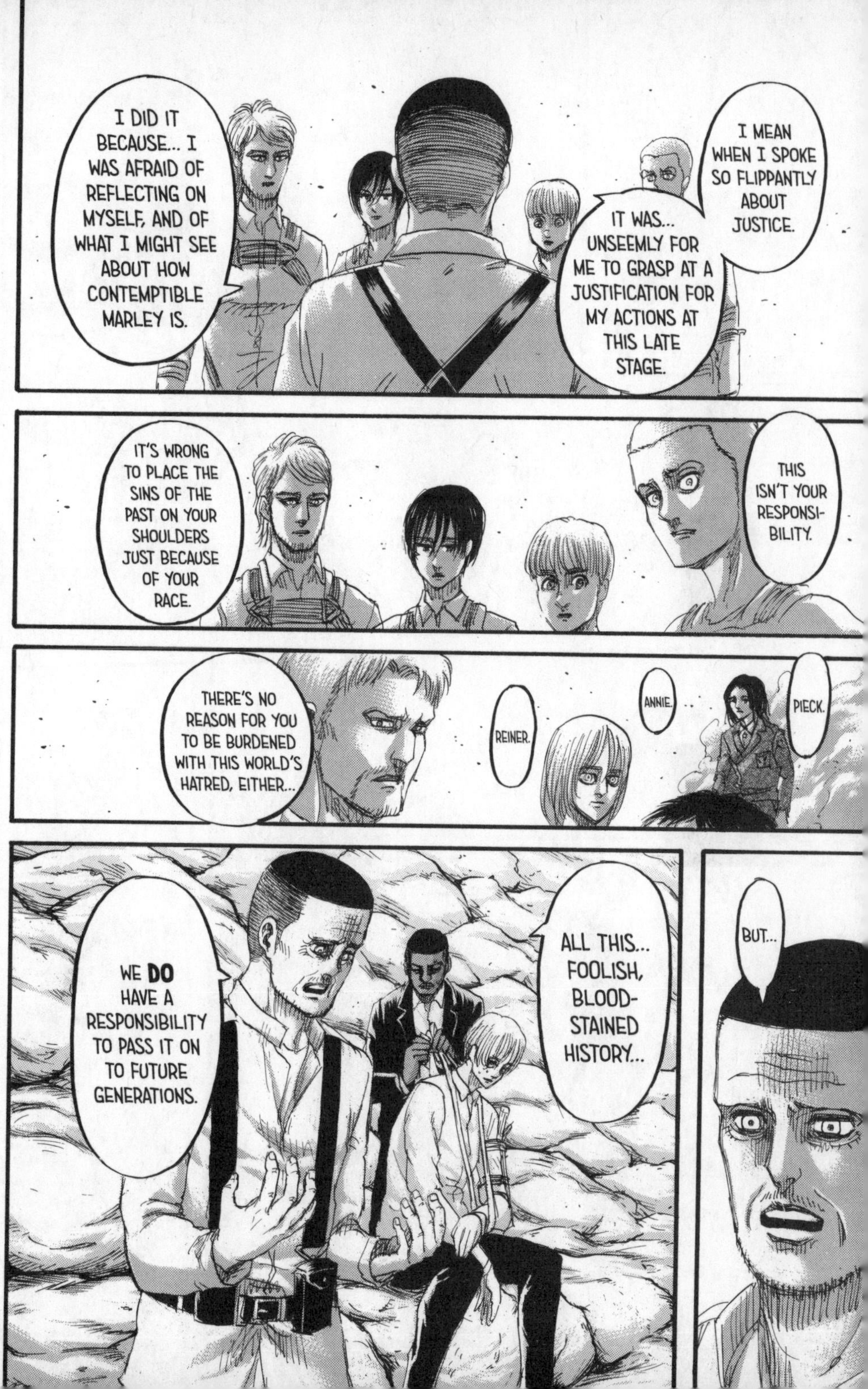
I MEAN WHEN I SPOKE SO FLIPPANTLY ABOUT JUSTICE.
IT WAS... UNSEEMLY FOR ME TO GRASP AT A JUSTIFICATION FOR MY ACTIONS AT THIS LATE STAGE.
I DID IT BECAUSE... I WAS AFRAID OF REFLECTING ON MYSELF, AND OF WHAT I MIGHT SEE ABOUT HOW CONTEMPTIBLE MARLEY IS.
THIS ISN'T YOUR RESPONSIBILITY.
IT'S WRONG TO PLACE THE SINS OF THE PAST ON YOUR SHOULDERS JUST BECAUSE OF YOUR RACE.
PIECK.
ANNIE.
REINER.
THERE'S NO REASON FOR YOU TO BE BURDENED WITH THIS WORLD'S HATRED, EITHER...
BUT...
ALL THIS... FOOLISH, BLOOD-STAINED HISTORY...
WE **DO** HAVE A RESPONSIBILITY TO PASS IT ON TO FUTURE GENERATIONS.

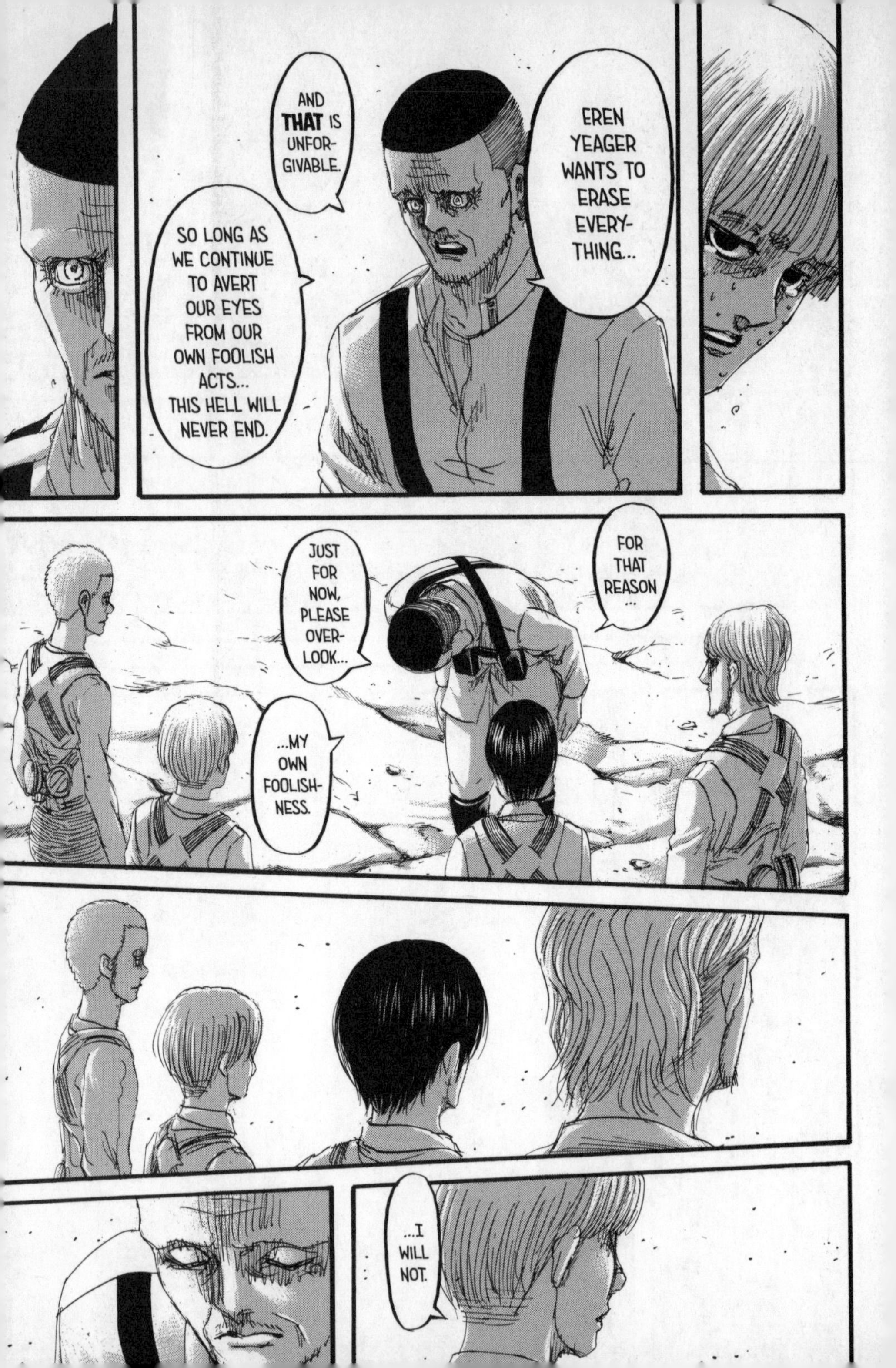
EREN YEAGER WANTS TO ERASE EVERYTHING...
AND **THAT** IS UNFORGIVABLE.
SO LONG AS WE CONTINUE TO AVERT OUR EYES FROM OUR OWN FOOLISH ACTS... THIS HELL WILL NEVER END.
FOR THAT REASON ...
JUST FOR NOW, PLEASE OVERLOOK...
...MY OWN FOOLISHNESS.
...I WILL NOT.

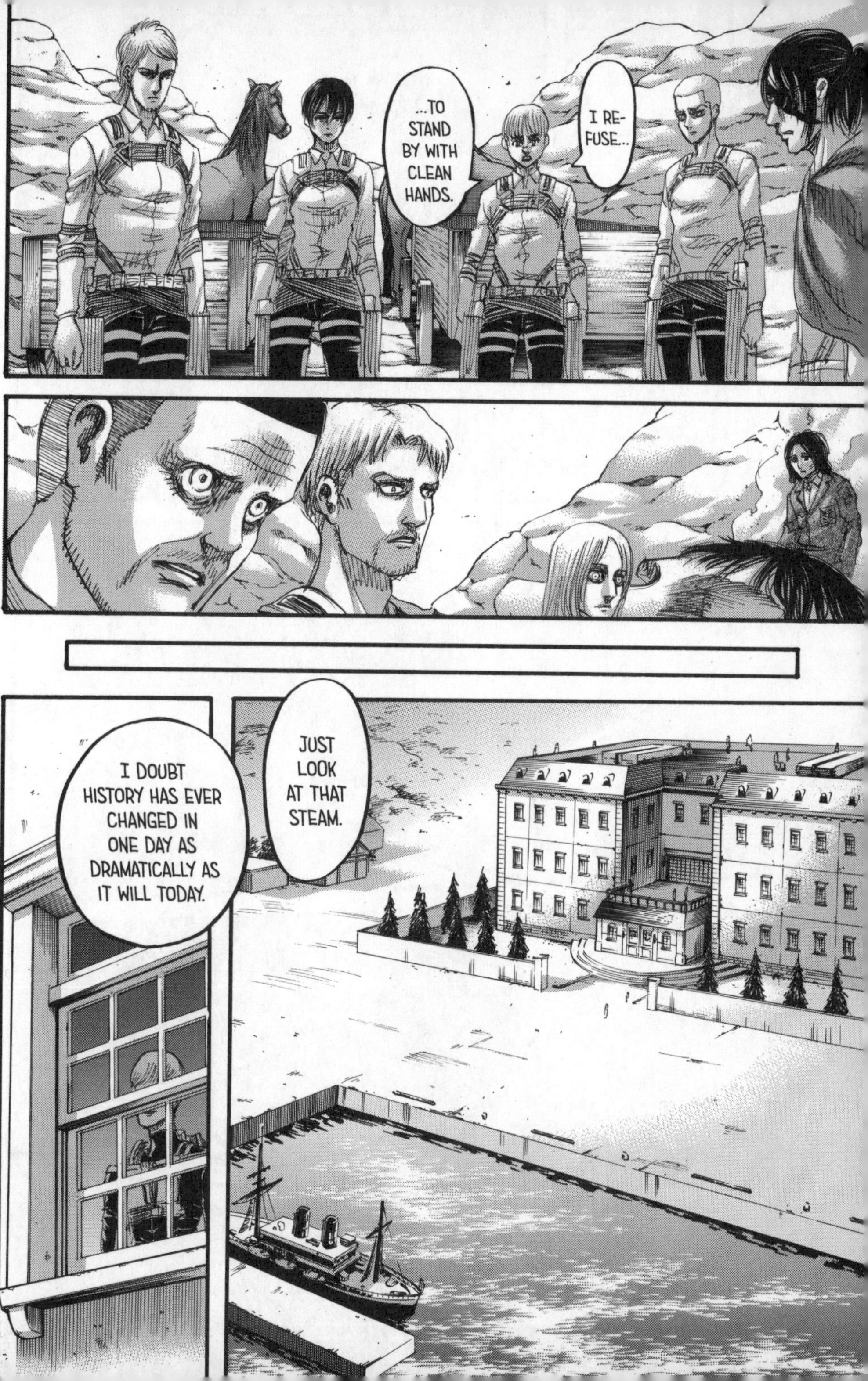
I REFUSE...
...TO STAND BY WITH CLEAN HANDS.
JUST LOOK AT THAT STEAM.
I DOUBT HISTORY HAS EVER CHANGED IN ONE DAY AS DRAMATICALLY AS IT WILL TODAY.

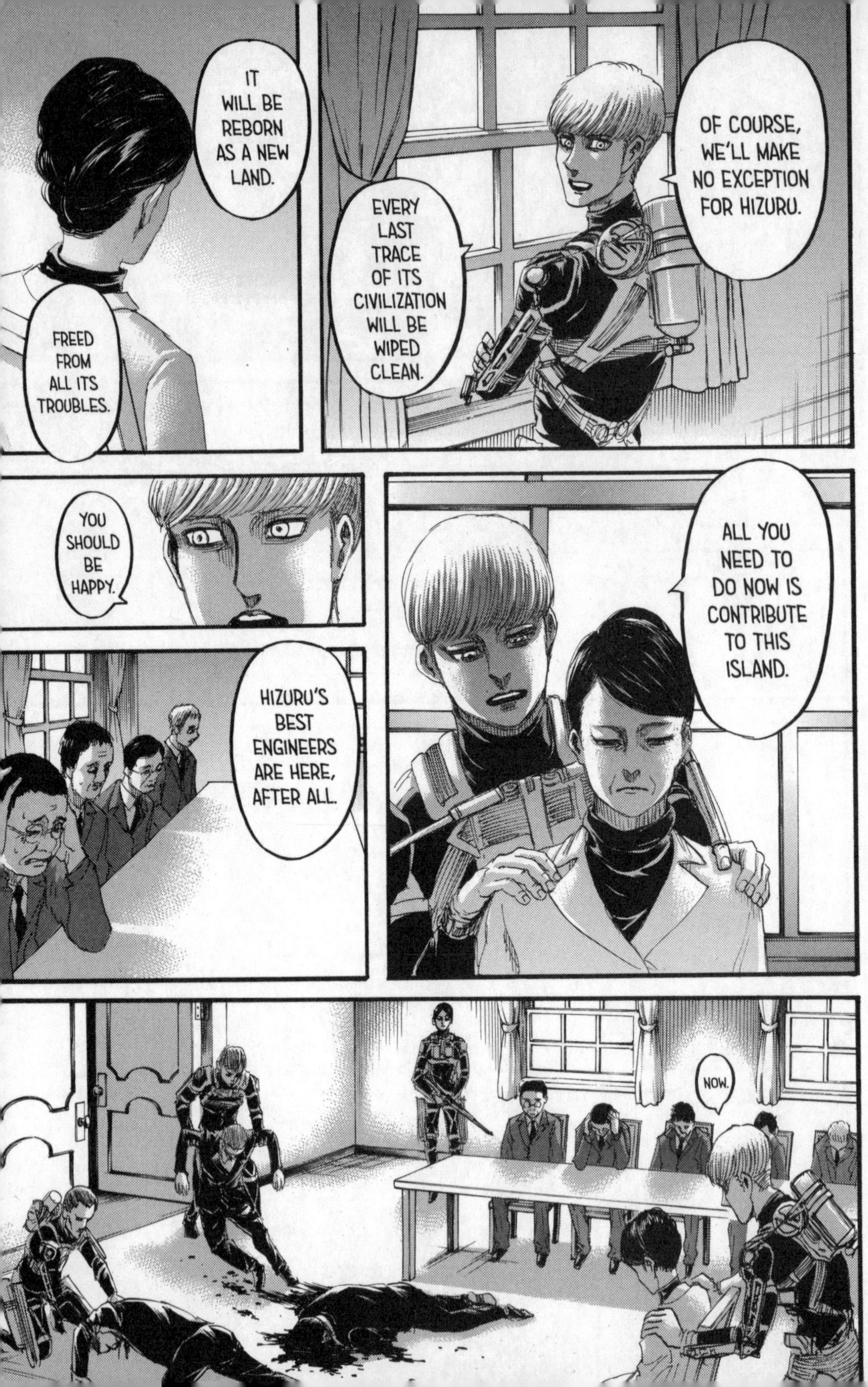

OF COURSE, WE'LL MAKE NO EXCEPTION FOR HIZURU.
EVERY LAST TRACE OF ITS CIVILIZATION WILL BE WIPED CLEAN.
IT WILL BE REBORN AS A NEW LAND.
FREED FROM ALL ITS TROUBLES.
ALL YOU NEED TO DO NOW IS CONTRIBUTE TO THIS ISLAND.
YOU SHOULD BE HAPPY.
HIZURU'S BEST ENGINEERS ARE HERE, AFTER ALL.
NOW.

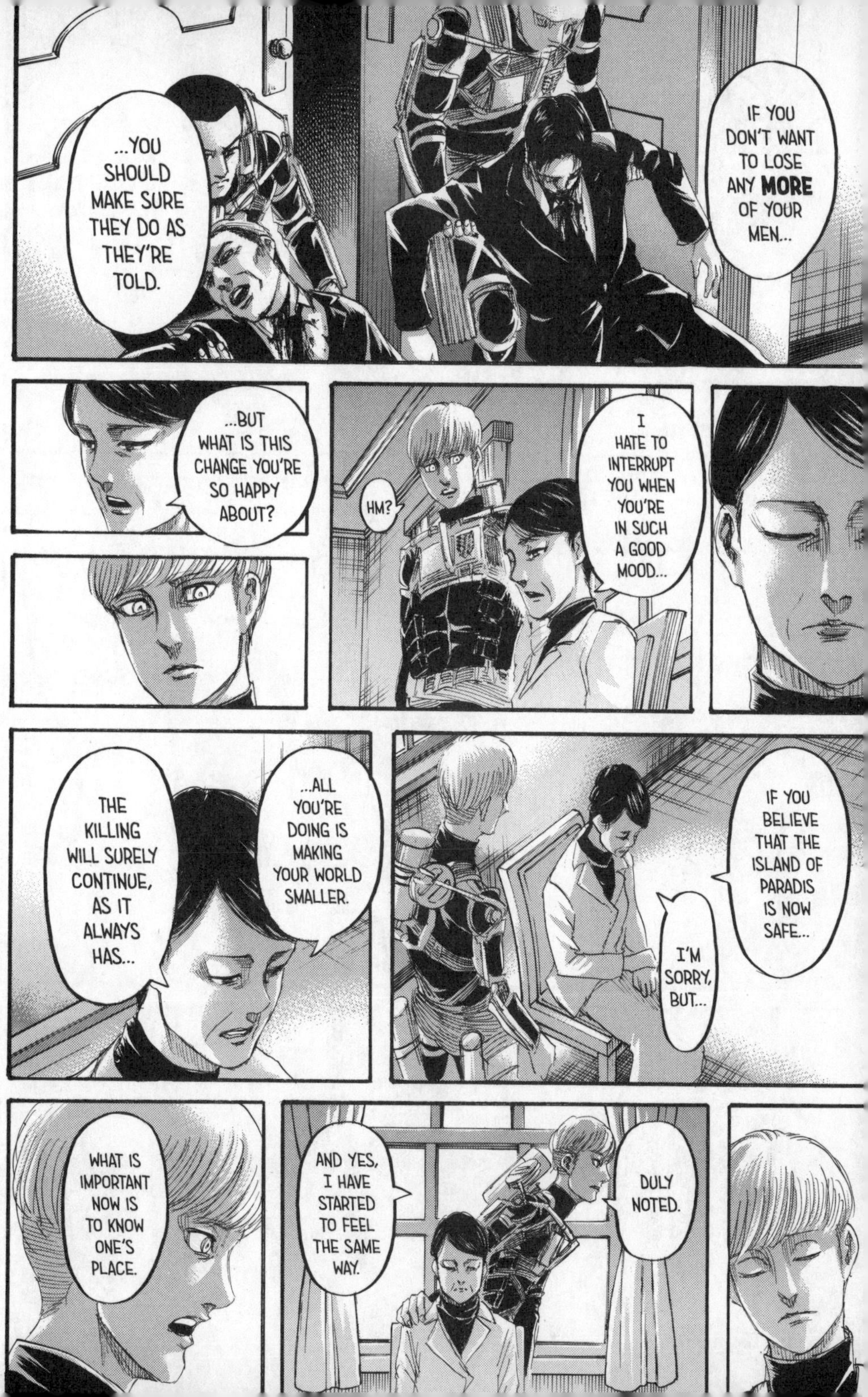
IF YOU DON'T WANT TO LOSE ANY **MORE** OF YOUR MEN...
...YOU SHOULD MAKE SURE THEY DO AS THEY'RE TOLD.
I HATE TO INTERRUPT YOU WHEN YOU'RE IN SUCH A GOOD MOOD...
HM?
...BUT WHAT IS THIS CHANGE YOU'RE SO HAPPY ABOUT?
IF YOU BELIEVE THAT THE ISLAND OF PARADIS IS NOW SAFE...
I'M SORRY, BUT...
...ALL YOU'RE DOING IS MAKING YOUR WORLD SMALLER.
THE KILLING WILL SURELY CONTINUE, AS IT ALWAYS HAS...
DULY NOTED.
AND YES, I HAVE STARTED TO FEEL THE SAME WAY.
WHAT IS IMPORTANT NOW IS TO KNOW ONE'S PLACE.

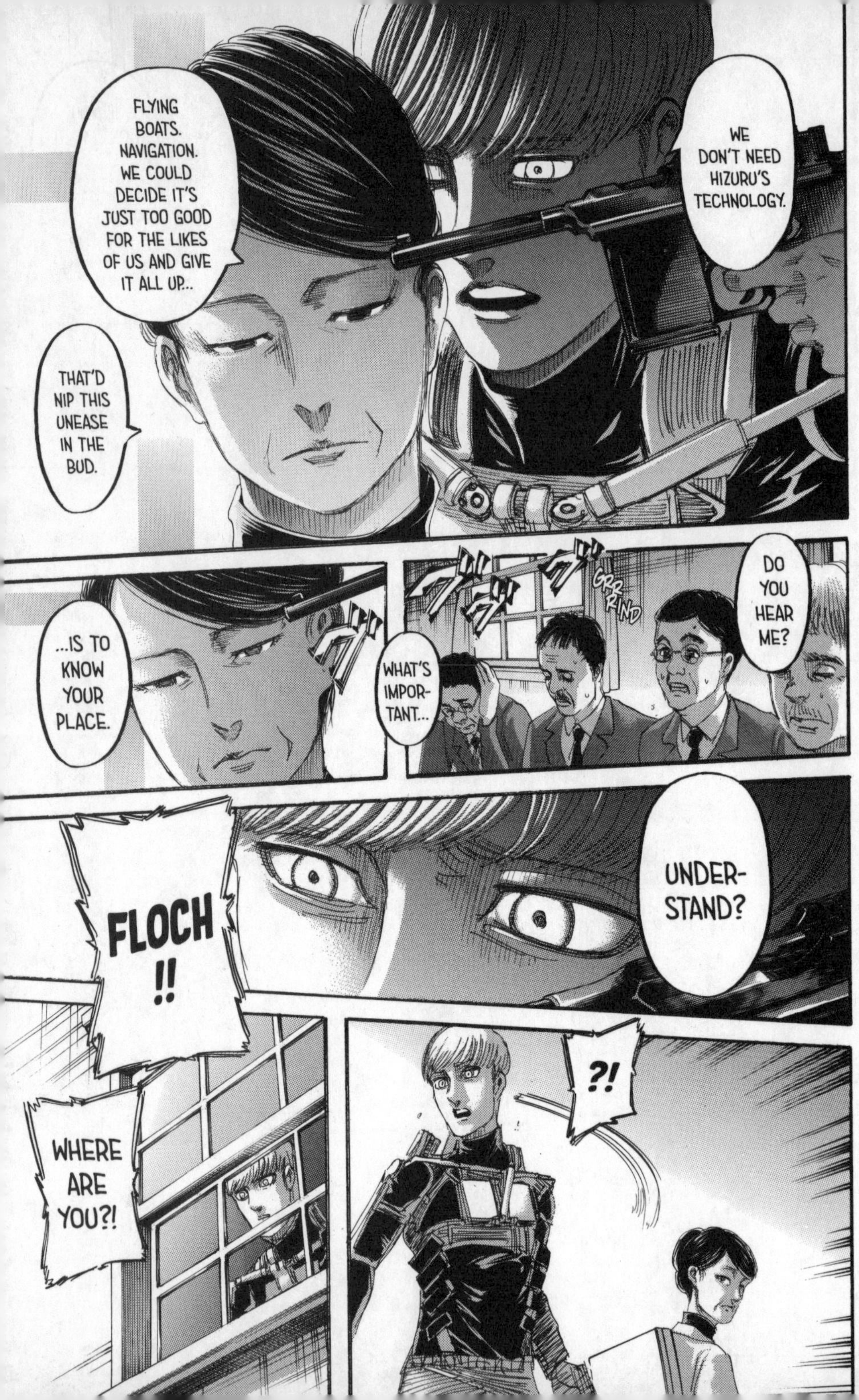
WE DON'T NEED HIZURU'S TECHNOLOGY.
FLYING BOATS. NAVIGATION. WE COULD DECIDE IT'S JUST TOO GOOD FOR THE LIKES OF US AND GIVE IT ALL UP...
THAT'D NIP THIS UNEASE IN THE BUD.
DO YOU HEAR ME?
GRRRIND
WHAT'S IMPORTANT...
...IS TO KNOW YOUR PLACE.
UNDERSTAND?
FLOCH!!
?!
WHERE ARE YOU?!

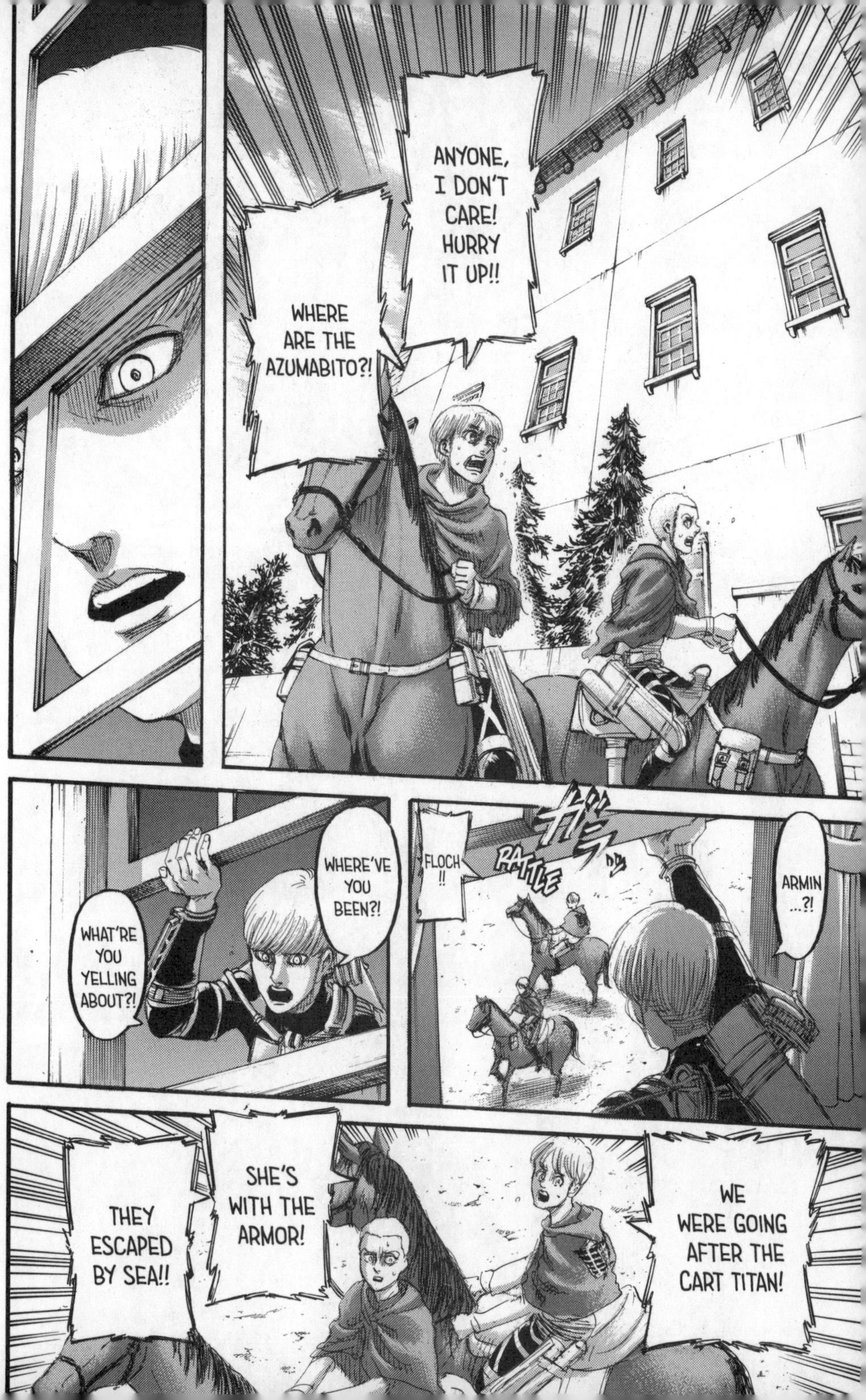

ANYONE, I DON'T CARE! HURRY IT UP!!
WHERE ARE THE AZUMABITO?!
ARMIN ...?!
FLOCH !!
RATTLE
WHERE'VE YOU BEEN?!
WHAT'RE YOU YELLING ABOUT?!
WE WERE GOING AFTER THE CART TITAN!
SHE'S WITH THE ARMOR!
THEY ESCAPED BY SEA!!

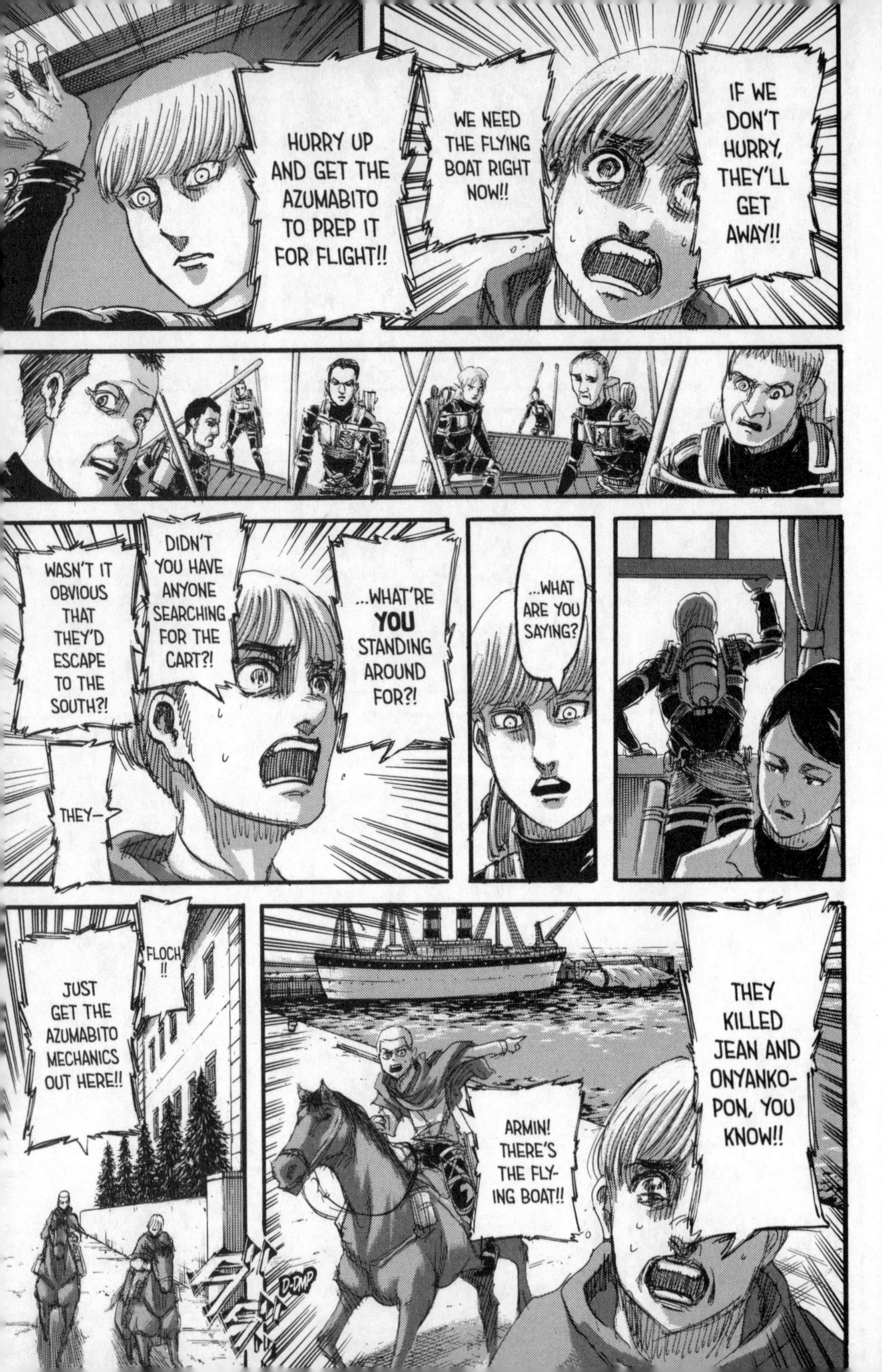
IF WE DON'T HURRY, THEY'LL GET AWAY!!
WE NEED THE FLYING BOAT RIGHT NOW!!
HURRY UP AND GET THE AZUMABITO TO PREP IT FOR FLIGHT!!
...WHAT ARE YOU SAYING?
...WHAT'RE YOU STANDING AROUND FOR?!
DIDN'T YOU HAVE ANYONE SEARCHING FOR THE CART?!
WASN'T IT OBVIOUS THAT THEY'D ESCAPE TO THE SOUTH?!
THEY—
THEY KILLED JEAN AND ONYANKO-PON, YOU KNOW!!
ARMIN! THERE'S THE FLY-ING BOAT!!
D-DMP
FLOCH!!
JUST GET THE AZUMABITO MECHANICS OUT HERE!!

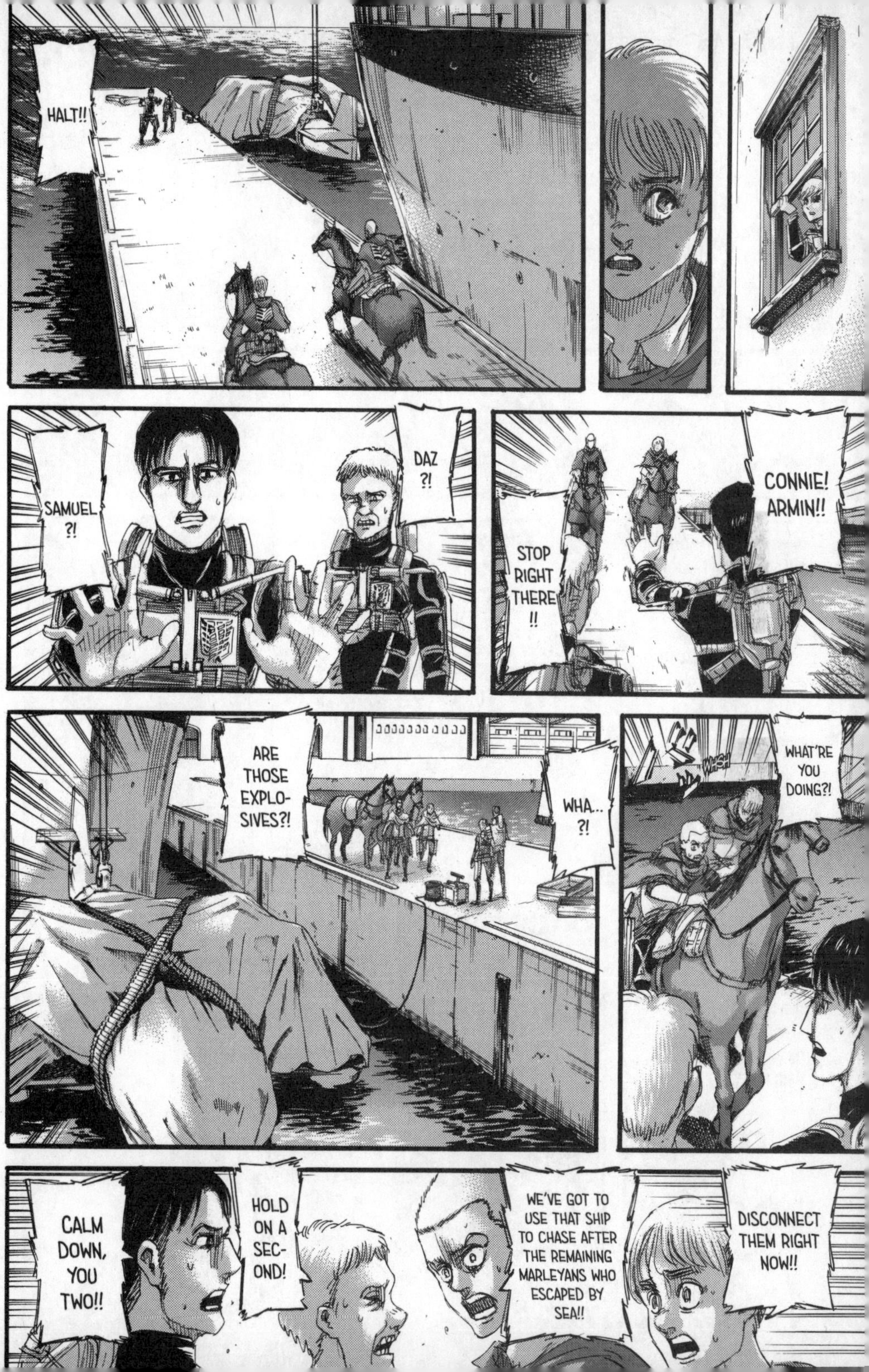
HALT!!
CONNIE! ARMIN!!
STOP RIGHT THERE!!
DAZ ?!
SAMUEL ?!
WHAT'RE YOU DOING?!
WHA... ?!
ARE THOSE EXPLOSIVES?!
DISCONNECT THEM RIGHT NOW!!
WE'VE GOT TO USE THAT SHIP TO CHASE AFTER THE REMAINING MARLEYANS WHO ESCAPED BY SEA!!
HOLD ON A SEC-OND!
CALM DOWN, YOU TWO!!

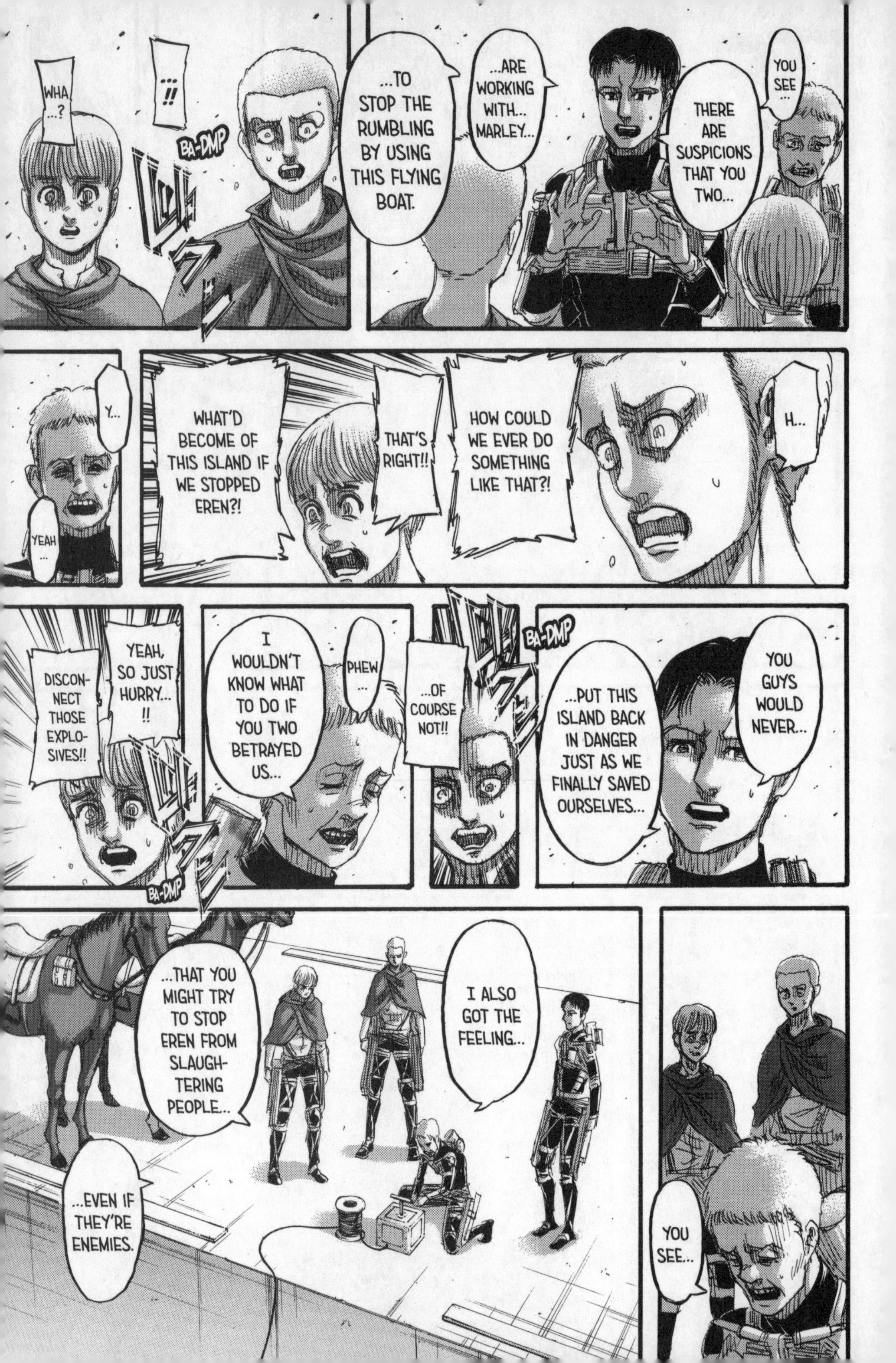
YOU SEE...
THERE ARE SUSPICIONS THAT YOU TWO...
...ARE WORKING WITH... MARLEY...
...TO STOP THE RUMBLING BY USING THIS FLYING BOAT.
...!!
BA-DMP
WHA...?
H...
HOW COULD WE EVER DO SOMETHING LIKE THAT?!
THAT'S RIGHT!!
WHAT'D BECOME OF THIS ISLAND IF WE STOPPED EREN?!
Y...
YEAH...
YOU GUYS WOULD NEVER...
...PUT THIS ISLAND BACK IN DANGER JUST AS WE FINALLY SAVED OURSELVES...
BA-DMP
...OF COURSE NOT!!
PHEW...
I WOULDN'T KNOW WHAT TO DO IF YOU TWO BETRAYED US...
YEAH, SO JUST HURRY...!!
DISCONNECT THOSE EXPLOSIVES!!
BA-DMP
YOU SEE...
I ALSO GOT THE FEELING...
...THAT YOU MIGHT TRY TO STOP EREN FROM SLAUGHTERING PEOPLE...
...EVEN IF THEY'RE ENEMIES.

WHAT'S WRONG?

SPLOOSH

WE DISCONNECTED THE DETONATOR.

IF THAT ALL WORKS OUT...

...THERE WON'T NEED TO BE ANY POINTLESS BLOODSHED.

THEN, ONCE THE FLYING BOAT IS READY... WE NEED TO SOMEHOW GET EVERYONE ON IT... AND LEAVE THIS PLACE.

...IS FOR FLOCH TO HAND OVER THE AZUMABITO MECHANICS...

ALL THAT'S LEFT...

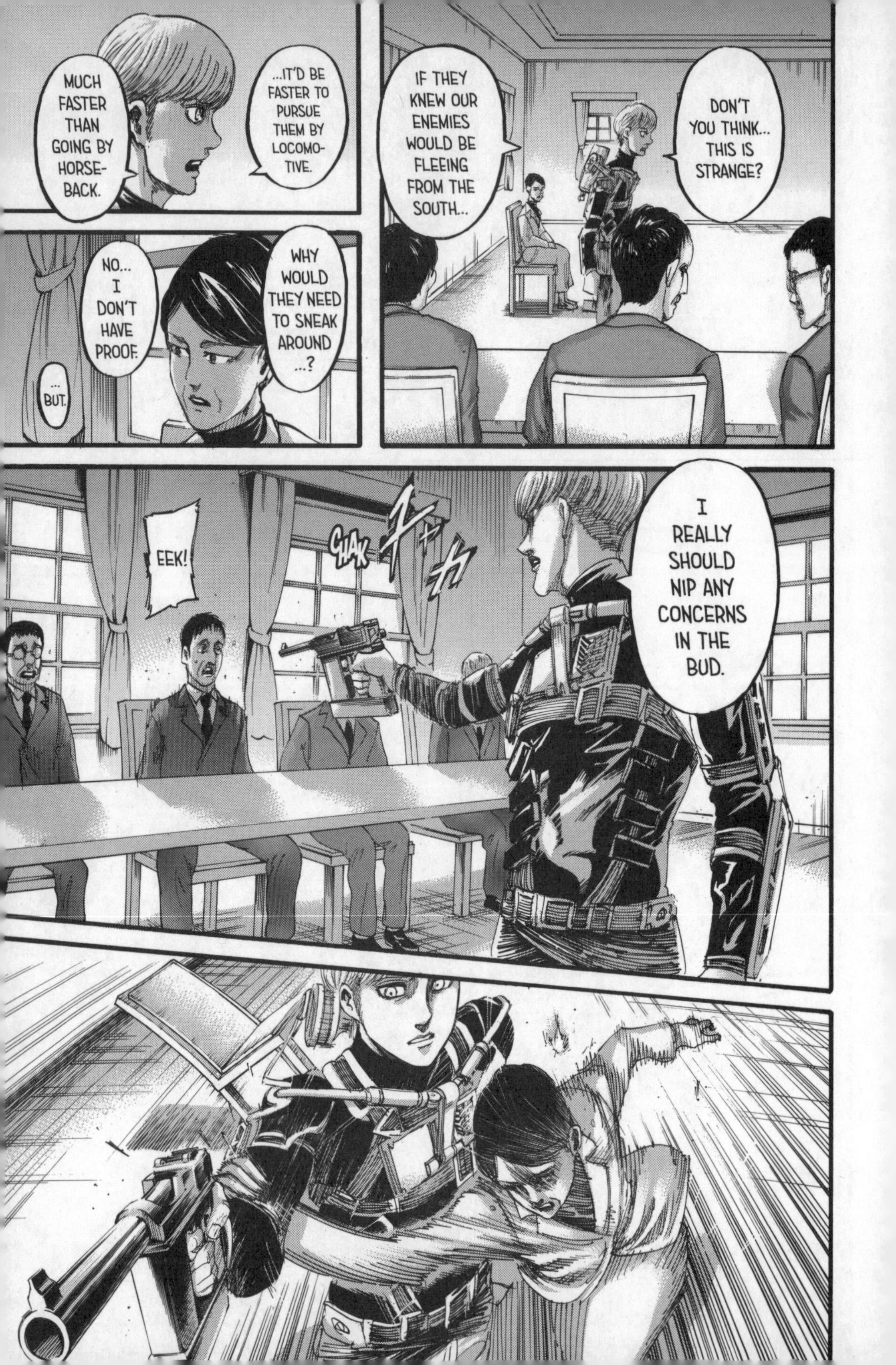
DON'T YOU THINK... THIS IS STRANGE?
IF THEY KNEW OUR ENEMIES WOULD BE FLEEING FROM THE SOUTH...
...IT'D BE FASTER TO PURSUE THEM BY LOCOMOTIVE.
MUCH FASTER THAN GOING BY HORSEBACK.
WHY WOULD THEY NEED TO SNEAK AROUND...?
NO... I DON'T HAVE PROOF.
...BUT.
I REALLY SHOULD NIP ANY CONCERNS IN THE BUD.
CHAK
EEK!

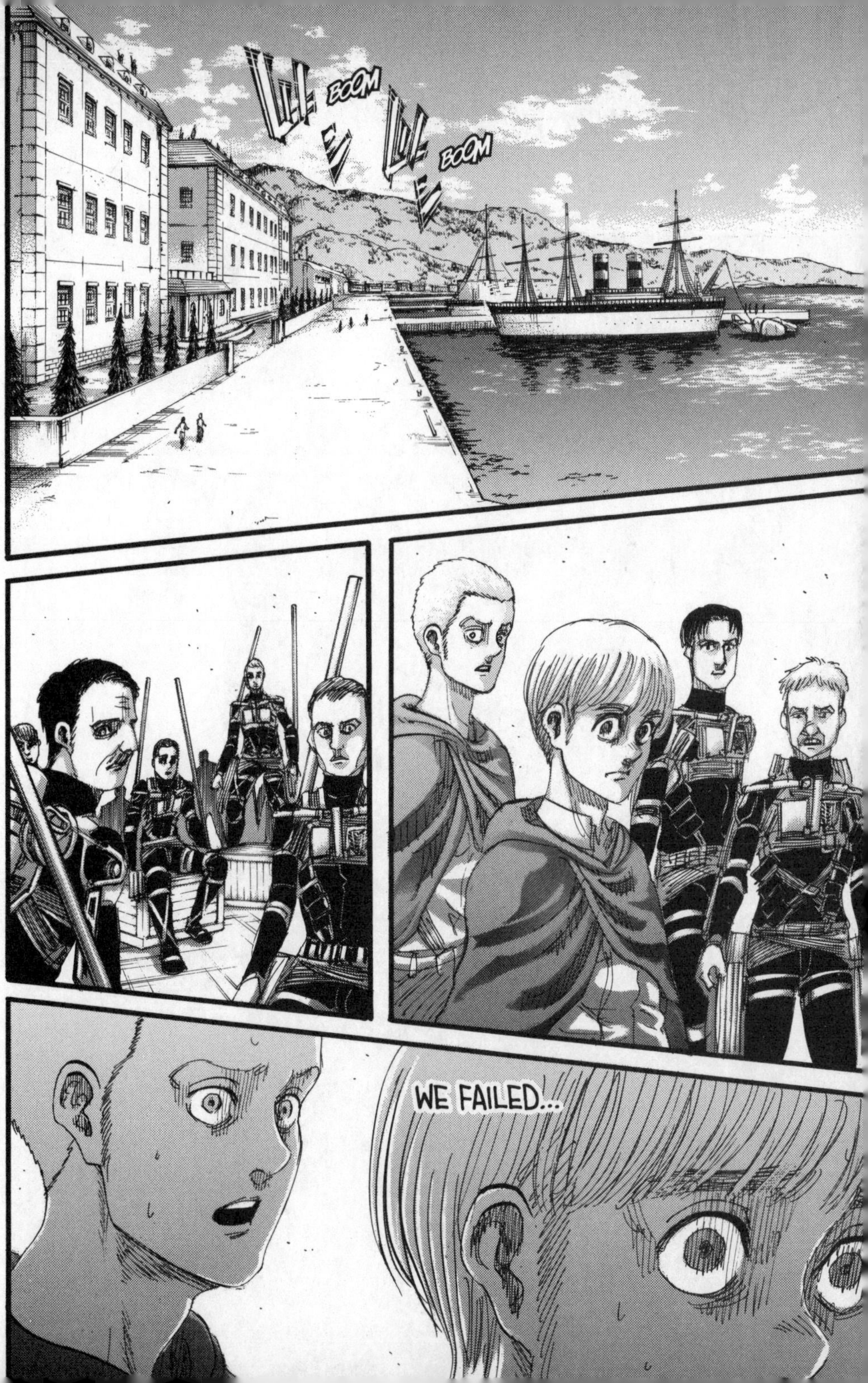
BOOM
BOOM
WE FAILED...

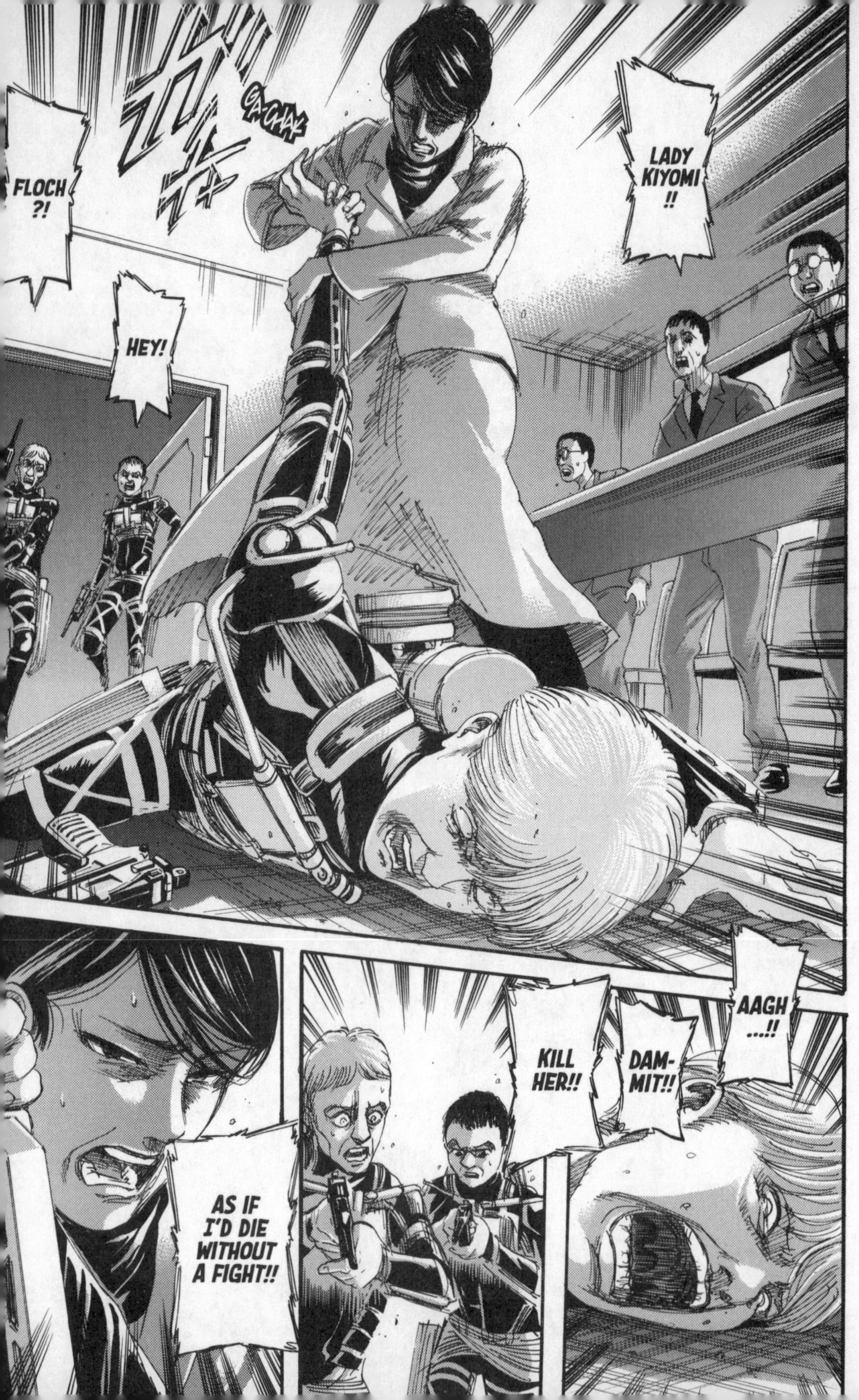
LADY KIYOMI!!
GA-CHAK
FLOCH ?!
HEY!
AAGH ...!!
DAM-MIT!!
KILL HER!!
AS IF I'D DIE WITHOUT A FIGHT!!

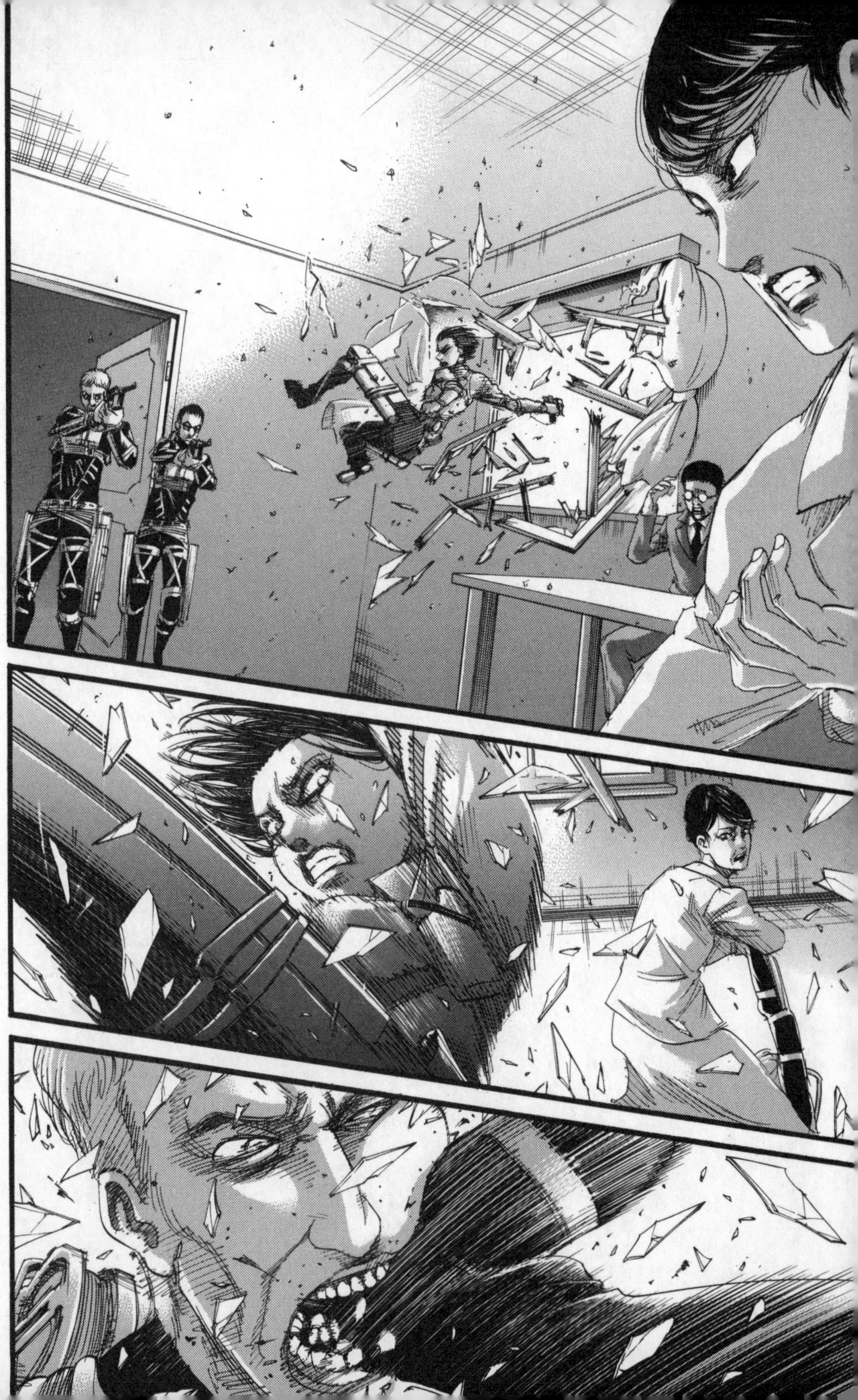

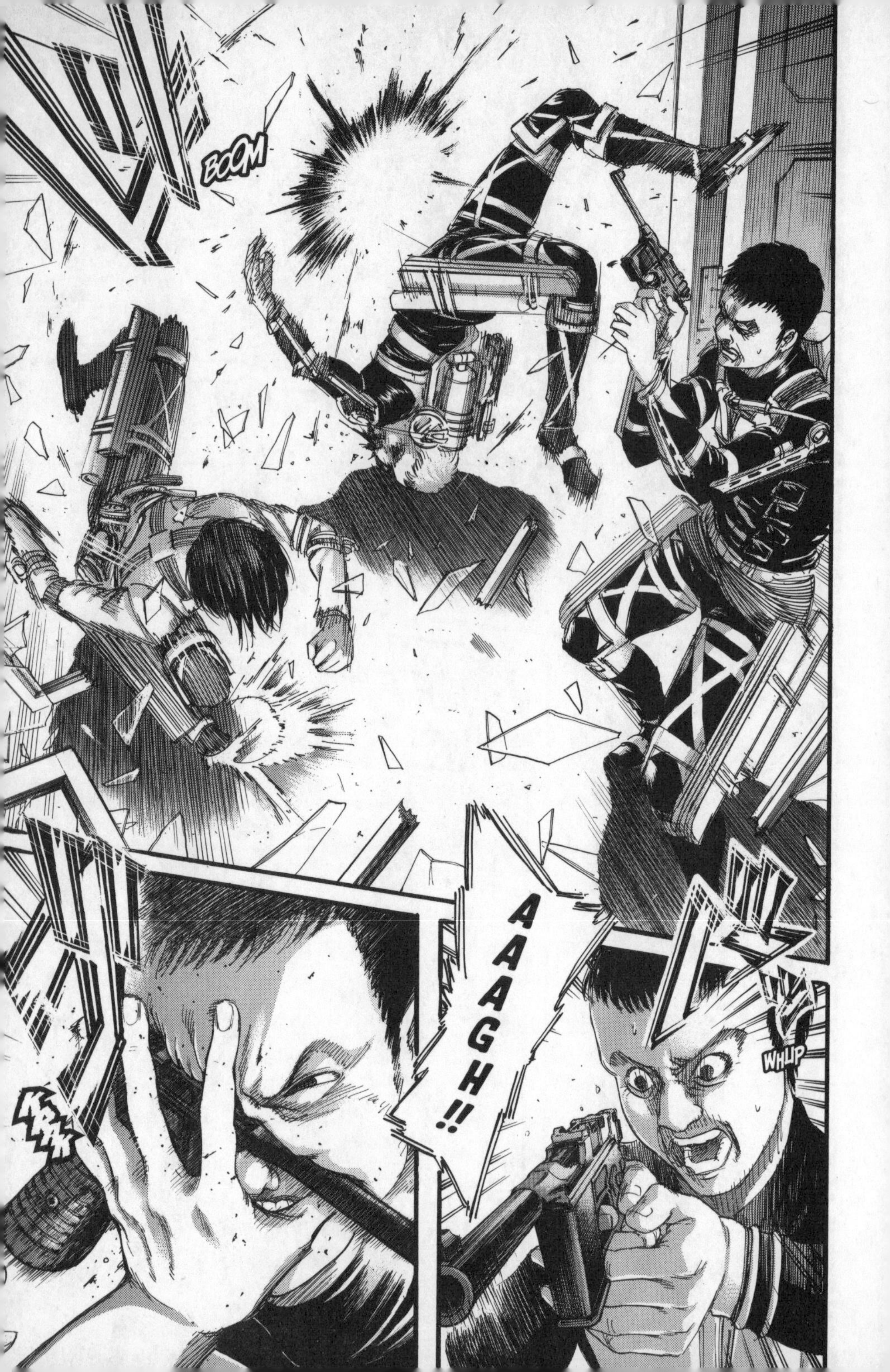
BOOM
WHUP
AAAAGH!!
KRAK

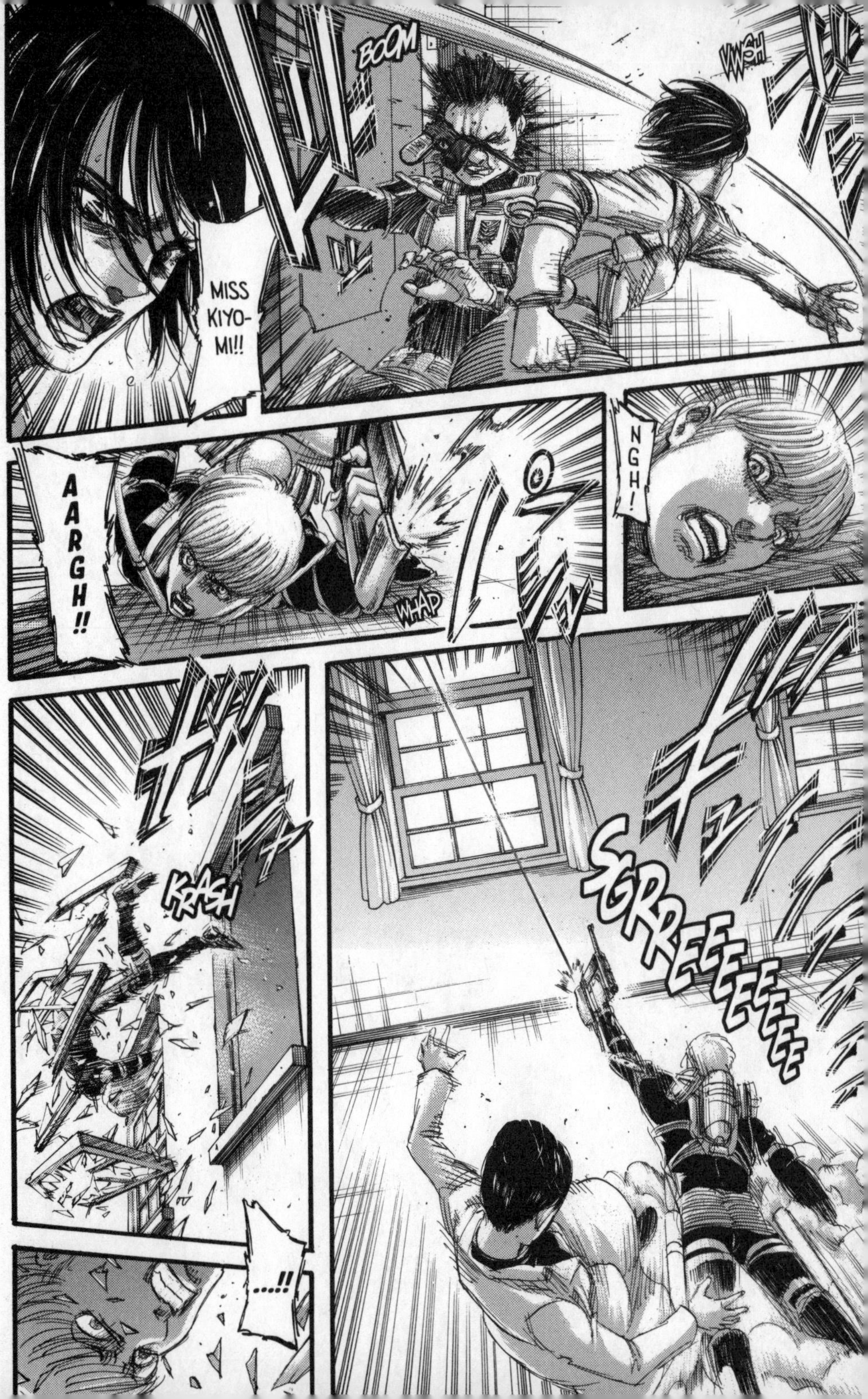
VWSH
BOOM
MISS KIYO-MI!!
NGH!
WHAP
AARGH!!
SCREEEEEEEEE
KRASH
...!!

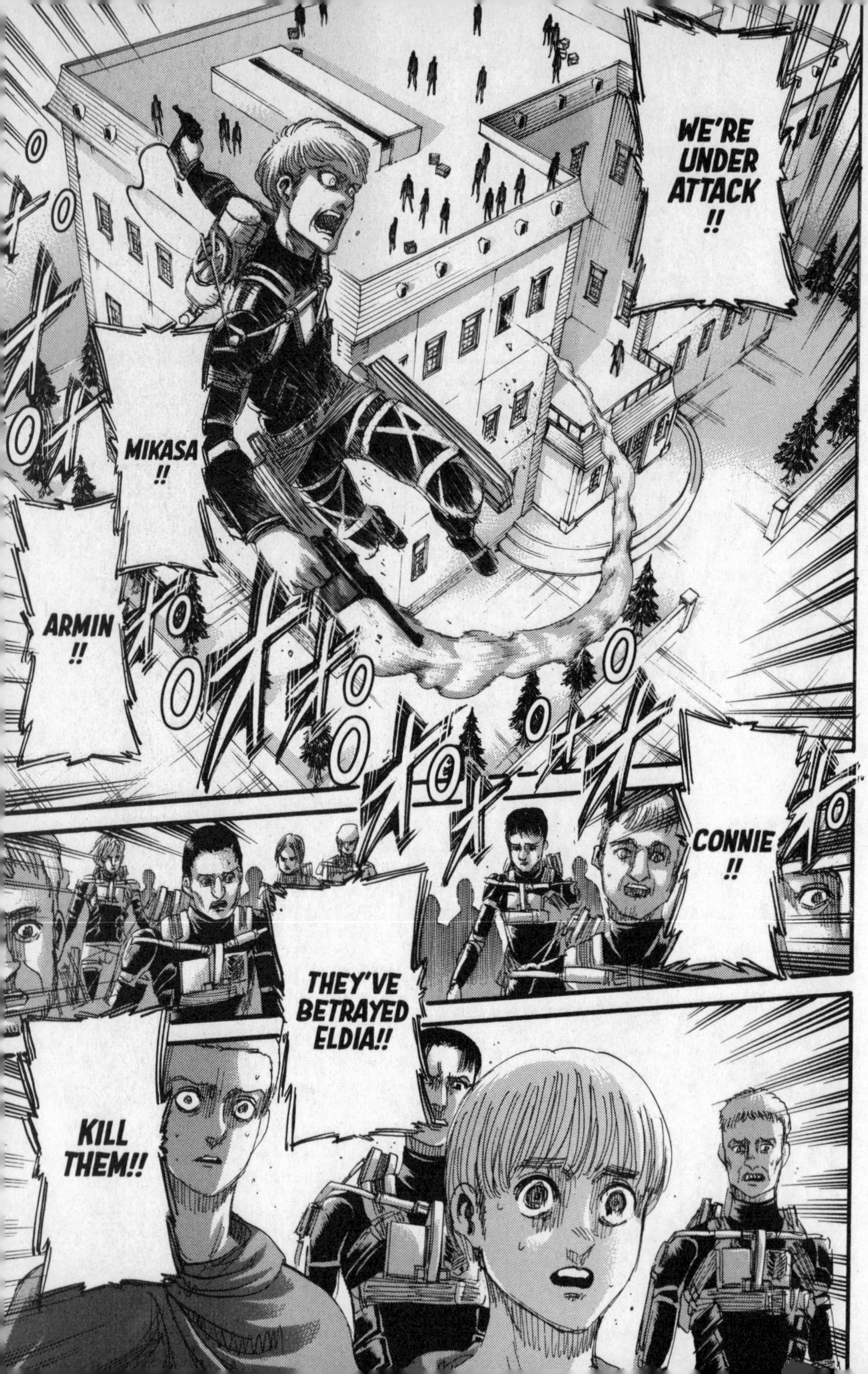
WE'RE UNDER ATTACK!!
MIKASA!!
ARMIN!!
CONNIE!!
THEY'VE BETRAYED ELDIA!!
KILL THEM!!

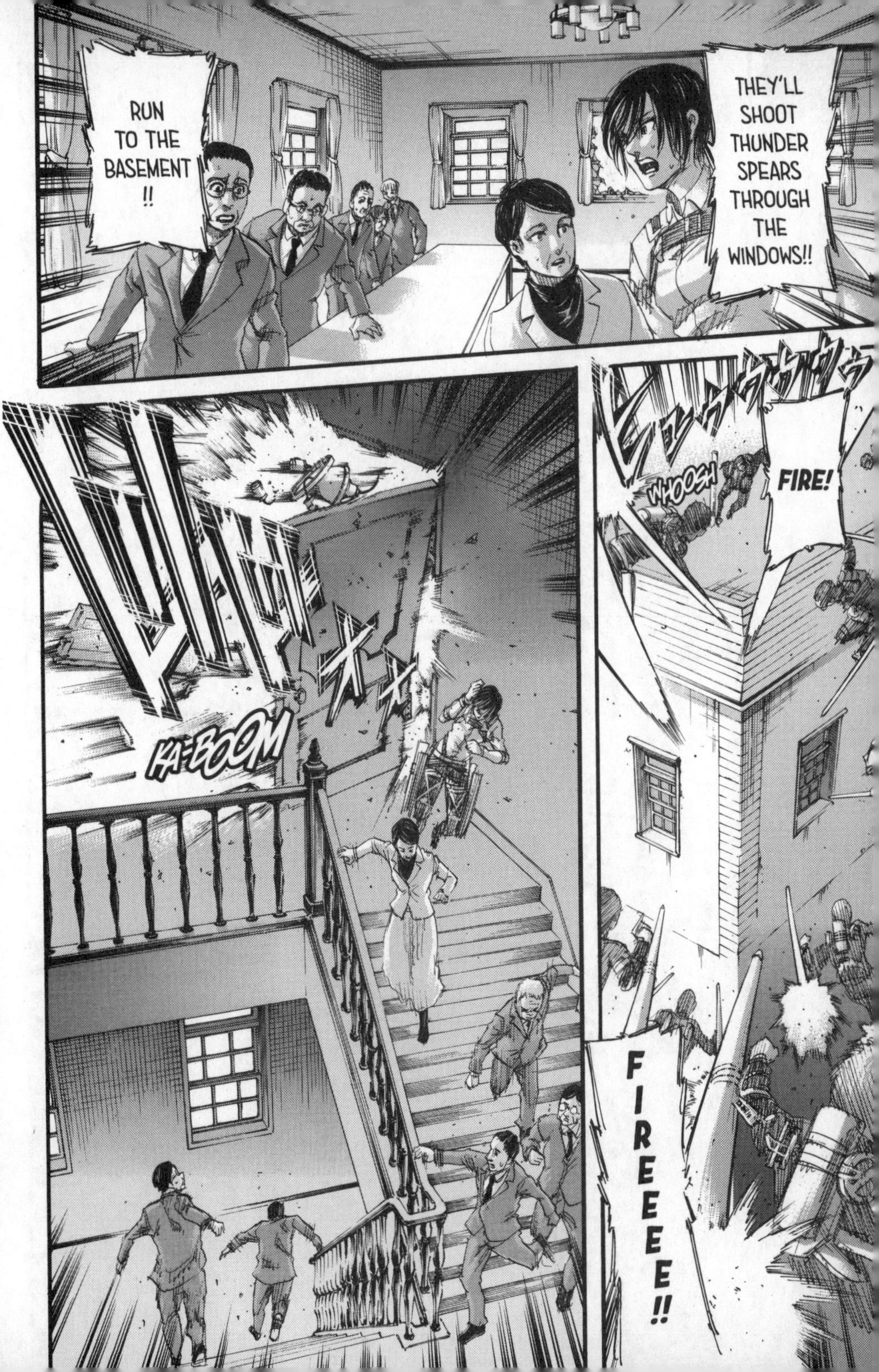
THEY'LL SHOOT THUNDER SPEARS THROUGH THE WINDOWS!!
RUN TO THE BASEMENT!!
FIRE!
WHOOSH
FIREEEEE!!
KA-BOOM

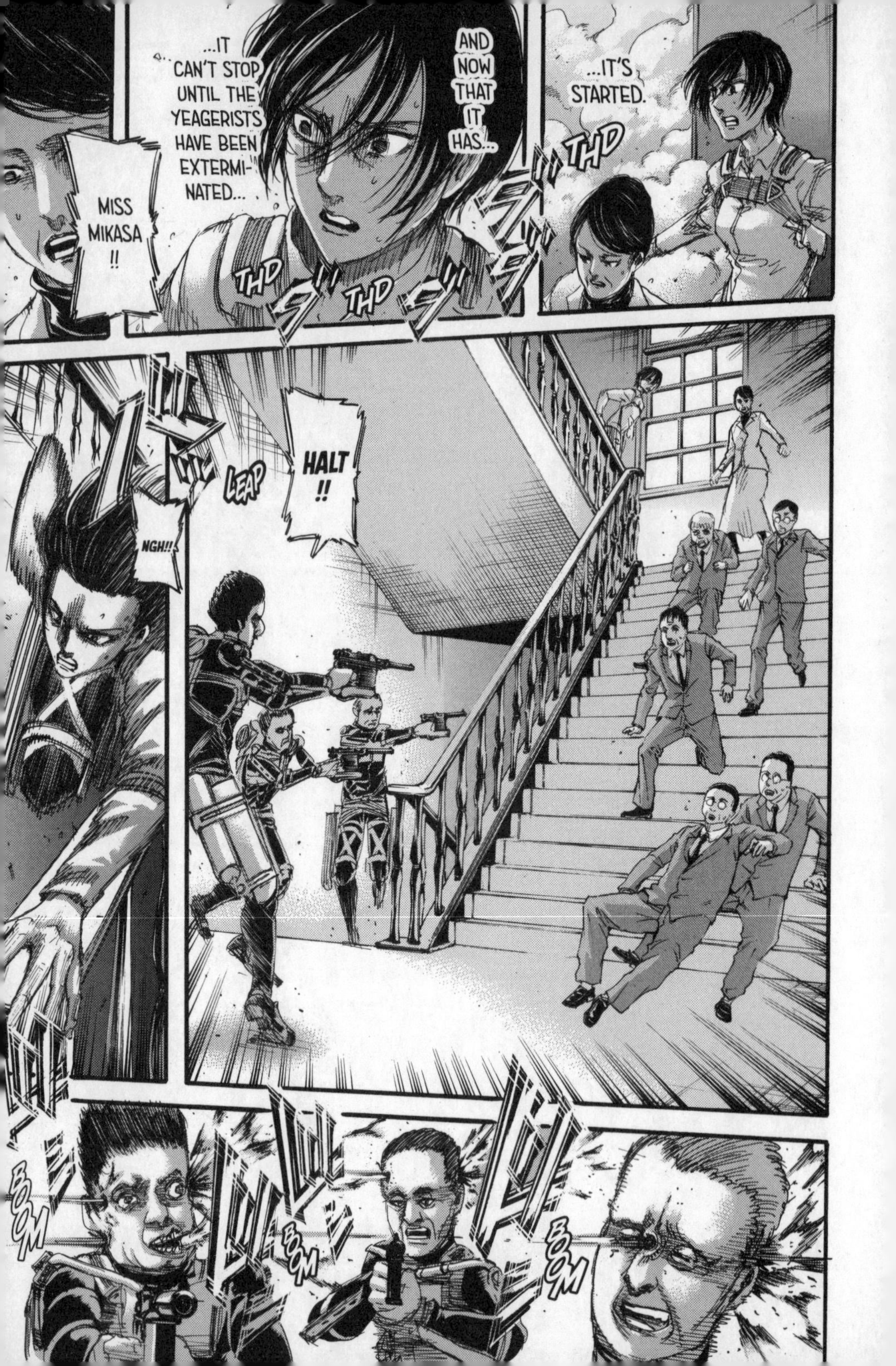
...IT'S STARTED.
THD
AND NOW THAT IT HAS...
...IT CAN'T STOP UNTIL THE YEAGERISTS HAVE BEEN EXTERMINATED...
THD
THD
MISS MIKASA !!
HALT !!
LEAP
NGH!!
BOOM
BOOM
BOOM

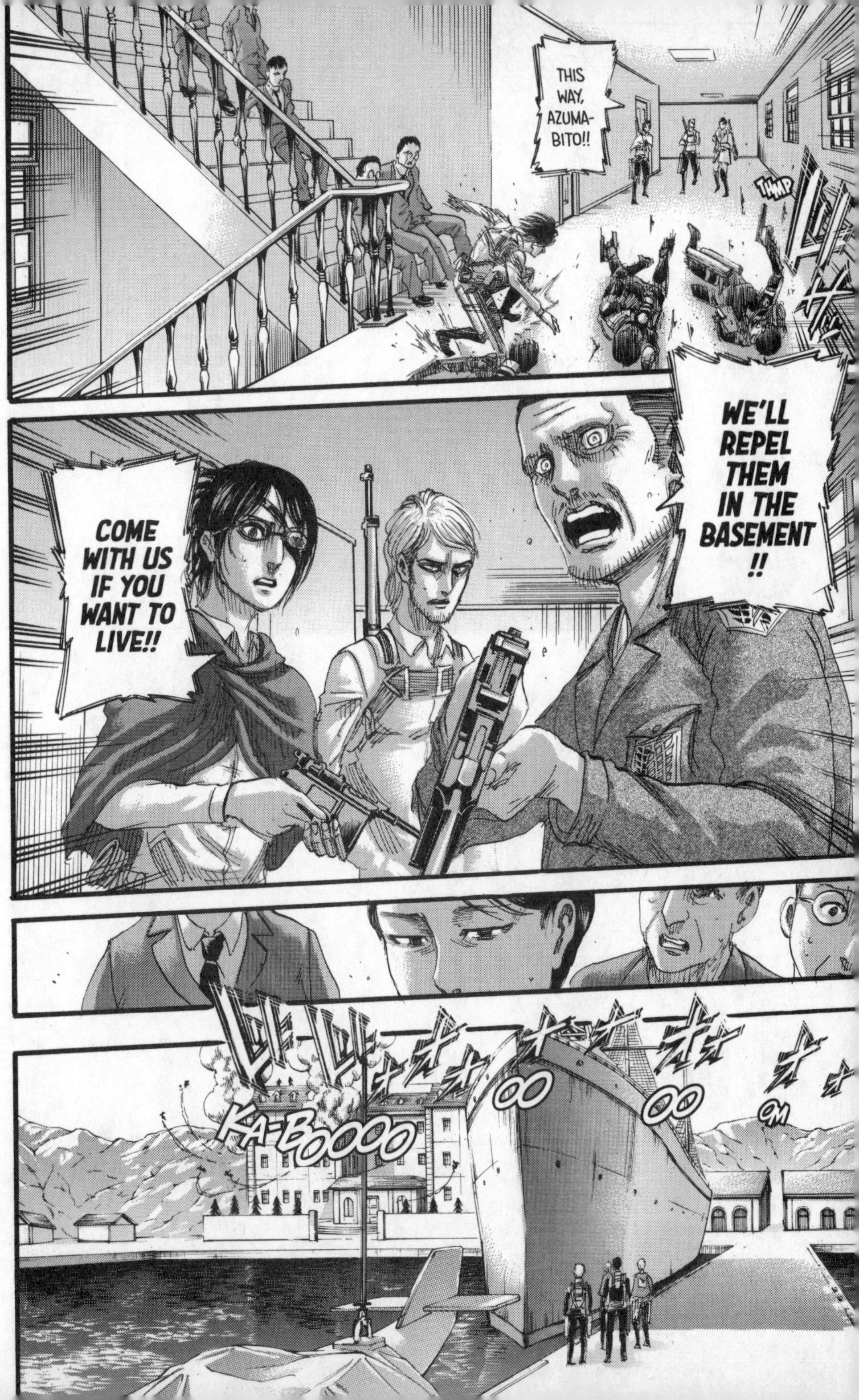
THIS WAY, AZUMA-BITO!!
THMP
WE'LL REPEL THEM IN THE BASEMENT!!
COME WITH US IF YOU WANT TO LIVE!!
KA-BOOOOO OO OOM

WHAT ARE YOU...

...HEY.

?!

STOP!!

DAZ!!

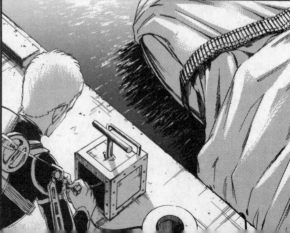

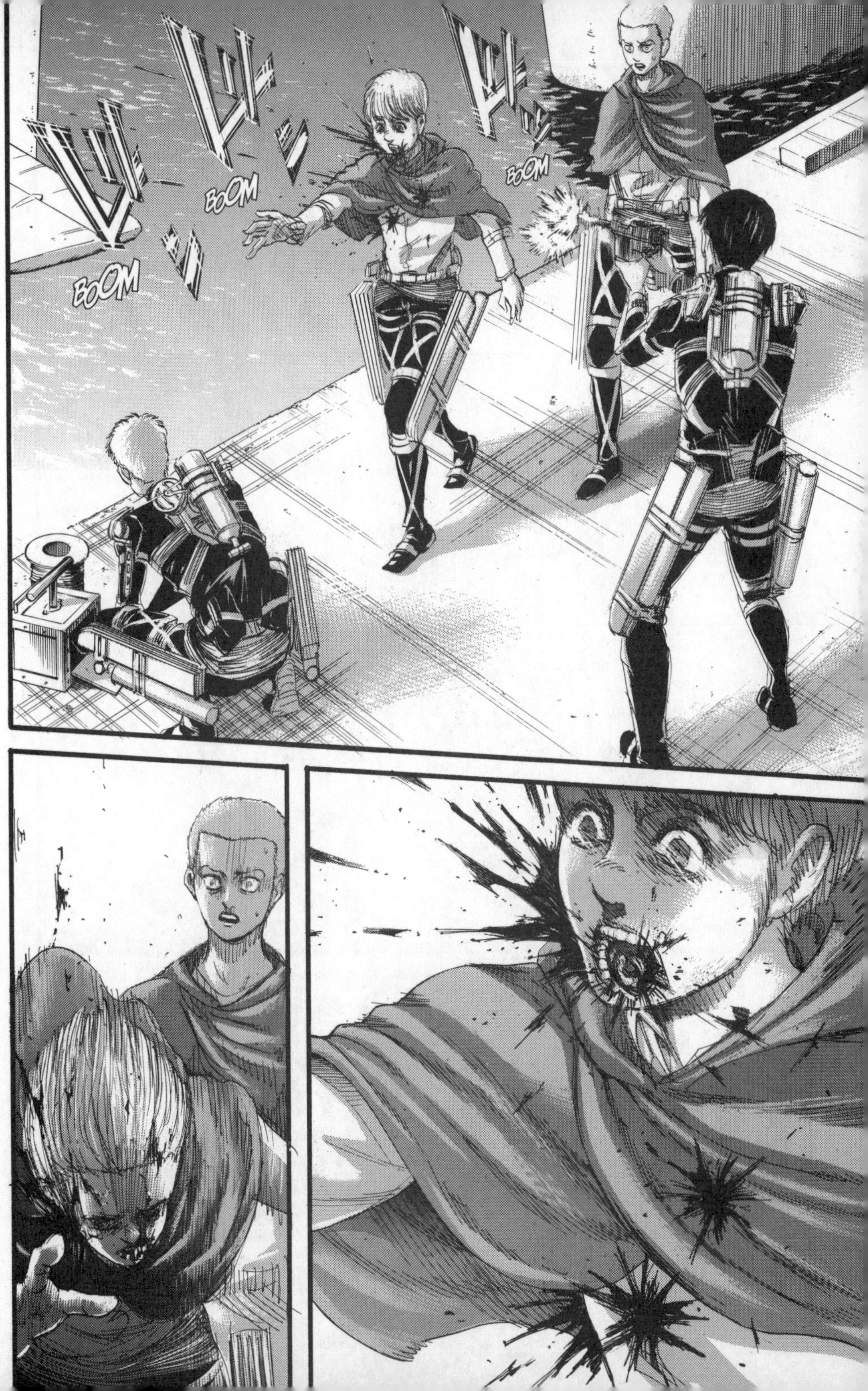
BOOM
BOOM
BOOM

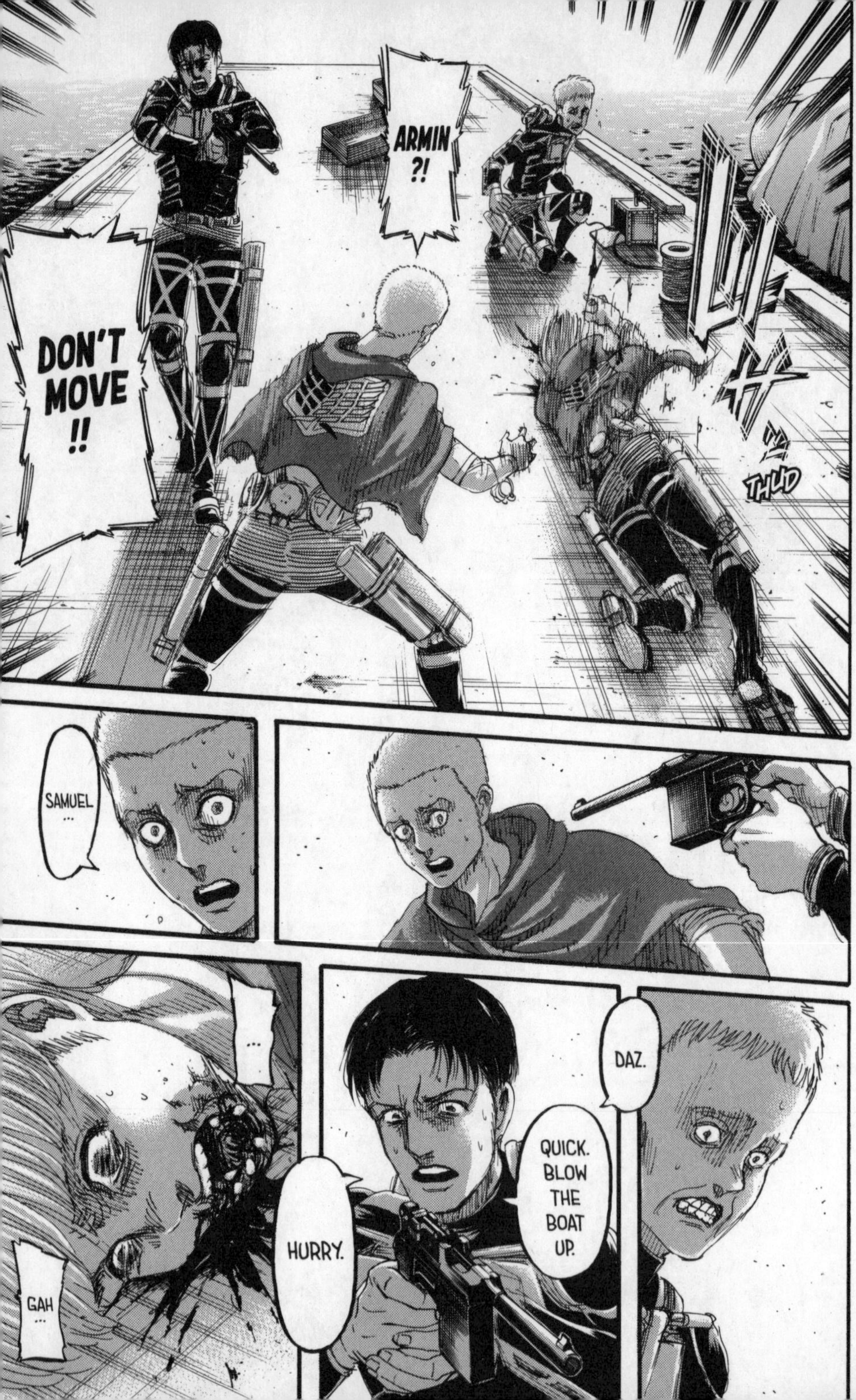
THUD
ARMIN ?!
DON'T MOVE !!
SAMUEL ...
DAZ.
QUICK. BLOW THE BOAT UP.
HURRY.
...
GAH ...

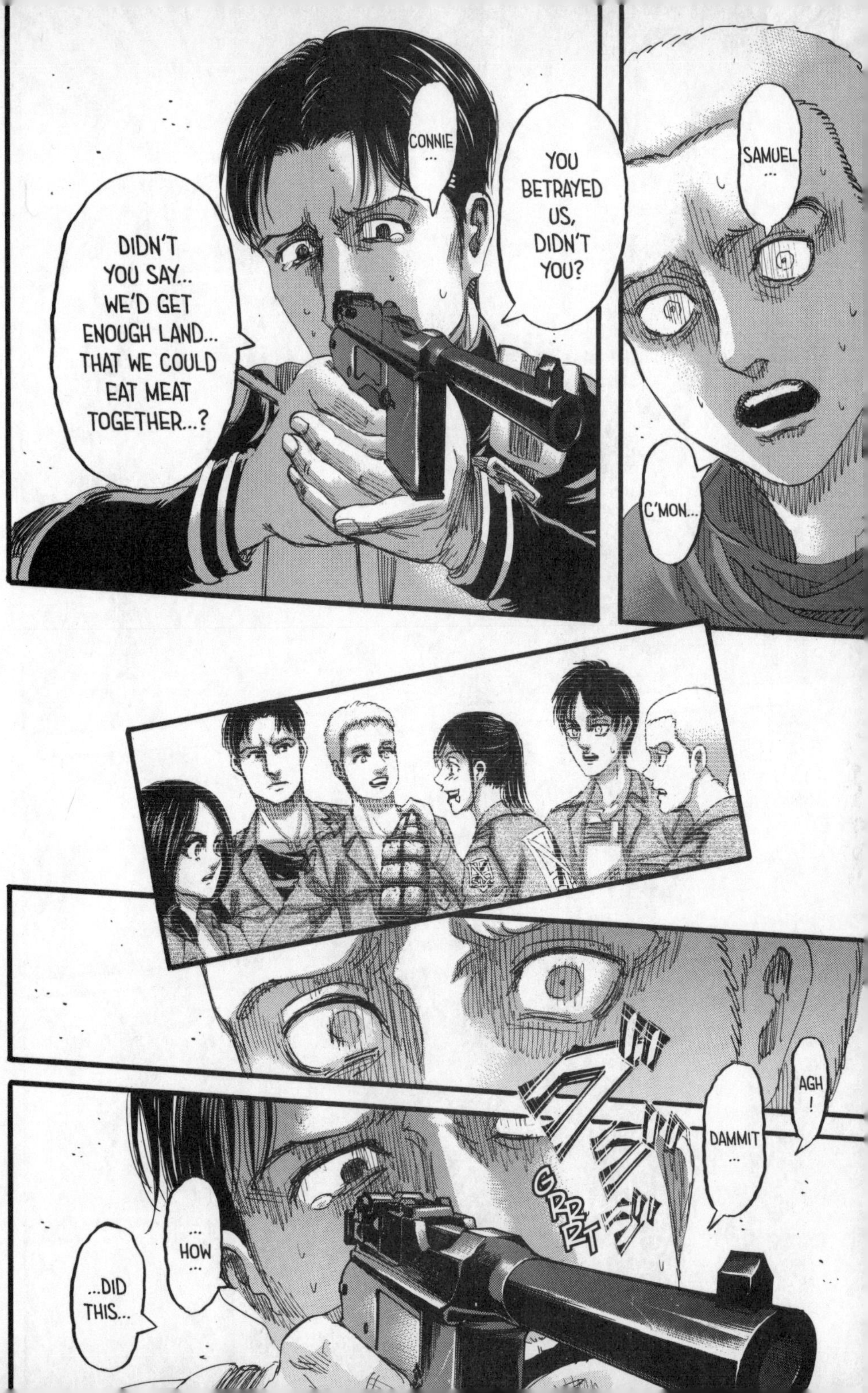
SAMUEL...
C'MON...
CONNIE...
YOU BETRAYED US, DIDN'T YOU?
DIDN'T YOU SAY... WE'D GET ENOUGH LAND... THAT WE COULD EAT MEAT TOGETHER...?
AGH!
DAMMIT...
GRRRT
...HOW...
...DID THIS...

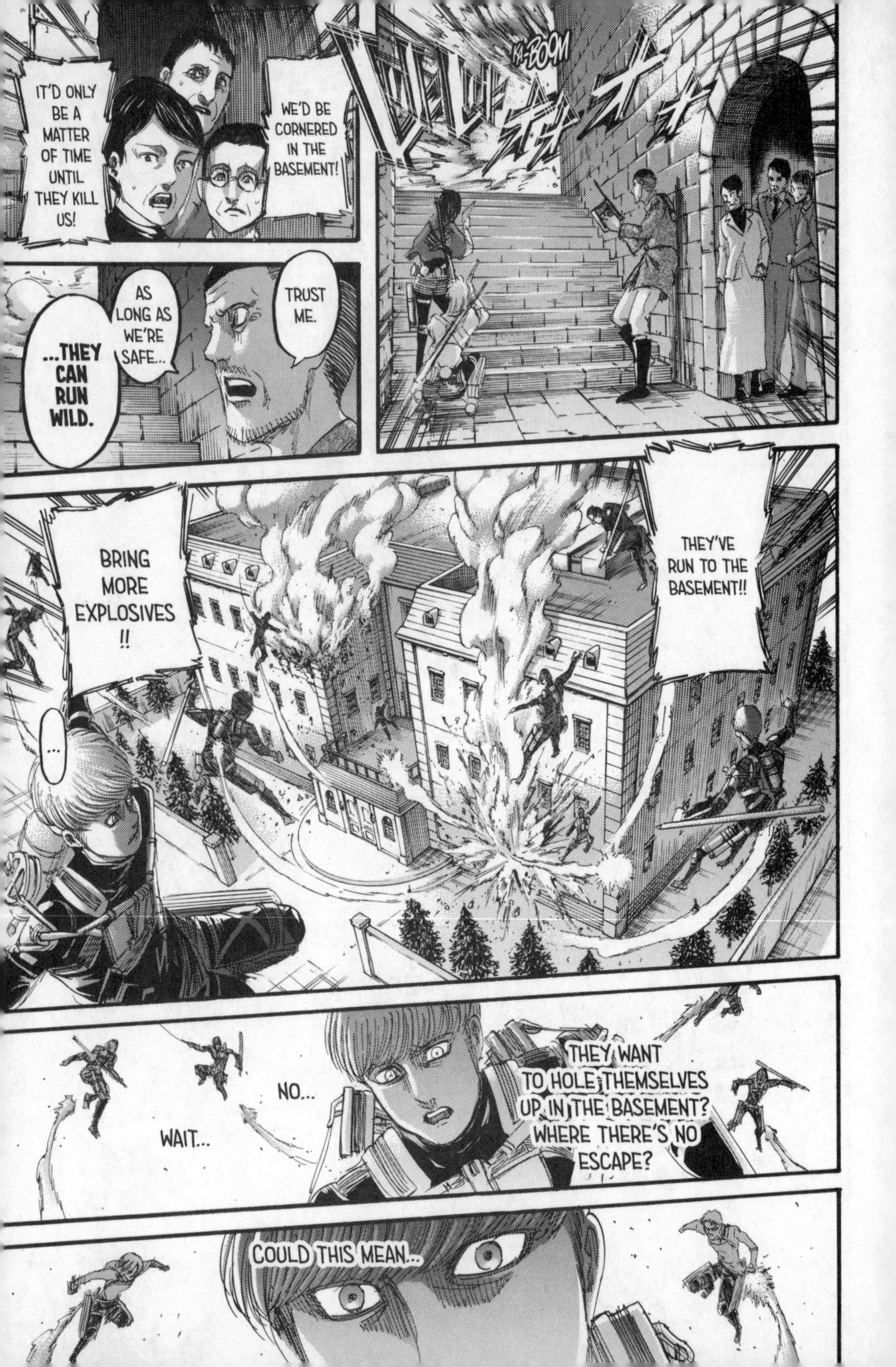
KA-BOOM
WE'D BE CORNERED IN THE BASEMENT!
IT'D ONLY BE A MATTER OF TIME UNTIL THEY KILL US!
TRUST ME.
AS LONG AS WE'RE SAFE...
...THEY CAN RUN WILD.
THEY'VE RUN TO THE BASEMENT!!
BRING MORE EXPLOSIVES !!
...
THEY WANT TO HOLE THEMSELVES UP IN THE BASEMENT? WHERE THERE'S NO ESCAPE?
NO...
WAIT...
COULD THIS MEAN...

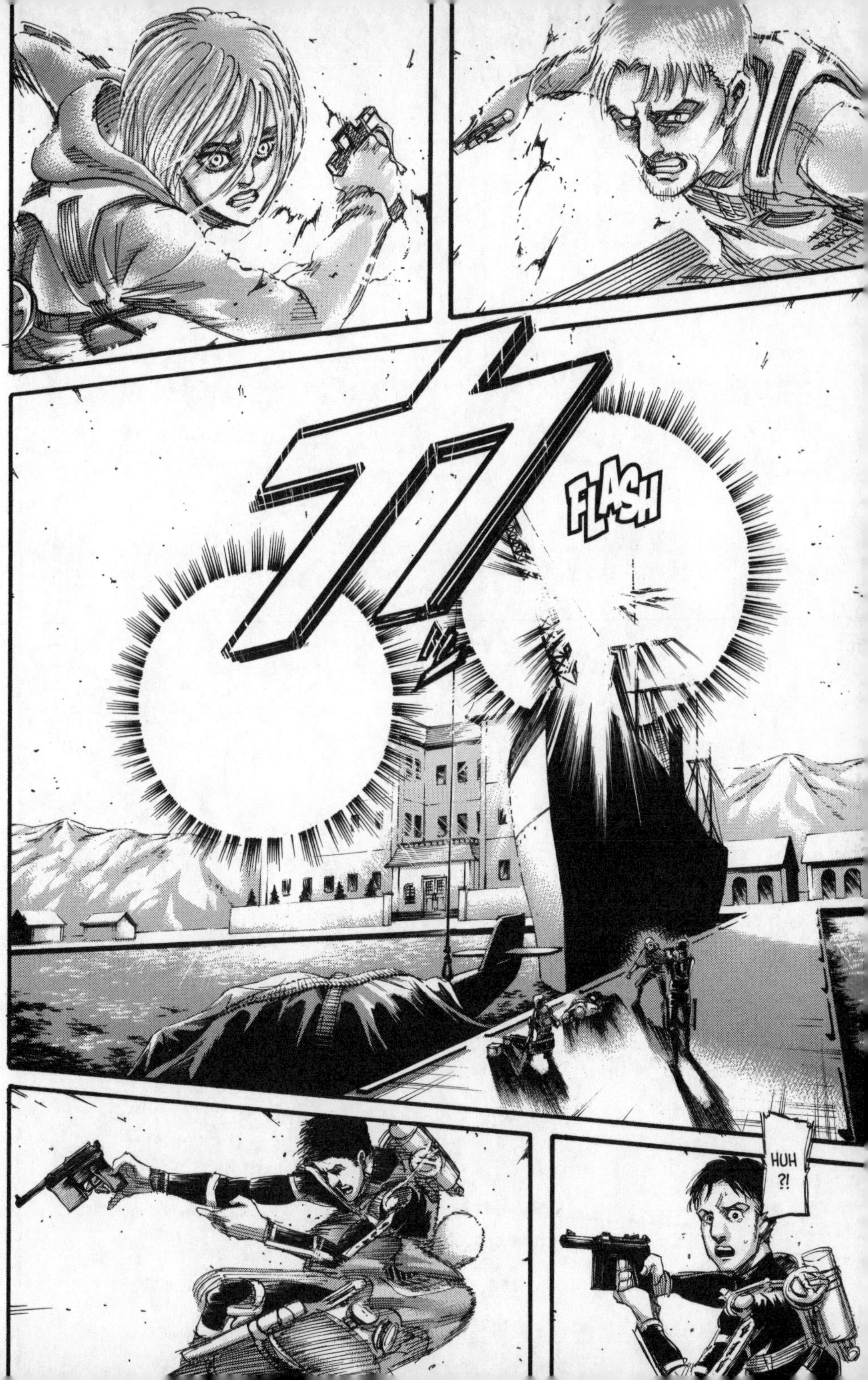
FLASH
HUH ?!

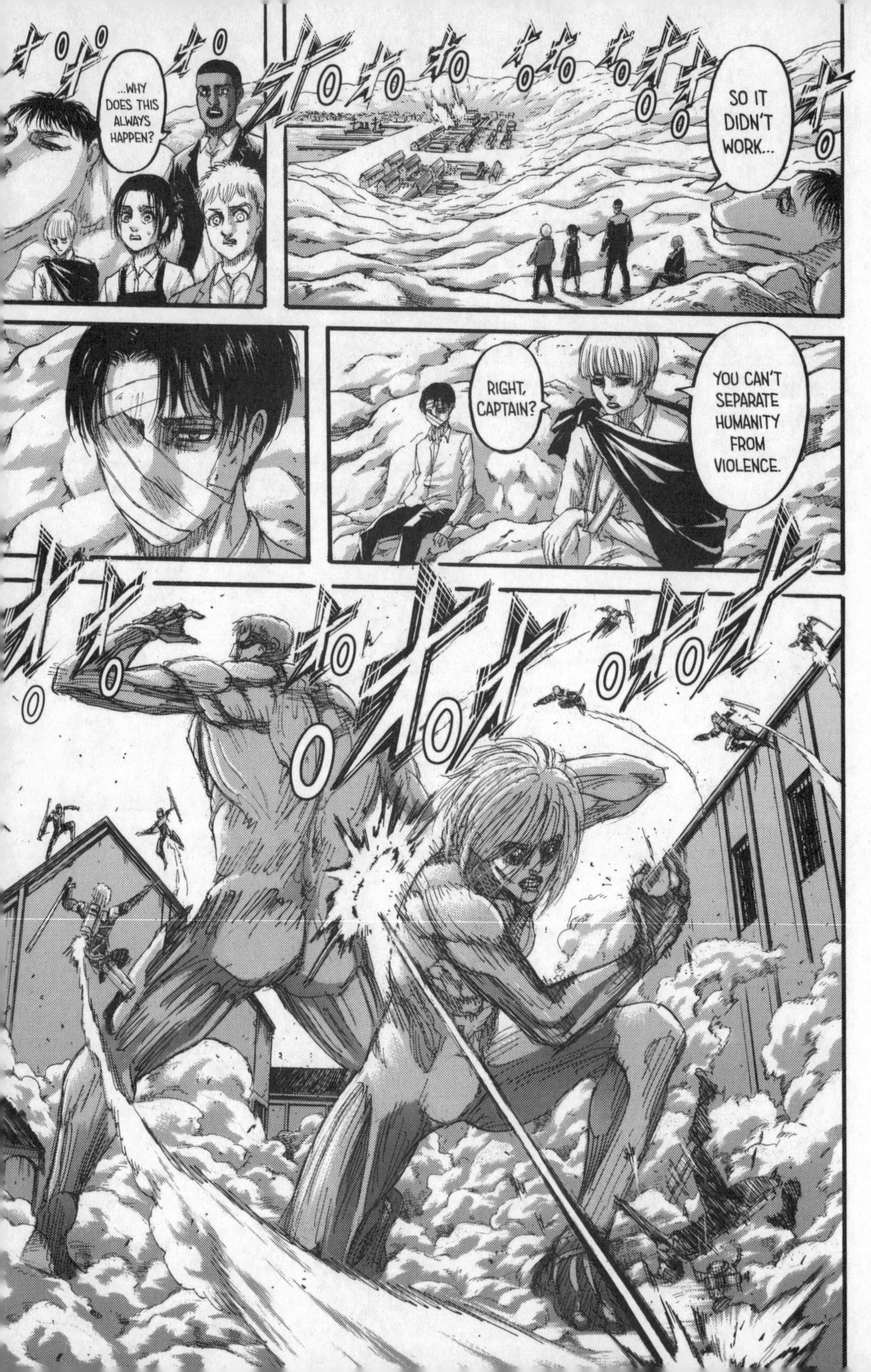
SO IT DIDN'T WORK...
...WHY DOES THIS ALWAYS HAPPEN?
YOU CAN'T SEPARATE HUMANITY FROM VIOLENCE.
RIGHT, CAPTAIN?

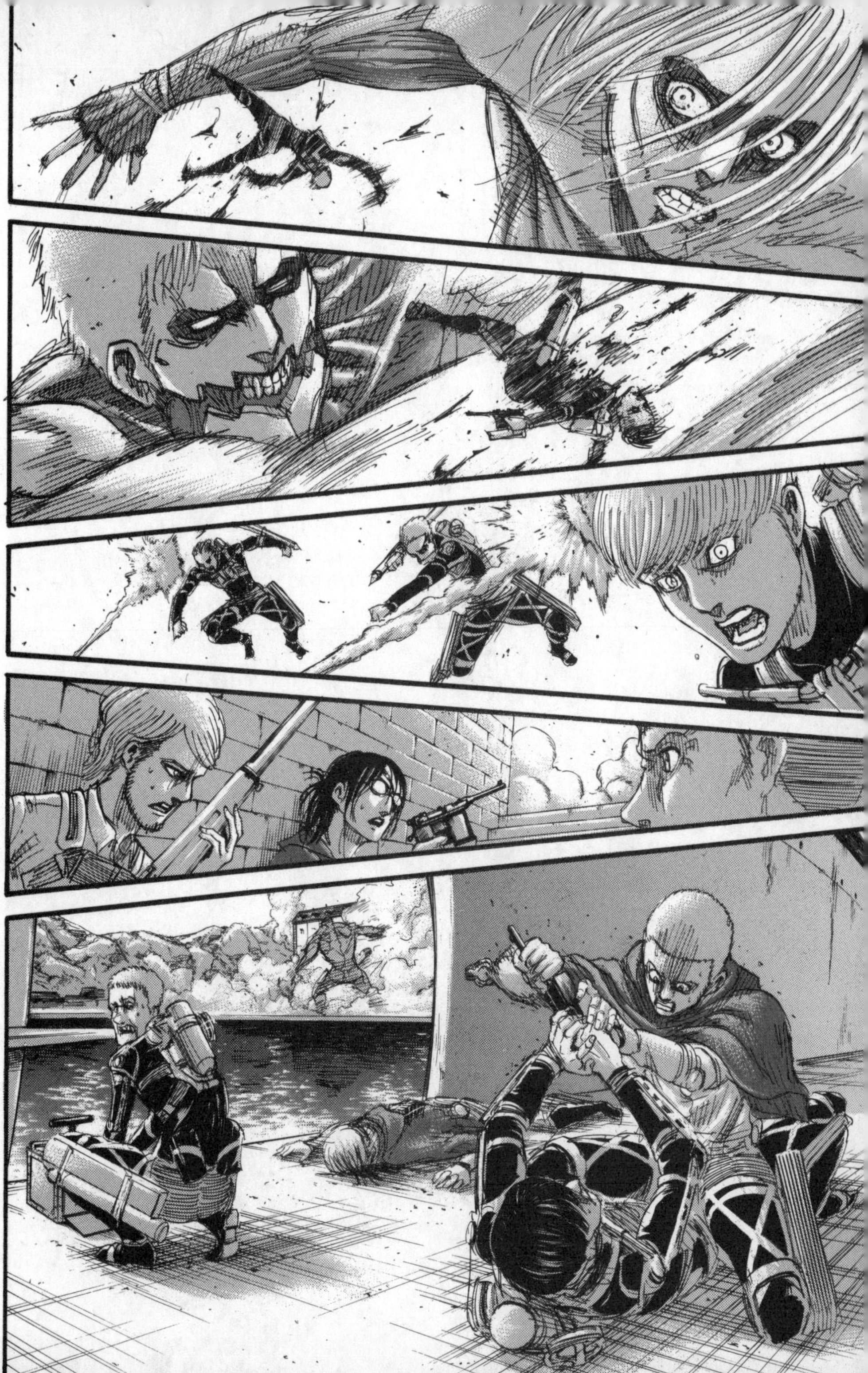

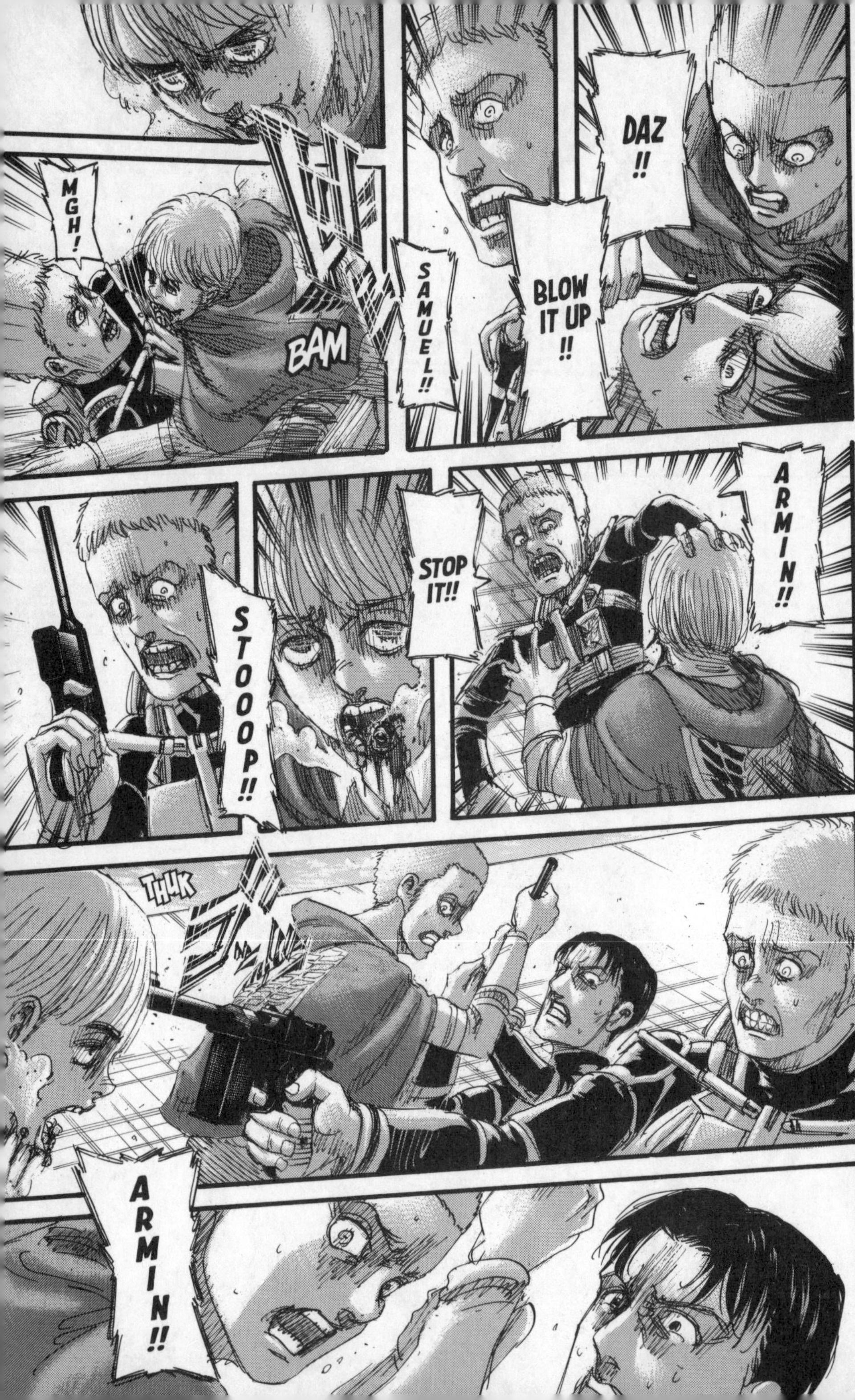

DAZ!!
BLOW IT UP!!
SAMUEL!!
MGH!
BAM
ARMIN!!
STOP IT!!
STOOOOP!!
THUK
ARMIN!!

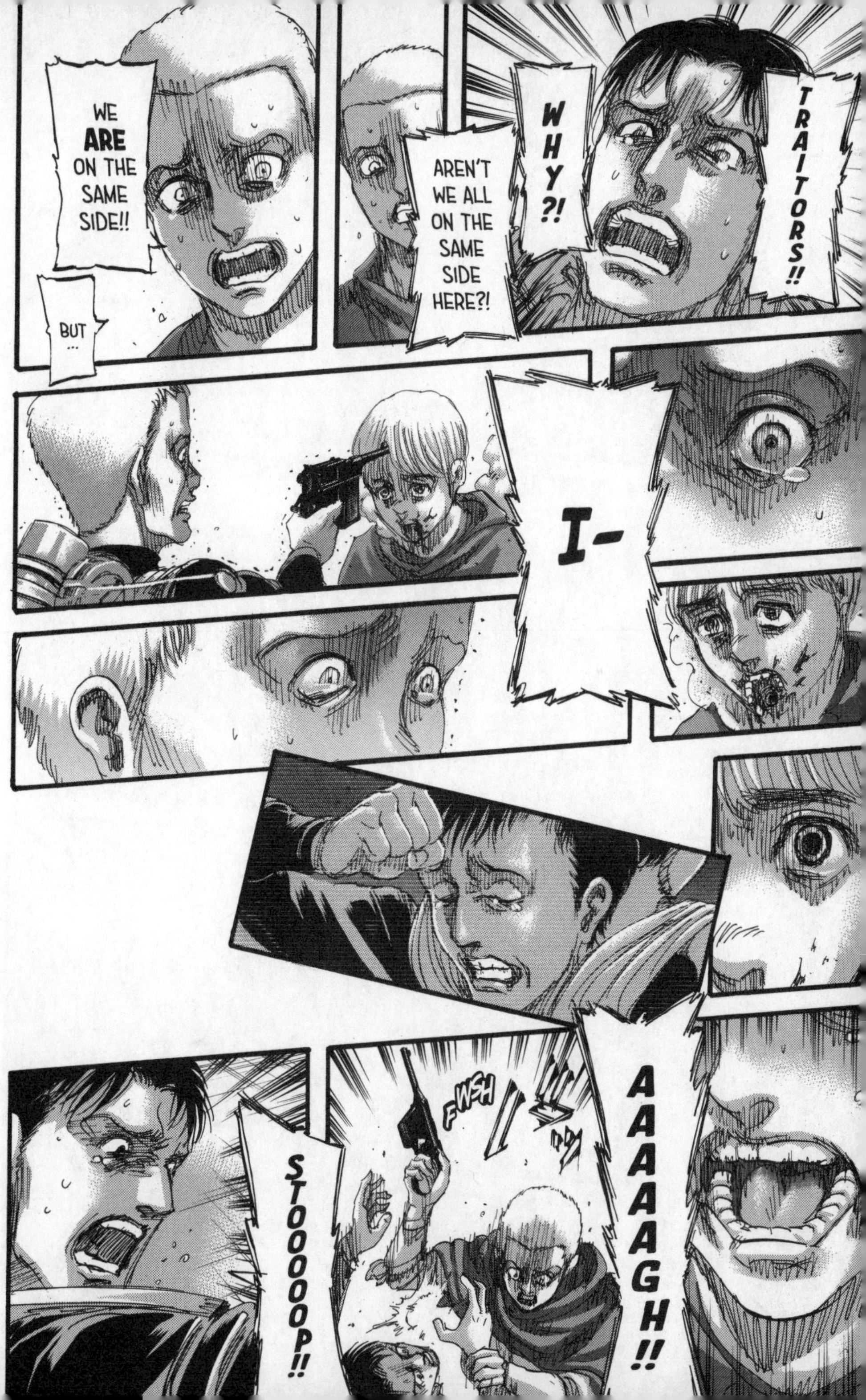

TRAITORS!!
WHY?!
AREN'T WE ALL ON THE SAME SIDE HERE?!
WE **ARE** ON THE SAME SIDE!!
BUT ...
I-
AAAAAAGH!!
FWSH
STOOOOOOP!!

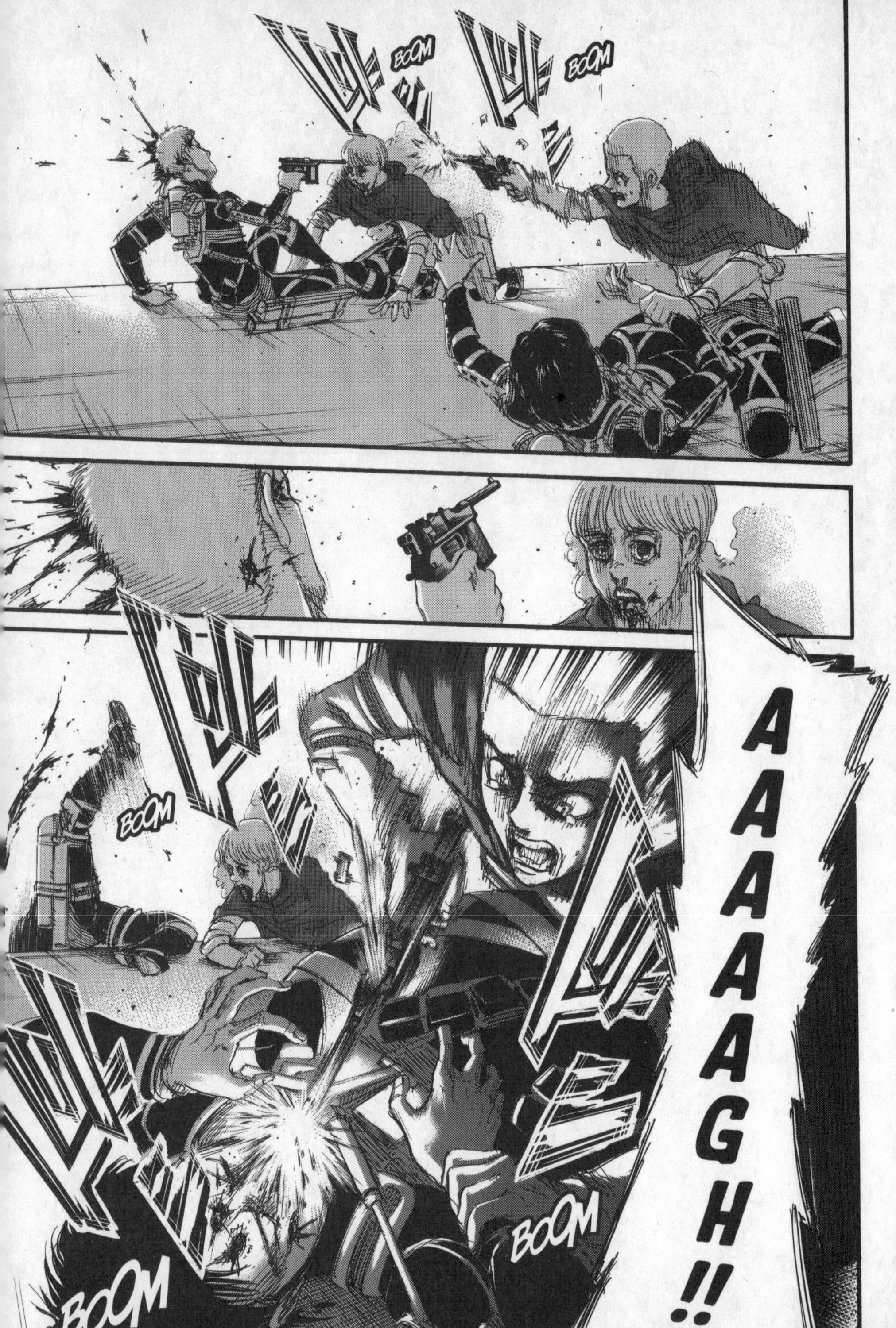
BOOM
BOOM
AAAAAGH!!
BOOM
BOOM
BOOM

ATTACK on TITAN

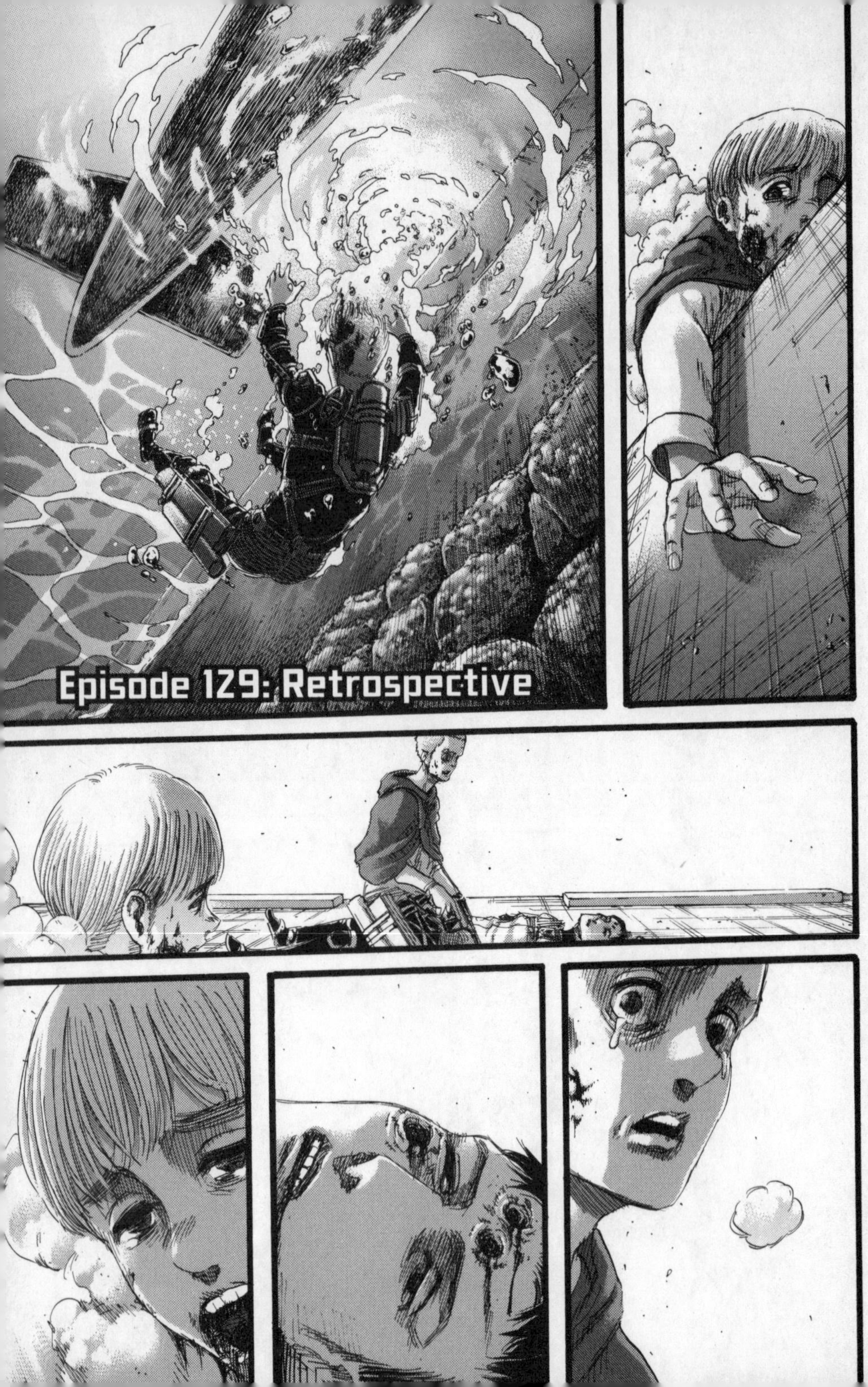
Episode 129: Retrospective

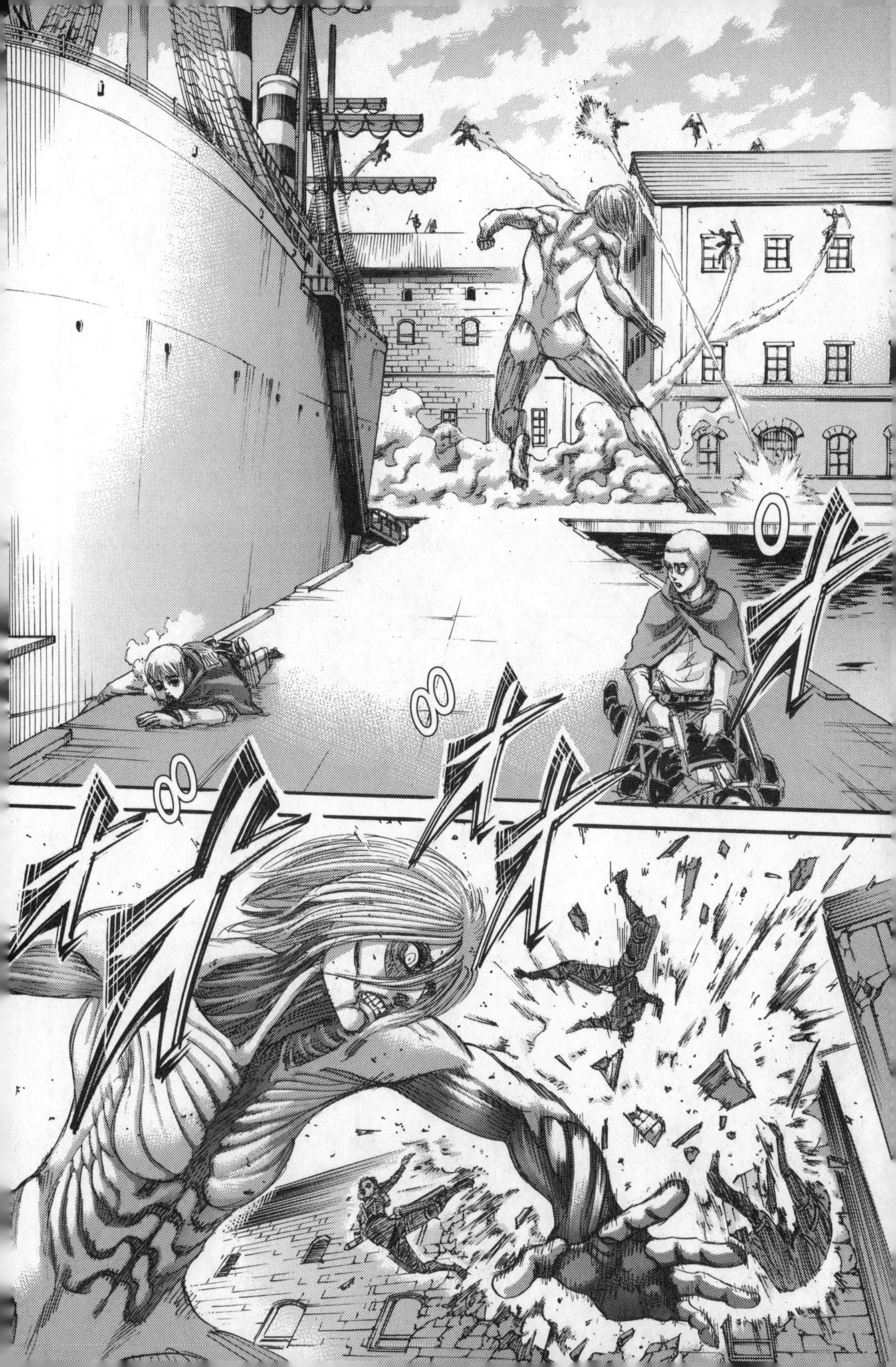

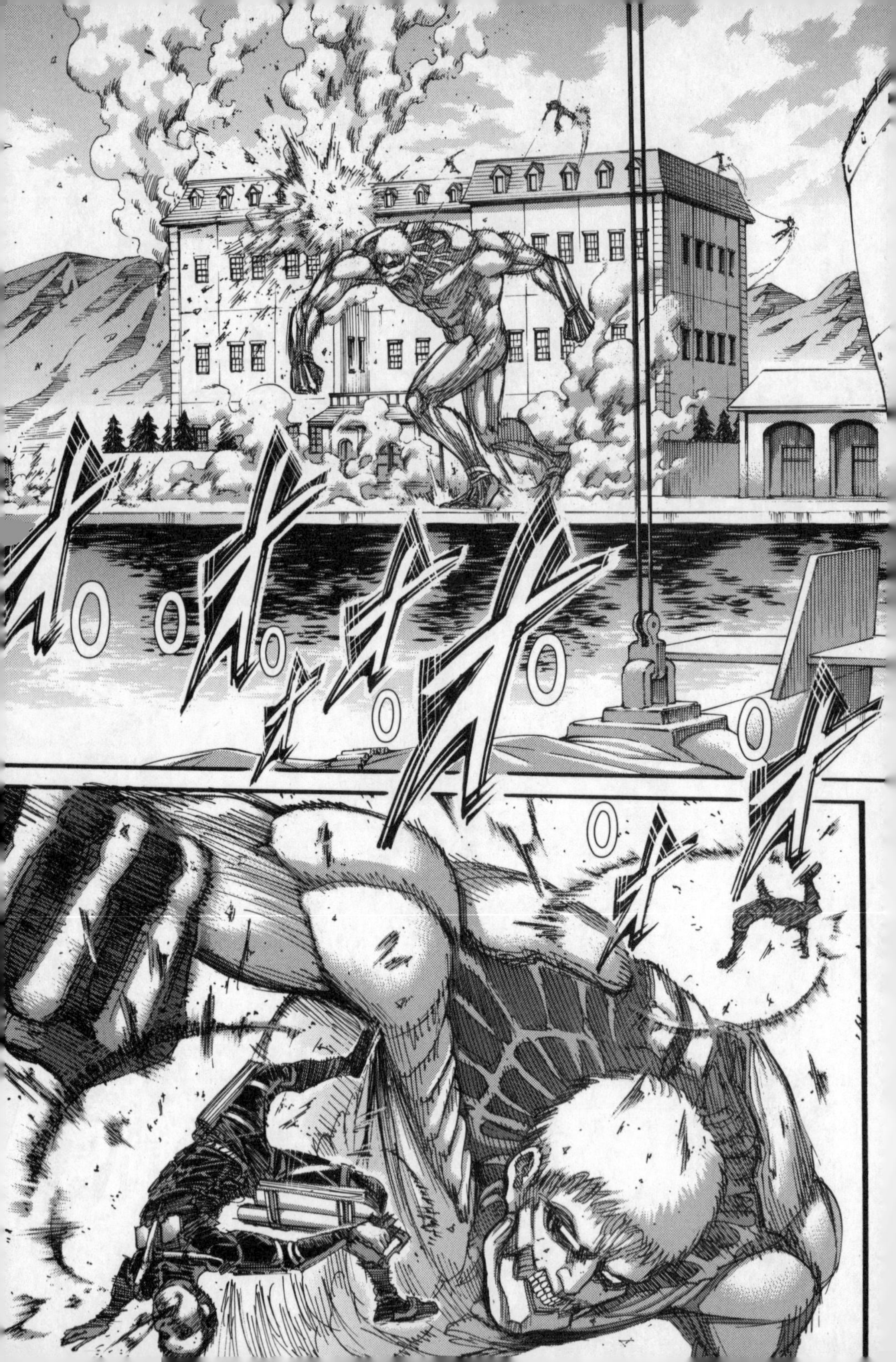

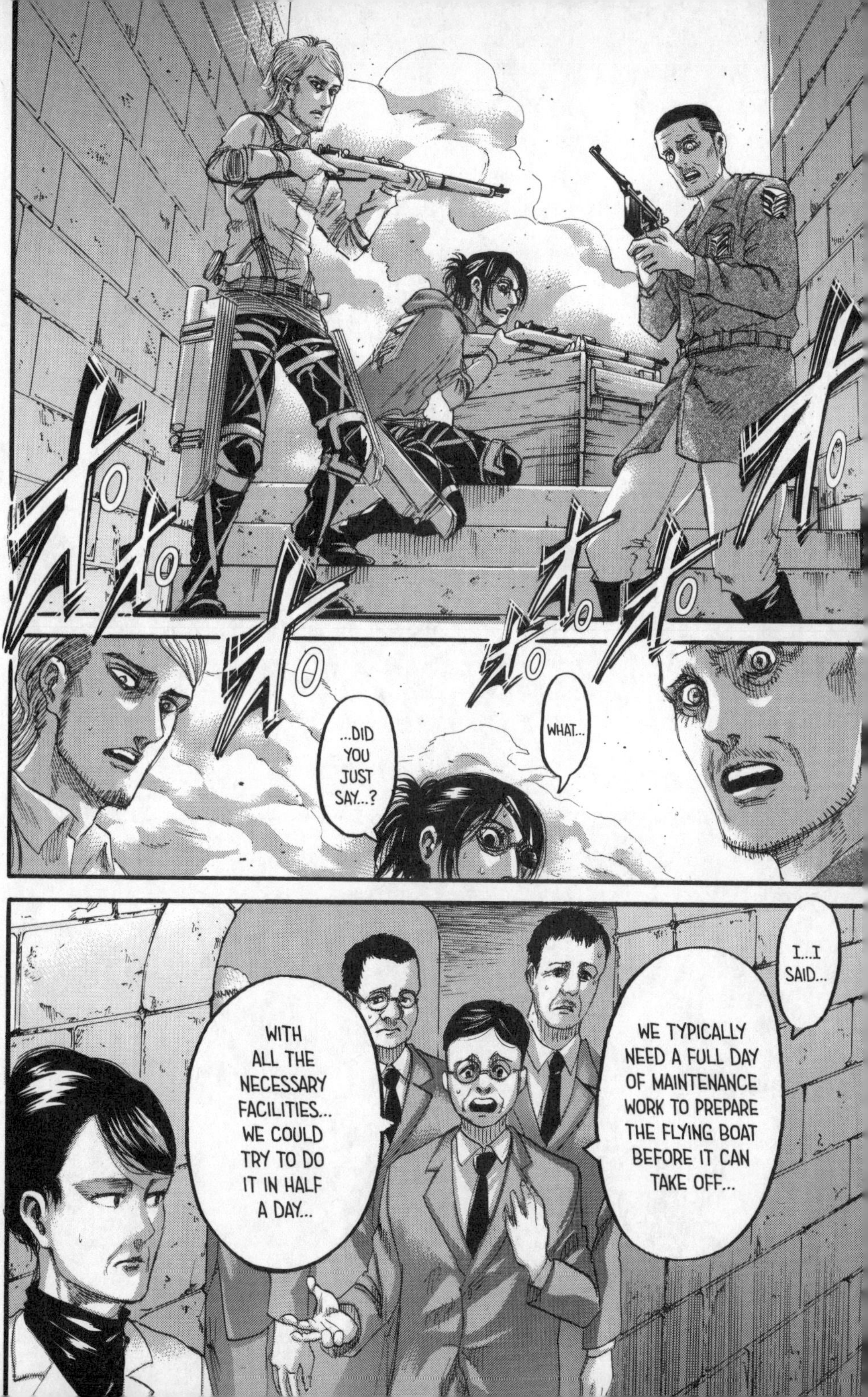
WHAT...
...DID YOU JUST SAY...?
I...I SAID...
WE TYPICALLY NEED A FULL DAY OF MAINTENANCE WORK TO PREPARE THE FLYING BOAT BEFORE IT CAN TAKE OFF...
WITH ALL THE NECESSARY FACILITIES... WE COULD TRY TO DO IT IN HALF A DAY...

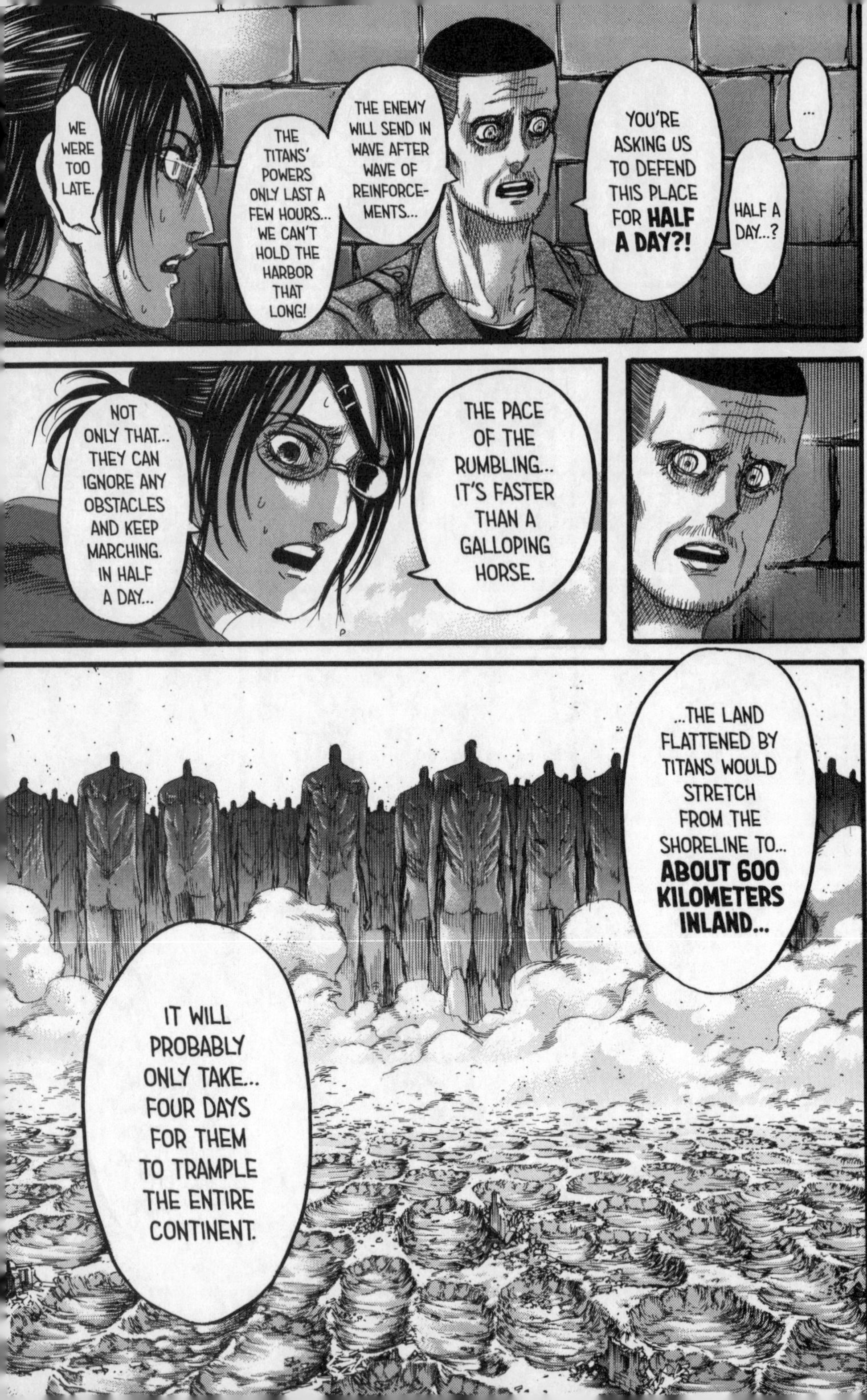
...
HALF A DAY...?
YOU'RE ASKING US TO DEFEND THIS PLACE FOR **HALF A DAY?!**
THE ENEMY WILL SEND IN WAVE AFTER WAVE OF REINFORCE- MENTS...
THE TITANS' POWERS ONLY LAST A FEW HOURS... WE CAN'T HOLD THE HARBOR THAT LONG!
WE WERE TOO LATE.
THE PACE OF THE RUMBLING... IT'S FASTER THAN A GALLOPING HORSE.
NOT ONLY THAT... THEY CAN IGNORE ANY OBSTACLES AND KEEP MARCHING. IN HALF A DAY...
...THE LAND FLATTENED BY TITANS WOULD STRETCH FROM THE SHORELINE TO... **ABOUT 600 KILOMETERS INLAND...**
IT WILL PROBABLY ONLY TAKE... FOUR DAYS FOR THEM TO TRAMPLE THE ENTIRE CONTINENT.

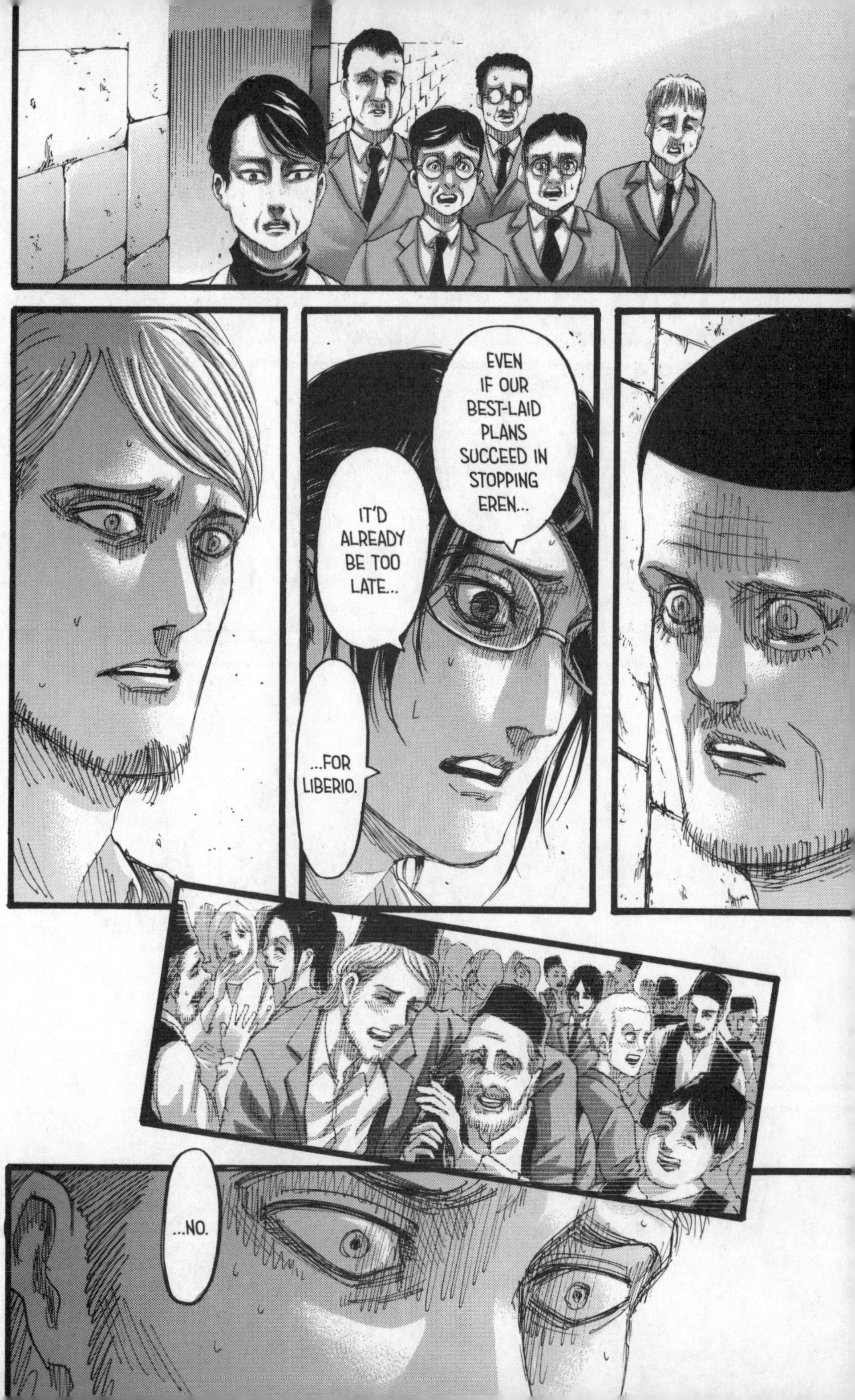
EVEN IF OUR BEST-LAID PLANS SUCCEED IN STOPPING EREN...
IT'D ALREADY BE TOO LATE...
...FOR LIBERIO.
...NO.

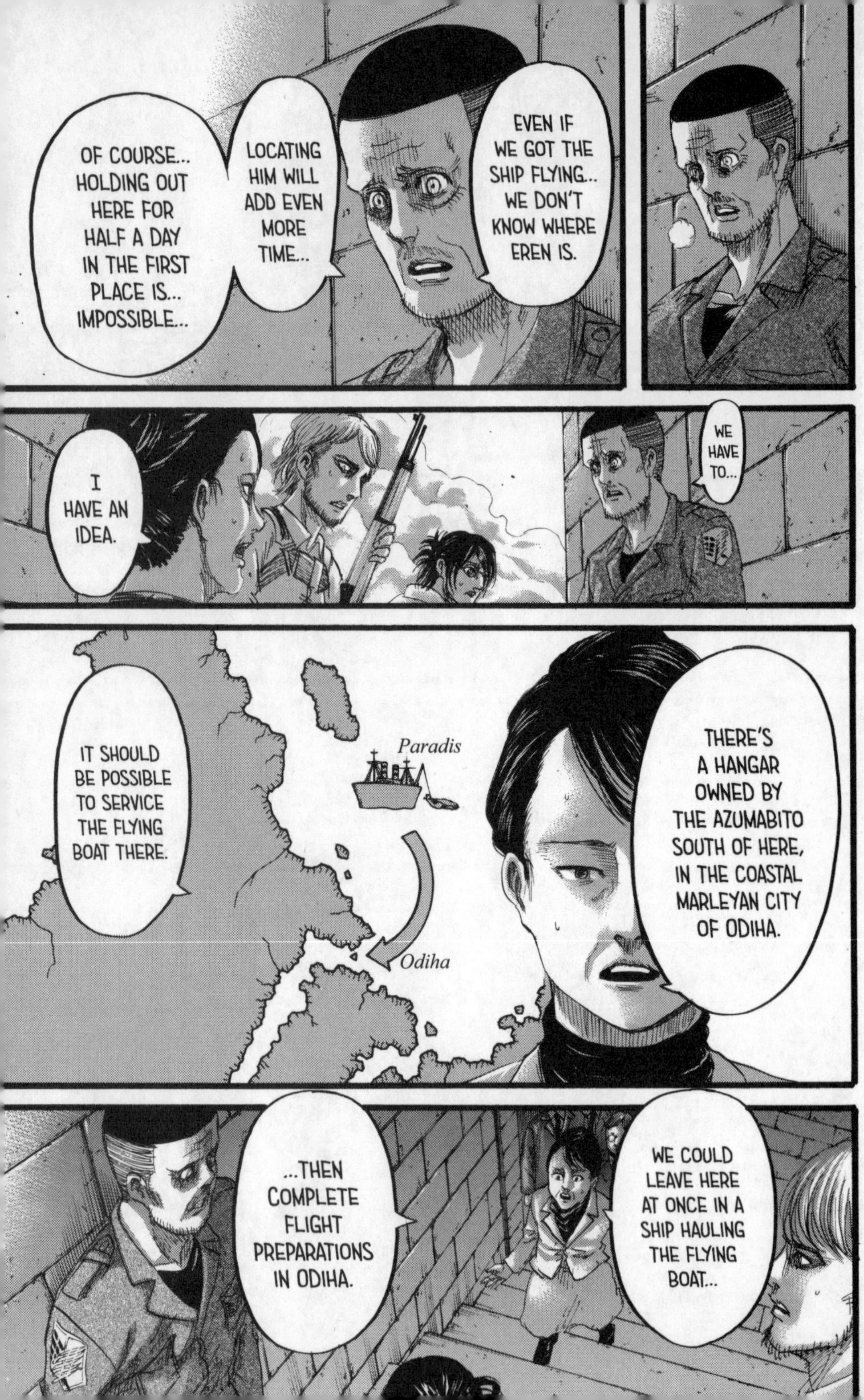
EVEN IF WE GOT THE SHIP FLYING... WE DON'T KNOW WHERE EREN IS.
LOCATING HIM WILL ADD EVEN MORE TIME...
OF COURSE... HOLDING OUT HERE FOR HALF A DAY IN THE FIRST PLACE IS... IMPOSSIBLE...
WE HAVE TO...
I HAVE AN IDEA.
THERE'S A HANGAR OWNED BY THE AZUMABITO SOUTH OF HERE, IN THE COASTAL MARLEYAN CITY OF ODIHA.
Paradis
Odiha
IT SHOULD BE POSSIBLE TO SERVICE THE FLYING BOAT THERE.
WE COULD LEAVE HERE AT ONCE IN A SHIP HAULING THE FLYING BOAT...
...THEN COMPLETE FLIGHT PREPARATIONS IN ODIHA.

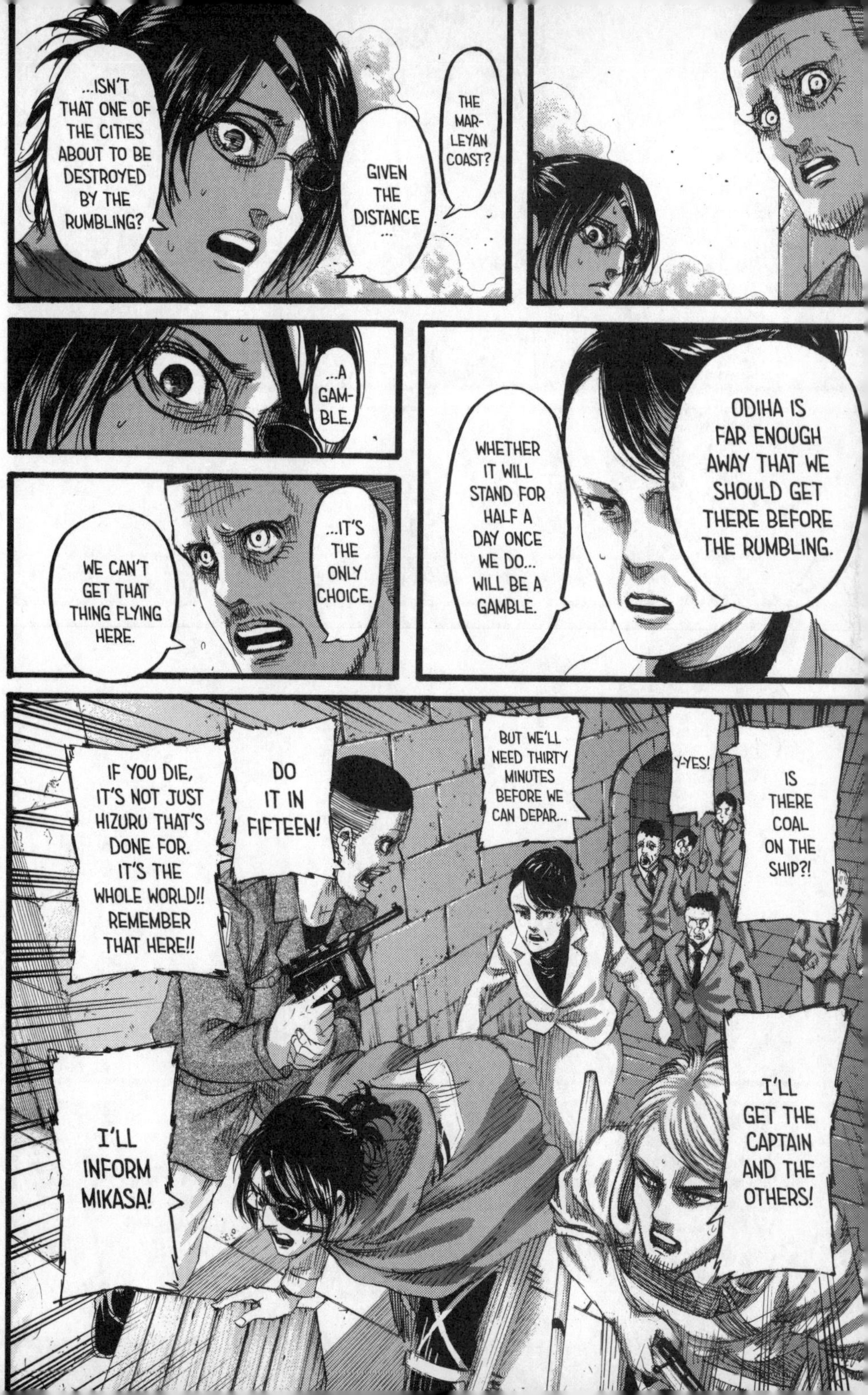
THE MARLEYAN COAST?
GIVEN THE DISTANCE ...
...ISN'T THAT ONE OF THE CITIES ABOUT TO BE DESTROYED BY THE RUMBLING?
ODIHA IS FAR ENOUGH AWAY THAT WE SHOULD GET THERE BEFORE THE RUMBLING.
WHETHER IT WILL STAND FOR HALF A DAY ONCE WE DO... WILL BE A GAMBLE.
...A GAMBLE.
...IT'S THE ONLY CHOICE.
WE CAN'T GET THAT THING FLYING HERE.
IS THERE COAL ON THE SHIP?!
Y-YES!
BUT WE'LL NEED THIRTY MINUTES BEFORE WE CAN DEPAR...
DO IT IN FIFTEEN!
IF YOU DIE, IT'S NOT JUST HIZURU THAT'S DONE FOR. IT'S THE WHOLE WORLD!! REMEMBER THAT HERE!!
I'LL GET THE CAPTAIN AND THE OTHERS!
I'LL INFORM MIKASA!

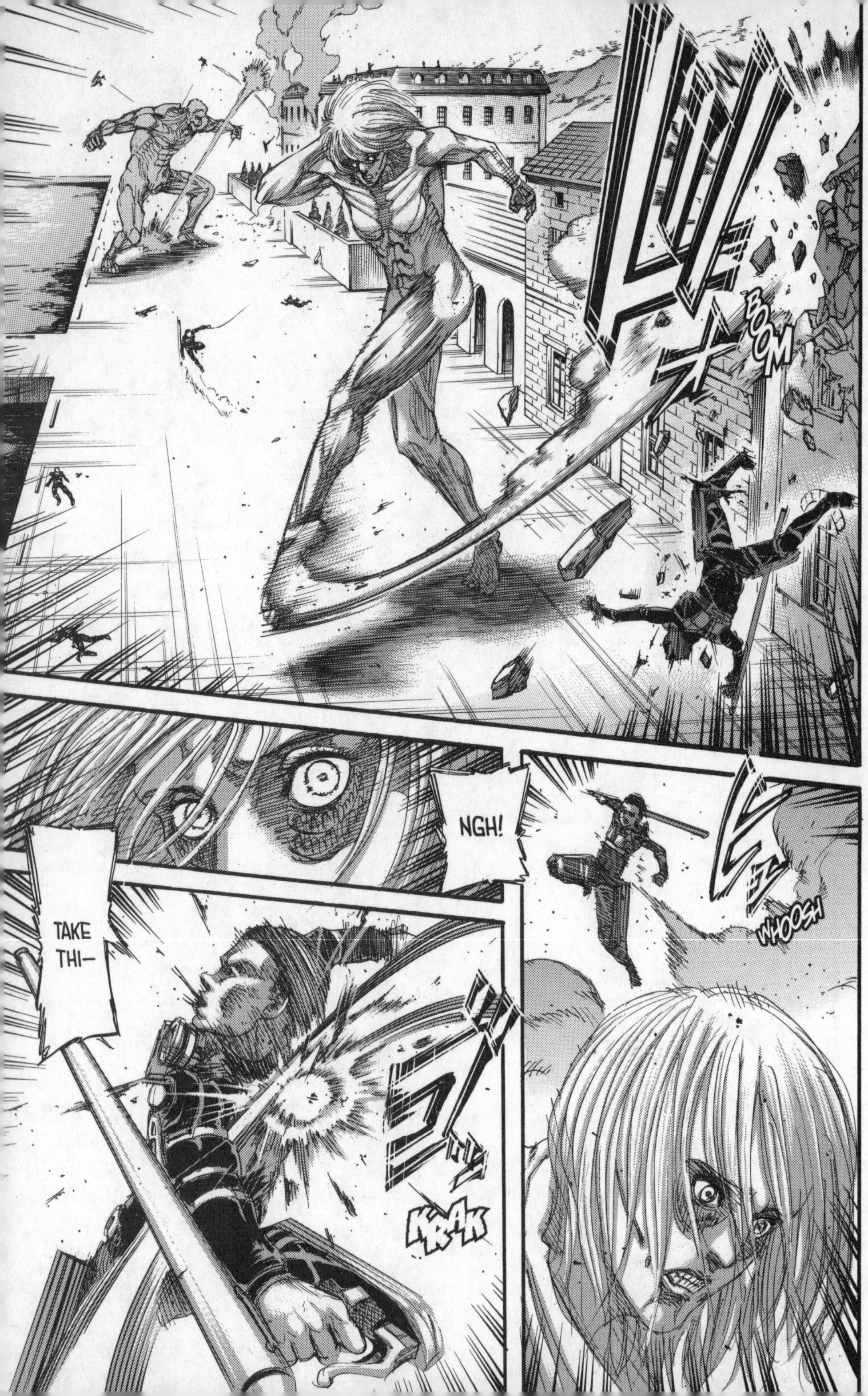
BOOM
WHOOSH
NGH!
TAKE THI—
KRAK

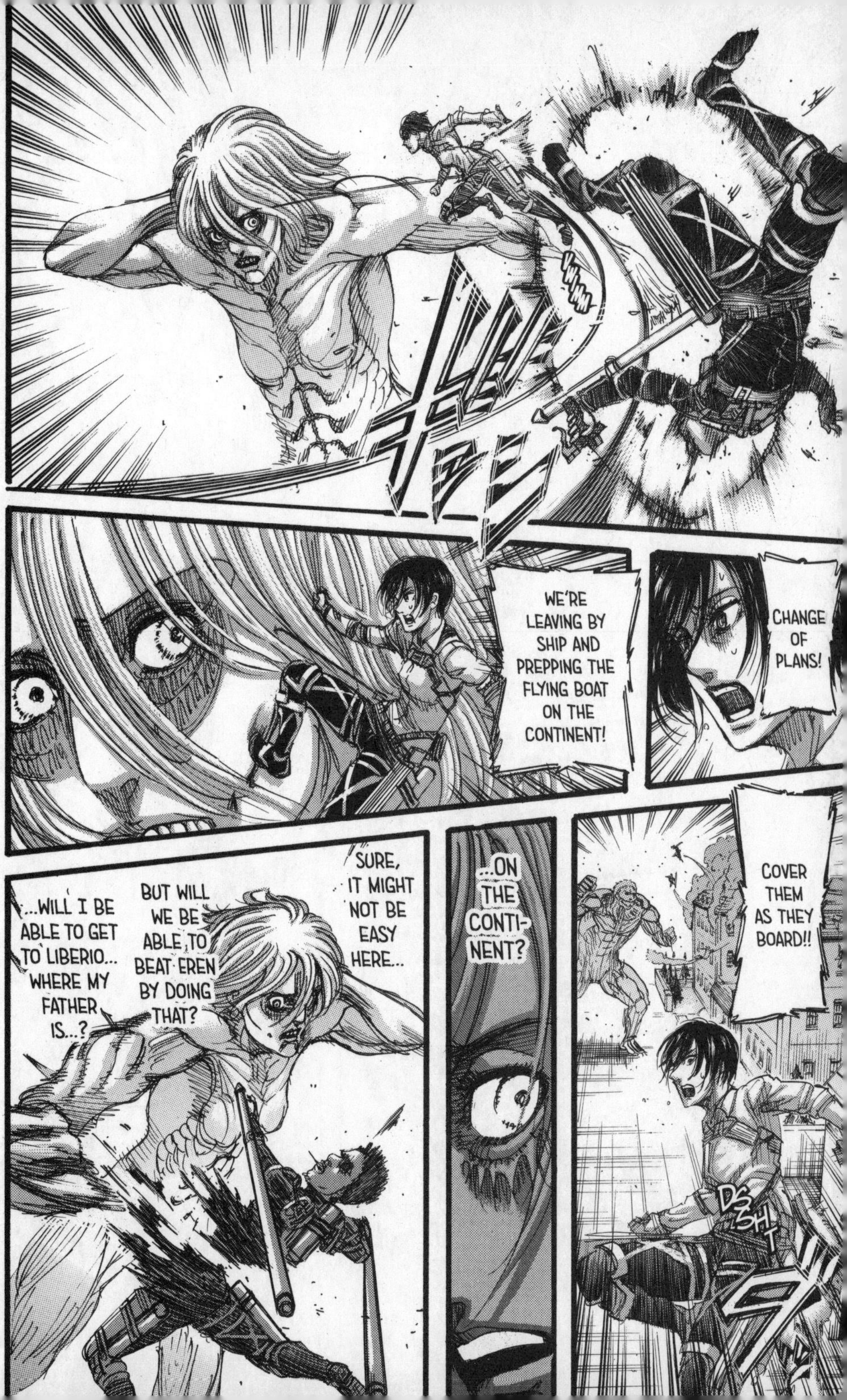
VWMM
CHANGE OF PLANS!
WE'RE LEAVING BY SHIP AND PREPPING THE FLYING BOAT ON THE CONTINENT!
COVER THEM AS THEY BOARD!!
DSSHT
...ON THE CONTI-NENT?
SURE, IT MIGHT NOT BE EASY HERE...
BUT WILL WE BE ABLE TO BEAT EREN BY DOING THAT?
...WILL I BE ABLE TO GET TO LIBERIO... WHERE MY FATHER IS...?

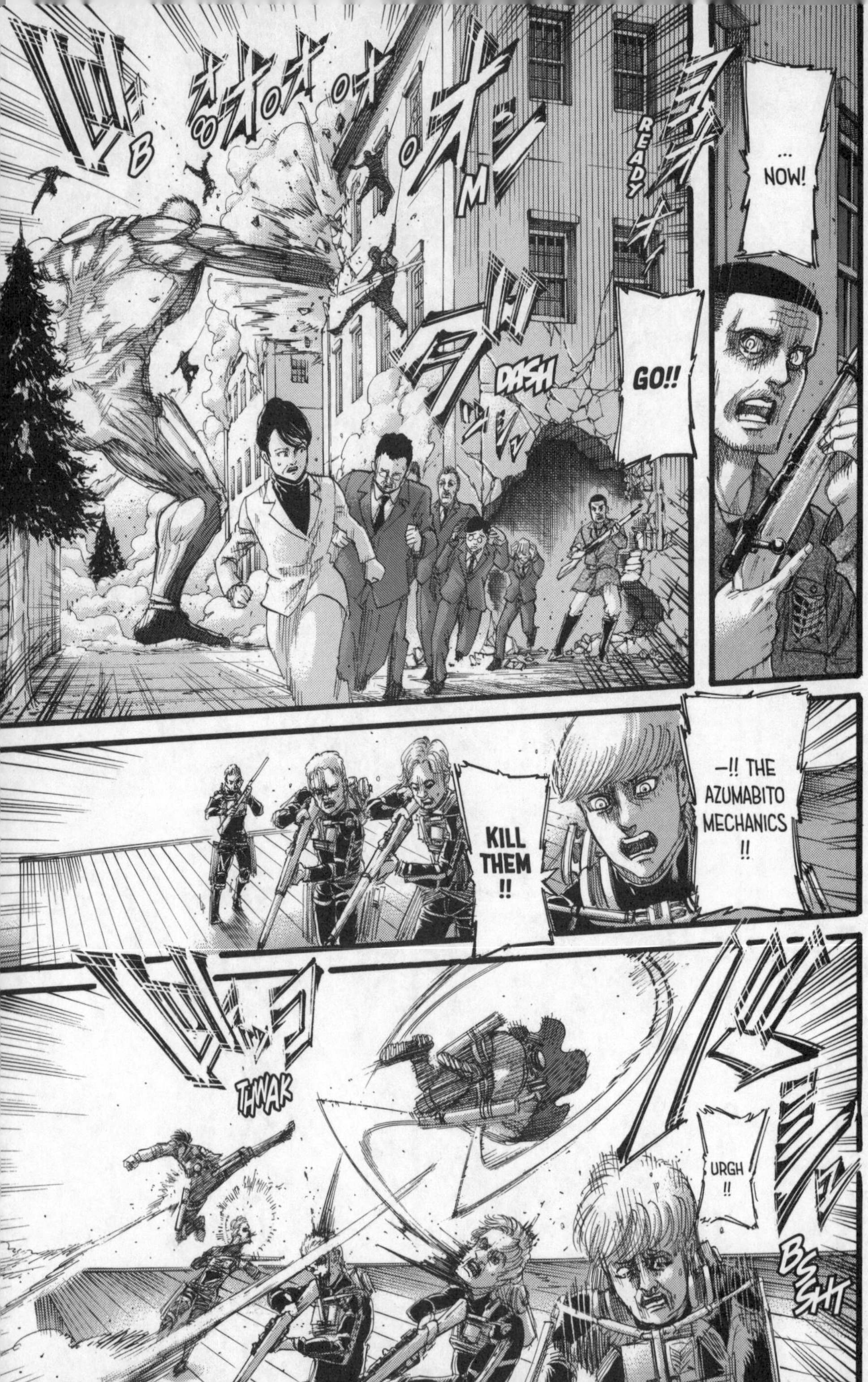
... NOW!
GO!!
READY
M
B
DASH
—!! THE AZUMABITO MECHANICS !!
KILL THEM !!
URGH !!
BSHT
THWAK

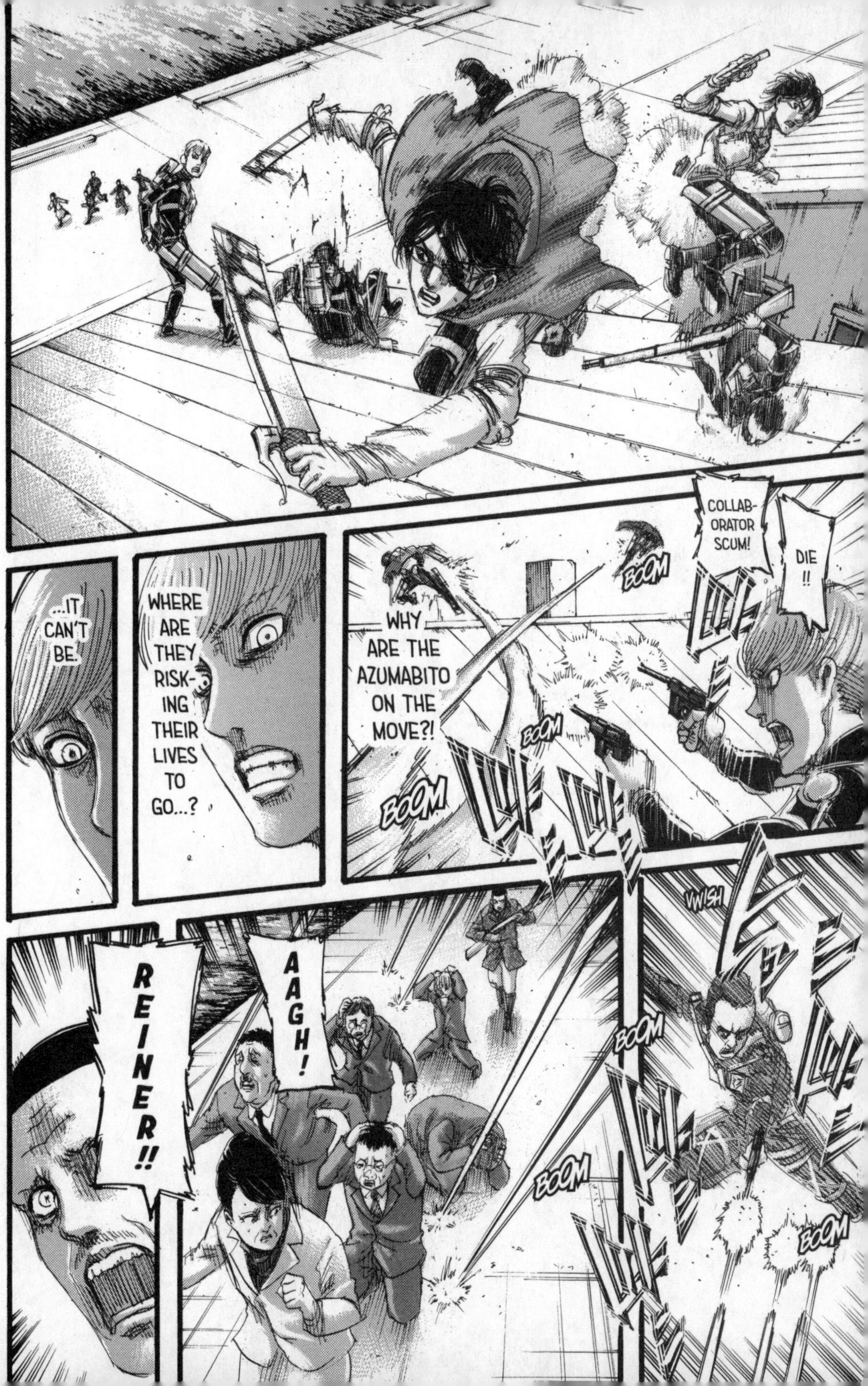
COLLAB-ORATOR SCUM!
DIE !!
BOOM
WHY ARE THE AZUMABITO ON THE MOVE?!
BOOM
BOOM
WHERE ARE THEY RISK-ING THEIR LIVES TO GO...?
...IT CAN'T BE.
VWISH
BOOM
BOOM
BOOM
AAGH!
REINER!!

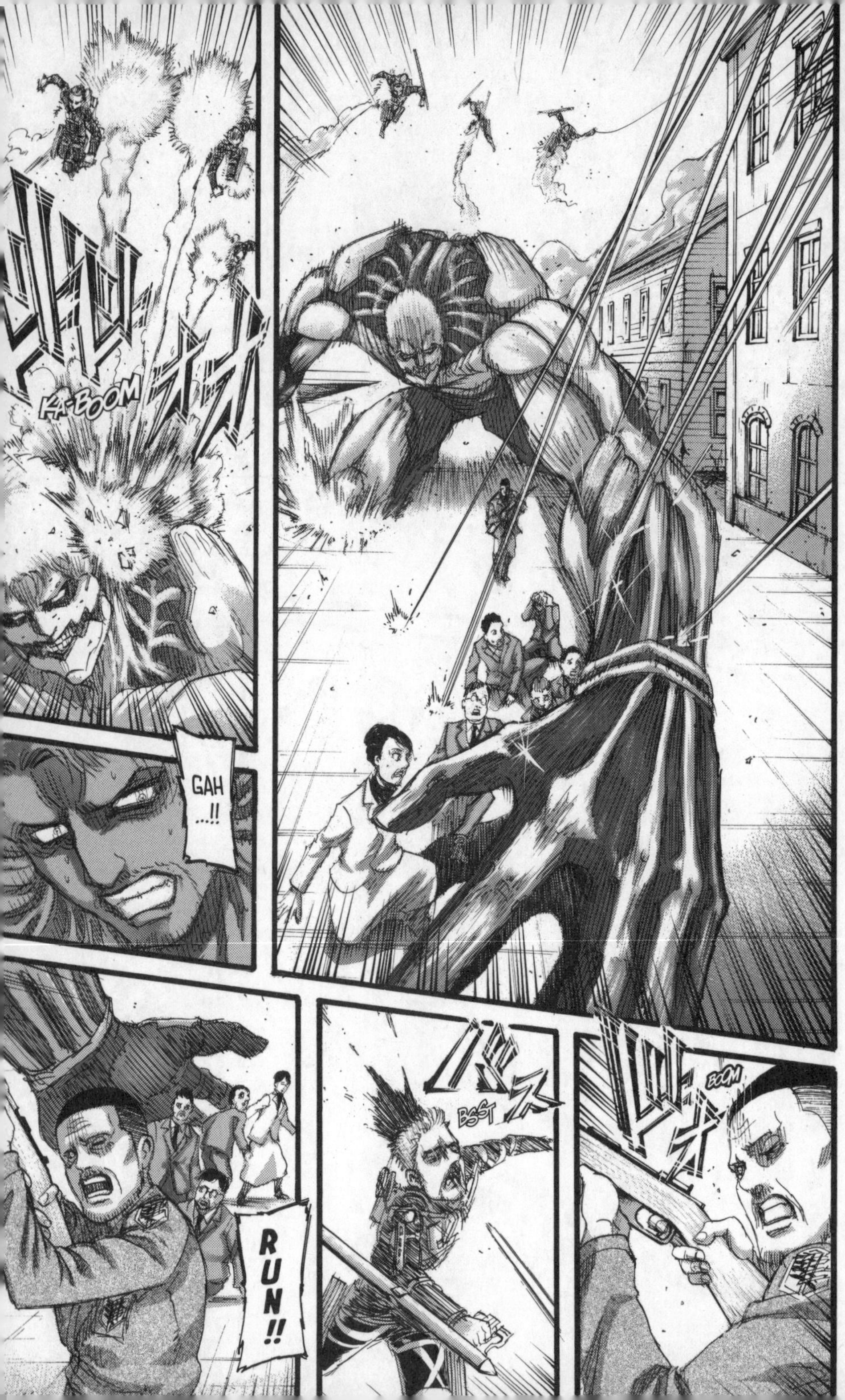
KA-BOOM
GAH ...!!
BOOM
BSST
RUN!!

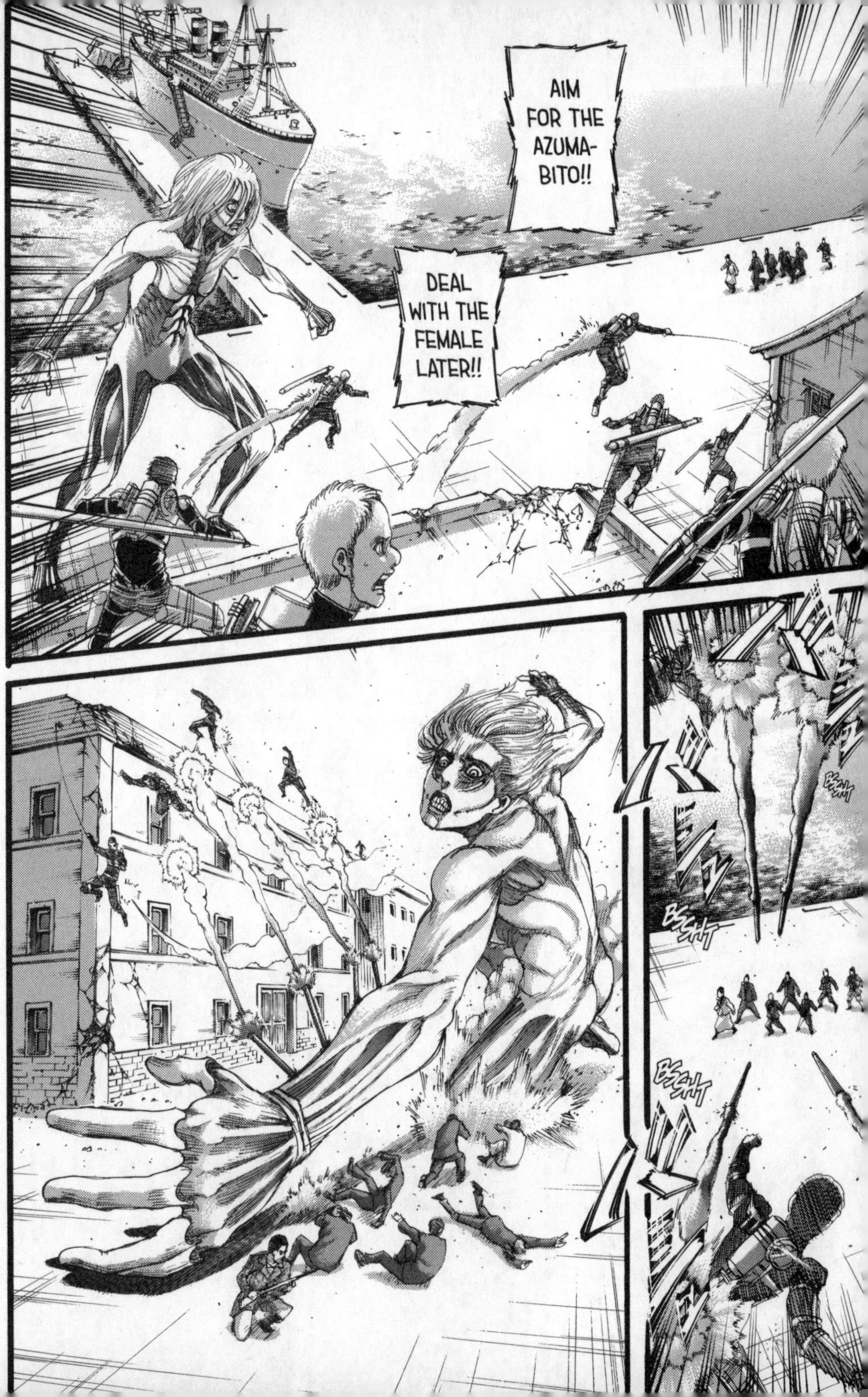
AIM FOR THE AZUMA-BITO!!
DEAL WITH THE FEMALE LATER!!
BSSHT
BSSHT
BSSHT

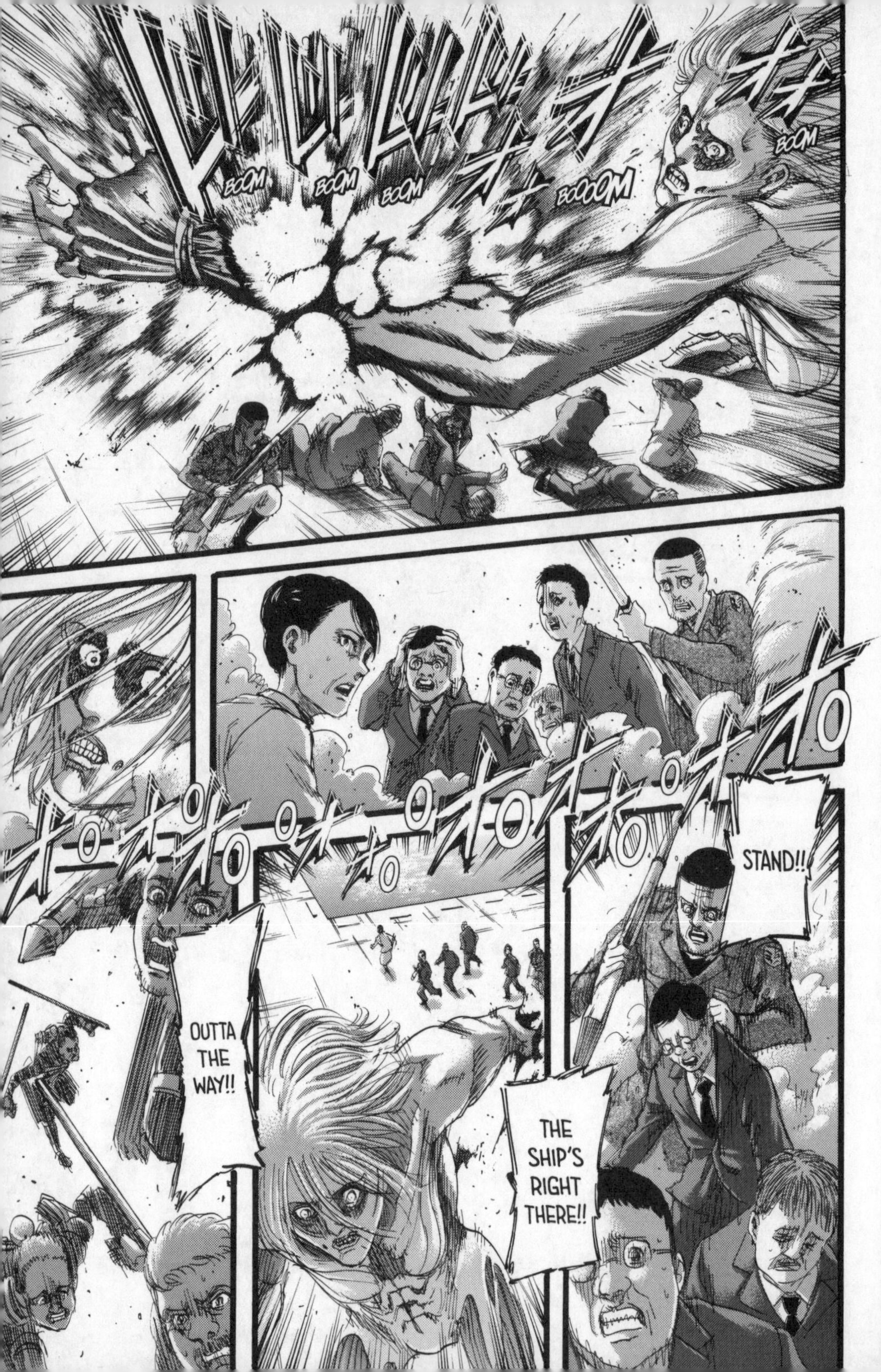
BOOM
BOOOOM
BOOM
BOOM
BOOM
STAND!!
THE SHIP'S RIGHT THERE!!
OUTTA THE WAY!!

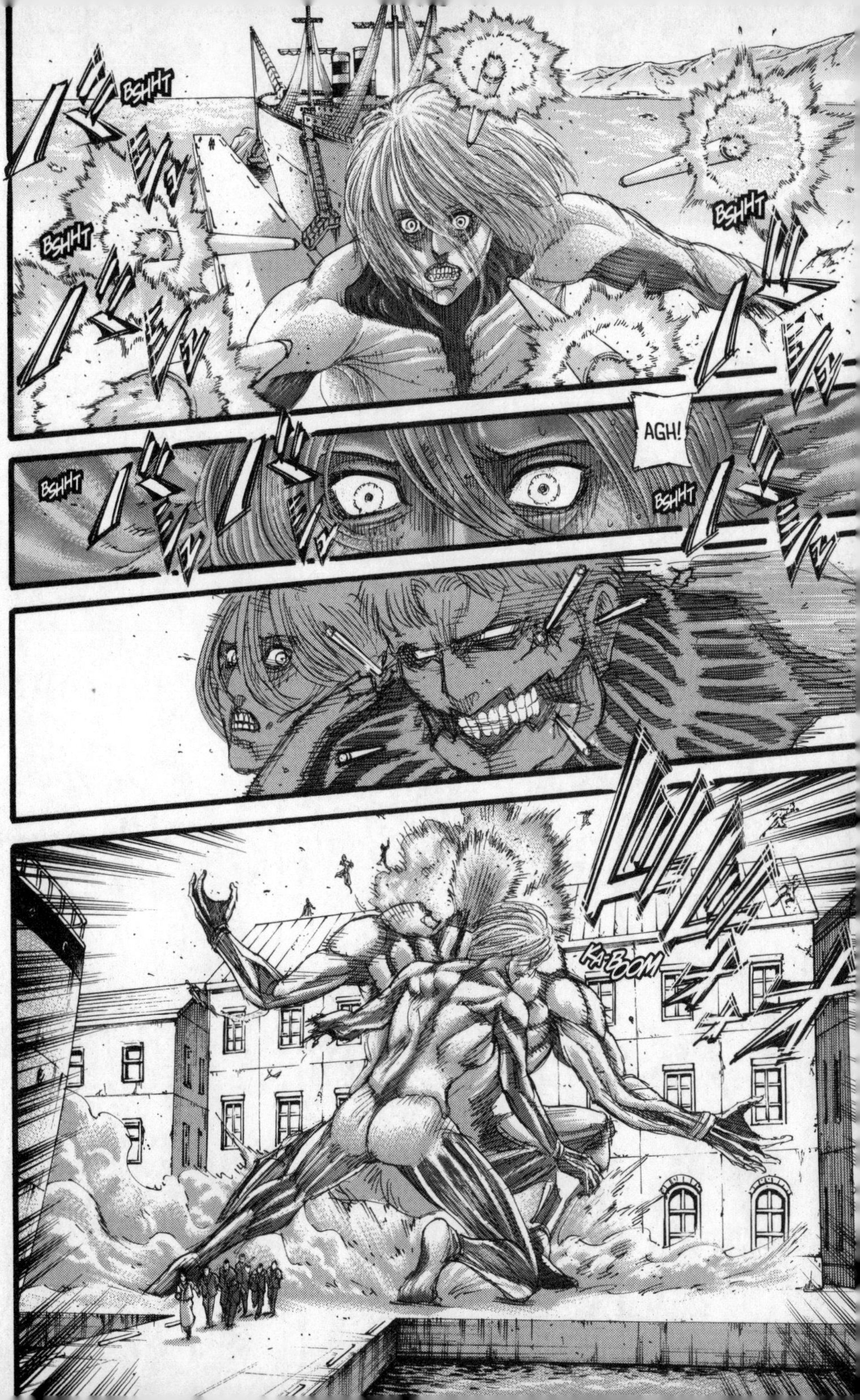
BSHHT
BSHHT
BSHHT
AGH!
BSHHT
BSHHT
KA-BOOM

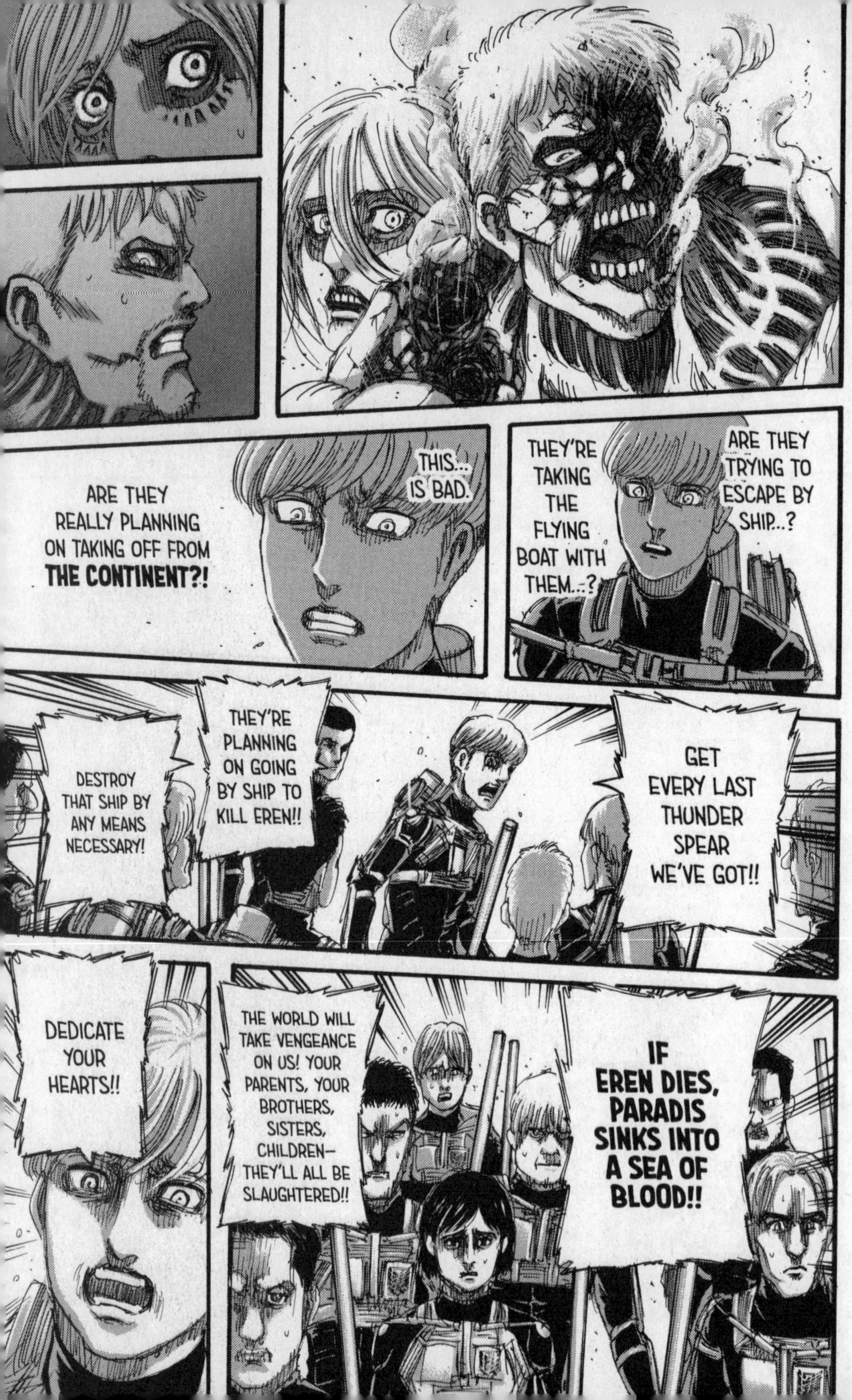
ARE THEY TRYING TO ESCAPE BY SHIP...?
THEY'RE TAKING THE FLYING BOAT WITH THEM...?
THIS... IS BAD.
ARE THEY REALLY PLANNING ON TAKING OFF FROM **THE CONTINENT?!**
GET EVERY LAST THUNDER SPEAR WE'VE GOT!!
THEY'RE PLANNING ON GOING BY SHIP TO KILL EREN!!
DESTROY THAT SHIP BY ANY MEANS NECESSARY!
IF EREN DIES, PARADIS SINKS INTO A SEA OF BLOOD!!
THE WORLD WILL TAKE VENGEANCE ON US! YOUR PARENTS, YOUR BROTHERS, SISTERS, CHILDREN— THEY'LL ALL BE SLAUGHTERED!!
DEDICATE YOUR HEARTS!!

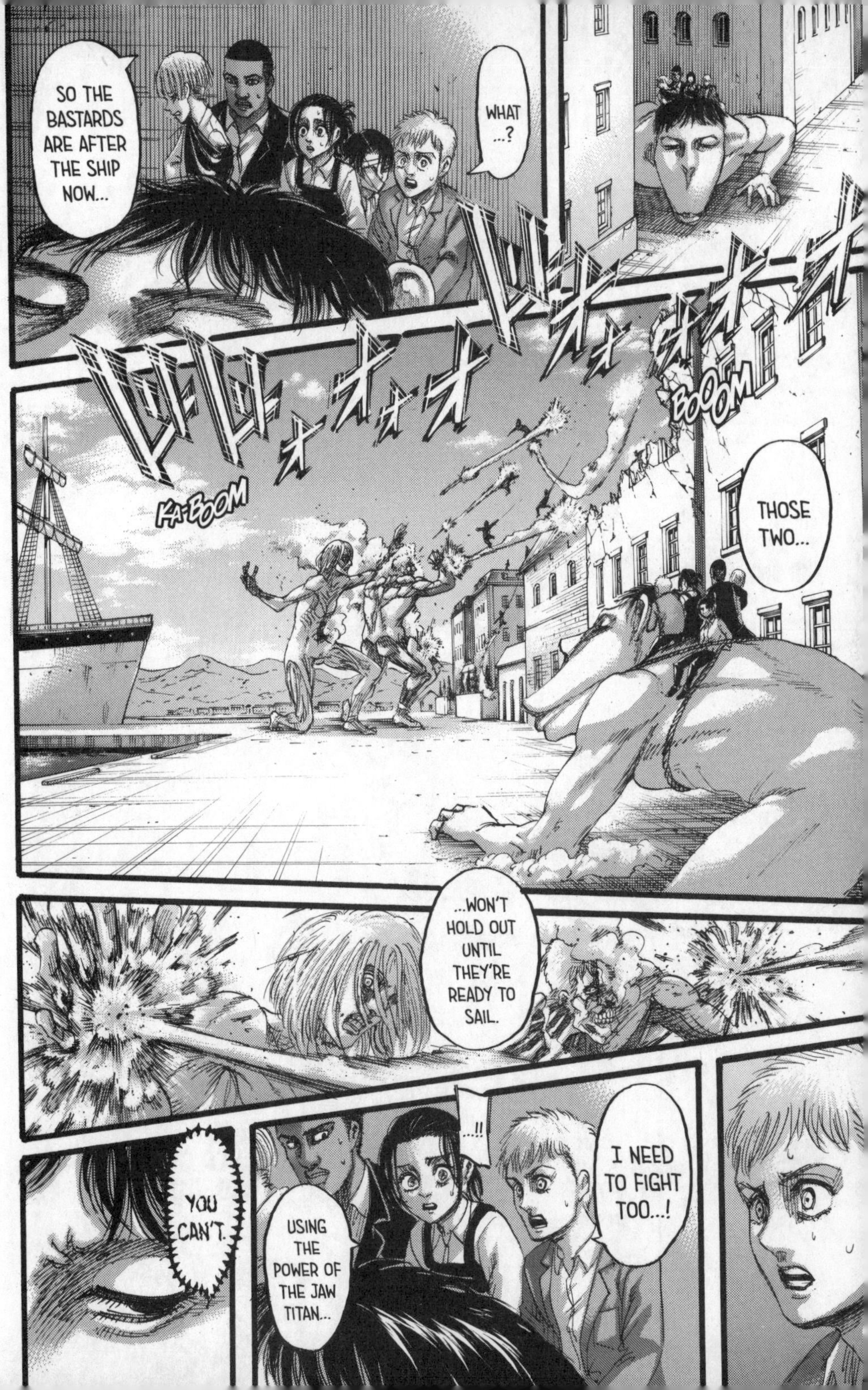

WHAT ...?
SO THE BASTARDS ARE AFTER THE SHIP NOW...
BOOOM
KA-BOOM
THOSE TWO...
...WON'T HOLD OUT UNTIL THEY'RE READY TO SAIL.
I NEED TO FIGHT TOO...!
...!!
USING THE POWER OF THE JAW TITAN...
YOU CAN'T.

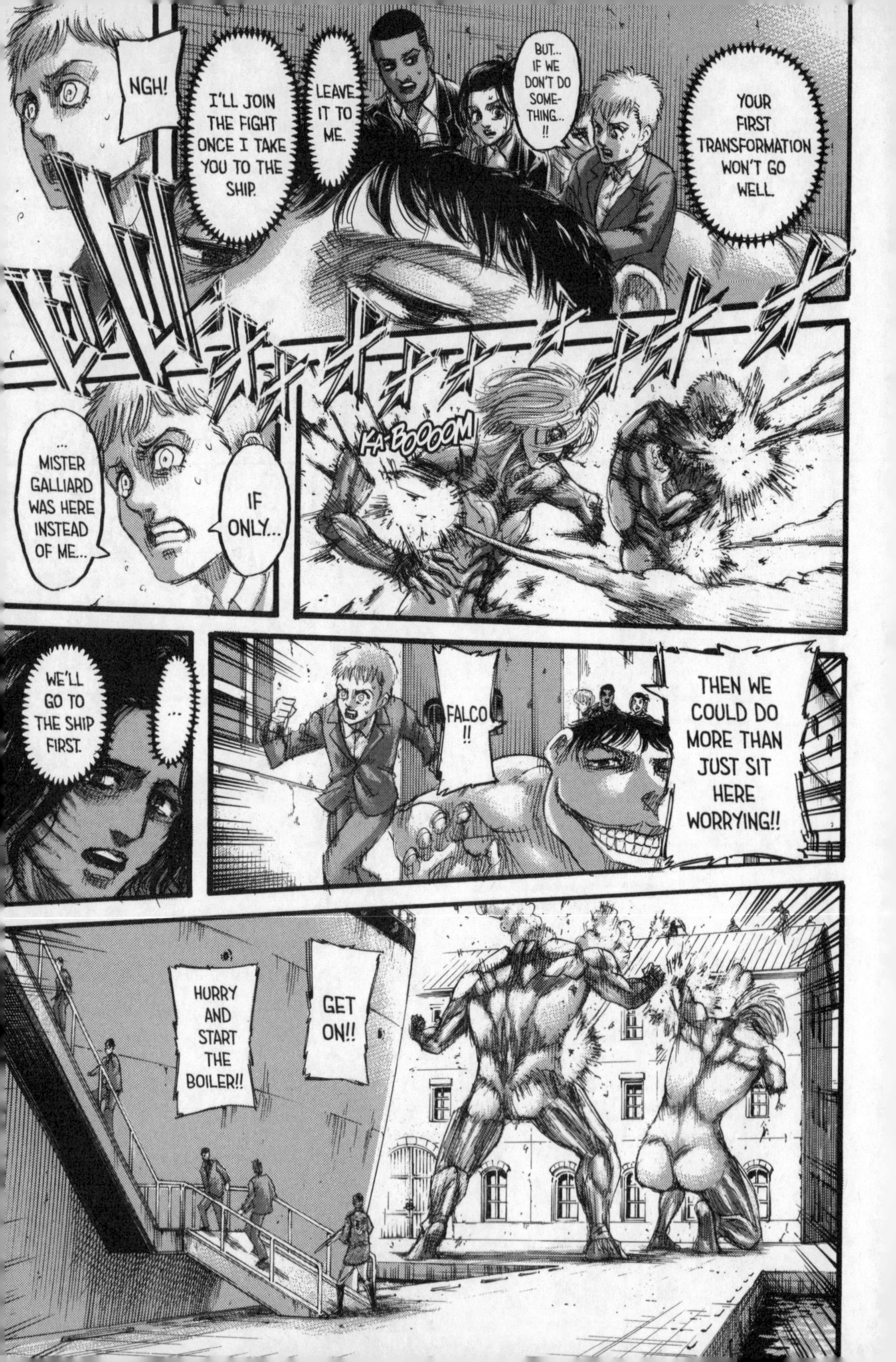
YOUR FIRST TRANSFORMATION WON'T GO WELL.
BUT... IF WE DON'T DO SOMETHING... !!
LEAVE IT TO ME.
I'LL JOIN THE FIGHT ONCE I TAKE YOU TO THE SHIP.
NGH!
KA-BOOOOM
IF ONLY...
... MISTER GALLIARD WAS HERE INSTEAD OF ME...
THEN WE COULD DO MORE THAN JUST SIT HERE WORRYING!!
FALCO !!
...
WE'LL GO TO THE SHIP FIRST.
GET ON!!
HURRY AND START THE BOILER!!

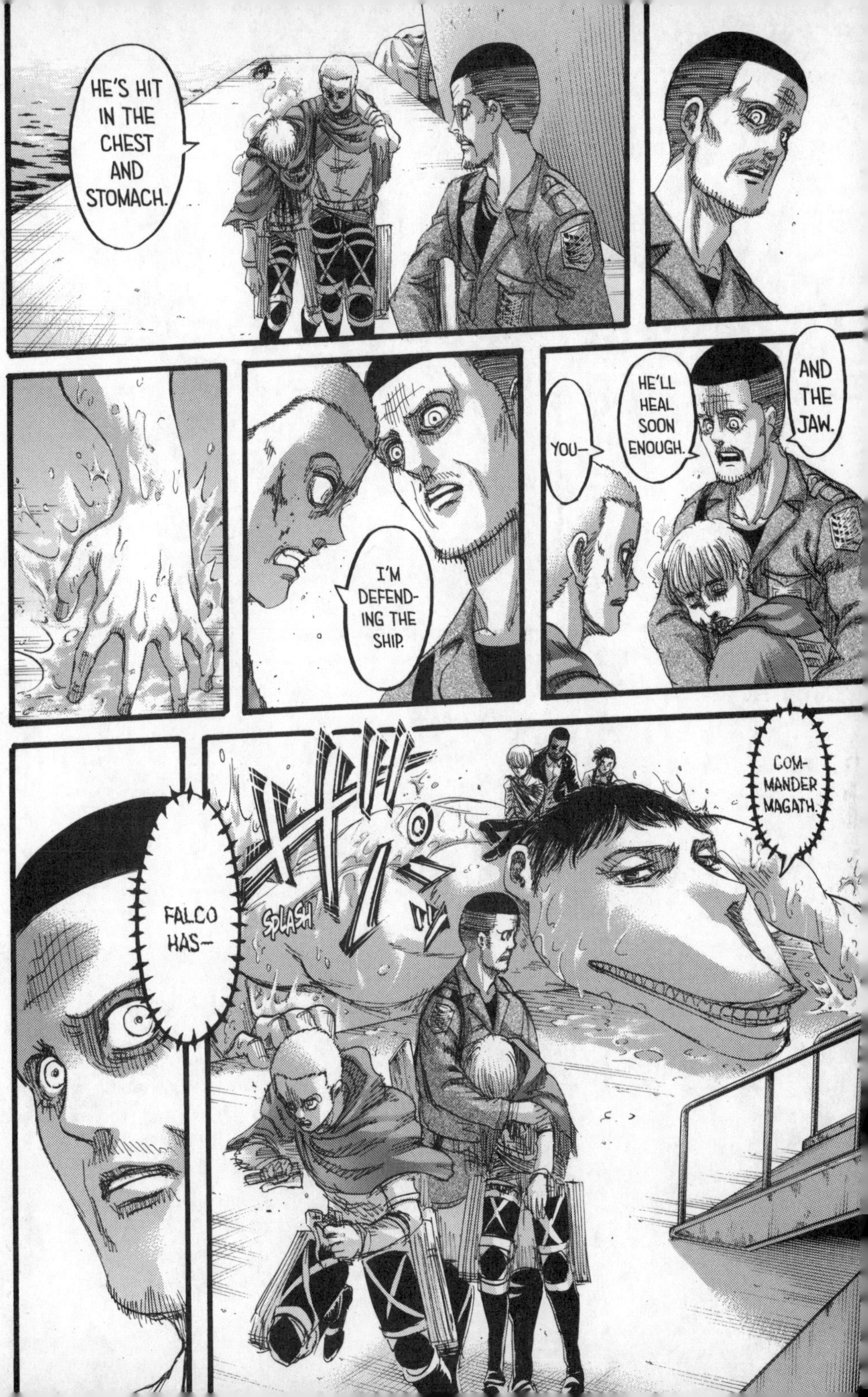
HE'S HIT IN THE CHEST AND STOMACH.
AND THE JAW.
HE'LL HEAL SOON ENOUGH.
YOU—
I'M DEFENDING THE SHIP.
COMMANDER MAGATH.
SPLASH
FALCO HAS—

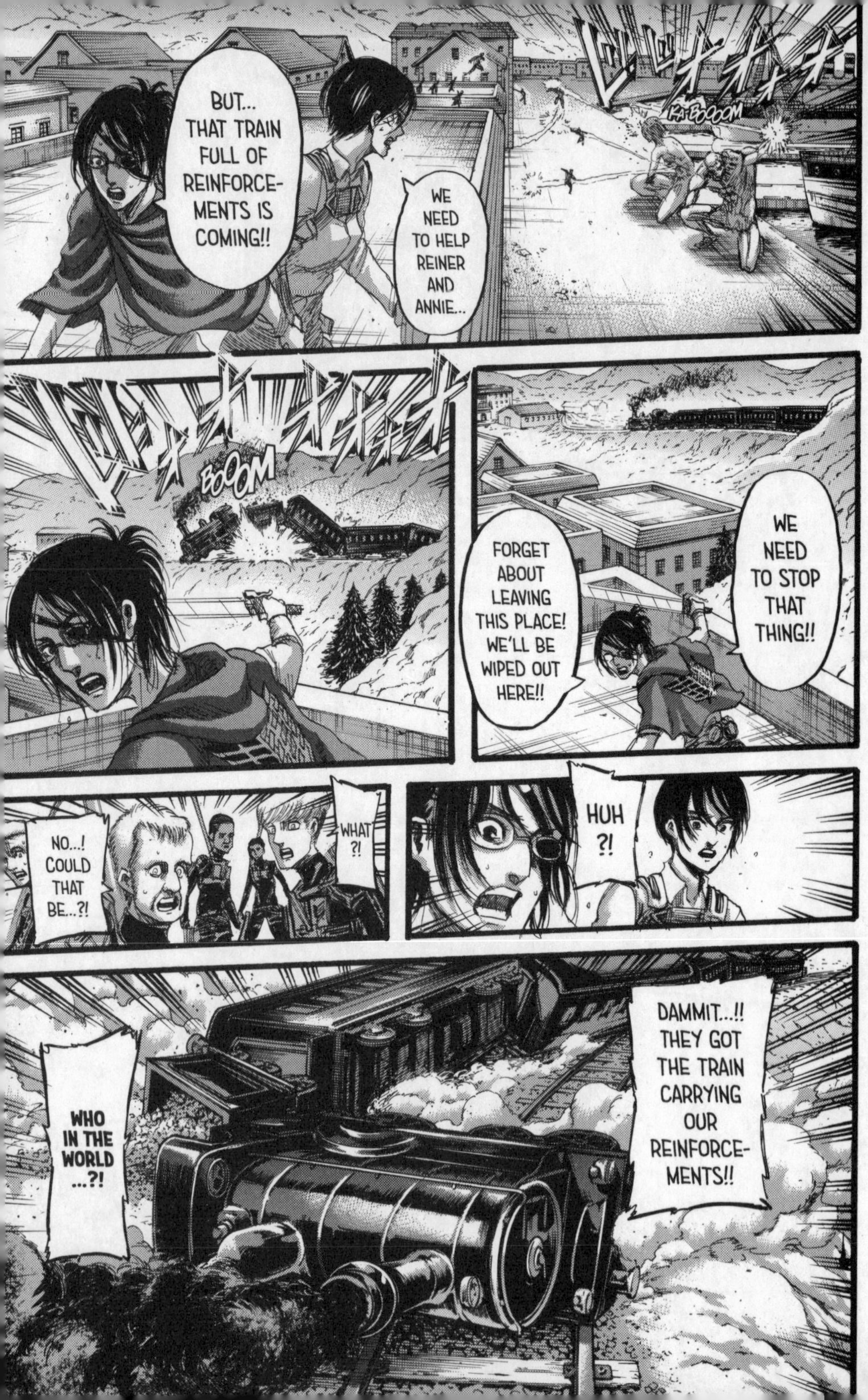
KA-BOOOM
WE NEED TO HELP REINER AND ANNIE...
BUT... THAT TRAIN FULL OF REINFORCEMENTS IS COMING!!
WE NEED TO STOP THAT THING!!
FORGET ABOUT LEAVING THIS PLACE! WE'LL BE WIPED OUT HERE!!
BOOOM
HUH ?!
WHAT ?!
NO...! COULD THAT BE...?!
DAMMIT...!! THEY GOT THE TRAIN CARRYING OUR REINFORCEMENTS!!
WHO IN THE WORLD ...?!

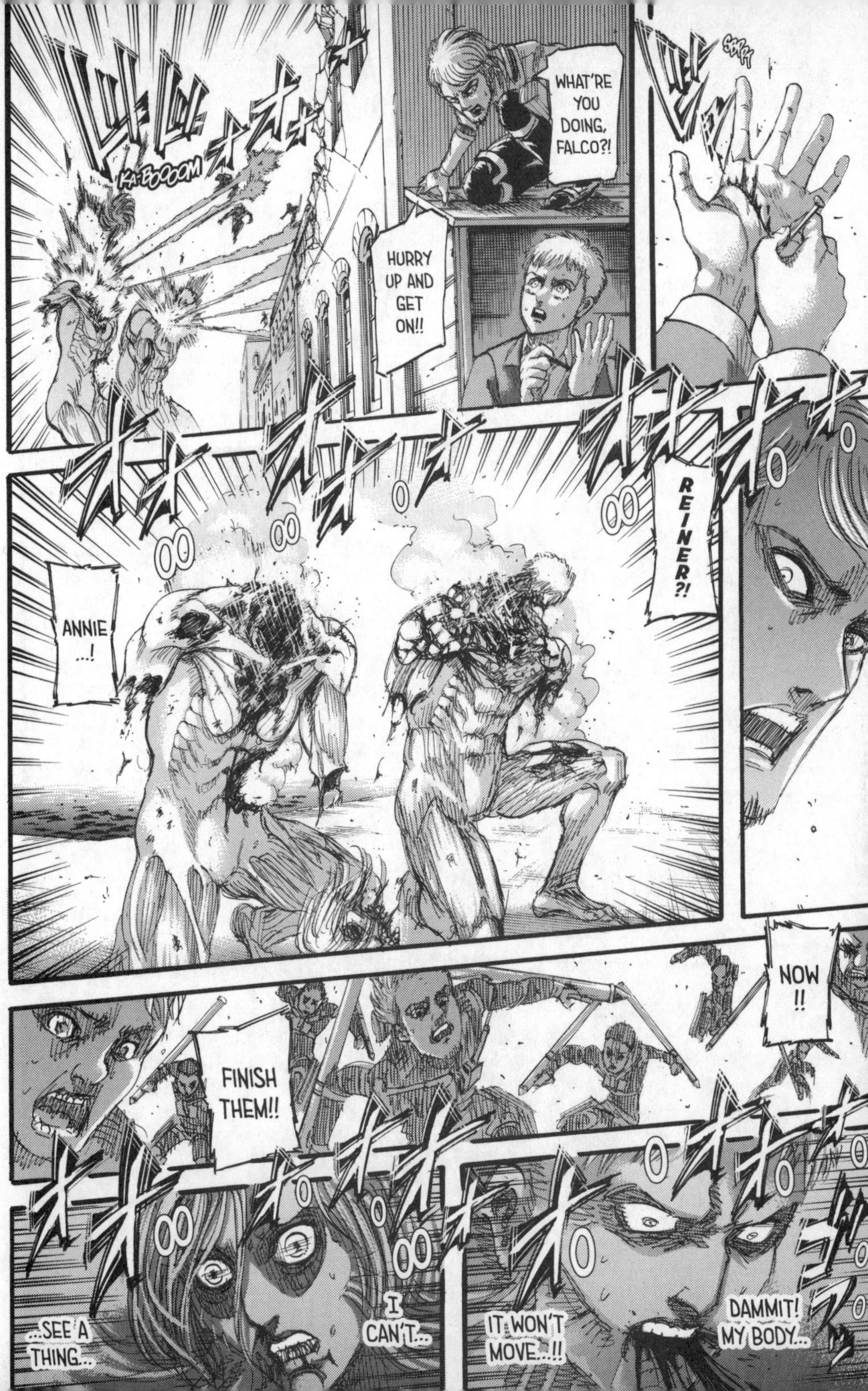
WHAT'RE YOU DOING, FALCO?!
HURRY UP AND GET ON!!
KA-BOOOOM
REINER?!
ANNIE ...!
NOW !!
FINISH THEM!!
DAMMIT! MY BODY...
IT WON'T MOVE...!!
I CAN'T...
...SEE A THING...

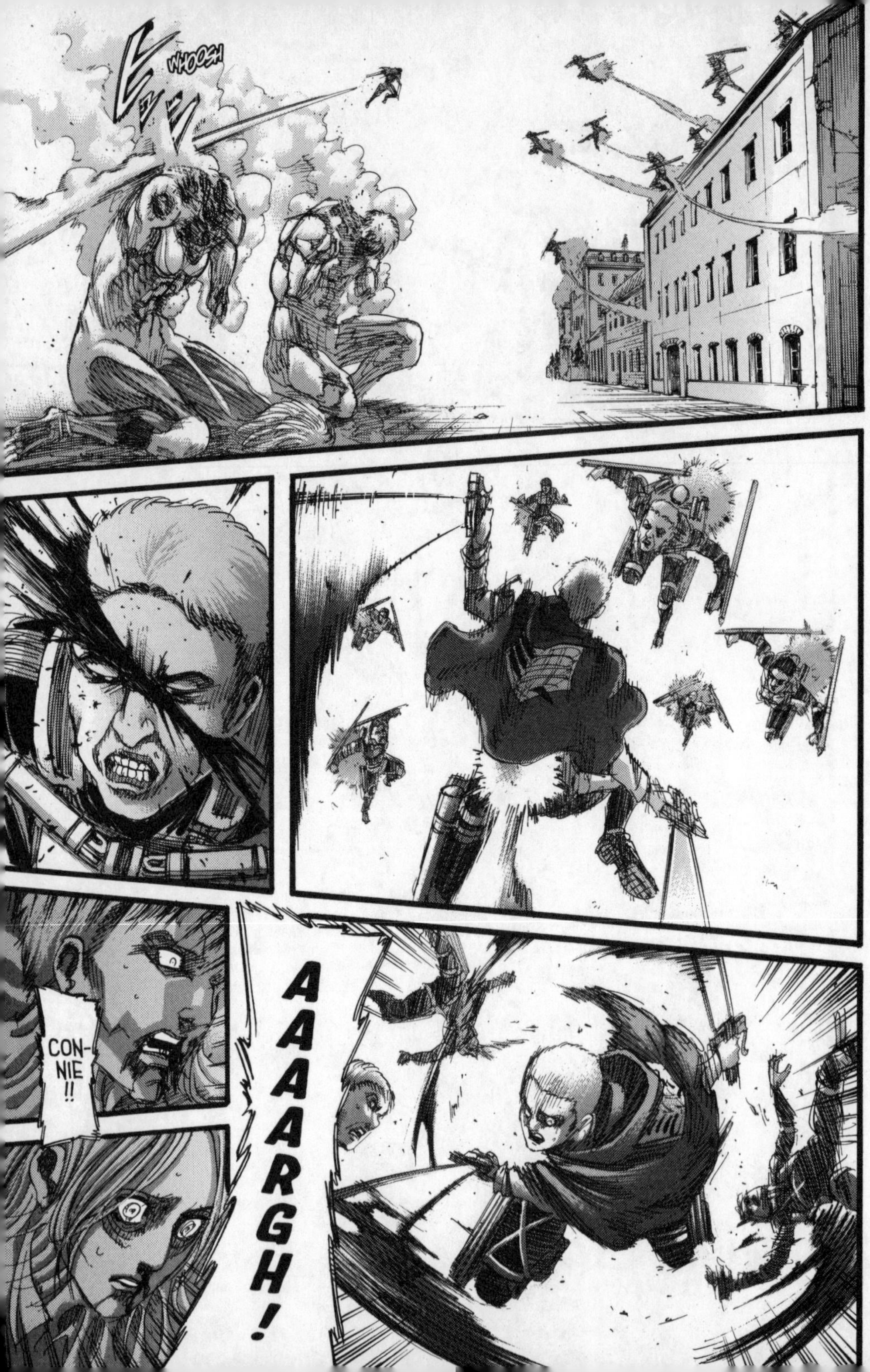
WHOOSH
AAAAARGH!
CON-NIE!!

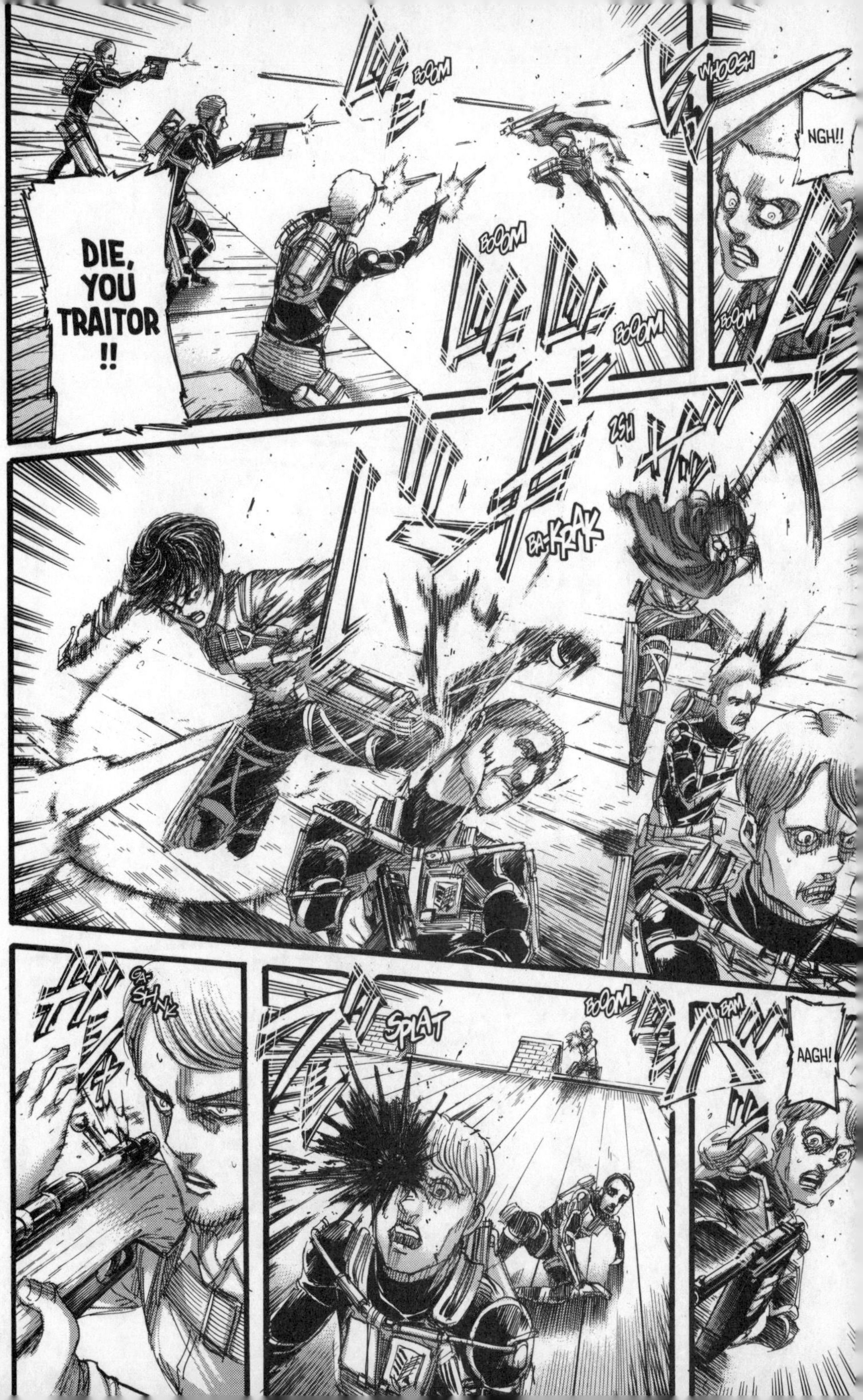
WHOOSH
NGH!!
BOOOM
BOOOM
BOOOM
BOOOM
DIE, YOU TRAITOR!!
ZSH
BA-KRAK
BAM
AAGH!
BOOOM
SPLAT
CA-SHNK

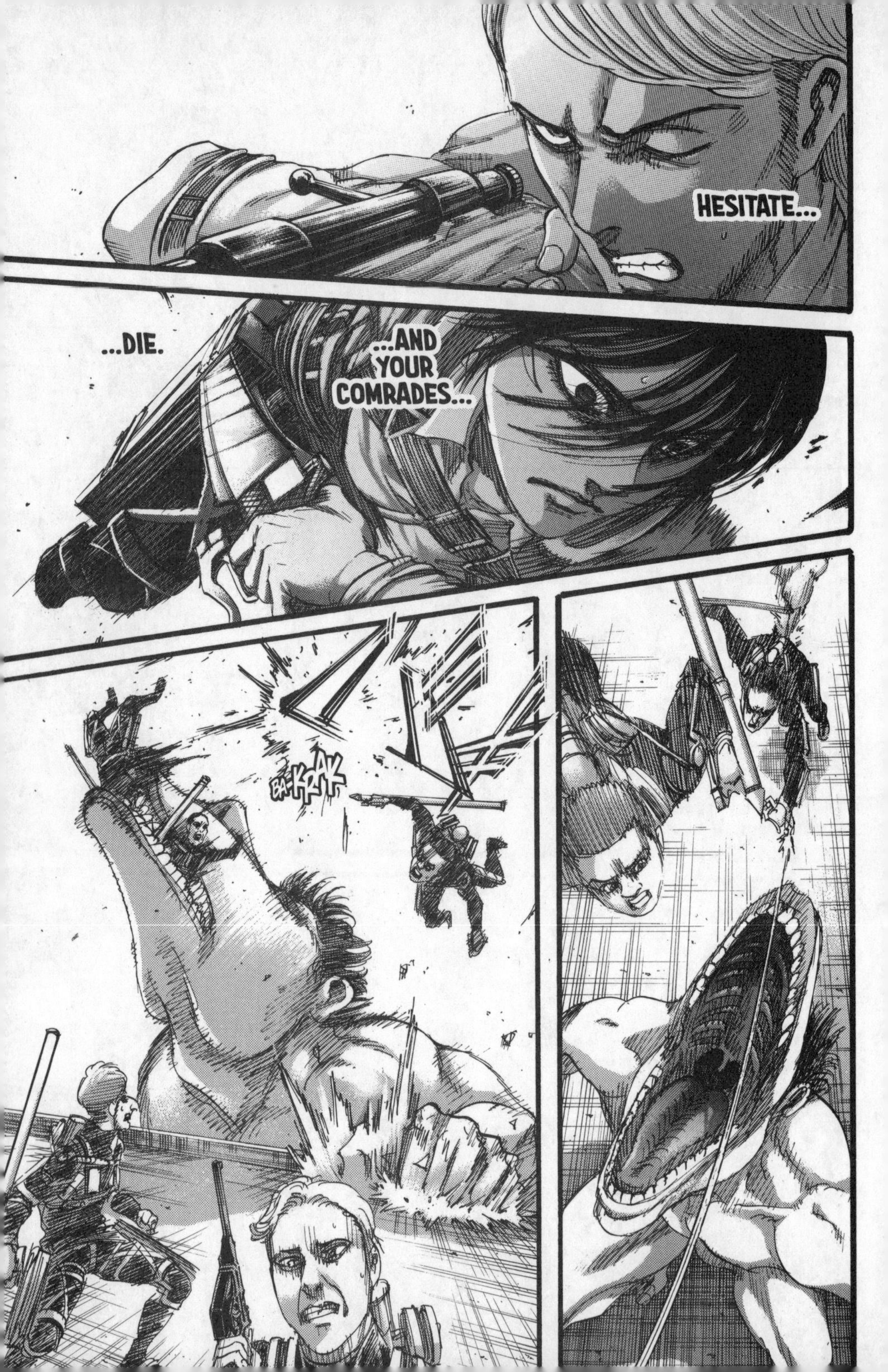
HESITATE...
...AND YOUR COMRADES...
...DIE.
BA-KRAK

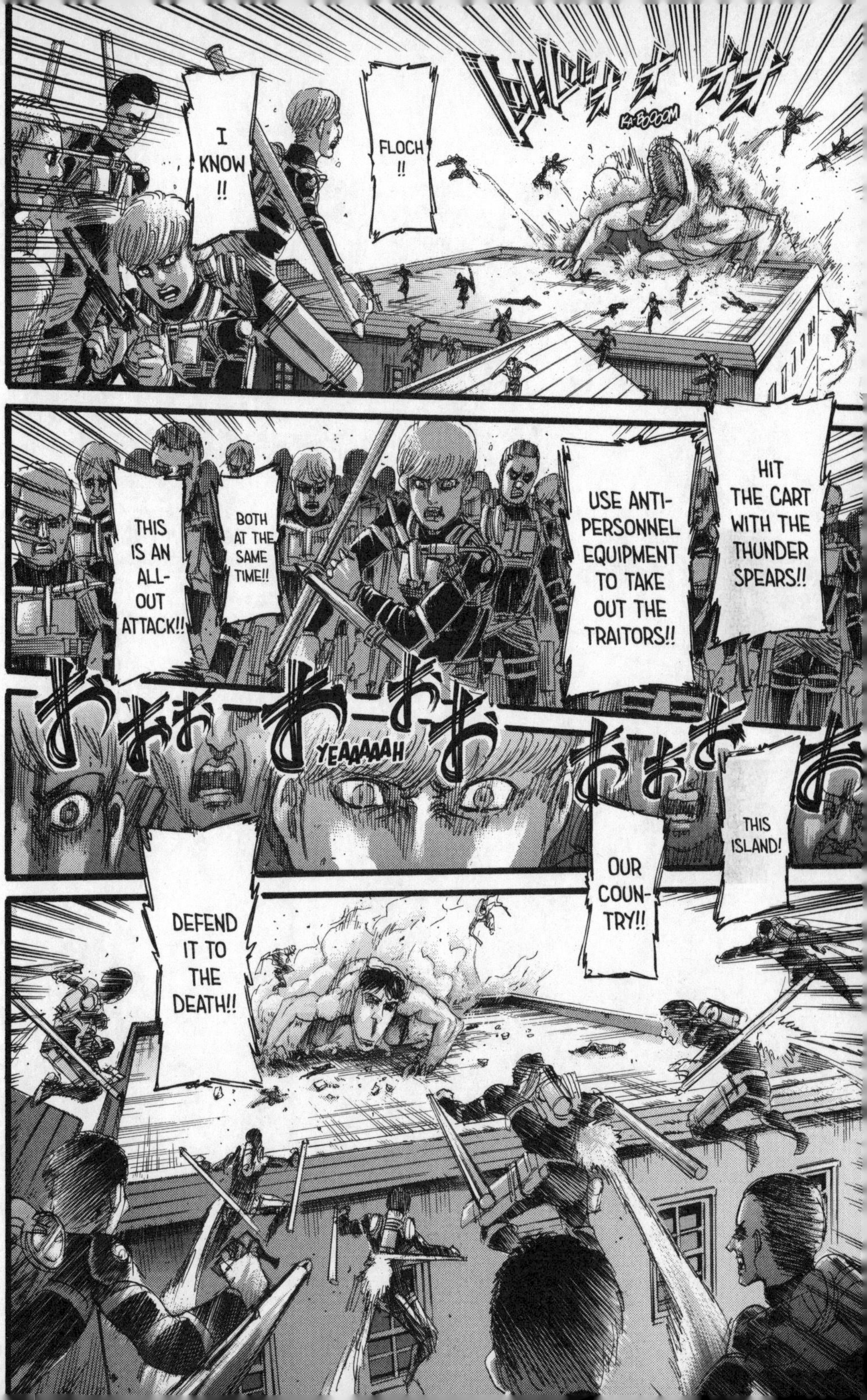
KA-BOOOM
FLOCH!!
I KNOW!!
HIT THE CART WITH THE THUNDER SPEARS!!
USE ANTI-PERSONNEL EQUIPMENT TO TAKE OUT THE TRAITORS!!
BOTH AT THE SAME TIME!!
THIS IS AN ALL-OUT ATTACK!!
YEAAAAAH
THIS ISLAND!
OUR COUNTRY!!
DEFEND IT TO THE DEATH!!

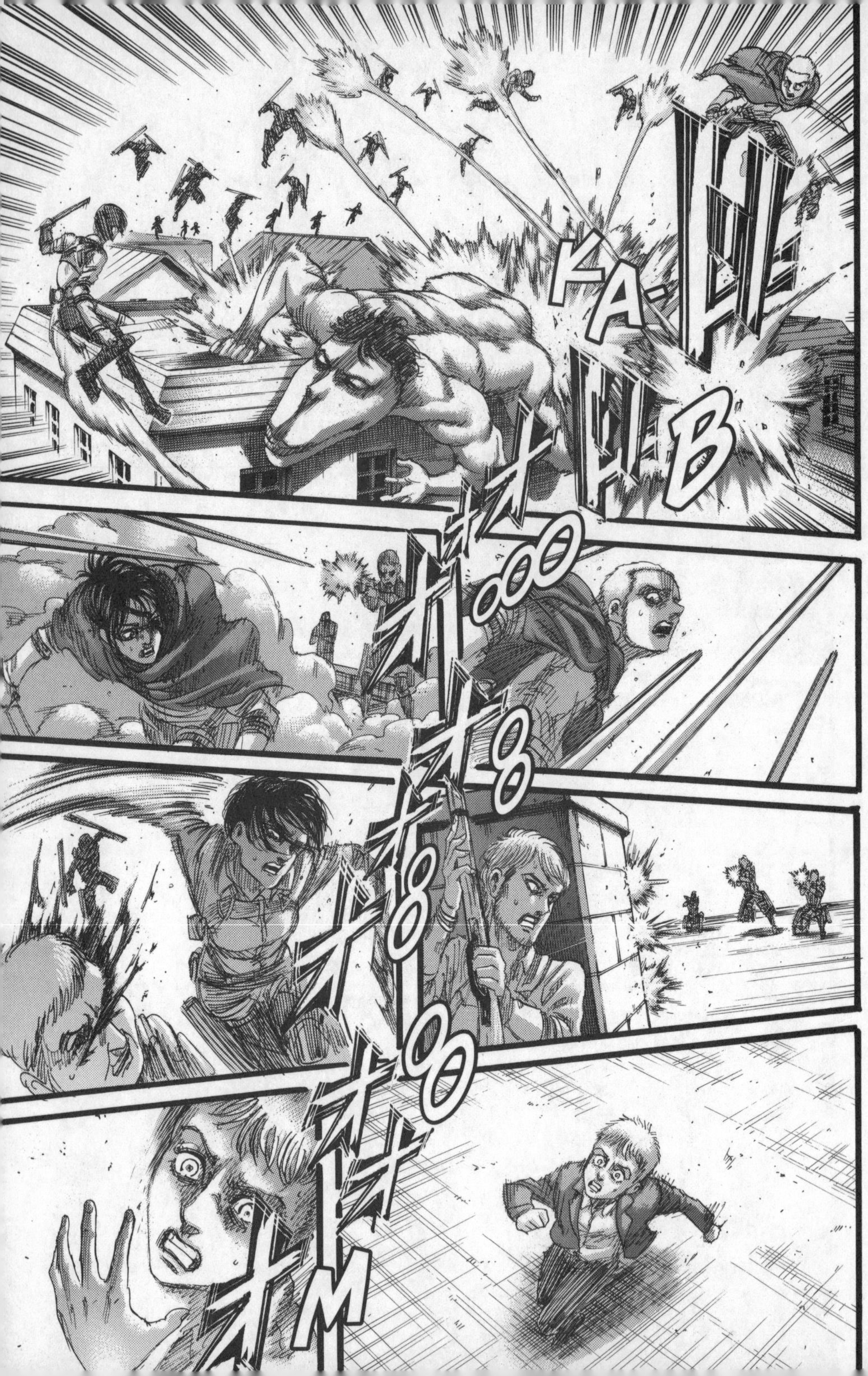
KA-BOOOOOM

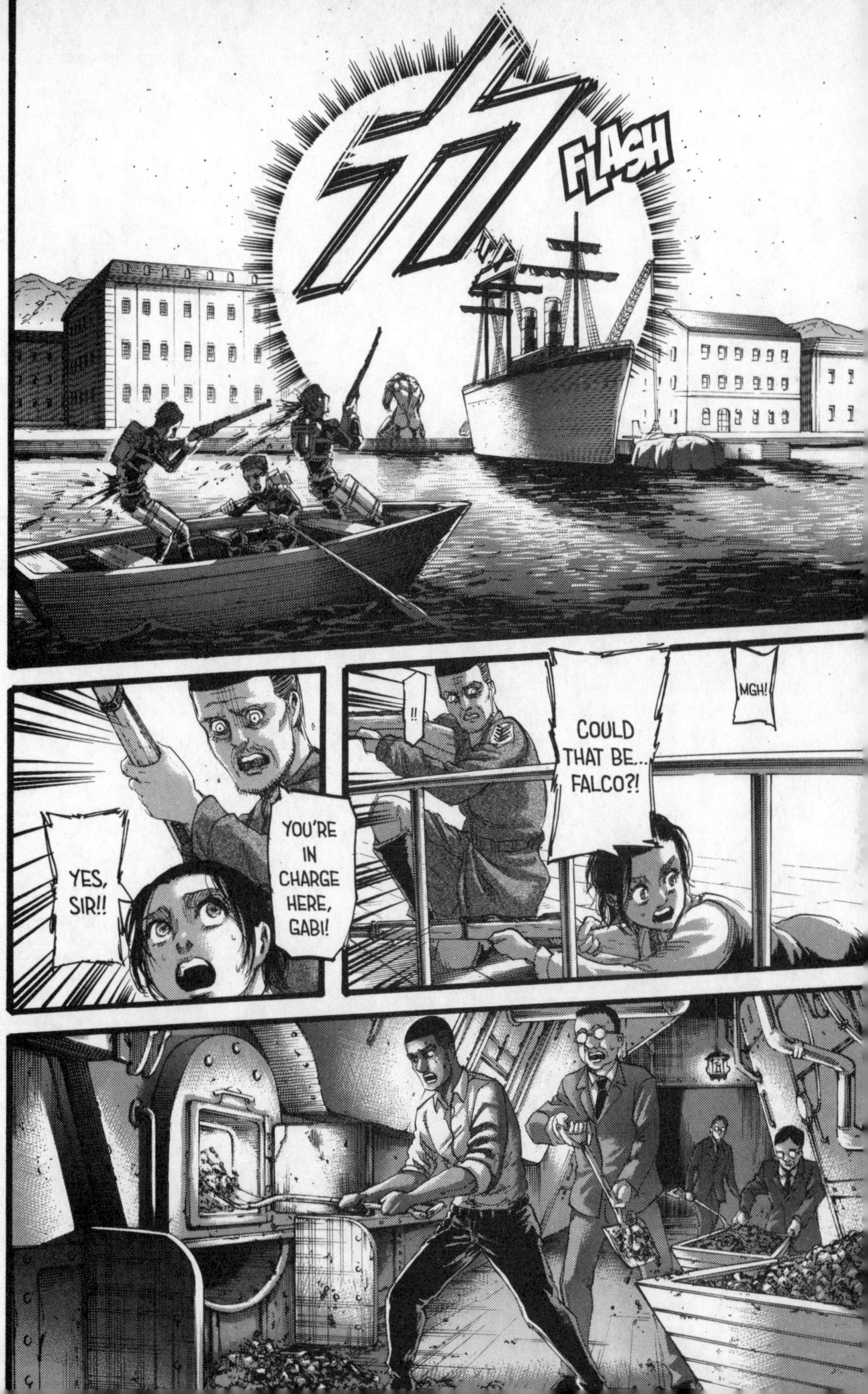
FLASH
MGH!
COULD THAT BE... FALCO?!
!!
YOU'RE IN CHARGE HERE, GABI!
YES, SIR!!

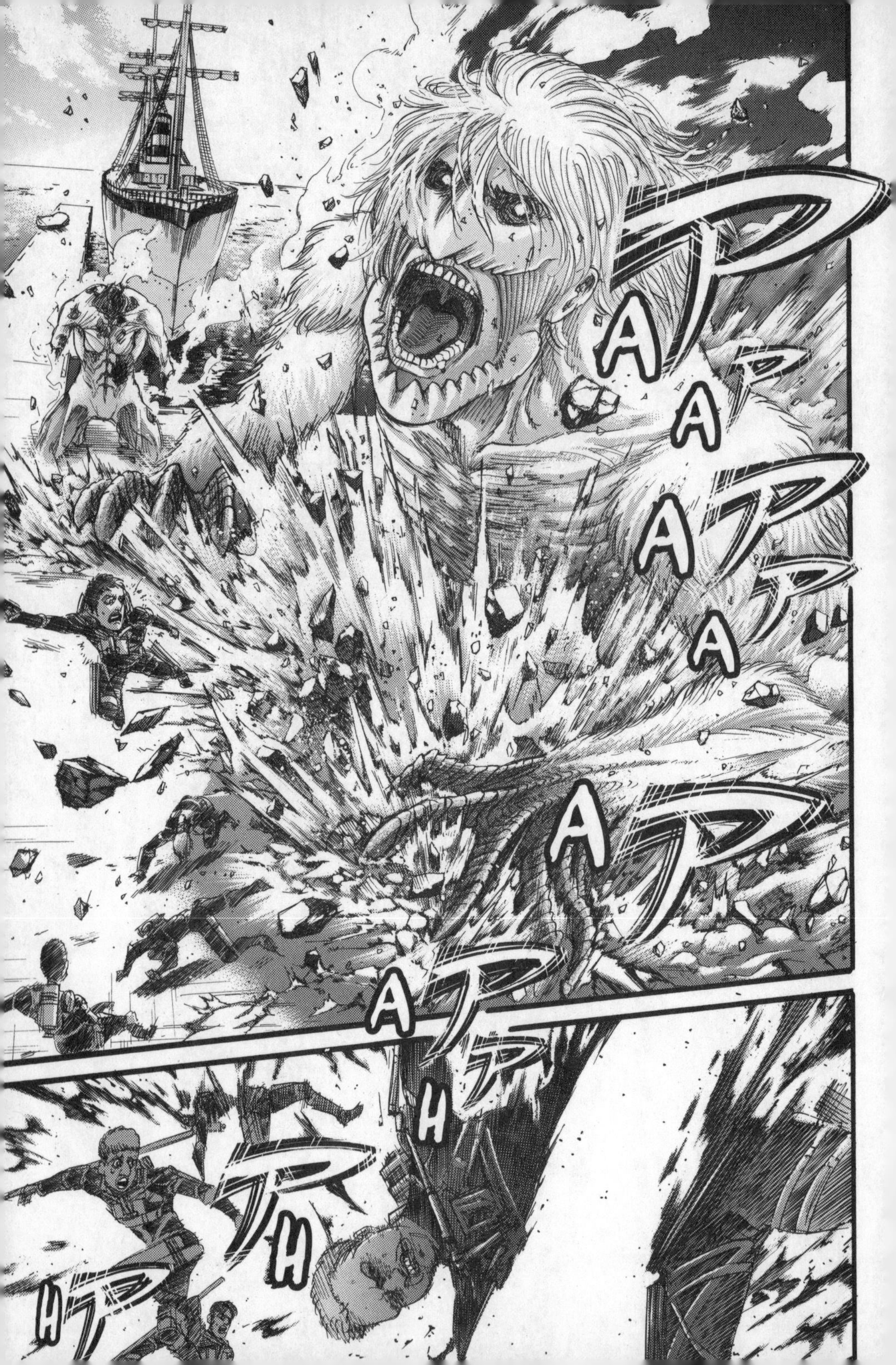

AAAAAAH
TH
H

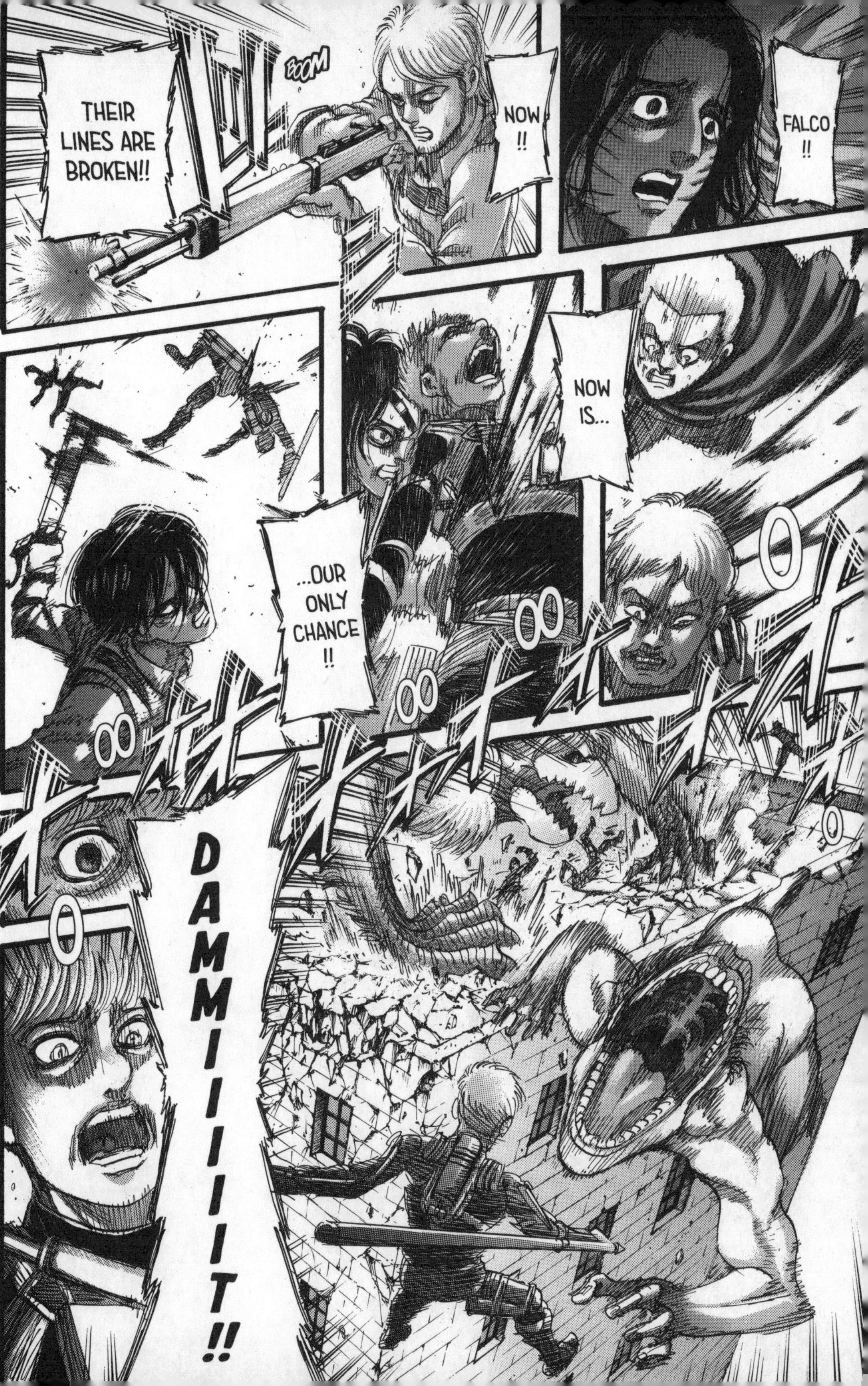
FALCO!!
NOW!!
BOOM
THEIR LINES ARE BROKEN!!
NOW IS...
...OUR ONLY CHANCE!!
DAMMIIIIIT!!

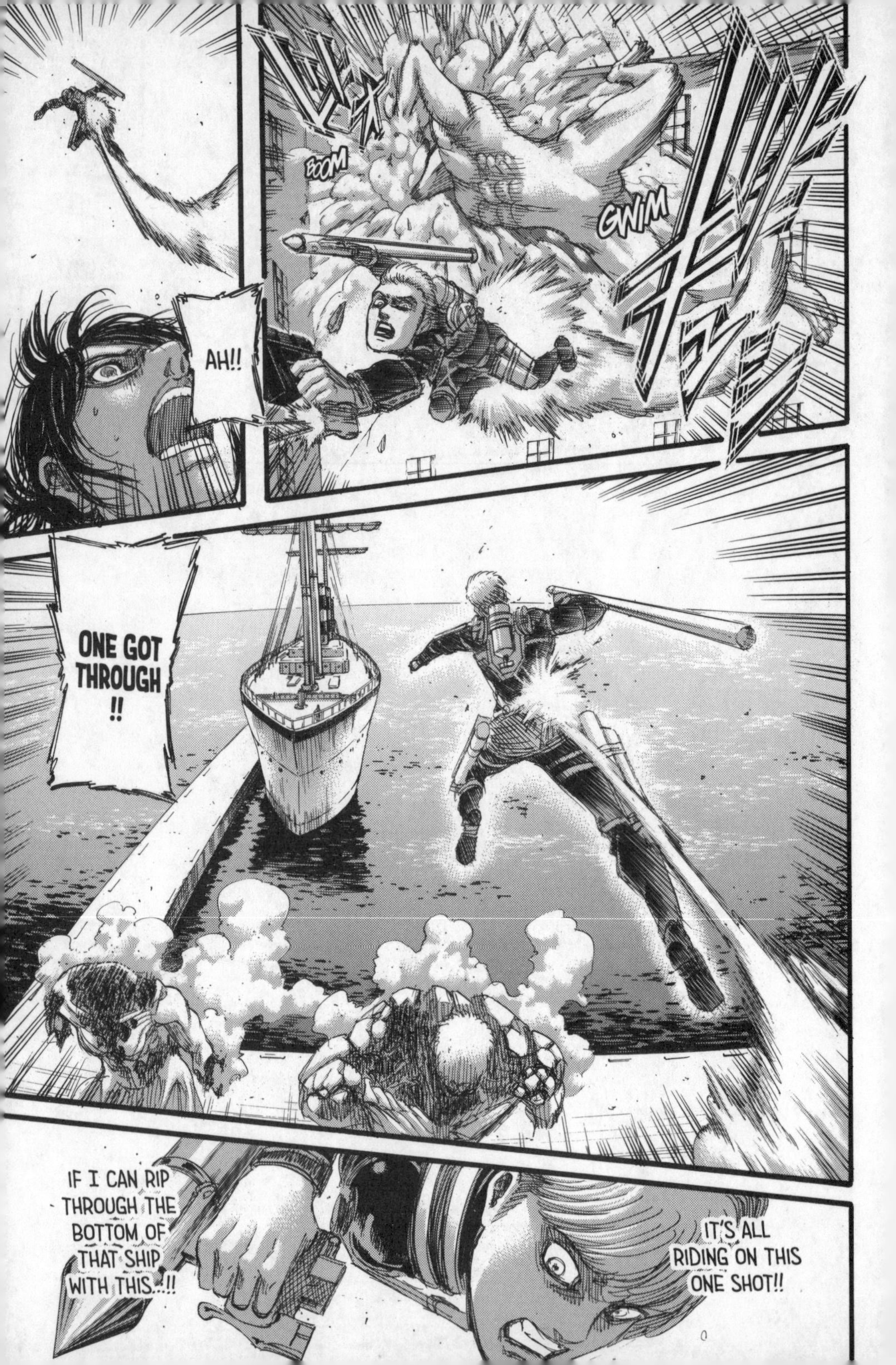
BOOM
GWIM
AH!!
ONE GOT THROUGH !!
IF I CAN RIP THROUGH THE BOTTOM OF THAT SHIP WITH THIS...!!
IT'S ALL RIDING ON THIS ONE SHOT!!

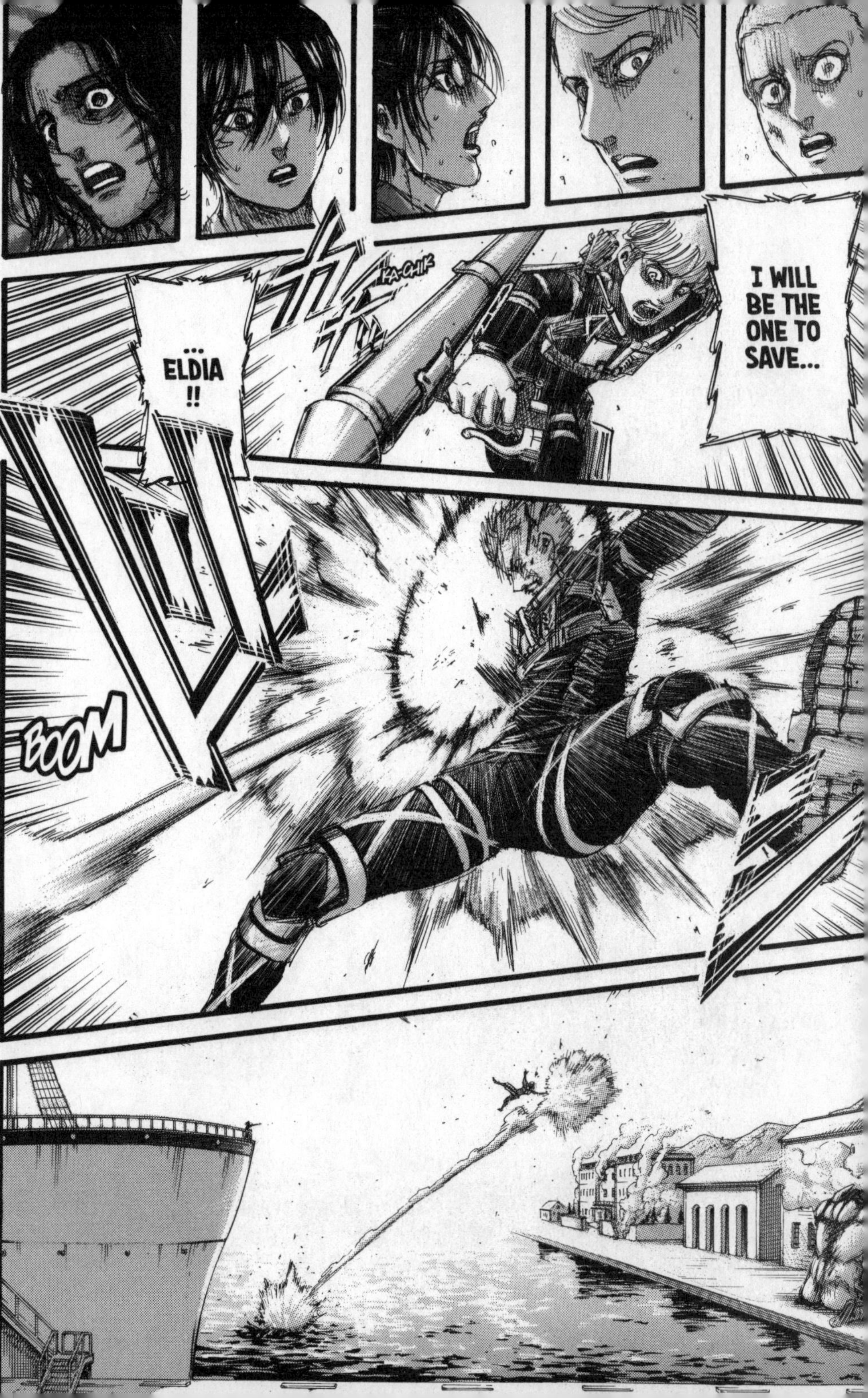
I WILL BE THE ONE TO SAVE...
KA-CHIK
...ELDIA!!
BOOM

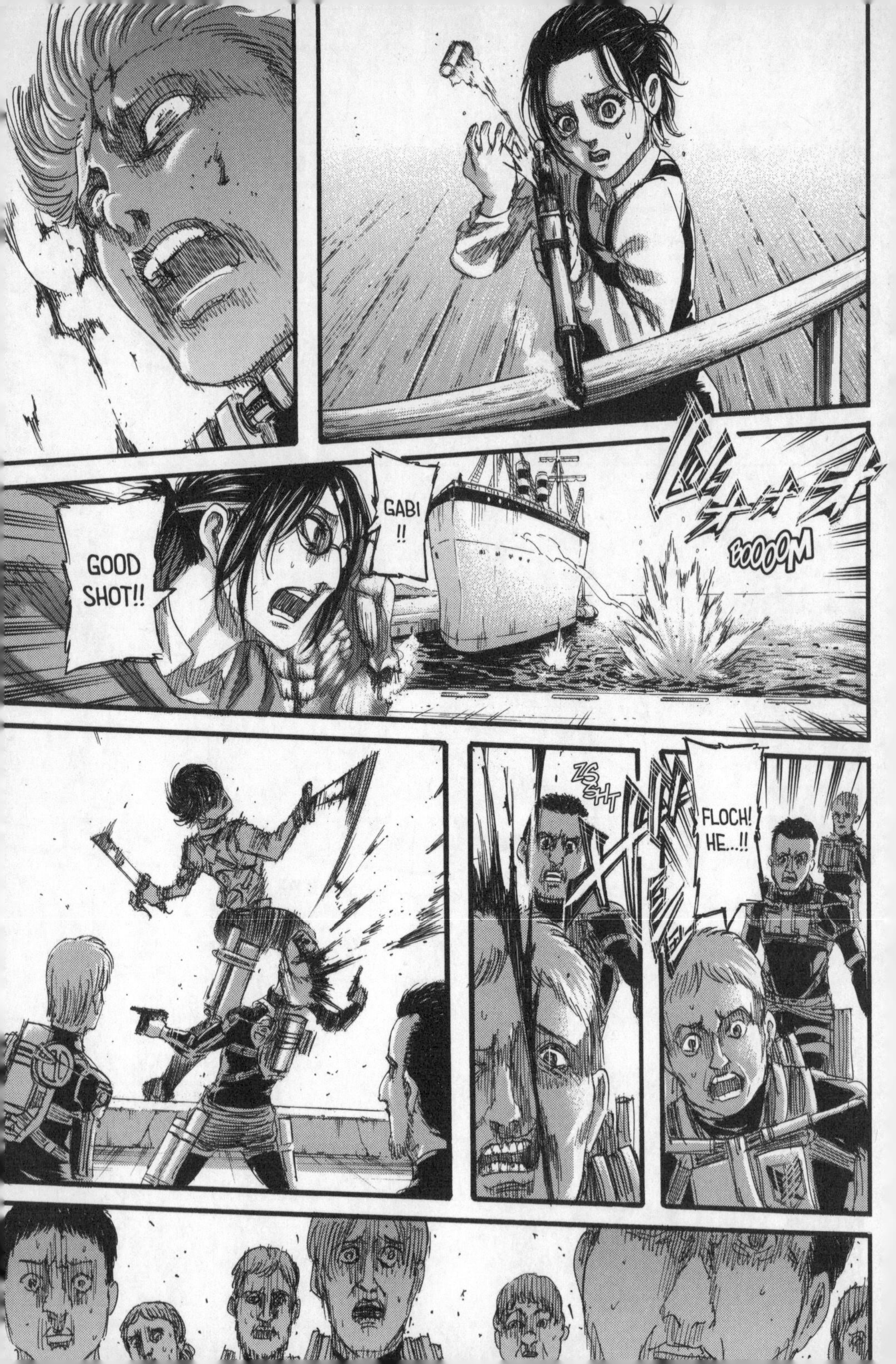
BOOOOM
GABI !!
GOOD SHOT!!
FLOCH! HE...!!
ZSHT

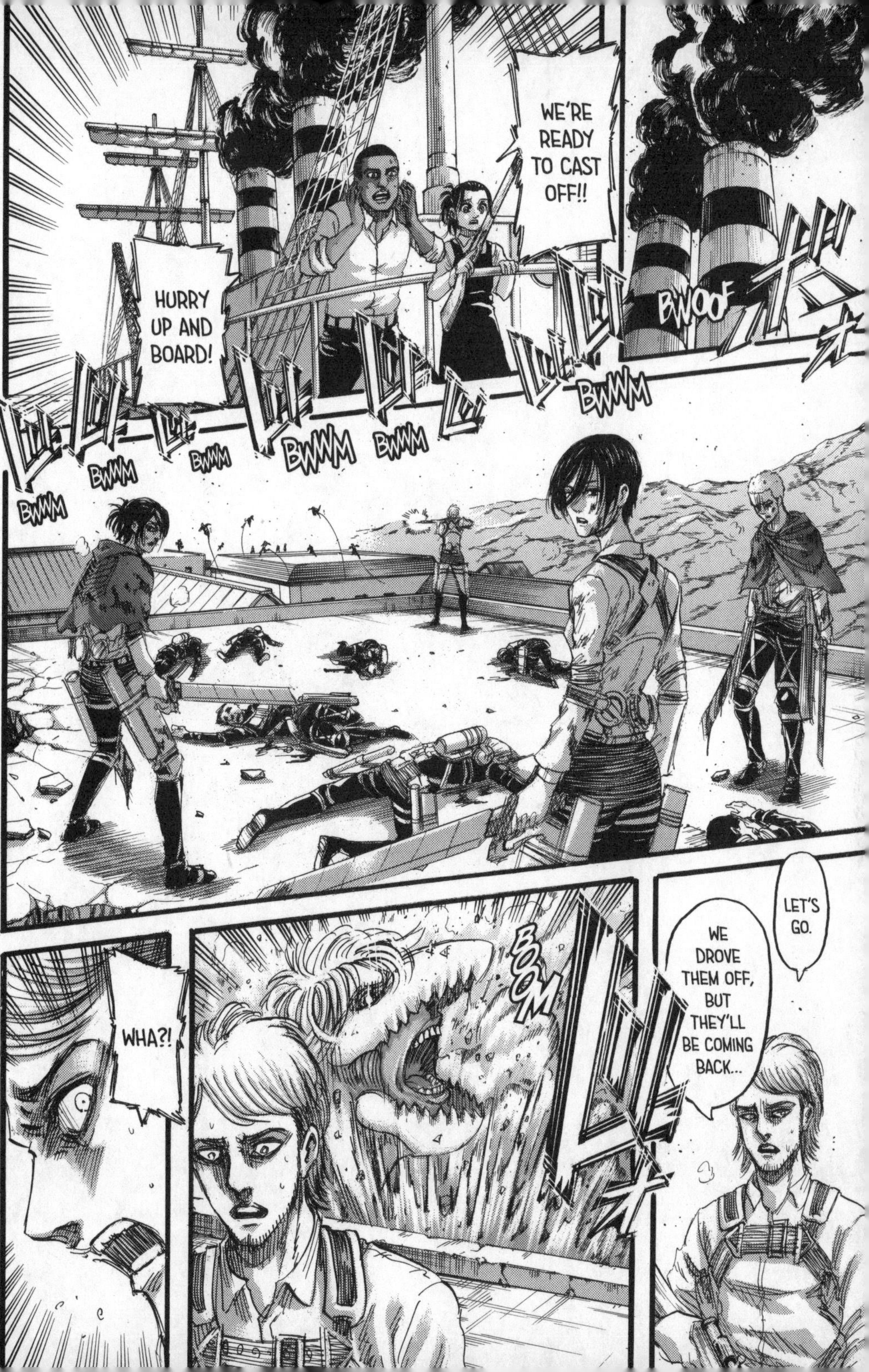

WE'RE READY TO CAST OFF!!
BWOOF
BWWM
HURRY UP AND BOARD!
BWWM
BWWM
BWWM
BWWM
BWWM
LET'S GO.
WE DROVE THEM OFF, BUT THEY'LL BE COMING BACK...
BOOM
WHA?!

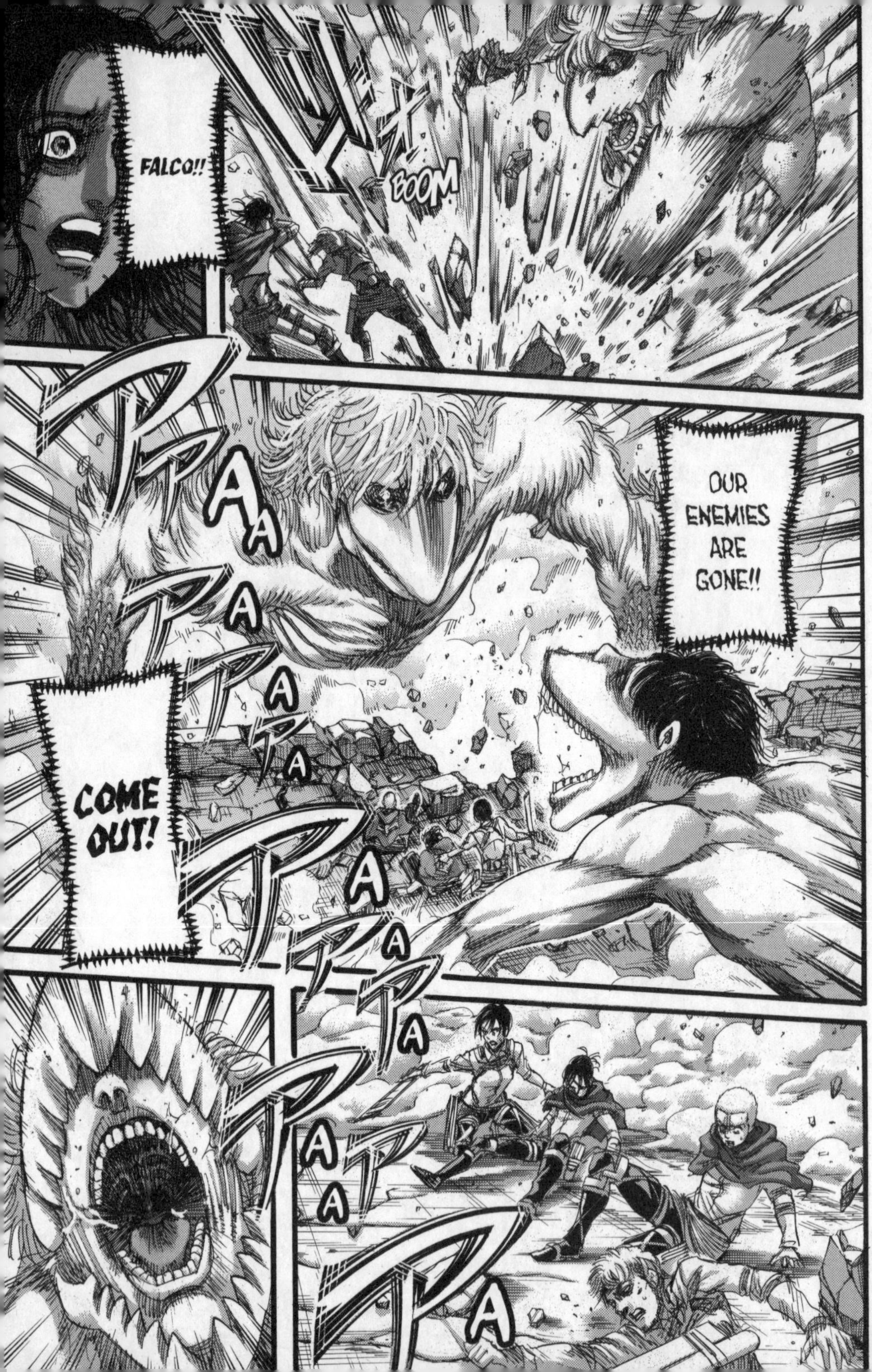
BOOM
FALCO!!
OUR ENEMIES ARE GONE!!
COME OUT!
AAAAAAAAAAAAAAA

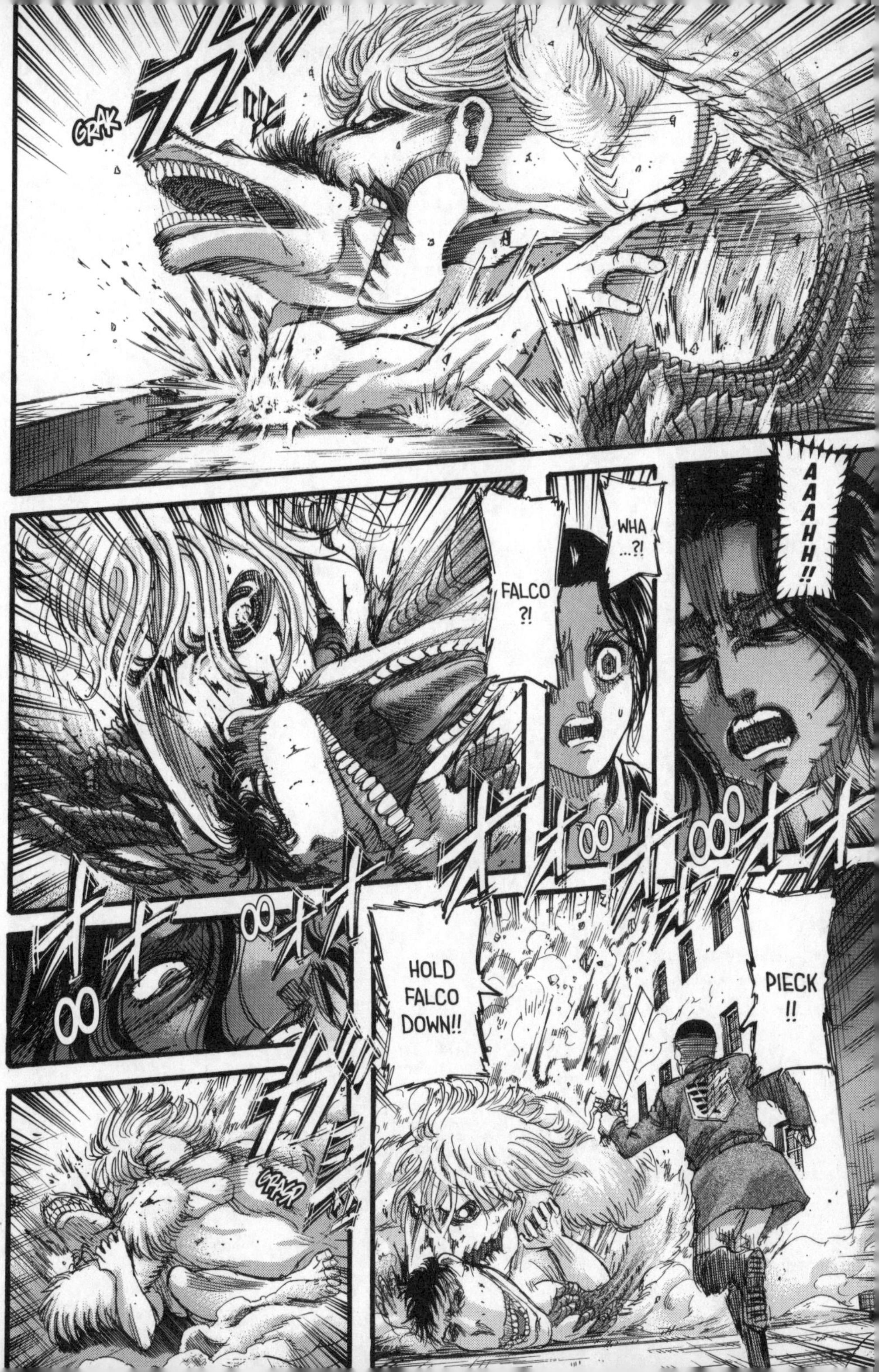
GRAK
AAAAHH!!
WHA ...?!
FALCO ?!
PIECK !!
HOLD FALCO DOWN!!
GRASP

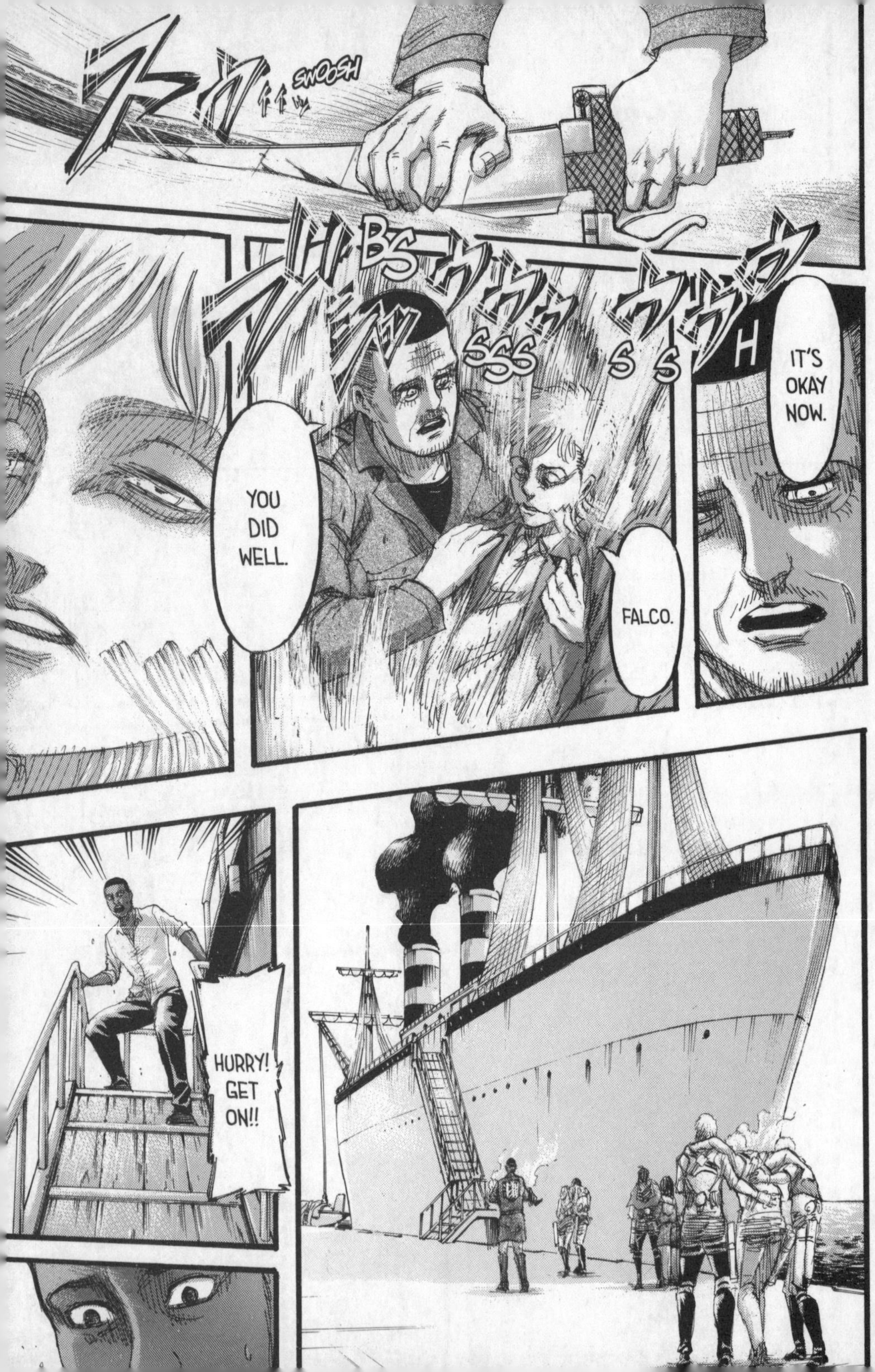
SWOOSH
BS SSS S S H
IT'S OKAY NOW.
FALCO.
YOU DID WELL.
HURRY! GET ON!!

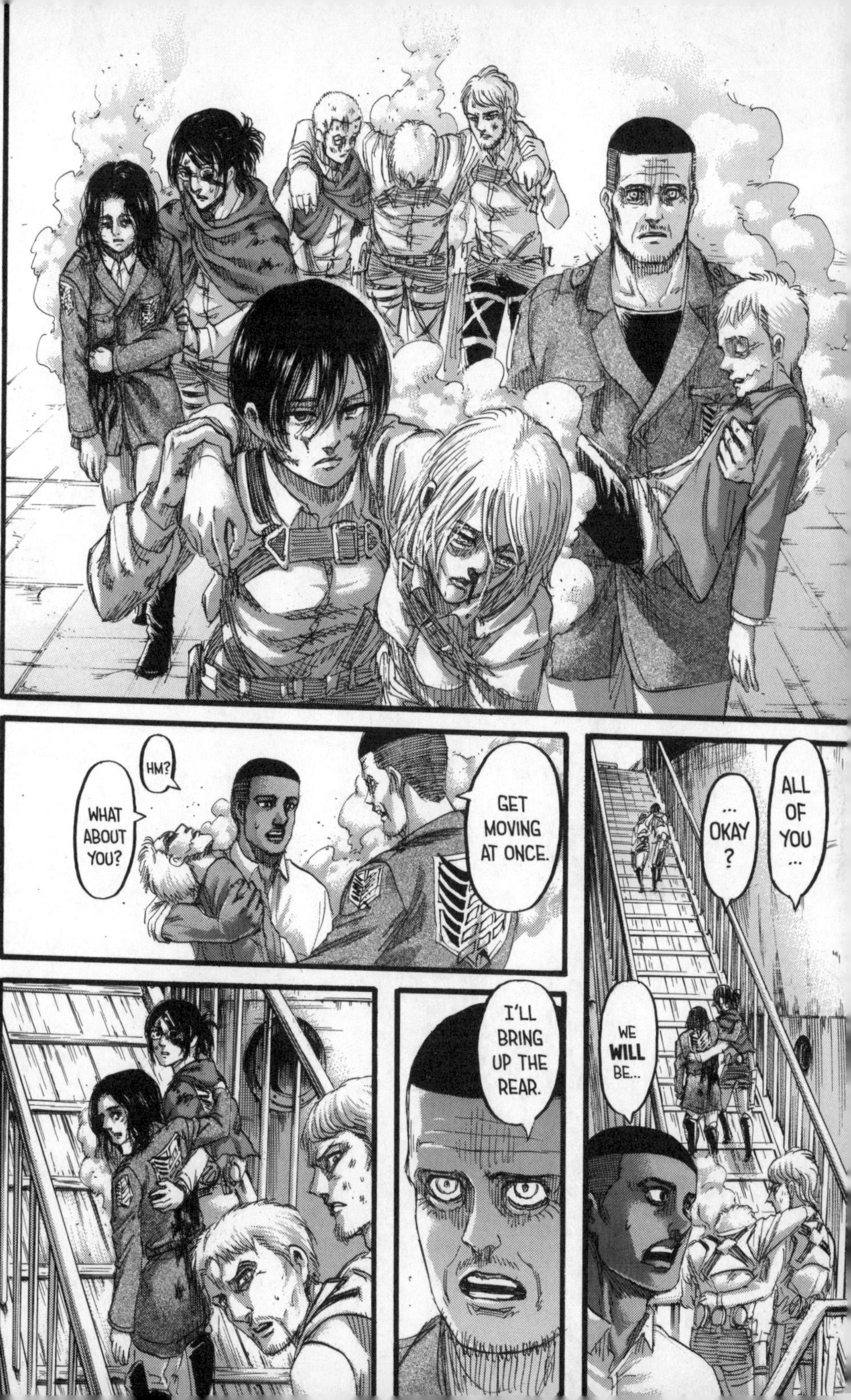
ALL OF YOU ...
... OKAY ?
WE **WILL** BE...
GET MOVING AT ONCE.
HM?
WHAT ABOUT YOU?
I'LL BRING UP THE REAR.

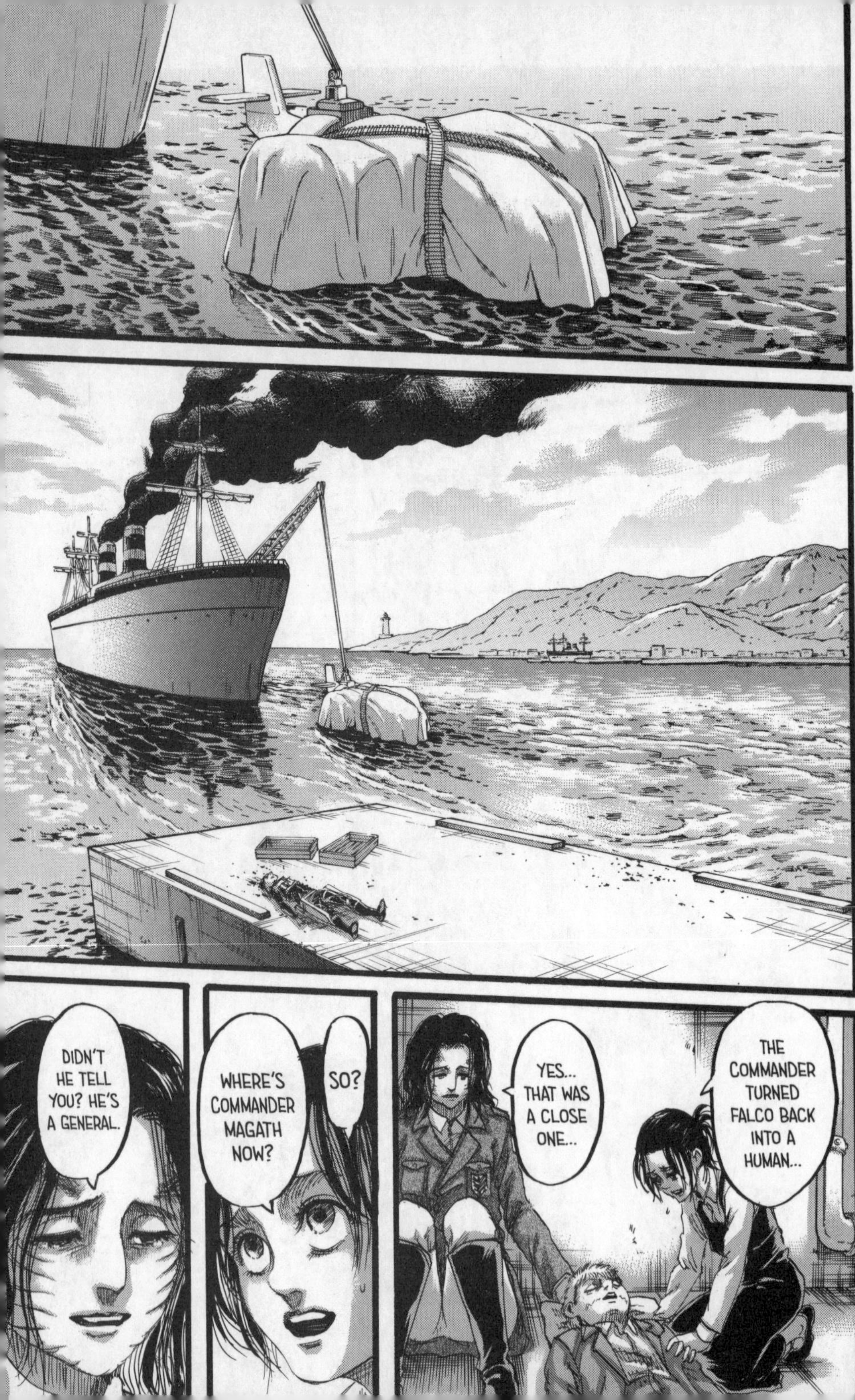
THE COMMANDER TURNED FALCO BACK INTO A HUMAN...
YES... THAT WAS A CLOSE ONE...
SO?
WHERE'S COMMANDER MAGATH NOW?
DIDN'T HE TELL YOU? HE'S A GENERAL.

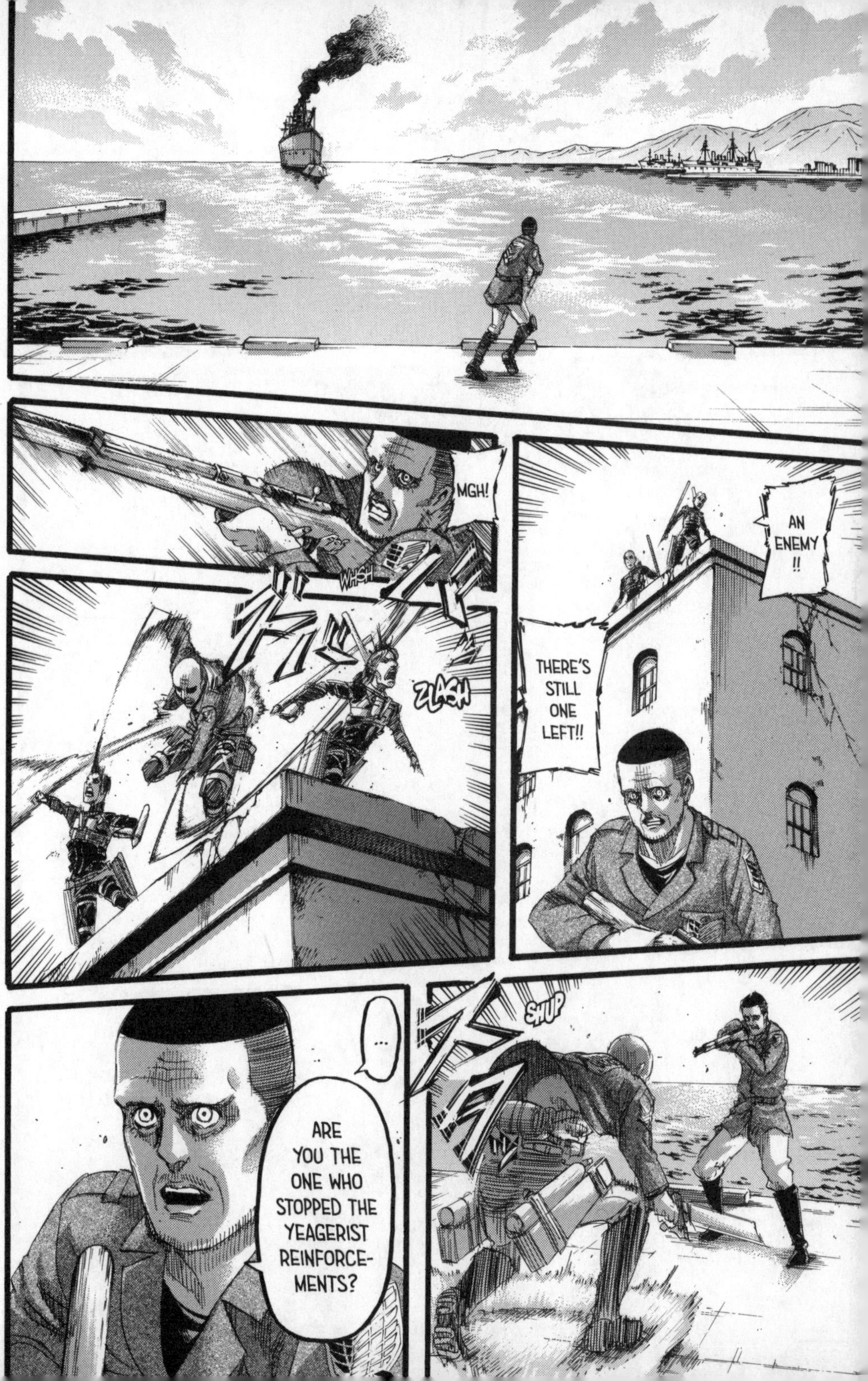
AN ENEMY !!
THERE'S STILL ONE LEFT!!
MGH!
WHSH
ZLASH
SHUP
...
ARE YOU THE ONE WHO STOPPED THE YEAGERIST REINFORCE-MENTS?

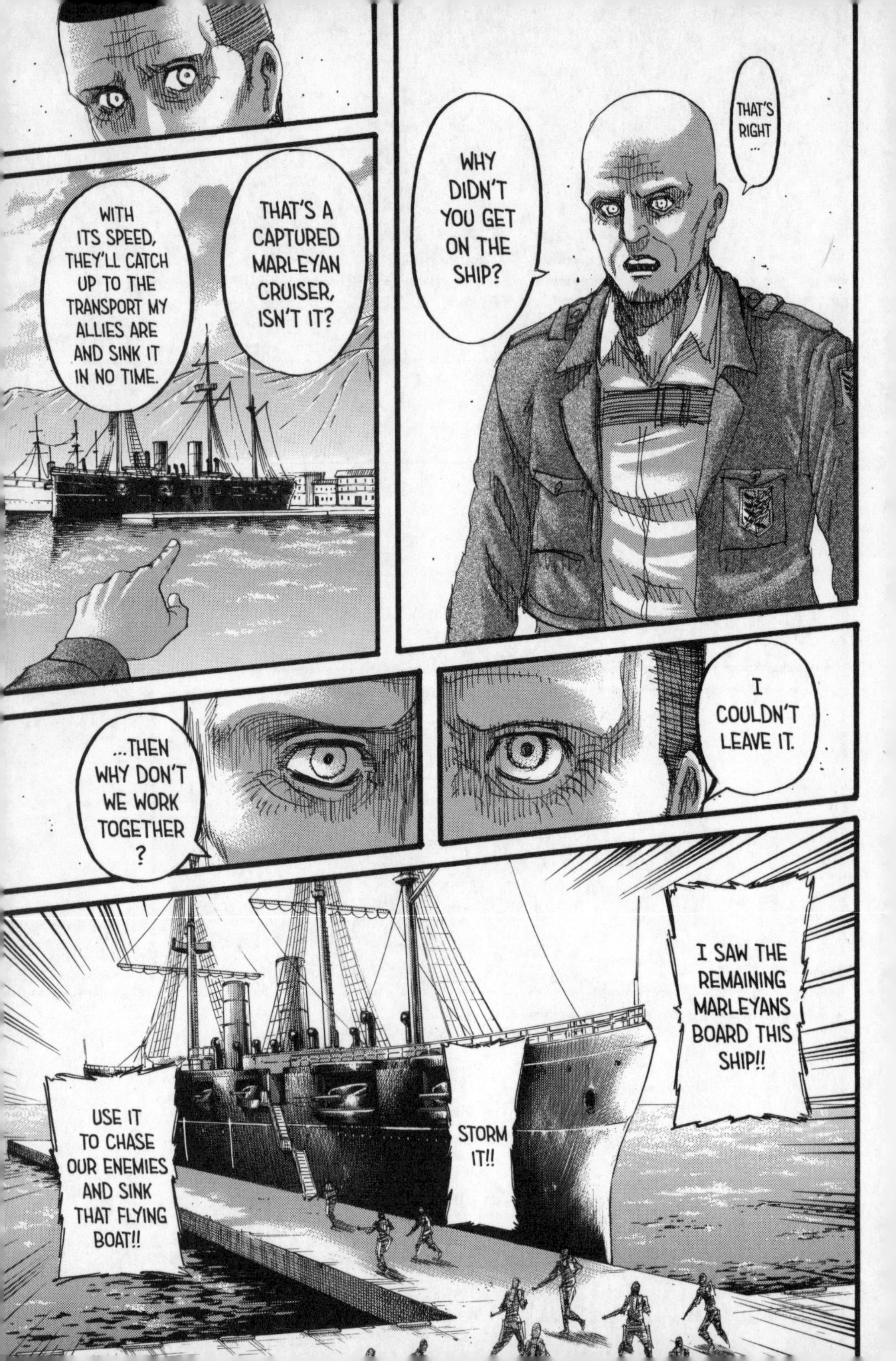
THAT'S RIGHT ...
WHY DIDN'T YOU GET ON THE SHIP?
THAT'S A CAPTURED MARLEYAN CRUISER, ISN'T IT?
WITH ITS SPEED, THEY'LL CATCH UP TO THE TRANSPORT MY ALLIES ARE AND SINK IT IN NO TIME.
I COULDN'T LEAVE IT.
...THEN WHY DON'T WE WORK TOGETHER ?
I SAW THE REMAINING MARLEYANS BOARD THIS SHIP!!
STORM IT!!
USE IT TO CHASE OUR ENEMIES AND SINK THAT FLYING BOAT!!

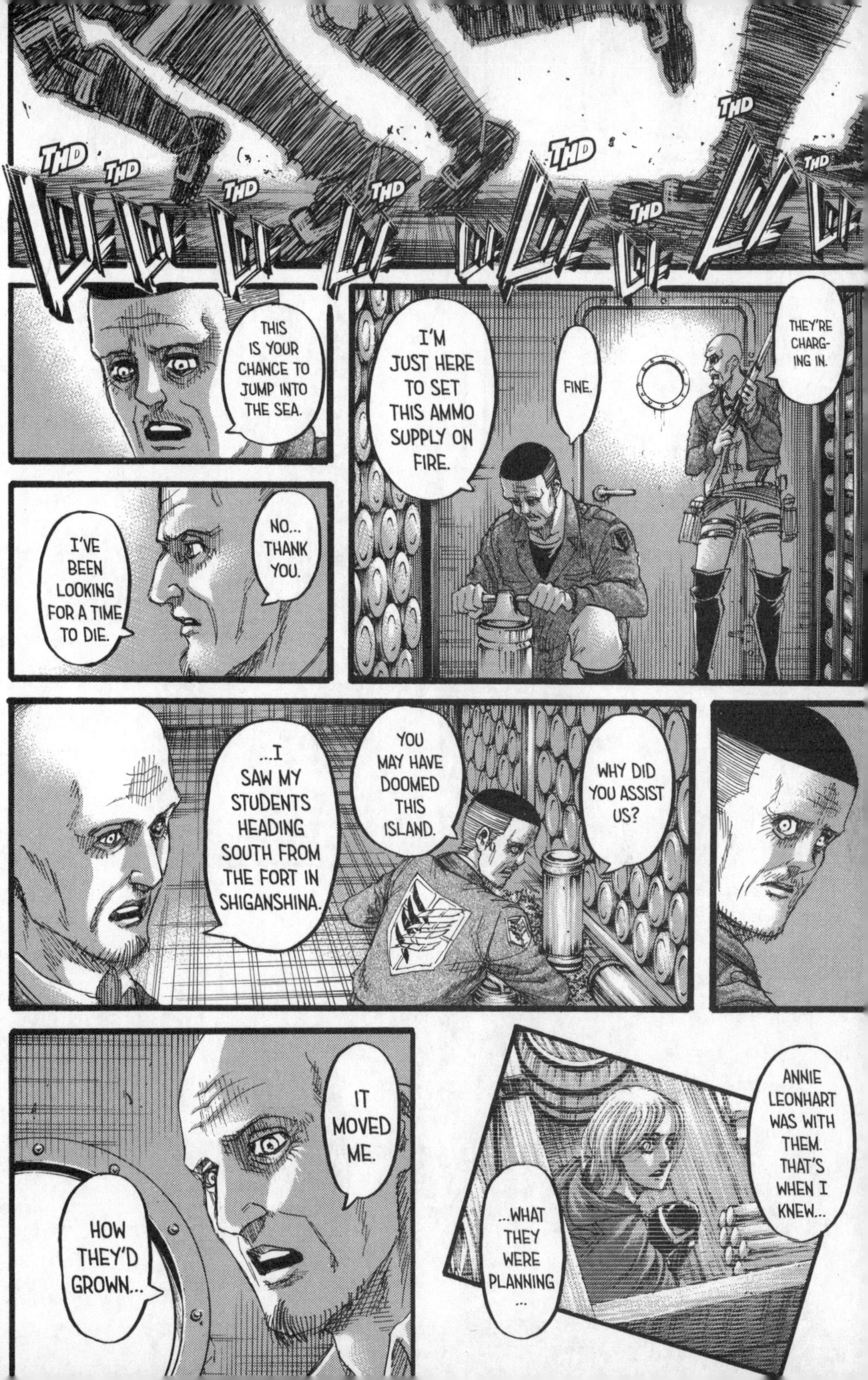
THD
THD
THD
THD
THD
THD
THD
THD
THD
THEY'RE CHARGING IN.
FINE.
I'M JUST HERE TO SET THIS AMMO SUPPLY ON FIRE.
THIS IS YOUR CHANCE TO JUMP INTO THE SEA.
NO... THANK YOU.
I'VE BEEN LOOKING FOR A TIME TO DIE.
WHY DID YOU ASSIST US?
YOU MAY HAVE DOOMED THIS ISLAND.
...I SAW MY STUDENTS HEADING SOUTH FROM THE FORT IN SHIGANSHINA.
ANNIE LEONHART WAS WITH THEM. THAT'S WHEN I KNEW...
...WHAT THEY WERE PLANNING...
IT MOVED ME.
HOW THEY'D GROWN...

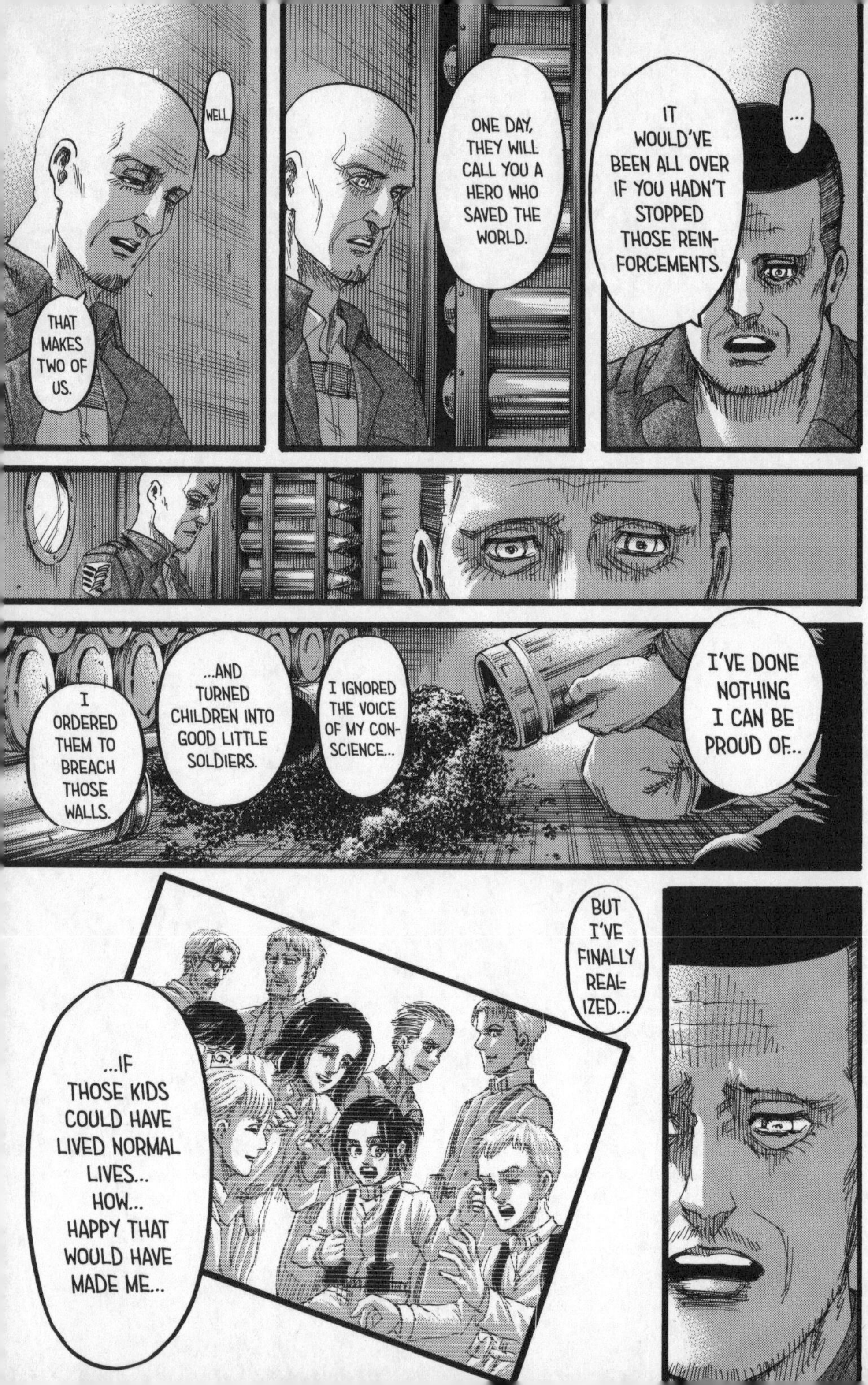
...
IT WOULD'VE BEEN ALL OVER IF YOU HADN'T STOPPED THOSE REINFORCEMENTS.
ONE DAY, THEY WILL CALL YOU A HERO WHO SAVED THE WORLD.
WELL.
THAT MAKES TWO OF US.
I'VE DONE NOTHING I CAN BE PROUD OF...
I IGNORED THE VOICE OF MY CONSCIENCE...
...AND TURNED CHILDREN INTO GOOD LITTLE SOLDIERS.
I ORDERED THEM TO BREACH THOSE WALLS.
BUT I'VE FINALLY REALIZED...
...IF THOSE KIDS COULD HAVE LIVED NORMAL LIVES... HOW... HAPPY THAT WOULD HAVE MADE ME...

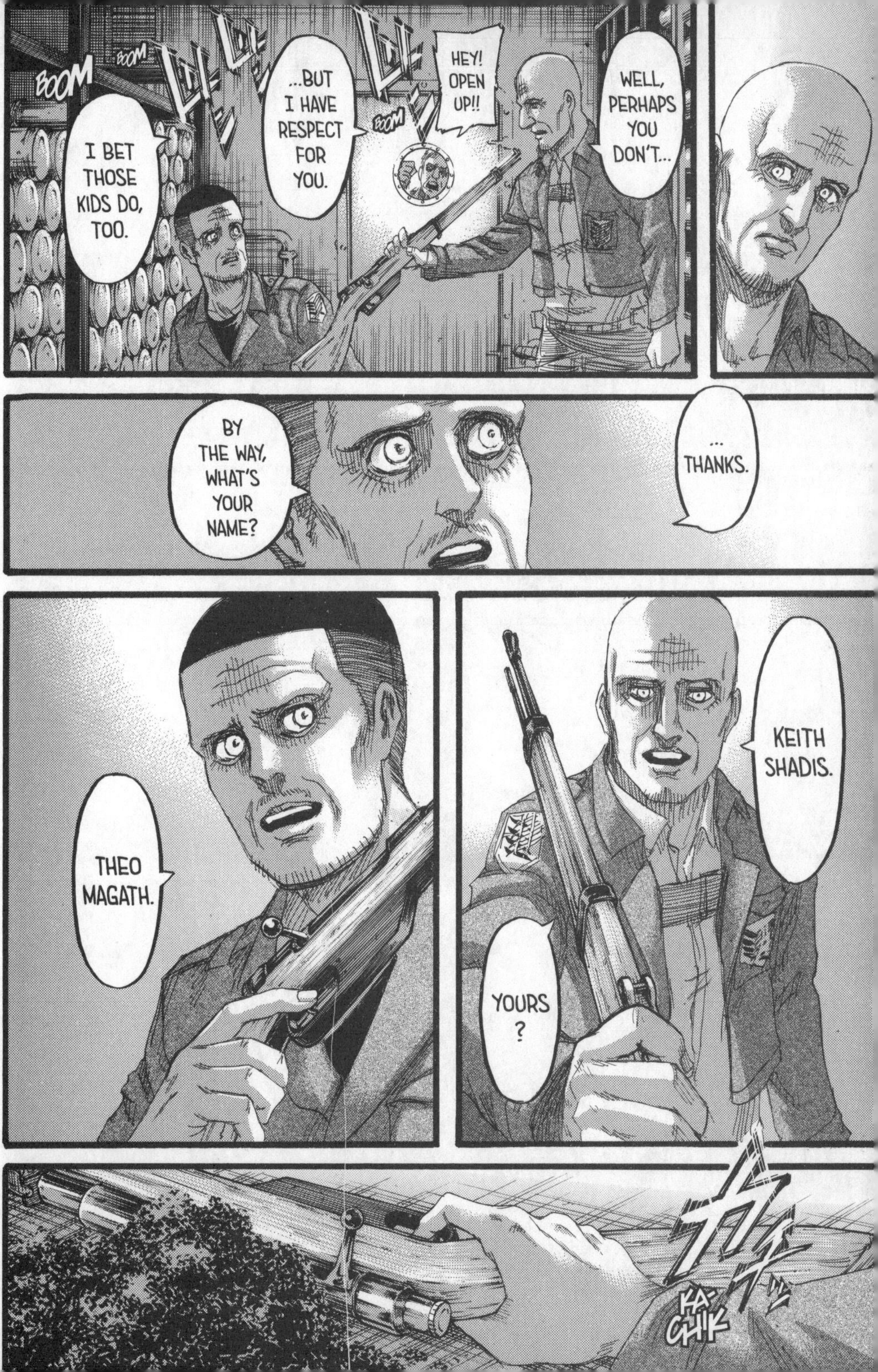
WELL, PERHAPS YOU DON'T...
HEY! OPEN UP!!
BOOM
...BUT I HAVE RESPECT FOR YOU.
BOOM
BOOM
I BET THOSE KIDS DO, TOO.
... THANKS.
BY THE WAY, WHAT'S YOUR NAME?
KEITH SHADIS.
YOURS?
THEO MAGATH.
KA-CHIK

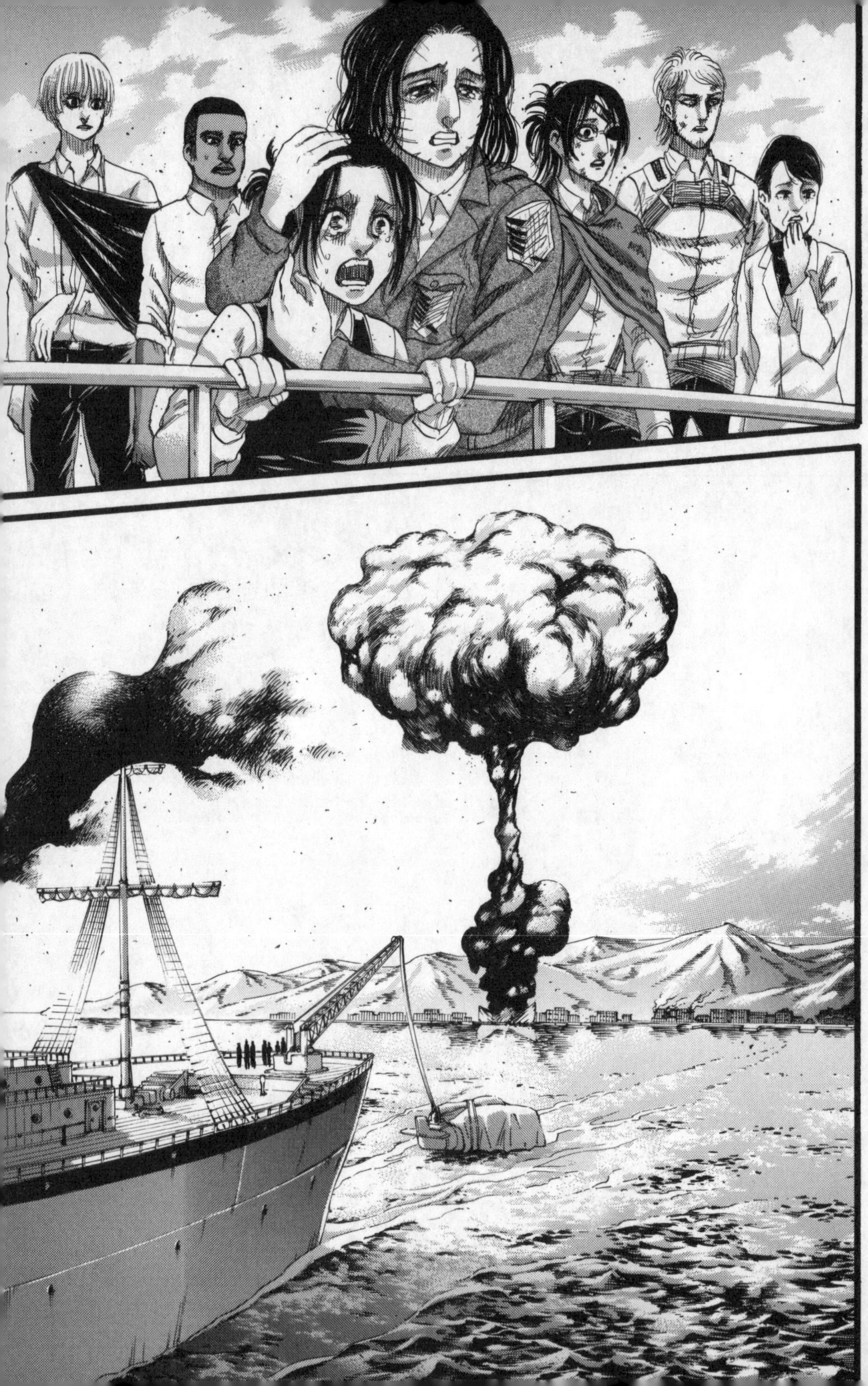

ATTACK on TITAN

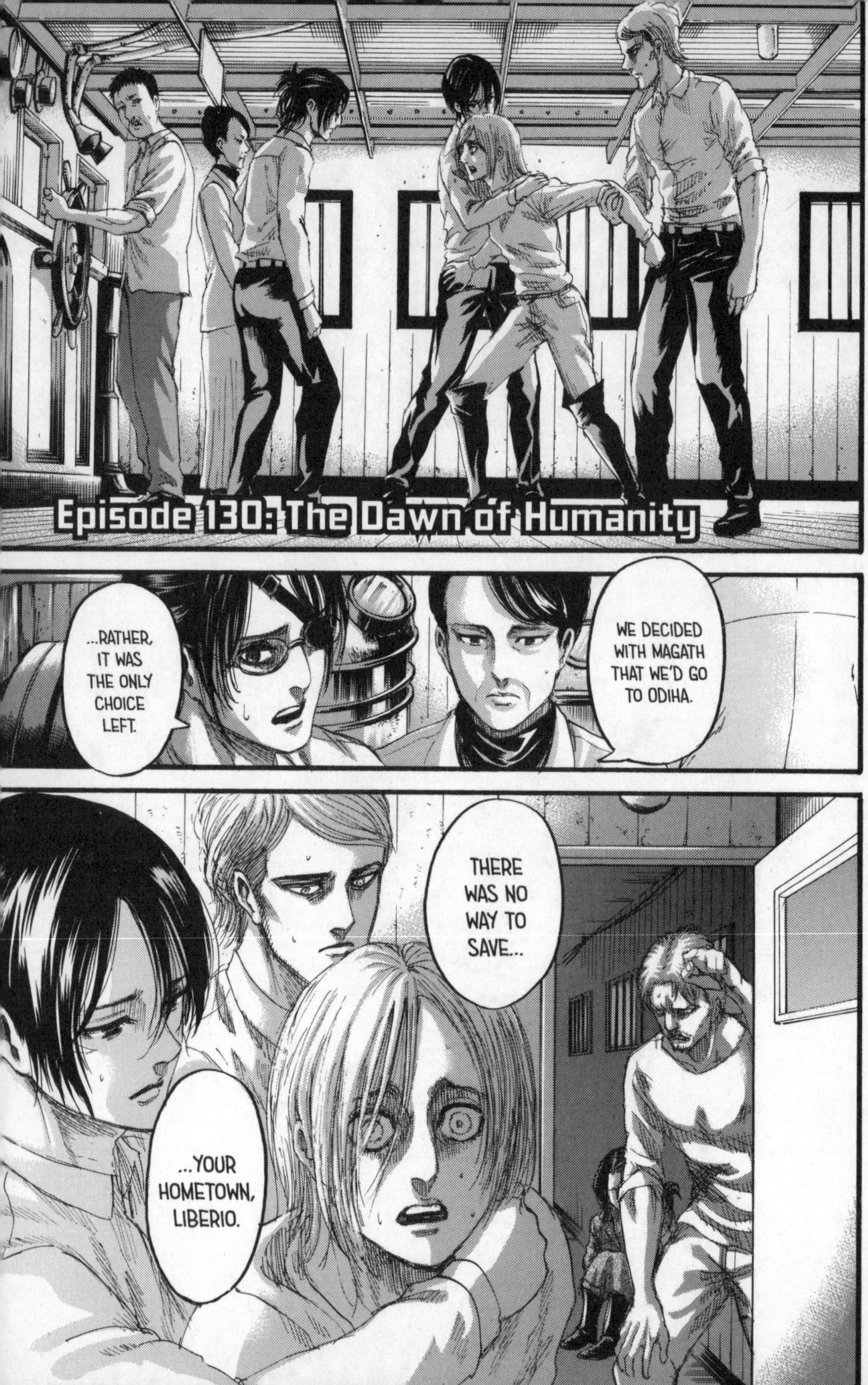
Episode 130: The Dawn of Humanity
WE DECIDED WITH MAGATH THAT WE'D GO TO ODIHA.
...RATHER, IT WAS THE ONLY CHOICE LEFT.
THERE WAS NO WAY TO SAVE...
...YOUR HOMETOWN, LIBERIO.

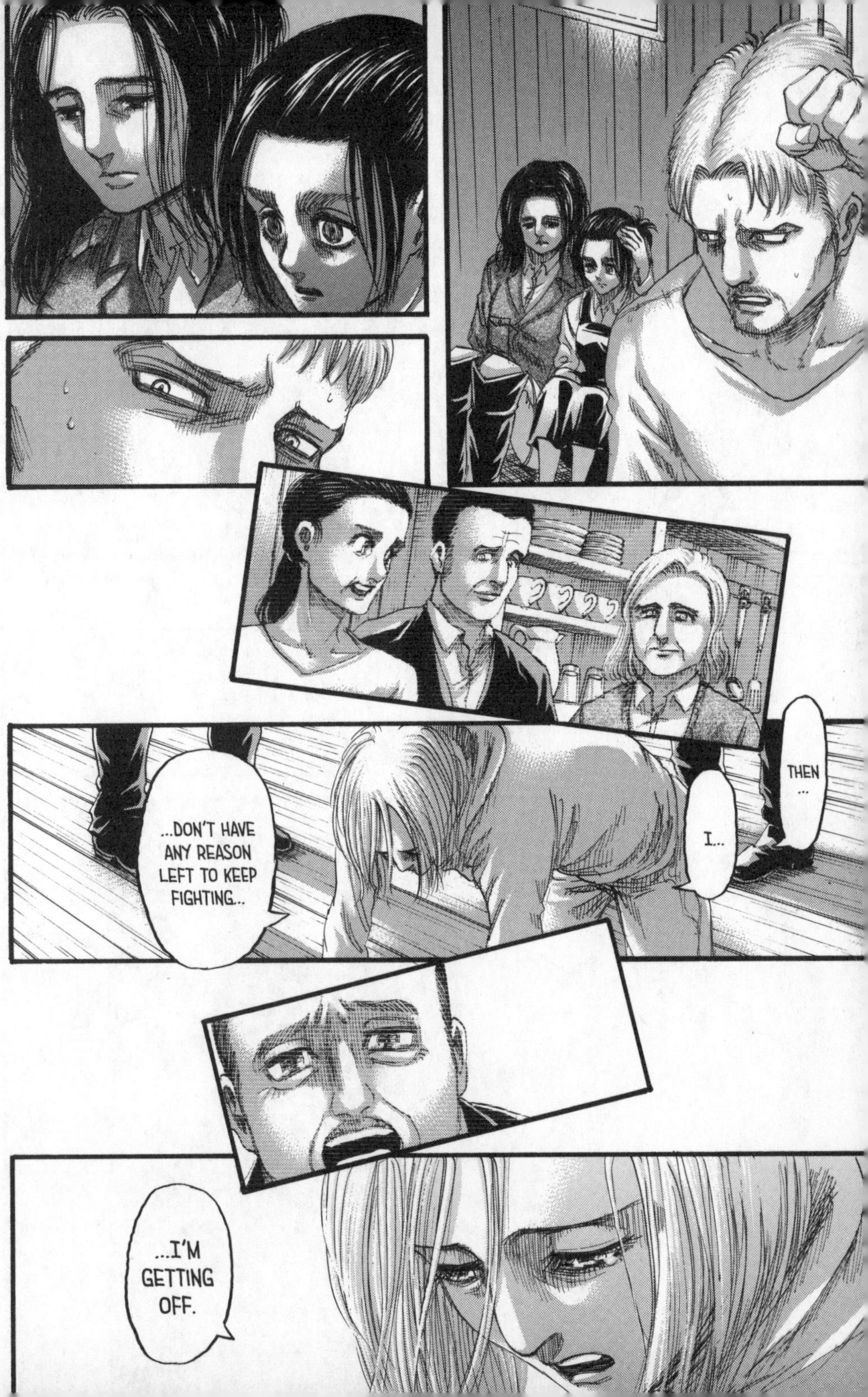
THEN...
I...
...DON'T HAVE ANY REASON LEFT TO KEEP FIGHTING...
...I'M GETTING OFF.

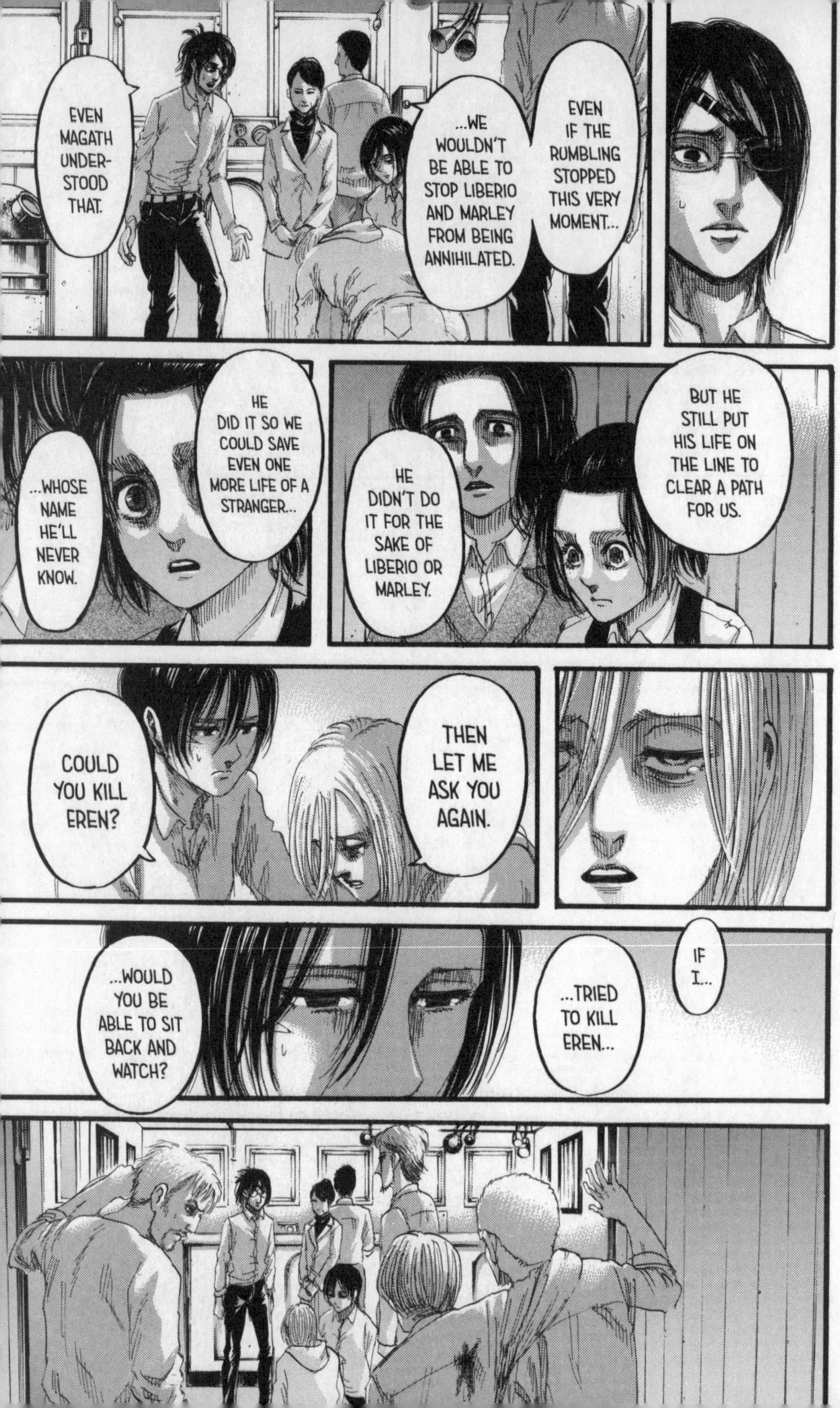
EVEN IF THE RUMBLING STOPPED THIS VERY MOMENT...
...WE WOULDN'T BE ABLE TO STOP LIBERIO AND MARLEY FROM BEING ANNIHILATED.
EVEN MAGATH UNDERSTOOD THAT.
BUT HE STILL PUT HIS LIFE ON THE LINE TO CLEAR A PATH FOR US.
HE DIDN'T DO IT FOR THE SAKE OF LIBERIO OR MARLEY.
HE DID IT SO WE COULD SAVE EVEN ONE MORE LIFE OF A STRANGER...
...WHOSE NAME HE'LL NEVER KNOW.
THEN LET ME ASK YOU AGAIN.
COULD YOU KILL EREN?
IF I...
...TRIED TO KILL EREN...
...WOULD YOU BE ABLE TO SIT BACK AND WATCH?

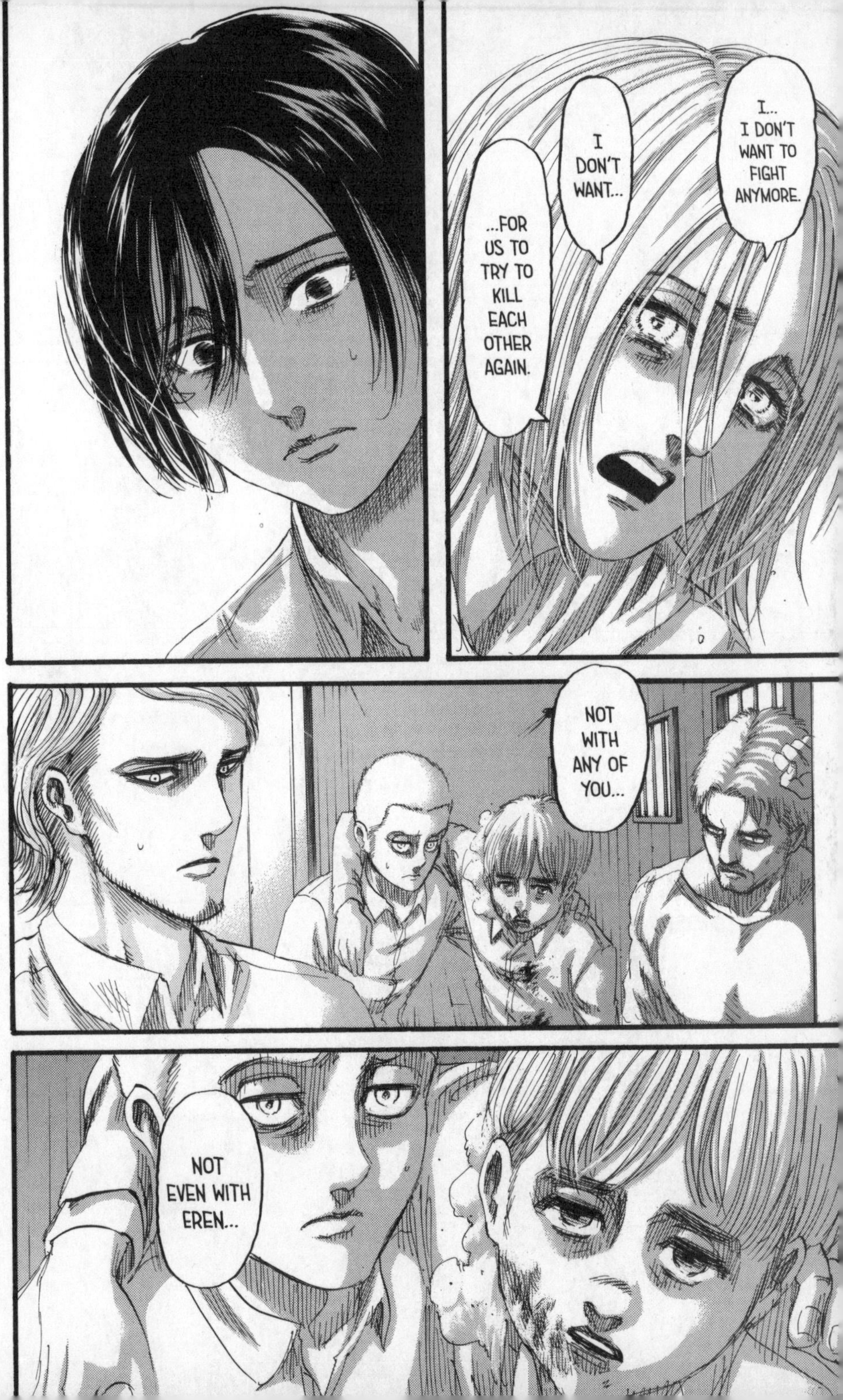
I... I DON'T WANT TO FIGHT ANYMORE.
I DON'T WANT...
...FOR US TO TRY TO KILL EACH OTHER AGAIN.
NOT WITH ANY OF YOU...
NOT EVEN WITH EREN...

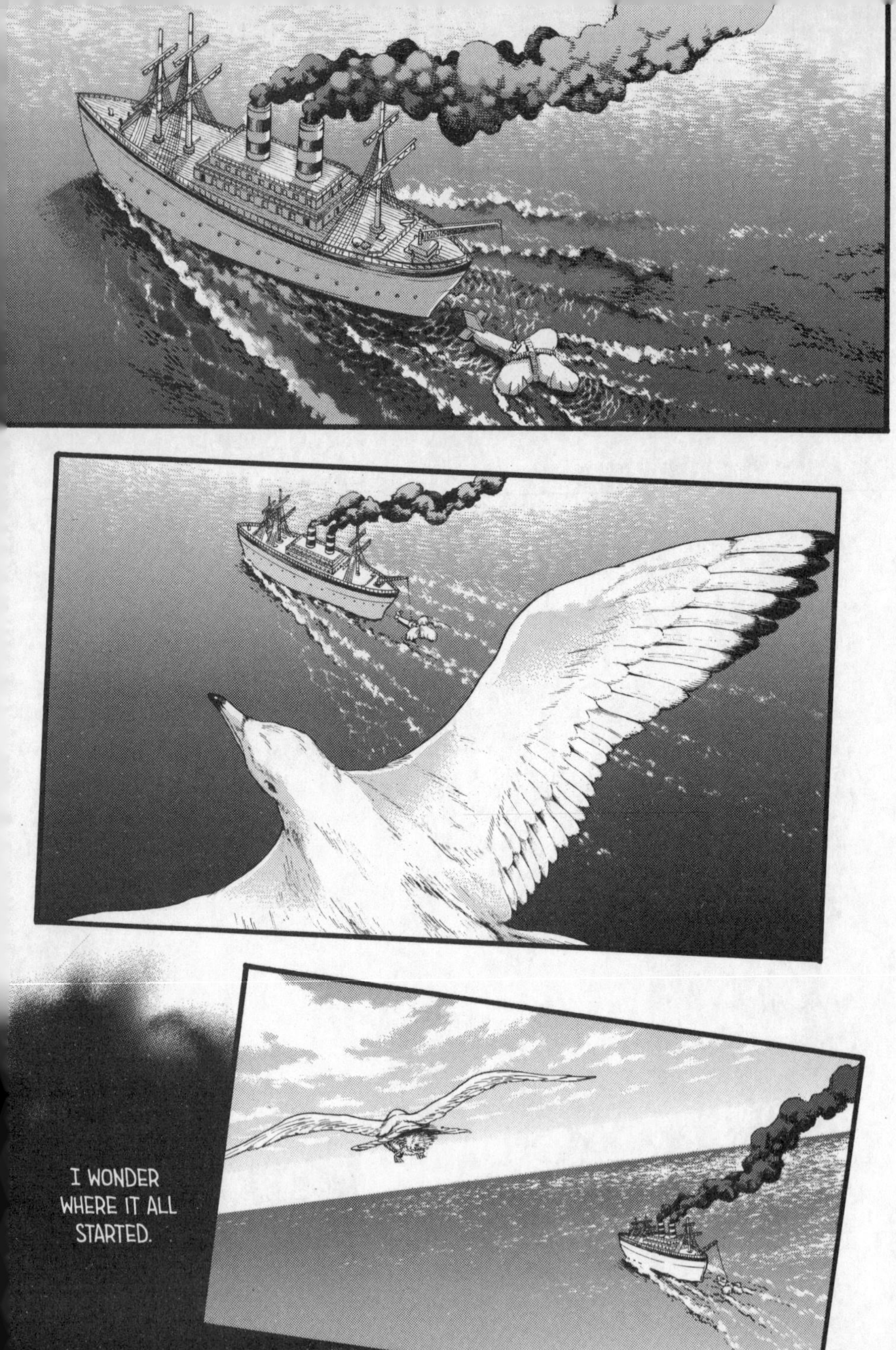
I WONDER WHERE IT ALL STARTED.

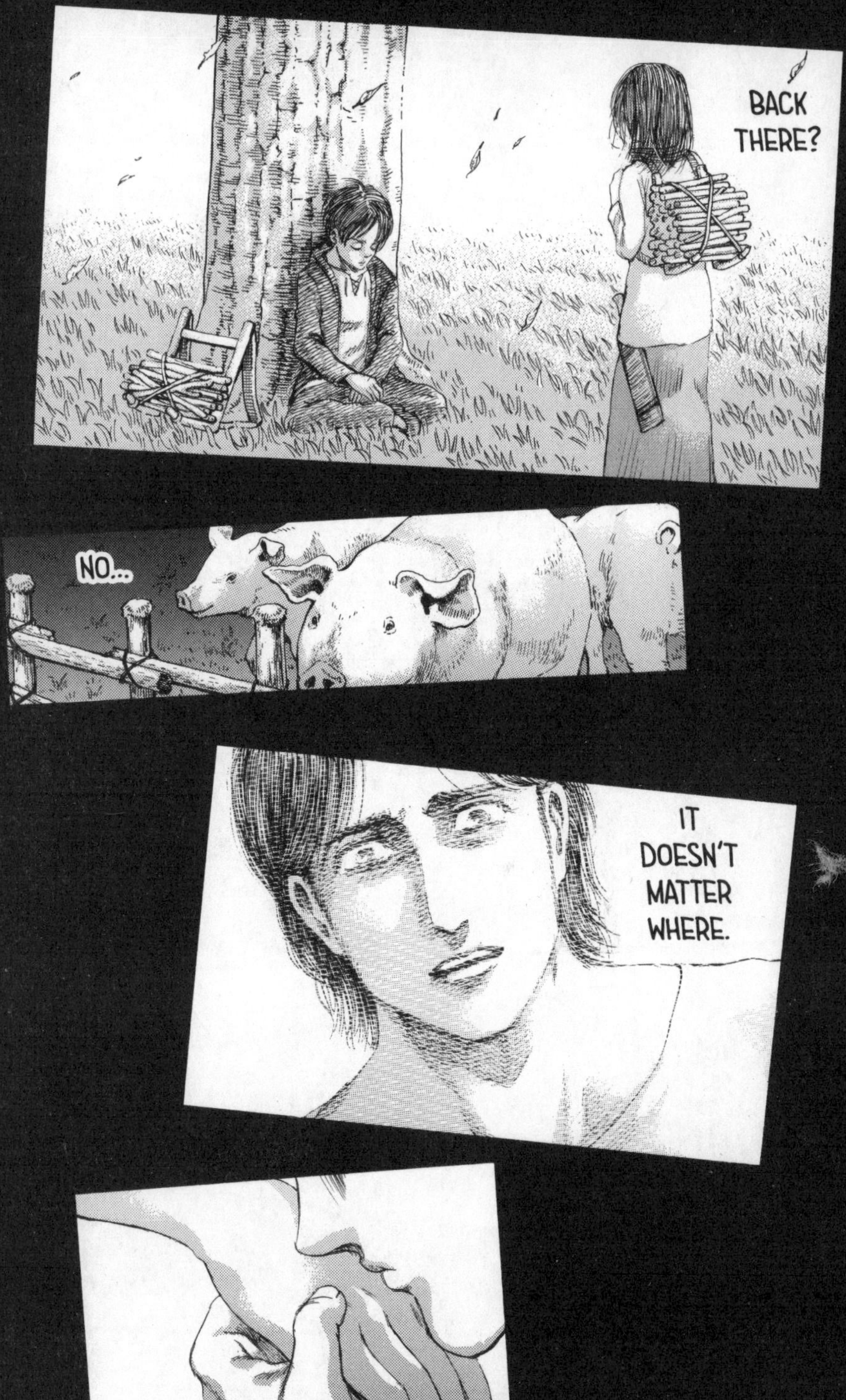
BACK THERE?
NO...
IT DOESN'T MATTER WHERE.

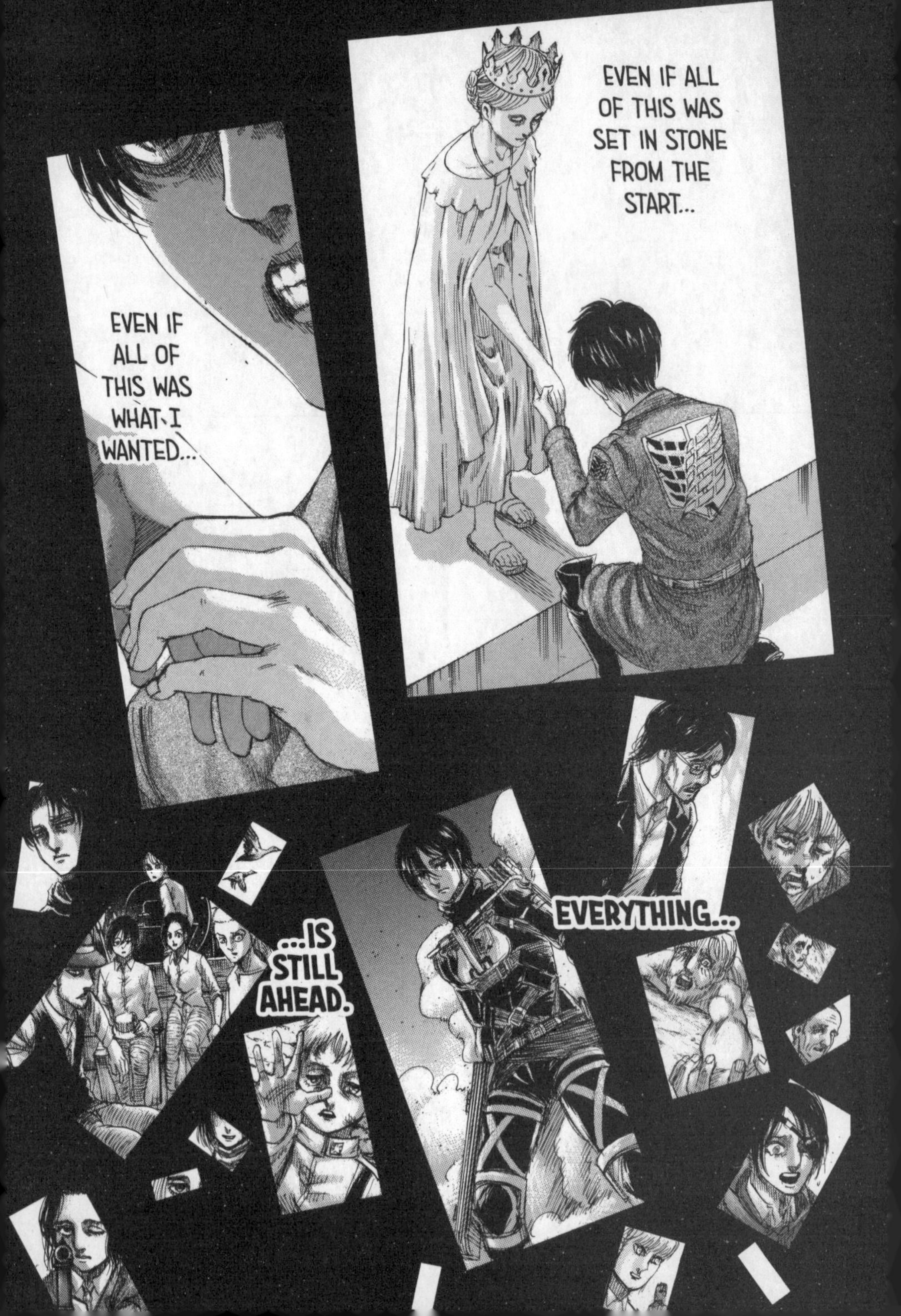
EVEN IF ALL OF THIS WAS SET IN STONE FROM THE START...
EVEN IF ALL OF THIS WAS WHAT I WANTED...
EVERYTHING...
...IS STILL AHEAD.

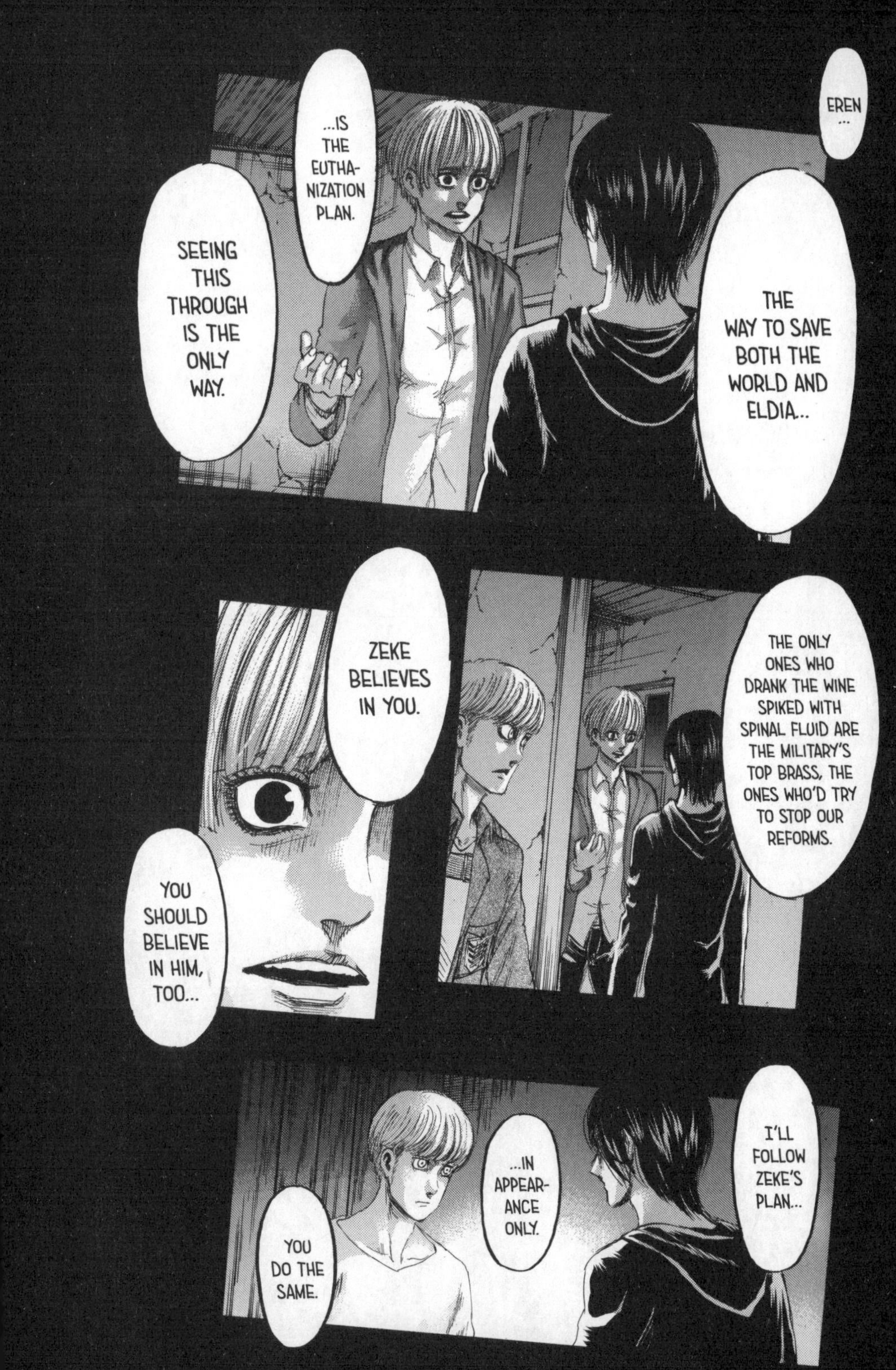
EREN...
THE WAY TO SAVE BOTH THE WORLD AND ELDIA...
...IS THE EUTHANIZATION PLAN.
SEEING THIS THROUGH IS THE ONLY WAY.
THE ONLY ONES WHO DRANK THE WINE SPIKED WITH SPINAL FLUID ARE THE MILITARY'S TOP BRASS, THE ONES WHO'D TRY TO STOP OUR REFORMS.
ZEKE BELIEVES IN YOU.
YOU SHOULD BELIEVE IN HIM, TOO...
I'LL FOLLOW ZEKE'S PLAN...
...IN APPEARANCE ONLY.
YOU DO THE SAME.

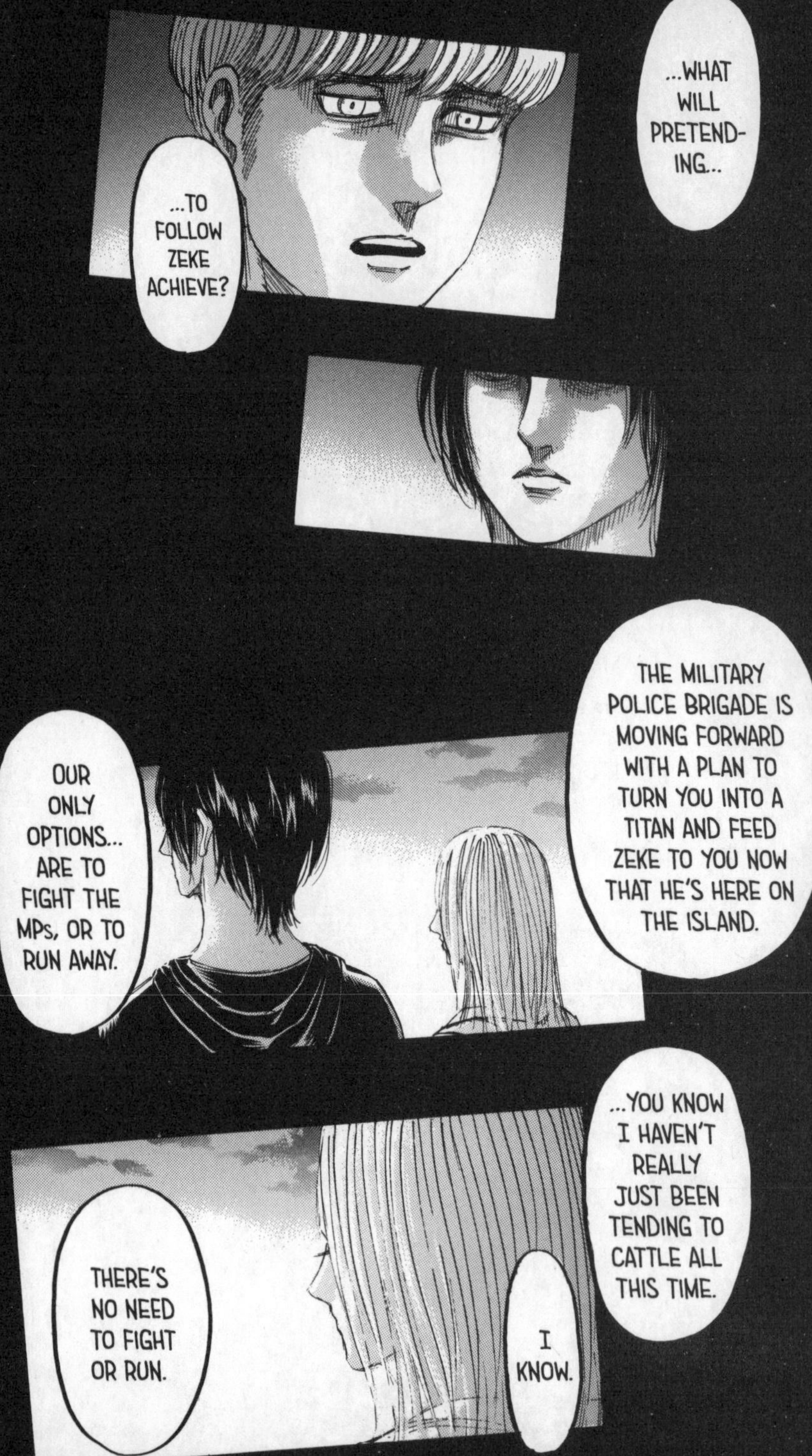
...WHAT WILL PRETEND-ING...
...TO FOLLOW ZEKE ACHIEVE?
THE MILITARY POLICE BRIGADE IS MOVING FORWARD WITH A PLAN TO TURN YOU INTO A TITAN AND FEED ZEKE TO YOU NOW THAT HE'S HERE ON THE ISLAND.
OUR ONLY OPTIONS... ARE TO FIGHT THE MPs, OR TO RUN AWAY.
...YOU KNOW I HAVEN'T REALLY JUST BEEN TENDING TO CATTLE ALL THIS TIME.
I KNOW.
THERE'S NO NEED TO FIGHT OR RUN.

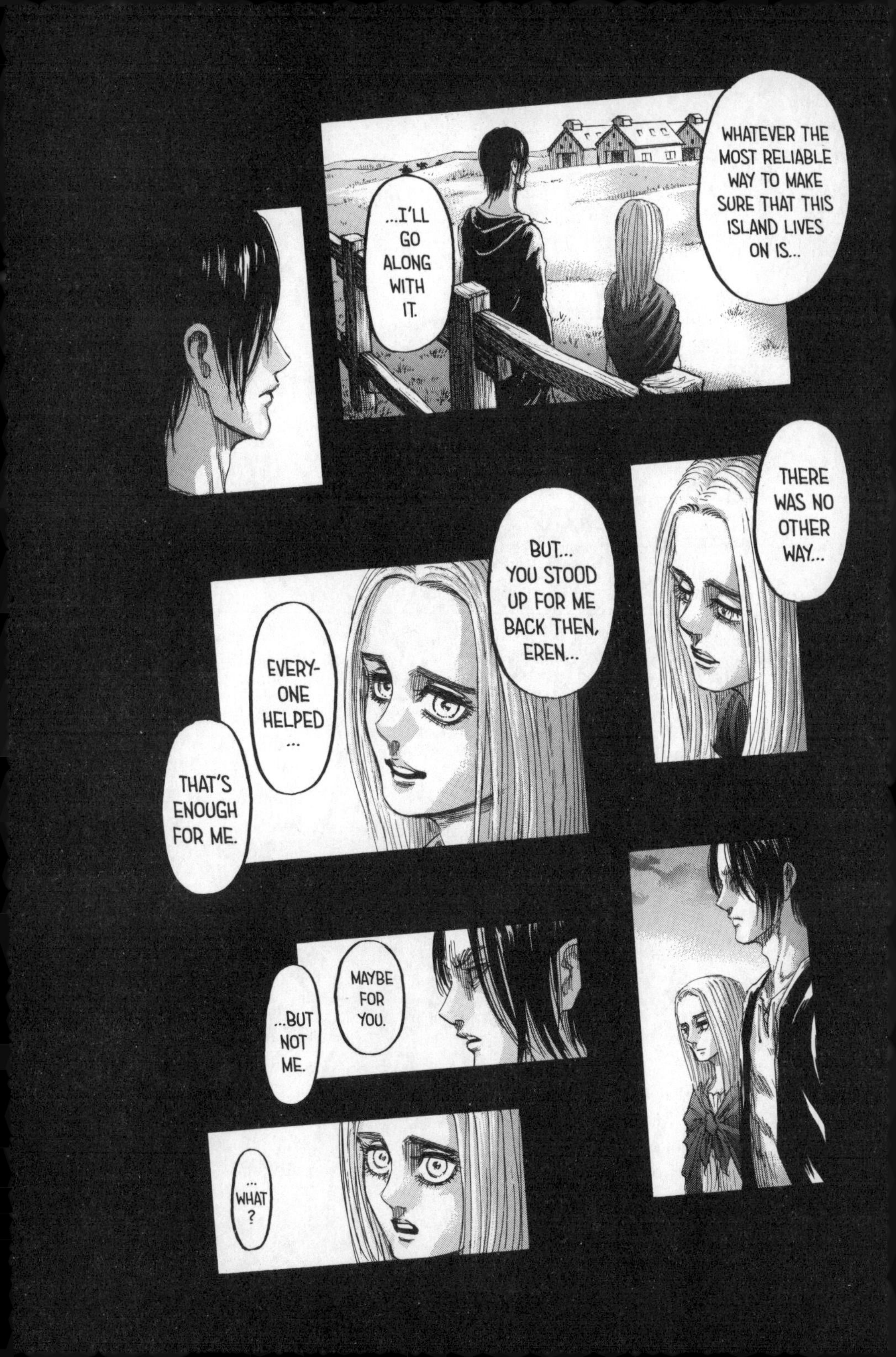
WHATEVER THE MOST RELIABLE WAY TO MAKE SURE THAT THIS ISLAND LIVES ON IS...
...I'LL GO ALONG WITH IT.
THERE WAS NO OTHER WAY...
BUT... YOU STOOD UP FOR ME BACK THEN, EREN...
EVERY-ONE HELPED ...
THAT'S ENOUGH FOR ME.
MAYBE FOR YOU.
...BUT NOT ME.
... WHAT ?

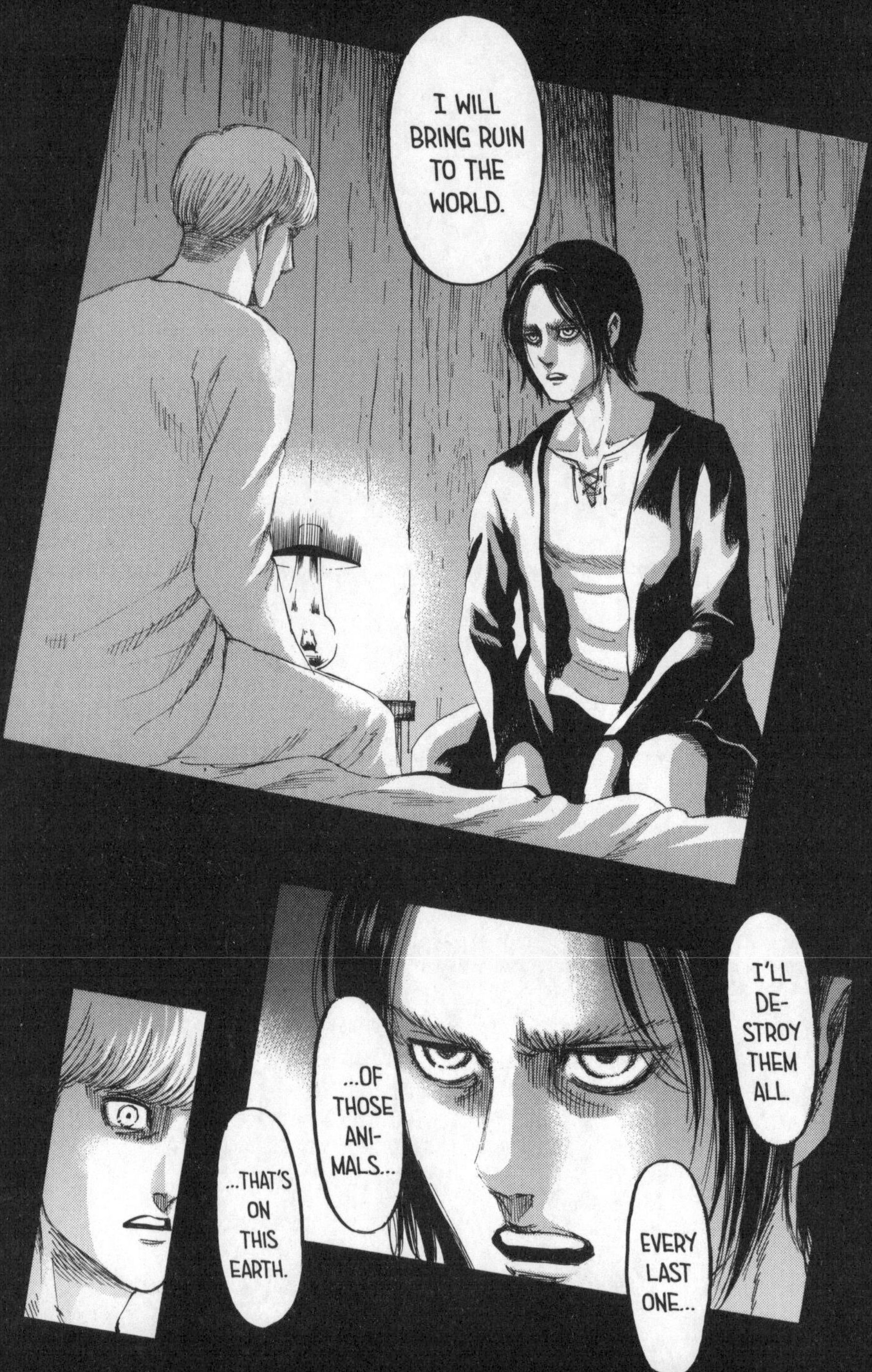
I WILL BRING RUIN TO THE WORLD.
I'LL DESTROY THEM ALL.
EVERY LAST ONE...
...OF THOSE ANIMALS...
...THAT'S ON THIS EARTH.

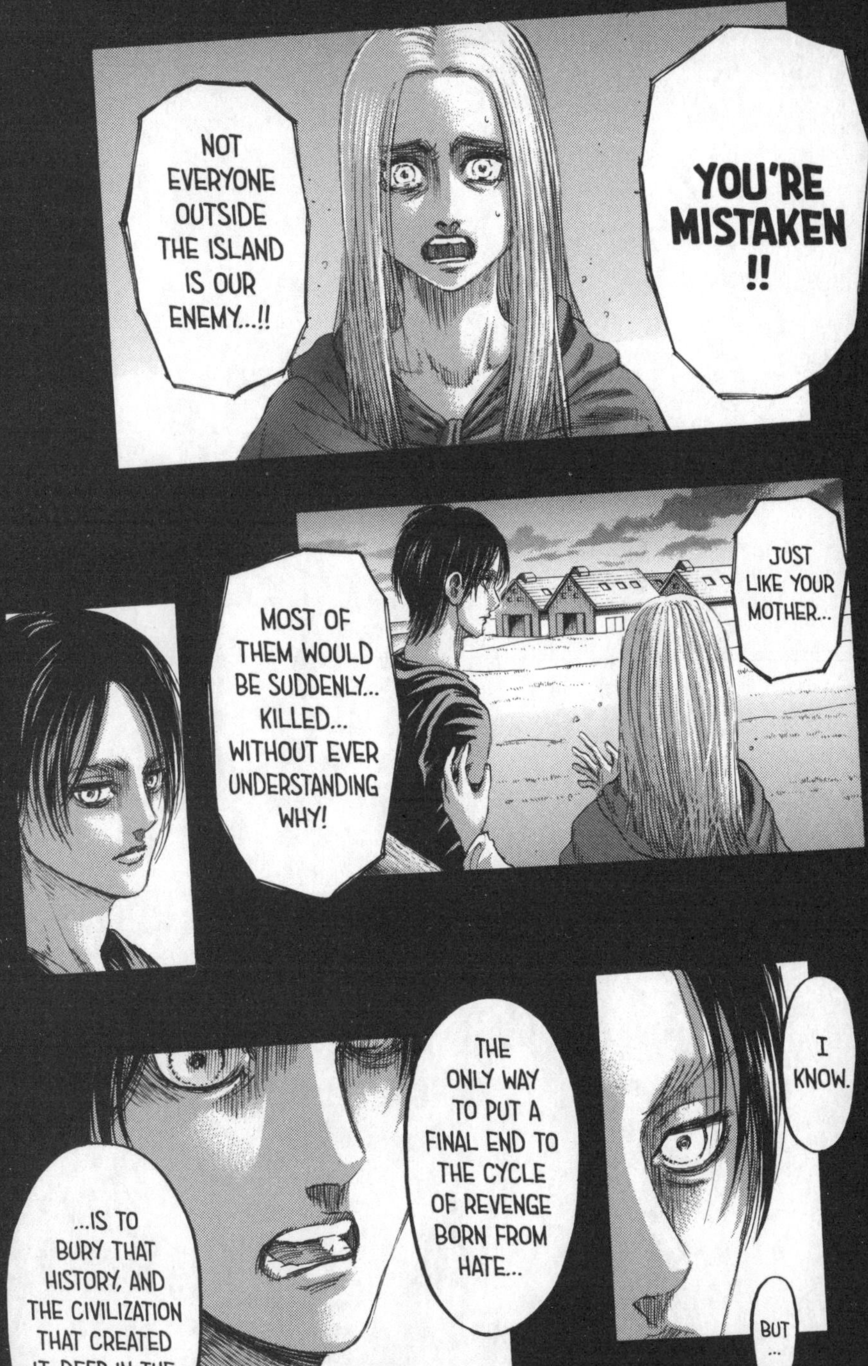
YOU'RE MISTAKEN !!
NOT EVERYONE OUTSIDE THE ISLAND IS OUR ENEMY...!!
JUST LIKE YOUR MOTHER...
MOST OF THEM WOULD BE SUDDENLY... KILLED... WITHOUT EVER UNDERSTANDING WHY!
I KNOW.
BUT ...
THE ONLY WAY TO PUT A FINAL END TO THE CYCLE OF REVENGE BORN FROM HATE...
...IS TO BURY THAT HISTORY, AND THE CIVILIZATION THAT CREATED IT, DEEP IN THE GROUND.

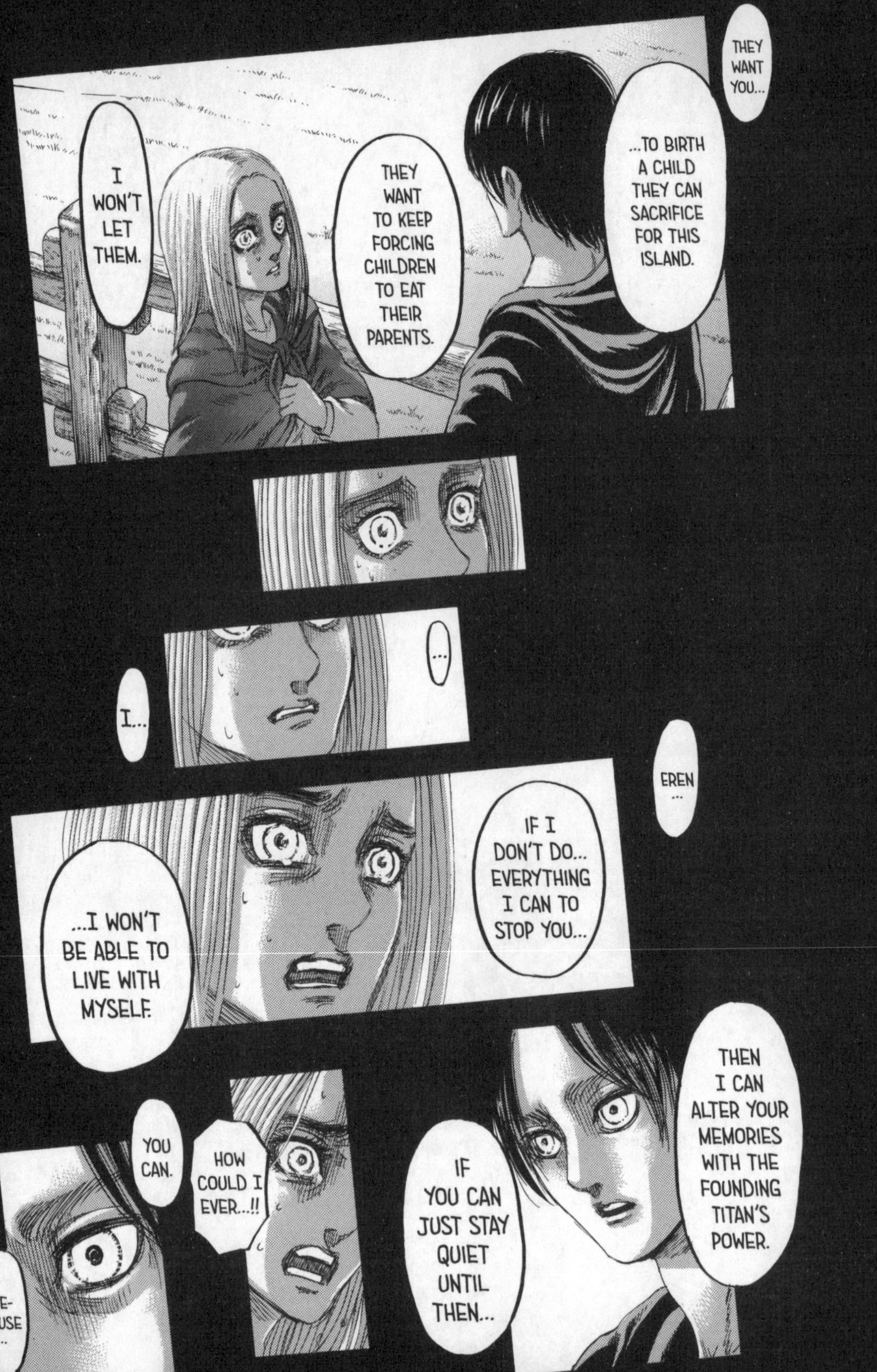
THEY WANT YOU...
...TO BIRTH A CHILD THEY CAN SACRIFICE FOR THIS ISLAND.
THEY WANT TO KEEP FORCING CHILDREN TO EAT THEIR PARENTS.
I WON'T LET THEM.
...
I...
EREN...
IF I DON'T DO... EVERYTHING I CAN TO STOP YOU...
...I WON'T BE ABLE TO LIVE WITH MYSELF.
THEN I CAN ALTER YOUR MEMORIES WITH THE FOUNDING TITAN'S POWER.
IF YOU CAN JUST STAY QUIET UNTIL THEN...
HOW COULD I EVER...!!
YOU CAN.
BE-CAUSE...

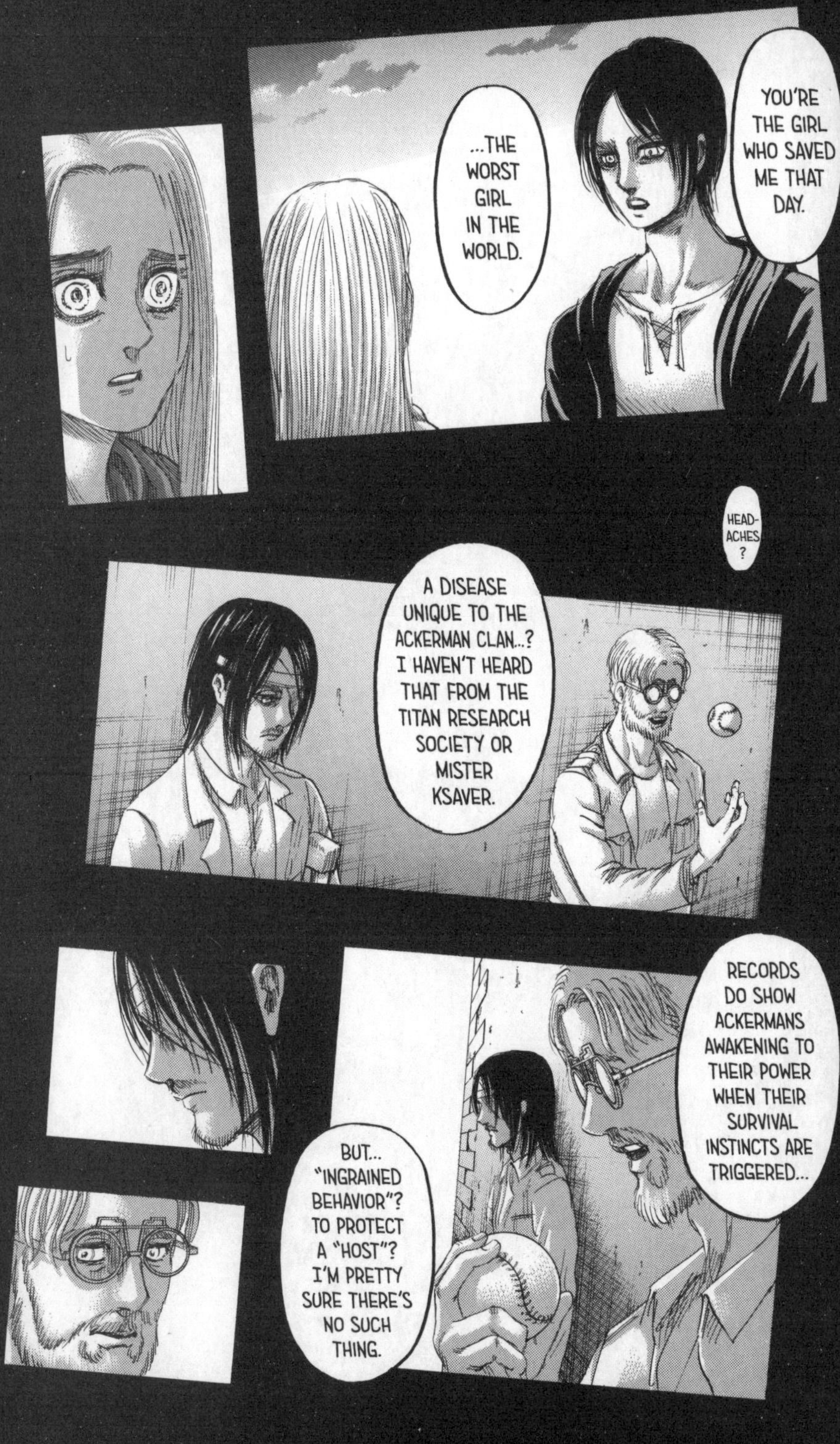
YOU'RE THE GIRL WHO SAVED ME THAT DAY.
...THE WORST GIRL IN THE WORLD.
HEAD-ACHES?
A DISEASE UNIQUE TO THE ACKERMAN CLAN...? I HAVEN'T HEARD THAT FROM THE TITAN RESEARCH SOCIETY OR MISTER KSAVER.
RECORDS DO SHOW ACKERMANS AWAKENING TO THEIR POWER WHEN THEIR SURVIVAL INSTINCTS ARE TRIGGERED...
BUT... "INGRAINED BEHAVIOR"? TO PROTECT A "HOST"? I'M PRETTY SURE THERE'S NO SUCH THING.

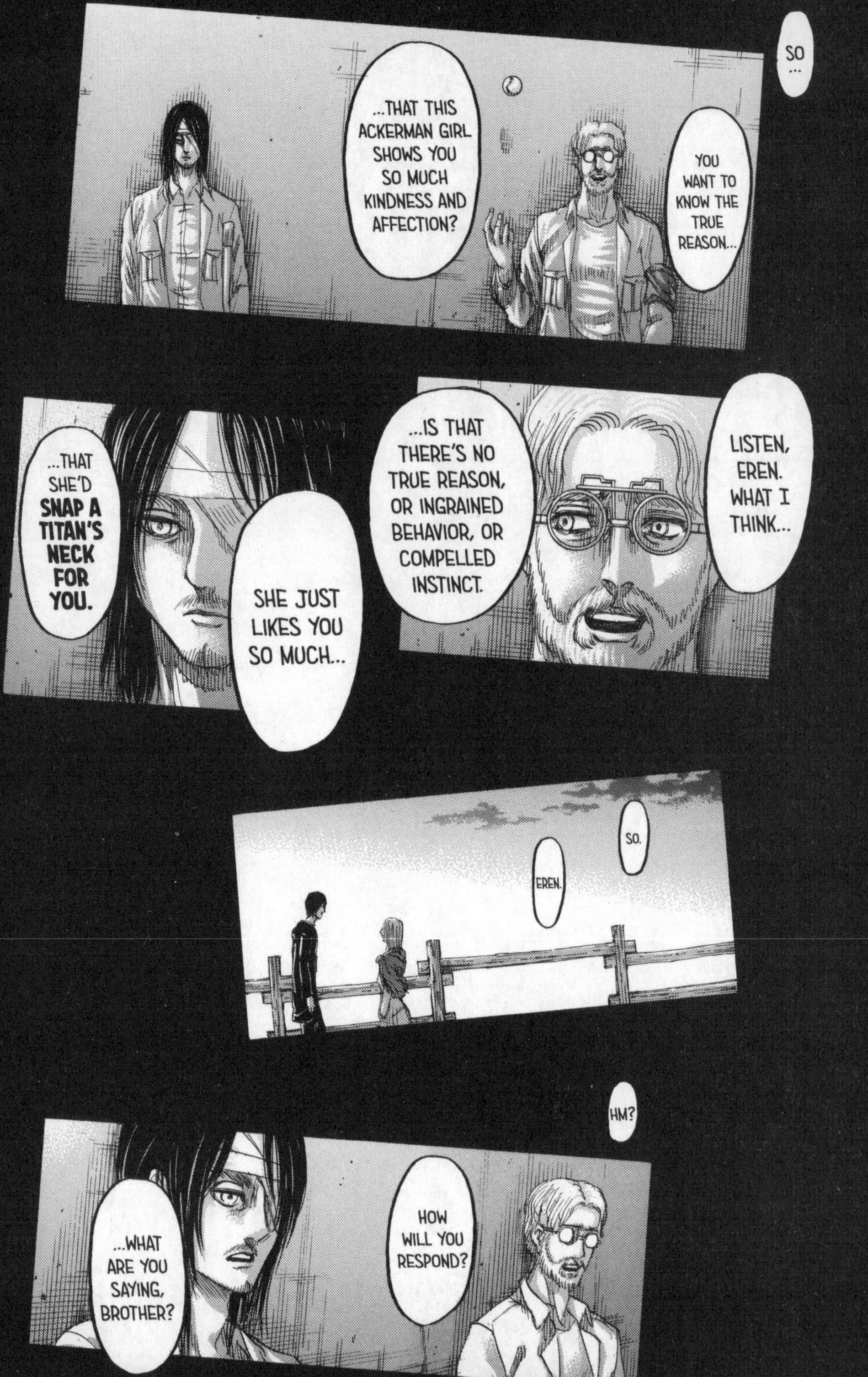
SO...
YOU WANT TO KNOW THE TRUE REASON...
...THAT THIS ACKERMAN GIRL SHOWS YOU SO MUCH KINDNESS AND AFFECTION?
LISTEN, EREN. WHAT I THINK...
...IS THAT THERE'S NO TRUE REASON, OR INGRAINED BEHAVIOR, OR COMPELLED INSTINCT.
SHE JUST LIKES YOU SO MUCH...
...THAT SHE'D **SNAP A TITAN'S NECK FOR YOU.**
SO.
EREN.
HM?
HOW WILL YOU RESPOND?
...WHAT ARE YOU SAYING, BROTHER?

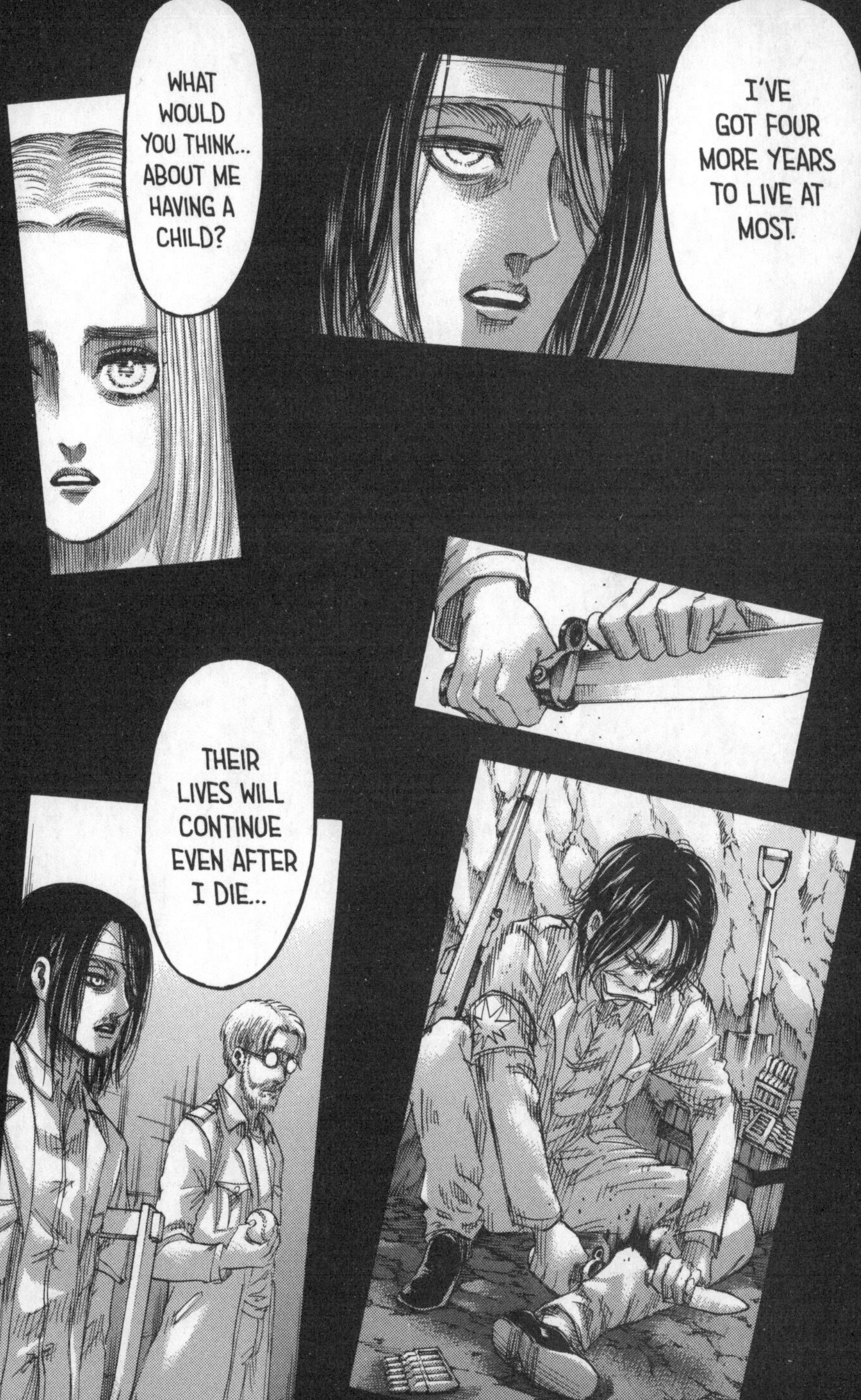
I'VE GOT FOUR MORE YEARS TO LIVE AT MOST.
WHAT WOULD YOU THINK... ABOUT ME HAVING A CHILD?
THEIR LIVES WILL CONTINUE EVEN AFTER I DIE...

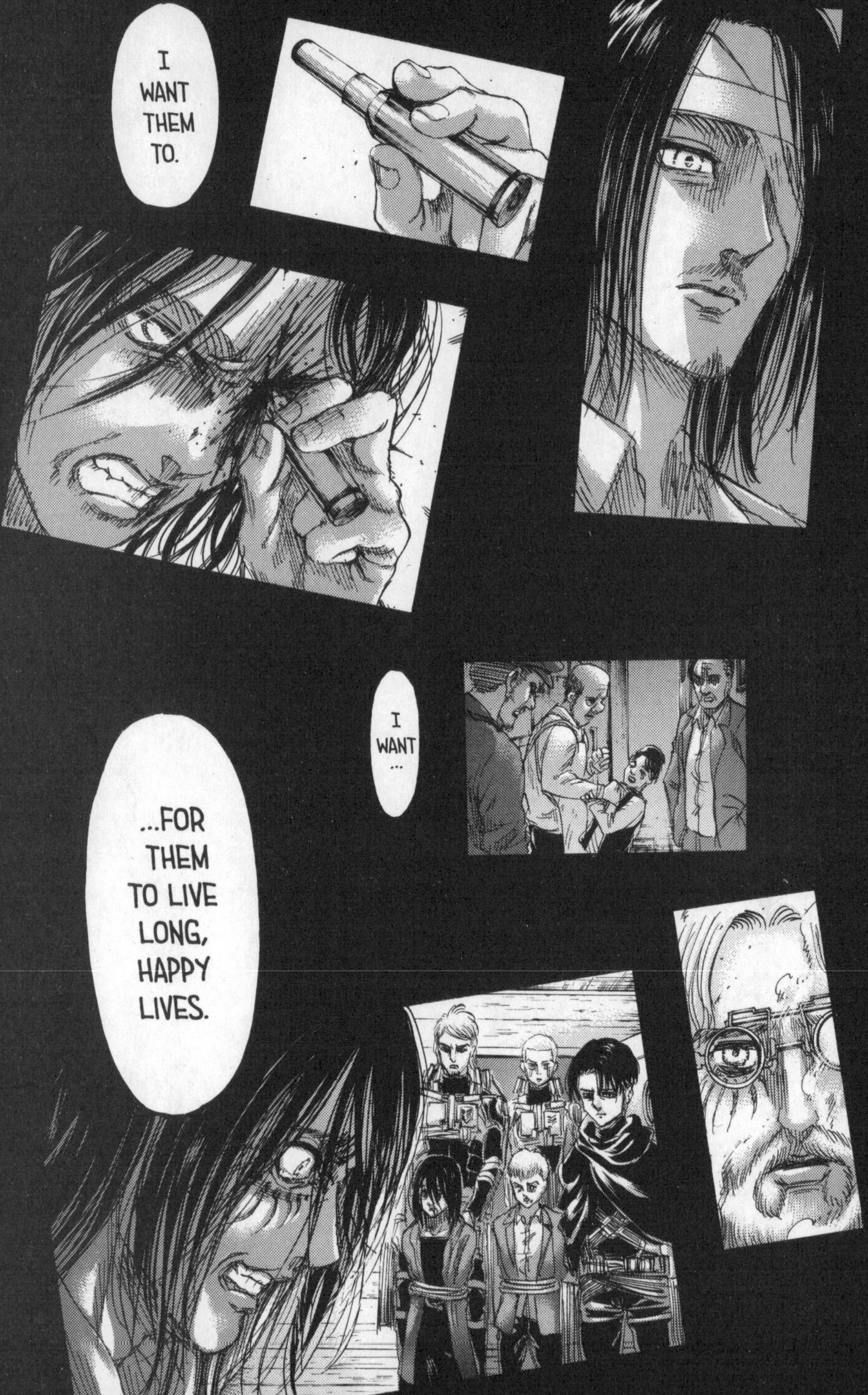
I WANT THEM TO.
I WANT...
...FOR THEM TO LIVE LONG, HAPPY LIVES.

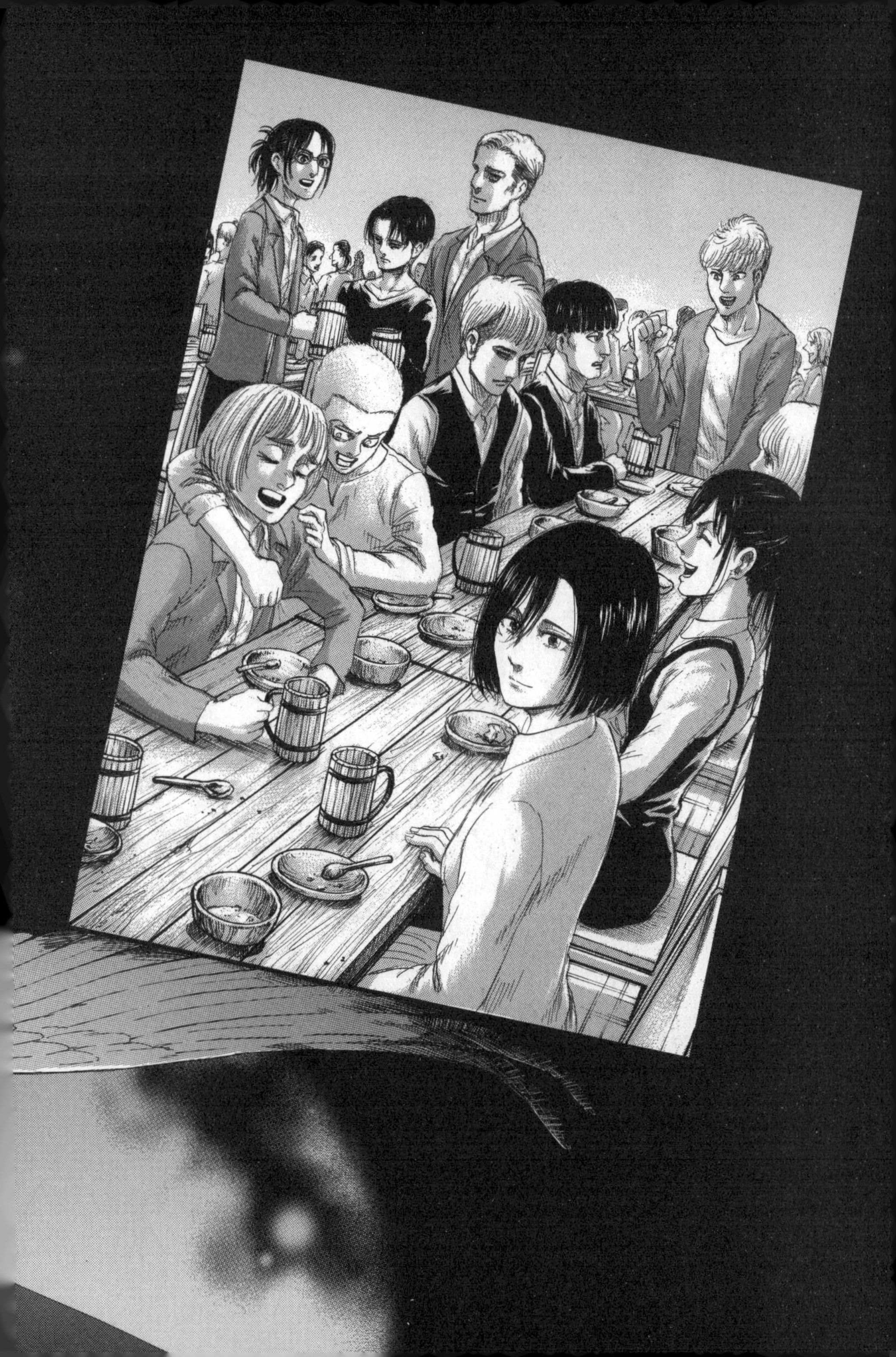

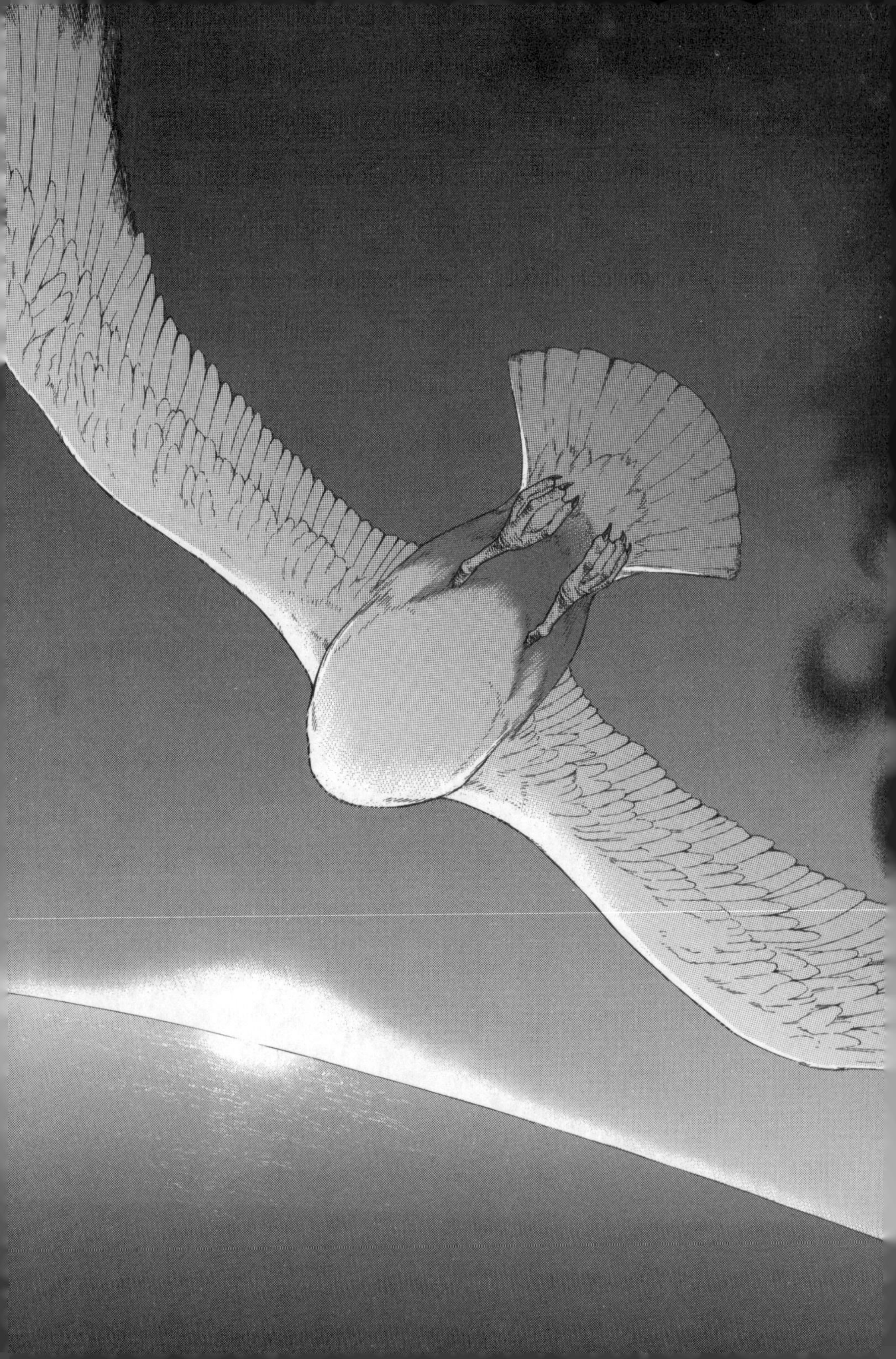

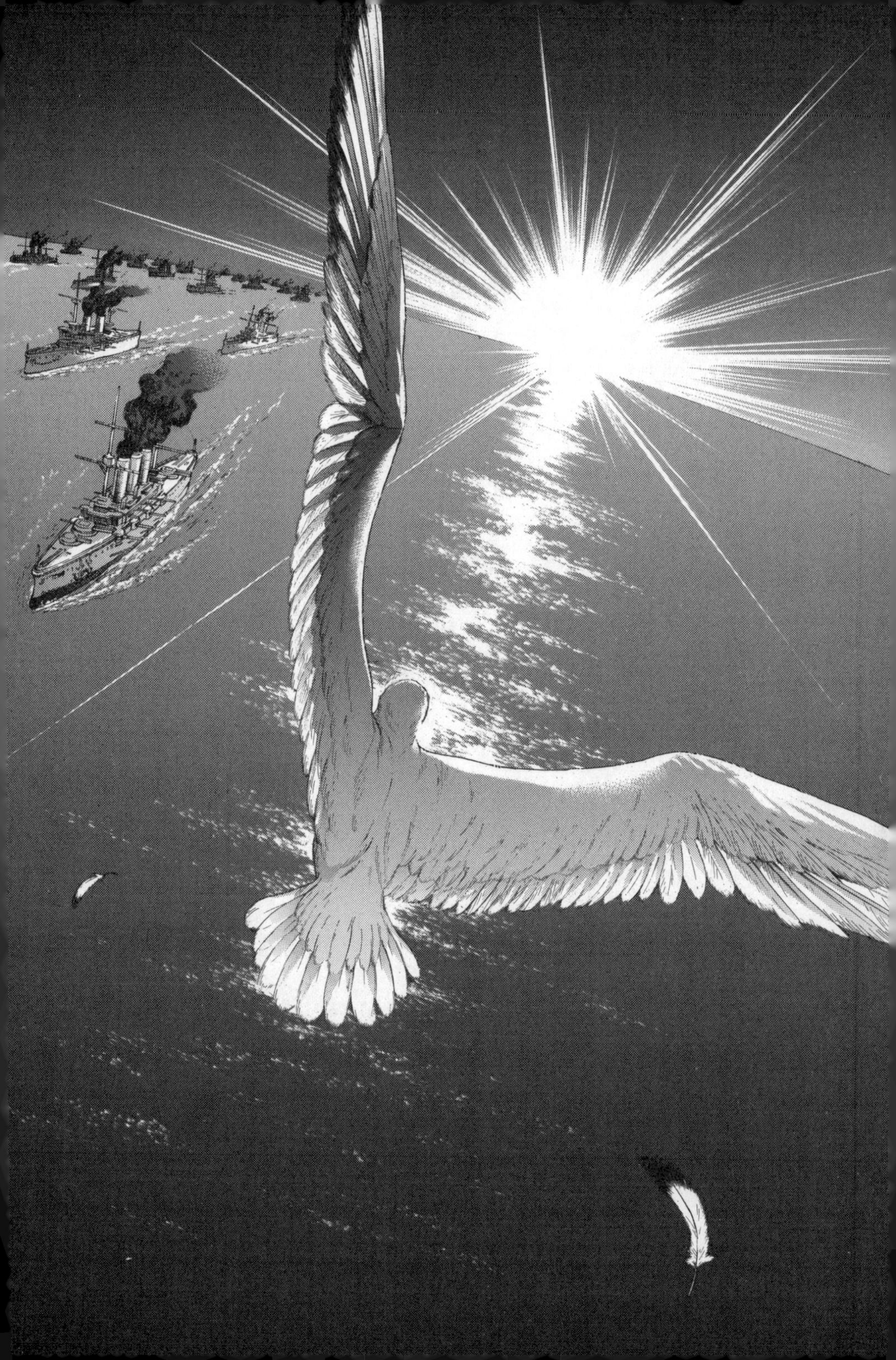

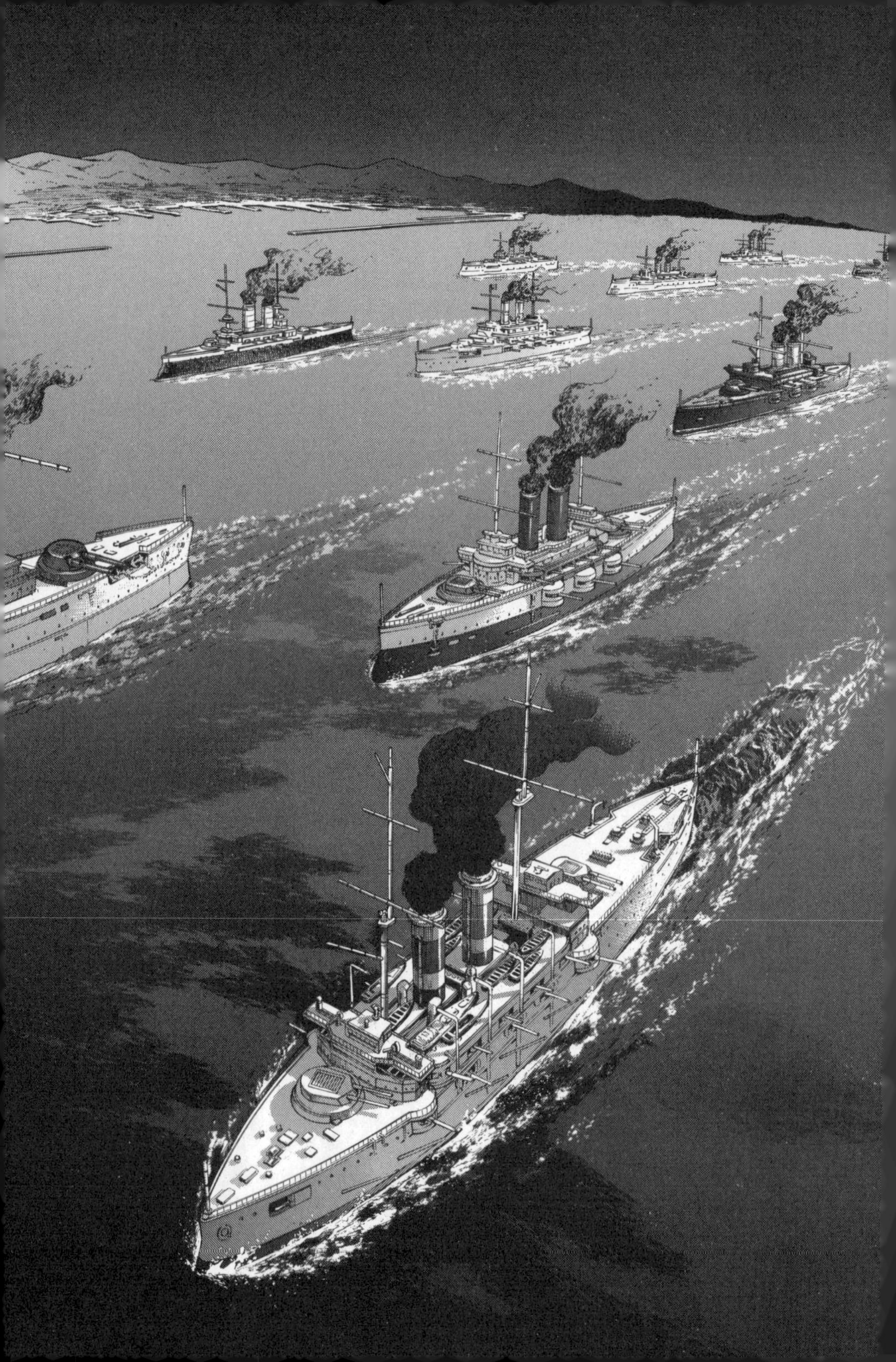

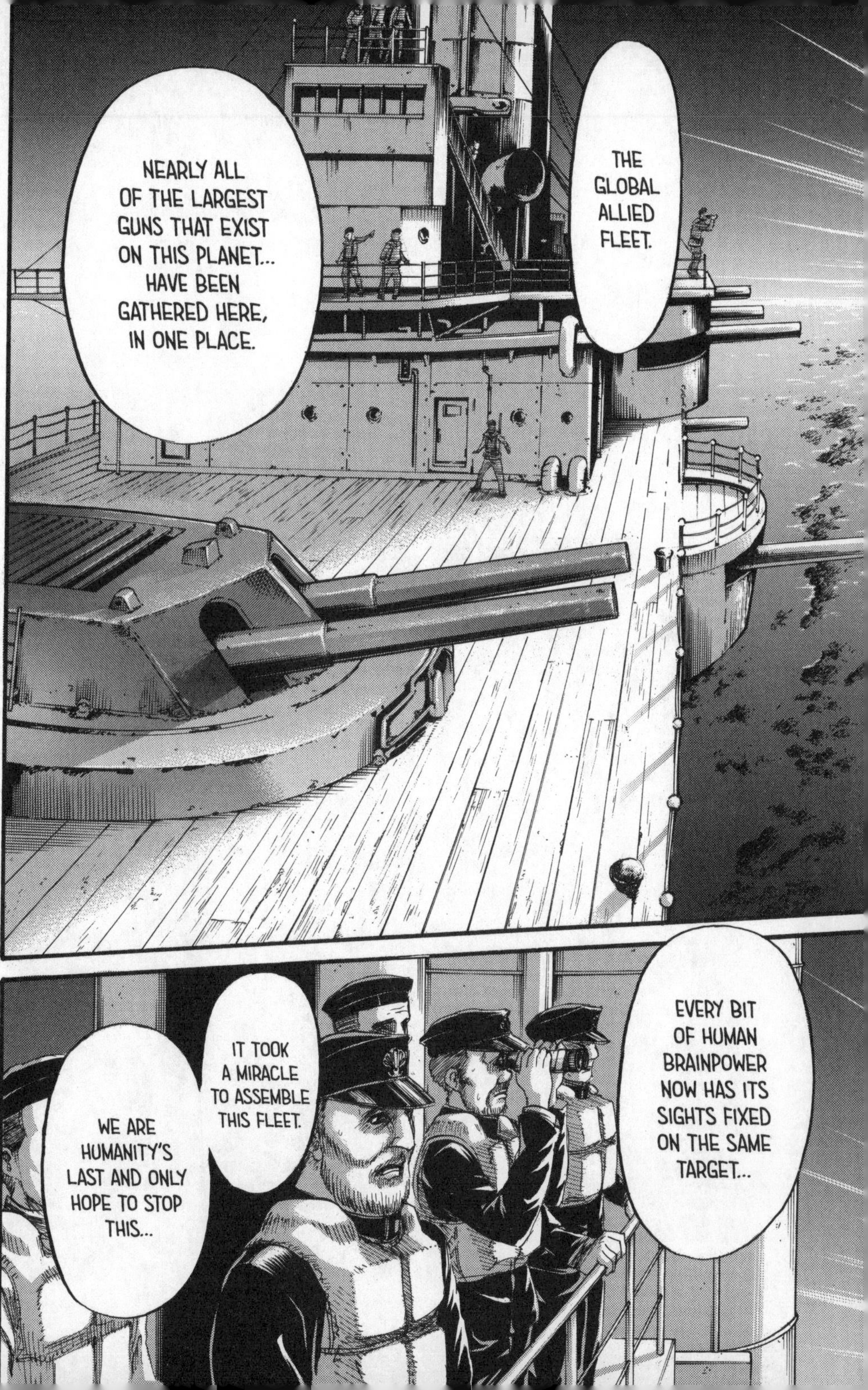
THE GLOBAL ALLIED FLEET.
NEARLY ALL OF THE LARGEST GUNS THAT EXIST ON THIS PLANET... HAVE BEEN GATHERED HERE, IN ONE PLACE.
EVERY BIT OF HUMAN BRAINPOWER NOW HAS ITS SIGHTS FIXED ON THE SAME TARGET...
IT TOOK A MIRACLE TO ASSEMBLE THIS FLEET.
WE ARE HUMANITY'S LAST AND ONLY HOPE TO STOP THIS...

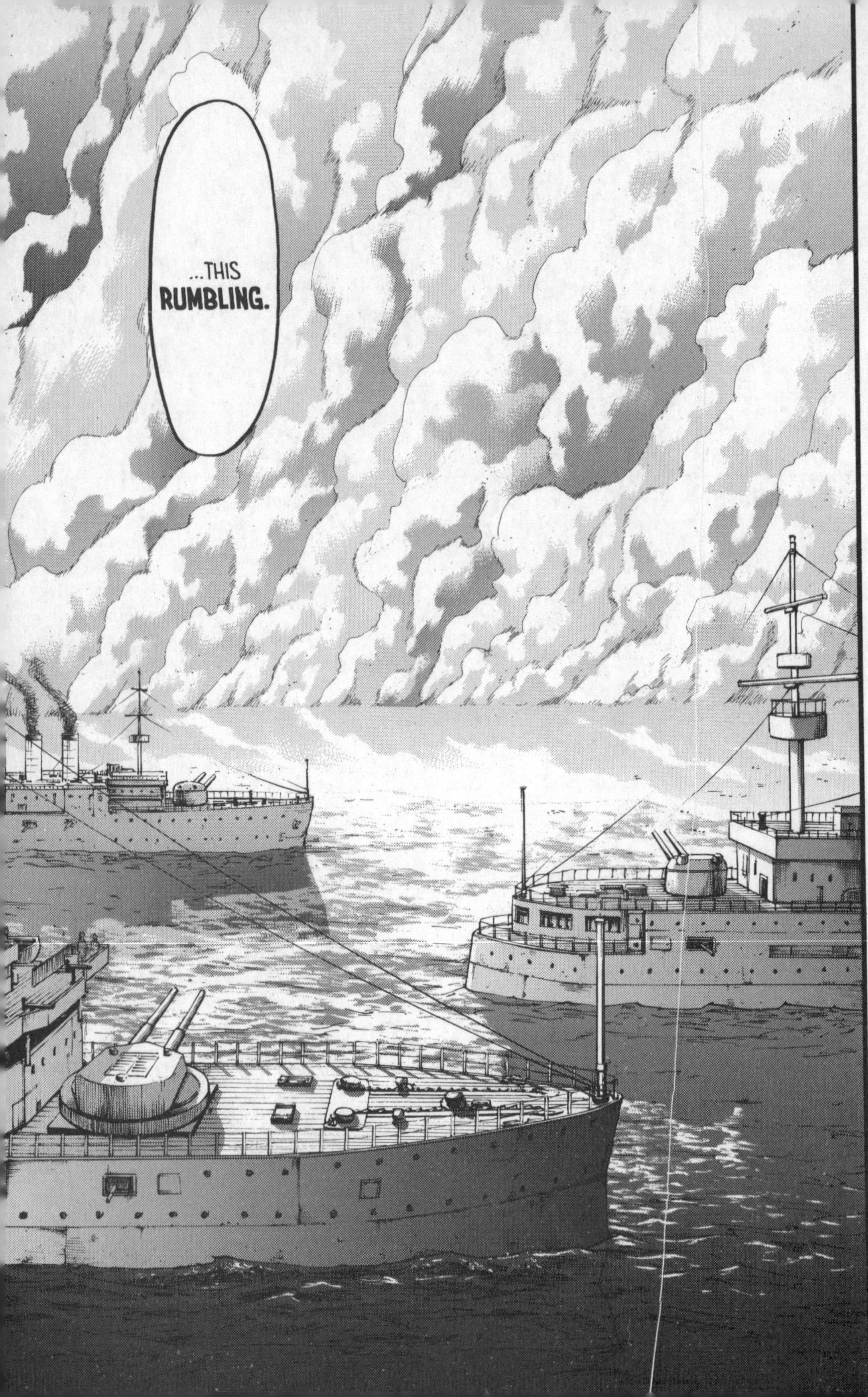
...THIS RUMBLING.

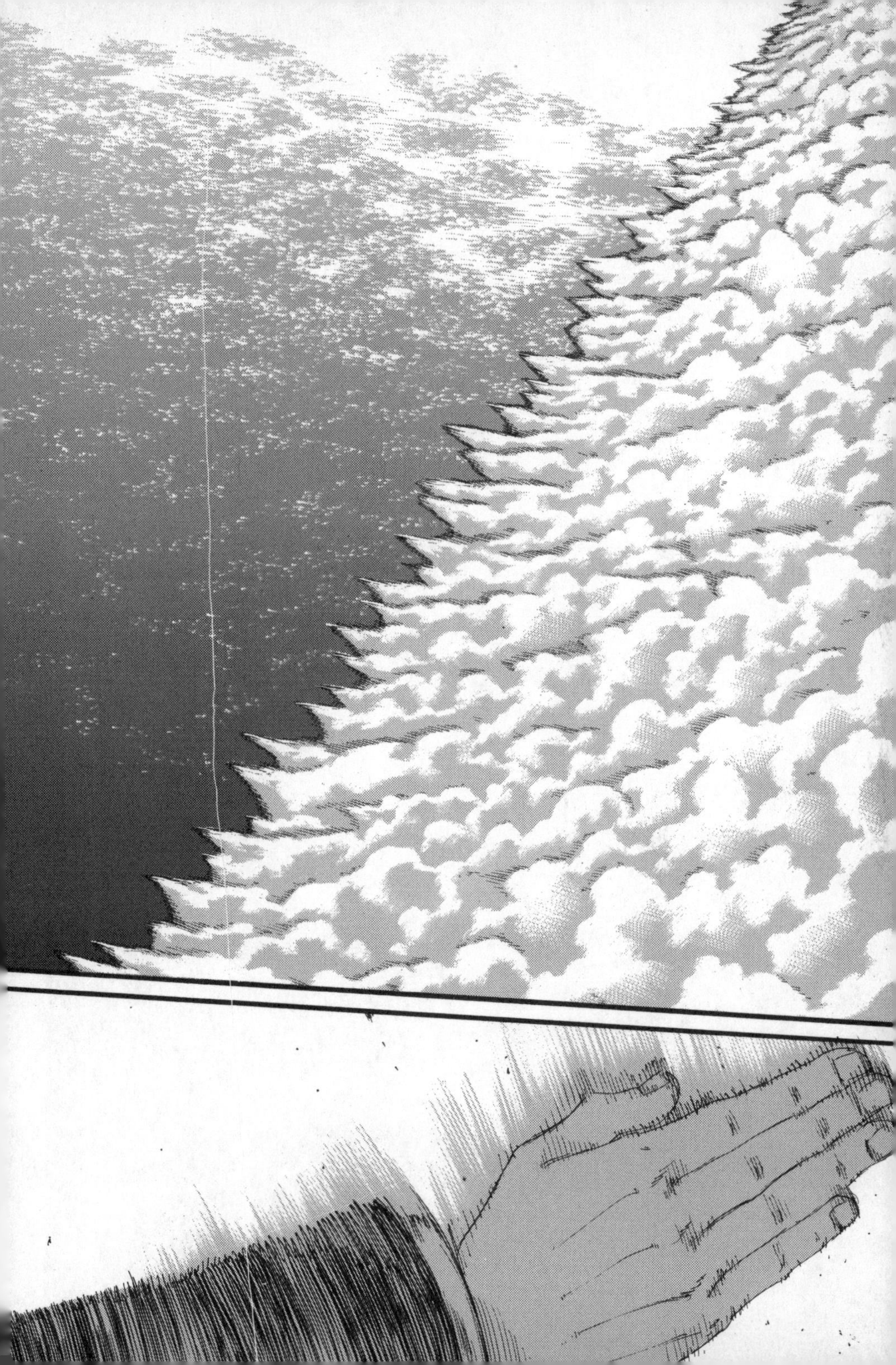

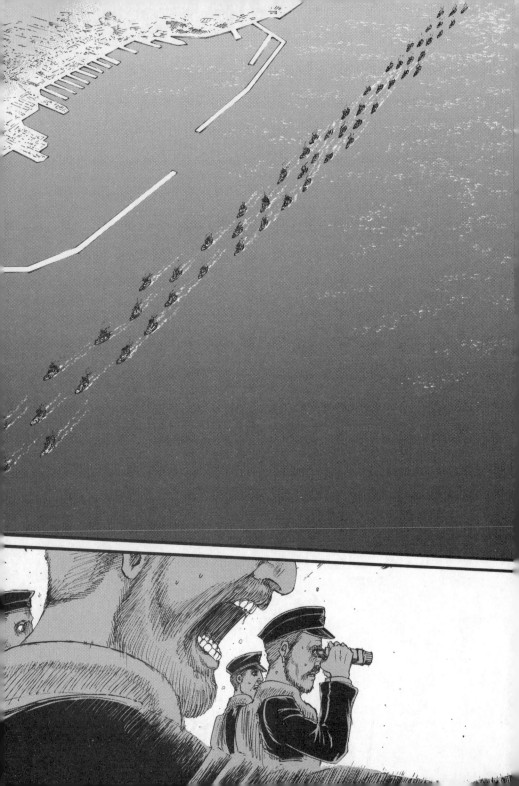

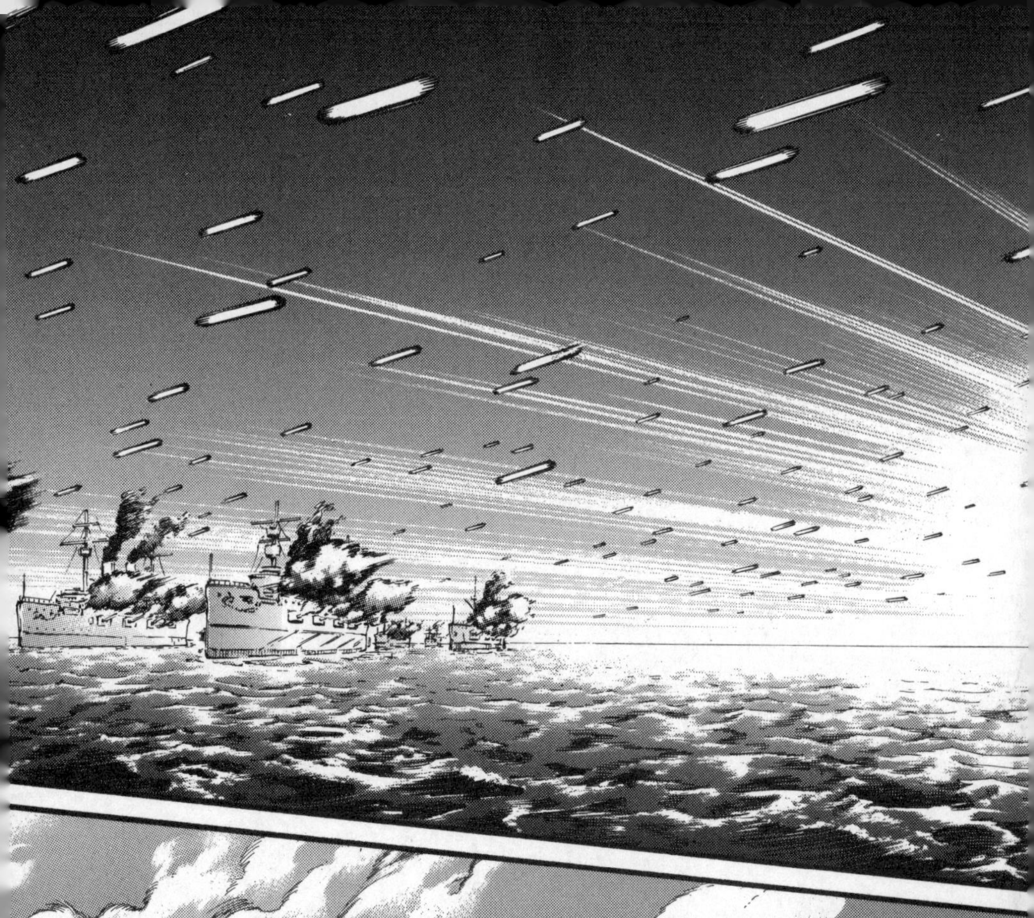
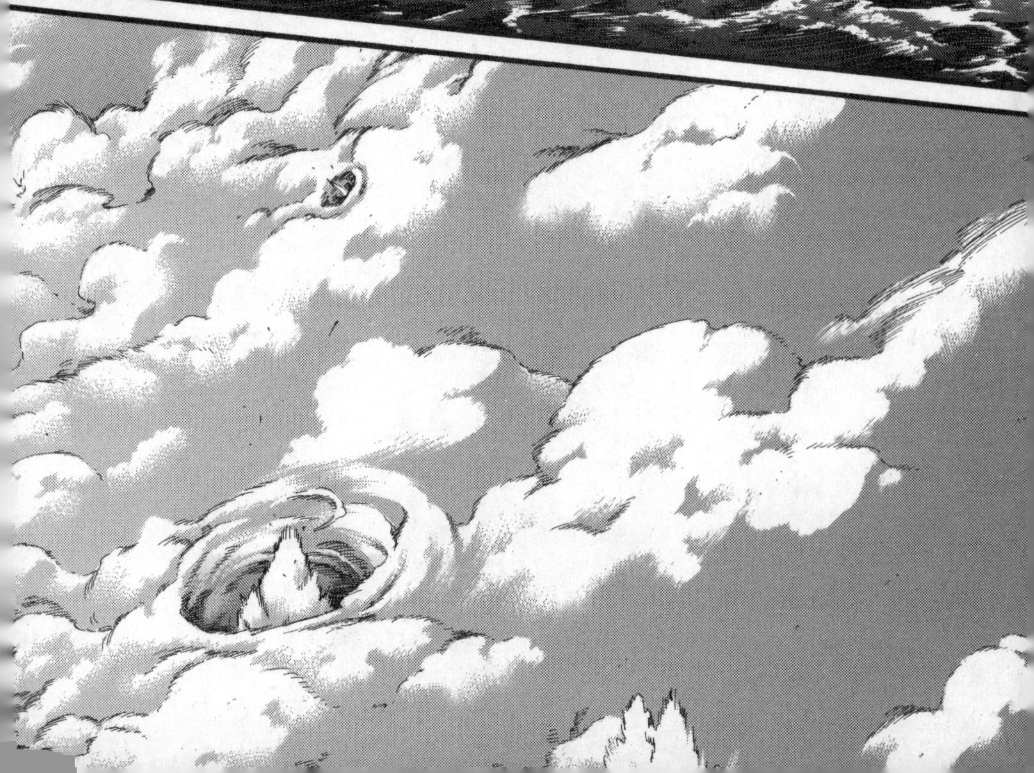

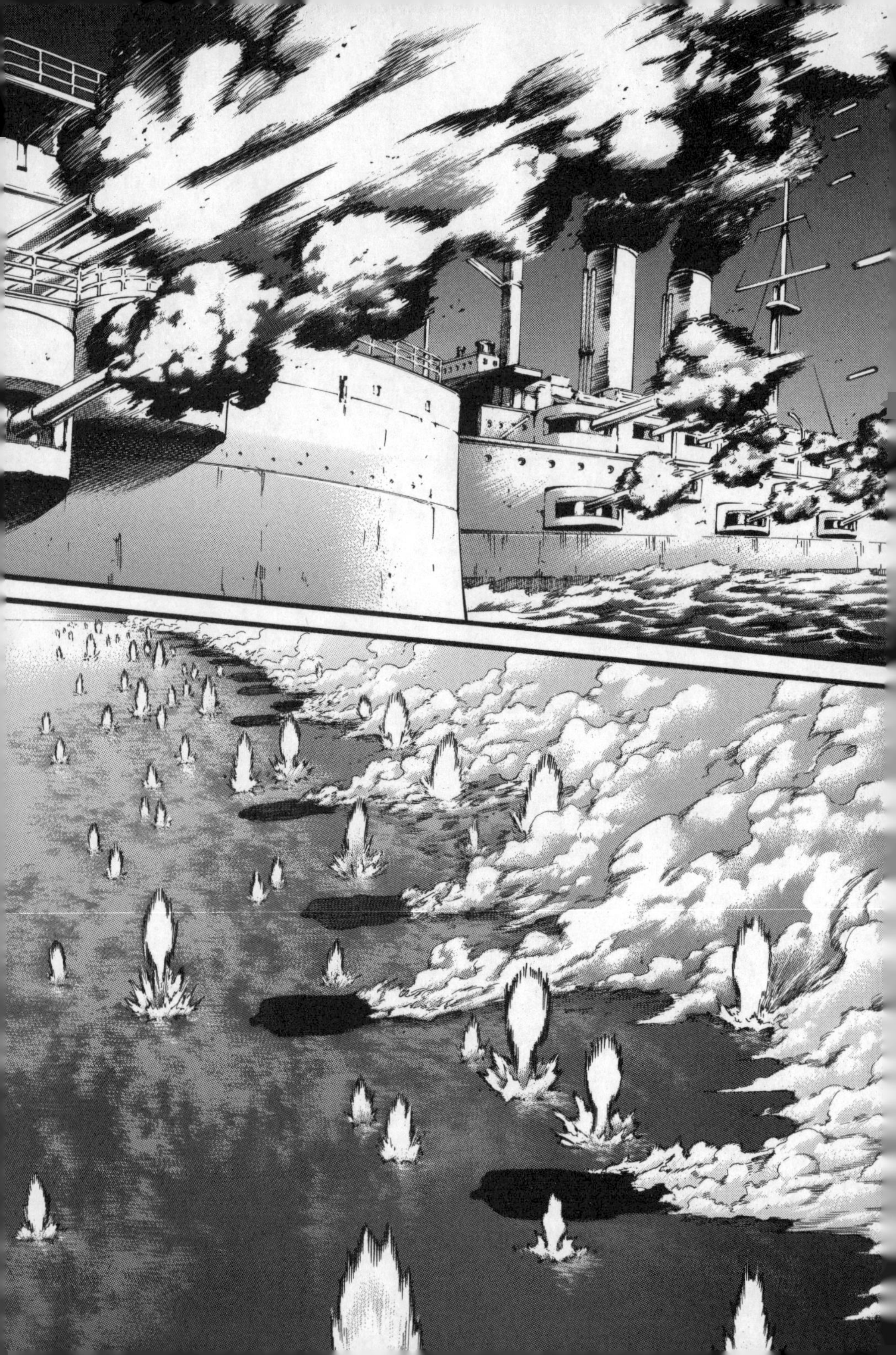

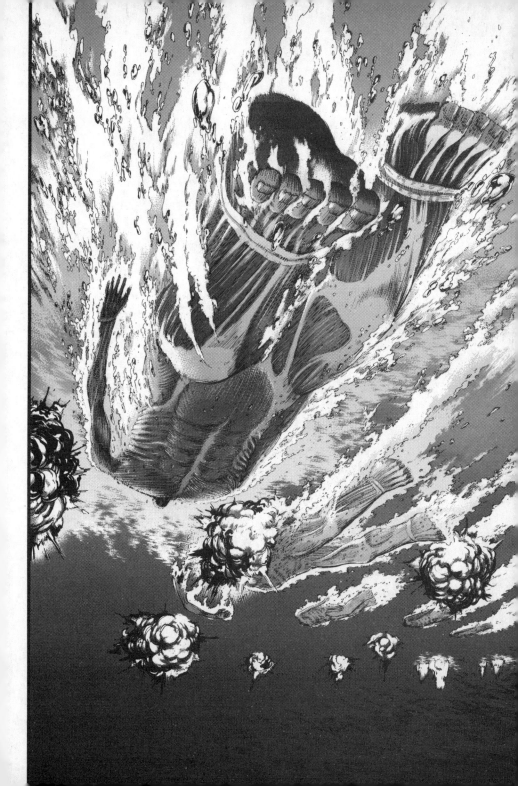

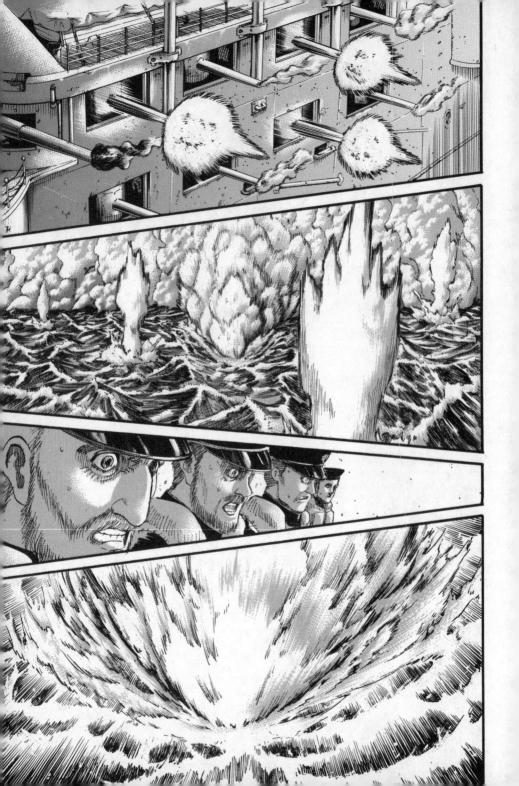

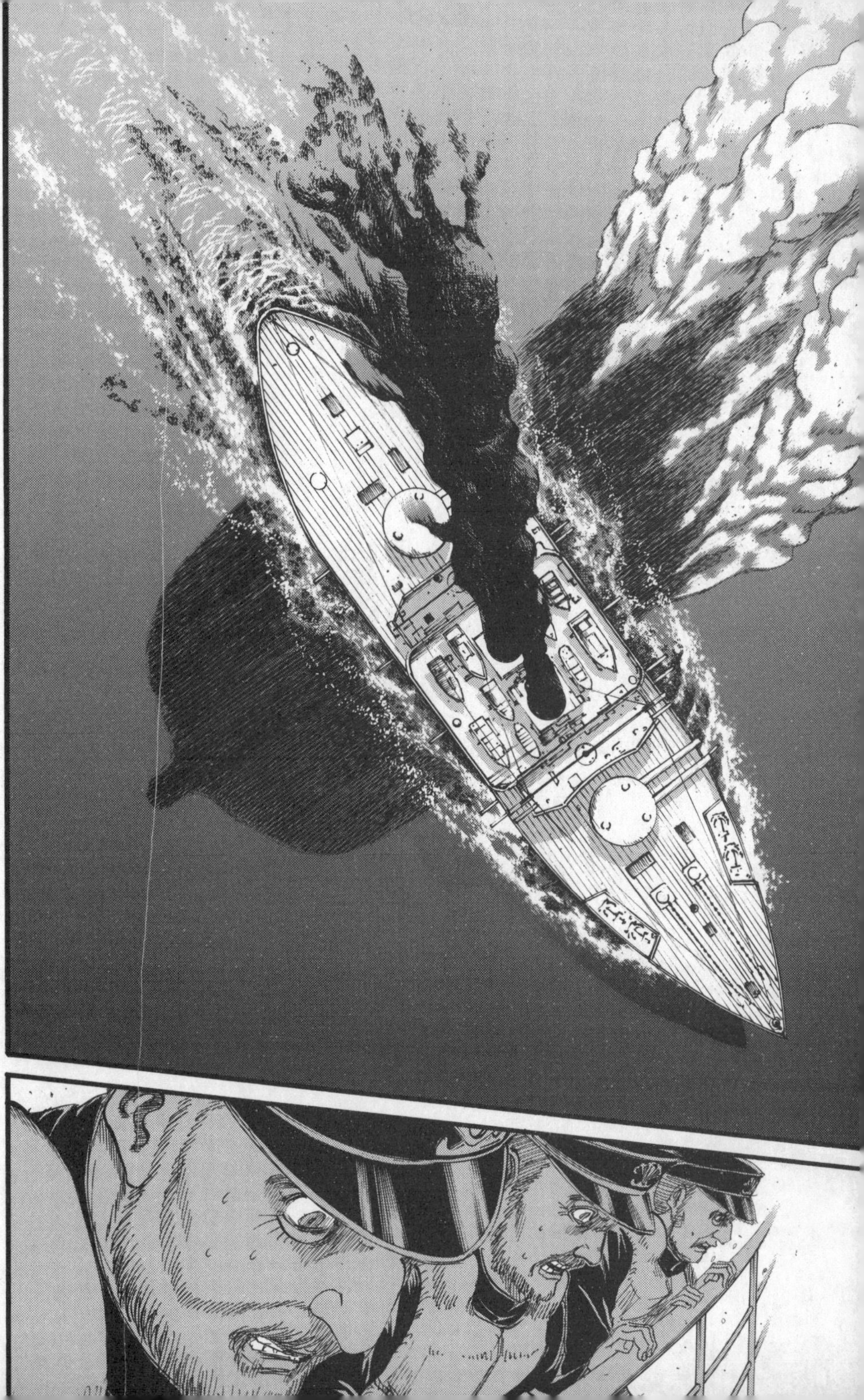

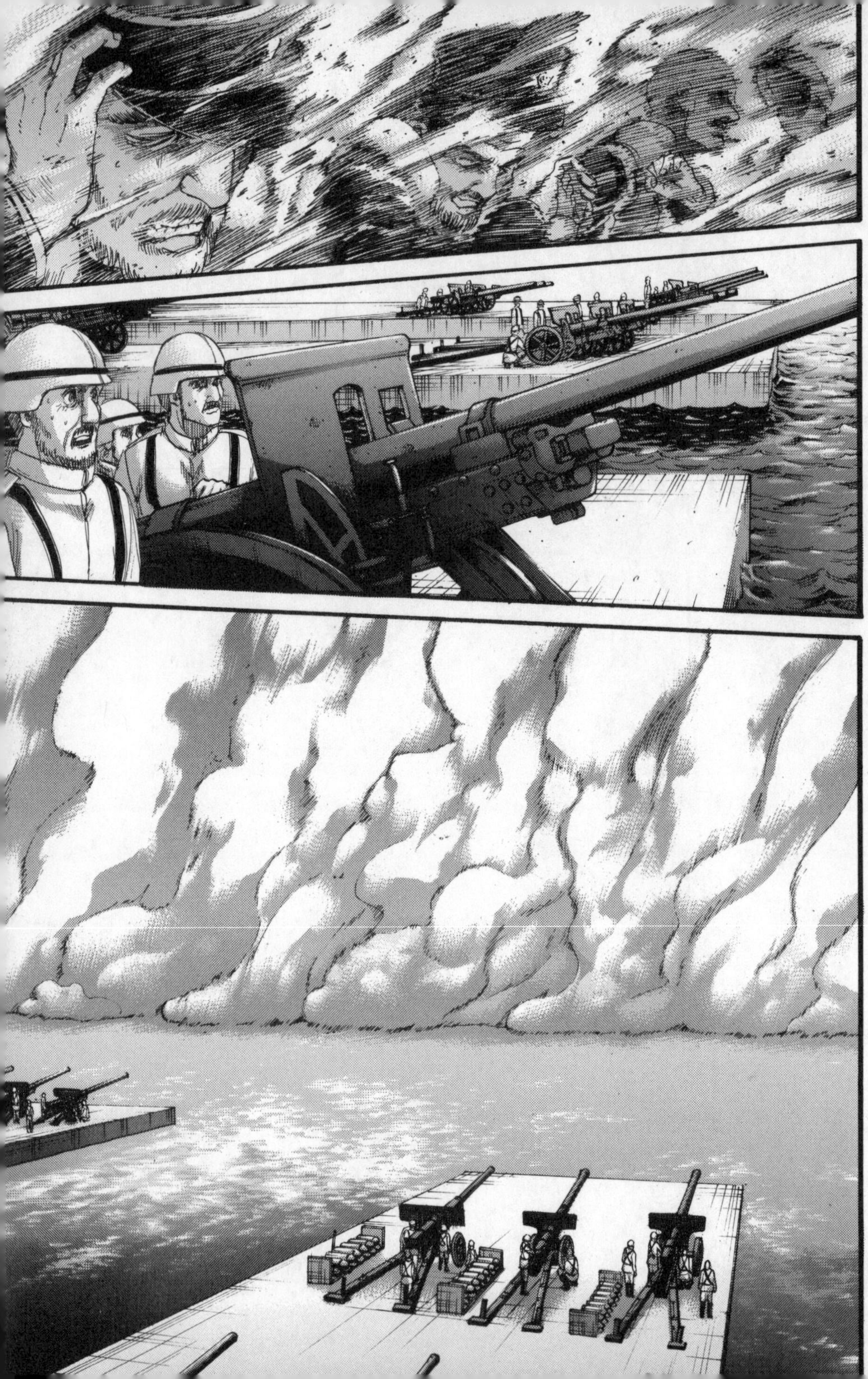

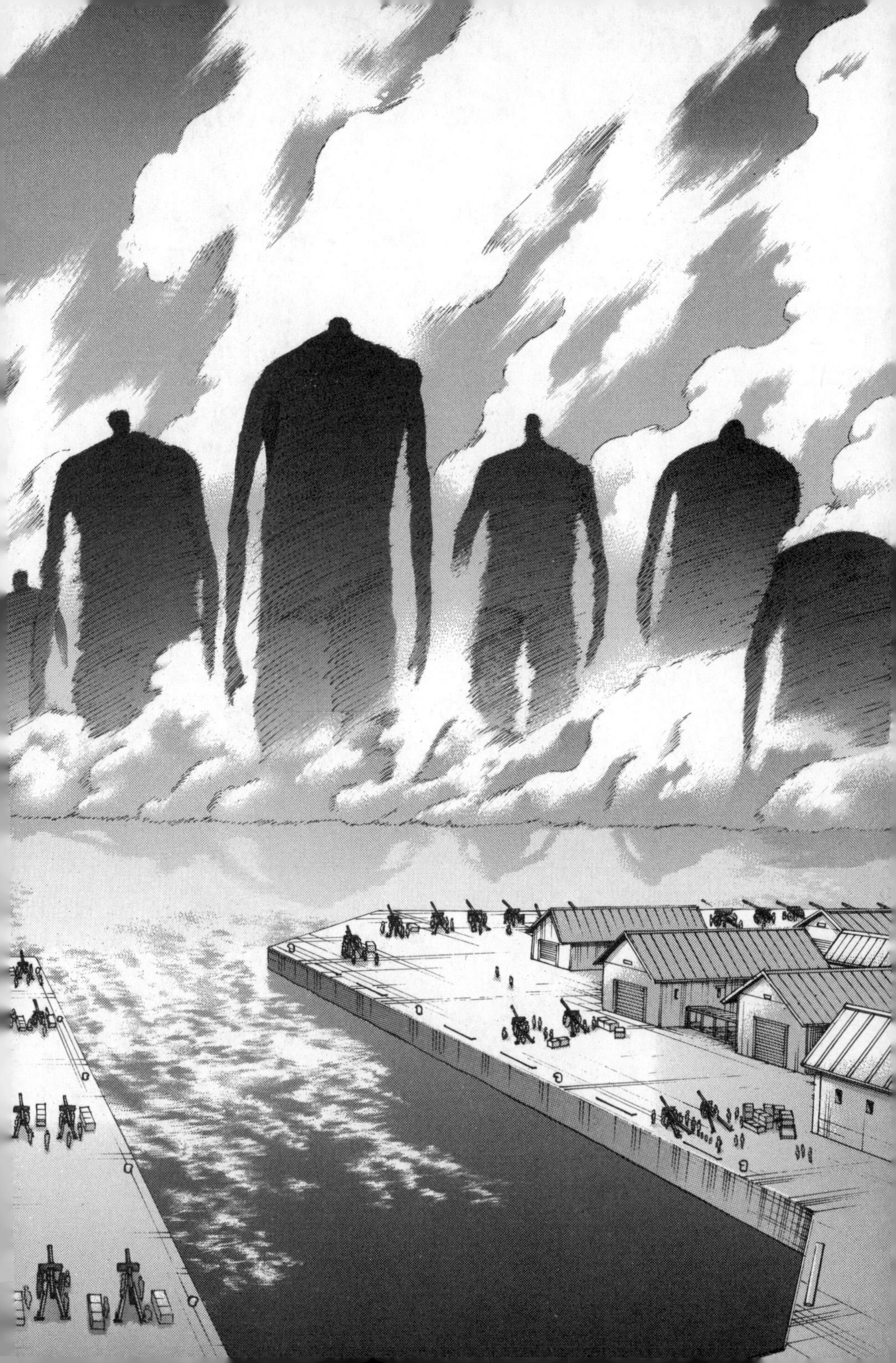

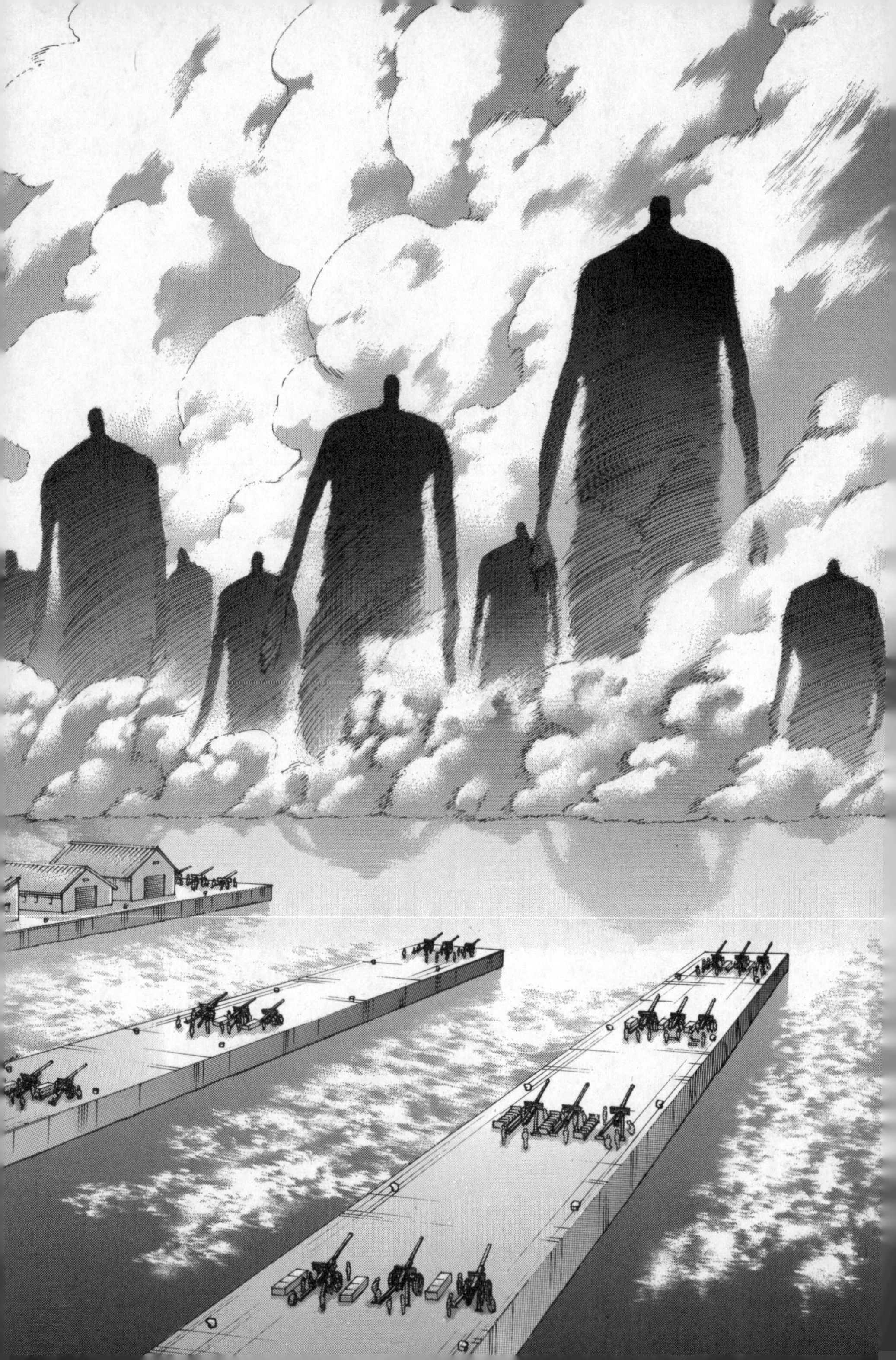

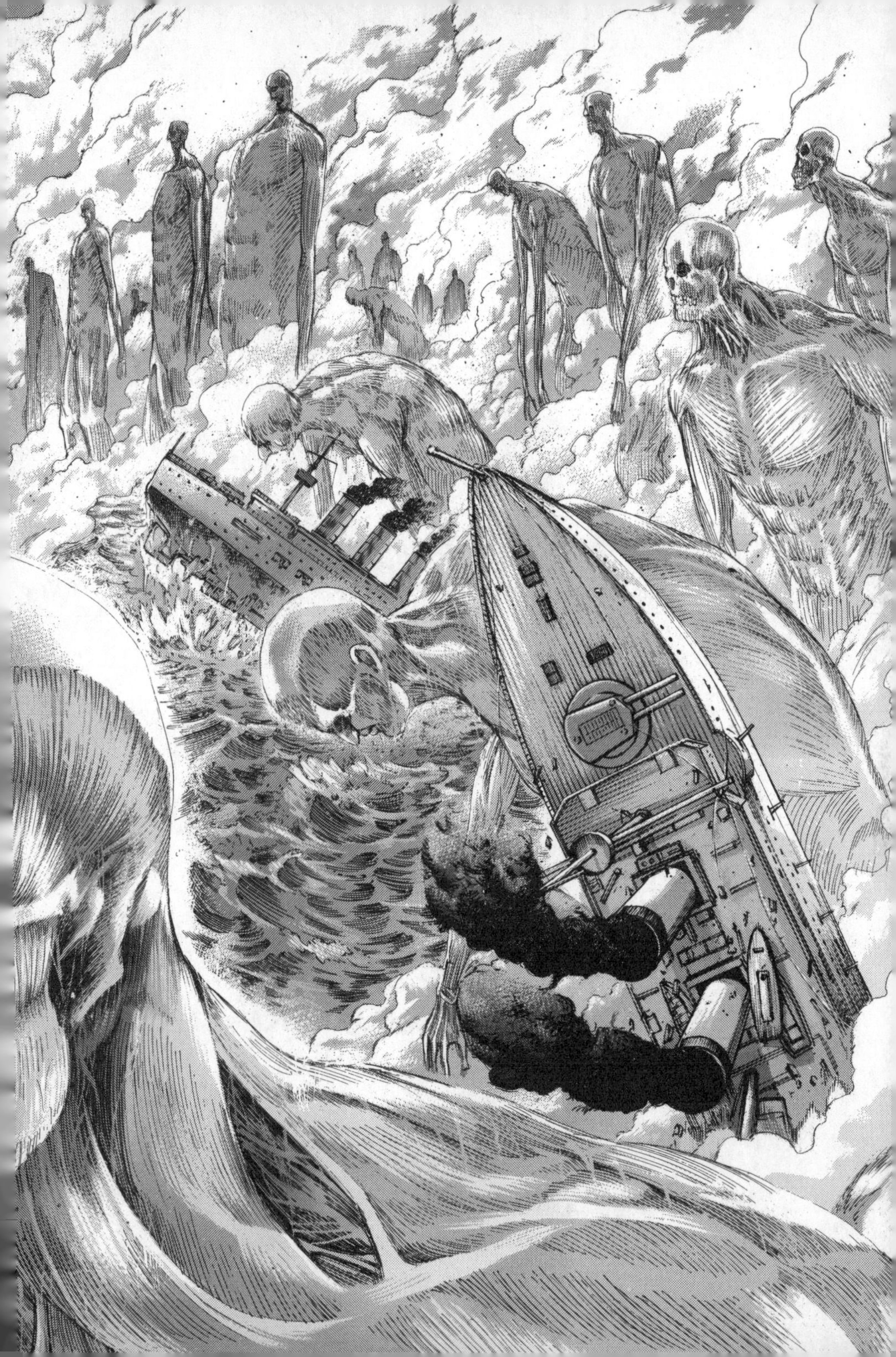

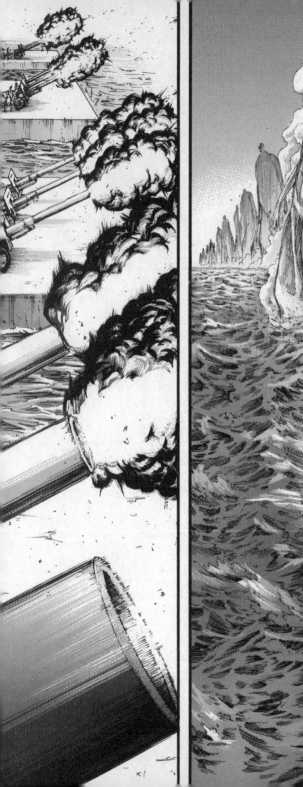

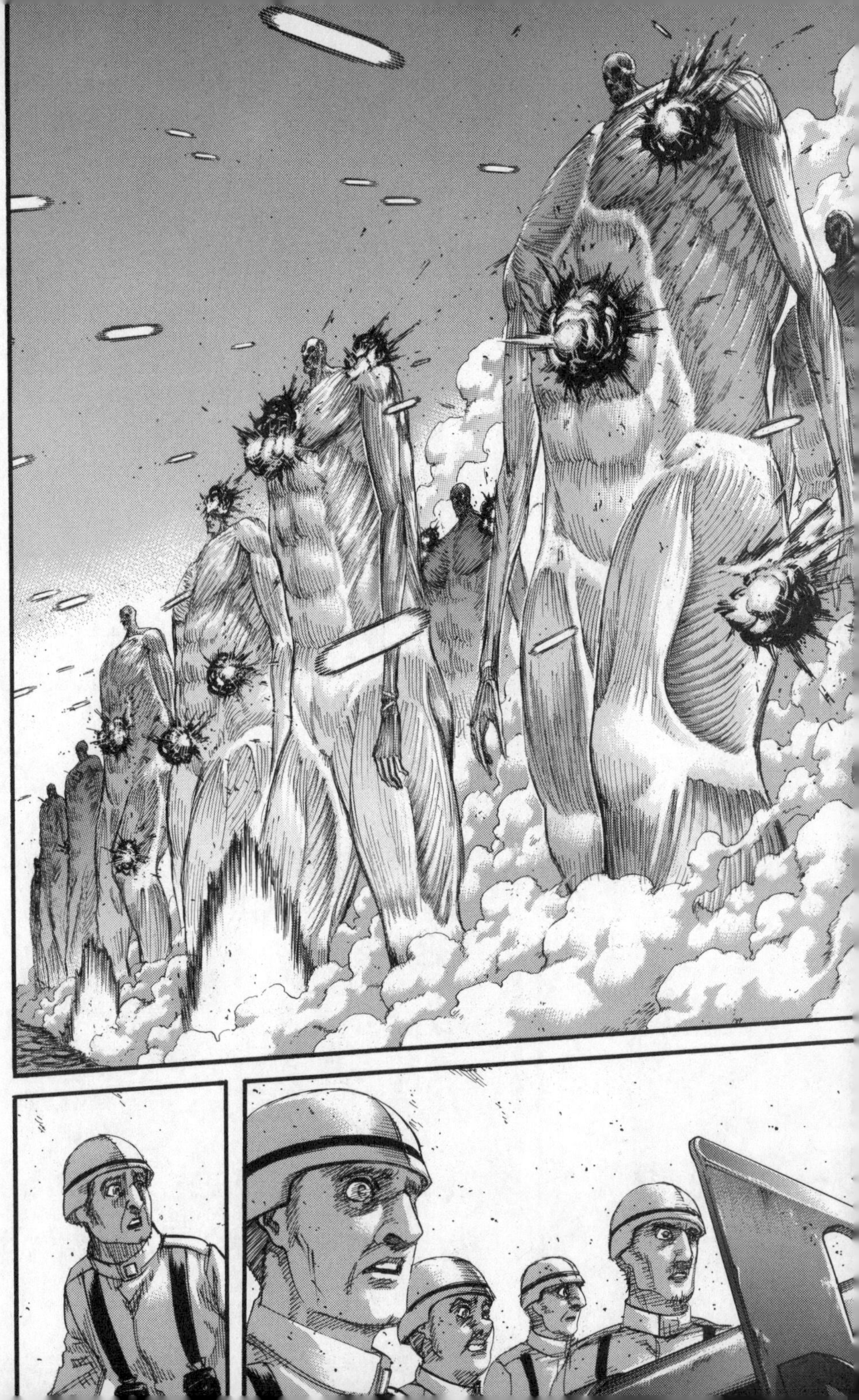

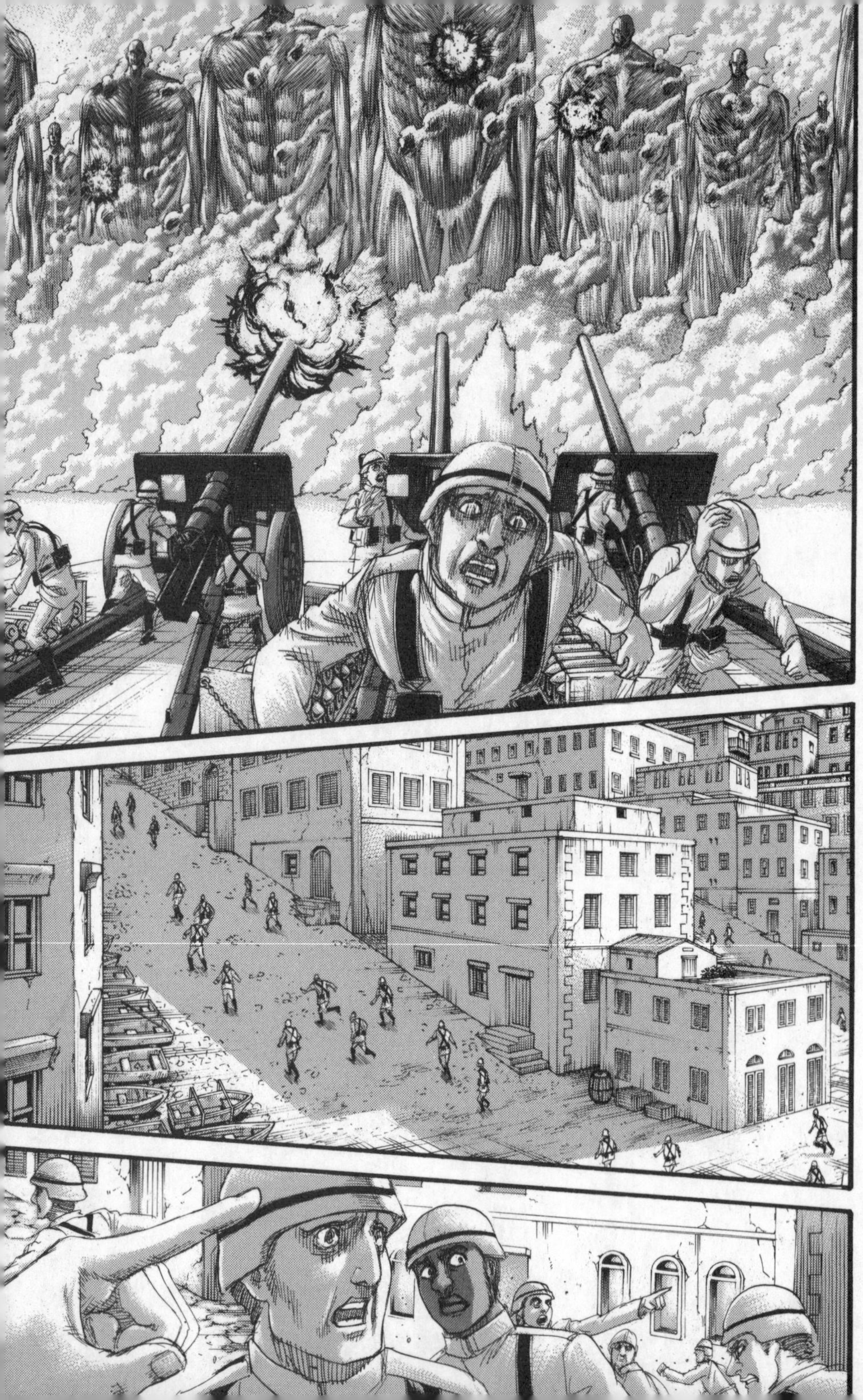

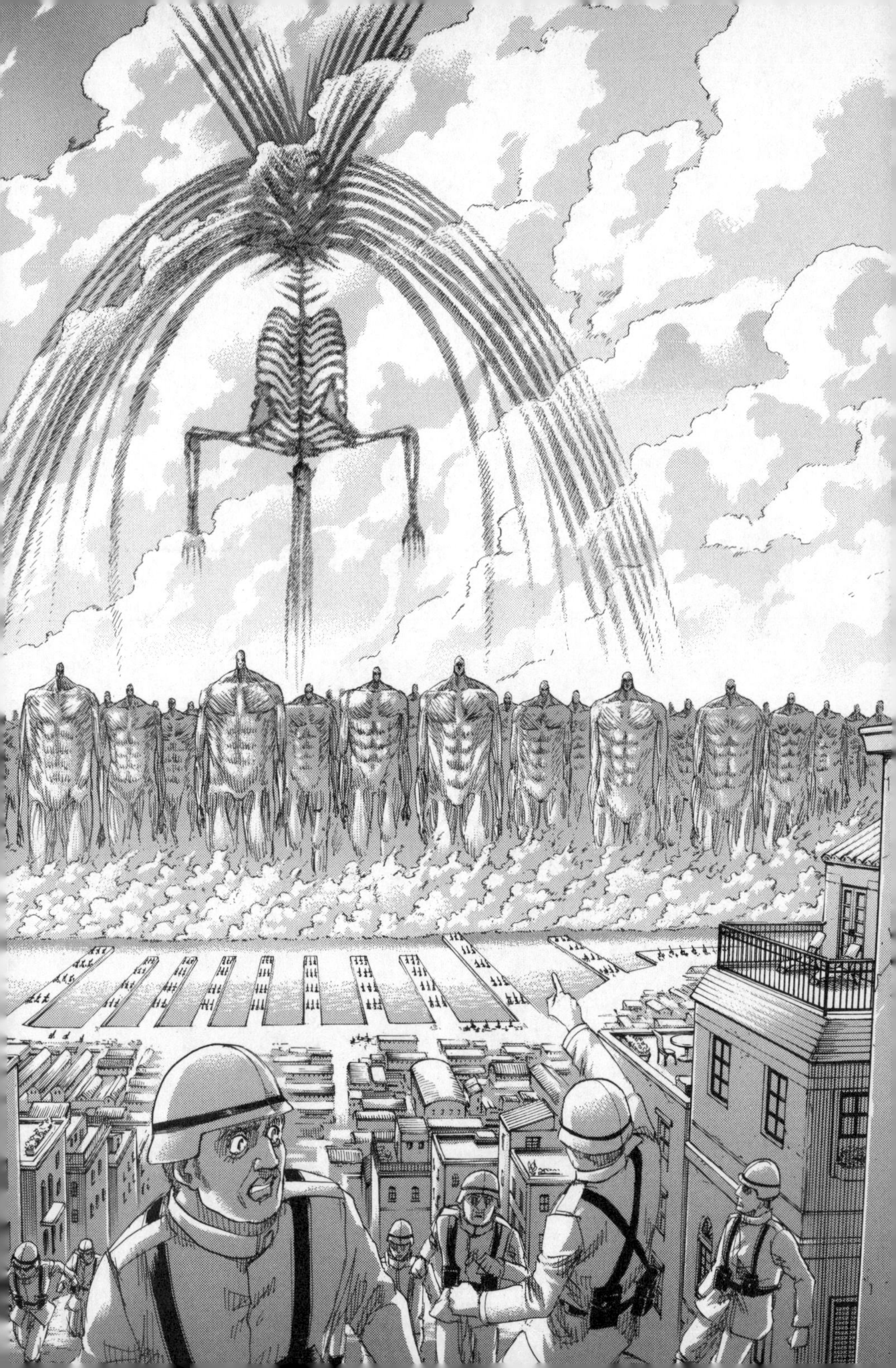

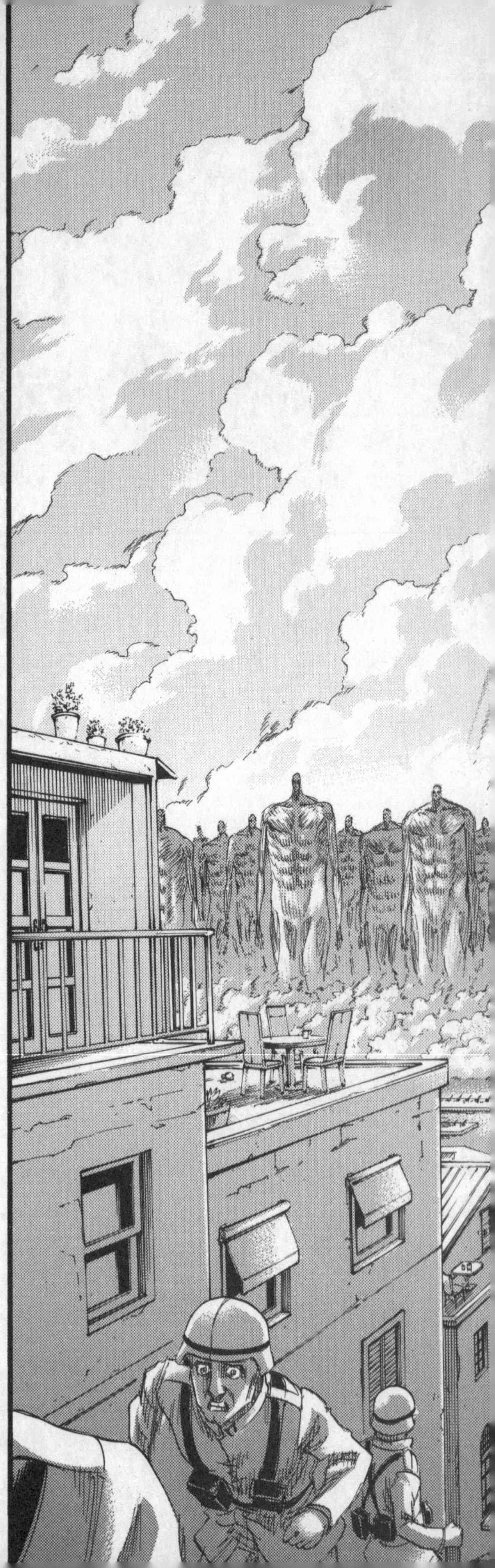

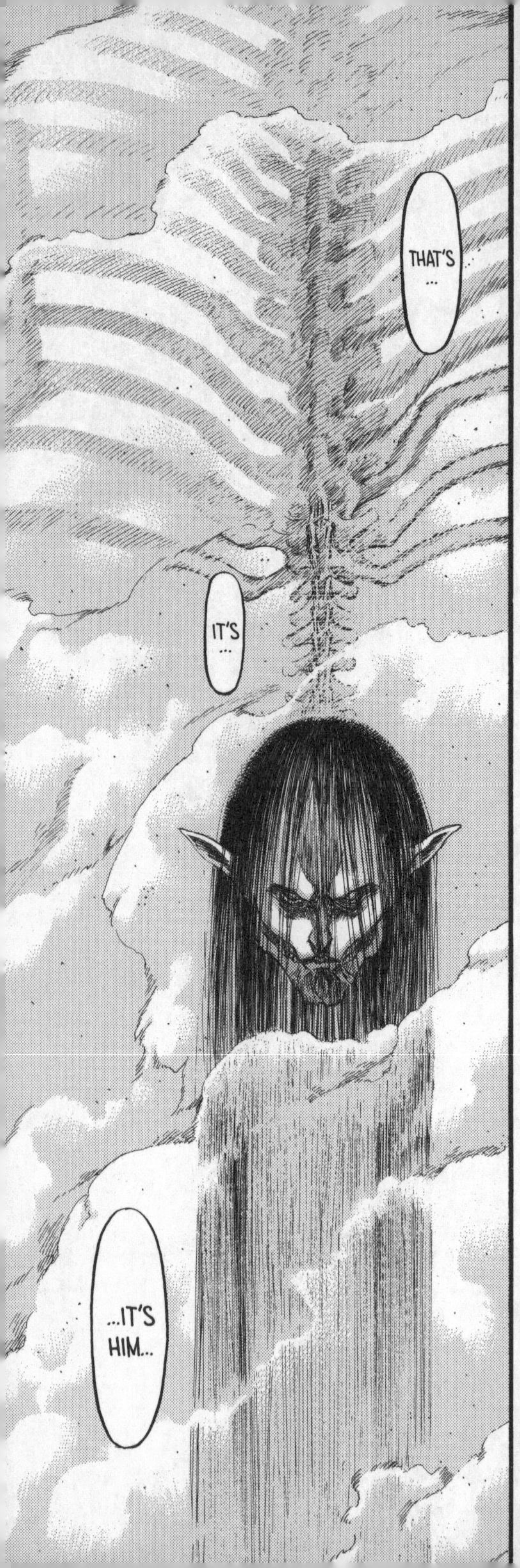
THAT'S ...
IT'S ...
...IT'S HIM...

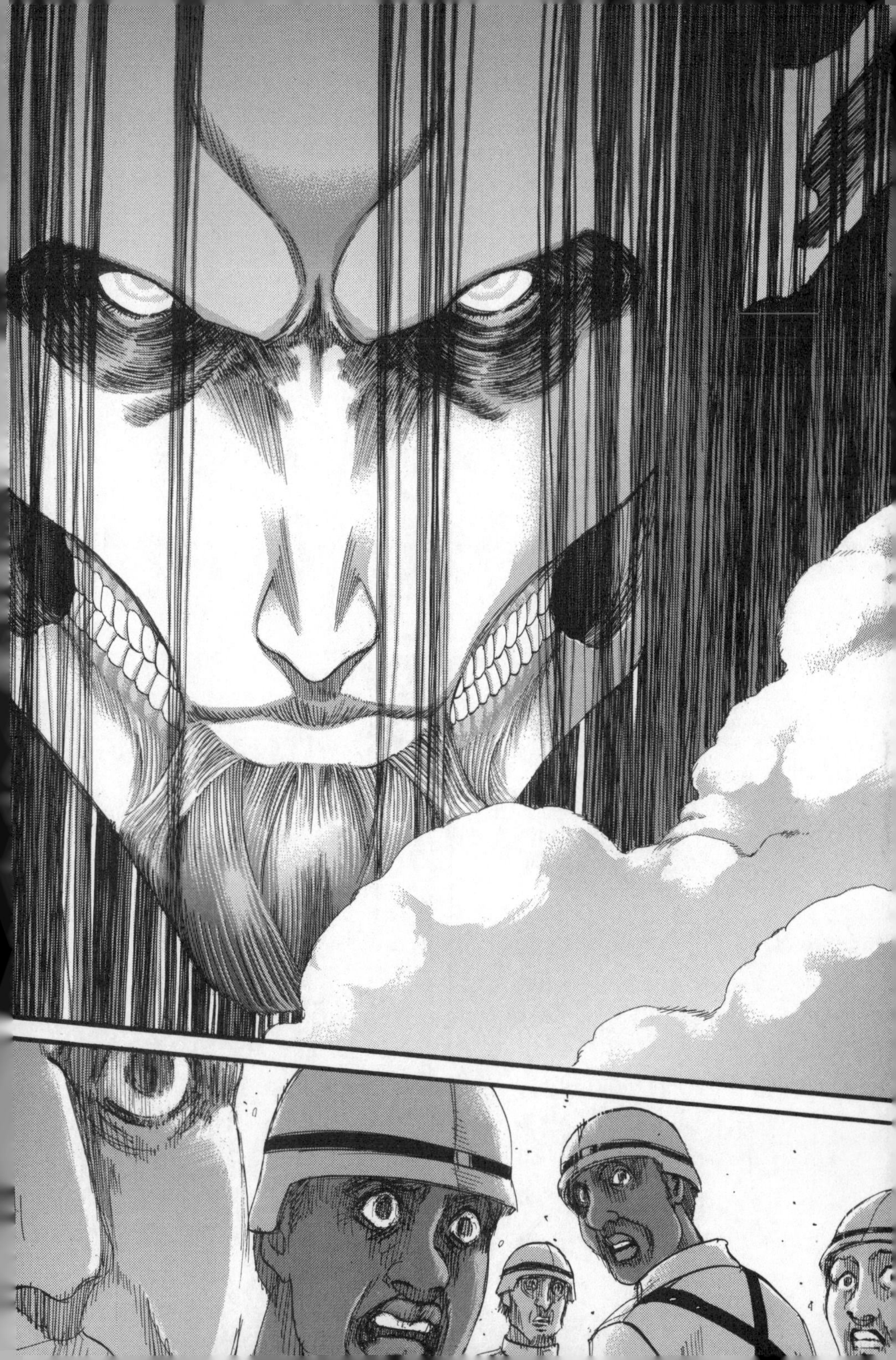

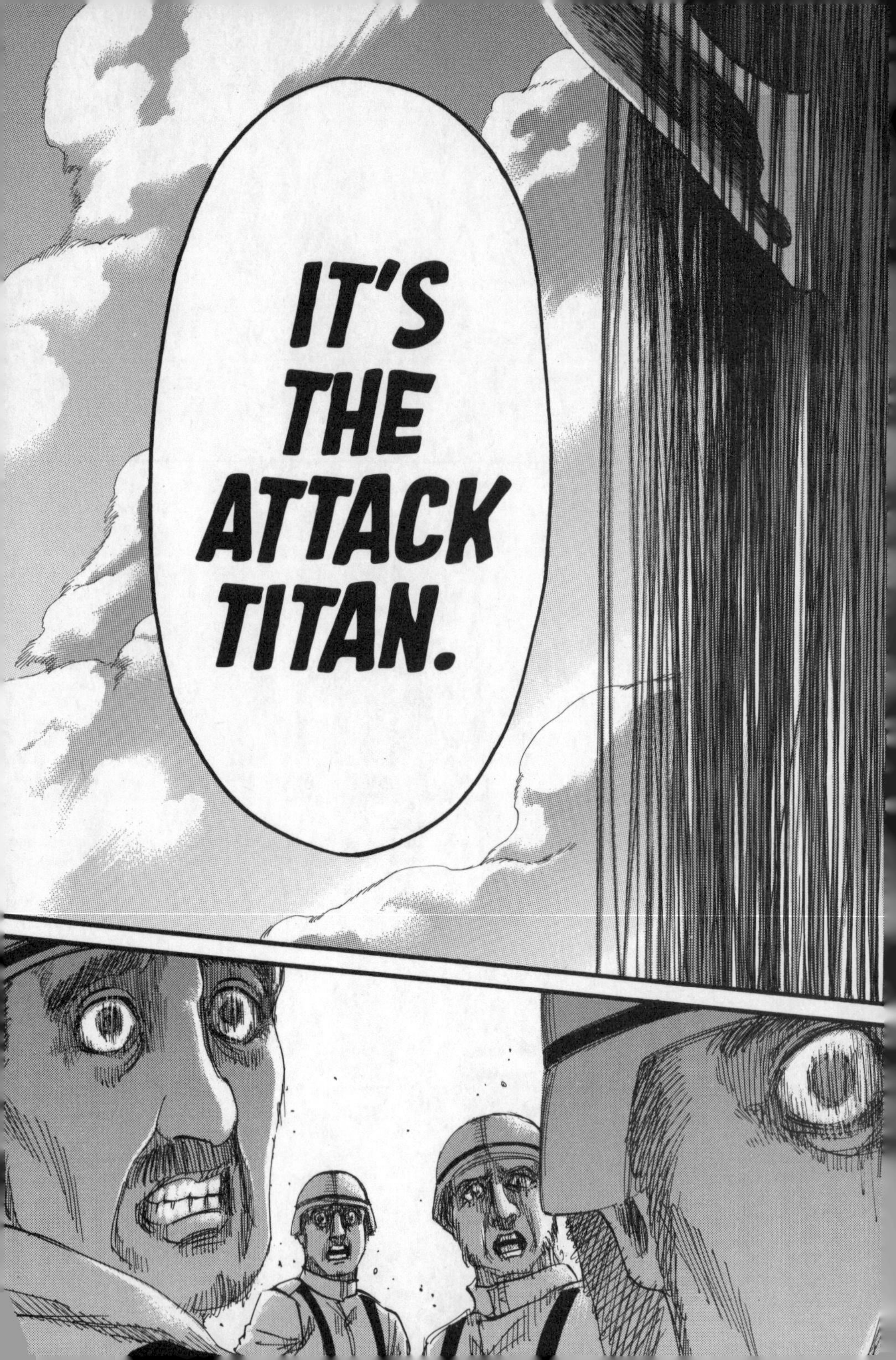
IT'S THE ATTACK TITAN.

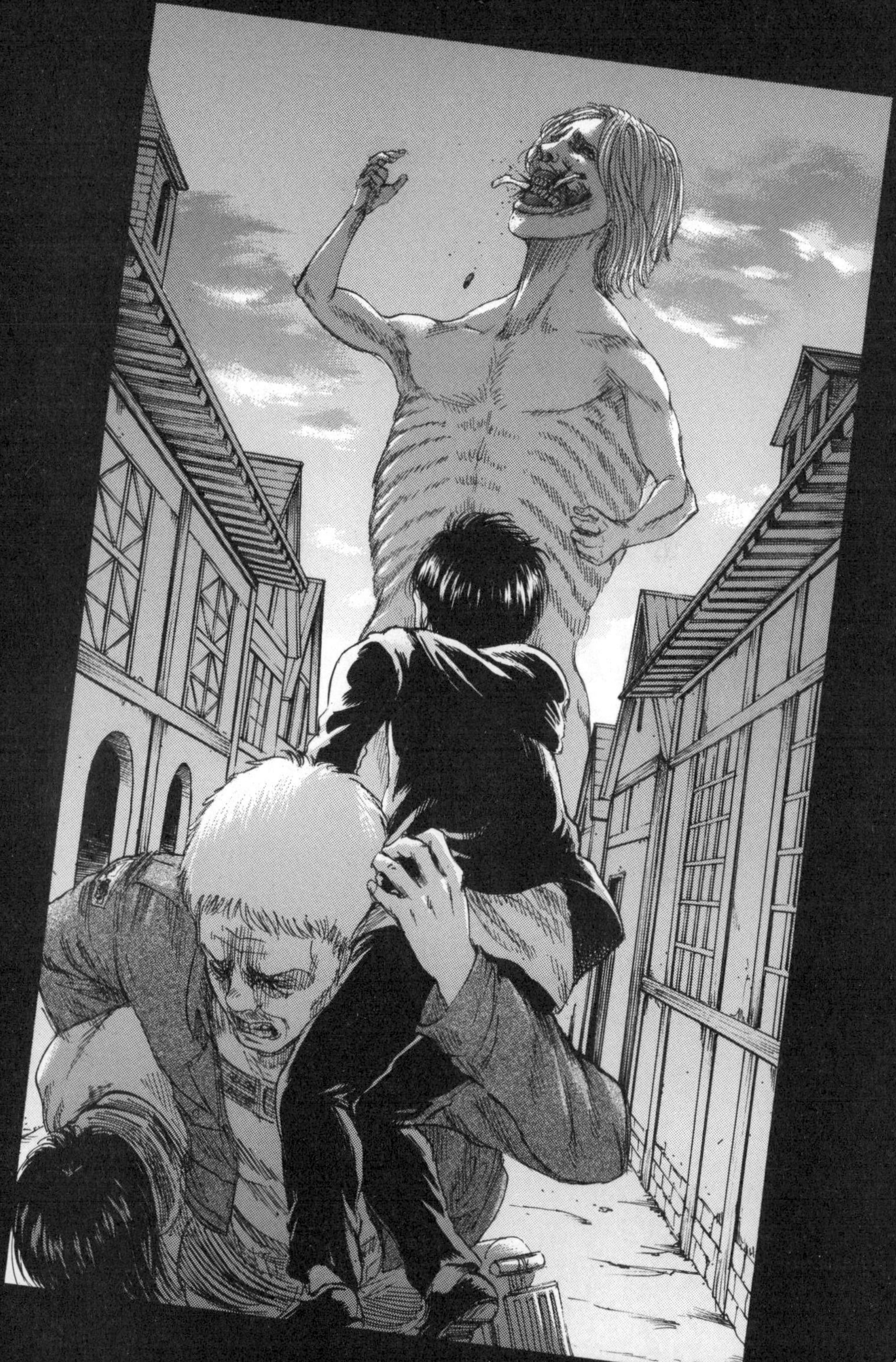

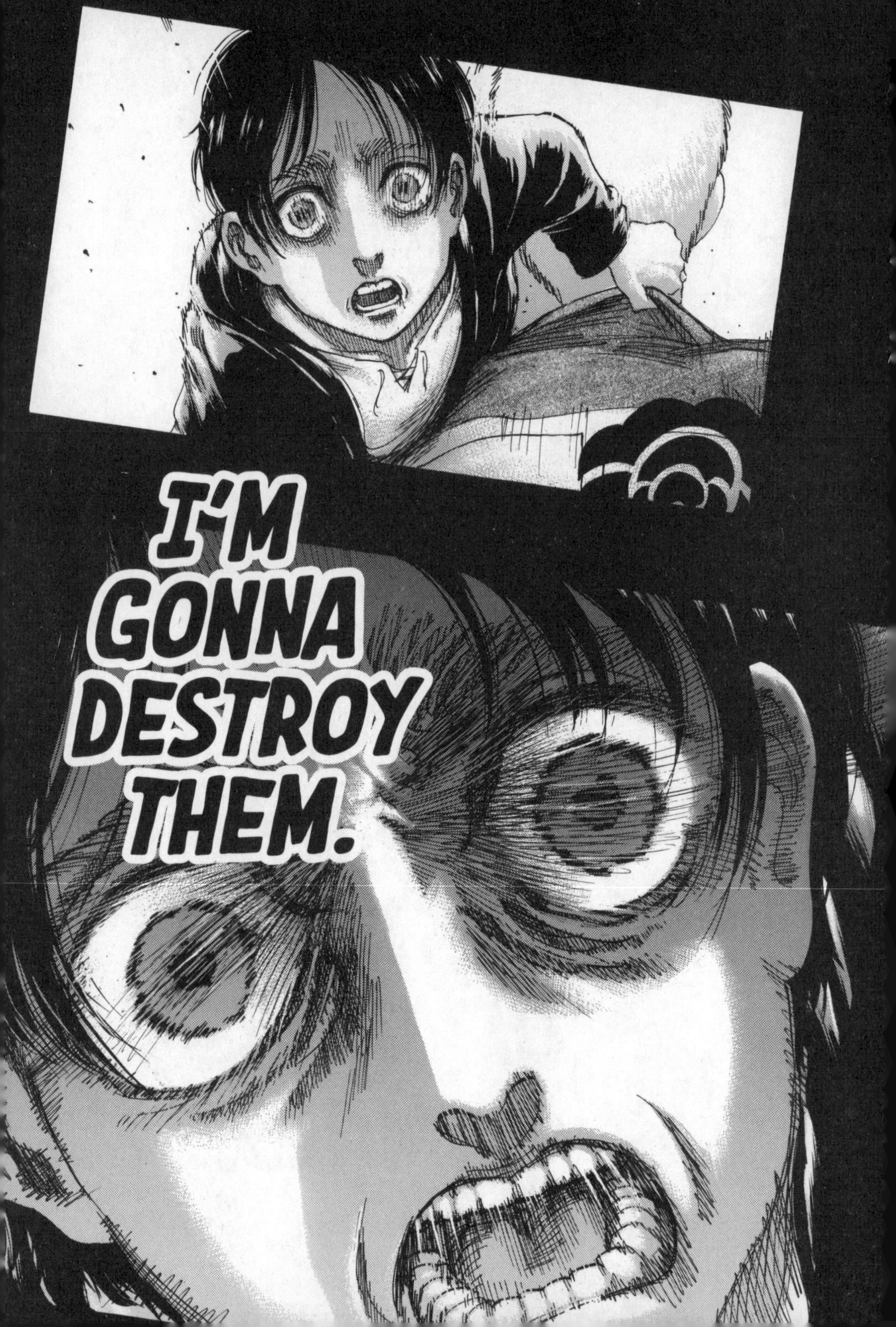
I'M GONNA DESTROY THEM.

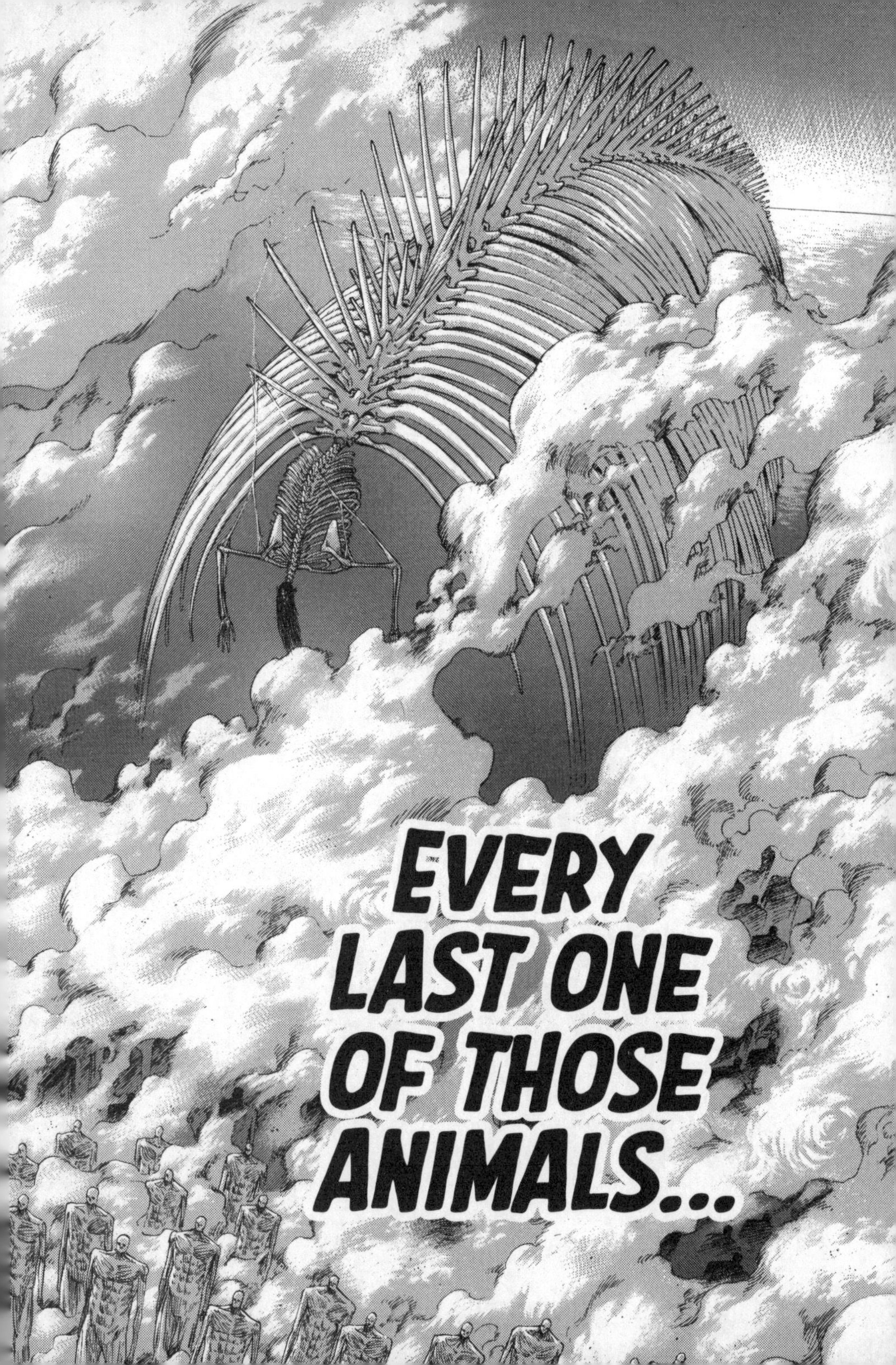
EVERY LAST ONE OF THOSE ANIMALS...

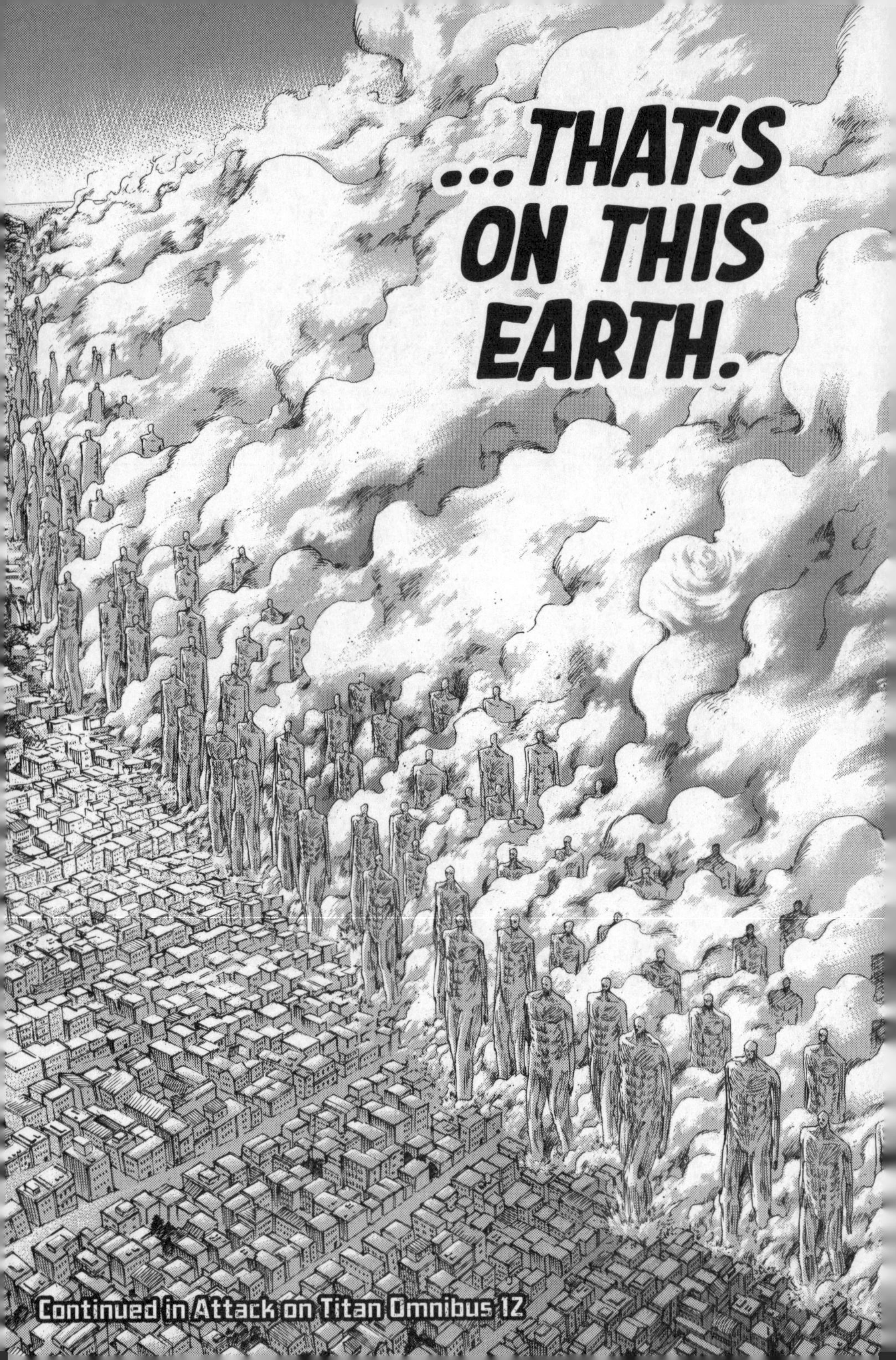
...THAT'S ON THIS EARTH.
Continued in Attack on Titan Omnibus 12

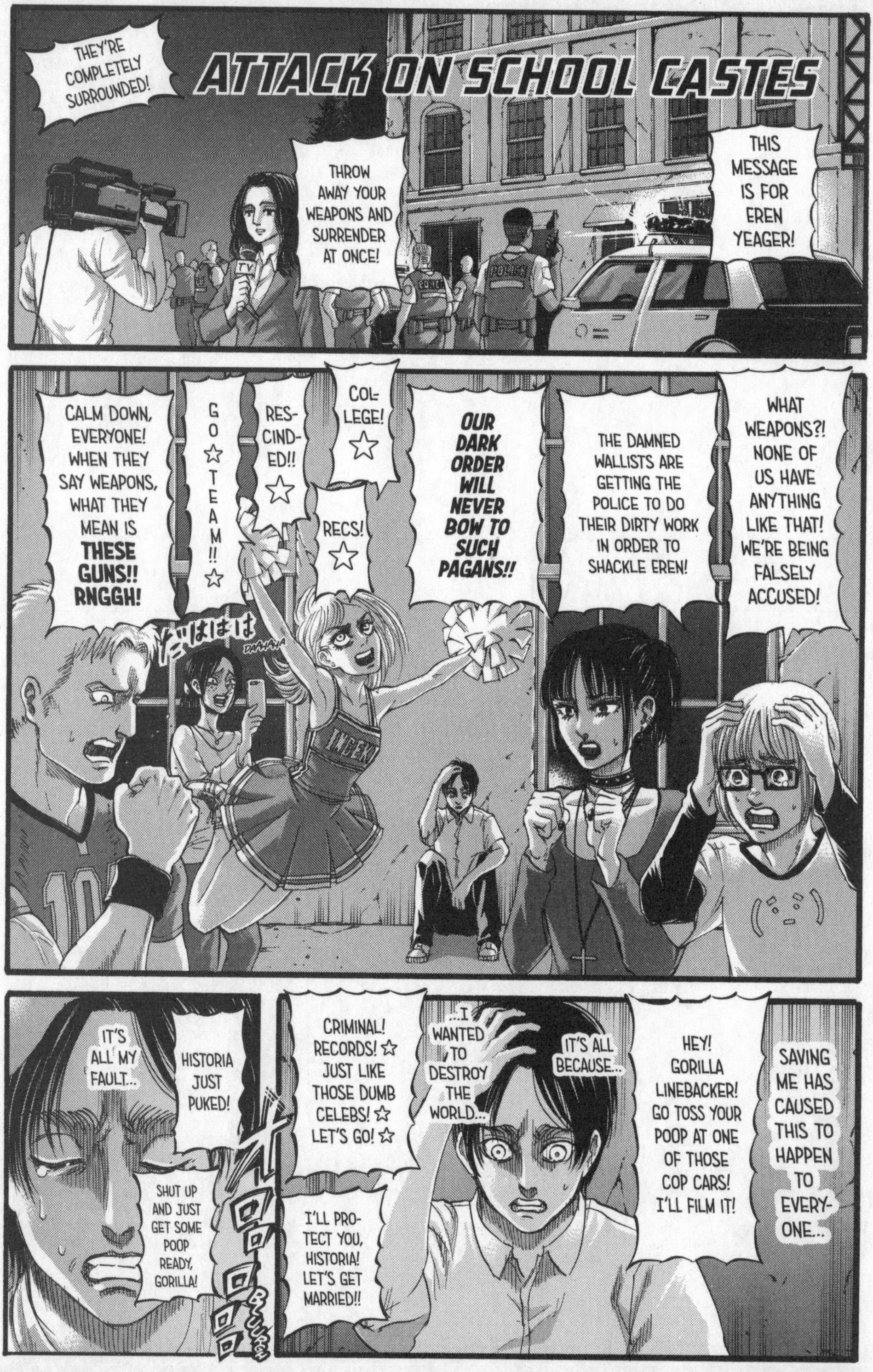
ATTACK ON SCHOOL CASTES
THIS MESSAGE IS FOR EREN YEAGER!
THROW AWAY YOUR WEAPONS AND SURRENDER AT ONCE!
THEY'RE COMPLETELY SURROUNDED!
WHAT WEAPONS?! NONE OF US HAVE ANYTHING LIKE THAT! WE'RE BEING FALSELY ACCUSED!
THE DAMNED WALLISTS ARE GETTING THE POLICE TO DO THEIR DIRTY WORK IN ORDER TO SHACKLE EREN!
OUR DARK ORDER WILL NEVER BOW TO SUCH PAGANS!!
COL-LEGE! ☆
RECS! ☆
RES-CIND-ED!! ☆
GO☆TEAM!!☆
CALM DOWN, EVERYONE! WHEN THEY SAY WEAPONS, WHAT THEY MEAN IS **THESE GUNS!! RNGGH!**
だはははは
DAHAHA
SAVING ME HAS CAUSED THIS TO HAPPEN TO EVERY-ONE...
HEY! GORILLA LINEBACKER! GO TOSS YOUR POOP AT ONE OF THOSE COP CARS! I'LL FILM IT!
IT'S ALL BECAUSE...
...I WANTED TO DESTROY THE WORLD...
CRIMINAL! RECORDS! ☆ JUST LIKE THOSE DUMB CELEBS! ☆ LET'S GO! ☆
I'LL PRO-TECT YOU, HISTORIA! LET'S GET MARRIED!!
HISTORIA JUST PUKED!
IT'S ALL MY FAULT...
SHUT UP AND JUST GET SOME POOP READY, GORILLA!
BLURGE

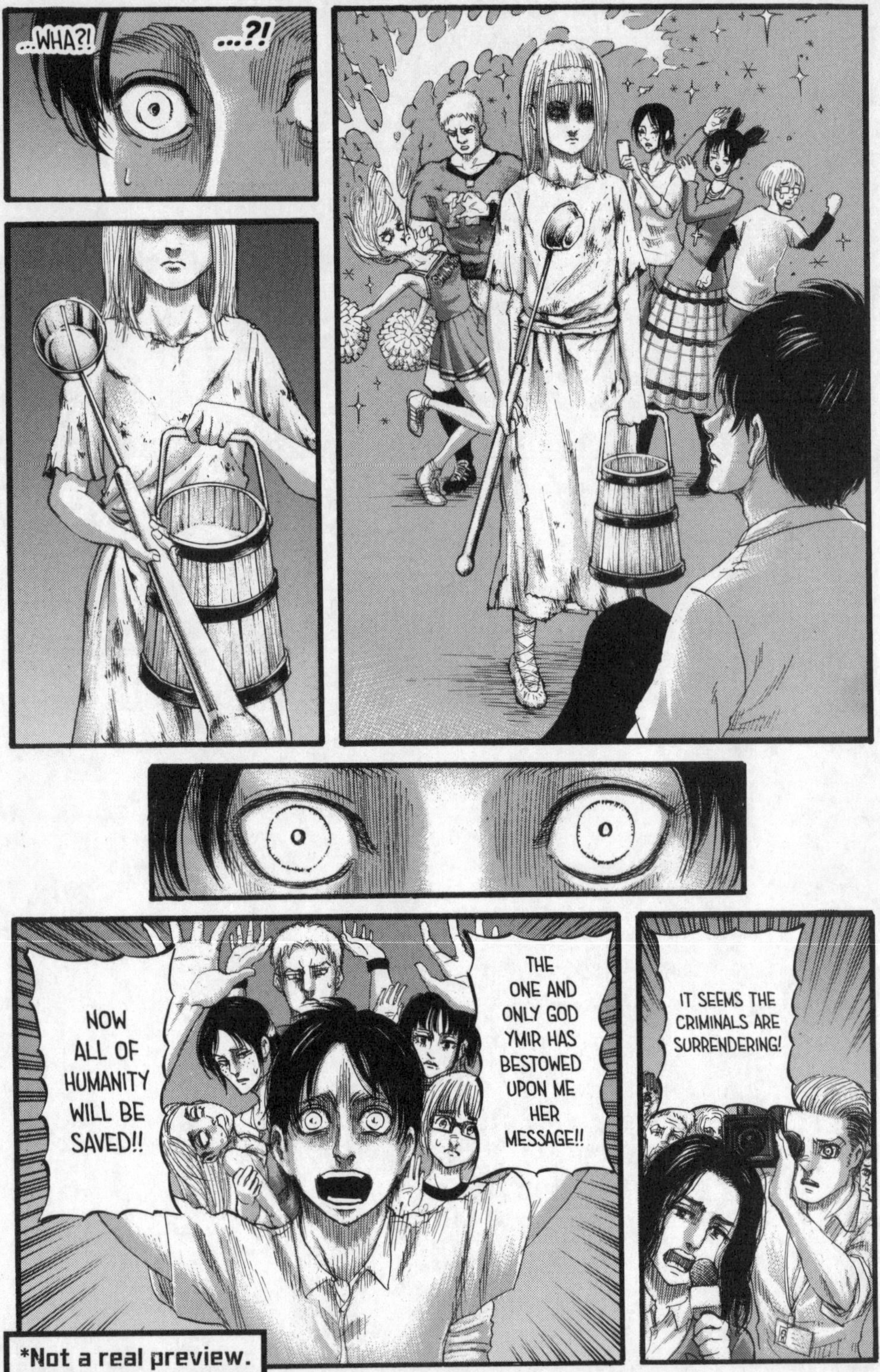
...?!
...WHA?!
IT SEEMS THE CRIMINALS ARE SURRENDERING!
THE ONE AND ONLY GOD YMIR HAS BESTOWED UPON ME HER MESSAGE!!
NOW ALL OF HUMANITY WILL BE SAVED!!
*Not a real preview.

ATTACK on TITAN